Competitive Social Media Marketing Strategies

Wilson Ozuem
University of Gloucestershire, UK

Gordon Bowen
Regent's University London, UK

A volume in the Advances in Marketing, Customer Relationship Management, and E-Services (AMCRMES) Book Series

BUSINESS SCIENCE *Reference*
An Imprint of IGI Global

Published in the United States of America by
Business Science Reference (an imprint of IGI Global)
701 E. Chocolate Avenue
Hershey PA, USA 17033
Tel: 717-533-8845
Fax: 717-533-8661
E-mail: cust@igi-global.com
Web site: http://www.igi-global.com

Library of Congress Cataloging-in-Publication Data

Names: Bowen, Gordon, 1950- editor. | Ozuem, Wilson, 1974- editor.
Title: Competitive social media marketing strategies / Gordon Bowen and Wilson Ozuem, editors.
Description: Hershey, PA : Business Science Reference, [2016] | Includes bibliographical references and index.
Identifiers: LCCN 2015041982| ISBN 9781466697768 (hardcover) | ISBN 9781466697775 (ebook)
Subjects: LCSH: Internet marketing--Social aspects. | Online social networks. | Social media. | Marketing--Social aspects.
Classification: LCC HF5415.1265 .C6544 2016 | DDC 658.8/72--dc23 LC record available at http://lccn.loc.gov/2015041982

This book is published in the IGI Global book series Advances in Marketing, Customer Relationship Management, and E-Services (AMCRMES) (ISSN: 2327-5502; eISSN: 2327-5529)

British Cataloguing in Publication Data
A Cataloguing in Publication record for this book is available from the British Library.

Advances in Marketing, Customer Relationship Management, and E-Services (AMCRMES) Book Series

Eldon Y. Li
National Chengchi University, Taiwan & California Polytechnic State University, USA

ISSN: 2327-5502
EISSN: 2327-5529

Mission

Business processes, services, and communications are important factors in the management of good customer relationship, which is the foundation of any well organized business. Technology continues to play a vital role in the organization and automation of business processes for marketing, sales, and customer service. These features aid in the attraction of new clients and maintaining existing relationships.

The Advances in Marketing, Customer Relationship Management, and E-Services (AMCRMES) Book Series addresses success factors for customer relationship management, marketing, and electronic services and its performance outcomes. This collection of reference source covers aspects of consumer behavior and marketing business strategies aiming towards researchers, scholars, and practitioners in the fields of marketing management.

Coverage

- Ethical Considerations in E-Marketing
- B2B marketing
- Customer Retention
- Data mining and marketing
- Web Mining and Marketing
- Cases on Electronic Services
- Telemarketing
- Online Community Management and Behavior
- CRM strategies
- Relationship marketing

The Advances in Marketing, Customer Relationship Management, and E-Services (AMCRMES) Book Series (ISSN 2327-5502) is published by IGI Global, 701 E. Chocolate Avenue, Hershey, PA 17033-1240, USA, www.igi-global.com. This series is composed of titles available for purchase individually; each title is edited to be contextually exclusive from any other title within the series. For pricing and ordering information please visit http://www.igi-global.com/book-series/advances-marketing-customer-relationship-management/37150. Postmaster: Send all address changes to above address.

Titles in this Series

For a list of additional titles in this series, please visit: www.igi-global.com

Product Innovation through Knowledge Management and Social Media Strategies
Alok Kumar Goel (CSIR Human Resource Development Centre, India) and Puja Singhal (Amity University, India)
Business Science Reference • copyright 2016 • 421pp • H/C (ISBN: 9781466696075) • US $205.00 (our price)

Fuzzy Optimization and Multi-Criteria Decision Making in Digital Marketing
Anil Kumar (ABV-Indian Institute of Information Technology & Management, India) and Manoj Kumar Dash (ABV-Indian Institute of Information Technology & Management, India)
Business Science Reference • copyright 2016 • 368pp • H/C (ISBN: 9781466688087) • US $200.00 (our price)

Trends and Innovations in Marketing Information Systems
Theodosios Tsiakis (Alexander Technological Educational Institute of Thessaloniki, Greece)
Business Science Reference • copyright 2015 • 454pp • H/C (ISBN: 9781466684591) • US $225.00 (our price)

Capturing, Analyzing, and Managing Word-of-Mouth in the Digital Marketplace
Sumangla Rathore (Sir Padampat Singhania University, India) and Avinash Panwar (Sir Padampat Singhania University, India)
Business Science Reference • copyright 2016 • 339pp • H/C (ISBN: 9781466694491) • US $200.00 (our price)

Strategic Customer Relationship Management in the Age of Social Media
Amir Khanlari (University of Tehran, Iran)
Business Science Reference • copyright 2015 • 332pp • H/C (ISBN: 9781466685864) • US $200.00 (our price)

Maximizing Commerce and Marketing Strategies through Micro-Blogging
Janée N. Burkhalter (Saint Joseph's University, USA) and Natalie T. Wood (Saint Joseph's University, USA & Edith Cowan University, Australia)
Business Science Reference • copyright 2015 • 380pp • H/C (ISBN: 9781466684089) • US $225.00 (our price)

Analyzing the Cultural Diversity of Consumers in the Global Marketplace
Juan Miguel Alcántara-Pilar (University of Granada, Spain) Salvador del Barrio-García (University of Granada, Spain) Esmeralda Crespo-Almendros (University of Granada, Spain) and Lucia Porcu (University of Granada, Spain)
Business Science Reference • copyright 2015 • 403pp • H/C (ISBN: 9781466682627) • US $200.00 (our price)

Engaging Consumers through Branded Entertainment and Convergent Media
Jose Marti Parreno (Universidad Europea de Valencia, Spain) Carla Ruiz Mafe (Universidad de Valencia, Spain) and Lisa Scribner (University of North Carolina Wilmington, USA)
Business Science Reference • copyright 2015 • 353pp • H/C (ISBN: 9781466683426) • US $205.00 (our price)

IGI GLOBAL
DISSEMINATOR OF KNOWLEDGE
www.igi-global.com

701 E. Chocolate Ave., Hershey, PA 17033
Order online at www.igi-global.com or call 717-533-8845 x100
To place a standing order for titles released in this series, contact: cust@igi-global.com
Mon-Fri 8:00 am - 5:00 pm (est) or fax 24 hours a day 717-533-8661

Editorial Advisory Board

List of Reviewers

Table of Contents

Detailed Table of Contents

Integration of digital marketing into overall business strategy is no longer an option, it is imperative for success. Yet, not all have tapped into this. Another opportunity that could leverage an organisation in today's competitive environment is affinity marketing. Successful implementation of affinity marketing has the potential to enhance participation, raise revenue, increase retention and provide a mutually beneficial arrangement for the partners involved. Yet, despite its appeal and the popularity it achieved in the late 1980s and early 1990s, uptake of the scheme has slowed down. Whilst some affinity partners have embraced digital marketing to an extent, most are not using it effectively to drive and sustain their affinity marketing scheme. Cognisant that affinity marketing is still a lucrative area, this chapter sets forth a digital marketing strategy for affinity marketing, e-affinity marketing, as this is where the added value for the 21st century customer is envisioned.

The role of social media as a contemporary Local Area Marketing (LAM) technique in Dialogue Marketing is not clearly defined. Dialogue Marketing focuses on a structured approach of ongoing interactive communication to form relationships with people (Allan Steinmetz, 1997). According to Webster and Hume (2015) contemporary LAM techniques refer to using digital marketing to build relationships with local community. Problems facing franchise businesses include how to use Dialogue Marketing as a contemporary LAM technique to maximise local community connections as well as to build essential relationships. Advancing previous work in LAM, this study analyses social media's role as a contemporary LAM technique in Dialogue Marketing. It explores the use of Dialogue Management as a tool to enhance

Dialogue Marketing for franchise businesses. It presents an integrated framework for the identification of social media adoption levels and how this can enhance franchise business success by providing an important contribution to the franchise industry sector. It concludes by offering a conceptual touchpoint channel model with a view to progressing discourse in the area and uniting current thinking.

The Internet has transformed social communications and social behaviours. Technology-aided interpersonal interactions have replaced traditional 'face-to-face' affiliations. The purpose of this chapter is to examine the effect of user-generated content on perceived customer value. In contrast to prior study mainly investigates the effect of two main areas, namely, customer and company, this study additionally widens the scope and influence of user-generated content on consumer-to-consumer communications. Our findings suggest that user-generated content mediates on consumer decision-making process, providing higher-order credibility beyond the conventional marketing communication programmes.

Always on the lookout for novelty and innovation, companies are using social networks, which now occupy an important place in our daily. Users of social networks constitute a new target for retailers looking to evolve their loyalty programs. Through Facebook or twitter accounts, the company can develop a profile of the user and have an idea regarding their interests... Therefore, companies have a lot of opportunities through social CRM, to communicate, to develop their relationship programs and, in fine, to retain their customer. Although the social CRM is perceived as a business strategy it requires a technology platform, rules, processes and social characteristics. To ensure interaction with these tools, the company should ensure that the consumer adopts them in an abundant manner. This paper aims at examining the emergence of interaction across internet tools, the importance of managing customer relationship through social CRM and the determinants of why consumers adopt these tools by studying the case of Facebook in emerging countries.

Social media is seen very much as a marketing tool and there is little in the literature that considers its use as a strategic decision making tool. This conceptual paper is an attempt to redress the balance. Social media user-generated content from blogs or consumer feedback are methods that social media can support effective strategic decision making. However, the business and organisational environments are influential on the effective of the data collected and ultimately its analysis. The decision making approach – single or multistage are significant influencers on the quality of the decisions. Multistage decision making is supportive of controversial decision making, which leads to better utilisation of the information and consequently, better decision making. Ultimately, robust decision making is underpinned by the effectiveness of the decision making process.

The Internet environment has transformed the concepts of service failure and recovery strategies from a dyadic customer-provider focus into a multidimensional web quality scope. In traditional encounters, the research spectrum of service failure and recovery strategies is very much developed from a customer service approach, and the responsibility of recovery has been traditionally assumed to be something that is assigned to the marketer. Studies pay little or no attention to the multidimensional nature of service failures contingent to recovery strategies in the evolving social media. To date, empirical studies have focused on service failures and recovery strategies in online marketing environments, but pay limited attention to social media platforms. This paper aims to provide some insights on the need for a broader conceptualisation of service failure and recovery strategies, incorporating social media platforms for the development of effective marketing communications programme.

In situations where government functions are in short supply as with most developing countries particularly Nigeria, issues concerning stakeholder engagement and stakeholder voice are usually on the back burner as a consequence. In this chapter, the authors argues that such landscape is midwifed and sustained by state fragility, which is a situation where government is incapacitated to provide basic social goods as well as infrastructures and enabling institutions that can facilitate corporate-stakeholder engagement and stakeholders' voice amplification. In the Nigerian petroleum industry, this contentious issue are redoubled, given the controversial dynamics of the sector. As this chapter contends, new media (as opposed to old media) has the potentials to facilitate better engagement in corporate-stakeholder dialectics, which can be a harbinger of amplification of stakeholders' voice for sustainable relations and engagement in the industry. In a fragile state, traditional media has a monopoly of information dissemination and sharing, which traditionally limits stakeholder engagement/voice thereby frustrating efforts towards ensuring corporate-stakeholder engagement, corporate responsibility and accountability. Thus, this dilemma can be surmounted with the aid of new media as it is a communication/engagement tool that democratises the discursive space for deliberative corporate-stakeholder relations. It is hoped that this contention will help to illuminate perspectives on how the lingering corporate-stakeholder Catch-22 in Nigeria's petroleum sector can be better managed. Methodologically, literature on main issues in this chapter will be explored and a conceptual framework – stakeholder voice amplification method (SVAM) – will be developed that has the potential to advance knowledge on better corporate-stakeholder engagement in a fragile state such as Nigeria.

Recent years have witnessed a rapid growth in internet-enabled devices, including smartphones which have facilitated the performance of many tasks online. One of the major activities taking place on such online platforms is shopping. Indeed, smartphones are redefining the landscape of consumption from visiting conventional physical shops to consuming products and services in a digital arena. Despite a proliferation of both theoretical and empirical studies on smartphones marketplace, there is still a paucity of studies on how mobile phone devices enhance and facilitate consumption from physical marketplace to online marketspace. This chapter aims to contribute to extant studies on how smartphones impact on the consumption process.

This chapter explains the roles of social media marketing and brand management in global marketing, thus describing the theoretical and practical concept of social media marketing, the overview of brand management, the significance of social media marketing, and the application of social media-related brand management in global marketing. The creation of social media marketing and brand management is necessary for modern organizations that seek to serve suppliers and customers, increase business performance, enhance competitiveness, and gain routine success in global business. Thus, it is vital for modern organizations to acknowledge their social media marketing and brand management utilization, establish a strategic plan to consistently evaluate their effective promotions, and immediately respond to social media marketing and brand management needs of customers. The chapter argues that applying social media marketing and brand management in global marketing has the potential to enhance organizational performance and achieve strategic goals in the digital age.

Social media provides companies innovative ways to market their products and services to their customers. The social media tools, such as Facebook, provides new ways to reach customers. With increasing number of people being connected to social media, businesses of all types are targeting social media as a new platform to reach their customers and strengthen customer relationships. Still, many companies are unsure as to how they can use social media for their advantage. There is lack of resources and fear of failure that hold many companies back from using social media in their marketing campaigns. Companies need a set of guidelines to understand how they can develop long-term, successful marketing strategies that involve social media as a significant component. This chapter analyzes use of social media marketing to suggest some ways companies can use social media to generate value both for them and their customers. This chapter also discusses how companies can develop a social media marketing strategy.

The most common feature of Search Engine Marketing (SEM) is the pay-per-click concept that outlines the conceptual understanding of the human-computer interaction (HCI) in marketing. In this type of marketing, the three active actors act simultaneously: the service provider, the search engine as the platform and the individual user base. On the assumption that technology will dominate future marketing channels, this study will explore the conceptualisations of SEM, in relation to HCI in tourism marketing. This paper asserts that strategically, a congenial and accepted level of interaction is much required between the service provider and consumers. Also, this is outlined that the customization of a tourism industry led application and adoption of SEM is possible on ground of the Unified theory of Acceptance and Use of Technology (UTAUT) where, factors like age, gender, experience and voluntariness of use are attached with performance expectancy (Venkatesh et al., 2003).

Debates regarding the ontological relationship between Social Media and customer retention have attracted considerable attention, particularly in the luxury beauty industry. The use of Social Media in the luxury beauty industry has caused many heated debates as it is seen as a form of interference in the exclusivity of luxury brands by limiting the physical and sensual contact between brand and customer. The purpose of this chapter is to provide some insights into how social media impacts on the cosmetics industry. Further, we provide evidence that the effective application of social media in the luxury beauty industry could lead to wider market share, and customer retention. The chapter concludes with some strategies that practitioners and researchers can adopt to develop effective marketing communication strategies, using social media platforms.

Foreword

Social media's enormously rapid development in just a few years has caught some businessmen/women on the hop! Marketing directors who grew up with what we now call traditional media are nervous of something new and to them untried, and perhaps rightly so. Should companies be investing money on digital marketing, or should they stay offline? As this book points out, an online presence is now imperative. Every organisation, large or small, public or private, commercial or not for profit, should now have a digital marketing strategy as an integral part of their marketing plan. A social media portfolio is becoming an increasingly important tool. However, fools rush in! This book guides the reader through strategic implications of digital marketing, pointing out its pitfalls as well as its potentials.

Building relationships has always been at the core of marketing (even if this went unrecognised for much of the 20th century). In *Relationship Marketing: Exploring Relational Strategies in Marketing*, first published in 2001, I argued that many organisations had lost sight of this and that the traditional 4Ps and transactional marketing strategies should be challenged. This was before the digital age really got going (four and five years before Facebook and Twitter, respectively), but it noted that technology offered an opportunity for relationship building. This current book argues that social media should be part of this strategy. Converging technologies mean that we have access at home or on the move. When I first travelled to work, it was newspapers that helped while away the commute. Today, while the odd (free) paper is still read, it's Facebook, Twitter, YouTube, Google+, LinkedIn, Pinterest, Instagram, and many more that are capturing the attention of the public.

This book guides the reader through a series of papers, outlining various strategy opportunities open to the organisation. It promotes local area marketing, which is particularly appropriate to franchise businesses who can maximise community-wide interaction whilst building relationships. It notes the behaviour-changing nature of technology and that technology, being interactive, has the ability to replace face-to-face contact without necessarily demeaning the social element. CRM (customer relationship management) has had its critics, but the book argues that with the appropriate platform, social CRM would enable organisations to interact across a range of Internet tools. It promotes analysis of user-generated content from consumers and influential bloggers and the lessons that can be learnt from them. A further consideration is the role of social media in situations where things have gone wrong. Service failure and recovery strategies are crucial. As research has shown, it is frequently not the original problem that really irritates customers but the organisations' response to it. Not every community, home or abroad, has the support services available. A coherent argument is made that, through stakeholder engagement, communities can encourage involvement through social media. The shopping (in its widest sense) environment is examined from the perspective of smart, often handheld devices such as smartphones. In addition to local communities, a chapter is devoted to brand management in a global context and how this can be built around social media. SEM (search-engine marketing) is not ignored in this debate; indeed, its importance is underlined. Finally, industry-specific uses (for example, in luxury categories) are examined and solutions proposed.

All in all, I recommend *Competitive Social Media Strategies* to all of you interested in expanding your knowledge in this area. Whether you are a student or a seasoned professional, it has something to contribute to your learning.

John Egan
Regent's University London, UK

John Egan *is head of the Department of Marketing and Strategy at Regent's University London. Professor Egan is also chair of the Academy of Marketing.*

Foreword

It has been generally accepted that intrinsically motivated activities are enjoyed hedonically, because they appeal to outcomes which are derived directly from the behavior itself and satisfy psychological needs directly. On the other hand, the incentives for extrinsic motivation are more concerned with utilitarian consequences separated from behavior and thus have less direct effects on psychological satisfaction. According to the experiential perspective of participation, customers' motive of active participation can be substantially attributed to seeking intrinsic rewards, that is, the pleasure of participation in co-producing experiences, rather than simple extrinsic values based on utilitarian benefits and costs. In sum, consumers can make their experience more favorable by proactively, rather than passively, co-creating value derived from the experience.

For a modern marketer, how to design a platform where consumers can efficiently organize their resource project and thus maximize their value in the process of experience production-consumption is a critical issue to address. In this sense, social media in the era of digital marketing have been considered as an umbrella of solution which encompasses a variety of systematic instruments that enable users to co-create their experience value with new business models from consumption situations. As the level of customer' participation increases, they are more likely to manage consumption resources, such as time, skills, goods, and services, in a creative way, to generate intrinsically rewarding stimuli of experiences.

This book captures thoroughly the instrumental value of social media in building and maintaining a sustainable competitive advantage of business by articulating various perspectives and cases of application. Each chapter focuses on specific issues and industries which highlight the prominent role of social media in strategic market planning and implementation. Also, this book incorporates key concepts of social media, such as user generated content (UGC), Search Engine Marketing (SEM), affinity marketing, Local Area Marketing (LAM), Stakeholder Voice Amplification Method (SVAM), and human - computer interaction (HCI). They are well connected on the root of theories of consumer participation which suggests how they have been used to manage stakeholders, brands, customer loyalty, and service failure/recovery, in developing countries and a global marketing environment. The articles included in this book not only advance our understandings of business innovation, but also imply the efforts of marketers and businesses as a whole to socialize their customers by applying social media are rewarding both to the company and the customer.

Moreover, this book echoes the elaborative likelihood model (ELM) which contrasts instrumental values of use of cognitively based issue-relevant thinking—that is, central routes; and reliance on relatively little issue-relevant thinking—that is, peripheral routes as means of persuasion in social media interactions. In the same vein, belief-oriented and feeling-oriented approaches applied by social media are each intended to reflect fundamentally different means of persuasion. The former is seen as more issue-relevant such that dedicated cognitive effort is required for an evaluation, whereas the judgments associated with more peripheral feelings-based appeals are likely based on simple cues. Applying the ELM perspective suggests that audience with high or low involvement in a situation of social media interaction may either actively seek information regarding their decision making, or passively absorb the information over time. Information-saturated targets are likely to scan long-term memory for existing and decision-relevant information, which may provide them with a satisfactory course of action before they make judgements. Obviously, in such cases, it is not necessary for audience to collect additional information by way of peripheral routes. This mechanism contends that the impact of influence attempts is reduced by the duration of dyadic interactions, supporting the importance of continuous development of innovative social media. This book with vision provides a variety of ideas and guidelines which are useful for marketers to address current and future issues.

In summary, the authors of this book have done an excellent job of incorporating current and critical issues of social media management and leading them to strategic implications for practitioners in today's changing environments of marketing. Specifically, the book is highly recommended for academics to gain insights into social media from reviewing this book. I enjoyed the book and I think you all will as well.

Che-Jen Su
Fu Jen Catholic University, Taiwan

Che-Jen Su *is Professor of Restaurant, Hotel and Institutional Management at Fu Jen Catholic University, Taipei, Taiwan.*

Preface

The marketing environment battlefield is evolving from just offline battles to online offences. Organisations cannot expect to win and become successful by staying in the offline physical environment, the need for online presence is now an imperative for successful business performance. The issue is how to navigate the online environment successfully, which requires digital marketing strategies that evolve and sustain companies in the 21st Century. Digital marketing strategies need to acknowledge and incorporate social media techniques and activities in their marketing portfolio and link to the strategic planning process.

Social media activities and techniques span the whole business environment and thus can be leveraged by any size of business. Businesses now have social media tools that allow them to change the business and competitive landscapes to their advantage. Social media is a tool to enable change, but particularly disruptive change, leading to sustainability of the change. The marketing environment is becoming more volatile due to businesses need to adapt proactively and effectively to competitor actions. Social media is evolving, and has the potential counteract changes in the marketing environment and to a degree limit uncertainty and discover new business opportunities. Environmental scanning is one area that social media has a role that could facilitate marketing and strategic planning. Firms that fully engage with social media have a real opportunity to steal a march on their competitors and develop a sustainable advantage.

Competitive Social Media Marketing reference textbook is targeting marketing professionals, undergraduate and postgraduate students in business, marketing, digital marketing, and others students that want to understand the scope and potential of social media marketing. Furthermore, the other target groups are universities, libraries, business and management consultants, professional institutions, and individuals with an interest in digital marketing and in particular social media.

Scope of the book includes the use and application of user generated content (UGC) in a marketing and strategic context, affinity marketing progression e-affinity marketing for digital marketing, dialogue marketing in the context of Local Area Marketing (LAM), social media as a facilitator of building customer loyalty in the digital environment, service failure and recovery strategies in the Internet environment, social media as a tool to engage stakeholders in emerging and developing countries, smartphone phenomena and its influence on consumer consumption in the digital shopping landscape, social media as a mechanism to manage brands in a global marketing environment, search engine marketing human-computer interface in relation to the tourism marketing, social media as a competitive advantage tool, and social media platforms and their effectiveness in the cosmetic industry.

Chapter 1 argues that digital marketing must be an integral part of business strategy, but not all businesses realise the importance and as a lever of success. Affinity marketing is a resource to improve organisational financial performance by enhancing participation and improve retention rates all properties that are beneficial to the organisation and the partnerships. Although affinity marketing has a degree of popularity it has not been sufficient to propel its implementation. Traditional affinity marketing is being replaced by e-affinity marketing, which is more suited for the digital age. E-affinity marketing requires a digital marketing strategy, which is the aim of the chapter.

Chapter 2's role is to promote the discourse on Local Area Marketing (LAM) in the area of Dialogue Marketing, which is not clearly defined. Dialogue marketing focuses on structured interactive communications in marketing and LAM on digital marketing relationship building. One area that a LAM approach is of particular benefit is in the franchise businesses, because of the need to build relationships and maximise community-wide interaction and at the same time build relationships. This study develops the application of social media as a LAM technique in Dialogue Marketing. To this end one end product of this paper is the development of an integrated framework to identify adoption levels of social media within the LAM context and its potential to enhance franchising businesses.

Chapter 3 suggests that the internet is a transformational technology the changes social processes such as behaviour and communications. The nature of the technology, which is interactive enables it to substitute for face to face situations. To compensate for decrease in social interaction, this chapter maintains that user-generated content can be a proxy to perceived customer value. Specifically, the aim of the chapter is to broaden the scope of previous research in this area from the organisation and customer to consumer to consumer user generated content. There is a role for this type of user generated content in mediating in consumer decision making.

Chapter 4 makes the point that organisations are always looking for opportunities to innovate and social networks provide a method to achieve this. This chapter also further suggest users of social networks are another target for retailers to evolve and grow their loyalty base. Social networks allow firms to leverage social CRM to develop relationships programs and communicate. Social CRM is a strategy, but it needs to sit on a technology platform and use methods to interact. The strategic nature of social CRM requires users to interact across a wide range of internet tools such as Facebook, Twitter etc. The nature of this interaction is aim of this paper and how to manage customer relationships across these tools, but in the context of emerging countries.

Chapter 5 discusses the concept that social media is not only a marketing tool, but has potential to facilitate strategic decision making. The user generated content from blogs or consumer feedback are rich areas to analyse with a view to aid strategic decision making. The strategic decisions made on the basis of user generated content will still be influence by the prevail business and organisational environment, but improved quality of data collected will streamline the decision making process. Single stage decision making produces lower quality decisions than multistage decision making. However, the quality of the decision making is directly linked to the number of stages in the decision making process. Such decisions that are multi-stage are more controversial, but utilise information more effectively. Good quality information that has richness and a multi-stage approach to decision making are the ideal ingredients to making more robust strategic decisions.

Chapter 6 reflects on service failure and recovery strategies in an Internet environment and how it changes in the conventional environment. One consequence is that service failure is didactic experience (customer and provider) in the conventional environment, but is a multidimensional experience in the Internet environment, because of web quality variables. Conventional environments maintain that service failure and recovery strategies are engineered to the customer requirements and is assigned to marketers. There is a paucity of research on service failure and recovery strategies in the Internet environment and the multidimensional nature of service failure and the application of social media to recovery strategies.

The aim of the paper is to add to the literature on service failure and recovery strategies in the online environment, but with particular reference to the use of social media in this context. At the same time it will also provide a broad conceptualisation of service failure and recovery strategies.

Chapter 7 reviews the situation where governmental functions are in short supply, which is a familiar situation in developing countries, such as Nigeria. Consequently, stakeholder engagement and stakeholders' voice were less important. This paper argues that state fragility and inability to provide and distribute basic goods sustains the situation identified. Thus amplification of stakeholder engagement and stakeholder voices are facilitated when basic services and government services are functioning effectively. To overcome the lack of stakeholder engagement and stakeholders' voice an opportunity to apply social media in this context is a possible solution. Social media is an interactive communication tool and is more challenging to control than traditional media (old media). Social media democratises the space of stakeholder non-engagement and enables corporate – stakeholder engagement, raising corporate social responsibility, and corporate accountability. To achieve the interaction communications to minimise the non-engagement space a framework based on Stakeholder Voice Amplification Method (SVAM) is suggested based on research from the petroleum industry.

Chapter 8 considers the rapid growth in internet-enabled devices, with particular reference to smartphones. Internet-enabled devices facilitate online activities and an important area is shopping. Online shopping via smartphones is re-designing the shopping landscape and encroaching on the traditional shopping approach and experience. The shopping consumption landscape is undergoing change due to the digital arena and consequently, affecting shopping consumption in physical shops. This chapter is evolving the literature from just about smartphones in the marketplace to how the digital mobile phones can enhance and facilitate the move away from physical shopping and offline landscape to the digital mobile phone online landscape.

Chapter 9 discusses the role of social media marketing and brand management in a global marketing context. Its emphasis is on the theoretical and practical aspects of social media marketing on brand management in a global marketing environment. Social media marketing and brand management are becoming imperatives to serve suppliers and customers, thus enhancing organisational and business performance, leading to increasing competitiveness. Strategic plans need to incorporate ideas and activities relating to social media marketing and brand management, with the benefit that organisations that take this approach have improved promotional performance and are proactive in their response to customers' social media marketing and brand management needs. Thus the application of social marketing and brand management in a global marketing context will lead to improved organisational performance and align strategic goals in a digital age.

Chapter 10 focuses on how companies can develop effective social media strategies. Many companies understand that social media is beneficial to their business, but it is moving beyond this to developing innovative social media strategies. How to use platforms such as Facebook to reach their target market and build sustainable relationships is a sticking point for businesses. Companies do not allocate sufficient resources or there is fear of the unknown are factors, which affects the successful implementation of social media marketing. Firms need to set guidelines and develop successful social media marketing plans so the long-term benefits can be exploited. To this end a central aim of this paper is to assist companies to analyse and develop social media marketing strategies that add value to the firm and their customers.

Chapter 11 debates Search Engine Marketing (SEM) with reference to pay-per-click to conceptualise the human - computer interaction (HCI) in marketing. In SEM three actors are active simultaneously: the service provider, the search engine platform and the individual user. This study examines the SEM conceptualisation in relation to the HCI theory in tourism marketing. Underpinning the discussion is that technology will be the dominant factor in future marketing channels. The overarching assertion is that strategically a congenial and acceptable level of interaction is required between users and service providers. Also the assertion that the customisation of SEM can occur in the tourism industry by the application of the Unified Theory of Acceptance and Use of Technology (UTAUT) is part of the discussion.

Chapter 12 discusses the use of social media and customer retention in the beauty industry has stirred many debates. There is a feeling the social media has no place in the luxury industry such as beauty. Social media is felt to interfere with the exclusivity of the product by limiting the physical and sensual contact between the brand and the customer. The chapter aims to provide insight into how social media affects the cosmetic industry. Furthermore, the chapter provides evidence that the application of social media to the beauty industry can lead to wider market share and customer retention. Finally, the chapter concludes with marketing communication strategies for the beauty industry based on social media platforms.

Social media has a broad range of applications for business be they small, medium or gigantic. However, the application of social media to a business or industry will need refining to take account of their marketing environment. The challenge for marketers in the digital industry is to adapt, develop and engage with the new ideas and applications in social media to enable businesses to gain and maintain a sustainable competitive advantage.

Chapter 1
Digital Marketing Strategy for Affinity Marketing:
Utilising the New Marketing Arena

Aster Mekonnen
GSM London, UK

ABSTRACT

Integration of digital marketing into overall business strategy is no longer an option, it is imperative for success. Yet, not all have tapped into this. Another opportunity that could leverage an organisation in today's competitive environment is affinity marketing. Successful implementation of affinity marketing has the potential to enhance participation, raise revenue, increase retention and provide a mutually beneficial arrangement for the partners involved. Yet, despite its appeal and the popularity it achieved in the late 1980s and early 1990s, uptake of the scheme has slowed down. Whilst some affinity partners have embraced digital marketing to an extent, most are not using it effectively to drive and sustain their affinity marketing scheme. Cognisant that affinity marketing is still a lucrative area, this chapter sets forth a digital marketing strategy for affinity marketing, e-affinity marketing, as this is where the added value for the 21st century customer is envisioned.

INTRODUCTION

Businesses in the 21st century are hugely reliant on the internet to support the growth of their organisations. Whether one should integrate internet technology as part of their business plan is no longer questionable, but rather a matter of how it may be most effectively deployed (Michael Porter, 2001). The growth of and investment in digital marketing is astounding. For instance, an industry survey conducted by Pricewater house and Cooper (PwC) and sponsored by the Interactive Advertising Bureau (IAB) has shown that in US alone the revenue generated for half-year 2014 totalled $23.billion, 15% higher than the previous year (IAB, 2014). Coupled with the digital era, affinity marketing presents a unique opportunity for organisations to strengthen their competitiveness as well as build on their customer's loyalty. The internet presents the ultimate interactive and integrative communications system (Schultz, 1996). Given that affinity marketing (i.e. the triadic relationship between the affinity group, the customer and

DOI: 10.4018/978-1-4666-9776-8.ch001

the service provider) is said to be built on the affinity that customers already have with their affinity group, integrating and implementing digital marketing effectively has the potential to further enhance the customer-affinity group as well as the customer-service provider relationship.

Given the minimal integration of digital marketing in driving affinity marketing, the challenge is to determine the extent to which marketers are using it and to propose ways of enhancing usage. As noted above, unlike most media the internet is interactive and provides marketers with a wide variety of potential uses that range from marketing research to advertising and selling. One of the most significant contributions of the internet is that of value-added marketing – adding value to visitors' experience by allowing marketers to give them additional information as well as services. "The concept of value-added marketing creates loyalty to one or more homepage sites and consequently to the homepage sponsor. Such loyalty is the corner-stone of building lasting relationships with customers" (Husted & Whitehouse, Jr., 2002, p.4).

In the face of today's rapidly changing environment, with the advent of a technology revolution and associated trends such as social media, customers' needs and demands (and even decision making processes) are changing. Recent studies have elicited that companies which master the process of digital integration are 2.5 times more likely to convert their customers (Bughin, 2013). Unfortunately, affinity marketers have not risen to the challenge. The investigation by the author has shown that most affinity marketing schemes are not adequately visible on the internet, therefore failing to capitalise on the opportunity that the digital platform presents.

This chapter intends to provide a strategy that enables affinity partners to integrate their business plan with digital marketing as a key component to drive success. The rest of the chapter is organised under three main areas: the new marketing arena; affinity marketing and digital marketing; and strategic integration. The new marketing arena gives an overview of the 'technology behind digital marketing', looking at the impact of technology and the internet. It also introduces such concepts as e-business, e-commerce and e-marketing with a view to clarifying terminologies, as well as to help put digital marketing into context. The first section will also outline some of the popular 'digital marketing strategies' adopted by marketers to date. Part two on affinity marketing and digital marketing reviews the origins and core values of affinity marketing under the section 'affinity marketing – the big opportunity', highlighting some of the challenges faced by affinity marketers. It then explores how this could be utilised to formulate objectives for e-affinity marketing. Part three – 'strategic integration' – begins with an investigation into 'affinity marketing on the web', a key step in planning the process for e-affinity marketing strategy. This is followed by a discussion on 'knowing the customers', as understanding visitors' needs is an important step in determining what they are offered. Then the 'strategy to activity' proposes steps to help set appropriate strategy and related activities based on knowledge of the target group. The last step in the process – 'performance analysis' – is designed to review the effectiveness of the new initiatives.

1. THE NEW MARKETING ARENA

Aghaei et al. (2012) describes the four generations of the web as follows: Web 1.0 as a web of information connections, Web 2.0 as a web of people connections, Web 3.0 as a web of knowledge connections and Web 4.0 as a web of intelligence connections (the future). The internet has grown from strength to strength since its innovation phase 1964 - 1974 (creation of the fundamental building blocks), through the institutionalisation phase 1975 - 1995 (when large intuitions were provided funding and legitimisation), up to today's commercialisation phase 1995 – present (private corporations take over, expand the backbone of the internet and local services) (Laudon & Travis, 2013). By the end of 2014, the number of internet users in the world is predicted to reach almost 3 billion, with two-thirds of them coming from the developing world (ICT Publication, 2014). Today, the web provides a tremendous opportunity to reach customers directly. A recent survey of digital marketing spending indicated that up to 2.5% of a company's revenue is used in this area (Gartner, 2013). This report suggests that the three top digital activities key to marketing success are the operation of a corporate website, social marketing and digital advertising. Social media is undoubtedly gaining in prominence, with over 72% of internet users now active on social media. The likes of Facebook and Google+ now have over 1 billion users and the potential to attract more (Laudon & Travis, 2013).

Advances in technology and the evolution of marketing are inseparable. The printing press, radio, television and now the internet are all examples of major breakthroughs in technology that also advanced the field of marketing. Technology has the ability to open up new markets and to radically change existing ones. The rapidness of changes in technology makes it necessary to continuously study consumer behaviour. As soon as one thinks that they may have a grasp on what their archetypal consumer wants, those wants will have changed. In the developed world, the digital revolution is changing the way we choose and buy our products and services. People are now going online on a daily basis to fulfil needs such as banking, shopping, recreation and communication.

Some marketing principles never change. Companies must meet the needs of their customers, the need now is digital integration, which is further fuelled by digitally enabled social networking (more commonly known as social media).

The Technology behind Digital Marketing

The terms internet marketing, e-marketing and digital marketing are often used interchangeably. However, e-marketing is sometimes considered to have a broader scope than internet marketing since it refers to digital media such as web, e-mail and wireless media, but also includes management of digital customer data and electronic customer relationship management systems (E-CRM systems). The term 'digital marketing' was first used in the 1990s and was then described as 'the marketing of products or services using digital channels to reach consumers (Dorie 2012). The key objective is to promote brands through various forms of digital media. To help clarify these alternative terminologies and definitions, in collaboration with the Institute of Digital Marketing, Chaffey (2005) proposed an all-encompassing explanation of digital marketing, describing it as an activity that involves the application of technologies which form online channels to market; that's web, e-mail, databases, plus mobile/wireless and digital TV.

The internet began in the late 1950s in the military and was gradually advanced by computer scientists. The digital revolution, also called the third industrial revolution, is the change from analogue, mechanical, and electronic technology to digital technology (Ryan & Jones, 2012). The digital age as we know it now began with the internet and the Web 1.0 platforms of the early 1990s. This was a rather static world in which users could get the information they desired but it could not be shared on the web. There was no such thing as interaction, as the only activity was reading of content. In 1993, we saw the entrance of the first clickable banner ad and by the next year online magazine Hotwired had begun to purchase huge numbers of banner ads. This was the first step towards shifting the market into a new digital age.

Web 1.0 then slowly progressed into Web 2.0. This is not a new version of Web 1.0; it is about enhancing how people use technology. People were no longer passively taking in information, but instead the internet became a sort of super-highway where users could directly interact with both other users and businesses, the collaborative potential enabling users to share, interact and communicate via rich media content such as Facebook, Instagram, YouTube, FaceTime, Skype and many more. In the early 2000s, supported by the capabilities of broadband and fibre optics, numerous networks and social platforms were developed. This finally enabled Web 2.0 to become truly social. Social media has now become a thriving entity.

In the 2000s and the 2010s, as digital marketing continued to get more sophisticated, it became recognised as an effective technology to enable and foster a relationship with more concisely targeted consumers. With this came the need to formulate a strategy specifically tailored to meet the demands of the internet audience. Digital marketing has changed drastically since its conception in the early 1990s and will continue to change.

Which Digital Marketing Strategy?

Although the term 'strategy' has been used in many different contexts, they are all synonymous in being described as the means to achieve a goal. One simple definition is that it is "a plan of action designed to achieve a long-term or overall aim" (Strauss & Frost, 2014, p. 72). In comparison to traditional strategy, e-business strategy is described as "the deployment of enterprise resources to capitalise on technologies for reaching specified objectives that ultimately improve performance and create sustainable competitive advantage" (Strauss & Frost, 2014). This is inclusive of information technology components such as the internet, digital data, databases, etc.

There are several tools that have been developed or adapted by marketers in their effort to integrate digital marketing strategy into their overall business strategy. Chaffey and Chadwick's generic digital marketing strategy development process (2006, 2012); Chaffey and Smith's 'SOSTAC© Planning Framework for e-Marketing' (2012); and Strauss and Frost's 'E-Marketing Plan' (2014) being amongst such theories. The foundation of these strategies is traditional marketing with common elements, such as; assessing the marketplace; defining objectives; selecting a strategic approach; implementing actions or activities; measuring results or performance (being comparable).

When considering the formulation of a strategic plan suitable for e-affinity marketing, first and foremost one has to examine the unique features inherent to affinity marketing. The review of generic and specific digital marketing strategies, as well as current best practice, can also aid the building of an e-affinity marketing strategy as it will undoubtedly unveil some of the most essential elements required in order to develop a robust digital marketing strategy. Therefore, highlights from some of the notable literature mentioned in the subject area are discussed below.

In a comprehensive study on internet marketing, Chaffey and Chadwick (2006) suggest that the internet marketing strategy should follow a similar form to the traditional strategic marketing planning process and should include: goal setting, situation review, strategy formulation and resource allocation and monitoring. The authors highlight that this plan should also take into consideration external and internal factors that could affect the organisation. In their discussion of digital marketing, the authors further outline three key steps that need to be followed: defining the online opportunity, selecting the strategic approach and delivering results online.

A similar concept was proposed in in the late 1990s by PR Smith, who developed a marketing planning system represented by SOSTAC©, which stands for situation, objectives, strategy, tactics, actions and control. This model was voted as the third most popular marketing model by the Chartered Institute of Marketing (CIM). This could be attributed to its simple, all-encompassing features. At a later date, in 2008, Chaffey and Smith proposed an overall strategy process model for strategic internet marketing - the SOSTAC© planning framework for digital marketing strategy development, which incorporated unique features and capabilities of the internet.

The environment, strategy and performance (ESP) model created by Strauss and Frost (2014) is an alternative approach to e-marketing strategy, which builds on the idea that businesses need a well formulated process on which to determine the success of their strategy. ESP is supported by key marketing tools such as the SWOT (strength, weakness, opportunity and threat), and e-marketing mix to create a comprehensive strategy.

Deviating from the process or plan orientated approaches described above, Ryan and Jones (2012) identified five key components that generally form the foundation of a digital marketing strategy as follows; knowing your business; knowing your competition; knowing the customer; knowing what you want to achieve and knowing how you are going to do it. The authors argue that this process "forces you to sit down and analyse the market in which you are operating in with a critical eye, and to really think about the different components of your business and how digital marketing can help you to achieve your business goal" (Ryan & Jones, 2012, p.23).

Another recent work with an alternative focus is Scott's (2013) investigation of the use of social media, in which he discusses the importance of setting a clear goal when building a digital marketing and PR plan. Here, the author places emphasis on a buyer orientated focus in the context of the organisational goals. Scott suggests that organisations should learn as much as they can about their buyers and segment them into groups identified by 'buyers' persona'. This, he notes, should be the first and single most important step that an organisation needs to take in creating a digital marketing plan. Scott also explained other components that need to be included in the overall planning, such as tactics for the implementation and measurement of the marketing effort and success.

What is clear from the review is that the digital marketing strategy must support and be integrated with the overall business and marketing plans. The review has also shown that there is no single common approach to building a digital marketing strategy, nor should there be one. But, there are essential elements that every marketing strategy must have. This should include (but not be exclusive to); setting digital goals or objectives; analysing the situation; knowing one's customer; setting the strategy and tactics by which to execute it and having a control mechanism for evaluating performance. To the same effect, one must design a strategy or plan that is well structured and comprehensive in the context of the specified sector. With an informative overview of the key components required to build a digital marketing strategy, let us now turn to the context in which we want to develop it for – affinity marketing.

2. AFFINITY MARKETING AND DIGITAL MARKETING

Affinity marketing is widely recognised as a scheme that:

Involves customers who already have sympathy to one brand (be it commercial, not-for-profit or another membership organisation) being sold another service, by another organisation, with the endorsement of the affinity organisation and using its channels of communication. (Mintel, 2000)

Considering how affinity marketing fits within the broader field of services marketing, while most of the studies to date placed it within the context of relationship marketing, associations of the topic have also been made with cause-related marketing. The first time affinity marketing appeared in association with cause-related marketing was in Varadarajan and Menon's (1988) work on the concepts of cause-related marketing. In this work, the authors described affinity marketing as an extreme type of highly targeted cause-related marketing. Varadarajan and Menon (1988) defined cause-related marketing as:

The process of formulating and implementing marketing activities that are characterised by an offer from the firm to contribute a specified amount to a designated cause when customers engage in revenue-providing exchanges that satisfy organisational and individual objectives. (Varadarajan & Menon, 1988, p. 123)

Similarly, Macchiette and Roy (1992) suggested in their study of affinity marketing that the revenue generated by affinity could be seen as cause-related marketing. Soon after, in Schlegelmilch and Woodruffe's (1995) comparative analysis of the affinity card markets (the most popular affinity marketing scheme in the USA and the UK) it was suggested that affinity credit cards fit with cause-related marketing because a firm (the card issuing service provider) uses an association with a designated cause (for example a charity) to market its product or service. Another view that follows the same line of discussion is Worthington and Horne's (1992) proposal that affinity marketing is a sub-set of cause-related marketing, representing a step-change in the nature and intensity of the triadic relationship between the commercial and non-profit partners and consumers. Both cause-related marketing and affinity marketing are premised on the idea that linking specific products to a credible and respected cause or non-profit organisation (in return for a contribution to that cause or organisation) will make the product offering more attractive to consumers (Ross et al, 1992).

Currently, there is growing interest in the use of cause-related marketing as a corporate communication strategy in encouraging sales and as a tool for competitive differentiation (Bigné et al., 2012). Therefore, due to their similarity, equal interest could be expected for affinity marketing. Moreover, one should also note that the role of information communication technology in philanthropy is growing. There is a new culture of generosity, for instance in the UK, between 2007 and 2008 online donations almost doubled, rising from 4% to 7% of UK wide giving (Honoré, 2011). In light of the role of technology and the 'big opportunity' presented through affinity marketing, this section starts with an in-depth review of affinity marketing, highlighting the key principles underpinning its foundation. It then explores how this could be utilised to formulate 'objectives for e-affinity marketing'.

Affinity Marketing: The 'BIG' Opportunity

The first significant academic perspective of affinity marketing was offered by Macchiette and Roy (1992), who described it as a blending of affinity and existing marketing concepts. Affinity, they suggest, is "an individual level of cohesiveness, social bonding, identification and conformity to the norms and standards of a particular reference group" (p.48), while the marketing concept focuses on the "expectation of benefit for the individual, satisfying consumer wants and needs" (p.48). Therefore, the main component in affinity marketing is the customer/affinity group relationship, upon which the affinity marketing scheme is leveraged. Affinity marketing is therefore based upon a strategic partnership between complementary brands, in which a mutually beneficial triadic relationship is formed between the group, the members of the group and the service provider of the product being used for marketing purposes.

There were several organisations linked to affinity marketing schemes. For example, work related organisations, charities, educational institutes and leisure clubs could all be linked to such a scheme. It is worth noting that different types of affinity groups are likely to exhibit differing types of relationships (Worthington, 2001; Laing et al., 2004). This is suggestive that each type of group is influenced by different sets of values that could potentially affect an individual's decision making process with regards to an affinity product. Popular industries that utilise affinity schemes include financial services (often related to the issuance of credit cards), insurance, communications, travel and tourism.

In examining affinity relationships and related schemes, one also needs to be aware that strength of these relationships may vary. Consequently the strength may influence customers' decision making processes and levels of engagement with the affinity group and associated partners, be it offline or online. In addition, the nature of the customer - service provider relationship needs to be taken in to consideration in order to get a full picture of the triadic relationship. This will enable us to gauge why and how the relationship developed, the extent to which the affinity group affects the relationship and how this could aid in the development of a digital strategy.

As previously noted, the affinity marketing partnership (described as a triadic relationship) is based on Macchiette and Roy's (1992) 'affinity interaction model'. The model depicts the triadic relationship formed between the consumer, the affinity group and the commercial organisation. Varied adaptations of the triadic relationship have since been proposed (Mekonnen, 2012, Worthington. 1997). In a triadic relationship it is assumed that a long-term ongoing relationship is formed. Moreover, it is believed that value is created to all partners involved in the triad, provided the relationships are managed well (Worthington, 2001). The triadic relationship provides tangible and non-tangible benefits to all the partners involved (i.e. the customer, the affinity group and the service provider). A summary of these benefits are illustrated in Figure 1.

Figure 1. Triadic relationship and associated benefits: The case of affinity credit cards
Key: T- Tangible benefit NT- Non-tangible benefit

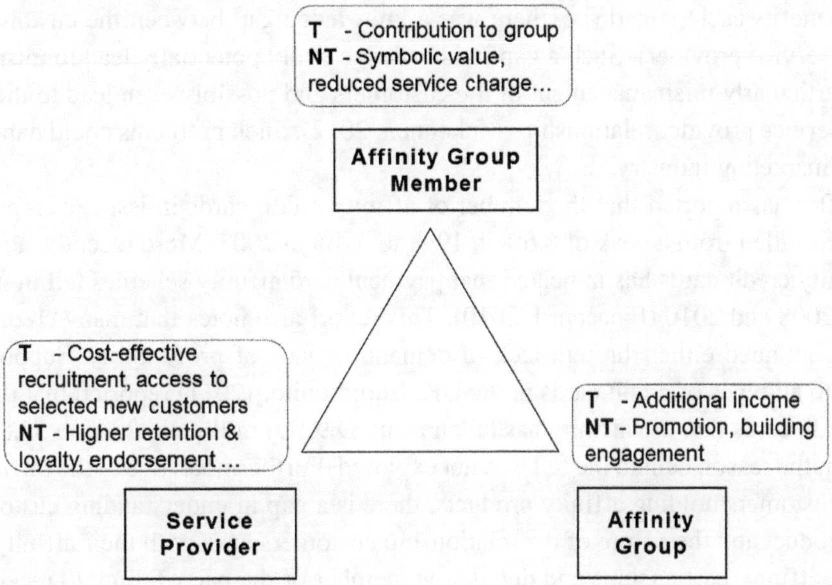

Utilising the concept of affinity marketing, affinity credit cards provided the main focal point for affinity schemes, especially in the early days of the development and growth of affinity marketing. Consequently, most of the literature on the subject is based on affinity credit cards. Affinity cards were also the earliest adopted and have been perhaps one of the most successful affinity products. Therefore some of the examples in this chapter may draw on affinity credit cards to demonstrate key concepts in relation to digital marketing

Affinity credit cards are like conventional credit cards for the most part, except that they are affiliated to particular affinity groups and it is therefore presumed that they are taken out by people with common interests. Usually, an affinity credit card will display the logo of the particular affinity group, along with the name of the service provider and the card scheme mark (Visa or MasterCard). The key difference between the affinity credit card and the generic bank card is that when a member or supporter of the affinity group signs up for the card, a payment is made by the affinity credit card service provider to the affinity group. Most affinity credit card agreements include both an initial donation from the service provider to the affinity partner (ranging from £5 to £10 per card issued) and an ongoing turnover related payment (usually around 20p to 25p per £100 spent on the card). The USA is the leader of affinity marketing and can often serve as a useful indicator for the UK market. A recent report on credit cards conducted by the USA's Government of Accountability Office (GAO, 2014) indicated that the University of California received about $1.5 million through its agreement with FIA card services, the largest payment to an institute of higher education in 2012. The University of Cambridge, whose alumni affinity credit card launched in 1993, had 10,000 card holders by 1999 and had generated over £250,000 for the university by that date (Mintel, 2000). Thus, there is undoubtedly a 'big opportunity' to raise funds and promote the standing of an organisation or a cause through affinity marketing.

Affinity Marketing Challenges

Looking at the affinity card industry in particular, despite sounding like the ideal partnership, the decline in the number of charity credit cards available is a sure sign that these partnerships have encountered some problems. Horne et al. (2000) have shown that there was a gap in how the affinity partners understood the benefits each gained (i.e. there was a knowledge gap between the customer, the affinity group and the service provider). Such a gap in knowledge could potentially lead to mismanagement of the scheme, particularly mismanagement of the customers and possibly even lead to the dissolution of the customer-service provider relationship (Mekonnen, 2012). Such problems could hamper the growth of the affinity marketing industry.

Mintel (2004) has reported that the number of affinity credit cards in issue, as a proportion of all credit cards, has fallen from a peak of 8.6% in 1998 to 3.4% in 2003. More recently, a market research report on affinity credit cards has indicated that payment card affinity schemes fell in number by over 25% between 2008 and 2010 (Finaccord, 2010). This report also notes that many credit card schemes have been discontinued either through lack of demand or lack of profitability. Supporting this, in a study relating to all types of credit cards in the UK, Euromonitor (2011) reported that the total number of personal credit cards that use affinity has fallen from 69,927.4 million in 2005 to 55,894.3 million in 2010. However, the reason behind the fall was not explored. Furthermore, due to the difficulty in obtaining access to customers holding affinity products, there is a gap in understanding customers' attitudes towards this product and the nature of the relationship customers have with their affinity groups. More often than not, affinity partnerships end due to one member of the party failing to receive comparable benefits to the other (Bumell, 2013). A recent example of this can be seen in the demise of the Lloyds Banking Group's partnerships with charities such as Cancer Research UK, the NSPCC and the Scottish SPCA. In the case of Cancer Research UK, Lloyds ceased offering their charity credit card in 2012 after a 23-year partnership which raised a total of £14.5 million for the charity (Howard, 2012).

There is no known study to date that explains why the growth of affinity marketing schemes has stagnated, or any that have considered why there is limited integration of affinity marketing in the digital landscape. Yet the coupling of these two areas has huge potential in capturing a unique market. Having reviewed alternative digital strategies for business and the core concepts of affinity marketing, let's now turn to the setting of a plan for e-affinity marketing in the 21st Century.

3. STRATEGIC INTEGRATION

This strategic integration identifies the key steps required for planning a digital marketing strategy for affinity marketing. The 'E-Affinity Marketing Planning Process' presented in Figure 2 illustrates the step-by-step process for creating an e-affinity marketing plan. Each step is not necessarily conducted in isolation and there is likely to be an iterative process of back and forth to fine-tune essential elements that need to be reviewed within each step.

Setting E-affinity Marketing Objective

One main area highlighted in relation to planning a digital marketing strategy is the need to clearly identify the goal or objective desired from the digital channel. It is important that organisations build on

Figure 2. E-Affinity Marketing Planning Process

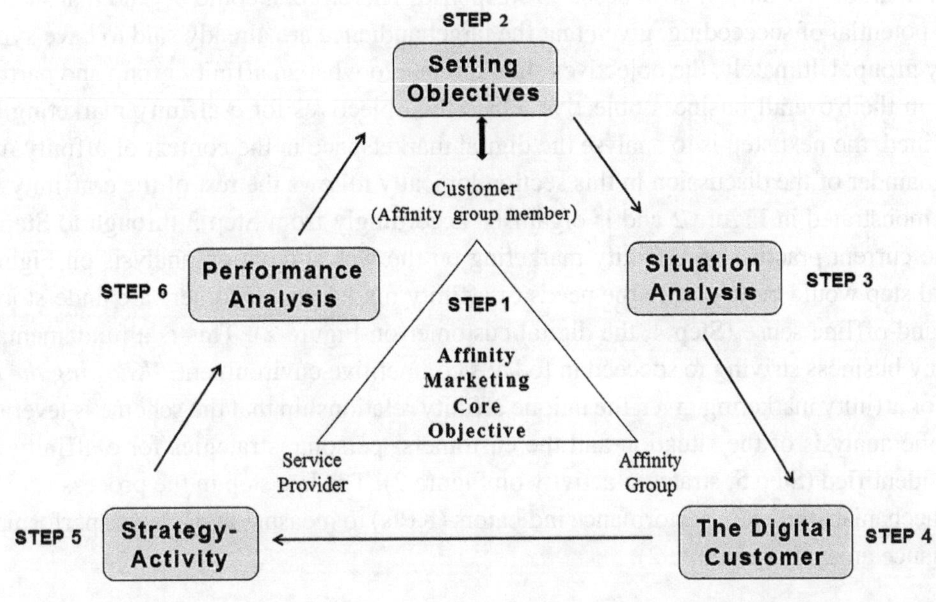

their overarching objectives in the advent of digital integration. Likewise, affinity marketing schemes should follow the same ethos, as it is an extension of the channel or means by which the organisation reaches customers. Therefore, to help create objectives for e-affinity marketing, the recommendation is to initially evaluate the core values related to the scheme and then consider how this can be enhanced or achieved via digital channels. Informed by knowledge of the core objective, the next step in the process is setting e-affinity marketing objectives (Step 2).

A review of digital marketing strategies to date indicates that most of the e-marketing planning tools proposed begin with an evaluation of the environment before commencing with the designated steps. However, given the nature of affinity relationships and the overarching aims and principles underpinning affinity marketing, this paper opted to diverge from this approach as it was felt necessary that the digital objectives for e-affinity marketing should be defined from the outset.

In the SOSTAC© model for digital planning, the objective is denoted by the statement "Where do we want to be?" It is further noted that the model can be used to identify what a business wants to achieve through online channels, as well as to question what the benefits might be (Chaffey & Smith, 2008). This model is encompassed by five broad benefits of, reasons for or objectives of e-marketing: 1) to grow sales 2) to add value 3) to get closer to customers 4) to save costs and 5) to extend the brand online. What is striking about these objectives is that most of it is already aligned with the principles and aims underpinning affinity marketing.

In digital marketing, there are a number of different objectives that can be set; for example, lead generation, acquisition, engagement or retention. In previous studies it has been proposed that an *explorer* could be converted to a *supporter* – thereby strengthening the customer-affinity group relationship as well as the customer-service provider relationship (Mekonnen, 2012). Therefore, if one was to consider a charity group seeking to raise more donations through long-term commitment, one objective could be to convert x% of its episodic donors or members on the newsletter mailing list to the affinity credit card scheme by July 2016. As shown by Mintel's 2000 report, customer acquisition through affinity-based direct mail communication to a 'warm' audience may yield a 6% to 7% response, whereas direct mail into the mass 'cold' market may only yield at best a 1% response. Therefore, it could be said that such a strategy has a high potential of succeeding, given that the target audience are already said to have sympathy for the affinity group. Ultimately, the objectives should relate to what an affinity group and partner aspires to achieve in their overall business objective. Once the objectives for e-affinity marketing have been clearly defined, the next step is to analyse the digital marketspace in the context of affinity marketing.

The remainder of the discussion in this section logically follows the rest of the e-affinity marketing process demonstrated in Figure 2 and is organised accordingly from Step 3 through to Step 6. Step 3 reviews the current practice of 'Affinity marketing on the web' (situation analysis on Figure 2). The next logical step would be to ensure the needs of affinity marketing customers are understood, in both an online and offline sense (Step 4, the digital customer on Figure 2). This is a fundamental requirement for any business striving to succeed in today's competitive environment. *'Knowing the customer'* is crucial for affinity marketing given the unique affinity relationship that the scheme is leveraged upon. Based on the analysis of the situation and the customers' persona, strategies for e-affinity marketing need to be identified (Step 5, strategic-activity on Figure 2). The last step in the process is to formulate a control mechanism with key performance indicators (KPIs) to measure and analyse performance (Step 6, performance analysis on Figure 2).

Affinity Marketing on the Web

The situation analysis (Step 3 of the process in Figure 2) should provide an overview of your organisation (who you are, what you do and how you interact and trade online) by addressing internal and external factors impacting on the business. For e-marketing, it is suggested that this analysis should include growth in users, changes in the market place as well as examples of good and bad e-marketing practices (Chaffey & Smith, 2013 and Strauss & Frost, 2014). Extending this, in the context of e-affinity marketing analysis an assessment of members or supporters' engagement with the group via the web should also be included.

It is important to have an honest and realistic baseline of your current capabilities and activities in order to define a meaningful digital marketing plan for the future. In order to analyse the situation in the first instance, affinity partners (in particular the affinity groups) should consider encompassing the following areas and answering related questions:

1. **Identification of the Digital Customer:** The affinity group needs to know who the digital customers are (with a demographics breakdown), how they interact with the brand, and what platform(s) they use.
2. **SWOT Analysis:** What are the strengths, weaknesses, opportunities and threats of digital integration in relation to the affinity scheme to the organisation as a whole. This should be inclusive of the affinity groups internal capabilities, skills and knowledge with respect to digital marketing.
3. **Competitor Analysis:** The affinity group should identify its competitors and assess how they compete. In terms of added value, to what extent have competitors incorporated an affinity scheme? Competitors overall product offering (i.e. inclusive of price, customer service, and their key differentiators). Furthermore, affinity groups should take this opportunity to assess their competitive position with respect to digital marketing in the industry they operate in and in relation to their close competitors.
4. **Digital Channels Analysis:** The affinity group should list the various digital channels used and success of each in different areas of the organisation. In other words the affinity groups should be able to assess the scope, depth and effectiveness of their current digital marketing activities across the range of digital channels.

Currently it is apparent that the main presence of affinity marketing on the web is on the affinity groups website. This could be attributed to the complicated nature of the triadic relationship and due to the fact that the initial contact with the affinity group members or supporters is often made via the affinity group. However, once the customer sign up to the affinity scheme, the affinity product provider is primarily in charge of the relationship, and subsequently the one that has regular contact with the member with regards to the scheme.

Taking the above into consideration, following on the affinity credit card theme, the author investigated the presence of the affinity marketing scheme on the websites of affinity groups. Past studies have shown charity, sports, and university affinity groups to be amongst the most popular ones from the array of affinity groups at present (Mintel, 2000 and Mekonnen et al., 2008). Therefore, the websites of 10-15 affinity groups within each of the above category were investigated to evaluate the current situation. Visibility and activity of each group in relation to the prominence of the scheme in the homepage as well as related sub-pages were examined.

An e-commerce presence map is one way of identifying presence in the context of the website, email, social media and offline media, with presence identified on different platforms including the traditional desktop, tablet, and mobile (Laudon & Traver, 2013). Activities one should look for when evaluating presence should include search, display, newsletter, conversation, engagement and sharing. Ideally an extensive investigation of all of the above would be recommended, but in this case the author had already uncovered that current digital integration of affinity marketing to be minimal. Therefore, the information the researcher was able to unearth was limited.

The key findings from the investigation into affinity scheme presence on the web include the following:

1. In extreme cases there were affinity groups with a robust website dedicated to the main function, but they did not have a page on their website for the affinity schemes which they are participating in offline. Therefore, in these cases no further investigation could be conducted.
2. With the affinity groups who had their affinity scheme represented on the website, at the time the investigation was conducted, with the exception of a few the affinity schemes were not visible at all on the homepage. In a few of the cases where it appeared on the homepage, it was only visible as a side banner ad.
3. Where the affinity groups had incorporated the affinity scheme in their website, it was noted that there was no link associated to the scheme on the homepage. This suggests that affinity schemes may not be ranked highly in terms of the organisation's priority for digital integration.
4. In most cases it is evident that unless a potential digital customer actively searches for the affinity scheme, with existing knowledge the scheme, there was not much chance of the customer finding out about the scheme whilst navigating through the homepage. For the most part, there does not appear to be any consistency as to how the affinity groups are leading potential customers to the site dedicated to the affinity scheme. Out of the three categories investigated, universities appear to have adopted a relatively similar step for customers to reach the site dedicated to the affinity scheme. They all appear to lead their members or supporter to the page hosting the affinity scheme via the alumni page, for which the link is often visible on the homepage.
5. Once customers reach the page related to the affinity scheme, if they wish to proceed with signing up for the scheme, they will then be directed to the partner's (affinity product provider) website to complete the registration.

On the whole, all the affinity groups investigated appear to have the technological capability to fully integrate the affinity scheme as part of their digital activities, as can be evidenced by the depth of the activities they have integrated for some of the functions relating to the organisation's main offerings. For example, the University of Cambridge's magazine page gives visitors several opportunities to interact, e.g. play crosswords, download the magazine, link to the CAM reader app, etc. In comparison, the page related to the affinity scheme only has general information and a link to the service provider. Generally speaking, there is no indication to show that the same level of effort is exerted for affinity schemes. For many of the affinity groups, although the affinity scheme may not be their main priority in relation to their overarching business objective, if harnessed it has the potential to add value to the customers experience and consequently build a long-term relationship for all parties involved.

Knowing Your Customer

Once the overarching e-affinity marketing objective has been derived from the core values underpinning affinity marketing (Step 1 and 2) and the situation analysed (Step 3), the affinity groups needs to focus on their customer (Step 4) and work towards an appropriate digital strategy that meets customer's demands.

Identification of digital customers in situation analysis looked at a more generic set of information exploring their demographic breakdown, how they interact with the brand, and what platform(s) they use However, here the emphasis is to extend this knowledge and get a deeper understanding of customers' value in relation to their affinity relationship and the affinity scheme, with a view towards building a persona for the digital customer. A better understanding of how affinity group members or supporters perceive their group's unique qualities, social status and size may provide a way of assessing the strength of their 'affinity', therefore analysing their receptivity to affinity marketing. When an organisation considers the design of their site, they need to understand the differing mind sets of the visitors in order to reach them by building an effective content strategy (Scott, 2013). Scott demonstrates this point by explaining how a college website could have multiple goals such as: 1) Keeping alumni happy so that they donate money to their Alma matter (differentiating between the young and the older alumni), 2) Recruiting students (with sites that need to be tailored for both high school students who may be considering the college as well as the parents reviewing the college, with different information needs), 3) keeping current students happy. In total, five groups are identified here. By understanding the persona of these five groups, the college can create appropriate content to cater for each set of visitors. Similarly, when considering creating of an effective e-affinity marketing site, affinity groups needs to first understand the behaviour of each group of customers that are likely to visit the site.

With e-affinity marketing the affinity group can start by segmenting potential customers based on existing knowledge of the characteristics exhibited by members of the affinity group. For instance, three types of affinity marketing customers - *communicators, supporters* and *explorers* were identified in a recent study related to understanding their relationship with affinity marketing (Mekonnen, 2012). Explorers were primarily driven by opportunities in the marketplace (benefit sought: individual-functional). For communicators, conveying their profession as part of their identity was a strong influencing factor when considering an affinity scheme such as an affinity credit card. For supporters, the functional benefits (donations) were the main reason for acquiring the affinity product. With this knowledge in mind, for example, a professional group's website could place emphasis on the symbolic value of the affinity product on the page dedicated to the affinity scheme. Furthermore, the group could also promote the symbolic value of the scheme on its homepage as one of its online value propositions.

It is also important to recognise that the strength of relationships varies and customers with different strength of relationships (for instance high, medium or low) will require different levels of engagement. Once the organisation has a clear picture of its potential e-affinity marketing customers, it then needs to plan its digital strategy with these groups in mind. Subsequently, the marketing channels used, message, content, layout and structure, as well as wording and language intended to describe what the affinity group provides, should be guided by the defined persona (Scott, 2013).

Strategy to Activity

Having recognised the 'big opportunity', defined digital objectives in line with the organisation's core values and objectives (Step 1 and 2), conducted a situation analysis to assess the affinity scheme's presence on the web (Step 3) and defined the digital audience in relation to the affinity scheme (Step 4), the next step in the process is to set out a strategy and set of related activities (Step 5). This should be formulated to enable the affinity marketing partners to fulfil the objectives set.

Affinity partners should consider the following three steps in setting and implementing the strategy:

1. Initially, affinity partners need to clearly specify what they want to achieve. Strategy is the long-term vision and should be set for a defined period. There should also be an approved budget allocation. For example (continuing on the theme of the affinity credit card), if we revisit the example used in Step 2, if the objective is 'to convert x% of the members on the mailing list for newsletter to the affinity credit card scheme by July 2016', the strategy could be to send periodic communication to the target audience, from the mailing list. In this strategy the affinity group should strive to understand the existing customer database and learn how it interacts with the website. In addition the strategy should also question how the affinity group is currently communicating with its existing customer database?
2. The next step is the tactic. Tactics are the detailed plans to implement the strategy and tend to be short-term and flexible (Chaffey & Smith, 2012 and Strauss & Frost, 2013). Continuing on the theme of the affinity card example from Point 1 above, at this stage the affinity group can determine the exact online activities or communication channels suitable for each target identified. Furthermore, decision regarding the content and frequency of the communication can also be taken.
3. In the final stage the partners need to specify how each activity will be managed. Given the complexity of the scheme, partners may have different objectives and levels of responsibility at different stages in the relationship. This includes everything from the promotion, to the sales and on to the maintenance of the scheme. This is evident if we look at the nature of the triadic relationship demonstrated by the infographic diagram (Figure 1), which indicates the variety of benefits to be gained by each partner. The process of building the affinity scheme also demonstrates different levels of responsibility. For instance, whilst the introductory and initiation of customers often falls upon the affinity group, the signing up of customers is the affinity product provider's responsibility.

Earlier studies have already indicated that there has been a gap in how the affinity partners understood the benefits each gained by each (Horne et al., 2000). Mintel (2004) has also reported how the complex nature of triadic relationship might lead to a problem in relation to how the customers are managed. Technically, the affinity groups might feel that they should have a say in the relationship, since it is assumed that the customer will be a member or supporter of their organisation. Besides, it is assumed that the affinity group would obviously have been the host group that provided the service provider with details of the customers' names and addresses in the first instance. However, in reality it generally tends to be the service provider that takes control of the customer relationship in affinity marketing schemes. For example, with affinity credit cards, the service providers know who the card holders are, they speak or communicate with them regularly via email and the monthly statement; ultimately, they provide the customer service to their card holders. Moreover, due to data protection requirements, the affinity groups were not even always told which of their members have actually arranged a financial product via the scheme (Mintel, 2004). Therefore, when devising and implementing the e-affinity marketing strategy it is critical that both partners are involved in the design, management and maintenance of each tactical e-tool, as both will benefit if the site is fully optimised.

Performance and Analysis

The final step in the process of strategic integration is 'performance and analysis' (Step 6, Figure 2). This is designed to measure and analyse the performance of the website in order to determine the success of the strategies and the plans. As the result is intended help future developments of the site, this is indicated as an iterative process with the final arrow pointing back to e-affinity marketing objectives.

Performance analysis is primarily led by the objectives set at the outset, with the help of web analytics. Web analytics is the measurement, collection, analysis and reporting of the internet data for purposes of understanding and optimising web usage (Web Analytics Association WWW, 2008, p.3). Analytics is not just a tool for measuring web traffic, but can be used as a tool for business and market research, and to assess and improve the effectiveness of a website. The partners involved in the triadic relationship should be able to measure, monitor and review their e-affinity marketing campaign, updating and modifying elements as required.

Often the objectives set at the beginning should guide the identification of KPI at the start of the process. Other areas that need to be considered are the frequency of reporting and the analysis of performance, questioning why it is happening. Furthermore given the complex nature of the triadic relationship partners should also determine who measures what and reports to whom and finally who takes appropriate actions arising (what should be done about it). As with the previous step (strategies – activities) this is another area where the responsibilities and terms performance and analysis need to be clearly defined and agreed between the affinity scheme partners.

CONCLUSION

This paper was inspired by the dearth of literature and lack of practical guide on optimising affinity marketing schemes through digital integration. There is no known study to data that explains why the growth of affinity marketing scheme has stagnated or one that looks at why there is limited integration of the scheme in the digital landscape. Yet the coupling of these two areas has huge potential in capturing a unique market. The Internet is an ideal platform to target and engage customers, consequently encouraging a long term relationship. Moreover it has been shown that the role of information communication technology in philanthropy is growing, with donation via the internet nearly doubling between 2007 and 2008 (Honoré, 2011).

This paper proposes a strategic integration plan which identifies six key steps required for planning a digital marketing strategy for affinity marketing, 'E-Affinity Marketing Planning Process'. Initially, the core values related to the scheme needs to be evaluated (Step 1) as this will enable clear and concise e-affinity marketing objectives to be set (Step 2). Then the current situation or current practice of affinity marketing on the web needs to be reviewed (Step 3). The next step is to understand affinity marketing customers' persona (Step 4). Knowing the customer is fundamental for any business striving to succeed in today's competitive environment. Following this based on the situation analysis and the customers' persona, strategies and activities for e-affinity marketing need to be identified (Step 5). Finally the last step in the process is to formulate a control mechanism with KPIs to measure and analyse the performance of the scheme (Step 6).

On the whole all the affinity groups investigated appear to have the technology capability to successfully integrate affinity scheme as part of their digital activities, as evident by the depth of the activities they have integrated for some of the functions relating to the organisations main offerings. But the activities supporting the affinity scheme appears to be limited. Thus it is apparent that affinity groups are not exerting the same level of effort on their affinity schemes digitally as they are doing so in other areas of their website. There may be a number of factors contributing to the lack of the schemes presence on the web. For instance lack of digital collaboration between the affinity partners and not having a clearly defined responsibility with regards to the management of the scheme online could be possible reasons worth exploring.

Knowledge and understanding of customer is an asset for any organisation for better segmenting and management. As Scott (2013) has suggested, if organisations can segment their customers into distinct groups then it makes it easier to create content targeted to each group identified. As it stands the affinity scheme sites investigated did not exhibit segmentation or targeting. Yet there are some known characteristics associated with affinity marketing customers (Laing et al., 2004, Mekonnen, 2012; Worhington, 2001). For instance the typologies identified as 'explorer', 'communicator' and 'supporter' can give good insight as to what affinity marketing customers associated with a professional or a charity group would expect from an affinity scheme such as an affinity credit card. Such knowledge could be used as a starting point when formulating personas for e-affinity marketing customers in different sectors.

It is undeniable that all partners involved in the triadic relationship could benefit given that the digital integration is implemented and managed correctly. Specifying clear strategies guided by the digital objectives aligned with the core values underpinning affinity marketing is crucial to the success of the scheme. The strategy then needs to be implemented and executed properly with tactics formulated that takes into consideration partners responsibility. In the past affinity marketing schemes had faced some challenges with regards to customer ownership and responsibility. This needs to be clarified as failure to do so could impair successful digital integration. Whilst the initial engagement of the customers may primarily fall under the affinity group, management of the scheme is often undertaken by the affinity scheme service provider. With regards to converging and conflicting interests relating to customer ownership the affinity group and the affinity service provider should have an agreement in place as to how to manage the customers in the event where the terms of the partnership have to be altered or if the partnership has to end. This is strongly tied with good communication, sharing information, and collaborative working without compromising customers' confidentiality. Affinity partners' efforts in promoting the scheme to customers need to be aligned. Without breaching confidentiality, a possible plan of action for the service provider could be to collaborate with the affinity group in providing periodic updates to the customers. From the customers' perspective, lack of informative continuous communication could lead to relationship weakening (Mekonnen, 2012). This relates to communication during the periods when the customer-service provider relationship was stable as well as during the process of dissolution (Mekonnen, 2012). To avoid such pitfall the digital integration of affinity scheme, needs to ensure that there is a schedule or plan in place to harness communication online. Furthermore affinity partners need to understand the nature of communication desired by different segments.

Through performance analysis continuous improvement and sustainable growth could be achieved. Web analytics will bring this to life. The right KPI need to be set for this to be effective. Affinity marketing on the web has been explored to a degree but for the most part an untapped area.

REFERENCES

Aghaei, S., Nematbakhsh, A. N., & Farsani, H. K. (2012). Evolution of the World Wide Web: From Web 1.0 to Web 4.0. *International Journal of Web & Semantic Technology*, *3*(1), 1–10. doi:10.5121/ijwest.2012.3101

Bigné-Alcañiz, E., Currás-Pérez, R., Ruiz-Mafé, C., & Sanz-Blas, S. (2012). Cause-related marketing influence on consumer responses: The Moderating effect of Cause-brand fit. *Journal of Marketing Communications*, *18*(4), 265–283. doi:10.1080/13527266.2010.521358

Bughin, J. (2013). Brand success in the era of digital Darwinism. *Journal of Brand Strategy*, *2*(4), 355–365.

Bumell, P. (2013). What happened to charity credit cards? *News archive*. Retrieved from http://www.affinitymarketing.co.uk

Chaffey, D., Ellis-Chadwick, F., Johnson, K., & Mayer, R. (2006). *Internet Marketing Strategy, Implementation and Practice* (3rd ed.). Harlow, UK: Prentice Hall FT.

Chaffey, D., Ellis-Chadwick, F., Johnson, K., & Mayer, R. (2012). *Internet Marketing Strategy, Implementation and Practice* (5th ed.). Harlow, UK: Prentice Hall FT.

Chaffey, D., & Smith, P. R. (2008). *EMarketing Excellence Planning and optimizing your digital marketing* (3rd ed.). London, UK: Elsevier.

Chaffey, D., & Smith, P. R. (2013). *EMarketing Excellence Planning and optimizing your digital marketing* (4th ed.). New York, NY: Routledge.

Dorie, C. (2012). The End of the Expert: Why no one in marketing knows what they are doing. *Forbes News archive*. Retrieved from http://www.forbes.com

Euromonitor International. (2011, March). Global Market Information Database GMID - Country Sector Briefing – credit cards London, UK.

Finaccord. (2010). *Affinity and Partnership Marketing in UK Payment Cards and Consumer Finance*. London: UK. April 2010

Gartner. (2013). *Gartner Survey Shows U.S. Digital Marketing Budgets Average 2.5 Percent of Company Revenue*, Stamford, CT, USA. Retrieved from http://www.gartner.com/newsroom/archive/

Honoré E. (2011). *The role of Information Communication Technology in Philanthropy*, Centre of charitable giving and philanthropy NCVO/CAF.

Horne, S., Naudé, P., & Worthington, S. (2000). Knowledge Gaps between Participants in a Triadic Relationship. *International Journal of Bank Marketing*, *18*(6), 287–293. doi:10.1108/02652320010358706

Howard, B. (2012, January 28). Cancer charity loses out as bank ends credit card deal. BBC News – Business. London, UK.

Husted, S. W., & Whitehouse, F. R. Jr. (2002). Cause-Related Marketing via the World Wide Web: A Relationship Marketing Strategy. *Journal of Nonprofit & Public Sector Marketing*, *10*(1), 3–22. doi:10.1300/J054v10n01_02

International Advertising Bureau IBA. (2014). Advertising Revenue Report HY 2014 DOC.

Laing, A., Harris, F., & Mekonnen, A. (2004). Deconstructing affinity relationships: Consumers and affinity marketing. *Journal of Customer Behaviour*, *3*(2), 215–228. doi:10.1362/1475392041829500

Laudon, K., & Travis, C. (2013). *E-Commerce 2013: Global Edition* (9th ed.). Harlow, UK: Pearson Education.

Macchiette, B., & Roy, A. (1992). Affinity Marketing: What is it and How does it Work? *Journal of Services Marketing*, *6*(3), 47–67. doi:10.1108/08876049210035935

Mekonnen, A. (2012). *Customer-service provider relationship dissolution: the case of affinity marketing*. Thesis ((Doctoral dissertation). Open University, UK. Available from ProQuest Dissertations and Theses database. (U581639)

Mekonnen, A., Harris, F., & Laing, A. (2008). Linking products to a cause or affinity group: Does this really make them more attractive to consumers? *European Journal of Marketing*, *42*(1/2), 135–153. doi:10.1108/03090560810840943

Mintel. (2000). *Affinity and Store Cards October 2000*. London, UK Mintel.

Mintel. (2004). *Affinity Marketing UK 2004*. London, UK: Mintel.

Porter, M. E. (2001). Strategy and the Internet. *Harvard Business Review*, *79*(3), 62–78. PMID:11246925

Ross, J. K., Patterson, L., & Stutts, M. A. (1992). Consumer Perceptions of Organisations that Use Cause-Related Marketing. *Journal of the Academy of Marketing Science*, *20*(1), 93–97. doi:10.1007/BF02723480

Ryan, D., & Jones, C. (2012). *Understanding Digital Marketing* (2nd ed.). London, UK: Kogan Page.

Sanou, B. (2014). *ICT Facts and Figures, International Telecommunication Union (ICT)*. Publication.

Schlegelmilch, B. B., & Woodruffe, H. (1995). A comparative analysis of the affinity card market in the USA and the UK. *International Journal of Bank Marketing*, *13*(5), 12–23. doi:10.1108/02652329510092176

Schultz, D.E., (1996, December 18). Integration and the Internet. *Marketing News*, No. 12.

Scott, D. M. (2011). *The New Rules of Marketing & PR*. Hoboken, NJ: Wiley.

Storbacka, K., Strandvik, T., & Grönroos, C. (1994). Managing Customer Relationships for Profit: The Dynamics of Relationship Quality. *International Journal of Service Industry Management*, *5*(5), 21–38. doi:10.1108/09564239410074358

Strauss, J., & Frost, R. (2014). *E-marketing* (6th ed.). New Jersey: Pearson Education Limited.

United States Government Accountability Office. (2014). CREDIT CARDS: Marketing to College Students Appears to Have Declined (GAO-14-225).

Varadarajan, P., & Menon, A. (1988). Cause-Related Marketing: A Coalignment of Marketing Strategy and Corporate Philanthropy. *Journal of Marketing*, *52*(3), 58–74. doi:10.2307/1251450

Vela-McConnell, J. A. (1999). *Who is my neighbour?: Social affinity in a modern world*. Albany, NY: New York Press.

Web Analytics Association (2008), *Web Analytics Definitions*. Draft for Public Comment, September 22nd 2008.

Worthington, S. (1997). Affinity Credit Card Issuers and their Relationship with their Alumni Affinity Group Partners. *International Journal of Bank Marketing*, *15*(2), 39–47. doi:10.1108/02652329710160448

Worthington, S. (2001). Affinity credit cards: A critical review. *International Journal of Retail & Distribution Management*, *29*(11), 485–512. doi:10.1108/EUM0000000006174

Worthington, S., & Horne, S. (1992). Affinity Credit Cards in the United Kingdom – Card Issuer Strategies and Affinity Group Aspirations. *International Journal of Bank Marketing*, *10*(7), 3–10. doi:10.1108/02652329210021113

KEY TERMS AND DEFINITIONS

Affinity Relationship: A relationship built on the notion of cohesiveness, bonding, liking, identification and related concepts.

Affinity Scheme: A way of adding value through differentiation by designing a product that is of interest to members, employees and supporters of the said affinity group.

Cause-Related Marketing: A marketing activity where by a product is linked to a cause or non-profit organisation in return for a contribution to that cause or organisation and to make the product offering more attractive to consumers.

Digital Integration: In the context of marketing, this refers to integrating online efforts and aligning it with overall business objective.

E-Affinity Marketing: Refers to the promotion and sales of products endorsed by affinity groups through the internet.

Chapter 2
Analysing the Role of Social Media in Dialogue Marketing and Management as a Contemporary Franchising Local Area Marketing Technique

Geoffrey B. Webster
Central Queensland University, Australia

Margee Hume
Central Queensland University, Australia

ABSTRACT

The role of social media as a contemporary Local Area Marketing (LAM) technique in Dialogue Marketing is not clearly defined. Dialogue Marketing focuses on a structured approach of ongoing interactive communication to form relationships with people (Allan Steinmetz, 1997). According to Webster and Hume (2015) contemporary LAM techniques refer to using digital marketing to build relationships with local community. Problems facing franchise businesses include how to use Dialogue Marketing as a contemporary LAM technique to maximise local community connections as well as to build essential relationships. Advancing previous work in LAM, this study analyses social media's role as a contemporary LAM technique in Dialogue Marketing. It explores the use of Dialogue Management as a tool to enhance Dialogue Marketing for franchise businesses. It presents an integrated framework for the identification of social media adoption levels and how this can enhance franchise business success by providing an important contribution to the franchise industry sector. It concludes by offering a conceptual touchpoint channel model with a view to progressing discourse in the area and uniting current thinking.

RESEARCH RATIONALE

This research is significant in that it is not only exploring dialogue management strategy choices as contemporary franchise local area marketing (LAM) techniques in the social media platform hierarchy

DOI: 10.4018/978-1-4666-9776-8.ch002

but also the extent to which dialogue marketing is embedded in social networking. It is also examining further the consistency of LAM techniques used to engage with their online communities.

This chapter will highlight how franchises create and retain their customers with social media using dialogue management strategies. This chapter examines 3 distinct problems. These problems include:

Problem 1: The lack of objective investigation into how franchises make dialogue management strategy choices for their contemporary LAM techniques: Often franchisees are provided with limited marketing training (Webster & Hume, 2015), resulting in poor or inadequate dialogue management strategy choices given their social media involvement. This research will advance discussion into this problem and highlight optimal strategy choices.

Problem 2: Lack of objective reporting into the extent franchises have embedded dialogue marketing into their social networking strategies. Social networking is typically undertaken at a franchisor level rather than at the franchisee level resulting in a standardised approach as opposed to a customised one.

Problem 3: The lack of an enhanced theoretical framework or model that incorporates the dialogue marketing process in the formation of relationships with customers and consumers: A proposed social media engagement model outlines the categories of the relationships but not specifically how dialogue marketing leads people to form relationships using social media platforms. This work will incorporate the notion of dialogue marketing and advance the model.

RESEARCH METHOD

As this work is initially exploratory, a qualitative approach was considered relevant to define the problems the researchers are seeking to examine (Boyce, 2002). The research aim encompassed undertaking exploratory research to ascertain the suitability of conducting a more robust examination and to enlarge the researcher's knowledge about the issues and problems described earlier (Kumar, 1996). An extensive literature review, incorporating 'internet' sources and 'academic business journal databases' was conducted. As Kumar (1996) points out, a literature review can assist a researcher in widening their base of knowledge for their area of research, offering focus and definition to the research problem as well as improving their research methodology. To search academic journal databases, keyword terms the researchers used included *social media engagement*, *touchpoints* and *social media measurement*. Internet search engines, 'Google' and 'Bing' were utilised by the researchers to unearth supplementary information, in particular, practitioner white papers, forum reviews, content articles, industry survey reports and advocacy group websites for the keyword terms, *customer engagement*, *content marketing*, *social analytics* and *touchpoints*.

Following the literature review pertaining to the topic areas, "Franchise Dialogue Marketing" and "Dialogue Marketing in Social Media", further information was collected through a structured observation. A structured observation was conducted in the shape of an internet marketing images review for the keyword, "touchpoints". The reason a structured observation method was considered as an approach for because it increased data reliability and lowers the chance of observer bias (Kinnear & Taylor, 1998). A convenience sampling methodology was employed to select the internet marketing images to study. In exploratory research situations, convenience or 'haphazard sampling' is the most preferred approach as it is easy as well as quick to implement and to administer, given tight deadlines (Zikmund, Ward, Lowe & Winzar, 2007). As the research aims to investigate how businesses, in particular franchise businesses embed dialogue marketing into their social networking strategies as well as to form and build relationships, the data analysis undertaken was a 'descriptive analysis' (Kinnear & Taylor, 1998) which was applicable given the nature of the research.

DATA COLLECTION

As described above, two instruments, a literature review and researcher observations were used to collect data on the role of social media in dialogue marketing and management. Reporting time constraints required only exploratory and descriptive research to be undertaken. Completing the literature review was important for a number of reasons. It brought focus and clarity to shaping the research problems as well as understanding the relationship between the existing body of knowledge on social media and dialogue marketing and identified gaps.

The second instrument was the recording of researcher observations from primary sources in the form of touchpoint images. Details about the first 31 images observed on the Google Images website were recorded. Image rankings based on image use frequency was the reason for selecting the first 31 touchpoint images. Given the exploratory nature of this research, data findings tabulations were limited to frequency and percentage distributions only without statistical analysis.

INTRODUCTION

In July 2010, Amazon, the giant American on-line book retailer sold more ebooks than paperbacks. Also, ebooks accounted for triple the number of sales of hardcovers according to Amazon CEO, Jeff Bezos. In the publishing industry, this was a huge milestone (Ostrow, 2011). Bradley Johnson (2014) from Ad Age, reported that in 2013, digital marketing accounted for 35.3% of all U.S. advertising agency revenue but this growth is slowing. Traditional marketing still has the dominant position with over 57% of advertising revenue with television advertising (40%) the significant player (Marketingcharts.com, April 2014). Traditional television viewing though especially amongst young American adults (18-24 year olds) remains in steady decline. Other age demographic groups, including 25-34 year olds, 35-49 year olds and 50-64 year olds appear to be reducing their levels of traditional television consumption as well (Marketingcharts.com, September 2014). In a recent IAB survey (2014), it is also reported that increases in digital video advertising will be funded by shifting money away from television advertising. It predicts that within five years, digital marketing will at least be the same as television. In the latest 2014 CMO Survey, respondents have indicated that social media spending would account for over 21% of a business's overall marketing budget within the next five years. This highlights at least a doubling of social media spending budgets in a five year period (CMOSurvey.org, 2014). So how does this paradigm shift relate to 'Dialogue Marketing'?

It was the 'digital revolution' that has made dialogue marketing possible. Dialogue marketing is firstly establishing the consumers attention, whilst at the same time, learning all about them including their motive or intent and then secondly to engage with them on an individual basis through various appropriate online experiences. Such engagement means developing experiences across a range of brand communication channels such as e-mails, point-of-purchase (POP), mobile messaging and social networks. The goal is to have the consumer create an emotional bond with the organisation's brand (Koreatimes.co.kr, 2013).

This chapter investigates the dialogue components of contemporary local area marketing (LAM) and how they are managed by businesses including franchises. The chapter will also analyse the reasons and causes of dialogue engagement levels used in social media and the contribution of this knowledge to further enhance a proposed theoretical social media engagement model. Understanding the role of dialogue management in social media to form online customer relationships is crucial in being able to further enhance this proposed theoretical social media engagement framework.

The objective of this research is to report on how businesses especially franchisees and their social media marketers market and manage dialogue within the social media context as a contemporary local area marketing (LAM) technique for building relationships with prospects and customers. This will provide a better understanding on how franchisees manage their online dialogue for different levels of engagement.

The intended contribution to the franchise industry specifically is to provide an integrated framework for the application of social media as a LAM and community based dialogue marketing technique to increase awareness and ultimately enhance franchise brand success using dialogue management strategies to engage with prospects and customers.

BACKGROUND

Dialogue Marketing is a term that refers to a structured approach of ongoing interactive communication to form relationships with people (Allan Steinmetz, 1997). Social networks are a key component in 'Dialogue Marketing' as it is this strategy that organisations leverage to induce sales with customer prospects (Financial-dictionary.thefreedictionary.com, 2012). Ellie Selby (2012) defines dialogue marketing also as social networking. She further states that of the 90% of businesses who use social media as their social networking tool, only 50% of them use it effectively. This assessment is supported by survey results from the CMO Survey conducted once every four years in conjunction with the American Duke University, Fuqua School of Business. From this survey, 45% of respondents believed social media had not had any significant impact on their business (CMOsurvey.org, 2014). This supports the research conducted by Webster and Hume (2015) into franchise businesses where they found that 77% of Australian franchises appeared to receive minimal benefits from their social media engagement. Cooper Smith from Business Insider (2014) also reported associated findings in a recent survey stating that only 23% of marketers thought their promotional social media efforts were effective. Negative social media feedback often stimulates further discussion on social networks which could have devastating consequences for franchise businesses (Corstjens & Umblijs, 2012). This may not be the major reason though. Sensis Yellow Pages Australia (2014, p.59) reported the main reasons why businesses did not have a social media presence were that, "it took too much time, it did not provide a return on investment, a feeling that it was too open to tampering as well as to adverse comments and there had been a lack of interest in it."

These reasons were echoed to much extent in the annual Digital Readiness Survey (Table 1) conducted by Chambers of Commerce and Industry Queensland (CCIQ) (2012) (2013), the top reason was "time and resources". A close second was "not relevant to my customers" but this was down 6.5% from last year, suggesting more businesses may have believed that social media is now more relevant. This is supported too by respondents indicating only a minimal positive change (+ 2%) to the "See little value"

Table 1. Business Social Media non-usage

Survey Question: Why do you not use social media in your business?			
Response Option	**2012**	**2013**	**% Change**
See little value	25%	27.0%	+ 2%
Not relevant to my customers	45%	38.5%	- 6.5%
Time and resources	35%	41.0%	+ 6%
Don't understand social media	15%	22.6%	+ 7.6%
Fear of negative exposure and feedback	10%	19.5%	+ 9.5%

reason option. As for the reason "fear of negative exposure and feedback" receiving the largest positive percentage change (+9.5%), it was still ranked bottom of all the likely reasons.

According to Australian public relations specialist Rebecca Stalker (2010), franchise businesses in how they use social media, focus on strong word-of-mouth recommendations as well as enhancing and increasing brand awareness.

Findings from the annual CCIQ Digital Readiness Survey (2012) (2013), on how Queensland businesses use social media in their business (Table 2) would support Stalker's earlier assertion. 'Communication with clients', 'Marketing' and 'PR' have increased in significance and appear to be the stand-out likely reasons. According to Sensis Yellow Pages Australia (2014), for small to medium businesses the most common use of social media was to invite online comments, ratings or reviews whilst for large businesses it was for interactive communication with contacts or customers (Table 3). Of interest here for further research is the percentage of businesses offering incentives, coupons and discounts being the lowest even though consumers saw these as their key reason to connect.

Table 2. Business Social Media usage

Survey Question: How do you use social media in your business?			
Response Option	**2012**	**2013**	**% Change**
Communication with clients	70%	75.0%	+ 5.0%
Communication with suppliers	20%	20.0%	-
Research/information gathering	40%	35.9%	- 4.1%
Marketing	70%	78.2%	+ 8.2%
PR	55%	61.5%	+ 6.5%
Communicate internally	20%	15%	- 5%

Table 3. 2014 Business use of Social Media (Sensis Yellow Pages Australia)

Key Reasons	Large	Medium	Small
Offer incentives to consumers via social media	41%	43%	28%
Use social media for interactive communication with customers and contacts	61%	55%	45%
Invite online comments, ratings and reviews on SM sites	53%	59%	46%

In relation to 'social media for interactive communication', a survey of Australian franchise businesses (2012 Franchising Australia Report) into the most common social media communication methods used highlighted Facebook 63.5%, Franchisee intranet 58.7%, Twitter 38.9%, LinkedIn 27% and Posing and responding to Franchisee blogs 14.3%. No details as to the emphasis of the communication was reported. Ironically, in the latest Franchising Australia Report (2014, p.3) on the topic of social media communication methods, there is no survey question or discussion even though there is a report sub-section, *"Franchisor Online Communication & Sales Strategies"*. The focus is purely on online sales. This would suggest a gap in the understanding by franchise businesses as to what is social media and its rising power as a dialogue marketing tool.

SOCIAL MEDIA

Social media fundamentality is a form of two-way social communication that is evolving through new applications and categories (Nations, 2014). It's alive, organic and dynamic. Social media was defined early in its evolution as "a category of online media where people are talking, participating, sharing, networking, and bookmarking online. Most social media services encourage discussion, feedback, voting, comments, and sharing of information from all interested parties." (Jones, 2009) He suggested that social media used various conduits to develop two-conversations. These conduits included such categories as 'social news' (people reading and voting on news articles and topics), 'social sharing' (people creating and uploading content such as photos and videos), 'social networks' (people connecting and maintaining connections with family, friends, family as well as associates and social bookmarking' (people flagging interesting information and content and sharing these with other people.

Kaplan and Haenlein (2010) classified social media as a ranking by level of personal interaction:

1. Virtual social worlds (e.g. Second Life),
2. Virtual game worlds (e.g. World of Warcraft),
3. Social networking sites (e.g. Facebook),
4. Content communities (e.g. YouTube),
5. Blogs and microbloggs (e.g. Twitter),
6. Collaborative projects (e.g. Wikipedia).

This ranking suggested a higher emphasis on social media as a vehicle for social communities given its interactive conversational focus as opposed to a content one. A classic example of the power of social media community was when Dave Carroll used social media to complain about United Airlines breaking his guitar in 2008 The world quickly knew about that. For the global community, social media has shifted the scales and taken brand communication power away from organisations (Kietzmann, Hermkens, McCarthy, Silvestre, 2011). Organisations and businesses are increasing faced with the dilemma of embracing social media or ignoring it.

Kietzmann et al. (2011) argue that organisations have been hesitant to engage appropriately with social media. A possible reason for this could be their lack of understanding about social media ecology (Kaplan and Haenlein, 2010). For organisations to understand their social media audience and engagement needs, Kietzmann et al. (2011) developed a seven building block honeycomb (Table 4).

Table 4. The Honeycomb of Social Media (Kietzmann, Hermkens, McCarthy, Silvestre, 2011, p. 243)

Functionality	Description	Implications
Conversations	The extent to which users communicate with each other	Conversation velocity, and the risks of sharing and joining
Groups	The extent to which users are ordered or form communities	Membership rules and protocols
Identity	The extent to which users reveal themselves	Data privacy controls, and tools for user self-promotion
Presence	The extent to which users know if others are available	Creating and managing the reality, intimacy and immediacy of the content
Relationships	The extent to which users relate to each other	Managing the structural and flow properties in a network of relationships
Reputation	The extent to which users know the social standing of others and content	Monitoring the strength, passion, sentiment, and reach of users and brands
Sharing	The extent to which users exchange, distribute and receive content	Content management system and social graph

Each building block represents a specific social media function. By analysing the 'building blocks' of individual social media platforms and their implications, organisations can determine their applicability and suitability fit. This framework can also provide useful criteria in analysing the social media platform choices of organisations, specifically franchise businesses which will be the subject of future explanatory research.

Accompanying this framework is a set of guidelines, for organisations to navigate through the social media maze. Kietzmann et al. (2011) coincidently referred to these guidelines as their 4 C's, Cognize (review and identification of suitable social media platforms), Congruity (alignment of suitable social media platforms with organisational goals), Curate (management of social media engagement by level and frequency of involvement) and Chase (monitoring the social media environment for changes that would impact on the organisation.) These guidelines are meant to provide the foundations for the monitoring, understanding and responding to actions generated from those target social media sites that form the basis of an organisation's social media strategy. These four steps coincidently appear to model the PDCA continuous improvement cycle process developed by quality management experts, Edwards Deming and Walter Shewhart (Pearson, Larson & Gray, 2013).

With the predicted rise in digital marketing as reported earlier, so marketing budgets will change to reflect increases in spending on social media spending. For example, according to the 2014 Sensis Yellow Pages Australia Report, social media spending in 2014 was as an average, $4,560 for small businesses (16% of marketing budget) and $38,800 (12% of marketing budget). In 2013, for small business it was $1,970 (15% of marketing budget) and for medium sized businesses it was $11,780 (9% of marketing budget) (2014 Sensis Yellow Pages Australia Report).

An important characteristic of any effective social media strategy is measurability. When it comes to how well Australian businesses measure the success of social media investment, the statistics are shocking. Only 17% of small businesses and 28% of medium businesses explicitly measure their social media investment returns. The most frequent measure used by these businesses was to monitor the level of social media responses. Most of these businesses however did not know what the level was. The other concern raised as well in the 2014 Sensis Yellow Pages Australia Report apart from the majority of businesses not formally measuring their social media ROI, many also were not clear as to the ingredients of a successful social media strategy. From these findings, there appears to be gap of knowledge in this area that warrants further investigation.

Without suitable metrics, it is hard to monitor its effectiveness (Willis, 2011). According to Natalie Burg of Forbes (2013), no social media return-on-investment (ROI) measurement is perfect or comprehensive but it is possible. The key is to use a combination of methods such as metric tools, interactions and traffic analysis over time to develop suitable benchmarks against which future social media strategies and efforts can be measured (CMOsurvey.org, 2014). This means better integration of data, strategies, automation technologies and analytics tools in the form of Dialogue Management (Koreatimes.co.kr, 2013). In relation to 'metrics', one of the interesting trends identified in the CMO survey (2014) is that businesses are now shifting away from pure 'financial' metrics such as sales level, revenue per customer, customer retention costs and profit per customer toward more referral and text measures ('soft' metrics) such as hits per page, number of followers or friends, repeat visits and buzz indicators (web mentions)

Dialogue management in a marketing context involves monitoring various social media platforms to identify how people are engaging in communication and conversations. In other words, identifying what and how the dialogue is being used. With social media, it's all about the relationship and the quality of that relationship. In a social media context therefore, dialogue management involves using various dialogue marketing techniques to leverage marketing strategies. For franchise businesses, this would mean embedding dialogue management into their franchise marketing efforts.

Franchise Marketing is the dialogue of a franchise business's most important relationship, which is the one between themselves and their customers (Franchisemarketingsystems.com, 2014). An issue often raised by franchisee's that affect this dialogue, is the social media restrictions and lack of marketing support provided by franchisor's to their local operations. These social media restrictions make it hard for the local franchise business to drive customer engagement, local awareness, the feeling of belonging and connectedness as well as prospect traffic. (Rubin, 2014)

DIALOGUE MARKETING

Dialogue Marketing according to Allan Steinmetz (1997, p.1), is "a structured program of ongoing two-way communication". He explains that it works due to its roots in human nature, i.e. people are more likely to communicate with those people who they know and trust. Even though the communication will be highly customized, there are 4 stages to dialogue marketing, these being:

Stage 1: Recognise the business.
Stage 2: Know the business.
Stage 3: Want to use the business.
Stage 4: Maintain an ongoing relationship with the business (Steinmetz, 1997).

These stages align closely to the customer strategy stages outlined by McColl-Kennedy & Keil (2000) for developing and building customer loyalty. The key element with the customer strategy stages methodology is the understanding of customer retention economics, sometimes described as "customer-focussed marketing". Being "customer-centric" means focussing on customer outcomes through achieving customer satisfaction and loyalty. Creating, maintaining and enhancing customer relationships are

Table 5. Social Media dialogue marketing relationship strategies

Dialogue Marketing Stage	Recognise the Business	Know the Business	Want to Use the Business	Maintain Business Relationship
Social Media Category	*Customer Awareness*	*Customer Acquisition*	*Customer Retention/ Service*	*Customer Loyalty*
Social Media	√	√	√	√
Social Networking	√	√	√	√
Social News		√	√	√
Social Bookmarking			√	√
Social Sharing				√
Wiki Authoring				√

the essence of the relationship marketing process (Kotler, Brown, Adam, Burton & Armstrong, 2007). Table 5 outlines the integration of dialogue marketing stages to both the social media categories (Nations, 2014) and relationship marketing process. (Webster & Hume, 2015).

Nations (2014) social media categories definitions are:

- **Social Media:** Two-way social communication between people,
- **Social Networking:** People connecting and staying in touch with friends, relatives and colleagues,
- **Social News:** People reading and voting on news topics and articles,
- **Social Bookmarking:** People finding, flagging and sharing online information,
- **Social Sharing:** People creating, uploading and sharing their creations, and
- **Wiki Authoring:** People collaboratively adding and editing articles for websites and/or databases.

Customer-centric focused businesses using technology are able to more easily identify, differentiate and engage with their customers as well as communicate more personally with them (Stone and Jacobs, 2001, p.49). Technology in this sense includes online channels that support the overall customer relationship strategy (Petersen, Grone, Kammer, Kirscheneder, 2010, p.4).

To investigate the role of Dialogue Marketing further, it is important to also consider its rise to prominence as a marketing concept. According to Tahir Wafi (2014), initially there was the Marketing Mix concept originally developed by Borden (1964) which consisted of 14 elements. Jerome McCarthy refined to the concept to 4 P's (Product, Price, Place and Promotion) which subsequently appeared in a book by Philip Kotler, 'Principles of Marketing' published in 1967. The first marketing mix concept to offer a customer-centric approach was developed by Lauterborn (1990).

To understand the shifts in consumer behaviour coinciding with the rise in consumer power, Bob Lauterborn proposed a consumer marketing mix model, the '4 C's'. He reasoned that marketers needed to view the marketing mix from the consumer's perspective, i.e. 'walking in their shoes'. This meant describing, 'product' in terms of 'consumer needs and wants', 'price' as the 'cost' to satisfy consumers wants and needs, 'place' as in the 'convenience' for consumers to buy and 'promotion' being the 'communication' marketers have with consumers. Lauterborn himself says, "All good advertising creates a dialogue".

So how could dialogue marketing be used by businesses to build relationships, add value to the experience and lead to product recommendations? Steinmetz (1997) has outlined 10 guiding principles behind successful dialogue marketing. These principles are:

- Develop a clear objectives statement
- Ensure consumers can select their own entry points
- Create a channel where consumers can respond and share information about themselves
- Don't be in a rush
- Appreciate the benefit and value of the interaction
- Continue maintaining contact
- Adopt a sequenced approach with the communication
- Based on consumer information gained, customise responses and modify tactics to suit
- Ensure the marketing database is comprehensive for dialogue marketing
- Be creative with the communication.

Table 6 compares the two marketing mix concepts with Dialogue Marketing principles and how they align. Between the Lauterborn model and the Steinmetz model, there appears to be quite a strong correlation. In understanding consumer's wants and needs, this would require businesses to 'listen'. Customised responses would be the outcome of the data collected. The cost of a successful outcome is not only money but 'time' for the customer to feel satisfied with the outcome. Steinmetz believed that customer satisfaction could be gauged through maintaining regular communication with the customer. He also believed that by providing multiple entry points and a variety of channels through which to communication was possible accentuated consumer 'convenience.' It's about making it easy for the customer to eventually buy. To maintain ongoing 'communication' also means not letting the message and the content get stale in the eyes of the consumer. Regular communication involves a systematic approach. Steinmetz's underlying premise for the dialogue marketing model was that people tended to interact more with those they already knew and trusted.

The premise, according to Steinmetz (1997) of what makes dialogue marketing work is the basic human nature principle. A relationship is built up over time through communication leading to a form of behavioural response. In advertising this is referred to as the 'Hierarchy of Effects Model' (or purchase funnel), one of the traditional learning response hierarchy models (Belch, Belch, Kerr & Powell, 2009).

Table 6. Marketing mix elements comparison

4 Marketing Mix P's	4 Marketing Mix C's	Dialogue Marketing Principles
Product	Consumer Wants & Needs	Objectives, Customised responses, Comprehensive data
Price	Consumer's Cost to Satisfy	Time, Contact continuity
Place	Convenience to Buy	Entry points, Channels
Promotion	Communication	Sequenced approach, Creativity
Source: McCarthy (1964)	Source: Lauterborn (1990)	Source: Steinmetz (1997)

DIGITAL MARKETING MIX

In the ongoing refinement of the marketing mix concept, various contemporary models incorporating 'digital marketing' have emerged. Digital Marketing involves using various digital media, such as email, mobile phones and social networks for promotional purposes (Inwise.com, 2011). Contemporary LAM techniques used by franchise businesses include email, mobile and search engine marketing, online advertising, forums and directories as well as blogs (Webster & Hume, 2015). These techniques are in essence, digital media channels forming part of the 'digital marketing mix'.

So what would constitute the 'digital marketing mix' and what would be its elements? Various models have been proposed to describe such a mix. In 2005, the SIVA model was created by Dev and Schultz. This was enhanced to the SAVE model in 2013 by Richard Ettensen, Eduardo Conrado and Jonathon Knowles and has since then been gaining marketing practitioner traction.

The key SAVE model elements are:

- **Solutions:** Offerings defined by needs met,
- **Access:** Integrated cross-channel presence that takes into account the customer's complete purchase journey,
- **Value:** Benefits received relative to purchase price, and
- **Education:** Providing information relevant to customer's specific needs at every purchase cycle point.

The SAVE model was originally developed to explain the B2B market and the only difference between SIVA and SAVE was that the earlier model emphasises 'Information' instead of 'Education'. Information in this context related to one-way communication whereas with 'Education', the wording is two-way, meaning that information is given and received with feedback and recommendations being included to close the customer purchase cycle (Wafi, 2014).

Several years prior to the SAVE model, Fetherstonhaugh (2009) developed his 4E's model in response to what he saw as the 'information age' and improvements in technology. His 4E's model related to:

- **Experience:** How the product makes the consumer feel,
- **Everyplace:** Trialling new methods of distribution,
- **Exchange:** Perception of product value, rather than cost to buy, and
- **Evangelism:** Belief in the product, sharing the emotion with others.

Although his model was primarily designed to explain 'e-commerce', it could also be applied in non-technological environments (Wafi, 2014). Interestingly, in these contemporary marketing concept models, social media appears is not specifically mentioned even though the 4E's and SAVE models were developed after the advent of social media. In 2013, Leslie Nuccio developed the '4C's of Social Media Marketing Model specifically for social media. The elements in this 4C's model include:

- **Communities:** Social communities made up of intertwined social networks with common interests,
- **Conversations:** Social conversations around personal community interests,
- **Channels:** Various social media channels, and
- **Campaigns:** Social media campaigns.

Table 7. Digital marketing mix model comparison

4 E's Model	SAVE Model	4 Social Media Marketing C's
Experience	Solutions	Communities
Everyplace	Access	Channels
Exchange	Value	Campaigns
Evangelism	Education	Conversations
Source: Fetherstonhaugh (2009)	Source: Ettensen, et. al. (2013)	Source: Nuccio (2013)

With this model, the common thread appears to be the emphasis on information sharing and the value of the information being shared through reciprocity. For a business, the success of its social media would depend on choosing the right social media channels to conduct the ideal conversations. Successful social media strategies involve closely aligning social media community interests with relevant business goals and then fostering the right conversations that will be reciprocated by the community (Siddiqi, 2014).

In Table 7, the two digital marketing mix models are compared to the 4C's Social Media Marketing model. There appears to be an effective synergy of stages, however with social media there is the level of engagement context. In this regard, the Social Media Honeycomb framework (Keitzmann, et. al., 2011) might be a viable option but would warrant further research. Wafi (2014) believes that the SAVE model aligns with the relationship management concept because, as it steps customers through the purchase process, the relationship is continually being built. It could be argued that the 4 E's and SAVE models are not purely 'customer-centric' as there is a product emphasis in the initial stages, 'Experience' and 'Solutions' in contrast to the business engaging with its customer community first with the 4C's Social Media model. Even in the 'Value' and 'Exchange' stages, the notion of a business justifying product value appears to be at odds with fostering community interests.

Reciprocity is often the provision of first-party referrals or endorsements as part of the feedback process, as well as third-party testimonials from reliable sources. In a social media context, this would be considered 'social bookmarking' (Webster & Hume 2015). Conversations begin and are maintained, through reciprocity and sharing. At the core of the 4C's of Social Media Marketing is the sales funnel, the same one described by Lauterborn (1990), or otherwise known as the "Hierarchy of Effects model (Belch, Belch, Kerr & Powell, 2009).

HIERARCHY OF EFFECTS MODEL

Being the basis for both Steinmetz's Dialogue Marketing model (1997) and Nuccio's 4C's of Social Media Marketing model (2013), why does the Hierarchy of Effects model still have appeal as a concept? Interestingly, as reported by Belch et al. (2009) this model is also the foundation for the measuring the effects of advertising in many decision making processes as well as for setting objectives. Lavidge and Steiner (1961) who developed the Hierarchy of Effects model discussed how each the three functions of advertising, 1) awareness and knowledge, 2) liking and preference and 3) conviction and purchase directly aligned with each of three psychological behavioural components, a) cognitive (thoughts), b) affective (emotions) and c) conative (motives). They likened their process to a flight of stairs and the evaluation as to the effectiveness of advertising would indicate measures of progression on the staircase. The logic behind the staircase analogy, Lavidge and Steiner (1961) claim is that the effects of advertising are cumulative and therefore measurement needs to consider the residual 'long-term' effects.

Leslie Nuccio (2013) in the 4C's of Social Media Marketing explains this process as the customer purchase funnel, similarly with six steps, these being: awareness, consideration, preference, purchase, loyalty and advocacy. It is part of relationship marketing which is a nurturing type model. That is, marketers need to be aware online customers will require numerous 'touches' and 'impressions' before they feel comfortable to purchase. Nuccio refers to this as 'social dialogue marketing' or in its basic form, word-of-mouth sharing. The 4C's of Social Media Marketing model was developed to provide an approach to transition from traditional marketing to social media marketing. The first step in this transition is 'social listening' which involves using social media technologies and tools (i.e. social media networks) to understand more about the target community to be pursued. This information is then used to generate meaningful and appropriate word-of-mouth conversations that can be easily shared.

Social media networks emit enhanced persona through the provision of current, authentic and focussed communication tailored to the receiver according to Artegic.com (2014), a German digital marketing firm. For businesses to embrace online dialogue marketing, they need to be open to criticism and see it as an opportunity for improvement. In the social media space, this means being a good 'listener' and tailoring personalised responses as part of two-way communication. Interestingly, Artegic.com describes the engagement process as being customer-centred. They explain the approach as one where relevant 'teaser' information is provided through social networks, encouraging people to engage through subscribing, opting-in or signing up to get the 'full version'. Another approach is to embed reward incentives for engagement, such as competition prizes directly into the specific social media platforms to elicit this engagement. In terms of measurability, they recommend lead tracking from specific social media networks.

Leslie Nuccio (2013) contends that measuring social media success can best be achieved using 'action' oriented metrics, i.e. disguised clicks in the form of shares, emails, likes, tweets and other aptly named counts. This can be likened to 'impressions' used to measure performance in traditional public relations and advertising campaigns. Given that for brand recognition, as a heuristic, it has to be seen at least seven times before it makes an 'impression', tracking these is a good metric option.

According to Nuccio (2013), where social media comes its own as a method of communication is through the combination of the personal selling dialogue (information sharing) with the enormity of traditional broadcast advertising. Using 'impressions' in tandem with 'actions' forms the basis of 'social dialogue marketing' and makes compelling sense as an indicator of solid communication channel strategy (Nuccio 2013). This sounds straightforward in theory, however for Australian SME's measuring social media success is an issue. Could Dialogue Management be a solution?

DIALOGUE MANAGEMENT

Dialogue management involves identifying and monitoring how people engage in communication and conversations within the social media networking context. The emphasis is on determining the strength and quality of that relationship and how it's managed/leveraged. Technology is the key to driving dialogue management. In a recent Economist Intelligence Unit (2014, p.8) survey report titled, "Customer Service,

Marketing and Technology: Mastering the Customer Journey", which surveyed 272 customer service and marketing executives, the 5 top technologies identified as changing the way businesses operate were:

1. Mobile Technology
2. Cloud Computing
3. Social Media
4. Big Data
5. E-Commerce

For mobile technology popularity, this reinforces the 2013 Australian research that reports the percentage of social media users who accessed their accounts on smartphones and tablets increased sharply in 2013. Up from 53% the previous year, sixty-seven percent of social users surveyed accessed their accounts via smartphone, which was the highest of all the devices (eMarketer.com, 2013). According to Don Springer of Oracle (clickzintel, 2014a) businesses using cloud computing only have to store and maintain the data that is essential to them. Data will be hosted in the cloud by third parties but with the business maintaining the data.

Cloud-based data services are rapidly gaining momentum in the market, with a choice of two delivery options, a) 'emerging': this option is an "appliance" service that provides a single, reliable source of accurate business data, alongside social information about accounts, leads, contacts, etc. The second option b) 'exchange' is where premium datasets are sold in exchange for providing a rich set of Web interfaces to ease data integration, like a 'market exchange'.

'Big data' is simply a term to describe the large volume of structure, semi-structured and un-structured data that is capable of being mined. (Rouse, 2014). E-commerce technologies relate to various internet reliant functions such as text messages, emails, shopping carts, data exchanges and web based services used to conduct business over the internet (Beal, 2014). For franchise businesses, ecommerce brings with it certain issues. For one, it can change brand awareness and perception and therefore significantly influence franchise brand value. For any franchise business, brand name is everything. Territory conflict is another issue for those franchise businesses that benefit from a designated territory. Internet sales from the franchisor or other franchise businesses is often viewed as 'unfair competition' and 'territory encroachment' (Perrigot & Penart, 2013).

This may only be a concern of the franchise businesses but not their customers. An emerging platform in ecommerce that has developed out of the popularity of social media is 'social commerce.' It's using social networking sites to share information socially (social sharing) with friends about their sales or intended purchases. Consultation with social communities for purchasing decision advice is also conducted by consumers. Website functions make it easy to share this information with friends as well. Such recommendation from friends are more valuable as it strongly influences a friend's online purchases (Liang, Ho, Li & Turtan, 2011).

For businesses, it's a matter of channeling this social commerce into a single source where it can be synthesised and analysed, i.e. converting this social media communication into 'social data'. This social data is then used to provide insights about the businesses social community, their contributions, history and activities (Gross, 2012). Listening to the social commerce is the first step in the 'social relationship management' process. It is hearing what people are saying about the business, its products and its people on various social media channels.

The social relationship management (SRM) process consists of 6 steps, Listen, Engage, Create, Publish, Manage and Analyse according to Oracle (clickzintel, 2014a, p.5). 'Engage' is where a business actually interacts with its fans and followers in ways prompting further community engagement, such as with questions, proving feedback to comments, and answering posts, etc. 'Create' is about developing resources, such as online content and web applications based on engagement feedback to maintain the engagement cycle. These resources are then published across social media channels. The 'Manage' step in the SRM process focuses on ensuring the business communicates with its community in a consistent manner. With the 'Analyse' step, its emphasis is on the metrics and outcomes and where can improve on social performance.

This is where the integration of social technologies within a CRM system becomes an effective business tool. According to Paul Greenberg from Oracle (clickzintel, 2014b, p.6) in response to customer's controlling conversations, 'social CRM' has emerged as a tool to engage customers in mutually beneficial interactive conversations. He states that, "social CRM is a philosophy and a business strategy supported by a technology platform, business rules and characteristics." Again, all good in theory but when it's reported that 75% of SMEs do not have a CRM system and only 39% have a digital marketing plan (CCIQ Digital Readiness Survey, 2013), then the goalposts blur. When it came to use of various technologies, nearly 60% of respondents who didn't indicated it was due to a lack of knowledge or understanding about them. They were unsure as to which technologies to adopt and they didn't know what they really wanted in terms of outcomes. On top of that, over 50% of businesses were worried about the shortage of digital skills to drive and manage these technologies. Given that 98% of all Australian businesses are responsible for their own online presence (Sensis Yellow Pages Australia, 2014), it would be reasonable to assume based on the various survey findings that they have become overwhelmed with all this current emphasis on technology.

A more holistic approach to identifying and monitoring how people engage in communication and conversations with businesses would be to analyse business contact points. Contact points for franchise businesses would be the LAM techniques, both traditional (direct marketing) and contemporary (digital marketing channels) they use to engage with their local community (Webster & Hume, 2015). For businesses in general, these contact points would be all those interactions (human and physical) where they keep in 'touch' with their customers during the life of their relationship (Bradbury & Coons, 2007).

TOUCHPOINTS

Given the focus of this chapter, contact points or 'touchpoints' will be viewed from a digital marketing channel perspective. Using the SRM process, how can businesses communicate with their communities in a consistent manner? It is contended that this could be achieved through Dialogue Marketing and an integrated customer loyalty strategy approach. Online marketing expert Joanna Lord (Bigdoor, 2014, p.16) believes that customer loyalty should start for a business when an online community member first discovers the business. At every step of the customer journey, businesses should be creating opportunities to seed customer loyalty. Alex Gonzalez (2014) agrees that online consumers are now more social about their purchasing decision making and are increasingly going online for their advice, ideas and inspiration. Consumers are now, "critics, experts, advocates and influencers" states Gonzalez, co-founder of Chatalog. Social media and content strategist Jay Baer (Convinceandconvert.com, 2014), suggests that the goal for businesses should be to increase the variety of ways they can connect with people who have an interest in them through maximising social connection 'touchpoints' to gain maximum connection possibilities.

According to J-P De Clerck (2014), it's more than just increasing the number of digital marketing channels, its aligning experiences, goals, intent/purpose, context and channels to some tangible value for the customer within a context where touchpoints are activated through interest. This he asserts is the basis for 'touchpoint marketing'. Rather than focussing on 'content' alone as the prime marketing strategy, De Clerck maintains it is understanding the confines as to why people engage, i.e. their individual customer experiences and the specific touchpoint relevance where a business should concentrate its marketing efforts. As De Clerck (2014) states, "consistent customer experiences across channels lead to recommendations, retention and loyalty." Touchpoints can be either direct, indirect or invisible. Examples of direct touchpoints would be having some personal experience with a business such as, 'filling in a form', or 'clicking on a link', i.e. direct contact. Indirect touchpoints are those social interactions, word-of-mouth and value sharing contributions whereas invisible are those experiences that are non-visible, i.e. from the other four senses (sound, taste, smell and feeling) that are sometimes passed off as being random or by chance.

So what makes up a touchpoint? From J-P De Clerck's (2014) perspective it involves subject (interacting with people), intent (purpose of the interaction), social object (interaction creation content), and context (social environment). These elements together become the catalyst for a common significance convergence where businesses have the opportunity for conversion. Gonzalez (2014) believes there are 8 touchpoints that consumers use as part of their online decision making process.

These 8 touchpoints he lists as are:

- **Discovery Platforms:** For product ideas and inspiration,
- **Influencers and Bloggers:** For trusted opinions from expert sources,
- **Affinity Groups and Communities:** For opinions/feedback from reliable third party sources,
- **Social Networks:** For opinions from most trusted friends,
- **Social Media Platforms:** For additional influencer perceptions,
- **Consumer Reviews:** Relevant purchaser comments,
- **Direct Communication:** Live business contact,
- **In-Store via Mobile:** Live purchase decision feedback.

Gambetti and Graffigna (2010) in their research on consumer engagement refer to context as the ninth touchpoint, 'Social Environment', i.e. locations where people socialise that can nurture the growth of consumer engagement. As these are 'consumer touchpoints', according to Li and Kannan (2014), they are typically consumer initiated in their search for information. Business initiated touchpoints on the other hand are business marketing strategies, such as targeting potential customers through email marketing or advertising.

Business initiated brand touchpoints according to Di Marca (2012) are those contact points that interface the customer with the business's brand. They are the 'moments of truth' in the battle to position a business's brand in the minds of consumers. Brand reputation and trust is built on customer's experiences with these touchpoints having the power to spark dialogue and build relationships by creating consistently motivating and positive images, emotions and associations.

What Are Brand Touchpoints?

Scott Davis and Tina Longoria (2003, p.1) define brand touchpoints as, "all the different ways a brand interacts with and makes an impression with customers, employees and other stakeholders. Every action, tactic and strategy your brand has with customers or stakeholders whether it's through advertising, a merchandising display or a customer service call, it is a brand touchpoint."

Davis and Longoria (2003) segment brand touchpoints by customer experience in terms of 'pre-purchase', 'purchase' or 'post-purchase'. Examples of brand touchpoints in these segments include:

- **Pre-Purchase:** Advertising, direct mail/samples, coupons and incentives, deals and coupons,
- **Purchase:** Sales people, store and shelf placement, P-O-P displays, packaging, and
- **Post-Purchase:** Loyalty programs, newsletters, customer service, product and package performance.

Michael Paffenback (n.d.) in his Touchpointers.com blog similarly views brand touchpoints in three stages, pre-purchase, purchase and post-purchase. Jonas Persson (2012) based his Brand Touchpoint Matrix, on the belief that brand touchpoints should lead customers through the: consider, evaluate, buy, enjoy/advocate/bond phases and create increasing levels of value as they travel along the 'consumer decision journey'.

Steve Yastrow (n.d.) suggests that brand touchpoints fall into four categories:

1. When customer learns about the product (brand),
2. When the customer goes through product buying process,
3. When the customer maintains and uses the product (brand), and
4. When the customer informs other people about the product (brand) or merely thinks doing so.

This he describes as the customer relationship lifecycle with the product.

What Are Customer Touchpoints?

SurveyMonkey.com (2014) define 'customer touchpoints' as a "brands point of customer contact, from start to finish". They go on to further define it as "any time a potential customer or customer comes in contact with your brand – before, during and after they purchase something from you". SurveyMonkey even provide a list of touchpoints under the categories of 'before purchase', 'during purchase' and 'after purchase'.

The major conclusions to be drawn from this discussion are that, a) 'brand touchpoints' and 'customer touchpoints are essentially the same thing, 'touchpoints', b) there appears to be marketing practitioner consensus over the categorising of touchpoints and c) touchpoint customer lifecycles appear to follow a customer loyalty approach. To further elaborate on touchpoint categories, Denise Lee Yohn (2013-14) groups the three brand touchpoint segments as 'interactions' with customers. Brand touchpoints such advertising and packaging she refers to as 'static'. Call centres and sales people Denise labels as 'people' touchpoints whilst social media and websites she denotes as 'interactive' touchpoints.

Touchpoints, Jeannie Walters (2013) claims are mistakenly described. Most touchpoints are in fact conduits or channels indicating the connection method, not the actual interaction undertaken. These touchpoint channels are business oriented not customer-centric focused. An example of the distinction between the two would be, touchpoint channel: 'social media', touchpoint: 'Facebook chat'. The touchpoint is the action or experience from engaging with the touchpoint channel.

An additional perspective to the defining of 'touchpoints', is this notion of touchpoint 'affective commitment'. Iglesias, Singh and Batista-Foguet (2011) argue consumers with increased experiences are more likely to develop heightened levels of customer loyalty due to their propensity for affective commitment. In their research they define affective commitment (Allen & Meyer 1990) as the level of consumer emotional attachment to a specific brand or business based on brand recognition. Wilson and Morgan (2011) refer to this as a 'state of resonance' brand consumer bond. They suggest that sense of intimacy generated stems from brands being human personified. Brand contact intimacy is therefore the emotional mirror existing where consumers also project and graft their own emotions onto brands. Valued brand experience, is what Jonas Persson (2012) considered were the keys to a businesses success which is in agreement with the Iglesias, Singh and Batista-Foguet assertions. Given the diversity of touchpoints, Yandav and Pavlou (2014) argue that even if the businesses offline and online emphasis differed in context, the consumer's underlying behavioural processes will most likely be similar.

So where is this leading to? Businesses when analysing the value of their touchpoints need to consider a) channel, b) action response and c) emotional attachment.

From an academic perspective, has there been any consistency in how marketing practitioners view 'touchpoints' or 'touchpoint channels'? For ease of continuing discussion, 'touchpoint channels' have been described under the term 'touchpoints'.

TOUCHPOINTS REVIEW

One of the authors, Geoff Webster conducted an internet review over 2 days analysing images for the keyword term, 'touchpoints' in Google images. As a convenience sample, he selected for his review the first 31 images that appeared. The review considered; a) industry focus, b) touchpoints present, c) touchpoint categories and d) theoretical model connectivity. Review observation questions included:

- Was there an industry focus present?
- How many touchpoints could be observed?
- Were these touchpoints categorised in some way?
- Was there reference to a theoretical model?

Where there was a reference to a theoretical model, appropriate identifications were sought. For 'Response Process', this included any of the Response Process models such as AIDA model and the Hierarchy of Effects model (Belch, Belch, Kerr & Powell, 2009). Steinmetz (1997) in describing his Dialogue Marketing Principles discussed earlier, notes that the centre of Dialogue Marketing is the Hierarchy of Effects model or 'Purchase Funnel'. With 'Decision Making Process', this included any of the purchase involvement and types of consumer decision making models (Neal, Quester and Hawkins,

2002). Relationship Marketing included any reference the customer relationship stages, awareness, acquisition, retention/service and loyalty emphasising a customer-centric approach as also earlier discussed.

In summary, from the Touchpoint Review (Table 8), 39% had an industry focus, 87% had a touchpoint presence, 48% had touchpoints categorised, and 32% were linked to theoretical models.

Table 8. Touchpoints review

Image	Industry Focus	Touchpoints	Categories	Theoretical Model
1	-	24	√	Response Process
2	Small Business	18	√	-
3	Retail	17	-	-
4	-	10	-	-
5	-	4	√	-
6	-	17	-	-
7	-	17	√	Response Process
8	Supplier	-	-	-
9	-	8	-	Decision Making Process
10	Healthcare	4	√	-
11	-	33	√	-
12	Baby Care	16	√	-
13	-	11	-	-
14	Beer Brewing	21	√	Decision Making Process
15	-	10	√	-
16	Travel	8	-	-
17	-	47	√	Response Process
18	Finance	19	√	-
19	-	21	-	Decision Making Process
20	-	16	-	Decision Making Process
21	-	11	√	-
22	-	9	√	-
23	Small Business	9	-	-
24	Childcare	-	-	-
25	-	15	√	Decision Making Process
26	-	13	√	Relationship Marketing Stages
27	-	-	-	-
28	Furniture	23	-	Decision Making Process
29	-	33	-	-
30	Art	-	-	-
31	-	21	-	-
No.	**12**	**455**	**15**	**10**

Industry Focus

It is noted that 61% were not industry specific, suggesting the images were to serve a generic purpose. The industries depicted also were quite diverse.

Touchpoints

Even though a significant number listed touchpoints (87%), there were still 13% that included no touchpoints even though the images were about touchpoints. The average number of touchpoints was just under 17 and the range was quite wide from 0 - 47. The nature of the specific touchpoints did vary widely from image to image and would provide excellent subject material for future research.

Touchpoint Categories

About half of the images (48%) had categorised their touchpoints. Similarly, the specific categories also varied widely across the image array additionally offering ideal data for future research.

Theoretical Model Connectivity

What is interesting here is that of the 32% that linked to a theoretical model only 2 images (6%) also had an industry focus. When identifying theoretical model connectivity, 60% (6) connected to the Decision Making Process, whilst 30% (3) connected to the 'Response Process' and 10% (1) only related to the Relationship Marketing Stages.

From the researcher's observations, the overwhelming emphasis with the touchpoints appears to be on a 'purchase' onus, i.e. response process and decision making process rather than one on 'relationship', i.e. relationship marketing stages. Also, of the images reviewed in Table 7, 19% (6) only indicated touchpoints and an additional 16% (5) had touchpoints and categories, making up a total of 35% of images being purely generic in nature meaning they relate to nothing specifically. This would indicate disconcerting fragmentation amongst marketing practitioners as to their interpretation and application of touchpoints. Further evidence of this divide is coming from marketing practitioners themselves where they distinguish between 'marketers' and 'modern marketers' as well as in the use of buzz phrases such marketing qualified leads, digital body language and lead scoring (clickzintel, 2014b).

Frequencies reported in the form of Yes/Number count.

In observing the touchpoint images, a significant proportion were depicted as being a a) pie/circle, b) mind map, c) matrix or d) cycle. Many of the images represented as a cycle included linkages to the customer strategy stages, i.e. the Hierarchy of Effects Model (Lavidge & Steiner, 1961) or more commonly the "Purchase Funnel". The descriptions of these customer strategy stages differed slightly image to image, but the contexts are essentially the same. A comparison of the first five cycle images with linked customer strategy stages has been compiled in Table 9 to highlight the similarities in descriptions.

The table also shows how these customer strategy stages fit within Steinmetz's (1997) Dialogue Marketing stages. From the observations it was noted that within the cycle images some of the touchpoints were repeated. This suggested a model for collating and categorising touchpoints on the basis of engagement was warranted.

Table 9. Touchpoint cycles comparison

Customer Strategy Stage Descriptions								Source
Pre-purchase				*Purchase*	*Post-purchase*			Michael Paffenback (n.d)
Awareness			Consideration	Purchase		Service	Loyalty	B2bstories.com
Awareness			Consideration	Purchase		Retention	Advocacy	Garymagnone.com
	Discover	Compare	Consider	Commit		Retain		Bigdoor.com
Awareness		Evaluation		Purchase	Usage	Repurchase	Advocacy	Ecommercemanagers.com
Awareness	Discovery			Engagement	Active client	Successful client	Refer	Nickmangham.wordpress.com
Recognise the business		*Know the business*		*Use the business*		*Maintain business relationship*		Steinmetz (1997)

PROPOSED TOUCHPOINT CHANNEL ENGAGEMENT MODEL

In the previous discussion about touchpoints and touchpoint channels, researchers were divided on how to categorise them. For example, Davis and Longoria (2003) suggested segmenting touchpoints by "experience". Denise Lee Yohn (2013-14) proposed that they should be segmented by "interactions". Li and Kannan (2014) and Di Marcia (2012) outlined classifying touchpoints by who "initiated" them. Webster and Hume (2015) when describing traditional and contemporary LAM techniques used by franchise businesses profiled touchpoints by their "type" as either physical or digital in form. De Clerck (2014) portrayed touchpoints as being "direct" or "indirect" by their engagement with people.

Based on the Jeannie Walters (2013) concept of touchpoint channels, a model to categorise these channels is proposed. The proposed Touchpoint Channel Engagement Model allows segmentation of touchpoint channels. With segmentation, a business can determine whether it has the correct mix and balance of touchpoint channels for engagement with its community. This requires a two step process. Step 1 involves creating an inventory list of a business's touchpoint channels. As an example, a touchpoint channel such as, 'Facebook' would be listed on the inventory list as shown in Table 10.

In Step 2, each of the "Touchpoint Channels" would be mapped to a "Touchpoint Channel Triangle" (Figure 1) on the basis of 'Type', 'Initiation' and 'Experience'. The 'Form' description would be denoted with the number of the touchpoint channel, i.e. 1I (Social Media – Facebook), 2D (Billboard). The intention is to develop a touchpoint channel mix based on engagement segmentation. With the touchpoint channel mix mapped, the Touchpoint Channel Triangle could then be used as a gap analysis tool to determine if businesses have the right balance of touchpoint channels. This would also form the basis for ongoing touchpoint channel testing.

Table 10. Touchpoint channel inventory list

No	Description	Form		Type		Initiation		Experience	
		Direct	Indirect	Physical	Digital	Consumer	Business	Interactive	Static
1	Social Media – Facebook		√		√	√		√	
2	Billboard	√		√			√		√

Figure 1. Touchpoint channel triangle

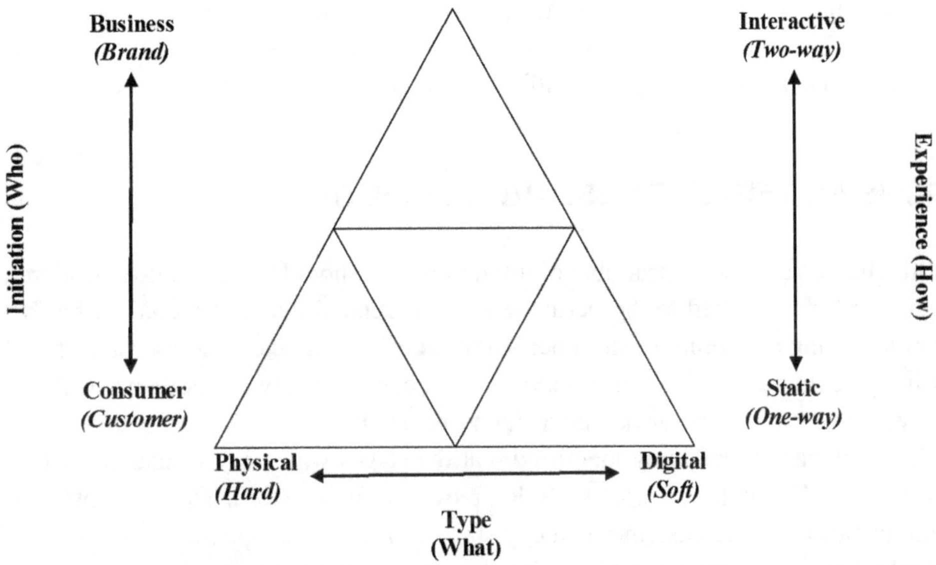

This proposed model is theoretical only and field testing is yet to be undertaken. It is envisaged that this will occur as part of future research.

CONTRIBUTIONS OF THIS MODEL

This conceptual research furthers the discourse into the role of local area marketing techniques or more commonly known as touchpoints and how they relate to dialogue marketing and management. The particular emphasis was initially on franchise businesses with small to medium enterprises (SMEs) in the broader context, given the limited academic material available on LAM and social media engagement techniques for franchise businesses. It reflected on various areas of digital marketing including, marketing mix, digital revolution impacts on dialogue marketing, ROI emphasis shift from 'hard' to 'soft' metric options, functions of social media and implications, social media marketing mix alignment to Hierarchy of Effects Model, uptake of social customer relationship management strategies using dialogue management techniques, researching and reviewing touchpoints as a means of interactive community engagement and understanding dialogue marketing in the customer strategy process. It considered these theories as a system of relationships not previously examined and by doing so has conceptualised a new and original approach to touchpoints and community engagement. A touchpoint channel engagement model has been proposed integrating various touchpoint segmentation methods including by type, experience, initiation and form into an easy to understand triangular matrix that business can use as a map.

Continuing this study to analyse the role of Social Media in Dialogue Marketing as a contemporary Local Area Marketing (LAM) technique has enabled the authors to propose a model that may provide a missing link for marketing practitioners and advance the area of knowledge with respect to touchpoints. The study identified knowledge gaps in the application of touchpoints especially amongst marketing practitioners. Locating these voids has led to a better understanding of touchpoints and touchpoint channels. This now heightens the need for a consistent approach to classifying and categorising touchpoint channels and touchpoint engagement. The touchpoint review confirmed the reciprocity concept as to not only providing the basis for a business, in particular franchise businesses to identify their social media level standing but also outline gap opportunities to further engage with its community.

LIMITATIONS AND FUTURE RESEARCH DIRECTIONS

In reading this chapter, there were a number of limitations that should be taken into consideration. Firstly, qualitative research was limited to the perusing of topic related material including business industry white papers including marketing practitioner survey reports and academic journals as well as online touchpoint image convenience sample observations. Secondly, this work is theoretical only in nature with testing yet to occur. This is earmarked as future research.

Research into dialogue marketing identified that the stages were very similar to customer strategy stages as well as the Hierarchy of Effects Model, purchase funnel steps. This prompted a comparison of touchpoint cycles featuring customer strategy stages. From the sample, there were a number of images observed where touchpoints were associated with various customer strategy stages. Confirming the strength of these associations especially to social media categories could be the subject of future research. Several contemporary digital marketing mix concepts were compared with a potential social marketing mix being possibly identified. Another avenue for future research would be research into a digital marketing mix that incorporates social media as well as dialogue management technologies.

An online touchpoint image review was undertaken observing how touchpoints were represented. The review focused on what images were industry specific, the number of touchpoint examples listed, the relevance of touchpoint channel categories and justification linkages to decision inducing theoretical models, i.e. for sales, customer loyalty, decision making, etc. Of the 31 images observed, 61% had no industry focus, 52% did not listing touchpoints by category and 68% without being justified by a theoretical model. Given that this was a preliminary study, the findings suggest an inconsistent application and that further research to be undertaken. This research will include an investigation into social media touchpoint channel audience engagement and the implications on business through the application of the Social Media Honeycomb (Kietzmann, et. al., 2011).

Future research will be examining social media metrics especially to identify those that reflect social engagement trends and the most appropriate dialogue management technologies. Even though there is a trend toward referral and text measures for social media metrics, a goal for future research would be establish industry benchmarks. Industry benchmark metrics would provide a comparison when monitoring data on content engagement, conversations, touchpoint channels and social media campaigns. From a business perspective it's vital to understand which dialogue management technologies are more profitable. For a franchise business, it's important to know which touchpoints or local area marketing techniques and dialogue marketing strategies are working to build relationships as well as identifying any contact gaps. With social media marketing, it is understanding which touchpoint channels provide the best levels of engagement. Given that digital marketing expenditure and mobile broadband penetration increasing, knowing where to focus local area marketing efforts is essential for survival. The question would be then does digital marketing provide value to a business. It is estimated that by 2016, more internet searches will be undertaken by mobile devices than by desktop computers warranting increased research and understanding into dialogue management. From a cultural context, is there a trend to using regional based technologies (i.e. geographic based search engines) and how might such a development affect social media engagement? Future research into the impact of digital body language and its influence on touchpoints could be of benefit.

Determining the success of touchpoints to create emotional attachment with a brand or a business is currently a popular topic amongst marketing practitioners and warrants academic attention. A focus of this research would relate to the type of emotional attachment that has the most success in engaging people, i.e. is it emotional bonding through image association, brand persona, character personality or narrative. Typically it's connected with brand/product positioning. As a benchmark for emotional attachment, a recent development for franchise businesses, the Vende Social Franchise Social Index (FSI) ranks on a weekly basis how well franchise industry brands are engaging on social media sites such as Facebook and Twitter. Further research into the effectiveness of such indexes to flag trends when mapped against a social media marketing mix would be worthwhile.

Being able to map touchpoint channels is just one component in the process of measuring the value of customer contacts or engagement. Kaplan and Haenlein (2010) alluded to where business might go with their social media strategies in the future and that would be into virtual worlds. Given the sophistication of Enterprise Resource Planning (ERP) tools, it is not too implausible to think about simulated business environments in virtual worlds where business and marketing strategies are tested as well as new products and services being developed, all though the use of social media with real data (i.e. customer demographics and preferences). As for future social media research, there is no doubt it will continue.

CONCLUSION

This research furthers the discourse into the role of local area marketing techniques as it relates to dialogue marketing and management with particular emphasis on franchise businesses. The following conclusions can be drawn from this study. There is no standardised approach in the identification of a business's level of social media adoption. Marketing practitioners also appear to be divided over which applicable methods are applicable in determining appropriate touchpoint channels. There is an implicit assertion that dialogue marketing has consensus as a relationship building strategy. As technology evolves, especially mobile technology, dialogue management strategies such as online environmental diagnostic tools are becoming more prevalent as a preferred option to manage touchpoints. Although businesses are using touchpoints to engage with communities and customers, there appears to be minimal research into the value of these connections (i.e. frequency and level), albeit due to a lack of industry focus or theoretical supporting framework.

The chapter proposed a Touchpoint Channel Engagement Model (Touchpoint Channel Triangle) to better understand how businesses manage their dialogue and to identify potential contact gaps. This model provided linkages to the marking, digital marketing and social media mixes through the perceptual mapping of a business's touchpoints. Such mapping would enable testing of alternate touchpoint mixes to identify potential implications for business and determine suitable mix balances. For social media touchpoint testing, the use of the Social Media Honeycomb (Kietzmann, et. al., 2011) could be appropriate.

The chapter identified that digital marketing expenditure is trending upwards to the point of exceeding traditional marketing within the near future. The question for small to medium size businesses is how can they sustain and subsequently justify the associated cost increases to maintain their online presence. This chapter outlines areas for future research into social media including metrics benchmarks, the affects of mobile technology penetration and the subsequent impacts on digital marketing budgets. Any future research into Dialogue Marketing should also cover the personification of business brands and the creation of emotional attachment to prompt enhanced touchpoint engagement.

REFERENCES

Allen, N. J., & Meyer, J. P. (1990). The measurement and antecedents of affective, continuance and normative commitment to the organization. *Journal of Occupational Psychology*, 63(1).

Artegic.com. (2014). *What Social Media Can Do for Your Dialogue Marketing*. Retrieved from https://www.artegic.com/eCRM/0,215645635f6964092d0933333734/EN/news/d0.html

Beal, V. (2014). *Electronic Commerce (ecommerce)*. Retrieved from http://www.webopedia.com/TERM/E/electronic_commerce.html

Belch, G. E., Belch, M. A., Kerr, G., & Powell, I. (2009). *Advertising and Promotion: An Integrated Marketing Communication Perspective*. Sydney, Australia: McGraw Hill.

Bigdoor.com. (2014). *A Marketers Guide to Customer Loyalty*. Retrieved from http://bigdoor.com/resources/marketers-guide-to-customer-loyalty/

Borden, N. H. (1964). The Concept of the Marketing Mix. In G. Schwartz (Ed.), Science in Marketing. New York, NJ: John Wiley.

Boyce, J. (2002). *Market Research in Practice*. Sydney, Australia: McGraw Hill.

Bradbury, T., & Coons, D. (2007). *Customer Touchpoints – Your Brand in Action*. Retrieved from http://www.thesmartbuilder.com/whitepapers/SMART_Whitepaper_-_Touchpoints.pdf

Burg, N. (2013). *How to Measure Your Social Media Return on Investment*. Retrieved from http://www.forbes.com/sites/capitalonespark/2013/04/25/how-to-measure-your-social-media-return-on-investment/

Cciq.com.au. (2012). *2012 Digital Readiness Study*. Retrieved from http://www.cciq.com.au/assets/Documents/Digital/DigitalReadiness-Report-final-web.pdf

Cciq.com.au. (2013). *2013 Digital Readiness Survey*. Retrieved from http://www.cciq.com.au/industries/technology/digital-readiness-study/

Clickzintel.com. 2014a. *The Value of Social Data*. Retrieved from http://www.clickzintel.com/download/getting-true-value-social-20281

Clickzintel.com. 2014b. *Conversion: Along the Suspect to Advocate Journey*. Retrieved from http://www.clickzintel.com/abstract/conversion-suspect-advocate-journey-22997

CMOSurvey.org. (2014). *CMO Survey Report: Highlights and Insights, August 2014*. Retrieved from http://cmosurvey.org/files/2014/09/The_CMO_Survey-Highlights_and_Insights-Aug-2014.pdf

Convinceandconvert.com. (2014). *Social Circles Use Social Media to Build a Touchpoint Corral*. Retrieved from http://www.convinceandconvert.com/social-media-strategy/social-circles-use-social-media-to-build-a-touchpoint-corral/

Corstjens, M. & Umblijs, A. (2012). The Power of Evil – The Damage of Negative Social Media Strongly Outweigh Positive Contributions. *Journal of Advertising Research*, December, 52(4), 433-449.

Davis, S., & Longoria, T. (2003). *Harmonizing your Touchpoints*. Retrieved October 16, 2014, from https://www.prophet.com/downloads/articles/Harmonizing%20Your%20Touchpoints%20(SD%20TL).pdf

De Clerck, J.-P. (2014). *Is Touchpoint Marketing the Only Marketing Left?* Retrieved from http://www.i-scoop.eu/touchpoint-marketing-marketing-left/

Dimarca.com.au. (2012). *Build the Brand Experience Through Touch Points*. Retrieved from http://www.dimarca.com.au/brand-touch-points.aspx

Economist Intelligence Unit. (2014). *EIU Survey Report: Customer Service, Marketing and Technology: Mastering the Customer Journey*. Retrieved from http://www.cio.co.uk/cmsdata/whitepapers/3508924/Customer_service_marketing_and_technology_Mastering_the_customer_journey.pdf

eMarketer.com. (2014). *In Australia, Mobile Propels More Time Spent on Social*. Retrieved from http://www.emarketer.com/Articles/Print.aspx?R=1009951

Ettenson, R. Eduardo, C. & Knowles, J. (2013). Rethinking the 4Ps. *Harvard Business Review*, 91(1), 26.

Fetherstonhaugh, B. (2009). *The 4Ps are out, the 4Es are in*. OgilvyOne worldwide- New York, Retrieved from http//www.ogilvyone.com.ph/downloads/The4PsAreOutthe4EsAreIn.pdf

Financial-dictionary.thefreedictionary.com. (2014). *Dialogue Marketing*. Retrieved from http://financial-dictionary.thefreedictionary.com/Dialogue+Marketing

Franchise.edu.au. (2014). *2014 Franchising Australia Report*. Retrieved from https://www.franchise.edu.au/__data/assets/pdf_file/0009/657063/FranchisingAustralia2014_webversion.pdf?bustCache=93366477&webSyncID=ab0cfc4d-39e7-41ad-b380-0eda5d1b3503&sessionGUID=08846ed5-e354-4c7e-aa14-4a24feb9b611

Franchisemarketingsystems.com. (2014). *Franchise Marketing Systems will sell your franchise for you*. Retrieved from http://www.franchisemarketingsystems.com/services/franchise-sales/

Frazer, L., Weaven, S., & Bodey, K. (2012). *Franchising Australia 2012 Report*. Retrieved from http://www.franchise.org.au/images/FranchisingAustralia2012fullreport.pdf

Gambetti, R. C., & Graffigna, G. (2010). The concept of Engagement: A Systematic Analysis of the Ongoing Marketing Debate. *International Journal of Market Research*, *52*(6), 801–826. doi:10.2501/S147078531020166

Gonzales, A. (2014). *The Eight Touchpoints of a Customers Consideration Phase*. Retrieved from http://www.marketingprofs.com/opinions/2014/24455/the-eight-touchpoints-of-a-customers-consideration-phase

Griffith.edu.au. (2012). *2012 Franchising Australia Report*. Retrieved from https://www.griffith.edu.au/__data/assets/pdf_file/0005/571793/Franchising-Australia-2012-full-report-compressed.pdf

Gross, T. S. (2012). *Social Relationship Management …Is In Your Future*. Retrieved from http://www.forbes.com/sites/prospernow/2012/02/20/social-relationship-management-is-in-your-future/

Iab.net. (2014). *Digital Content Newfronts: Video Ads Spend Study April 2014*. Retrieved from http://www.iab.net/media/file/2014_IAB_Digital_NewFronts.pdf

Iglesias, O., Singh, J., & Batista-Foguet, J. (2011). The role of brand experience and affective commitment in determining brand loyalty. *Journal of Brand Management*, *18*(8), 570–582. doi:10.1057/bm.2010.58

Inwise.com. (2011). *What is Digital Marketing?* Retrieved from http://www.inwise.com/about/what's-digital-marketing.aspx

Johnson, B. (2014). *Revenue, Staffing, Stocks and Digital Show Growth for Agencies in 2014 Report*. Retrieved from http://adage.com/article/agency-news/2014-agency-report-revenue-staffing-stocks-digital/292849/

Jones, R. (2009). *Social Media Marketing 101, Part 1*. Retrieved from http://sbinfocanada.about.com/gi/o.htm?zi=1/XJ&zTi=1&sdn=sbinfocanada&cdn=money&tm=1059&gps=451_10_1887_1024&f=00&tt=8&bt=6&bts=6&zu=http%3A//searchenginewatch.com/3632809

Kaplan, A. M., & Haenlein, M. (2010). Users of the world, unite! The challenges and opportunities of Social Media. *Business Horizons*, *53*(1), 59–68. doi:10.1016/j.bushor.2009.09.003

Kietzmann, J. H., Hermkens, K., McCarthy, I. P., & Silvestre, B. S. (2011). Social Media? Get serious! Understanding the functional building blocks of social media. *Business Horizons*, *54*(3), 241–251. doi:10.1016/j.bushor.2011.01.005

Kinnear, T. C., & Taylor, J. R. (1988). *Marketing Research: An Applied Approach* (3rd ed.). Singapore: McGraw Hill.

Koreatimes.co.kr. (2013). *Dialogue Marketing: Having a Two-way Conversation*. Retrieved from http://www.koreatimes.co.kr/www/news/biz/2014/03/331_131812.html

Kotler, P., Brown, L., Adam, S., Burton, S., & Armstrong, G. (2007). *Marketing* (7th ed.). Sydney, Australia: Pearson Education.

Kumar, R. (1996). *Research Methodology: A Step-by-Step Guide for Beginners*. Melbourne, Australia: Addison Wesley Longman.

Lauterborn, R. (1990). New Marketing Litany: 4Ps Passé; C-Words Take Over. *Advertising Age*, *61*(41), 26–28.

Lavidge, R. J., & Steiner, G. A. (1961). A Model for Predictive Measurements of Advertising Effectiveness. *Journal of Marketing*, *25*(6), 59–62. doi:10.2307/1248516

Lee Yahn, D. (2013). *Brand Touchpoint Wheel – Worksheet*. Retrieved from http://deniseleeyohn.com/wp-content/uploads/2013/12/WGBD-Download-Brand-Touchpoint-Wheel-Worksheet.pdf

Li, H., & Kannan, P. K. (2014). Attributing Conversions in a Multichannel Online Marketing Environment: An Empirical Model and a Field Experiment. *JMR, Journal of Marketing Research*, *51*(1), 40–56. doi:10.1509/jmr.13.0050

Liang, T., Ho, Y., Li, Y. & Turton E. (2011). What Drives Social Commerce: The Role of Social Support and Relationship Quality. *International Journal of Electronic Commerce,* 16(2), 69–90.

Marketingcharts.com. (2014a). *Marketing Budget Shifts from Traditional to Digital Media Might be Slowing*. Retrieved from http://www.marketingcharts.com/online/marketing-budget-shifts-from-traditional-to-digital-media-may-be-slowing-42159/

Marketingcharts.com. (2014b). *Are Young People Watching less TV?* Retrieved from http://www.marketingcharts.com/television/are-young-people-watching-less-tv-24817/

McColl-Kennedy, J. R., & Kiel, G. C. (2000). *Marketing – A Strategic Approach*. Melbourne, Australia: Nelson Thompson Learning.

Nations, D. (2014). *What is Social Media?* Retrieved from http://webtrends.about.com/od/web20/a/social-media.htm

Neal, C., Quester, P. G., & Hawkins, D. (2002). *Consumer Behaviour – Implications for Marketing Strategy* (3rd ed.). Sydney, Australia: McGraw-Hill Irwin.

Nuccio, L. (2013). *Social Dialogue Marketing Metrics Drives Word-of-Mouth*. Retrieved from http://www.meltwater.com/social-media-blog/social-dialogue-marketing/

Ostrow, A. (2011). *Kindle Books Now Outselling Paperbacks at Amazon*. Retrieved from http://mashable.com/2011/01/27/kindle-books-outselling-paperbacks/

Paffenback, M. (2011). *How To Identify Your Brand Touchpoints*. Retrieved from http://www.touchpointers.com/2011/10/11/how-to-identify-your-brand-touchpoints/

Pearson, N., Larson, E. W., & Gray, C. F. (2013). *Project Management in Practice* (1st ed.). Sydney, Australia: McGraw-Hill Education.

Perrigot, R., & Penard, T. (2013, Spring). Determinants of Economic Strategy in Franchising: A Resources –Based View in Franchising. *International Journal of Electronic Commerce*, *17*(3), 109–130. doi:10.2753/JEC1086-4415170305

Persson, J. (2012). *Brand Touchpoint Matrix*. Retrieved from http://brandtouchpointmatrix.com/

Petersen, M., Grone, F., Kammer, K., & Kirscheneder, J. (2010). *Multi-Channel Customer Management: Delighting Consumers, Driving Efficiency*. Retrieved from http://www.strategyand.pwc.com/media/uploads/Multi-Channel_Customer_Management.pdf

Rouse, M. (2014). *Big Data*. Retrieved from http://searchcloudcomputing.techtarget.com/definition/big-data-Big-Data

Rubin, G. (2014). *Effective National Marketing Policies for Your Local Franchisees*. Retrieved from http://www.franchising.com/articles/effective_national_marketing_policies_for_your_local_franchisees.html

Selby, E. (2014). *The Big Misunderstanding About Social Media Marketing*. Retrieved from http://www.maxxdesignblog.co.uk/integrated-marketing/social-media-marketing/social-media-berkshire/

Sensis.com.au. (2014). *Yellow Social Media Report*. Retrieved from https://www.sensis.com.au/content/dam/sas/PDFdirectory/Yellow-Social-Media-Report-2014.pdf

Siddiqi, A. (2014). *From Monologue to Dialogue With the Right Technology and the 4 C's of Social Media Marketing*. Retrieved from http://www.mediabuzz.com.sg/asian-emarketing/Social-Media/1855-from-monologue-to-dialogue-with-the-right-technology-and-the-four-cs-of-social-media-marketing

Smith, C. (2014). *One-Third of Marketers Generate a Return on Their Social Media Efforts*. Retrieved from http://www.businessinsider.com.au/one-third-of-marketers-generate-a-return-on-their-social-media-efforts-2014-1

Stalker, R. (2010). *The Rise and Rise of Social Media*. Retrieved from http://www.franchise.net.au/issues/the-rise-and-rise-of-social-media

Steinmetz, A. (1997). *The Art of Conversation: Dialogue Marketing and the Business-to-Business Relationship*. Retrieved from http://www.adlittle.com/downloads/tx_adlprism/1997_q4_27-32.pdf

Stone, R., & Jacobs, R. (2001). *Successful Direct Marketing Methods* (7th ed.). New York, NJ: McGraw Hill.

SurveyMonkey.com. (2014). *How To Identify Your Customer Touchpoints*. Retrieved October 17, 2014, from https://www.surveymonkey.com/blog/en/identify-customer-touchpoints/

Wafi, T. (2014). *From 4Ps to SAVE – A Theoretical Analysis of Various Marketing Mix Models*. Retrieved from http://www.academia.edu/3834304/FROM_4PS_TO_SAVE_A_THEORITICAL_ANALYSIS_OF_VARIOUS_MARKETING_MIX_MODELS

Walters, J. (2013). *What is a Customer Touchpoint?* Retrieved from http://360connext.com/customer-touchpoint/

Webster, G. B., & Hume, M. (2015). Defining the Role of Social Media as a Contemporary LAM Technique in Franchising. In G. Bowen & W. Ozuem (Eds.), *Computer-mediated strategies: social media and online brand communities* (pp. 223–251). Hershey, PA: IGI Global.

Willis, J. (2011). *8 Characteristics of Effective Social Media Campaigns*. Retrieved from http://www.searchenginepeople.com/blog/effective-social-media-campaigns.html

Wilson, J. J., & Morgan, J. E. (2011). Friends or Freeloaders? Encouraging brand conscience and introducing the concept of emotion-based consumer loss mitigation. *Journal of Brand Management*, *18*(9), 659–676. doi:10.1057/bm.2011.4

Yadav, M. S., & Pavlou, P. A. (2014). Marketing in Computer-Mediated Environments: Research Synthesis and New Directions. *Journal of Marketing*, *78*(1), 20–40. doi:10.1509/jm.12.0020

Yastrow, S. (n. d.). *Touchpoint Mapping Exercise*. Retrieved from http://www.yastrow.com/downloads/touchpoint-map.pdf

Zikmund, W. G., Ward, S., Lowe, B., & Winzar, H. (2007). *Marketing Research* (A. Pacific, Ed.). Melbourne, Australia: Thomson Learning.

ADDITIONAL READING

Harrison, F. (2013). Digging Deeper Down into the Empirical Generalization of Brand Recall: Adding Owned and Earned Media to Paid-Media Touchpoints. *Journal of Advertising Research*, *53*(2), 181–185. doi:10.2501/JAR-53-2-181-185

Trainor, K.J. (2012). Relating Social Media Technologies to Performance: A Capabilities-Based Perspective. *Journal of Personal Selling & Sales Management*, 32(3), 317-331.

Webcertain.com. (2014). *The Webcertain Global Mobile Report 2014*. Retrieved from http://internationaldigitalhub.com/en/publications/the-2014-webcertain-global-mobile-report

KEY TERMS AND DEFINITIONS

Brand Touchpoints: Points of contact where people interface with a business brand or product.

Consumer Touchpoints: Consumer initiated points of contact in search of information.

Dialogue Management: Identifying and monitoring of the dialogue people use to engage in communities as well as conversations and maneuvering this dialogue to build relationships.

Dialogue Marketing: A structured approach of ongoing interactive communication to form relationships with people.

Digital Marketing: The use of digital media channels and electronic devices to market products and services.

Social Commerce: Using social media to share information with friends about purchases or planned purchases.

Social Dialogue Marketing: The use of social media in a structured way to engage in ongoing interactive communication to form relationships with people.

Social Marketing: Maximising the connections with people who share a common interest through social media.

Social Relationship Management: Monitoring of a business's social media mentions to better manage their online presence.

Chapter 3
User-Generated Content and Perceived Customer Value

Wilson Ozuem
University of Gloucestershire, UK

Celia Almeida Pinho
University of West London, UK

Yllka Azemi
Cardiff Metropolitan University, UK

ABSTRACT

The Internet has transformed social communications and social behaviours. Technology-aided interpersonal interactions have replaced traditional 'face-to-face' affiliations. The purpose of this chapter is to examine the effect of user-generated content on perceived customer value. In contrast to prior study mainly investigates the effect of two main areas, namely, customer and company, this study additionally widens the scope and influence of user-generated content on consumer-to-consumer communications. Our findings suggest that user-generated content mediates on consumer decision-making process, providing higher-order credibility beyond the conventional marketing communication programmes.

INTRODUCTION

The Internet has transformed social communications and social behaviours. Technology-aided interpersonal interactions have replaced traditional 'face-to-face' affiliations (Muniz and O'Guinn, 2001). Xue and Reynolds (2010) noted that the increase in online activity has changed social and behavioural characteristics. Li and Bernoff (2008) suggested digital consumers have five different types of social behaviours: creators (e.g., publish, maintain and upload), critics (e.g., comment and rate), collectors (e.g., save and share), joiners (e.g., connect and unite) and spectators (e.g., read). These social behaviours consequently influence the social relationships and interactions between peers, that is, consumer-to-consumer (C2C) relationships, as well as between product and service providers, that is, business-to-consumer (B2C) relationships (Bratucu et al., 2014). Prahalad and Ramaswamy (2004) argued that the

DOI: 10.4018/978-1-4666-9776-8.ch003

role of the consumer has shifted from being isolated, unaware and passive to being connected, informed and active. Increasingly people are engaged in more online activities, such as social media and online shopping (Azemi and Ozuem, 2015). Based on the Internet Society's Global Internet User Survey in 2012, 96% of users access the Internet at least once a day.

Of these, 98% believe it is essential for their access to knowledge and education, while 80% believe the Internet plays a positive role for both the individual and the society as a whole. According to Prahalad and Ramaswamy (2004, p. 10), consumers are increasingly engaging in the process of both 'defining and creating value'. Consumers use their experiences as a means to offer advice and opinions about goods and services (Li and Zhan, 2011). Studies suggest that computer-mediated communications, such as websites, forums and newsgroups, are increasingly used by consumers to share information which will help them and others make better decisions on product and service choices (Man Yee et al., 2009; Li and Zhan, 2011; Bratucu et al., 2014). Electronic word of mouth (eWOM) is perceived as more trustworthy and credible than traditional marketing advertising as they are peer-generated messages (Bickart and Schindler, 2001). eWOM has the advantage of having a lower cost base than traditional WOM, and it spreads at an unprecedented speed (Li and Zhan, 2011). King et al. (2014, p. 167) argued that eWOM, 'the preferred method of communication', and its importance as a research area should not be understated.

THEORETICAL FOUNDATIONS AND CONTEXT

A review of the extant literature provides divergent notions and interpretations on the computer-mediated content created by consumers, such as user-generated content (Hautz et al., 2013; Chen et al., 2011), eWOM (Thorsten Hennig-Thuran et al., 2004), computer-mediated content, C2C communications (Adjei, Noble and Noble, 2010), consumer-generated media (Blackshaw and Nazzaro, 2004) and C2C exchange (Gruen, Osmobekov and Czaplewski, 2007). The concepts of CGC and eWOM are similar, and some researchers have applied these concepts interchangeably (Kozinets et al., 2010; Ozuem, Howell and Lancaster 2008).

Thorsten Hennig-Thuran et al. (2004, p. 39) defined eWOM as 'any positive or negative statement made by potential, actual, or former customers about a product or company, which is made available to a multitude of people and institutions via the Internet'. This definition appears truncated in that customers' interactions and discussions are not only limited to a product or company as 'other issues' are taken into account when examining consumer knowledge sharing. For instance, when you consider consumer interactions within (both online and offline) therapeutic communities, such as Weight Watchers, peers within the community can, through sharing experiences, teach and support one another in incremental learning that may promote a change in attitudes, values and behaviour (Tian et al., 2014; Ozuem, O'Keeffe and Lancaster, 2015). Xun and Reynold (2010, p. 21) defined eWOM as a 'dynamic and ongoing information exchange process'. Traditional communication theories consider the concept of WOM to have a powerful influence on consumer behaviour, particularly in information search, evaluations and subsequent decision making (Brown et al., 2007). Due to the conceptual closeness between traditional WOM and eWOM, previous studies on the latter have been built and developed on the former (Thorsten Hennig-Thuran et al., 2004). Nevertheless, owing to the complex computer-mediated context in which eWOM is generated and consumed, the concept has distinct and unique characteristics from traditional WOM (King et al., 2014; Brown et al., 2007).

Contrary to WOM, which traditionally happens in a face-to-face or one-on-one context, participants of eWOM and online CGC engage in communication with a network of people and are nongeographically bound (Kozinets et al., 2010; De Valck, Van Bruggen and Wierenga, 2009). Consumers have developed computer-mediated communities otherwise known as 'virtual communities' or online communities. According to Hagel and Armstrong (1997), these virtual communities are the 'coffeehouses' of the online environment and have influential effects on many aspects of social behaviour, including consumer behaviour. Consequently, these social groups have a 'real' existence for their participants (Kozinets, 1999). For Kozinets, online interactions of consumption-related online communities are based upon shared enthusiasm and knowledge for a specific consumption activity or group-related activities. Similarly, Bratucu et al. (2014) suggested that when viewed from a consumer perspective, online communities have certain particularities, which include a sense of belong to a community, bonding and shared interest among other peers.

In addition, contrary to traditional WOM, eWOM's potential reach and volume is 'unparalleled' (Dellarocas, 2003), as multiple exchanges of one eWOM message have potentially the ability to influence many receivers (Bratucu et al., 2014). Furthermore, as online CGC remains in the public domain, it can be easily accessed (Kozinets, 2002). Studies have found that online eWOM influences consumer purchase behaviour (Duan, Gu and Whinston, 2008; Bickart and Schindler, 2001). Chintagunta, Gopinath and Venkataraman's (2010) findings indicate that although high volumes of eWOM can lead to greater awareness for consumers, it does not necessarily mean it leads to eWOM adoption.

Traditional communication theories affirm that informational factors, which include a source, a message and a receiver, are major elements that affect information evaluation (Wathen and Burkell, 2002). Brown et al. (2007) suggested that depending on the nature of the message content, consumers process message differently. Hence, the same content can create different responses in different recipients depending on their perceptions and experiences. As the actual influence of the information depends on the recipient, the present study seeks to apply communication and information theories to understand how people are influenced.

Informational Influences

Several theories have been applied to understand how people are influenced by information and adopting ideas, knowledge or information. For instance, Petty and Cacioppo's (1986) Elaboration Likelihood Model (ELM) posits people's attitudes and behaviours are influenced either centrally (through the nature of arguments in the message) or peripherally (through other issues not directly related to the topic of the message). This theory focuses on how different levels/depths of processing affect persuasion communications. Other dual process theories have been used to explain how different types of influences, informational and normative factors, work together to 'shape the readers information-credibility judgement' (Man Yee et al., 2009, p. 13). Informational influences arise from information obtained as evidence of reality and is based on a receiver's self-judgement of the received information (Man Yee et al., 2009, p. 13). By implications, the content and the receiver are relevant components of information and thus important sources of influence. Conversely, normative influences stem from the norms/expectations of others that are implicit or explicit in the choice preference (Man Yee et al., 2009, p. 13). Both the levels/depths of information processing and the different types of influences are important in understanding and evaluating the current phenomenon of CGC, consequently relevant to the study at hand. Cheung et al. (2008) noted that information seeking and information adoption depend on source credibility and information quality. In a recent study, King et al. (2014) argued that the evaluation of eWOM's credibility and usefulness by consumers is driven by source characteristics and the textual content of the message.

Source credibility and source bias are important factors to consider when evaluating eWOM messages. Kelman and Hovland (1953), cited in Li and Zhan (2011, p. 240), suggested that source credibility refers to 'the perceived ability and motivation of a message source to provide accurate, truthful information'. According to source credibility theory, the credibility and the receiver's acceptance of a message are affected by source expertise and source bias (Buda and Zhang, 2000). Previous studies (Hovland et al., 1953, cited in Li and Zhan 2011) suggest source expertise to be the perceived knowledge and experience of the source providing the information and the extent to which the source is perceived to have valid assertions. Similarly, Ohanian (1990) contended that multiple constructs of the expertise dimensions included expert, experienced, knowledgeable, qualified and skilled; whereas trustworthiness dimensions include the constructs of dependable, honest, reliable, sincere and trustworthy. On the other hand, source bias, or source trustworthiness, refers to the potential bias/incentive that may be revealed in the source's information and is related to the motives of the source providing the information (Li and Zhan, 2011). Brown et al. (2007) averred that credibility evaluations appear to be made, in part, on the basis of the information seekers' involvement with the website and prior experiences. In addition, several studies have shown (Dhar and Chang, 2009) that recommendations originating from consumers have a much stronger influence on purchasing behaviour compared with traditional advertising sources, as message receivers identify with sources they perceive to be more similar to themselves, such as other consumers and noncommercial sources (Bickart and Schindler, 2001).

Brown et al. (2007) demonstrated that a source would be perceived as being more credible when it possesses greater expertise and is less disposed to bias. However, research carried out by Thorsten Hennig-Thuran et al. (2004) suggested there are several motivations for senders to engage in eWOM. Based on their quantitative study on the motivation behind consumers engaging in eWOM on a web-based consumer-opinion platform, they argued that there are motivational reasons why senders engage in e-WOM. The authors extended Balasubramanian and Mahajan's (2001) three types of social interaction utility, namely, focus-related utility, consumption utility, and approval utility framework, to include two additional consumer utilities, namely, moderator-related utility and homeostasis utility. Four motives for focused-related utility were identified by the authors, namely, 'concern for other consumers, helping the company, social benefits and exerting power' (Thorsten Hennig-Thuran et al. 2004, p. 42). Within the consumption utility, the authors identified writing comments and post-purchase advise-seeking as consumer motives, and the motives of 'self-enhancement' and 'economic rewards' were identified within the approval utility. Lastly, the research added the motives of 'convenience' and 'problem-solving support' under the moderator-related utility and identified two motives of expressing positive emotions and venting negative feelings as motives associated with homeostasis utility. The 11 district motivations were then empirically tested using an online questionnaire, with a sample size of 2,063. The data collated were analysed using a content analysis of participants' self-reported behaviour on antecedents of online product reviews. The authors' analysis suggested the primary factors leading to eWOM behaviour were consumers' desire for social interaction, desire for economic incentives, concern for other consumers and the potential to enhance their own self-worth. Thorsten Hennig-Thuran et al. (2004) also identified four potential consumer segments, namely, self-interested helpers, multiple-motive, consumer advocates and true altruists. Of these, self-interested consumers were found by the authors to form the biggest generators of eWOM. However, the authors' findings could only be drawn at an aggregated level. Consequently, it was difficult to detect differences between different kinds of goods and services. In addition, the participants of their studies were predominately male. The female participants only accounted for 36.7% of the sample size. This factor could potentially affect the current findings, particularly on the biggest consumer segments identified. Nevertheless, Thorsten Hennig-Thuran et al.'s (2004) findings highlight the unique characteristics of eWOM within online communities and provide practical implications, thereby serving as a basis for understanding eWOM communication motives within the present research on eWOM.

The concept of source credibility and its relevance as a key element to understanding CGC has been established. As suggested by Hautz et al. (2013), consumers are more likely to be persuaded by a message when the source is perceived as credible; and this in turn, as suggested by Keller (2007), has a direct effect on the persuasiveness of a message and consequently the receiver's behaviour. However, the actual message itself is also a relevant key element in understanding CGC and its perceived value. Consequently, information quality and information adoption will be discussed next.

Information Quality and Information Adoption

According to Bhattacherjee and Sanford (2006), quality refers to the persuasive strength of arguments contained in an informational message. Within the online context, numerous information quality dimensions have been identified, for instance, accuracy, relevance, understandability, completeness, currency, dynamism and variety and information content, accuracy, format and timeliness (Cheung et al. 2008). Consumers' acceptance of a communicator message is an effective measure for WOM adoption (Ozuem, Borrelli and Lancaster, 2015).

Sussman and Siegal (2003) adopted the ELM and proposed a theoretical model to explain how people are influenced to adopt information posted in online contexts. This study specifically focused on how knowledge workers are influenced to adopt the advice they receive in mediated contexts. Sussman and Siegal (2003) considered two key propositions in their information adoption model, namely, argument quality (information quality) as the central influence and source credibility as the peripheral influence. The model was tested both qualitatively and quantitatively, the former through interviews and the latter through a survey. Content analyses of 46 (18% response rate) interview data were performed to understand the extent to which they reflected prior theoretical model and explore conditions in which the theory might not be applicable. The model was found to be sufficiently supported, and a confirmatory phase was conducted using quantitative survey. The survey of 63 (35% response rate) was analysed. However, the results were reported on a sample size of 59. The results indicated both information usefulness and argument quality and source adoption influence adoption intention. Although the response rate is low, the findings support the model, indicating that it can be used to understand knowledge transfer using computer-mediated communication. This study is focused on an organisation, and data are collated based on participants' perceptions of e-mails consisting of advice and recommendations received from colleagues. The findings indicate that both argument quality and source credibility were positively related to perceived helpfulness. Consequently, the recipients who perceived the message as credible had more confidence in accepting and adopting the advice given, in the same way consumers who perceive an eWOM credible make judgements about its believability.

Cheung, Lee and Rabjohn (2008) further developed Sussman and Siegal's (2003) model and empirically tested their theory-driven information adoption model, seeking to examine the extent to which opinion seekers are willing to accept and adopt online consumer reviews and defining factors which encourage the adoption of CGC. The model sought to explain the determinants of information adoption within an online consumer community by examining the individual relationships between argument quality, source credibility, information usefulness and information adoption. Perceived usefulness was determined by the authors as key to information adoption. The authors considered relevance, timeliness, accuracy and comprehensiveness as determinants of argument quality and source expertise and source trustworthiness as determinants of source credibility. Their study did not examine actual CGC content/ consumer reviews, neither did they consider other potential components of argument quality, such as consumers' perceived functional, hedonic, symbolic and cost/sacrifice value (Smith and Colgate, 2007) of the evaluated product. The authors empirically tested the model using a sample of 154 users. Their findings indicate that comprehensiveness and relevance are the most effective components of argument quality, suggesting these are key influences in information adoption. Although the authors have examined and tested several components of argument quality, their study noted only 46% of variance is explained by the constructs. Consequently, they concluded information usefulness is the only factor in motivating information adoption. This study highlights that other constructs rather than information usefulness need to be taken into consideration when examining factors of eWOM adoption.

Adjei, Noble and Noble (2010), in line with other researchers (Sussman and Siegal, 2003; Cheung et al., 2008), considered the nature and quality of communications to be of central importance. The researchers developed and empirically tested a model to understand the influence of online brand communities on relationships and purchases. Their model considers online communication quality as the most fundamental driver of uncertainty reduction. Adjei et al. (2010) considered, in particular, the extent to which uncertainties are reduced in C2C exchange within online member communities. Their findings suggest online brand communities, whether they are company or independently owned websites, are effective tools for influencing sales. This finding is contrary to the findings suggested by Xue and Phelps (2004). Furthermore, their results demonstrate asymmetrical effects of positive and negative information, whereby the former has a stronger moderating influence than the latter on purchase behaviour. However, the authors limit their dimensions of communication quality to relevance, frequency, duration and timeliness of the exchanged information and do not take into consideration customer value dimensions, such as functional, hedonic, symbolic and cost/sacrifice value (Smith and Colgate, 2007) expressed in the C2C exchange. Furthermore, the forums evaluated in the research had products with relatively high price points between $1,000 and $20,000. The results may be different when lower-priced items are considered. The current study seeks to address alternative dimensions of communication quality focusing on relatively low-price-point weight management product category.

Mudambi and Schuff (2010) developed and tested a model of customer review helpfulness, addressing the issue of what makes customer reviews helpful to a consumer in the decision-making process. The authors interpreted helpfulness as a measure of perceived value and defined a helpful customer review as 'a peer-generated product evaluation that facilitates the consumer's purchase decision process' (Mudambi and Schuff, 2010). Information quality is viewed as critical in reducing uncertainty (similar to Adjei et al.'s study [2010] discussed above); consequently, the authors' model of customer review helpfulness begins with the assumption that consumers have a need to reduce purchase uncertainty. The authors considered review extremity and review depth as two important factors consumers take into account to determine helpfulness. The former addresses whether the review is positive, negative or neutral, whereas the latter addresses the extensiveness of a reviewer's comments (Mudambi and Schuff, 2010). Previous studies on reviews have provided conflicting implications on review extremity and star ratings. For example, Eisend (2006) indicated that two-sided messages enhance source credibility and brand attitude in consumer communications, implying moderate reviews are more helpful than extreme reviews. By contrast, Mudambi and Schuff (2010), found extreme ratings of eBay sellers to be more influential than moderate ratings; and Forman et al. (2008) cited in Mudambi and Schuff (2010), found moderate book reviews to be less helpful than extreme reviews. Consequently, contrary to prior research, the authors took into consideration the nature of the products within their model. Considering different product types can have differing information needs. Hence, these could potentially affect consumer reviews and ratings. The authors hypothesised the difference between search and experience goods had the potential to inform understanding of the helpfulness of an online review. Experience goods were considered as those which consumers are required to sample or purchase in order to evaluate quality, whereas search goods are those which consumers are able to evaluate product quality prior to purchase. Mudambi and Schuff's (2010) qualitative analysis of 1587 reviews from Amazon.com, across six products, indicated review extremity, review depth and product type affect the perceived helpfulness of the review. Furthermore, their findings suggest product type moderates the effect of extremity on the helpfulness of the review. Review depth was found to have a positive effect on the helpfulness of both product types, reviews with extreme ratings were found to be less helpful for experience goods and review depth was found to have a greater positive effect on the helpfulness for search goods than experience goods. Although the authors' research provides insights into understanding what makes a review helpful to consumers for different product types, the measures used, that is, review extremity (star rating) and review depth (word count), were based on a quantitative data-driven approach without considering the actual text of the reviewer and if their content corroborated with the star rating. Mudambi and Schuff's (2010) study is relevant for the current study in three aspects: Firstly, it enabled the current researcher to identify the nature of the product under consideration. Consequently, weight management products are thus defined within the current study as experience goods as they require sampling or purchase in order to fully evaluate the product. In addition, Mudambi and Schuff (2010, p. 187) identified that perceived quality of an experience good depends more on subjective attributes that are based on personal taste. Consequently, it's a unique consideration for the current study. Lastly, the current study will use both a qualitative approach to analyse the actual CGC using several informational value dimensions and a quantitative approach to analyse review extremity (star rating) and review depth (word count) to see if these corroborate.

Li and Zhan (2011) conducted a study examining how message features influence WOM adoption. Specifically, the authors investigated how language style, organisational structure and other content features affect the perceived helpfulness of online product reviews. The researchers carried out two studies. The first study was conducted using content analysis of a dataset of online product reviews of a consumer electronic device. It identified content characteristics shared by helpful reviews. The authors' second study involved an experimental approach to examine the boundary conditions under which specific content features potentially could influence review helpfulness. The studies use review 'helpfulness ratings' as a proxy for review adoption. The authors developed a new set of measures for argument quality and source credibility which would be more applicable to online-review analysis. Li and Zhan's (2011) theoretical framework identified argument quality measures as ease of comprehension, evidence presence, opposing viewpoints and comprehensiveness. As comprehension is an antecedent of persuasion and positively related to acceptance, ease of comprehension was therefore classified as an important factor; information credibility was identified as relevant information or anecdotal evidence that supports the reviewer's claims; messages containing opposing viewpoints were classified as two-sided as opposed to one-sided messages and comprehensiveness was related to the review length and the number of product features discussed. The authors' theoretical framework identified product usage and language intensity as measures of source credibility. As consumer usage of products is inferred to as product expertise, review readers can consequently assess the reviewer's usage experience with the product. Li and Zhan (2011) identified language intensity as associated to source trustworthiness, revealing extreme position through the use of intense language and emotion-laden words negatively affects the perceived source competence and consequentially can reduce persuasion power, particularly when the recipient's position is in conflict with the reviewer. Their findings in the first study suggest showing positive emotions increases review helpfulness. Review readers preferred comprehensive and easy-to-read reviews, valued opinions from product users and required supporting evidence. However, their second study did not replicate the first. Nevertheless, their results suggest recipients respond much more favourably to strong positive emotions rather than negative ones, especially when consumer involvement is high. The authors argued that as most consumers do not refer to product reviews unless they are considering a product purchase, they are likely to be highly involved when they access online reviews. The second study also revealed review readers with positive prior attitudes towards the product tended to prefer positive reviews over negative ones. Similarly, those having negative prior attitudes also evaluated positive reviews more favourable when they were highly involved. Their finding suggests reviews with strong positive emotions gain higher rating. Although Li and Zhan's (2011) study is not representative, it does provide some insight into how persuasion is accomplished in the virtual community.

Man Yee et al. (2009) conducted a study examining the informational and normative determinants of the perceived credibility of eWOM, identifying factors which contribute to consumer message adoption. Their study examined how receivers' perceived source credibility affected perceived recommendation credibility by applying a dual-process theory of information processing to examine how consumer reviews are evaluated. Specifically, their study focused on two primary aspects: informational and normative influences which reflect online social aggregation mechanisms which affect the persuasiveness of customer reviews. The former involves receivers' self-judgement, and the latter is more based on the position of other consumers and their opinions. Informational determinants were based on the content of reviews; argument strength (review is convincing and has valid supporting arguments); recommendation framing (i.e., valence of review, praise message positively framed or complaint message negatively framed); recommendation sidedness, either a one-sided message which reflects either a positive or a negative feature of a product or service or a two-sided message which has both positive and negative elements; source credibility as rated by other eWOM users, i.e., reviewers' reputation rating; and confirmation of receivers' prior belief is concerned with whether the perceived information received is consistent with the receivers' prior knowledge or expectations. Normative determinants were based on recommendation consistency (congruency of messages) and recommendation rating (others' overall perception of the reviewer message). The authors' study found informational-based determinants, specifically argument strength and source credibility. The confirmation with receivers' prior beliefs significantly influenced perceived eWOM credibility. The authors asserted that receivers do no simply follow comments blindly. Instead, in the presence of normative information, only opinions based on strong and valid arguments are accepted. Having said that, Man Yee et al. (2009) suggested that normative influence cues do significantly affect how people determine the credibility of the online recommendations. They found out that involvement significantly moderates the relationship between recommendation consistency and perceived review credibility. The study helps the current research as it confirms both informational and normative influences must be taken into account in order to understand the usage or influence of eWOM and to evaluate eWOM.

Fan, Miao, Fang and Lin (2013) conducted a study examining the perceived eWOM credibility in an online consumer's decision-making process and identified source credibility, eWOM quantity and quality to significantly affect consumers' perceived eWOM credibility. Source credibility was considered a key factor in helping consumers judge online information, whereas eWOM volume quantity was considered to reduce consumer anxiety, as others have already purchased the product. Hence, the messages represented the popularity of the product, helping in making a purchase decision. For Fan et al. (2013), low-quality eWOM was defined as providing more emotional descriptions, whereas high-quality eWOM was defined as providing a more pragmatic description relating to product attributes. The authors also proposed customer expertise and customer involvement in their conceptual model. Higher customer involvement was perceived to motivate consumers to understand the products and read others' opinions to gather more information, whereas customer expertise enabled a reader to evaluate information according to their experience and knowledge. Their findings provide evidence that perceived eWOM credibility significantly affects eWOM adoption. The quality of eWOM was found to be the most significant factor positively affecting their perceived credibility, and the quantity of eWOM was also found to have a positive influence. Fan et al. (2013) concluded that customer expertise and customer involvement had no significant effect on eWOM credibility. Their findings provide empirical evidence that eWOM plays a significant role in the consumer decision-making process. Consequently, for organisations, consumer opinions are important factors to consider. Although their conceptual model only provides evidence of three instead of five factors, their study is of relevance to the current research as it provides factors relevant in predicting consumers' perceived eWOM credibility. Consequently, these factors can be applied to the current research, when evaluating actual CGC. Increasingly, consumers turn to online social networks and in particular eWOM networks to utilise product information to make purchasing decisions (Man Yee et al., 2009). However, as indicated by Chintagunta, Gopinath and Venkataraman (2010), high volume does not indicate automatic adoption. Furthermore, the process by which consumers evaluate the credibility of online recommendations is of interest due to the relative facelessness of the Internet medium compared with WOM. Consequently, Mudambi and Schuff (2010) suggested that as CGC becomes more prevalent, there is a growing need to focus on the quality rather than the quantity.

CONCLUSION AND MANAGERIAL IMPLICATIONS

As CGC becomes more mainstream, it is of interest to further understand its significance and relevance in different contents of consumers' consumption experiences. The current study, at a macro level, takes into consideration the present popularity of CGC as well as the growing epidemic relating to excess weight issues and the consequent health problems people are experiencing.

The first macro level to be considered is CGC. Irrefutably through web 2.0 technologies, the 'voice' of the consumer has evolved, creating the electronic version of eWOM communications (Williams et al., 2012) with consumers no longer limited by geographical boundaries. According to Prahalad and Ramaswamy (2004, p. 137), 'Value is now centred in the experiences of consumers rather than being rooted in goods and services'. Consequently, consumers today are described as 'self-reflective', are narrative agents (Caru and Cova, 2008; Ozuem, Thomas and Lancaster, 2015) and produce wide-ranging amounts of self-generated content over various platforms, sharing their opinions and experiences. As a result, consumer CGC is a rapidly growing trend for brand discussions and consumer insights. For instance, recent empirical evidence reveals 39% of millennials discuss products/brands on a daily basis (Crowdtap, 2014). They consider CGC 35% more memorable than other media, and they trust it 50% more than other forms of media other media (Crowdtap, 2014). Williams et al. (2012) noted that consumers' persuasive power is due to their noncommercial interest. Consequently, evidence suggests that

CGC is influential, and brand perceptions are increasingly shaped by consumers and not by companies and marketing executives. Thus, from a marketing perspective, it is therefore important for marketers to understand consumers' online content creation and its potential influence on their brands. From a consumer's perspective, CGC offers a peer perspective potentially free from commercial interest.

The second macro level considered is consumer health, which is a concern of everyone. Currently the level of excess weight is on an upward trend, and in the last 25 years, the number of people with obesity in the UK has trebled and is reaching 'epidemic' proportions (BBC, 2014b). Furthermore, according to the National Obesity Forum, more than half of the UK population is estimated to be obese by 2050 (BBC, 2014a). In addition, being significantly overweight has been linked to further health issues, such as diabetes, heart disease, high blood pressure, stress, anxiety and depression (BBC, 2014b). Consequently, health issues, especially those related to weight issues, are frequently discussed both offline and online. According to Euromonitor International (2014), the global obesity epidemic has increased the weight management market industry to US$14.3bn in 2013. The weight loss management category includes meal replacement options, medication and supplements especially formulated and marketed for weight loss or weight control; and it also includes meal plans, such as Weight Watchers, Slimming World, Jenny Craig and Nutrisystem (Euromonitor International, 2014). However, despite the increase in weight management products and supplements to help consumers, the industry has been plagued by false advertising and false claims. For example, Sensa Products were fined US$26.5m by the Federal Trade Commission for false advertising (Catillo, 2014), and Dr Oz faced an investigation with regard to his promotion of weight loss supplements (Euromonitor International, 2014). The increased availability of information through computer-mediated communications could potentially empower consumers to make more educated decisions, simultaneously improving their health literacy (Euromonitor International, 2014).

Having established the popularity and growth of CGC as well as the current global epidemic of weight management issue, this study identifies these interlinked issues as a relevant topic of interest. Understanding how effective CGC is in helping other consumers understand health issues relating to weight management products is an interesting research question at a macro level. However, this study seeks to explore, at a micro level, the key elements of CGC and examine the extent to which these elements provide value based on communication and information theories. Although the phenomenon of CGC has been explored, it is a relatively new research topic; and due to its constant mutable nature, there is a need to further extend research in this area. Effective CGC could potentially assist the formation of effective health and marketing campaigns, which could in turn benefit governments, as well as companies and brands, in creating healthier and more desirable products which would take into account consumer health issues. Consequently, this could benefit consumers by providing health awareness and healthier consumption choices.

REFERENCES

Adjei, M., Noble, S., & Noble, C. (2010). The influence of C2C communications in online brand communities on customer purchase behavior. *Journal of the Academy of Marketing Science*, *38*(5), 634–653. doi:10.1007/s11747-009-0178-5

Azemi, Y., & Ozuem, W. (2015). Social media and SMEs in transition countries. In G. Bowen & W. Ozuem (Eds.), *Computer-mediated marketing strategies: social media and online brand communities* (pp. 114–133). Hershey, PA: IGI Global. doi:10.4018/978-1-4666-6595-8.ch005

Balasubramanian, S., & Mahajan, V. (2001). The economic leverage of the virtual community. *International Journal of Electronic Commerce*, *5*(3), 103–138.

BBC. (2014a). Obesity crisis: Future projections 'underestimated'. Retrieved from http://www.bbc.co.uk/news/health-25708278

BBC. (2014b). What are the health risks of obesity? Retrieved from http://www.bbc.co.uk/science/0/21702372

Bhattacherjee, A., & Sanford, C. (2006). Influence processes for information technology acceptance: An elaboration likelihood model. *Management Information Systems Quarterly*, *30*(4), 805–825.

Bickart, B., & Schindler, R. (2001). Internet forums as influential sources of consumer information. *Advances in Consumer Research. Association for Consumer Research (U. S.)*, *28*(1), 134.

Blackshaw, P., & Nazzaro, M. (2004). *Consumer-generated media (CGM) 101: Word-of-mouth in the age of the Web fortified consumer*. Retrieved from http://www.nielsen-online.com/downloads/us/buzz/nbzm_wp_CGM101.pdf

Bratucu, R., Gheorghe, I. R., Radu, A., & Purcarea, V. L. (2014). The relevance of netnography to the harness of Romanian health care electronic word-of-mouth. *Journal of Medicine and Life*, *7*(3), 363–367. PMID:25408755

Brown, J., Broderick, A., & Lee, N. (2007). Word of mouth communication within online communities: Conceptualizing the online social network. *Journal of Interactive Marketing*, *21*(3), 2–20. doi:10.1002/dir.20082

Buda, R., & Zhang, Y. (2000). Consumer product evaluation: The interactive effect of message framing, presentation order, and source credibility. *Journal of Product and Brand Management*, *9*(4), 229–242. doi:10.1108/10610420010344022

Caru, A., & Cova, B. (2008). Small versus big stories in framing consumption experiences. *Qualitative Market Research: An International Journal*, *11*(2), 166–176. doi:10.1108/13522750810864422

Catillo, M. (2014). Sensa, L'Occitane, LeanSpa, HGG Diet Direct fined by FTC for false advertising. Retrieved from http://www.cbsnews.com/news/sensa-loccitane-leanspa-hcg-diet-direct-fined-by-ftc-for-false-advertising/

Chen, J., Xu, H., & Whinston, A. (2011). Moderated online communities and quality of user-generated content. *Journal of Management Information Systems*, *28*(2), 237–268. doi:10.2753/MIS0742-1222280209

Cheung, C., Lee, M., & Rabjohn, N. (2008). The impact of electronic word-of-mouth: The adoption of online opinions in online customer communities. *Internet Research*, *18*(3), 229–247. doi:10.1108/10662240810883290

Cheung, M. Y., Luo, C., Sia, C. L., & Chen, H. (2009). Credibility of electronic word-of-mouth: Informational and normative determinants of on-line consumer recommendations. *International Journal of Electronic Commerce*, *13*(4), 9–38. doi:10.2753/JEC1086-4415130402

Chintagunta, P. K., Gopinath, S., & Venkataraman, S. (2010). The effects of online user reviews on movie box office performance: Accounting for sequential rollout and aggregation across local markets. *Marketing Science*, *29*(5), 944–957. doi:10.1287/mksc.1100.0572

Crowdtap (2014). Millennials heart UGC. Retrieved from http://blog.crowdtap.it/2014/04/millennials-heart-ugc-infographic/

De Valck, K., Van Bruggen, G., & Wierenga, B. (2009). Virtual communities: A marketing perspective. *Decision Support Systems*, *47*(3), 185–203. doi:10.1016/j.dss.2009.02.008

Dellarocas, C. (2003). The digitization of word of mouth: Promise and challenges of online feedback mechanisms. *Management Science*, *49*(10), 1407–1424. doi:10.1287/mnsc.49.10.1407.17308

Dhar, V., & Chang, E. (2009). Does chatter matter? The impact of user-generated content on music sales. *Journal of Interactive Marketing*, *23*(4), 300–307. doi:10.1016/j.intmar.2009.07.004

Duan, W., Gu, B., & Whinston, A. B. (2008). The dynamics of online word-of-mouth and product sales: An empirical investigation of the movie industry. *Journal of Retailing*, *84*(2), 233–242. doi:10.1016/j.jretai.2008.04.005

Eisend, M. (2006). Source credibility dimensions in marketing communication – A generalized solution. *Journal of Empirical Generalisations in Marketing*. Retrieved from http://www.empgens.com/resources/SourceCredibility.pdf

Euromonitor International. (2014). Consumer health trends, developments and prospects. Retrieved from http://www.euromonitor.com/consumer-health-trends-developments-and-prospects/report

Fan, Y., Miao, Y., Fang, Y., & Lin, R. (2013). Establishing the adoption of electronic word-of-mouth through consumers' perceived credibility. *International Business Research, 6*(3). Retrieved from http://ccsenet.org/journal/index.php/ibr/article/view/24217/15334

Gruen, T., Osmonbekov, T., & Czaplewski, A. (2007). Customer-to-customer exchange: Its MOA antecedents and its impact on value creation and loyalty. *Journal of the Academy of Marketing Science*, *35*(4), 537–549. doi:10.1007/s11747-006-0012-2

Hagel, J., & Armstrong, A. G. (1997). *Net gain: Expanding markets through virtual communities*. Boston, MA: Harvard Business School.

Hautz, J., Füller, J., Hutter, K., & Thürridl, C. (2013). Let users generate your video ads? The impact of video source and quality on consumers' perceptions and intended behaviors. *Journal of Interactive Marketing*, *28*(1), 1–15. doi:10.1016/j.intmar.2013.06.003

Hennig-Thurau, T., Gwinner, K., Walsh, G., & Gremler, D. (2004). Electronic word-of-mouth via consumer-opinion platforms: What motivates consumers to articulate themselves on the Internet? *Journal of Interactive Marketing*, *18*(1), 38–52. doi:10.1002/dir.10073

Internet Society. (2015). Global Internet user survey 2012. Retrieved from https://www.internetsociety.org/internet/global-internet-user-survey-2012

Keller, E. (2007). Unleashing the power of word of mouth: Creating brand advocacy to drive growth. *Journal of Advertising Research, 47*(4), 448–452. doi:10.2501/S0021849907070468

King, R., Racherla, P., & Bush, V. (2014). What we know and don't know about online word-of-mouth: A review and synthesis of the literature. *Journal of Interactive Marketing, 28*(3), 167–183. doi:10.1016/j.intmar.2014.02.001

Kozinets, R. V. (1999). E-tribalized marketing?: The strategic implications of virtual communities of consumption. *European Management Journal, 17*(3), 252–264. doi:10.1016/S0263-2373(99)00004-3

Kozinets, R. V. (2002). The field behind the screen: Using netnography for marketing research in online communities. *JMR, Journal of Marketing Research, 39*(1), 61–72. doi:10.1509/jmkr.39.1.61.18935

Kozinets, R. V., de Valck, K., Wojnicki, A. C., & Wilner, S. J. S. (2010). Networked narratives: Understanding word-of-mouth marketing in online communities. *Journal of Marketing, 74*(2), 71–89. doi:10.1509/jmkg.74.2.71

Li, C., & Bernoff, J. (2008). *Groundswell: Winning in a world transformed by social technologies*. Boston, MA: Forrester Research, Inc.

Li, J., & Zhan, L. (2011). Online persuasion: How the written word drives WOM—Evidence from consumer-generated product reviews. *Journal of Advertising Research, 51*(1), 239–257. doi:10.2501/JAR-51-1-239-257

Mudambi, S., & Schuff, D. (2010). What makes a helpful online review? A study of customer reviews on amazon.com. *Management Information Systems Quarterly, 34*(1), 185–200.

Muniz, A. M. Jr, & O'Guinn, T. C. (2001). Brand Community. *The Journal of Consumer Research, 27*(4), 412–432. Retrieved from http://search.ebscohost.com/login.aspx?direct=true&AuthType=ip,shib&db=buh&AN=5244454&site=ehost-live doi:10.1086/319618

Ohanian, R. (1990). Construction and validation of a scale to measure celebrity endorsers' perceived expertise, trustworthiness, and attractiveness. *Journal of Advertising, 19*(3), 39–52. doi:10.1080/00913367.1990.10673191

Ozuem, W., Borrelli, M., & Lancaster, G. (2015). Leveraging the co-evolution of offline and online video games: An empirical study. *Journal of Strategic Marketing*. doi:10.1080/0965254X.2015.1076883

Ozuem, W., Howell, K. E., & Lancaster, G. (2008). Communicating in the new interactive marketspace. *European Journal of Marketing, 42*(9/10), 1059–1083. doi:10.1108/03090560810891145

Ozuem, W., & Lancaster, G. (2014). Recovery strategies in on-line service failure. In A. Ghorbani (Ed.), *Marketing in the cyber era: strategies and emerging trends* (pp. 143–159). Hershey, PA: IGI Global. doi:10.4018/978-1-4666-4864-7.ch010

Ozuem, W., O'Keeffe, A., & Lancaster, G. (2015). Leadership Marketing: An exploratory study. *Journal of Strategic Marketing*. doi:10.1080/0965254X.2014.1001867

Ozuem, W., Thomas, T., & Lancaster, G. (2015). The influence of customer loyalty on small island economies: An empirical and exploratory study. *Journal of Strategic Marketing*. doi:10.1080/0965254X.2015.1011205

Petty, R. E., & Cacioppo, J. T. (1986). *Communication and persuasion: Central and peripheral routes to attitude change*. New York, NY: Springer-Verlag. doi:10.1007/978-1-4612-4964-1

Prahalad, C. K., & Ramaswamy, V. (2004). *The future of competition: Co-creating unique value with customers*. Boston, MA: Harvard Business School Press.

Prahalad, C. K., & Ramaswamy, V. (2004). Co-creation experiences: The next practice in value creation. *Journal of Interactive Marketing*, *18*(3), 5–14. doi:10.1002/dir.20015

Smith, J. B., & Colgate, M. (2007). Customer value creation: A practical framework. *Journal of Marketing Theory and Practice*, *15*(1), 7–23. doi:10.2753/MTP1069-6679150101

Sussman, S., & Siegal, W. (2003). Informational influence in organizations: An integrated approach to knowledge adoption. *Information Systems Research*, *14*(1), 47–65. doi:10.1287/isre.14.1.47.14767

Tian, K., Sautter, P., Fisher, D., Fischbach, S., Luna-Nevarez, C., Boberg, K., & Vann, R. et al. (2014). Transforming health care: Empowering therapeutic communities through technology-enhanced narratives. *The Journal of Consumer Research*, *41*(2), 237–260. doi:10.1086/676311

Wathen, C. N., & Burkell, J. (2002). Believe it or not: Factors influencing credibility on the Web. *Journal of the American Society for Information Science and Technology*, *53*(2), 134–144. doi:10.1002/asi.10016

Williams, D., Crittenden, V., Keo, T., & McCarty, P. (2012). The use of social media: An exploratory study of usage among digital natives. *Journal of Public Affairs*, *12*(2), 127–136. doi:10.1002/pa.1414

Xue, F., & Phelps, J. (2004). Internet-facilitated consumer-to-consumer communication: The moderating role of receiver characteristics. *International Journal of Internet Marketing and Advertising*, *1*(2), 121–136. doi:10.1504/IJIMA.2004.004016

Xun, J., & Reynolds, J. (2010). Applying netnography to market research: The case of the online forum. *Journal of Targeting. Measurement and Analysis for Marketing*, *18*(1), 17–31. doi:10.1057/jt.2009.29

KEY WORDS AND DEFINITIONS

Advertising: A message that companies reveal to inform the audience about a product or service.
Computer-Mediated Communications: Individuals' communication through electronic devices.
Consumer: An individual who buys from a company (i.e., goods or services).
eWOM: The online communication across parties (i.e., individuals and customers).
Perceived Customer Value: The benefit that a customer gets from the purchase.
Social Media: An online platform where people communicate and share information.
User-Generated Content: A personal platform developed and revealed online (e.g., video).

Chapter 4
Loyalty Strategy and Social-CRM:
How Consumers Adhere to the Tools

Nedra Bahri-Ammari
IHEC of Carthage, Tunisia

Slim Mraidi
ESC of Manouba, Tunisia

ABSTRACT

Always on the lookout for novelty and innovation, companies are using social networks, which now occupy an important place in our daily. Users of social networks constitute a new target for retailers looking to evolve their loyalty programs. Through Facebook or twitter accounts, the company can develop a profile of the user and have an idea regarding their interests... Therefore, companies have a lot of opportunities through social CRM, to communicate, to develop their relationship programs and, in fine, to retain their customer. Although the social CRM is perceived as a business strategy it requires a technology platform, rules, processes and social characteristics. To ensure interaction with these tools, the company should ensure that the consumer adopts them in an abundant manner. This paper aims at examining the emergence of interaction across internet tools, the importance of managing customer relationship through social CRM and the determinants of why consumers adopt these tools by studying the case of Facebook in emerging countries.

INTRODUCTION

The current abundance in supply forces businesses to react by implementing a customer relationship management strategy whose goal is customer loyalty (Bahri-Ammari, 2014; Vesel & Zabkar, 2009). Such a strategy, that considers all interactions with customers, is essential for the creation of a close relationship with customers, at least with the most profitable ones. This strategy is defined as the company's ability to offer tailored services or products for a particular customer. It involves an ongoing ability to understand and anticipate customers' needs, and therefore considers the relationship with them as a

DOI: 10.4018/978-1-4666-9776-8.ch004

business object. The customer is attracted by a valuable offer because it allows him/her to spare certain time-consuming market activities, notably costly.

CRM, as an interactive technology, allows the company to track competitors' reactions and be responsive to consumer needs. Responding quickly to needs by providing services with high added value is now the challenge for most companies. CRM is the process that manages those expectations to ensure long-term relationships and meet consumers' dynamic needs. To be always in tandem with the changing environment and to provide the expected benefits, CRM was able to adapt itself to technological progress. The advent of internet has given birth to e-CRM which Alhaiou et al. (2009) presents as the online usage of CRM. Dominance of Internet in modern life gives e-CRM an important place in the company's vision, which has a new channel to carry its retention strategy.

In addition to the electronic channel, the company can now use mobiles as a channel to manage relationships with its customers. According to Valsecchi et al. (2007), mobile CRM (m-CRM) is CRM performed by a mobile support such as a mobile phone. The company may therefore develop an application that allows users to keep in touch with it and allows access to interactive content as part of the company's relationship policy.

Being always on the lookout for novelty and innovation, CRM professionals have benefited from the emergence of social networks and integrated their success and enthusiasm into their relationship strategies, which gave birth to Social CRM (S-CRM). That puts the customer at the center of business strategy. Now, customers are no longer passive receivers who simply receive information from the company, they rather contribute to its development by discussing and collaborating with the brand. Companies rely on this way to build close relationships with their customers in view of promoting their commitment to the brand and make them potential ambassadors. This is the view of Baird and Parasnis (2011) who argue that the main objective of classic CRM was to take the best possible customer value throughout the life of their relationship with the company while S-CRM aims at managing the dialog with the customer.

Social networks have revolutionized and facilitated communication between people, inspiring and encouraging customer relationship management professionals to integrate this new tool in their relational strategies because it provides opportunities for a targeting based on specific criteria, not possible before. Using Facebook as part of its S-CRM strategy (Zarella, 2010), the company can for example use this channel to communicate with fans and disseminate information concerning news about the brand, products / services, answer questions from its customers and keep in touch with them. All these new forms of CRM are not in conflict, and one does not cancel the other. Rather, they are a subset of the overall CRM business strategy. Therefore, they should be complementary and coherent for the company that has several channels that can be used to carry S-CRM policy (Weinberg, 2009). To ensure interaction with these tools, the company should ensure that the consumer adopts them in an abundant manner. Thus, the interest carried to the TAM model which can explain the intention to use technology. TAM was specifically tailored to model user acceptance of IS with the aim of explaining the intention to use of an information system. It includes two essential variables: perceived usefulness (PU), perceived of ease of use (PEU), attitude and intention. This study aims to measure the importance of managing customer relationship through social CRM and to examine Internet users' behavior towards adoption of technology (Facebook). Also to study customers' acceptance technology behavior to determine the factors which influence their intention to adopt Facebook in emerging countries. This research will help managers to highlight the predicted factors which really affect Internet users (Venkatesh & Davis, 2003; Ellison et al. 2007). The results could serve to determine the variables which urge Internet users to use Facebook. These variables will be studied to help brands and marketers in their communication strategies.

LITERATURE REVIEW

IT, Marketing Function, and Customer Relationship Management

The interest given to combining information technologies and marketing function by some authors is understood on the ground that... *information technologies are powerful in marketing because they allow organizations to build strong personalized relationships with their consumers and to understand their needs* (Abbot et al. 2001). In marketing, they are tools of analysis and of tactical and operational solutions (Leverick et al. 1997). The success of implementing any system should be adequate with the firm's objectives and organizational structure. The objectives relate to the development of a relationship with the customer (Schitz et Rovner, 1992), a better efficiency or optimization of resources and improvement of return on investment. The structure should be adapted accordingly by having a back office and Front-service systems. Given the increase of available information on consumers, only information technologies will be able to analyze and treat them in an efficient way (Fletcher, 1995; Arnold et Penn, 1987; Wightman, 1987; Kumar et Vrat, 1989). "The recognition of the contribution of information technologies in the firm is due to the quick development of ICT which gave visibility and credibility for the relationship marketing paradigm (Crosby et al. 1990)". The firm should incorporate a relationship-based vision that makes the success of implemented technologies easier to achieve (Bahri-Ammari, 2014).

Information Technologies and the Relationship Marketing Paradigm

"New" marketing needs a perspective that should be based on integrative relationships to guarantee retention of customers (Jolley et al. 2006).

According to some authors, there should be a paradigm for marketing conception and implementation (Gummesson, 1995). Others prefer practicing transactional marketing with a variety of relationship marketing tools (Brodie et al. 1997). Proposals in the literature agree on developing a link between relationship marketing and information technology. The inexistence of links between these two concepts has nevertheless been the object of some studies (Ford et al. 1998). They are four stages that justify this link: transactional marketing, relationship marketing, databases marketing, interactive marketing and network marketing (Brodie et al. 1997).

Information Technologies changed the role of consumers, communicational and interactivity relationships (Zineldin, 2000). These IT mechanisms assign to the relationship perspective the possibility of satisfying and maintaining customers loyal to the firm (Lindon & Jallat, 2002). They are currently among the most decisive factors for the creation, development and strengthening of relationships. Technologies implemented with the existing information systems allow for an increasing and a complete evolution of industries by creating new competitiveness sources (Venkatraman, 1997).

Relationship Marketing and Marketing Information Systems

Information systems provide the company with the ability to understand the specific needs of each customer segment, and define an offer adapted to each of them (product characteristics, price adjustment, definition of appropriate service).

The provided information overcomes the communication problems of the two parties.

Designing the most appropriate and targeted communication strategy allows for building long-term relationships between the customer and the firm (Pawar & Sharda, 1997).

- More communication with customers

It allows for a better valorization and retention of customer. Retention needs, on the one hand, monitoring customers, and on the other hand, the thoughtful use of databases for its changing needs. The firm should establish an ICT-based approach (Law et al. 2003), and anticipate possible changes. They should also review their management methods and restructure their strategies. This is about valorizing a wealth that is still little exploited: customer capital.

A marketing information system provides continuous information to users on customer behavior. Once processed and communicated, they help to establish loyalty programs specific to each segment, with the aim of anticipating customer demand; generating demand, generating prospective buyers, developing customer value and transforming potential customers into acquired customers and keeping them (Bahri & Mzoughi, 2007).

As for the firm, the aim is to promote "cross selling" between different products or services, to promote communication of information within the firm and to spare sales people and provide them with computer tools.

Currently, relationships based on information technology allow the organization to integrate consumer demand so they it is properly analyzed and processed. These demands are for the information technology sharing, collaborative planning and coordination systems (Godfrey, 1993). Freedom of movement of information involves information on consumers, products, performance of service, logistics, competitive comparison, suppliers, costs and critical funding for the creation, development and promotion of long-term relationships (Hamon et al. 2004). If information technology is the basis of relationship marketing, information systems are powerful catalyst structures whose need is the flow and sharing of information. Some companies believe that knowledge and information are the most important acquisitions if they are properly exploited. The company is now forced to use communicative means such as Internet, Intranet, Extranet, and EDI, to share and disseminate information to ensure the proper management of its relationships (Zineldin, 2000).

Technologicalship Marketing

This new type of marketing allows putting in effect any relationship marketing strategy, through technologies. It is particularly interested in supporting the link between the internal environment and the process of interaction with customers, and putting into interaction information technology, consumer and organization (Zineldin, 2000). The company puts all its resources available to consumers in order to retain them and build their loyalty. These resources relate to implementing information technology as well as its supporting tools (Jordan and Krumwiede, 1999). This new concept provides different types of solutions, interactions and relationships with various consumers. The technologicalship consumer provides a new variety of relationships and solutions appropriate to different needs (Buckinx & Poel, 2005). Being fully integrated into marketing, it combines activities and marketing tools in a single operation. However, its success depends on the development and use of technology and the development of relationships between involved parties (Hamon et al. 2004). These relationships will be built and developed whenever technology changes or is replicated through novelty (Larivière & VanDen,

2004). A customer follow-up service is now essential to detect changes that may take place and be able to respond in real time.

This type of marketing is a strategic factor for companies that adopt a customer-oriented approach and a competitiveness and differentiation factor of ten stronger than products quality themselves. Accordingly, a marketing information system should present information that will form the basis for the design of a CRM software and exceed at the same time customer expectations (Larivière & VanDen, 2004). This is done through adopting communicative means and defining a quality service modulated in tune with customer value (Yuan & Chang, 2001). Likewise, is it necessary that the company should be able to identify these requirements? The following table illustrates the difference between relationship marketing and technologicalship marketing in terms of marketing key success factors. In view of these results, we can assume that the role of Customer Relationship Management (CRM) as a technology is to retain and maintain relationships with customers (table 1).

Table 1. Relationship marketing and technologicalship marketing (Zineldin, 2000)

Category	Relationship Marketing	Technologicalship Marketing
The marketing environment	The role of the marketing is relatively clear and constant, defined; · The market is relatively limited by alliances and the network; · The niches of markets are easy to identify; · The relations are dyadic confrontation, interpersonal contact based on the commitment and the trust; · A marketing "pullover" and " push " for the consumer; The cost is raised for the promotion as well as for the construction of relation and preservation of the customers; · The importance of the level of the information to enable the marketing information system.	· The role of the marketing is in continuous evolution, moved forward by the technologies; · The market is less affected by the defects; · niches are easily identified and categorized; · The contact is personal; · The marketing is "pull" and " push " for the consumer; · The cost of the promotion is low as well as that of the creation of relation and preservation of the customers; · The importance of the level of the information to enable the marketing information system, the marketing groups become more important when there is integration of the TI.
Marketing success factors	· to Maintain the existing customers, the retention is considered as a success; · Focused on the consumer satisfaction; · An existing relative consciousness for the customers; · The received value is essential to succeed · The business alliances are essential for the marketing; · The creativity is important for the differentiation on the long term, the adaptation, to put the consumer in the center of the organization is a source of differentiation; · An interactivity raised with the consumers.	· to Maintain and to attract new customers is the success of companies; · Focused on the consumer satisfaction and the TI; · A consciousness is existing for the customers; · The valuable perception is essential to succeed; · The work should be structured in chain between the company, his consumers and his partners to find relevant solutions. This coordination allows the marketers to go towards the consumer and to influence their practices and routines; · The innovation became essential for the differentiation every time the number and the type of competitors increase. The technology (Internet) offers various axes of innovations in this particular case the personalization; · A high interactivity is considerable with the consumers
The position of the organization	The decision is focused on the relation between firms in network and in individual; The relations between firms lead to the development of the product; The existing marketing groups are as an umbrella for the organization.	· The decision is focused on the product / leading and the consumers with the aim of reaching defined markets by using the technological progress and the capacity to create a relational exchange; · The marketing and the information systems lead to the decisions on products; · The marketing groups become more integrated with other technological groups.

Development of a CRM Strategy

A CRM strategy has the merit of developing a company's loyalty base by setting up a system that looks for understanding customer needs and market dynamics, measuring and optimizing quality and key dimensions of customer service, decrypting and managing the key elements of satisfaction and segmenting customers and designing loyalty-building strategies (Abdelmoula et al. 2007, Ben Issa, 2011). It is considered decisive because of its capacity to give a mutual advantage to the customer and the firm (Gronroos, 1996). Opinions on the contributions of CRM are for most researchers certain, but uncertain for some others.

Customer Relationship Management (CRM): Definition

It is a process that manages customer expectations to ensure long-term relationships and serve consumers' dynamic needs (Burez & VanDen, 2007). The CRM is to increase customer acquisition and company profitability, since it is less expensive for the company to retain an existing customer than to acquire a new one (Hamon et al. 2004). CRM applications involves also activities that have a significant impact on profitability (Wong & Hong, 2006).

For some authors, CRM seeks to establish a long-term commitment, trust (Khalil and Pearson, 2007) and cooperation relationship with customers (Lars, 2007). This relationship is characterized by openness and sincerity in delivering a high quality service, responding to consumer input, and by a predisposition of the company to sacrifice short-term gain for long-term gain. CRM gives the company the ability to establish a relationship marketing strategy having as a basis the building of a long-term cooperation relationship and a mutual dependence between the two parties (Kinard & Capella, 2006; Kim, 2008).

CRM, considered also to be a management approach, identifies, attracts and increases the retention of the most profitable customers. Its deployment introduces a considerable impact on firm activity since it answers to one or several strategic needs. Moreover, seen as a process that helps to analyze a gigantic data warehouse to provide the necessary information to understand each customer separately, its implementation offers advantages in terms of improved sales, changes in market share, consumer satisfaction and reducing attrition rate or customer flight (Burez & Van-Den, 2007). The firm, on the basis of these data, will be able to adopt a variety of treatments for consumers' different segments. Thus, this is the clear objective of CRM, i.e. creating faithful long-term relationships between the firm and its customers. This sets out the processor activities that help build profitable long-term relationships with consumers.

However, CRM adoption may lead the company to experience unexpected results because 75% to 85% of implemented CRM applications fail. Some authors find that failure of an application is the result of a lack of development of a CRM vision, and a lack of robust approaches to its implementation. Setting up an efficient CRM requires the presence of an information technology which, on the one hand, is needed to implement CRM for decision-making applications, and on the other hand to assist in retaining and maintaining relationships with customers, namely CRM performance. It is "a customer-oriented business philosophy, which includes the analysis, planning and control of customer relationships by means of information technologies and modern communication" (Grabner-Kraeuter & Moedritscher, 2002; Zulkifli & Tahir, 2012). CRM is a strategy framed in methodology and supported by technology. The fact that it relies on technology, CRM supports technological development and incorporates these changes in its operating procedures. We are witnessing the emergence of new forms of CRM whose basics are found in the possibilities offered by new technologies. There are mainly two innovations that have offered new opportunities for CRM strategies. These are the advent of Internet and mobile telephony.

E-CRM

Internet dominance in modern life gave e-CRM an important place in the company's strategy (Harrison-Walker & Neely, 2004). E-CRM solutions directly related to the company's information system furnish a significant contribution in data collection which, once cross-treated, contributes to improving customer knowledge (Cinquin et al. 2002). In addition, e-CRM provides the company with a new channel to promote its loyalty-promoting strategy. This channel has low costs for web-based campaigns. Moreover, the company has total control over its spending. If the company finds out that their campaigns missed their targets, it can change or stop them. In addition, e-CRM enables the company to obtain immediate feedback and advice from its customers.

The benefits of an e-CRM strategy are noticeable for both company and user who notices an improvement in the company's services. The tangible benefits of e-CRM are criteria to measure the contribution of this strategy (Namchul, 2005).

Meet the needs of a demanding user among the objectives of e-CRM is the response to customer expectations. User expectations vis-à-vis popular website shave by and then changed. The user uses Internet in search of an immediate interest relevant to real life (time saving, superior or a unique quality, lowest price). The ergonomics of the web page, in this case, should be well adapted to attract the user to browse the site. However, usage improvement is the minimal service that users expect, while customization allows tailored changes in the offered services.

Satisfaction and customer loyalty; loyalty strategy on Internet aims essentially at fostering users' loyalty by offering them an enriching added value and a navigation experience during the course of their visits and their actions. The essential precondition is to know users to determine their different interactions with the site, or even with the entire firm.

Obtain a "tailored" product or service; the company's interest to "customize" the offered service is to make it unique for each user interacting with the site. Thus, the user who visits the Dell website wants the supplier to remember that he/she is a great lover of video games. Therefore, the computer that will be proposed by default should incorporate the latest generation video cards with a discount on the price of premium brands. In this ultra-personalized relationship lies the future of Internet and the potential of e-CRM.

Quickly find the searched products and services; customer relationship management tools are designed to detect the needs and expectations of customers. By knowing their interests, it is possible to effectively guide the user to what he/she is likely to consult or buy. The advisory role of the site is all the more determined that the average amount of information available on each site increases dramatically (Hwang & Kim, 2007).

Capitalize on previous visits; the results of the various visits allow companies to increase the chances of customer loyalty. The site will highlight specific products or services based on information that customers themselves provided, directly or indirectly, during their previous, visits. The US tour operator www.travelocity.com allows users to "customize" its services. Customers may well indicate their usual starting city, airline loyalty cards they hold, and their favorite current al companies. Capitalizing on visits may be done implicitly through data collected from databases or information systems.

Table 2.

Loading Time of the Page	Percentage of User Leaving the Session
10 seconds	16%
15 seconds	49%
20 seconds	74%
30 seconds	95%
Prefer not to say	5%

Have a versatile service; the more the site is complex and dynamic, the more the time needed to generate the page increases. Relying on strong infrastructure and optimized mechanisms, customization tools provide pages that are dynamically generated without disrupting the overall performance of the site. According to a study by *eMarketer*, patience of a user when downloading a page vanishes very quickly.

Example: According to Zona Research, after 8 seconds, half of net users already leave a web site to go surfing on another.

A fluid and automatic customer management: the firm which implements an e-CRM strategy on its site disposes of a very important advantage: answering to customer expectations. A satisfied user is the one who visits again the site and who regularly uses or consumes products or services. This is a loyal user, which is priceless.

Improve the knowledge of customers/prospects: e-CRM allows for better knowing the user in a win-win exchange basis. Thanks to exchanging information between both parties, the firm will be able to determine the service or the product adapted to customer needs. The knowledge of customers or prospects is often very delicate to obtain by traditional ways/channels. There are many reasons to explain this:1) the company uses a network of retailers that blocks and prevents access to customers; 2) customers or prospects cannot be identified during their interactions with the company; 3) interaction is only fragmentary. The customer asks the seller of a store for advice. The loyalty card is used to identify customers and allows for making the connection with their purchases; 4) the product is difficult to access or retail networks are hostile to this type of initiative. With internet users, the firm is able to gather statistics to profile every customer individually.

Relieve companies from some tasks: e-CRM also allows the company to relieve companies from some tasks. Internet users perceive as better service the ability to run themselves tasks usually performed by the company.

An example would be an online bank that operates this kind of approach because it allows the customer to makes transfers, edit RIB and place stock market orders.

Customization is the key to this approach as it facilitates access to the functions they actually need in a given context, and allows for a control on personal data. Customization of tasks allows for important productivity gains. Cisco and Dell took advantage of this approach.

Automate customer relationship: automating the relationship is considerably interesting for the company because it allows users to obtain information without the need for human resources. In other words, e-commerce sites inform their customers of the stages of their ordering system by e-mail or via the web. The cost of managing customer relationship is then reduced. Sales teams and customer care personnel, free from routine interactions, can fully focus on functions with higher added value services. They might be strategies for some and advice for others (Table 3).

Table 3. CRM Dimensions (Karimi et al. 2001)

The CRM Dimensions	Main Ideas	Main Technologies
Operational CRM	√A combination of technologies allowing to collect all information coming from correlations between clients and the firm; √Represent the direct interface of the firm with its clients and aims to improve the correlations with the clients; √Amplify the need to build an culture centric client and give a better effectiveness of the services of marketing, sales and client (Crosby and Johnson, on 2001)	The base of data client, the centre of call, GED, CSS, management automated by orders, telephone system, fax, SFA, the Web
Collaboratif CRM	√ Used to make correlations easier between the organisation and its partners of exchanges to promote better communications and coordination and to allow so the clients retention √Work with a view to establishing correlations thanks to the inquiries of satisfaction, of letter of claim … √ « Undid the organisation to know the precise needs of its directed segments in information and to answer the clients in a quick and definite way» (Crosby and Johnson, on 2001)	Workflow, the E-mail
Analytical CRM	√ Uses in operational CRM and in collective CRM to constitute warehouses of data which gather all information collected on the partners of exchanges (m-triologix, on 2001) √ Analyse data to serve as a basis for the training of profiles clients, to define segments of market and to develop predictive models of future clients' behaviours (Crosby and al. On 2002) √ Make easier the task of marketers in the location of the profitable clients and the identification of the not profitable clients; √Try to find tendencies and general rules by extrapolating data coming from past experiences to try to arrest the future (Crosby and Johnson, on 2001).	The datawarehouse, the datamining

Be responsive: according to Cinquin et al. (2002), responsiveness is a direct result of automating relationships. These latter will depend on delay between receiving the order on the front page and its processing by back-office management systems. E-CRM, in this case, offers high level interfaces which managers can leverage to obtain a real-time control of certain elements of the site.

Control the processes of customer relationship: the implementation and development of management software needs reengineering of industrial processes and the development of quality standards. Software packages promote the design and dissemination of standardized business management processes. Operationalization of decision-making into processes needs a suitable infrastructure, an opening of systems to exchange information and a complete reconfiguration of the company. Hence, the need for a reengineering of processes.

S-CRM

The advent of Web 2.0has changed digital communication enabling better responsiveness, better exchange and sharing of information on the internet. Social networks are pushing more the net boundaries to break the static aspect of websites and present a dynamic content open to sharing, and exchange among users. Thus, and in general, the notion of social networks refers to all websites that build a network of friends or business contacts. These sites allow their members to interact, communicate and share content.

In these terms, the concept of Social CRM (S-CRM) is considered, like m-CRM and e-CRM, a subset of CRM using a new medium, namely social networks integrated with CRM tools. This allows the company to spread(widen) the reach(impact) of its CRM strategy by exploiting this tool whose important audiences makeup a marketing support that should be exploited by companies in their building relationship strategies. The most known social networks are Twitter, LinkedIn and Facebook.

Presentation of S-CRM

Social CRM is a subset of a company's CRM strategy. Resulting from the incorporation of technology in CRM, S-CRM promotes interaction with customers to gain their commitment. S-CRM as "a philosophy and a business strategy, supported by a technology platform, business rules, workflow, social processes and characteristics, designed to engage the customer in a collaborative conversation to provide mutually beneficial value in a reliable and transparent business environment" (see table). It is the company's response to customer's control of communication (Alhaiou et al. 2009).

More developed than conventional CRM where there is no cooperation and interaction with the customer, S-CRM puts the customer at the center of business strategy. Now the customer is no longer a passive receiver who simply receives information from the company, but he/she contributes to its development by discussing and collaborating with the brand. Companies hope to build this kind of close relationship with their customers to promote their commitment to the brand and make them potential ambassadors. The main objective of classic CRM was to take the best possible value from customers throughout their relationship with the company (Barry et al. 2011). In contrast, S-CRM is to manage communication and not the customer. The following table shows the differences between CRM and S-CRM (table 4).

S-CRM is thus an extension of CRM which uses technological tools to establish long-term relationships with each customer. This will increase interaction and engagement of both parties.

Contribution of S-CRM

Social networks offer companies a new field to exploit. Communication through traditional media needs a large budget from the company, which seeks to spread its message on a larger scale. Conventional communicative options (television advertising, display), however, may have a limited time-bound im-

Table 4. Comparison between CRM and S-CRM

	Traditional CRM	Social CRM
Interlocutors	Concerned department	All collaborators
Sense of communication	Undertaken ⟺client	Undertaken ⟺client
Correlations	Working timetables	24h / 24 7j / 7
Objectives	Sell right away	Establish relations
Origin of data	The collaborators	Clients and firm
Channels of communication	Traditional (RDV, Tél …)	Social media
Who can intervene	Commissioner persons	All in the firm
The most important	The firm and the product	The client and his needs
Control of communication	Total	Partial
Enrichment of database	Internal trainings	Internal and social media

pact. This can be extended by opting for the integration of social networks that allow the company to constantly broadcast creative, relevant, personalized and interactive content. This content attracts more attention and encourages targeted customers to exchange and share information. According to some studies, customers committed to businesses via social media are more loyal and spend 40% more than the rest of the customers (Barry et al. 2011).

A case in point on the influence of social networks on customers is also highlighted by Adidas, which reported during the "WFA /RVD Global Advertiser Conference" conference in 2010 that it has attracted 200,000 fans on its Facebook page with one short campaign. This success has benefited the company with an estimated earnings of more than 22million dollars annually.

Therefore, we can conclude that S-CRM is a new opportunity which companies have to seize to be in tandem with the new expectations and new lifestyles of customers whom Alhaiou et al. (2009) qualified as " social consumers". According to this author, consumers who user social networks are not any more the traditional customers. Indeed, social consumer trusts his/her circle of acquaintances, in particular his peers with whom he/she is in permanent contact thanks to internet. This new consumer expects that the information he/she looks for is available on his/her demand while disposing of tools and the desire to share with others.

Integration of technology within the company needs nevertheless adapting management practices. It is the case for CRM and S-CRM whose implementation needs that the various structures and the various participants in the company are adapted. As it is about a subset of the company's global CRM strategy, S-CRM completes CRM thanks to the data collected on the social networks. There is interest in aligning an S-CRM strategy to an existing CRM strategy since the passage on social networks is going to generate a series of new interaction models with customers and these models will then be integrated into the CRM processes already in position. S-CRM is considered in the literature as a direct marketing tool appropriate to CRM.

S-CRM grants customers more importance by placing them at the heart of the company's strategy and by making them pass from a simple target to a real collaborator. Therefore, we witness a change in the company's communication which moves from a commercial message having as its only objective increasing sales, to a message that complies with customer needs and expectations because they contribute themselves to its elaboration. Establishing an on-line presence is simple, but the difficulty lies in attracting the audience, their preservation and their enrichment. Therefore, companies should learn to communicate with their customers, to answer questions, to assist them and without necessarily trying to put the products a priority. The quality and originality of the content of messages are essential, to allow for a group of interests to adjust their ideas and thinking on the brand, without this one being necessarily a focal point. Establishing a true relationship with its present audience on social networks which became the privileged space of communication through which consumers express and share their desires, their opinions, and their experiments.

This can be made to the customer's circle of friends and can spread to reach a high number of people.

Baird and Parasnis (2011) maintain that "social CRM includes the dynamic community of the consumers who communicate through social media" (Meyer-Waden, 2007; Wiedmann et al. 2007). It is a tool that delegated the control of relationships to the customer who has now the power to influence other consumers through social networks. It is, however, necessary that the firm keeps a permanent contact with its customers through social networks which give the possibility of reaching consumers everywhere and at any time to establish a contact, to transmit a message or to answer their questions. This directed communication also allows for an instantaneous and strong return of information, and can therefore be an important source of information because people express themselves freely through social networks.

Contribution in Information

The firm can collect information on: customers' expectations, their opinions, their perception of its products/services, their aspirations, their exchange of information with other customers-users and their relationship with the firm. There is so much useful information than what the brand can provide at the different stages of its relationship with its customers. The instantaneous nature of social networks and the need to manage in the best way possible information that circulates in them need the attention from the company which should keep some control over delivered content to ensure its suitability with its strategy and customer expectations.

Who Should Manage This Task?

These web community managers or web advisers who are in a way the online spokespeople of business. It is a task thsat consists in enriching and in federating communities on the Internet for the benefit of a business or a brand. This task is deeply linked to web 2.0 and to the development of social networks. The community managers organize and enrich exchanges within the community while specifying their objectives; ensure the development of the brand image within virtual communities and maintaining and up keeping the good reputation of the mark; identify communities on the web that would promote the brand (blogs, forums, discussion platforms, groups) and monitor its e-reputation through awareness techniques of image or opinion; diversify actions to recruit new members; build loyalty and promote the already existing community by organizing online events (cats, interviews, newsletter, games, competition, etc.) and look after the respect of the general terms of use of the site.

Disadvantages

Although, social networks contribute to creating and maintaining a long-term relationship with their customers, firms express some reserve towards this customer relationship management tool. Indeed, IBM Institute for Business lists the main weaknesses linked to the use of social media, namely:

- Technological equipment may generate significant costs that the return on investment is uncertain for the company.
- Loss of control by the company as the content which circulates may damage its image if it contains false information. The company is, therefore, likely to suffer from poor visibility.
- Integration of new technology may compensate for the lack of competence of employees.
- Adding a new dimension to a company's CRM strategy may lead to a difficulty in controlling interaction between the different used channels.
- Cross channeling may also present difficulty in analyzing information from the different used channels.

As for customers, their first concern is the respect of their personal information as well as the availability of the researched information that should be clear, true and accessible at any time. In our study, we chose to focus on one of these social networks, Facebook, which is undoubtedly the most known and most used social network with 1, 28 thousand million active registered users every month (on April 23rd, 2014) and 752 million active daily users according to the site's statistics against 114 million users who publish tweets every month, for example.

CRM TOOLS: FACEBOOK

Presentation

Facebook is an on-line service that allows its users to publish and to view some content and interact with other users. Information published on this site allows its users to find other users sharing the same interests and to interact with them.

Example: according to ComScore, American companies specialized in Web statistics, Facebook is the second most visited site worldwide after Google. It was created in February, 2004 by Mark Elliot Zuckerberg at the Harvard University and was originally intended for the students of this university. It opened little by little at other universities before becoming accessible to the wide public in September, 2006.It met at once with a huge success because it managed to attract 1 million users in a less than year after its launch (in November, 2004). According to Technomic.com site, it needed thirty eight years for the radio to reach50 million users, thirteen years for television; internet took four years while Facebook reached this figure in two years only. This success results in particular from the change this site created in the communication and interaction habits of individuals. Indeed, Facebook allows building relationships with people all around the world, finding old friends, publishing and sharing some content (photos, videos, messages) in an instantaneous way. Thus, it facilitated contact and interaction without caring about time or geographical constraints.

Facebook as a Support to S-CRM

The ease of communication of this tool inspired professionals of customer relationship management and encouraged them to promote their relationship strategies because it provided them with targeting possibilities according to definite criteria until then inconceivable. For example, Facebook puts at the disposal of advertisers all information declared by its users (gender, age, CSP, education). Therefore, businesses can adapt the contents of its messages, its products and its services according to the needs and interests of its customers.

However, the relational and social aspect prevails in this exchange as it is a matter of customer relationship management. The company could benefit from a recommendation, an advice, and a story coming from one of its customers more than from the product or the brand itself. Users often report on a friend's experience with such or such a brand or such or such an application. Then, it is not any more a matter of directly promoting its brand as much as letting friends of users making it for them. It is simply a question of word of mouth or informal communication. Once Facebook adopted in the framework of an S-CRM strategy, the company can answer customers' questions, exchange information on its brand, its products / services.... It can also communicate on an event like the launching of a new product or an opening of a new outlet, all of this in an immediate way.

Integrating Facebook within the company's S-CRM strategy also allows it to put its customers at the heart of this strategy and to make them real collaborators. Moreover, this is the very objectives of e-CRM. Indeed, a Facebook customer can unconsciously become "a relay". Customers subscribed to the company's Facebook page may have access to accurate information on the company, the products, the provided services, the manufacturing process, packaging … etc. Therefore, information circulates in both directions, from the company to the customer to communicate and emit its messages, as well as from the customer to the company so that this latter enriches its customer knowledge base. The collected data may serve to segment customers, to conduct surveys, in particular as part of a study on products perception, on customers' expectations, or to brainstorm for the conception of a new product or a new product name.

Analysis of this data, thanks to Facebook Insight, allows then the company to optimize its page but also to collect information on customer expectations, their distribution and much more useful data, which helps the company to proceed to a neat targeting of its customers. This data also allows the company to target prospects likely to subscribe to brand's Facebook page. To this effect, it has to study customers' acceptance technology behavior to determine the factors which influence their intention to adopt Facebook.

TECHNOLOGY ACCEPTANCE

The fact that a firm integrates ICT does not mean that these technologies will be adopted in a systematic way by consumers. Brangier and Hammes (2007) put down a series of questions as for the adoption of technology: what are the reasons which make that person uses a technology? Why do some people take pleasure in using a technology? Under which conditions, human and technological, do they form an efficient, competitive and satisfactory behavior? And why do people themselves refuse to try a technology that presents functions likely to help them? These questions thus urge us to think about the relationship that exists between the human being and technology as well as about how the former perceives technology.

Some authors consider that ICT revolutionized the ways with which we learn and reach information, allowing doing many things in a faster, easier, more flexible, and more efficient way. These opportunities are going to depend on the reaction that people have towards these technologies, i.e. the way human beings perceive, are satisfied, accept, refuse, and adopt. Several theoretical models tried to explain the relationship between users' attitudes, use satisfaction and intention to use ICT, of which the Technology Acceptance Model (TAM) is the most known model (Venkatesh et al. 2003).

Presentation of TAM

Users' use of a system reflects their acceptance of technology degree (Venkatesh et al. 2003). TAM is a fundamental conception of previous research on information systems (Davis et al. 1989; Mathieson, 1991; Adams et al. 1992; Gefen and Straub, 1997; Igbaria et al. 1997; Jackson et al. 1997). This model is an adaptation of TRA developed by Fishbein and Ajzen (1975). TAM was specifically tailored to model user acceptance of IS with the aim of explaining the intention to use of an information system. It includes two essential variables: perceived usefulness (PU) and perceived of ease of use (PEU) (figure 1). Davis, (2000) defines PU as "the degree to which a person believes that using a particular system would enhance his or her job performance." The author presents PEU as "the degree to which a person

Figure 1. The conceptual model

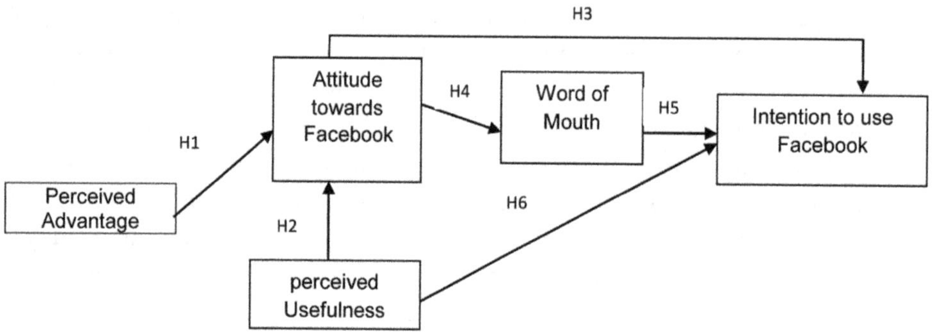

believes that using a particular system would be free." regarding the TAM model, acceptance behavior is explained, in addition to these two variables, by attitude toward using the system.

Venkatesh and Davis (2000) explain the determining role of these variables in understanding acceptance of the use of a new information technology system.

METHODOLOGY

Presentation of a Case Study

To answer the questions asked above, we are going to present model we adopted to explain how intention of adoption develops and under which processes? Our model includes TAM variables as well as other measures, in this particular perceived advantage and word of mouth (Venkatesh and Davis, 2003). These are determiners for the adoption of social networks.

Variables

The chosen variables to explain which one affected the online customer behavior are: perceived advantage, attitude towards Facebook, usefulness perception, Word of Mouth and intention to use Facebook.

Cognitive Factors and Attitude

According to the literature, we notice that the relation between the cognitive factors and the attitude was repeatedly treated. Davis et al. (1989) highlighted the effect of these factors on the attitude of the user of the technology.

Perceived Advantage and Attitude

Any object presented as new and innovative has to present an advantage which will incite individuals to adopt it. These individuals compare between the novelty which is presented to them and what already exists. Then, the relative advantage of this novelty rests on the additional features which it presents compared to the previous. Moreover, Mansfield, (1968) stipulated that "the rate of adoption of an innovation is a linear function of the profitability of the use of this novelty, the size of the investment required to use it and other unspecified variables."

This concept is defined as "the degree in which an innovation is perceived as being better than the one it replaces" (Rogers, 1995). The degree of perceived advantage is often expressed as economic profitability, social prestige, economy of time and effort, immediacy of the reward or other advantages. The nature of innovation determines which specific type of relative advantage (economic, social, etc.) is important for individuals who are going to adopt it. The characteristics of these potential individuals also determine which sub-dimensions of the relative advantage are the most important. The same author states that perceived advantage is one of the best indicators of innovation acceptability rate because it informs about the advantages and the resulting costs of innovation adaptation. The author also asserts that perceived advantage of an innovation positively correlates with its adoption rate.

Several studies distinguished between direct and indirect effects of perceived advantage. When consumers have the possibility to access some advantages among a multitude of alternatives, they will judge innovation on its usefulness. Then, they speak of indirect effects. (Nasco et al. 2007).

Nevertheless, perception of the usefulness of advantages differs from one consumer to another. Its influence on consumers' attitude towards adopting innovation is called the direct effect. Then, we can say that relative advantage plays a double role; it influences on the one hand attitude towards adoption of the new technology and on the other hand, it determines perceived usefulness of this new technology. Therefore, we can formulate the following hypothesis:

H1: The more the perceived advantage of the Facebook page, the more the attitude of its adoption supports via perceived usefulness increases.

Perceived Usefulness and Attitude

According to Davis (1989), the term "useful" means "capable of being used advantageously and profitably". The notion of usefulness refers to perceived benefit (Au & Enderwick 2000) and to the positive consequences of the behavior (Davis et al. 1989). Regarding the consumer behavioral models, perceived consequences influence behavior whether, directly and indirectly via attitudes (Malhotra & Mac Cort, 2001). For Senach (1990), «usefulness determines if the system allows the user to perform their task, if it is capable of realizing what is necessary for the user. Usefulness covers the functional capacity, performance of the system, and qualities of the audience". Davis et al. (1989) define perceived usefulness as "the degree in which a person believes that the use of a particular system would improve their efficiency at work." For these authors, perceived usefulness is considered as one of the most important components of the TAM model because it intervenes in determining users' behavior in a more influential way than other variables. Given this importance, the notion of perceived usefulness was the object of several studies. It is very present in literature and intervenes in several models resulting from the TAM model (Mathieson, 1991; Adam et al, 1992; Taylor and Todd, 1995; Igbaria et al, 1996; Jackson et al, 1997). Davis, (1989) assumes that perceived usefulness strongly correlates with users' acceptance behavior and should not be ignored by those who try to conceive or to apply a successful system". Perceived usefulness remains a determinant of the intention to use a system. For Nielsen (1993), perceived usefulness is the «fact of knowing if a system may be used to reach certain goals".

On the other hand, it is the degree in which innovation is perceived as offering an upper advantage and positive consequences (Chen and Wells, 2002, Rogers, 1995) that the organization thinks of benefiting from the use of Internet (Zaoui & Akremi, 2003).Therefore, perceived usefulness contributes to the development of an attitude in favor of the use of products offered by internet (Childers et al. 2001; Meuter et al. 2000; Chen et al. 2002; O'cass 2003; Bruner & Kumar, 2005; Dulyalak & Settapong, 2005). Other authors argue that perceived usefulness determines the attitude of using information technology (Mathieson, 1991; Taylor and Todd, 1995; Agarwal & Prasad, 1997; 1999). The second hypothesis:

H2: Perceived usefulness positively influences the attitude of using the brand Facebook page.

Attitude and Intention

Several recent studies agree to consider attitude as being an independent intention variable, which in its turn explains behavior variables. An attitude is defined as "an expressed psychological tendency following an evaluation of a particular entity with some degree of favor or of disfavor" (Eagly & Chaiken, 1993). Attitude expresses a positive *or a* negative assessment of commitment (Ajzen & Fishbein, 1980; Davis, 1989). Doob (1947) introduces attitude as "an implicit answer which influences the following answers." According to Campbell (1963), attitude is the "acquired predisposition towards a behavior." Eagly and Chaiken, (1993) define attitude towards technology as "an evaluation according to a degree of favor or of disfavor of the use of technology."

These various definitions emphasize the need to study attitude and its consequences on individuals' behavior. To determine and measure the effects of attitude, researchers evoked the hypothesis which stipulates that attitudes "guide, influence, manage and form or predict real behavior (Derbaix & Brée, 2000) ". This assumption originated in psychological theories. Indeed, researches and the various theories emerged in psychology insisted on the fact that human beings develop attitudes to objects and phenomena which they face, and it is these attitudes which condition their actions.

Furthermore, Wicker (1969) moves forward and assume that we cannot separate attitude from behavior, which remains valid in the context of adoption and use of technology (Nysveen et al. 2005; Bruner & Kumar, 2005; Curran & Meuter, 2005). Indeed, research on attitude stipulates that it influences in a direct and positive way the intention to adopt a new technology. Indeed, Moore and Benbasat (1991) as well as Rogers (1995) assert that individuals who do not use a new technology may develop an intention to adopt this technology influenced by social standards and not by the attributes of this technology. As for the people who have already adopted it, attitude determines by itself the intention to continue or not adopting technology

Several studies tried to highlight the fact that attitudes influence intentions (Ajzen & Fishbein, 1980; Fishbein & Ajzen, 1975). This relationship was well established in the literature on the use of the technology (Allen et al. 1992; Barki & Hartwick, 1994; Taylor & Todd, 1995; Dabholkar, 1996; Harrison et al. 1997). It was found out that attitudes are factors influencing behavioral intentions (Davis et al. 1989; Adam et al. 1992; Dabholkar 1994; Hebert and Benbasat 1994; Engel et al. 1995; Shim et al. 2001). This is what has been established in more recent research which has shown that attitude determines the intent to use technology (Davis et al. 1989; Dabholkar & Bagozzi, 2002; Chau & Hu 2002; Legris et al. 2003; Gong and Yu, 2004; Shih, 2004; Huang, 2005; Leroy et al. 2005; Limayem & Rowe, 2006; Khalil & Pearson, 2007; Jannouri & Gharbi, 2008). Thus, the third hypothesis:

H3: More the attitude of the customer towards the use of technology is favorable, the more its intention to adopt the Facebook page of the brand increases.

Word-of-Mouth, Attitude and Intention

Consumers have access to information through multiple communication channels, but interpersonal communication remains the most reliable and the most important source. Word-of-mouth is still considered the most credible source of information because it is a description of a really lived personal experience. This exchange of information between individuals influences their attitudes. Goyette et al. (2010) define word-of-mouth as "an informal oral communication from person to person, by phone, e-mail, mailing list or any other means of communication about a service or a product. The source of recommendation can be personal or impersonal." Anderson, (1998) defines word-of-mouth as "informal communication between private parties on the assessment of goods and services." Arndt, (1967) introduced word-of-mouth as "interpersonal oral communication between a receiver and a transmitter, that the receiver perceives as non-commercial, regarding a brand, a product or service." This definition highlighting their formal aspect of communication was originally advanced by definitions proposed later by Westbrook (1987), Bone (1992, 1995) and Silverman (2001).The same author considers word-of-mouth as "one of the oldest and more established means of advertising."

Moreover, Johnson (1999) presents word-of-mouth as "one of the most effective ways to attract and keep customers." A review of the literature allows us to conclude that this means of communication is more effective than advertising (Katz & Lazarsfeld, 1955; Traylor and Mathias, 1983; Buttle, 1998; Hinde, 1999; East et al. 2005). McDonnell, (2005) and Nielsen, (2007) assert that the modern consumer is less attentive to the traditional ways of advertising, what led companies to decrease spending dedicated to them.

According to Day (1971), word of mouth is nine times more efficient than advertising to change the consumers attitudes and to make them positive, while Morin, (1983) estimated that word of mouth is three times as efficient with respect to stimulating purchases.

Word-of-mouth may spread through several communication channels. Silverman (2001) cites: phone interviews, e-mails or other different means of communication. These information sources can be personal like friends, family or impersonal like press articles, discussion forums. (Brown & Reingen, 1987; Duhan et al. 1997). Brooks (1957) considers that friends and close relationships are the most influential information sources because the trust they inspire can have a positive impact on word of mouth (Ricard & Perrien, 1999; Ranaweera & Prabhu, 2003; Chen, 2006; Palmatier et al. 2007). Solomon, (2011) explains this reliability by familiarity with information transmitters.

Word-of-mouth can transmit an opinion which can be either positive or negative. The transmitter will then try to use a convincing language to clarify their point of view (Hennig-Thurau et al. 2004). This type of communication showed its impact by the persuasive potential it exerts on consumers (Stambouli & Briones, 2002). Lam and Mizerski, (2005) assume that word-of-mouth is an influential tool which can play in favor or against the brand. Indeed, Dichter, (1966) claims that people shape opinions. Furthermore, technological development and the emergence of new communication means gave more importance to word-of-mouth because of the appearance of new communication channels (Stambouli & Briones, 2002). Social networks allow people to post their opinions on products and companies in order to influence others (McCann, 2008, Dann, 2009), to contribute to the creation of the brand. Butlle,

(1998) assumed that word-of-mouth influences brand awareness, expectations, perceptions, attitudes, intentions and behavior. The following hypothesis:

H4: Consumer attitude toward the brand Facebook page positively influences Word-of-mouth.
H5: Word-of-mouth positively influences the intention to use the brand Facebook page.

Perceived Usefulness and Intention to Use Facebook

Rogers (1983) showed that the relative advantage of an innovation positively correlates with adoption rate. Davis et al. (1989) distinguished between pre-adoption and post-adoption phases. For these researchers, it is clear that perceived usefulness remains a determinant of intention to use a system during these two phases. Moreover, Szajna (1996) has empirically tested and validated the findings of Davis et al. (1989) and finally concluded that perceived usefulness determines intentions to use during these two phases. Thus, if consumers believe that the use of the brand's Facebook page will be of some usefulness to them, they will automatically adopt it. Therefore, perceived usefulness is a factor of the intention to use the page (figure 1).

H6: The perceived usefulness of the Facebook page influences positively the intention of its adoption by the consumer.

Sample Profile

48.5 percent of respondents were male and 51.5 percent were female. In terms of age, the majority of respondents (47.1 percent) were 25-44 years old, 40.5 percent were below 25 years and 12.3 percent were above 45 years. A total of 171 percent had attained superior level of education. The majority of respondents were executives (32.2 percent) and students (35.7 percent).

All the measurement scales were adopted from the literature and adjusted to our research setting. All the items were measured on a five point likert scale. To test our hypotheses, self-administrated questionnaires were used on a total of 300 customers. The target population included customers whose uses the Facebook page "Ooredoo Tunisia" and whose voluntarily agreed to answer the questionnaire. This page topped the ranking of brands whose pages are the most committed to their fans during the March-May 2014 period. A total of 227 complete and exploitable questionnaires was collected, with a 76% response rate. Sample size allows us to perform multiple data analysis packages (multivariate and SEM). An appropriate sample size should be ten times the number of items used in the questionnaire (Joreskog et al. 1999). In this study, sample size seems to be appropriate for SEM (227>21 items multiplied by 10).

RESULTS

Test Hypothesis

The two–step approach recommended by Anderson and Gerbing (1988) was used. The First step was performed to ensure the validity of the measurement model (CFA). Then, a path analysis was used to test the hypothetical causal relations of the research model. The values of the indices show an acceptable

Table 5. Results

Structural Path	Hypothesis	Student Test (CR)	Hypothesis Testing
Attitude towards Facebook ← Advantage perceived of Facebook	H1	(0,42) 5,863	Confirmed
Attitude towards Facebook ← Perceived Usefulness of Facebook	H2	(0,28) 6,005	Confirmed
Intention to use Facebook ← Attitude towards Facebook	H3	(0,70) 5,854	Confirmed
Word-of-Mouth ← Attitude towards Facebook	H4	(0,98) 11,228	Confirmed
Intention to use Facebook ← Word-of-Mouth	H5	(-0,09) -1,334	Rejected
Intention to use Facebook ← Perceived Usefulness of Facebook	H6	(0,35) 3.752	Confirmed

fit between the empirical and theoretical model (Khi² / dl=2.937; RMSEA= 0083; RMR=0.056; CFI= 0.918; GFI=0.992; AGFI=0.989).

In order to support our hypothesis, the standardized estimates and the significance of t test were examined for each path. The model tested six hypotheses by introducing perceived advantage, perceived usefulness, attitude towards Facebook, W-O-M and intention to use Facebook (Table 5).

As observed in table 4, the attitude to adopt Facebook is affected by perceived justice (H1) and perceived usefulness (H2). The relationship attitude/intention (H3) and attitude/WOM were also validated. However, the intention to use Facebook is not significantly predicted by the WOM (H5). Finally, perceived usefulness affected significantly the intention to adopt Facebook page (H6).

DISCUSSION AND IMPLICATIONS

This study is part of a relational logic highlighting the importance of introducing new technology-based customer relationship management. In order to show the impact and the effectiveness of the introduction of social networking in general and Facebook in particular on business relationship strategy, we studied the different variables considered important to strengthen any information exchange relationship between the customer and the company.

The results positively validate five of our six hypotheses and affirm that the use of the social network Facebook of a brand within the framework of its CRM strategy contributes to reinforcing brand commitment and loyalty (Henning et al. 2010; Kaplan & Haenlein, 2010; Van Doorn et al. 2010).

The perceived advantage of the Facebook page influences the attitude of its adoption. This result was also confirmed by Nasco et al. (2007). The higher the perception of the benefit of using the Facebook page, the higher the attitude of its adoption is favorable. According to the obtained results, perceived usefulness affects attitude to use the page. Thus, any user who perceives that the brand's Facebook page has a usefulness will develop a positive attitude towards it (Childers et al. 2001; Meuter et al. 2000; Chen et al. 2002; O'cass 2003; Bruner et Kumar 2005; Dulyalak et Settapong 2005; Porter et Donthu, 2006).

Customer attitude towards the use of technology and the intention to use the Facebook page are correlated. Indeed, more customer attitude towards the use of technology is favorable, more customer intention to adopt the brand's Facebook page increases. The same result was confirmed in the literature (Davis et al. 1989; Dabholkar et Bagozzi 2002; Chau et Hu 2002; Legris et al. 2003; Gong et Yu 2004; Shih 2004; Huang 2005; Leroy et al. 2005; Limayem & Rowe 2006; Khalil & Pearson 2007; Jannouri & Gharbi 2008).

Positive word-of-mouth on technology as informal communication positively influenced by customer attitude toward the Facebook page of the brand. However, the link between word-of-mouth and the intention to use the brand's Facebook page has not been validated (not significant test). This allows us to claim that the development of a positive intention is powered by attitude towards technology through word-of-mouth. These results are contrary to what was found in literature (Butlle, 1998; McCann, 2008; Dann, 2009; Qualmann, 2009). The results also showed that perceived usefulness of the Facebook page positively influences the intention of its adoption by the consumer. These outcome indicate that the factors considered in this study have helped reach significant results and validation of most hypotheses. In addition, they allowed us to explain user behavior towards the adoption of the brand's Facebook page (Davis et al. 1989; Szajna, 1996).

These results constitute promising ways for managers and CRM professionals to consider the adoption of a Facebook page as a management tool making it possible to exert a potential influence on customers' behavior (Harrigan & Choudhury, 2012).

The studied telecommunication brand attaches great significance to communication and interaction with its customers via its Facebook page by offering a multiplicity of services which contribute to improving management of its customer relationship. Thus, we can propose some recommendations.

Perceived advantage of the Facebook page has a significant effect on the attitude of its adoption by customers who will develop a positive attitude toward this page if they think it gives them an advantage Nasco et al. (2007). Thus, this page should provide all the services and information that may be useful to them and give them an advantage that will allow the company to distinguish itself from its competitors, and take advantage of integrating the social network Facebook in its CRM strategy. The company should ensure that its Facebook page offers useful features and services to customers to encourage them to adopt it. It should be able to access this page via various services offered by the company (news, promotions, FAQ, complaints...) without having to move or lose time. The Facebook page used by the company as a part of its social strategy should convey a good image in order to develop a favorable attitude among customers. This attitude influences their intention to adopt or not the page (Ellison et al. 2007; Choudhury & Harrigan, 2012). This latter should be able to impress them by its ergonomics, design, and ease of use. Word-of-mouth is a factor to be taken into account because it influences attitude of the customer towards the Facebook page of the brand. Thus, the company should ensure that its interaction with users of its page be a positive experience and ensure the flow of positive information between customers. Then, each one of them should feel treated in a privileged way in order to be satisfied. It may even offer gifts as a reward. Complaints of the user of the Facebook page should be treated promptly and clear and quick responses should be received. The goal is to satisfy the customer and to avoid poor information, which can harm company image. The content of the Facebook page should be clear and useful to develop in customers a favorable intention to use. Convenient services that encourage them to use should be found in this page. These may be FAQ that provide customers with answers to previous questions or web advisors that provide a quick answer if not an instant one. The Facebook page can also provide all services that do not require moving the customer and doing so could save a lot of time.

LIMITATION AND FUTURE RESEARCH

However, this work has some limitations. The Driving an online survey does not ensure a high response rate. So we had to send a large number of questionnaires for a number of respondents is less than him, but it was deemed satisfactory. In addition, one may experience some difficulty in understanding the questions or response items. The presence in front of him when responding is therefore important to assist him in case of trouble.

As futures researches, we recommend retailers, after implementation, to always study the attitude of consumers online through the integration of the variable as: belief, perception, influence of technologies adopted by the competition. Also to consider the gender, age, experience, social influence... as moderator variables will enhance the understanding some behaviors.

CONCLUSION

In an environment characterized by tough competition, every company, whether specialized or not, attempts to build an image allowing it to acquire and satisfy new customers and increase their loyalty and differentiate itself from other brands. Therefore, the customer is at the center of all desires. However, this relationship with a business has always been somewhat complicated by the fact that customers seek to satisfy their needs in the best way possible. Thus, there is a change in companies' strategies and their adoption of technological tools which prioritize customer satisfaction. Thus, the development of various loyalty programs has become essential for the company, which should include consumer behavior, motives and expectations in order to develop a suitable program and implement the ideal strategy. In this study, the passage from CRM, e-CRM to S-CRM was presented highlighting the importance of the relationship aspect in building loyalty and customer engagement through the company's social network. Then, integration of innovative technologies in general and in particular Facebook in their relationship strategy is needed to distinguish itself from the competition by providing customers with innovative value-added services that will attract consumers and, ultimately, increase their loyalty.

The results of the study in the telecommunications sector helped to highlight the influence of some determinants in forming favorable attitudes towards to the adoption of the Facebook page of the company and the development of loyalty towards the brand under study. These findings are promising for managers and Customer Relationship Management professionals. The studied variables (attitude, relative advantage, perceived usefulness) may have an impact on the intention to adopt and use the Facebook page as part of a relationship-building program. Therefore, we recommend retailers to integrate ICT and particularly the social network Facebook as a tool in their CRM strategy given its omnipresence in everyday life.

REFERENCES

Abdelmoula, S. N., Ben Lallouna, H. H., Skandrani, H., & Zghal, M. (2007). Transactionnel, relationnel ou hybride pour l'acquisition d'un avantage concurrentiel? Cas des entreprises tunisiennes. 75éme congrès de l'ACFAS, Québec.

Adams, D. A., Nelson, R. R., & Todd, P. A. (1992). Perceived usefulness, ease of use, and usage of information technology: A replication. *Management Information Systems Quarterly*, *16*(2), 227–247. doi:10.2307/249577

Agarwal, R., & Prasad, J. (1997). The role of innovation characteristics and perceived voluntariness in acceptance of information technologies. *Decision Sciences*, *28*(3), 557–582. doi:10.1111/j.1540-5915.1997.tb01322.x

Agarwal, R., & Prasad, J. (1999). Are individual differences germane to the acceptance of new information technologies? *Decision Sciences*, *30*(2), 361–391. doi:10.1111/j.1540-5915.1999.tb01614.x

Ajzen, I., & Fishbein, M. (1980). Understanding Attitudes and Predicting Social Behavior, Prentice-Hall Inc, NJ. Englewood Cliffs.

Alhaiou, T., Irani, Z., & Ali, M. (2009, July 13-14). The relationship between e-CRM implementation and e-loyalty at different adoption stages of transaction cycle: a conceptual framework and hypothesis. *Proceedings of the European and Mediterranean Conference on Information Systems EMCIS '09*, Izmir.

Au, K. M., & Enderwick, P. (2000). A cognitive model on attitude toward technology adoption. *Journal of Managerial Psychology*, *15*(4), 266–282. doi:10.1108/02683940010330957

Bahri, N., & Mzoughi, N. (2007). Impact of the Intranet on the Performance of Marketing Information System: Empirical Investigation in the Pharmaceutical Industry. *Online Journal of Management research, OJMR, e-Journal of PCTE.*

Bahri-Ammari, N. (2014). The Role of Loyalty Program (LP) in Establishing Brand Attachment and Word-of-Mouth Intentions: An Empirical Investigation in the Mobile Sector. *International Journal of Customer Relationship Marketing and Management*, *5*(3), 49–68. doi:10.4018/ijcrmm.2014070104

Baird, C. H., & Parasnis, G. (2011). From social media to Social CRM: Reinventing the customer relationship. *Strategy and Leadership*, *39*(6), 27–34. doi:10.1108/10878571111176600

Barki, H., & Hartwick, J. (1994). Measuring user participation, user involvement, and user attitude. *Management Information Systems Quarterly*, *18*(1), 59–82. doi:10.2307/249610

Barry, C., Markey, R., Almquist, E., & Brahm, C. (2011). Putting Social Media to work. Retrieved from http://www.bain.com/publications/articles/putting-social-media-to-work.aspx

Ben Issa, H. (2011). « Une approche socio-économique du maintien de la relation: Prestataire de service-Consommateur », Acte du 27éme Congrès de l'AFM, Bruxelles.

Bolton, R., Kannan, P. K., & Bramlett, M. (2000). Implications of loyalty program membership and service experiences for customer retention and value. *Journal of the Academy of Marketing Science*, *28*(1), 95–108. doi:10.1177/0092070300281009

Bone, P. F. (1992). Determinants of Word-of-Mouth communication during product consumption. *Advances in Consumer Research. Association for Consumer Research (U. S.)*, *19*, 579–583.

Bone, P. F. (1995). Word of Mouth effects on short-term and long-term product judgments. *Journal of Business Research*, *32*(3), 213–223. doi:10.1016/0148-2963(94)00047-I

Brodie, R., Coviello, R., Brookes, R., & Little, V. (1997). Towards a Paradigm Shift in Marketing? An Examination of Current Marketing Practices. *Journal of Marketing Management, 13*(5), 383–406. doi: 10.1080/0267257X.1997.9964481

Brodie, R., Coviello, R., Brookes, R., & Little, V. (1997). Towards a Paradigm Shift in Marketing? An Examination of Current Marketing Practices. *Journal of Marketing Management, 13*(5), 383–406. doi: 10.1080/0267257X.1997.9964481

Brown, J. J., & Reingen, P. H. (1987). Social ties and Word-of- Mouth referral behavior. *The Journal of Consumer Research, 14*(3), 350–362. doi:10.1086/209118

Bruner, G. C. II, & Kumar, A. (2005). Explaining consumer acceptance of handheld internet devices. *Journal of Business Research, 58*(5), 553–558. doi:10.1016/j.jbusres.2003.08.002

Buckinx, W., & Van-den Poel, D. (2005). Customer base analysis: Partial defection of behaviourally loyal clients in a non-contractual FMCG retail setting. *European Journal of Operational Research, 164*(1), 252–268. doi:10.1016/j.ejor.2003.12.010

Burez, J., & Van-den, Poel, D. (2007). CRM at a pay-TV company: Using analytical models to reduce customer attrition by targeted marketing for subscription services. *Expert Systems with Applications, 32*(2), 277–288. doi:10.1016/j.eswa.2005.11.037

Burez, J., & Van-den Poel, D. (2007). CRM at a pay-TV company: Using analytical models to reduce customer attrition by targeted marketing for subscription services. *Expert Systems with Applications, 32*(2), 277–288. doi:10.1016/j.eswa.2005.11.037

Buttle, A. F. (1998). Word-of-mouth: Understanding and managing referral marketing. *Journal of Strategic Marketing, 6*(3), 241–254. doi:10.1080/096525498346658

Campbell, D. T. (1963). C.W. Harris (Ed.), From descriptions to experimentation: interpreting trends as quasi experiments in Problems in measuring change. Madison university of Wisconsin.

Chau, P. Y. K., & Hu, P. (2004). Investigating health care professionals decisions to accept telemedicine technology: An empirical test of competing theories. *Information & Management, 39*(4), 705–719.

Chen, Q., & Wells, W. D. (2002). Attitude toward the site II: New information. *Journal of Advertising Research, 42*(2), 33–46.

Childers, T. L., Carr, C. L., Peck, J., & Carson, S. (2001). Hedonic and utilitarian motivations for online retail shopping behavior. *Journal of Retailing, 77*(4), 511–536. doi:10.1016/S0022-4359(01)00056-2

Choudhury, M. M., & Harrigan, P. (2012, July 2-4). Technology Acceptance Model and the Social CRM: A Model for Customer Engagement. Proceedings of the Academy of Marketing Conference, Southampton, UK.

Crosby, L. A., Evans, K. R., & Cowles, D. (1990). Relationship Quality in Services Selling: An Interpersonal Influence Perspective. *Journal of Marketing, 54*(3), 68–81. doi:10.2307/1251817

Curran, J. M., & Meuter, M. L. (2005). Self-service technology adoption: Comparing three technologies. *Journal of Services Marketing, 19*(2), 103–113. doi:10.1108/08876040510591411

Dabholkar, P. A., & Bagozzi, R. P. (2002). An attitudinal model of technology based self-service: Moderating effects of consumer traits and situational factors. *Journal of the Academy of Marketing Science*, *30*(3), 184–201. doi:10.1177/0092070302303001

Dann, S. (2010). Redefining social marketing with contemporary commercial marketing definitions. *Journal of Business Research*, *63*(2), 147–153. doi:10.1016/j.jbusres.2009.02.013

Davis, F. D. (1989). Perceived usefulness, perceived ease of use, and user acceptance of information technology. *Management Information Systems Quarterly*, *13*(3), 319–340. doi:10.2307/249008

Derbaix, C., & Brée, J. (2000). *Comportement du consommateur, présentation de textes choisis*. Paris: Editions Economica.

Dichter, E. (1966). How Word-of-Mouth Advertising Works. *Harvard Business Review*, *44*, 147–157.

Doob, L. W. (1947). The behavior of attitudes. *Psychological Review*, *54*(3), 135–156. doi:10.1037/h0058371 PMID:20240010

Duhan, D. F., Johnson, S. D., Wilcox, J. B., & Harrell, G. D. (1997). Influences on consumer use of Word-of-Mouth recommendation sources. *Journal of the Academy of Marketing Science*, *25*(4), 283–295. doi:10.1177/0092070397254001

Dulyalak, P., & Settapong, M. (2005, August 4-7). A study of behavioral intention for 3G mobile Internet technology: Preliminary research on mobile learning. *Proceedings* of *the second international conference on e-learning for knowledge based society*, Bangkok, Thailand.

Eagly, A. H., & Chaiken, S. (1993). *The psychology of attitudes*. Fort Worth, TX: Harcourt Bracce Jovanovich College Publishers.

Ellison, N., Steinfeld, C., & Lampe, C. (2007). The benefits of Facebook "friends": Social capital and college students' use of online social network sites. *Journal of Computer-Mediated Communication*, *12*(4), 1143–1168. doi:10.1111/j.1083-6101.2007.00367.x

Fishbein, M. A., & Ajzen, I. (1975). *Belief, attitude, intention and behavior: an introduction to theory and research, Reading*. MA: Addison Wesley.

Fletcher, K., & Wright, G. (1995). Organisational, Strategic and Technical Barriers to Successful Implementation of Database Marketing. *International Journal of Information Management*, *15*(2), 115–126. doi:10.1016/0268-4012(95)00005-R

Gefen, D., & Straub, D. W. (1997). Gender differences in perception and adoption of e-mail: An extension to the Technology Acceptance Model. *Management Information Systems Quarterly*, *21*(4), 389–400. doi:10.2307/249720

Gong, M. Y., & Yu, Y. (2004). An enhanced technology acceptance model for web-based learning. *Journal of Information Systems Education*, *15*(4), 365–374.

Goyette, I., L.Ricard, J. Bergeron et F. Marticotte (2010), « e-WOM scale: Une échelle de mesure du bouche-à-oreille dans un contexte de services électroniques », *Revue canadienne des sciences de l'administration,* 27: 5–23 (2010).

Grabner-Kraeuter, S., & Moedritscher, G. (2002). Alternative Approaches Toward Measuring CRM Performance. 6 th Research Conference on Relationship Marketing and Customer relationship Management, *Atlanta,* 9-12 Juin, 1-16.

Grabner-Kraeuter, S., & Moedritscher, G. (2002, June 9-12). Alternative Approaches Toward Measuring CRM Performance. *Proceedings of the 6th Research Conference on Relationship Marketing and Customer relationship Management*, Atlanta.

Grônroos, C. (1994). From marketing mix to relationship marketing: Towards a paradigm shift in marketing. *Australasian Marketing Journal*, *2*(August), 9–29. doi:10.1016/S1320-1646(94)70275-6

Grônroos, C. (1996). Relationship Marketing: Strategic and Tactical Implications. *Management*, 34/3, 5-14.

Gummesson, E. (1999). *Total Relationship Marketing*. Oxford: Butterworth Heinemann.

Hamon, C., Lézin, P., & Toullec, A. (2004). *Gestion des Clientèles*. Edition DUNOD.

Harrigan & Choudhury. M. M. (2012). *Social Media Technologies for CRM* (Working Paper). University of Southampton.

Hennig-Thurau, T., Gwinner, K. P., Walsh, G., & Gremler, D. D. (2004). Electronic word-of mouth via consumer opinion platforms: What motivates consumers to articulate themselves on the Internet. *Journal of Interactive Marketing*, *18*(1), 38–52. doi:10.1002/dir.10073

Hennig-Thurau, T., Malthouse, E. C., Friege, C., Gensler, S., Lobschat, L., Rangaswamy, A., & Skiera, B. (2010). The Impact of New Media on Customer Relationships. *Journal of Service Research*, *13*(3), 311–330. doi:10.1177/1094670510375460

Huang, E. (2005). The acceptance of women-centric web sites. *Journal of Computer Information Systems*, *45*(4), 75–83.

Igbaria, M., Parasuraman, S., & Baroudi, J. J. (1996). A motivational model of microcomputer usage. *Journal of Management Information Systems*, *13*(Summer), 127–143. doi:10.1080/07421222.1996.11518115

Jackson, C. M., Chow, S., & Leitch, R. A. (1997). Toward an understanding of the behavioral intention to use an information System. *Decision Sciences*, *28*(2), 357–389. doi:10.1111/j.1540-5915.1997.tb01315.x

Janouri, F., & Gharbi, J.E. (2008). Affrontement entre le risque perçu et le capital marque dans la formation de la confiance dans un site marchand.

Jolley, B., Mizerski, R., & Doina, O. (2006). How Habit and Satisfaction Affects Player Retention for Online Gambling. *Journal of Business Research*, *59*(12), 770–777. doi:10.1016/j.jbusres.2006.01.017

Jordan, W.G., & Krumwiede, K.R. (1999). ERP? Implementation, Beware. *Cost Management Update, (March),* 1-4.

Jöreskog, K. G., Sörbom, D., Du-Toit, S., & Du-Toit, M. (1999). *LISREL 8: NEW Statistical Feature.* Chicago, IL: Scientific Software International Inc.

Kaplan, A. M., & Haenlein, M. (2010). Users of the World, Unite! The Challenges and Opportunities of Social Media. *Business Horizons*, *53*(1), 59–68. doi:10.1016/j.bushor.2009.09.003

Katz, E., & Lazarsfeld, P. F. (1955). *Personal Influence, 2*. New York: The Free Press.

Khalil, M.N., & Pearson, J.M. (2007). The Influence of Trust on Internet Banking Acceptance. *Journal of internet banking and commerce*,12(2).

Kim, B. Y. (2008). Mediated Effects of Customer Orientation on Customer Relationship Management Performance. *International Journal of Hospitality & Tourism Administration*, *9*(2), 192–218. doi:10.1080/15256480801909089

Kinard, B. R., & Capella, M. L. (2006). Relationship marketing: The influence of consumer involvement on perceived benefits. *Journal of Services Marketing*, *20*(6), 359–368. doi:10.1108/08876040610691257

King, S. F., & Burgess, T. F. (2008). Understanding success and failure in customer relationship management. *Industrial Marketing Management*, *37*(4), 421–431. doi:10.1016/j.indmarman.2007.02.005

Lam, D., & Mizerski, D. (2005). The effects of locus of control on word-of-mouth communication. *Journal of Marketing Communications*, *11*(3), 215–228. doi:10.1080/1352726042000333180

Larivière, B., & Van-den Poel, D. (2005). Predicting Customer Retention and Profitability by Using Random Forests and Regression Forests Techniques. *Expert Systems with Applications*, *29*(2), 472–484. doi:10.1016/j.eswa.2005.04.043

Lars, M. W. (2007). The Effects of Loyalty Programs on Customer Lifetime Duration and Share of Wallet. *Journal of Retailing*, *83*(2), 223–236. doi:10.1016/j.jretai.2007.01.002

Le Roux, J.-B. (2013). Le nombre de smartphones dans le monde pourrait atteindre 3,3 milliards d'ici 2018. *Economiematin.fr*. Retrieved from http://www.economiematin.fr/ecoquick/item/3977-smartphones-utilisation-monde-reseau-operateurs-mobiles

Legris, P., Ingham, J., & Collerette, P. (2003). Why do people use information technology? A critical review of the technology acceptance mode. *Information & Management*, *40*(3), 191–204. doi:10.1016/S0378-7206(01)00143-4

Leroy, R. J. R., Marshall, G. W., & Stamps, M. B. (2005). Sales force use of technology: Antecedents to technology acceptance. *Journal of Business Research*, *58*(5), 553–280.

Limayem, M., & Rowe, F. (2006). Comparaison des facteurs influençant les intentions d'achat à partir du web à Hong Kong et en France: Influence sociale, risque et aversion pour la perte de contact. *Revue Française du Marketing*, *209*, 4–5.

Lindon, D., & Jallat, F. (2002). *Le Marketing*. Paris: Édition DUNOD.

Malhotra, N., & Mac, C. D. (2001). A cross-cultural comparison of behavioral intention models: Theoretical consideration and en empirical investigation. *International Marketing Review*, *18*(3), 235–269. doi:10.1108/02651330110396505

Mansfield, E. (1968). *Industrial Research and Technological innovation. New-York.* Norton.

Meyer-Waarden, L. (2007). The effects of loyalty programs on customer lifetime duration and share-of-wallet. *Journal of Retailing*, *83*(2), 223–236. doi:10.1016/j.jretai.2007.01.002

Moore, G. C., & Benbasat, I. (1991). Development of an instrument to measure the perceptions of adopting an information technology innovation. *Information Systems Research*, *2*(3), 192–222. doi:10.1287/isre.2.3.192

Morin, S. P. (1983, February 28). Influentials advising their friends to sell lots of high-tech gadgetry. *Wall Street Journal*, 30(8), 982-1003.

(n. d.). Retrieved from http://www.acxiom.fr/ideas-and-innovation/glossary/fid%C3%A9lisation-client

Nasco, S., Kulviwat, S., Kumar, A.G., & Bruner, C. (2008). The CAT model: extensions and moderators of dominance in technology acceptance. *Psychology & marketing*, 25(10), 987-1005.

(n.d.). Retrieved from http://www.escpap.net/conferences/marketing/2008_cp/Materiali/Paper/Fr/Janouri_Gharbi.pdf

Nielsen. (2007). Trust in advertising, a global Nielsen consumer report. Retrieved from www.nielsen.com/solutions/TrustinAdvertisingOct07.pdf

Nysveen, H., Perdersen, P. E., & Thorbjornsen, H. (2005). Explaining intention to use mobile services: Antecedents and cross-service comparisons. *Journal of the Academy of Marketing Science*, *33*(3), 330–346. doi:10.1177/0092070305276149

O'Cass, A., & French, T. (2003). Web Retailing Adoption: Exploring the nature of Internet Users Web Retailing Behaviour. *Journal of Retailing and Consumer Services*, *10*(2), 81–94. doi:10.1016/S0969-6989(02)00004-8

Pawar, B., & Sharda, R. (1997). Obtaining Business Intelligence on the Internet. *Long Range Planning*, *30*(1), 110–121. doi:10.1016/S0024-6301(96)00100-8

Ranaweera, C., & Prabhu, J. (2003). On the relative importance of customer satisfaction and trust as determinants of customer retention and positive word of mouth. *Journal of Targeting Measurement and Analysis of Marketing*, *12*(1), 82–90. doi:10.1057/palgrave.jt.5740100

Ricard, L., & Perrien, J. (1999). Explaining and evaluating the implementation of organizational relationship marketing in the banking industry: Clients' perception. *Journal of Business Research*, *45*(2), 199–209. doi:10.1016/S0148-2963(97)00226-9

Rogers, E. M. (1983). *Diffusion of Innovations* (3rd ed.). London: The Free Press.

Rogers, E. M. (1995). *Diffusion of innovations* (4th ed.). New York: Free Press.

Senach, B. (1990). Evaluation ergonomique des IHM. *Revue de la littérature*, rapport Inria N° 1180.

Stambouli, K., & Briones, E. (2002). *Buzz marketing: les stratégies de bouche à oreille*. Paris: Éditions d'Organisation.

Szajna, B. (1996). Empirical Evaluation of the Revised Technology Acceptance Model. *Management Science*, *42*(1), 85–92. doi:10.1287/mnsc.42.1.85

Taylor, S., & Todd, P. A. (1995). Understanding information technology usage: A test of competing models. *Information Systems Research*, *6*(2), 144–176. doi:10.1287/isre.6.2.144

Torsten, G. J., Rams, W., & Schindler, A. (2001). Customer Retention, Loyalty, and Satisfaction in the German Mobile Cellular Telecommunication Market. *Telecommunications Policy*, *25*(4), 249–269. doi:10.1016/S0308-5961(00)00097-5

Valsecchi, M., Renga, F. M., & Rangone, A. (2007). Mobile customer relationship management: An exploratory analysis of Italian applications. *Business Process Management Journal*, *13*(6), 755–770. doi:10.1108/14637150710834532

Van Doorn, J., Lemon, K. N., Mittal, V., Nass, S., Pick, D., Pirner, P., & Verhoef, P. C. (2010). Customer Engagement Behavior: Theoretical Foundations and Research Directions. *Journal of Service Research*, *13*(3), 253–266. doi:10.1177/1094670510375599

Venkatesh, V., & Davis, F. D. (2000). A theoretical extension of the technology acceptance model: Four longitudinal field studies. *Management Science*, *46*(2), 186–204. doi:10.1287/mnsc.46.2.186.11926

Venkatesh, V., & Davis, F. D.VenKkatesh. (1996). A Model of the perceived ease of use: Development and test. *Decision Sciences*, *27*(3), 451–481. doi:10.1111/j.1540-5915.1996.tb01822.x

Venkatesh, V., Morris, M. G., Davis, G. B., & Davis, F. D. (2003). User acceptance of information technology: Toward a unified view. *Management Information Systems Quarterly*, *27*(3), 25–47.

Vesel, P., & Zabkar, V. (2009). Managing customer loyalty through the mediating role of satisfaction in the DIY retail loyalty program. *Journal of Retailing and Consumer Services*, *16*(5), 396–406. doi:10.1016/j.jretconser.2009.05.002

Wang, H.-F., & Hong, W. (2006). Managing Customer Profitability in a Competitive Market by Continuous Data Mining. *Industrial Marketing Management*, *35*(6), 715–723. doi:10.1016/j.indmarman.2005.06.005

Weinberg, T. (2009). *The new community rules: Marketing on the social web*. Sebastopol, CA: O'Reilly Media, Inc.

Westbrook, R. A. (1987). Product/consumption-based affective responses and post-purchase processes. *JMR, Journal of Marketing Research*, *24*(3), 258–270. doi:10.2307/3151636

Wicker, A. W. (1969). Attitudes versus actions: The relationship of verbal overt behavioral responses to attitude objects. *The Journal of Social Issues*, *25*(4), 41–78. doi:10.1111/j.1540-4560.1969.tb00619.x

Wiedmann, K. P., Langner, S., & Hennings, N. (2007). Collaborated Marketing. In H. Bauer, D. Grosse-Leege, & J. Rösger (Eds.), Interactive Marketing in Web 2.0 – Konzepte und Anwendungen für ein erfolgreiches Marketing management in Internet. Munich: Vahlen.

Zaoui, I., & Akremi, A. E. (2003, May 21-23). l'intention d'achat du consommateur sur Internet: Déterminants et rôle modérateur de la confiance. Cas du site marchand du magasin général. Proceedings of the *8th AIM conference*, Grenoble, France.

Zarrella, D. (2010). *The social media marketing book.* Sebastopol, CA: O'Reilly Media, Inc.

Zineldin, M. (2000). Beyond relationship marketing: Technologicalship marketing. *Management Intelligence & planning*, 18(1), 9-23.

Zulkifli, Z., & Tahir, I. M. (2012). Developing and validating Customer Relationship Management (CRM) practices construct. *International Journal of Business and Behavioral Sciences*, *2*(1), 35–48.

Chapter 5 Social Media: Strategic Decision Making Tool

Gordon Bowen
Regent's University London, UK

Deidre Bowen
SHS Charity, UK

ABSTRACT

Social media is seen very much as a marketing tool and there is little in the literature that considers its use as a strategic decision making tool. This conceptual paper is an attempt to redress the balance. Social media user-generated content from blogs or consumer feedback are methods that social media can support effective strategic decision making. However, the business and organisational environments are influential on the effective of the data collected and ultimately its analysis. The decision making approach – single or multistage are significant influencers on the quality of the decisions. Multistage decision making is supportive of controversial decision making, which leads to better utilisation of the information and consequently, better decision making. Ultimately, robust decision making is underpinned by the effectiveness of the decision making process.

INTRODUCTION

Decision making is required by all organisations, however the approaches used to come to a decision will vary. Consequently, many books have been written on decision making, because of its importance to businesses and to organisational functioning (Hoy and Tarter, 2010; and Litchfield, 1956). Decision making is constraint by time and revisiting a decision is a bounded-process that is also time consuming (Hoy & Tarter, 2010). Decision making requires a degree of optimism and participation (Connolly & James, 2006; Gigerenzer, 2000; Gigerenzer et al., 1999). However, other authors view decision making as a non-optimistic process (Kahneman et al, 1982; and (Kahneman & Tversky, 1973). This does beg the question is social media more supportive of a particular approach to decision making or social media's role in decision making unrelated to the decision making approach. Decision making requires the identification of patterns and these patterns guide the individual especially in the formative years and they

DOI: 10.4018/978-1-4666-9776-8.ch005

become ingrained (Calabrese & Zepeda, 1999). Social media is a tool that can leverage the patterns and enhance the decision making process. Decision making assessment will require criteria referencing (Calabrese & Zepeda, 1999). Carroll and Johnson (1990) used criteria referencing to identify conflicting references points. Examples of these reference points are purposeful versus non-purposeful, consistent behaviour versus inconsistent behaviour and reasoning versus prone to error. Calabrese and Zepeda, (1999) suggest that a 'good' decision maker rarely makes a 'wrong' decision, because good decision maker keep an eye on the present and also on the future. This suggests the good decision maker have vision and can link current decisions to the future decisions. They understand how decisions today could impact future decisions. Knowledge is a key influencer on decision making and its ability to influence the cognitive pattern recognition is highly individualised (Calabrese & Zepeda, 1999). How the decision makers interact with the organisation, to form a dynamic relationship is influential on the decision making quality (Saiti & Eliophotou-Menon, 2009). Collaborative approaches to decision making is not easy and simple (Connolly & James, 2006).

Social media and marketing is becoming a prevalent tool for developing and maintaining engagement of customers and they have been found to influence purchase shopping behaviour (Ruane & Wallace, 2013). Traditional marketing is view as a unidirectional process, however, social media is a multi-interaction process (Scott, 2010). Social media is more effective for pull-marketing strategies, thus using social media to provide communication of information, knowledge, values and ethics about the product or service offerings (Lagrosen & Grund´en, 2014). The literature on social media focuses on marketing aspects such as marketing communications (Mount & Martinez, 2014; Lagrosen & Grund´en, 2014; Ruane & Wallace, 2013; LaPointe, 2012; Booth & Matic, 2011). Social media can be leveraged as a strategic tool and thus can improve decision making and leveraging social media to improve the level of decision making is scarcely covered in the literature. This conceptual paper contends that the application of social media as a strategic decision-making tool is neglected and social media has an important role in ensuring the robustness of decision making.

Theoretical Frameworks

Social Media

The research in social media became business focus from approximately around 2006 and one of the first studies was by McAfee (2006, 2009). McAfee coined the term Enterprise 2.0 to identify social media within or between companies, their partners or customers. McAfee's work focuses on the benefits for business (Deans, 2012). Marketing and social media is a popular area of investigation in the academic literature (Deans, 2012; Angel & Sexsmith, 2009; Baker 2009).

The social media framework (table 1) devised by Cook (2008) suggests the four C's categories are communication technologies, connection, co-operation and collaboration. The framework is a reference point for business and aids understanding of how to evaluate technology in the business environment and consider their business implications (Deans, 2012).

Cross-cultural communications play an important role in business decisions (Buderi and Huang, 2006; Huang, 2010). Experimentation with communication technologies across cross-cultural borders may alleviate business failures such as product launches, and outsourcing due to cultural misunderstandings (Ricks, 2006). Social media is changing communications across borders (Bernoff and Li, 2008). Social media will become a pervasive tool of communications as younger people enter the workplace

Table 1. 4C framework of social media technologies

Cooperation • Social Bookmarks • Media Sharing • Social Content • and Ranking Sites	**Communication** • Blogs • Twitter • Instant Messaging • Virtual Worlds
Connection • Social Networks • Mash-ups • Web RSS	**Collaboration** • Wikis • Conferencing/Teleconferencing • Electronic Meetings

Source: Cook, (2008)

in increasing numbers. They grown-up with social media. Western countries will need to communicate across cultural borders to engage the middle class in emerging countries, as an example (Deans and Miles, 2011). Strategy based on ideas or variety suggests that an abundance of ideas will help to improve the robustness of the strategy. Applying the communication advantages of social media to strategic decision making would help organisations to leverage their competitive advantage and update their strategic ideas more readily.

Connection technologies such as Facebook, LinkedIn or Twitter enable individuals to remain in contact in the workplace or socially. LinkedIn is a popular social network for business people to stay in contact. However, not all countries are supportive of social networks such as China. Mash-ups are potentially powerful by connecting or combining applications to develop new ones that provide added value (e.g. Zillow.com is a mash-up of real estate data and Google maps). Really Simple Syndication (RSS) is another connection tool that provides information feeds, thus connecting publishers with consumers. RSS feeds are an efficient and effective method to channel and distribute information (Cook, 2008). Decision making is reliant on information that is effective and efficiently directed and interactions between individuals, which is an attribute of social media's connectiveness (Cook, 2008; Calabrese & Zepeda, 1999; and Heck & Marcoulides, 1991).

The following framework (table 1) is a method to understand social media technology in an organisational and business contexts. Social media technologies that are classified under communication require interaction with people and focuses on relationships (Cook, 2008). This implies that supportive relationships are required to maximise 'interactivity' between people. Communication is important for cross-border activities by firms (Rifkin, 2006). Social media is a game changer for communications across borders (Bernoff & Li, 2008). Western companies will need to find new ways to communicate and connect with emerging middle classes in developing countries to promote their goods and to encourage consumers in these countries to purchase them (Deans & Miles, 2011). Social media technologies that are under the connection classification require little direct contact with people. Interaction takes place over time and individuals (Cook, 2008). Connection software is an approach to bring together friends, business colleagues and family. They allows global connections that are seamless, cost-effective and transparent. Mash-ups are a combination of online applications, such as real estate and use of Google maps (Cook, 2008). Co-operation technologies support group activities, but each contributors retain authority over their ownership of the information (Cook, 2008). The posting of information on video and photo-sharing sites are classed as co-operation social media technologies. It demonstrates the ability to relay information in real-time across the globe. Information is also shared in a timely manner (Deans,

2012). Business decisions require information that is timely and thus makes this technology valuable in the making of strategic decisions. The final dimension is collaboration technologies and this requires participants to have common goals and apply a coordinated approach to achieving tasks (Cook, 2008). Collaborative technologies facilitate 24/7 working and is extremely useful for bring a group of people in virtual locations together to solve a problem (Deans, 2012). These technologies reduce travel costs for firms that have heavy travel commitments and saving time (Heck, 2009). The social media technologies are have a role to play in decision making from improvement in the decision making process to informing the robustness of the information used.

SOCIAL MEDIA AND MARKETING STRATEGY

Social media assists in basic marketing techniques, however, the target market group must be defined. Segmentation in the online environment is easier than the offline environment (Scott, 2010). Weber (2009) argues that segmentation has changed, because of the advent of social media. Segmentation is focused on psychographic and behavioural characteristics, because of social media, which are ideally suited for the target group of young people. Crucially marketers can 'listen' (monitor) to the target group risk-free and for 24/7. Target groups can express their opinion openly facilitated by smartphones and mobile internet. (Smedescu, 2013). Listening to 'conversations' will help marketers to learn about specific problems on the brand, which face-to-face dialogue would not elicit. Listening to conversations is also known as 'Opinion mining' or 'Conversation sentiment analysis'. The purpose of the opinion mining is to detect the state of the conversation, i.e. positive, neutral or negative (Smedescu, 2013). Snyder and Barzlay, (2007) and Pang & Lee, (2012) have attempted to develop a more complex scale for conversation sentiment analysis. Sentiment analysis is learning through human interaction, but suffers from drawbacks such as the level of accuracy given language is complex and is influenced by cultural norms and context. However, the sentiment analysis does give a general idea of the feeling and general direction of the conversation. Recording the information will also give the impact of the conversation on social media and enable negative trends to be identified earlier. Monitoring of influencers e.g. Facebook friends and Twitter followers is an important aspect of monitoring (Smedescu, 2013).

Social media marketing is part of Internet marketing. Social media is a promotion tool and a sales support tool. The sales support activities of social media is normally referred to as 'social customer relationship management (sCRM). In the promotional role it assists in raising brand awareness and enables sharing of the latest product/service deals. This demonstrates the flexibility and multiple uses of social media (Smedescu, 2013). According to Stelzner, (2013) social media marketing is a tool to improve brand awareness, web site traffic, leads, market research, build fan brand loyalty, search ranking and grow useful business partnerships. Smedescu (2013) considers social media marketing to be new, where prompt customer-centric action is always required, because social media has given consumers increased power.

Firms should not think of social media as simply a marketing channel, but an approach to build beneficial relationships with their customers. Companies need to respect the voluntary nature of social media users and accentuate the positives and suppress the negatives. They should provide interesting issues that engage their users to produce relevant content and spread voluntarism (Lee, 2010).

Lee (2010) states that firms must be careful in the tone and manner of the delivery of the content. Developing a unique tone that is 'fun', 'sincere' and 'quick' is a good approach. This is important to communicate an effective message to their customers.

Lastly, Lee (2010) suggests that a cross-media strategy, so that social media is supported with other media and not considered an alternative. An integrated approach to social media is required to ensure a smooth communication process. A multi-facet approach to blogs is desirable such as the approach used by Intel, Twitter, Facebook and Youtube. Use of a multi-facet approach to blogs generates a richness of information that is diverse and can be shared with customers.

DECISION MAKING

The decision making is about doing the right thing (Beech, 1990). Individuals interactions drive the decision making process and these different interactions drive the overall decision making process, such as the direction of a business or school (Calabrese & Zepeda, 1999; Heck & Marcoulides, 1991). Simon (1960) suggests that decision making has three phases, which are finding a need for making a decision, define a course of action and selecting the course from the available actions identified. Decision making needs to be based on understanding and not based on prescriptive recipes (Richardson & Lane, 1994). Decision making in organisations are influenced directly by internal political concerns, beliefs about the process, organisational concerns and indirectly information collected by the decision makers by senior people such as a principal in a school (Heck et al, 1989). The expectation is that organisational context and size will influence the decision making process. However, Heck and Marcoulides, (1991); Monk, (1987), found that the size of an organisation does not affect the decision making process at least in a school. However, Salley et al (1979) found that school size was an important variable that influenced principals' attitudes about staffing. Decision making in schools is relatively uncertain (Heck et al,1990) and senior staff cannot have all the information required (Heck & Marcoulides, 1991). Uncertainty is affected by political conditions and the external environment and these become important factors in situational decision making (Heck & Marcoulides, 1991). A clear understanding of the context in which the decision choices are embedded is of significance in the understanding of organisational processes (Heck & Marcoulides, 1991).

Decision making assessment can be considered rational or normative and is associated with the decision maker following a logical and sequential set of steps. The other approach to decision making assessment is the descriptive approach, which focuses on what the decision maker is doing (Glasman & Fuller, 1992). An effective decision making process is a combination of the normative and descriptive approaches, with descriptive decision maker operating under an umbrella of ambiguity and complexity (Glasman & Fuller, 1992; Gorton, 1987). Rational decision making in environmental uncertainty was conducive to organisational outcomes such as schools (Glasman & Biniaminor, 1981). The principal's vision for the school and the conversion of the vision to expectations are attributes that effect positive organisational decision making (Glasman & Fuller, 1992). There are differences in decision making between effective principals and less effective principals, and one significant difference is how they acted to improve student improvement (Glasman & Fuller, 1992; Patterson, 1984). Glasman & Fuller, (1992) found differences in their perceptions to how their administrative roles relates to the delivery of the outcomes. Decision making should move away from a recipe approach for solving problems to "learning mentality" in the preparation of senior decision maker to use critical analysis (Richardson & Lane, 1994:14).

DECISION MAKING PROCESSES

Social media give customers and consumers increased power, because of its pervasiveness and young people are more active on social media networks (Smedescu, 2013; Deans & Miles, 2011). Is a central decision making process appropriate for organisations that intend to use social media as a strategic decision making tool? Instinctively the answer would be probably not. However, one needs to consider benefits and drawbacks of using centralised decision making. The guidelines are defined by the organisation for decision making, but the decision making process influences how the policies or strategy are determined (Saiti & Eliophotou-Menon, 2009).

Greater participating in decision making increases costs, several studies have supported decisions based on participation over hierarchical decision making, which are less effective than participative decision making (Deetz & Brown, 2004; Lawer, 1999). Diversity in the different perspectives encourages creativity leads to better and faster decisions. Problems tend to move from a low level of complexity to higher levels of complexity 'effective measures' need to be adopted such as participative decision making. The more complex the problem organisational buy-in becomes important (Saiti & Eliophotou-Menon, 2009: 447). Factors that support participatory decision making are the environment (political and social), the size, structure, departmentalisation of the organisation, and the characteristics of the decision makers such as their ability, dedication, and motivation (Miller and Lee, 2001). Connolly and Jones, (2006) suggest that collaborative working in educational institutions require participation at every level of the organisation. Furthermore, it demands flexibility, adaptability and fluency in communications. A study by Saiti & Eliophotou-Menon, (2009) on a school in the Greek educational system suggests that there is limited stakeholder involvement in the decision making process. The study identified a number of weaknesses with the Greek case of centralised decision making. Responsibility for decision making on Greek educational policy (design and implementation) are the sole responsibility of the Minister of Education. Final decision on educational policies are made by an administrative hierarchical system of the Ministry of Education. The centralised structure at the Ministry of Education inhibits diversity in participatory decision making. Given that educational is a major investment for a country, it would be expected that a collaborative approach to decision making would be a strong contender. Collaborative leadership is necessary to form inclusive relationships that bring in experience actors and smooth the successful implementation of the educational plans. Research by Drucker, (1993), Ghoshal and Bartlett, (1995) has demonstrated that most successful organisations harness the commitment and knowledge of their managers to create an environment that promotes creativity and speed implementation. The interaction between the organisation and the decision makers contribute to an effective decision making process (Saiti & Eliophotou-Menon, 2009).

The above analysis has implications for strategist that use social media as a decision making tool. Conversations from social media are voiced openly and the polarity of the information is typically honest and unbiased. This is because of the nature of the target group, who are young (Smedescu, 2013). In mature organisations the top decision makers tend to be older than the target groups and the application of a centralise decision making process would have similar consequences to the Greek educational case. Social media extends across global borders and operates 24/7 and gives customers and consumers increase power. This implies that decision making processes need to be responsive to customer-centric needs. Collaborative leadership aids decision making, which is responsive to customers' need, because it would be inclusive of actors with diverse experience and knowledgeable. However, decision making based on participative decision is slow and time consuming. There needs to be a trade-off between centralised decision making and participative decision making when decisions are made on social media sentiment analysis.

DECISION MAKING AND USER-GENERATED CONTENT (UGC)

One source of rich information for making strategic decision is the application of user-generated content (UGC) is social media and in particular blogs. It is important when developing strategy based on user-generated content from blogs to understand how it will affect decision making. Studies on user-generated content on decision making from blogs assumes it is a single stage process (Dellarocas et al. 2008 and Forman et al. 2008). Ignoring the multistage concept of decision making for information generated by blogs may introduce bias in the process and the parameters (Andrews & Manrai, 1998). The multistage process for decision making may generate managerial insights that are not offered in the single stage models (Gensch, 1987). Evaluation of the information is known as the screening stage, this is followed by the choice stage, which requires additional information for due diligence. The final stage is the contract stage, which in the case of venture capitalist (VC) discussing terms of finance. The stages identified are applicable to ventures seeking finance from venture capitalists (Tyebjee & Bruno, 1984).

Culman et al, (2010) identified the challenges faced by organisations implementing social media applications such as blogs to interact with customers. They found three factors – mindful adoption, community building and absorptive capacity are factors that influence the implementation of social media applications. Increase in negative posts attract additional readers and initially will rise exponentially and then stabilise at a point in time (Aggarwal et al. 2011). Readers of blogs exhibit a variety-seeking behaviour (Singh et al, 2010 and Huang et al, 2010). Traditional mass media was not as influential as social media applications such as blogs, Youtube and Myspace on U.S. presidential candidates' performance in the 2008 U.S. presidential race (Wattal, et al, 2010). To develop strategy the user-generated content should be representative of the users and the challenge is to encourage users to engage with the blogs. Firms need to ensure the implementation of the blogs are successful and be mindful of the three factors identified by Culman et al. (2010).

One of the earliest work on user-generated content is by Godes and Mayzlin, (2004) and they demonstrated that online conversations can measure user-generated content. The relationship between financial information associated with eWOM and final financing with data predominately from an online blog (VentureXpert) demonstrated the ability to create user-generated content from VentureXpert and its influence on the financing decision on new ventures (Aggarwal et al. 2012). Chevalier and Mayzlin, (2006) examined the relationship between online reviews on the relative sales of two online booksellers (Amazon.com and Barnes BN.com). Increase reviews on one site for a given led to an increase in sales compared to the other site, also negative reviews had a greater impact on sales than positive reviews. Forman et al, (2008) found that an increase in reviews leads to increase sales regards less of the state (positive or negative) of the reviews. Liu et al, (2010) investigated the forecasting accuracy of user-generated content on box office sales. The result demonstrated that the volume of user-generated content at different phases of the movie life cycle can significantly improve the accuracy of box office sales in the first week and total box office sales. Useful information can be elicit from user-generated content and they can be used for forecasting, which is a valuable attribute for developing strategy.

The next discussion is user-generated content on multistage decision making. Multistage decision making is used when limited resources are available and can reduce the high cognitive processing for large quantity of data (Roberts & Lattin, 1997). Screening is required where limited information is available and time is limited (Bettman et al 1998, Bettman & Park, 1980). One benefit of screening is that decision makers can reduce the processing required at the different levels and can spend more time actively seeking comprehensive information for each stage (Aggarwal & Singh, 2013). Research suggest that a multistage decision making process is more effective than single stage decision making. The influence of the attributes vary across the different stages (Roberts & Lattin, 1997 and Manrai 1995). Research by Roberts and Lattin (1997), Andrews and Srinivasan (1995) and Roberts and Lattin, (1991) suggests that multistage decision making improves the predictive accuracy over single stage decision making. Research by Aggarwal and Singh, (2013) on the influence of blogs on venture capital multistage decision making indicated that blog coverage helps with the screening phase and indirectly influences the final stage (contract in venture capital parlance). More decision makers help to create better alternatives to a negotiated agreement. The context of their research implies that wrong decisions lead to significant losses for the decision makers. It would appear that there is considerable motivation to collect and analyse information at the choice stage of decision making. Previous research suggest that the research context (positive or negative) does not lead to significant losses for the decision makers. The contradiction in the results may be that the decision makers in the previous studies were not highly motivated to collect data beyond the user-content generated information. Aggarwal and Singh (2013) work is applicable to situations where the motivation to avoid making a wrong decision is high. They give the example of car buying, but this is also true for strategic decisions. Work by (Aggarwal & Singh (2013) suggest that strategic decision making should gather user-generated content information and also gather additional information to improve the decision making process and minimise the risk of bad or wrong decisions. Strategist cannot rely only on user-generated content information and should use a process of triangulation to gather additional information to validate and expand the user-generated content information.

DECISION MAKING AND UNCERTAINTY

The uncertainty surrounding vital complex decisions in organisations has long become a barrier to effective decision making (Cohen and March, 1974). However, (Tjosvold et al, 2012) found from their research that uncertainty has a positive role (Kahnesman & Klein, 2010). When managers recognise uncertainty in decision making that recognision leads them to seek opposing views and ask questions from those with different views (Tjosvold, 2008, 1998). Tjosvold et al (2012) suggests that recognision of inadequacies in one views' can lead managers to seek controversial views in an organisational setting. In situations where uncertainty is decreasing will lead to less intellectual and emotional demand on managers and thus improve the effectiveness of the decision making (Berry, 2000 and Cohen and March, 1974). When managers recognise and experience uncertainty, this leads to the promotion of decision making (Tjosvold et al, 2012, Reynolds & Hrudey, (2006), and Bukszar, 2003). Notably, this uncertainty can lead managers to seek open-minded discussions of diverse ideas in order to develop solutions, which they consider to be effective (Tjosvold et al, 2012). Confidence that one is right can impede controversial seeking decision making ideas, but confidence that one can potentially understand the problem does not inhibit controversial seeking decision making ideas (Kahnesman & Klein, 2010).

Cooperative goals and uncertainty complement controversial seeking decision making. Managers that have cooperative relationships are disposed to controversial seeking decisions even when uncertainty is not much. Such managers may think conversations are productive even if they have confidence in their opinion. In a competitive environment managers need to feel unsure before openly conferring with colleagues (Tjosvold et al, 2012). Superiors see their views and goals as cooperative when approaching subordinates, but subordinates when approaching superiors are more likely to view their goals as competitive (Tjosvold et al, 2012 and Hogan et al, 1994). Individuals that adopt a constructive controversial and open-minded discussion of opposing views is an important antecedent for an effective individual manager decision making and has also shown to be an effective antecedent for team decision making (Tjosvold et al, 2012). Because of the nature of strategic decision making uncertainty is prevalent and the literature is suggesting that controversial seeking decision making will lead to more effective solutions.

Participants that are in a negative mood gathered, elaborated and processed information, more cautiously make decisions with more fluency and flexibility than participants in a positive mood. It would appear that negative moods give rise to a systematic approach to decision making. Positive moods induce heuristics processing. Participants exposed to negative mood states decreased their positive mood states and increased their negative mood states. Those inducted to positive mood states increased their positive mood state and decreased their negative mood state (Mohanty & Suar, 2014). Negative mood states increase the involvement in the problem (Mackie & Worth, 1989). User-generated content that is negative on organisation will induce better information processing, leading to more effective decision making. This assumes that the negative content will induce negative mood states. Should organisations using social media user-generated content look for negative outcomes and ignore positive outcomes to promote effective decision making? Does pessimism make for more effective decision making? Higher perceived uncertainty leads to lower behavioural intentions to undertake the activity. Perceived uncertainty is lowered if the actors in the environment play a role in decreasing the uncertainty (Yen, Hung & Liu, 2014). Top management need to articulate the benefits of the strategy to decrease the level of perceived uncertainty in the organisation (Yen, Hung & Liu, 2014). Uncertain outcomes sometimes generate negative evaluations and other times positive evaluations. Affective decisions are influenced by uncertainty, with consumers preferring uncertainty in the outcome over simply offering more to consumers. When promotions involve uncertainty increased information helps cognitive and affective decisions. The more gifts that are included in the promotion the greater the decrease in uncertainty for the consumer, but could be detrimental to consumer purchase behaviour. Cognitive decisions require information and consumers making such decisions view information as positive. However, consumers making affective decisions view uncertainty as positive (Laran & Tsiros, 2013).

Strategic decisions are made frequently, but not all are important or publicised. Some strategic decisions are data-driven (large quantity of historical data) and others are based on judgement and not based on historical data. The decision makers would have no measures to judge the uncertainties. Whether the combination of the above approaches or singularly judgement plays a crucial role. An emerging tool to help with judgemental strategic decision making is the prediction market. Prediction markets requires a market to be developed and a set of bets is placed by individuals based on their desired outcome. When the event occurs the market is closed. The individuals will buy a contract for less than a dollar, which equates to the probability of the outcome for the event. This approach is suitable for example on whether the elected US President will be a Democrat in the 2012 election (Borison & Hamm, 2010). The presentation of the information on certainty affects decision making and better ways of conveying estimation and presentation of uncertainty is paramount. Forecasts especially made on managerial judgement need to be conveyed clearly and effectively (Goodwin, 2014). Decision makers with more business experience are able to apply and adopt causation-based logic in making the decision than less experience managers. The manager's experience of the organisational environment affects the decision making process by influencing the interpretation of different schemas and allows him to make diverse interpretations and thus decisions on similar 'situations' (Nummela et al, 2014). The implication is that experience managers are better placed to make strategic decisions, as they have the knowledge to apply the 'what if' approach. Should only experience business managers make strategic decisions based on the user-generated content?

SOCIAL MEDIA AND BUSINESS PERFORMANCE

E-tailers use of social media draws upon social capital and social networks to promote their online business (Qu, Wang & Zhang, 2012). Social capital is defined as "...the sum of the actual and potential resources embedded within, available through, and derived from the network of relationships possessed by an individual or social unit..(Nahapiet & Ghoshal, 1998, p.243)." Embedded resources can be information and advice (Zagenczyk et al, 2008) and emotional support (Mehra et al, 2006) and reputation due their central position in the network (Balkundi & Harrison, 2006). These resources can lead to a competitive advantage (Brass et al, 2004). The addition of hyperlinks to other e-tailers storefronts undermine business performance of the focal e-tailer and hyperlinks pointing to the focal e-tailer's main storefronts boosts the e-tailer's business performance (Stephen & Toubia, 2010). However, Qu, Wang and Zhang, (2012) found that hyperlinks were beneficial to e-tailers' storefronts, because they reveal their social alliance network.

The number of inquiries is related to business performance. A high number of inquiries is a positive outcome for business performance. It should be noted that 80% of the inquiries were resolved satisfactorily. E-tailers seeking advice in online communities may cause social risk to the e-tailers, and they could be portrayed as incompetent and inexperience by potential buyers, which will undermine their business performance. Friendship ties (positive social relationship) have a positive effect on business performance. Bi-directional or unidirectional friendship ties are beneficial for business performance. Sharing information online is beneficial, seeking information without contributing undermines online business performance. Advice seeking should be balanced by advice giving (Qu, Wang & Zhang, 2012).

IMPLICATION TO MANAGEMENT

The decision making process requires the collection and analysis of information. However, the quality of decision making is improved and the robustness of the outcomes strengthened by using a multistage decision making process (Andrews & Manrai, 1998, Gensch, 1987, Simon, 1960). The implication is that strategic decisions should be based on a multistage approach and 'lesser' decision could be based on the single stage decision making process. Social media can help to unravel patterns and behaviour, which are valuable in spotting opportunities and trends. It is clear social media has a role in strategic decision making for online businesses. There is a level of risk when business environments exhibit uncertainty and this uncertainty will impact the decision making process. Businesses will always experience risks in the environment, so it is important to minimise the uncertainty risks in the decision making process.

One approach to minimising risks is to listen to conversations online. Conversations are open and unbiased in the online environment (Smedescu, 2013). Consequently, constant monitoring of social media will provide rich information that can be utilised in the strategic decision making process. If online information gained from social media is valuable for making strategic decisions this could imply that the decision making process should be near or at the top of the organisation. Centralisation of decision making is not necessarily a good thing and weakness have been identified with this method of decision making (Saiti & Eliophotou-Menon, 2009).

One source of information for assisting with the strategic decision making process is user-generated content, such as blogs and feedback (incoming and outgoing). The issue for management is decoding the information, because information is collected in an open environment does not necessarily mean patterns and trends are easy to discern or reliable. Although social media can provide valuable information for strategic decisions and strategic planning, a level of triangulation of the information is necessary. One approach is that user-generated content is subject to a multistage decision making process (Andrews & Manrai, 1998), which will improve decision making, because it will foster a collaborative and participative environment (Saiti & Eliophotou-Menon, 2009). In order for a participative and collaborative environment in an organisation requires all levels to be involved in the decision making process. This is approach to decision making is supportive of an organisational environment that uses an emergent approach to strategy development. The diversity of information used in developing emergent strategy should focus on the negative outcomes, will lead to effective involvement (Mackie & Worth, 1989). However, the positive and negative outcomes could be contradictory and thus is one method to condense the information, before focusing on the negative outcomes to facilitate decision making.

Decision making can be based on affective and cognitive approaches, both may be appropriate for environments that are subjected to uncertainty. Co-operative organisational environments complements uncertainty and can lead to controversial seeking decisions (Tjosvold et al, 2012). Strategic decision making in uncertain environments needs to be different and unique if business performance is to strengthen. There is no benefit in making strategic decisions that are similar to your competitors. User-generated contents provides additional information that minimises the effects of uncertainty in the business environments. Strategist analysing the user-generated contents should be of an optimistic temperament, because in this mood state the processing of information would be more effective and Nummela et al, (2014) found that experienced managers make better decisions. The use of social media as a tool to improve decision making and ultimately business performance gives rise to a positive outcome. However, if the information is not presented so that it is understandable and can be used for forecasting then no amount of tinkering with the decision making process can overcome this.

FUTURE RESEARCH AND RESEARCH LIMITATIONS

This paper is a conceptual paper and is thus as a consequence a research limitation. The work in the chapter could be developed by defining the different stages and roles in a multistage decision making process that uses user-generated content. The implementation of a multistage decision making process that is supportive of an emergent approach to strategy development is an area that is underdeveloped in the literature. Review of the literature supports a decentralised approach to the decision making process, but sometimes this is not always possible or desirable. Under what conditions is a centralised approached appropriate when using user-generated content?

CONCLUSION

The use of social media as part of the decision making process is an influencer on business performance. How the information derived from user-generated content is filtered and used will affect the significance of its usability. Information that is subjected to a multistage decision making process makes for better problem solving and controversial decision making. The mood of the persons in the strategic decision making is an influencer on the quality of the decision making. Decisions that are made in a collaborative and participatory business environment are factors that improve the decision making. The analysis suggests that controversial decision making depends on the organisational and business environments and leads to decision making that is effective and makes a difference to the organisation's business performance positively.

REFERENCES

Aggarwal, R., Gopal, R., Gupta, A., & Singh, H. (2012). Putting Money Where the Mouths Are: The Relation between Venture Financing and Electronic Word-of-Mouth. *Information Systems Research*, *23*(3), 976–992. doi:10.1287/isre.1110.0402

Aggarwal, R., Gopal, R., Sankaranarayanan, R., & Singh, P. V. (2012). Blog, Blogger, and the Firm: Can Negative Employee Posts Lead to Positive Outcomes? *Information Systems Research*, *23*(2), 306–322. doi:10.1287/isre.1110.0360

Aggarwal, R., & Singh, H. (2013). Differential Influence of Blogs across Different Stages OF Decision Making: The Case of Venture Capitalists. *Management Information Systems Quarterly*, *37*(4), 1093–1112.

Andrews, R. L., & Manrai, A. K. (1998). Simulation Experiments in Choice Simplification: The Effects of Task and Context on Forecasting. *JMR, Journal of Marketing Research*, *35*(2), 198–209. doi:10.2307/3151848

Andrews, R. L., & Srinivasan, T. C. (1995). Studying Consideration Effects in Empirical Choice Models Using Scanner Panel Data. *JMR, Journal of Marketing Research*, *32*(1), 30–41. doi:10.2307/3152108

Angel, R., & Sexsmith, J. (2009), Social networking: The view from the c-suite. *Ivey Business Journal Online*. Retrieved from http://www.iveybusinessjournal.com/topics/strategy/social-networking-theview-from-the-c-suite

Baker, B. (2009). Your customer is talking—to everyone: Social media is the new channel for customer connection. *Information Management Journal*, *19*(4), 20.

Balkundi, P., & Harrison, D. A. (2006). Ties, leaders, and time in teams: Strong inference about network structure's effects on team viability and performance. *Academy of Management Journal*, *49*(1), 49–68. doi:10.5465/AMJ.2006.20785500

Beech, L. (1990). *Image theory: Decision making in Personal and Organizational Contexts*. New York, NY: John Wiley and Sons.

Bernoff, J., & Li, C. (2008). Harnessing the power of the oh-so-social web. *Sloan Management Review*, *49*(3), 36–42.

Berry, A. J. (2000). Leadership in a new millennium: The challenge of the 'risk society'. *Leadership and Organization Development Journal*, *21*(1), 5–12. doi:10.1108/01437730010310686

Bettman, J. R., Luce, M. F., & Payne, J. W. (1998). Constructive Consumer Choice Processes. *The Journal of Consumer Research*, *25*(12), 187–217. doi:10.1086/209535

Bettman, J. R., & Park, C. W. (1980). Effects of Prior Knowledge and Experience and Phase of the Choice Process on Consumer Decision Processes: A Protocol Analysis. *The Journal of Consumer Research*, *7*(3), 234–248. doi:10.1086/208812

Booth, N., & Matic, J. A. (2011). Mapping and leveraging influencers in social media to shape corporate brand perceptions. *Corporate Communications: An International Journal*, *16*(3), 184–191. doi:10.1108/13563281111156853

Borison, A., & Hamm, G. (2010). Prediction Markets: A New Tool for Strategic Decision Making. *California Management Review*, *52*(4), 125–141. doi:10.1525/cmr.2010.52.4.125

Brass, D. J., Galaskiewicz, J., Greve, H. R., & Tsai, W. P. (2004). Taking stock of networks and organizations: A multilevel perspective. *Academy of Management Journal*, *47*(6), 795–817. doi:10.2307/20159624

Buderi, R., & Huang, G. T. (2006). Guanxi, New York: Simon & Schuster.

Bukszar, E. (2003). Does overconfidence lead to poor decisions? A comparison of decision making and judgment under uncertainty. *Journal of Business Management*, *9*, 33–43.

Calabrese, R. L., Sally, J., & Zepeda, S. J. (1999). Decision-making assessment: Improving principal performance. *International Journal of Educational Management*, *13*(1), 6–13. doi:10.1108/09513549910253428

Carroll, J., & Johnson, S. (1990). *Decision Research: A Field Guide*. Newbury Park, CA: Sage Press.

Chevalier, J. A., & Mayzlin, D. (2006). The Effect of Word of Mouth on Sales: Online Book Reviews. *JMR, Journal of Marketing Research*, *43*(3), 345–354. doi:10.1509/jmkr.43.3.345

Connolly, M., & James, C. (2006). Collaboration for school improvement: A resource dependency and institutional framework of analysis. *Educational Management Administration & Leadership*, *34*(1), 69–87. doi:10.1177/1741143206059540

Cook, N. (2008). *Enterprise 2.0*. Burlington, VT: Gower Publishing Limited.

Culnan, M. J., McHugh, P. J., & Zubillaga, J. I. (2010). How Large U.S. Companies Can Use Twitter and Other Social Media to Gain Business Value. *MIS Quarterly Executive*, *9*(4), 243–259.

Deans, P. C. (2012). Integration of Study Abroad with Social Media Technologies and Decision-making Applications. *Decision Sciences Journal of Innovative Education*, *10*(3), 299–336. doi:10.1111/j.1540-4609.2012.00344.x

Deans, P. C., & Miles, J. B. (2011), "A framework for understanding social media trends in China", Proceedings of the 11th International DSI and APDSI Joint Meeting, Taipei, Taiwan, July pp. 12–16.

Deetz, S., & Brown, D. (2004). Conceptualising involvement, participation and workplace decision processes – a communication theory perspective. In D. Tourish & O. Hargie (Eds.), *Key Issues in Organisational Communication* (pp. 172–187). London: Routledge.

Dellarocas, C., Zhang, X., & Awad, N. F. (2008). Exploring the Value of Online Product Reviews in Forecasting Sales: The Case of Motion Pictures. *Journal of Interactive Marketing*, *21*(4), 23–45. doi:10.1002/dir.20087

Drucker, P. F. (1993). *Post-capitalist Society*. New York, NY: Harper Collins.

Forman, C., Ghose, A., & Wiesenfeld, B. (2008). Examining the Relationship Between Reviews and Sales: The Role of Reviewer Identity Disclosure in Electronic Markets. *Information Systems Research*, *19*(3), 291–313. doi:10.1287/isre.1080.0193

Gensch, D. H. (1987). A Two-Stage Disaggregate Attribute Choice Model. *Marketing Science*, *6*(3), 223–239. doi:10.1287/mksc.6.3.223

Ghoshal, S., & Bartlett, C. A. (1995). Changing the role of the top management: Beyond structure to process. *Harvard Business Review*, (January-February): 86–96.

Gigerenzer, G. (2000). *Adaptive Thinking: Rationality in the Real World*. New York, NY: Oxford University Press.

Gigerenzer, G., & Todd, P. M.ABC Research Group. (1999). *Simple Heuristics that Make Us Smart*. New York, NY: Oxford University Press.

Glasman, N. S., & Biniaminov, I. (1981). Input-output Analyses of Schools. *Review of Educational Research*, *51*(4), 509–539. doi:10.3102/00346543051004509

Glasman, N. S., & Fuller, J. (1992). Assessing the Decisionmaking Patterns of School Principals. *International Journal of Educational Management*, *6*(3), 22–30. doi:10.1108/09513549210014178

Goodwin, P. (2014). Getting Real about Uncertainty. *Foresight*, *33*(Spring Iss.), 4–7.

Gorton, R. A. (1987). School Leadership and Administration. Brown, Wm C, Dubugne.

Heck, M. (2009). Telepresence shatters communication barriers. *Infoworld*. Retrieved from http://www.infoworld.com/d/ hardware/telepresence-shatters-communication-barriers-657

Heck, R., Larsen, T., & Marcoulides, G. (1990). Instructional Leadership and School Achievement: Validation of a Causal Model. *Educational Administration Quarterly*, *26*(2), 94–125. doi:10.1177/0013161X90026002002

Heck, R., Marcoulides, G., & Glasman, N. (1989). The Application of Causal Modeling Techniques to Administrative Decision-making: The Case of Teacher Allocation. *Educational Administration Quarterly*, *25*(3), 253–267. doi:10.1177/0013161X89025003003

Heck, R. S., & Marcoulides, G. A. (1991). The Effects of Organisational Size on Principal Decision Making. *International Journal of Educational Management*, *5*(1), 4–12. doi:10.1108/EUM0000000001966

Hogan, R., Curphy, G. J., & Hogan, J. (1994). What we know about leadership. *The American Journal of Psychology*, *49*(6), 493–504. doi:10.1037/0003-066X.49.6.493 PMID:8042818

Hoy, W. K., & Tarter, C. J. (2010). Swift and smart decision making: Heuristics that work. *International Journal of Educational Management*, *24*(4), 351–358. doi:10.1108/09513541011045272

Huang, L. (2010). Cross-cultural communication in business negotiations. *International Journal of Economics and Finance*, *2*(2), 196–199. doi:10.5539/ijef.v2n2p196

Huang, Y., Singh, P. V., & Ghose, A. (2010, December 12-15). Show Me the Incentives: A Dynamic Structural Model of Employee Blogging Behavior. *Proceedings of the 31st International Conference of Information Systems*, Saint Louis, MO, USA.

Kahneman, D., & Klein, G. (2010). Conditions for intuitive expertise: A failure to disagree. *The American Journal of Psychology*, *64*(6), 515–526. doi:10.1037/a0016755 PMID:19739881

Kahneman, D. K., Solvic, P., & Tversky, A. (1982). *Judgment under Uncertainty, Heuristics and Biases*. Cambridge: Cambridge University Press. doi:10.1017/CBO9780511809477

Kahneman, D. K., & Tversky, A. (1973). On the psychology of prediction. *Psychological Review*, *80*(4), 251–273. doi:10.1037/h0034747

Lagrosen, S. O., & Grunden, K. (2014). Social media marketing in the wellness industry. *The TQM Journal*, *26*(3), 253–260. doi:10.1108/TQM-12-2013-0129

LaPointe, P. (2012). Mind Over Metrics Measuring Facebook's Impact on Marketing The proverbial Hits the Fan. *Journal of Advertising Research*, *52*(3), 286–287. doi:10.2501/JAR-52-3-286-287

Laran, J., & Tsiros, M. (2013). An Investigation of the Effectiveness of Uncertainty in Marketing Promotions Involving Free Gifts. *Journal of Marketing*, *77*(2), 112–123. doi:10.1509/jm.11.0255

Lawer, E. (1999). Employee involvement makes a difference. *Journal for Quality and Participation*, *22*(5), 18–20.

Lee, D. (2010). *Korean Consumer Society Growing Popularity of Social Media and Business Strategy Samsung Economic Research Institute (SERI)* (pp. 112–117).

Litchfield, E. (1956). Notes on a general theory of administration. *Administrative Science Quarterly*, *1*(1), 3–29. doi:10.2307/2390838

Liu, Y., Chen, Y., Lusch, R. F., Chen, H., Zimbra, D., & Zeng, S. (2010). User-Generated Content on Social Media: Predicting New Product Market Success from Online Word-of-Mouth. *IEEE Intelligent Systems*, *25*(1), 75–78.

Mackie, D. M., & Worth, L. T. (1989). Processing deficits and the mediation of positive affect in persuasion. *Journal of Personality and Social Psychology*, *57*(1), 27–40. doi:10.1037/0022-3514.57.1.27 PMID:2754602

Manrai, A. K. (1995). Mathematical Models of Brand Choice Behavior. *European Journal of Operational Research*, *82*(1), 1–17. doi:10.1016/0377-2217(94)00236-6

McAfee, A. (2006). Enterprise 2.0: The dawn of emergent collaboration. *Sloan Management Review*, *47*(3), 21–28.

McAfee, A. (2009). Shattering the myths about Enterprise 2.0. *Harvard Business Review*, *87*(11), 120–124.

Mehra, A., Dixon, A. L., Brass, D. J., & Robertson, B. (2006). The social network ties of group leaders: Implications for group performance and leader reputation. *Organization Science*, *17*(1), 64–79. doi:10.1287/orsc.1050.0158

Miller, D., & Lee, J. (2001). The people make the process: Commitment to employees, decision making and performance. *Journal of Management*, *2*(2), 163–189. doi:10.1177/014920630102700203

Mohanty, S. N., & Suar, D. (2014). Decision Making Under Uncertainty and Information Processing In Positive and Negative Mood States. *Psychological Reports: Employment Psychology & Marketing*, *115*(1), 91–105. doi:10.2466/20.04.PR0.115c16z2 PMID:25153952

Monk, D. (1987). Assigning Elementary Pupils to their Teachers. *The Elementary School Journal*, *88*(2), 167–187. doi:10.1086/461531

Nahapiet, J., & Ghoshal, S. (1998). Social capital, intellectual capital, and the organizational advantage. *Academy of Management Review*, *23*(2), 242–266.

Nummela, N., Saarenketo, S., Jokela, P., & Loane, S. (2014). Strategic Decision-Making of a Born Global: A Comparative Study from Three Small Open Economies. *Management International Review*, *54*(4), 527–550. doi:10.1007/s11575-014-0211-x

Pang, B., & Lee, L. (2005). Seeing stars: Exploiting class relationships for sentiment categorization with respect to rating scales. Proceedings of the Association for Computational linguistics (pp. 115–124). Retrieved from http://www.cs.cornell.edu/home/llee/papers/pang-lee-stars.home.html doi:10.3115/1219840.1219855

Patterson, B. (1984). Perceptions of Efficacy in Effective and Ineffective Principals [Unpublished PhD dissertation]. University of California, Santa Barbara, CA, USA.

Qu, Z., Wang, Y., Wang, S., & Zhang, Y. (2013). Implications of online social activities for e-tailers' business performance. *European Journal of Management*, *47*(8), 1190–1212.

Reynolds, L. A., & Hrudey, S. E. (2006). Managing uncertainty in environmental decision-making: The risky business of establishing a relationship between science and law. *International Journal of Risk Assessment and Management*, *6*(1-3), 1–249. doi:10.1504/IJRAM.2006.007889

Richardson, M., & Lane, K. (1994). Reforming principal preparation from training to learning. Catalyst, Winter, 14-18.

Ricks, D. A. (2006). *Blunders in international business*. Malden, MA: Blackwell Publishing.

Rifkin, G. (2006). Building better global managers. Harvard Management Update, March, pp. 3–6.

Roberts, J. H., & Lattin, J. M. (1991). Development and Testing of a Model of Consideration Set Composition. *JMR, Journal of Marketing Research*, *28*(4), 429–440. doi:10.2307/3172783

Roberts, J. H., & Lattin, J. M. (1997). Consideration: Review of Research and Prospects for Future Insights. *JMR, Journal of Marketing Research*, *34*(3), 406–410. doi:10.2307/3151902

Ruane, L., & Wallace, E. (2013). Generation Y females online: Insights from brand narratives. *Qualitative Market Research: An International Journal*, *16*(3), 315–335. doi:10.1108/13522751311326125

Saiti, A., & Eliophotou-Menon, M. (2009). Educational decision making in a centralised system: The case of Greece. *International Journal of Educational Management*, *23*(6), 446–455. doi:10.1108/09513540910980998

Salley, C., McPherson, B., & Baehr, M. (1979). *National Occupational Analysis of the School Principalship*. Chicago: Industrial Relations Center, University of Chicago Press.

Scott, D. M. (2007). *The New Rules of Marketing and PR*. Hoboken, New Jersey: John Wiley & Sons, Inc.

Simon, H. A. (1960). *New Science of Management Decisions*. New York, NY: Harper and Row. doi:10.1037/13978-000

Singh, P. V., Sahoo, N., & Mukhopadhyay, T. (2010). Seeking Variety: A Dynamic Model of Employee Blog Reading Behavior. *Proceedings of the Workshop on Information Systems Economics*, Saint Louis, MO. doi:10.2139/ssrn.1617405

Smedescu, D. A. (2013). Social Media Marketing Tools. *Romanian Journal of Marketing*.

Snyder, B., & Barzilay, R. (2007). Multiple Aspect Ranking using the Cood Crief Algorithm. *Proceedings of the Joint Human Language Technology/North American Chapter of the ACL Conference* (HLT-NAACL) (pp. 300-307).

Stelzner, M. (2013). Social media marketing industry report: How Marketers Are Using Social Media to Grow Their Business. *Social Media Examiner.* Retrieved from http://www.socialmediaexaminer.com/socialmedia-marketing-report-2013

Stephen, A. T., & Toubia, O. (2010). Deriving value from social commerce networks. *JMR, Journal of Marketing Research*, *47*(2), 215–228. doi:10.1509/jmkr.47.2.215

Tjosvold, D., Peng, A. C., Chen, N. Y., & Fang, S. S. (2012). Individual Decision-Making in Organizations: Contribution of Uncertainty and Controversy in China.

Tyebjee, T. T., & Bruno, A. V. (1984). A Model of Venture Capitalist Investment Activity. *Management Science*, *30*(9), 1051–1066. doi:10.1287/mnsc.30.9.1051

Wattal, S., Schuff, D., Mandviwalla, M., & Williams, C. B. (2010). Web 2.0 and Politics: The 2008 U.S. Presidential Election and an E-Politics Research Agenda. *Management Information Systems Quarterly*, *34*(4), 669–688.

Weber, L. (2009). *Marketing To The Social Web: How Digital Customer Communities Build Your Business* (2nd ed.). Hoboken, New Jersey: John Wiley & Sons. doi:10.1002/9781118258125

Yen, T. F., Hung, C. J., & Liu, H. H. J. (2014). The Effects of Perceived Uncertainty on Tourists' Decision-Making to Agritourism in Taiwan. *The International Journal of Organizational Innovation*, *6*(4), 236–247.

Zagenczyk, T. J., Gibney, R., Murrell, A. J., & Boss, S. R. (2008). Friends don't make friends good citizens, but advisors do. *Group & Organization Management*, *33*(6), 760–780. doi:10.1177/1059601108326806

KEY TERMS AND DEFINITIONS

Marketing Strategy: Use of marketing to increase sales by achieving a sustainable competitive advantage.

Social Media: Online communications channels that allow community interaction content-sharing and collaboration.

Social Media and Business Performance: Use of social media to improve business processes in order to improve the organisation's performance.

UGC and Decision Making: The use of UGC to help clarify issues and enable solutions.

User-Generated Content (UGC): Material on websites and social media that is produced by the users of the websites and social media.

Chapter 6
Online Service Failure and Recovery Strategy:
The Mediating Role of Social Media

Yllka Azemi
Cardiff Metropolitan University, UK

Wilson Ozuem
University of Gloucestershire, UK

ABSTRACT

The Internet environment has transformed the concepts of service failure and recovery strategies from a dyadic customer-provider focus into a multidimensional web quality scope. In traditional encounters, the research spectrum of service failure and recovery strategies is very much developed from a customer service approach, and the responsibility of recovery has been traditionally assumed to be something that is assigned to the marketer. Studies pay little or no attention to the multidimensional nature of service failures contingent to recovery strategies in the evolving social media. To date, empirical studies have focused on service failures and recovery strategies in online marketing environments, but pay limited attention to social media platforms. This paper aims to provide some insights on the need for a broader conceptualisation of service failure and recovery strategies, incorporating social media platforms for the development of effective marketing communications programme.

INTRODUCTION

The Internet environment has transformed the concepts of service failure and recovery strategies from a dyadic customer-provider focus to a multidimensional web quality scope. In traditional encounters, the research spectrum of service failure and recovery strategies is very much developed from a customer service approach, and the responsibility of recovery has been traditionally assumed to be something that is assigned to the marketer, *ceteris paribus* (Bitner, Booms & Tetreault, 1990; Maxham & Netemeyer, 2002; Argo, White & Dahl, 2006; Roggeveen, Tsiros & Grewal; 2012; Sivakumar, Li & Dong, 2014). By contrast, research into online service failure and recovery strategies suggests that understanding is

DOI: 10.4018/978-1-4666-9776-8.ch006

limited to the spectrum of customer-website interactivity and less on the multidimensional nature of computer-mediated marketing environments (CMMEs) (Hoffman & Nowak, 1996; Ozuem, Howell & Lancaster, 2008).

CMME views online customer behaviour in a different way to traditional behaviour. Indeed, the online environment situates providers in an intense space of market competition, positioning the customer only a click away from switching providers in light of service failure (Y. S. Wang, Wu, Li & Y. Y. Wang, 2011). The CMME itself, together with the intensity of competition, serves as an indicator of very low customer switching and emotional costs (Forbes, Kelley & Hoffman, 2005). Consequently, online customers ignore postservice failure interactivity with the provider even though such activity is intended to recognise such failure and initiate service recovery. In such circumstances, customers can switch to alternative providers. In this fragile online environment, research into service failure and recovery strategies amongst online services has received more attention in understanding the causes of service failure rather than in understating customers' perception on service failure (Meuter et al., 2000; Holloway & Beatty, 2003).

A review of studies examines online service failure and recovery strategies from 2002 (Ozuem & Lancaster, 2014). Research into online service failure and recovery strategies has succeeded in assigning meaning to online service failures and categorising these into typologies (Forbes, Kelley & Hoffman, 2005; Kuo et al., 2011). Other scholars' attention was directed towards examining the online service failure and recovery strategies on lenses of traditional encounters' antecedents, though fewer antecedents are considered in the online failures (Wang et al., 2011; Ozuem & Lancaster, 2014). Such epistemological orientations limit the potential and opportunities inherent in CMME. Understanding service failure depends on individual expectations. Approaching the ontology of customers in the service failure and recovery process should be contextual rather than generic and standardised. Within this scope of approaching customers, Wang et al. (2011) examined their perceptions based on justice theory. The principles of justice theory lay on the equal fairness assessed from all the parties in a society (Mandle, 2009). In context to service recovery, Wang et al.'s (2011) defines justice 'as the customer's assessment of the fairness of the way in which service failures are handled' (p. 352). Their study reveals that customer perception of fairness is a reflection of the marketer's behaviour towards the customer. Zhu et al. (2013) sought to understand customer perceptions of what causes service failure (such as whether it is the customer's or the provider's fault) through attribution theory. Recently Ozuem & Lancaster (2014) utilised a constructivist perspective to comprehend customer recovery expectations and satisfaction. Studies pay little or no attention to the multidimensional nature of service failures contingent to recovery strategies in developing countries. To date, empirical studies have focused on service failures and recovery strategies in developed countries. This paper aims to provide some insights on the need for a context-specific development of recovery programmes and strategies in online marketing environments.

CONCEPTUAL BACKGROUND AND CONTEXT

The term 'service failure' has grown in popularity as a terminology used by both scholars and practitioners over the last two decades (Ozuem & Lancaster, 2014). Service failure has occurred in numerous research disciplines, including production and management (Craighead, Karwan & Miller, 2004), business (Choi & Mattila, 2008; Ozuem, O'Keeffe, and Lancaster 2015), marketing (Sivakumar, Li & Dong, 2014), consumer behaviour (Argo, White & Dahl, 2006) and the service industry (Chuang,

Cheng, Chang & Yang, 2012). Despite the uniqueness of these settings, if analysed together, it is clear that service failure is common to a range of commercial settings, and practical solutions must be attained to address service failures.

Various industries have been researched by scholars examining service failure and recoveries. These industries include fashion (Luo et al., 2012; Ozuem & Lancaster, 2014), the airline industry (Bitner, Booms & Tetreault, 1990; Ringberg, Odekerken-Schroder & Christensen, 2007; Bonifield & Cole, 2008; Roggeveen, Tsiros & Grewal, 2012; Tshin et al., 2014), medical care (Singh, 1990; Choi & Mattila, 2006), hospitality (Bitner, Booms & Tetreault, 1990; Smith, Bolton & Wagner, 1999; Smith & Bolton, 2002; Hess, Ganesan & Klein, 2003; Craighead, Karwan & Miller, 2004; Bonifield & Cole, 2008), grocery shopping (Singh, 1990), automotive repair (Singh, 1990; Craighead, Karwan & Miller, 2004) and the financial industry (Singh, 1990; Maxham & Netemeyer, 2002; Chuang, Cheng, Chang & Yang, 2012). Based on the reach of the analysis, it can be argued that the latter industry is perhaps the least researched area.

Service failure, as a term, can easily be conceptualised, and the definitions in the literature reflect a trajectory of meaning from common ground. Traced back to its early elucidation, Bell & Zemke (1987) stated that service failure 'happens every time our experience of service falls painfully short of expectations' (p. 32). They suggested that mismanaging the 'design and deployment of service with laser-like focus on the details' (p. 32) shapes the fluctuating of expectations, that is, service breakdown, which can be identified with two distinct labels. First is 'annoyance' embodied by irritated customers facing a slight shortage on what they have expected (i.e., a minor service failure). Second is 'victimisation' personified by customers encountering a major failure (Bell & Zemke, 1987, p. 33).

In terms of 'customer expectations', Sivakumar, Li & Dong (2014) proposed that 'service failure entails negative disconfirmation when service performance falls below expectations' (p. 46). To develop upon this idea, they imparted another perspective on service failure as follows: 'With the inherent heterogeneity of services, performance sometimes meets expectations, sometimes falls below expectations ("service failure"), and sometimes exceeds expectations ("service delight")' (p. 41). The term 'heterogeneity' used in the abovementioned definition refers to the multiple providers a customer can interface within the marketplace. It is therefore important to understand the complexity of behaviour amongst customers interfacing with service failures in terms of multiple choices in the market. The focus of this study is on the frequency, timing, proximity and sequence of service. Frequency is divided into two: concentrated and dispersed. The first refers to the failure or delight emerging from a single encounter. The second refers to multiple short failures or delights. Timing refers to the momentum of the failure or delight occurrence, whilst proximity is the interval amongst the failures or delights. Sequence compares a failure and a delight based on the importance of each in terms of their awakening series. Sivakumar et al. (2014) proposed that seriously perceived 'service failures' are those with 'dispersed breakdowns, long interludes among failures, and failures rather than delights situated in the closure of the encounter' (p. 53–54).

Yet service failure as a phenomenon is immensely complex and prone to misconceptions and gaps reflected in the literature and with some relevance for practitioners. The literature shows that scholars have been researching service failure from similar perspectives. Though research on service failure has enriched the literature, there is an unsolved puzzle in the extant research and an additional contribution is a necessity.

The primary idea that explains this complexity generates specifically from the differences amongst customer recovery expectations and that of myopic perception of customers' standpoints in terms of their prospects. In Bell & Zemke's (1987) delineation, the customer's expectation is associated with 'the zone of neutrality' (p.32), that is, the state of equality between what was expected and the gain. When the customer is satisfied with the experience, s/he is situated in the delighted zone. By contrast, when the customer is dissatisfied with the experience, s/he will be positioned in the undesirable one. 'On either side of the neutral zone is a memorable experience' (p. 32). The neutral zone identified by Bell & Zemke (1987) does not provide explanations on how to understand customers' expectations but rather provides the marketer with an overview on the ontological stance that they should take (i.e., the delight zone).

To develop upon this, the complexity in the nature of 'self' broadens when conceptualising service failure in the context of 'the delight experience', and this proposition has been advanced by authors such as Rust & Oliver (2000). They expressed a view of the 'counter customers' delighters'. The notion articulated in their study is that 'critics have suggested that delighting the customer "raises the bar" of customer expectations, making it more difficult to satisfy the customer in the next purchase cycle and hurting the firm in the long run' (p. 86). Here the perspective of the customer forgetting the delight was considered. The essence of customers forgetting the delight is that of not increasing the expectations of self in the sense that the provider is literally not forced to enhance their service above the standards they have already set. If this is the case and customers are not elastic in their choices but rather loyal to a single provider, Rust & Oliver (2000) concluded that delighting customers is a smart customer persuasion technique (p. 92). Some conceptualise the effect of delight on the customer and the provider based on how customers give meaning to delightful experiences. Intrinsically, to the latter group, customers are positioned under different perception grounds of delight, emphasising the enigma behind what a delightful experience is for a customer. Consequently, it is worth exploring how a provider should interact with a customer and what recovery strategy they should provide when service failure occurs.

An additional source of complexity in conceptualising service failure is the divergence within findings in relation to the effect that the 'customer-provider relationship' has on customer expectations and satisfaction when a failure awakens and recovery is provided. The lack of agreement around a structured paradigm as to how compact the relationship should be between the provider and the customer has led scholars and practitioners to debate these issues. Hess et al. (2003) suggested that the customer-provider relationship is complex and that customers interested in long-lasting relationships with a provider are more tolerant of failures, and have lower expectations. They are consequently more satisfied with perceptions of recovery (p. 140). It is suggested here that a more enduring customer-provider relationship is a positive outcome, particularly for providers, in the sense that less recovery effort is required. To the brilliance of irony, one may say, the sublime matter behind this study is the questioning of self. Are those findings presumptive yet superimpositions of prior studies, or do they reflect the absolute truth of the issue? Reiterating some truth in the ambiguity illustrated in the prior twofold question, the authors themselves accentuated generalisation of findings as an issue (Hess et al., 2003, p. 141).

The aforementioned study analysed customer responses to service failures in the context of prior service relationships, and Hui, Ho & Wan (2011) considered the issue of customer trust developed in terms of customer-provider encounter length. The outcome refers to 'trust' being the sublime indicator of how customers assign meaning whilst justifying responses to service failures. To illustrate this, the authors argue, 'Our studies show that it is not prior relationship per se but rather trust in the service provider that interacts with self-construal to influence consumer responses to service failures' (p. 74). In contrast to independent customers, it was evident that interdependent ones have less intention to switch and complain in the face of process and outcome failures, particularly if they trust the provider (p. 74). This emphasises trust building, particularly if the targeted customers are societal interdependent groups (p. 75). Note that if the customers do not complain, there is a downside for the company: that of the provider having tenuous information about the customer's stance towards the firm—an argument underlined when interdependent customers are considered (Hui et al., 2011, p. 76).

Craighead et al. (2004) called the time from failure occurrence to when the provider becomes aware of the failure 'the pre-recovery phase' (p. 309). Regardless of the attempt of marketers to develop the optimum scenario, that is, minimising the pre-recovery phase, and aiming to develop a pure recovery encounter with the customers—a concept explained by the literature as the ''service communality'' —they still face a state of unenviable 'commercial friendship' (see Ringberg et al., 2007, p. 194 for the original authors of concepts). One possible reason for the prolonged pre-recovery phase can probably be explained by the suggestion of Bougie, Pieters & Zeelenberg (2003). They proclaimed that 'most dissatisfied customers generally do not bother to complain' (p. 390). Therefore, it is difficult to conceptualise the customer's stance solely by making assumptions. It can be difficult for service employees to recognise dissatisfaction if the customer does not 'provide' a readable sign.

The idea advanced by Bougie et al. (2003) is the understanding of 'customer's behavioral responses to failed service encounters' (p. 377) subject to two emotional responses: dissatisfaction and anger. 'To explain dissatisfaction and anger, authors considered the following behavioural responses: switching, complaining, and negative word-of-mouth (WOM)' (p. 378). 'Dissatisfaction was found to be a significant predictor' (p.390) of the first response, whilst anger is significant to the entire list of responses (p.390). The authors suggested that 'findings appear to be in contrast with earlier work' (Bougie et al. 2003, p. 389) and create room to criticise how we understand the mental scope of customers following service failure behavioural responses. What they do not provide is an elaboration of the providers' ability to understand the mental state of the customer.

In terms of the emotional responses, the complexity in conceptualising service failures is subject to debate around two emotional approaches: variance-based and specific emotions (Zeelenberg & Pieters, 2004). The first approach typically situates perceptions of customers as either positive or negative, ignoring any explanation along this spectrum (pp. 445–446). By contrast, the latter approach considers literally everything about customer responses, from what they say through to their body language. All of these signs reveal much about customer mental perceptions, as illustrated in this study's discussions. The authors suggested that a specific emotions approach 'requires insight into the specific antecedents, phenomenology, and consequences of different emotions' (p. 446). They questioned the variance-based approach and argued that customer perceptions of failure should be analysed through the specific emotions approach elaborated upon through appraisal emotion theory (see Zeelenberg & Pieters, 2004, p. 446 for authors on appraisal emotion theory). They suggested that it is this approach that offers theory to comprehend the mental contour of customers. Here, the analysis of the specific emotions approach centres on two emotions, namely, regret and disappointment. They examined four behavioural responses, which they labelled switch, inertia, complaining and word-of-mouth based on these emotions. A synopsis of their findings suggests (1) switching and word-of-mouth are related to blended regret and disappointment; (2) complaining is related to disappointment although not to regret, and this variance is justified by the idea that customers assign their own responsibility to regret (p. 452); and (3) inertia has a modest relationship with regret and disappointment and can be considered unique in the context of this model. Complaining is perhaps the factor that exerts the greatest influence on mitigating customer perceptions of inertia (Zeelenberg & Pieters, 2004, p. 453).

Early literature relating to service marketing that focuses on analyses of role theory reflects a morphology outcome on customers and employees across common and blended responsibilities (Solomon et al., 1985). That is, not only employees are considered responsible for customer satisfaction, but the customers themselves are also considered in such discussions. Based on role theory, customers are more or less considered in terms of learned and systematic behaviour, identified as the *mindless* concept (p. 106), whereas the position of employees is explained across *intra-role congruence*, specifically 'the degree to which the service provider's concept of his/her role accords with the organization's conception of that role' (p. 104) and *inter-role congruence*, specifically 'the degree to which provider and client share a common definition of service roles (p. 104). It follows that the service provider expects from customers an equivalent response to prior responses and a change to their behaviour only when a service encounter deviation arises. The closer the employee is to the intra- and inter-roles, the more positive the provider-customer encounter will be. The salient interpretations that emerge from the abovementioned discussions (see Solomon et al. 1985) are as follows: First, regardless of the responsibility of customers, there are no 'rules' that spell out an ideal employee-customer interaction, and it is the employees' duty to design and influence service encounters and satisfaction. They must be able to understand customer expectations. Second, regardless of the degree to which a customer remains stable from one encounter to another, there is always the possibility of deviation, and the difficulty of managing service encounters remains problematic.

COMMON MISPERCEPTIONS AND MYTHS

In analysing a typology of service failures, a chronological reflection of the extant literature provides some elucidation on types of service failures. Several studies on this topic were conducted in the past, and the service failure types generated by subsequent studies are consistent with Bell & Zemke's (1987) twofold service failures: *process* and *outcome*. The former emphasises 'what getting the service should be like' (p. 32), and the latter refers to the means of the final outcome.

Based on the proposal of Bell & Zemke in the late 1980s, Bitner et al. (1990) developed a threefold service failure typology. The typology reflects the occurrence of failures in the employee-customer encounter and encompasses the following failure categories: (1) employee response to service delivery system failure, (2) employee response to customer needs and requests, and (3) unprompted and unsolicited employee actions (pp. 74-76). The core concept of this model accentuates the employee responsibilities in service encounter. Assuming that empowerment shapes employee behaviour, the service encounters, knowledge, and control components suggested by Bitner et al. (1990) must be acknowledged to avoid these three types of service failure. A formula to categorise service failure was also suggested by Keaveney (1995). The author identified two types of service breakdown: core service and service encounter. The core service failures include significant incidents with the service itself, grouped into three clusters, namely, mistakes, billing errors, and service catastrophes (p. 76). Meanwhile, the service encounter failures happen when employees show misleading behaviour (such as uncaring, impolite, unresponsive, and unknowledgeable employees) (Keaveney, 1995, p. 76).

An additional perspective on service failure classification was articulated by Choi and Mattila (2008). Although their study clearly sets out a unique conceptualisation, if a philosophical stance is taken, the authors have analysed service failure from two apexes directed towards a convergence that views service failure as having an effect on three components: overall satisfaction, word of mouth (WOM), and return intent. Under the first apex, 'controllability' affects the three components that generate a threefold service failure typology that encounters (1) failures caused by the firm, (2) failures caused partly by the customer, and (3) failures subject to some unknown causes. The authors suggest that customers tend to criticise companies that allow failures to occur and not always with good cause. They reflect, 'In other words, focal encounter, satisfaction, overall satisfaction, return intent, and positive word-of-mouth were significantly lower among these customers than among their counterparts in the self-blame or control condition (controllability unknown)' (p. 28). The authors further argue, 'people tend to blame others for negative outcomes and credit themselves for positive events' (p. 28). The second apex considers that service failure affects the three components subject to service expectations customers have had prior to service failure. Being set in a more liberal stand, customers who have higher expectations towards service express a greater forbearance when it comes to the postfailure experience that includes their overall satisfaction, subsequent propensity for WOM recommendations, and repurchase intentions (Choi and Mattila, 2008, p. 28).

A visual presentation of service failure typologies in traditional encounters explained above is presented in Figure 1, which shows the conceptualisation of this study. The outer circle presents the *general* classification on the causes of service failures (specifically, failures caused by the firm, partly by the customer, or by some other unknown factor). If failure is caused by the employee, a process or service encounter failure occurs, whereas if failure is caused by the customer or by another unknown cause, an outcome or a core service failure will happen. The author of the chapter retained all delineations presented by the original authors in a ceteris paribus stance rather than considering these delineations individually. Given the drawback of this adapted service failure classification model, further analysis on this model may provide a better conceptualisation of service failure typologies in the service literature.

In the context of self-service technologies (SST), and incorporating to some degree online services, subject to an analysis of customer dissatisfaction, Meuter, Ostrom, Roundtree & Bitner (2000) introduced the four-grounded service failure typology. The model is related to the virtual provider-customer encounter,

Figure 1. Traditional service failure typologies
Adapted from Bell & Zemke (1987), Bitner et al. (1990), Keaveney (1995), and Choi & Mattila (2008)

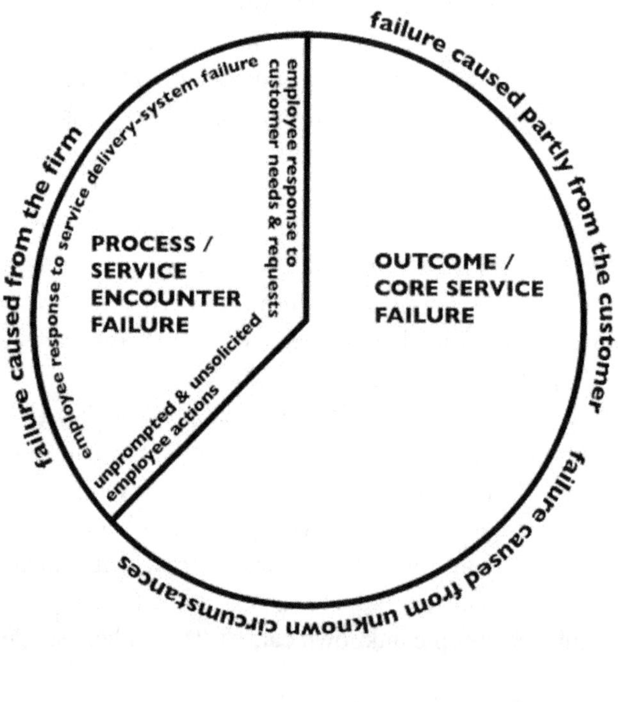

and it includes the following types of service failures: (1) technology failure, (2) process failure, (3) poor design, and (4) customer-driven failure (pp. 56-57). The original authors suggested, delineations with examples of each failure type as follows: (1) Technology failure—the interface medium breaks down and obstructs the use of services (for example, 'a broken ATM'). (2) Process failure—a failure that emerges after the customer has completed an interaction with a technological service medium. Most likely the customer will recognise the failure after some time has passed (for example, a customer has ordered and paid online for a product but didn't receive it). (3) Poor design—a technological failure occurs (for example, on a website or with an ATM) because there is a lack of clarity in terms of how to use it, and there is a service design problem with the service itself, rather than with the medium (for example, a prolonged period required for the money to be transferred from an ATM to a customer's account). (4) Customer-driven failure—failures can occur when the customer is 'at fault' (for example, a customer does not recall the personal identification number required to make an online transaction) (Meuter et al. 2000, p.57). Based on the abovementioned concept, customers tend to judge and assign the responsibility for failure to the provider (p. 60), and technology failures are considered the most catastrophic among the different types of failures (p. 59). It is suggested that 'recovery rarely occurs in SST context, because most firms have not figured out how to recover effectively' (Meuter et al., 2000, p. 60). Based on these ideas, customers are strict observers of online providers, and the provider must understand how customers assign meaning to the service failures to develop effective online recovery strategies.

An additional construct that categorises online service failures is the sixfold typology offered by Holloway & Beatty (2003). The authors reviewed the first two types of failure in parallel with the process, technology, and poor design failures of Meuter et al. (2000). They tackled the issue of online versus traditional service encounters and suggested that service failures also differ within these encounters. The failure typology suggested by them incorporates the following: (1) delivery, (2) website design, (3) payment, (4) security, (5) product quality, and (6) customer service problems (p. 95). This hierarchy of failure types has been set based on the frequency of occurrence—from the most frequent to the least frequent failure type (pp. 95–96). In analysing these failure types, the delivery problems the authors emphasised include problems such as 'the product arrived later than promised, the wrong product was delivered, merchandise was delivered to the wrong address' (p. 95). Website design problems include the following: the website did not open, the content was not user friendly, and the website was only available in one language (p. 96). Payment problems refer to customer perceptions of being 'charged more than they had expected' (p. 96). Security problems include fraud issues (p. 96). Problems with product quality mean failing to meet 'customer's expectations' (p. 96), and customer service problems occur because the provider does not respond to customer requests (p. 96). When contemplating the typology, the authors considered the behaviour of customers after online failure and suggested that 'customers may be more likely to complain online than in a traditional buying environment' (p. 102). This delineation, besides enriching the theoretical background of online research, provides an informative guide for the provider to identify their fallacies and a source to provide meaning to customer expectations. The study also suggests that the 'majority of consumers feel injustice following the firm's recovery effort' (p. 101). Holloway & Beatty (2003) accentuated the importance of providing customers with the ability to complain whilst providing 'toll-free numbers, e-mail addresses, and real-time chat rooms, as possible complaining channels' (p. 102).

A visualisation of online service failure typologies developed by Meuter et al. (2000) and Holloway & Beatty (2003) is shown in Figure 2. The two sets in Figure 2 represent the typologies of the original authors so that set A illustrates the service failure typology suggested by Meuter et al. (2000) and set B

Figure 2. Online service failure typologies
Adapted from Meuter et al. (2000) and Holloway & Beatty (2003)

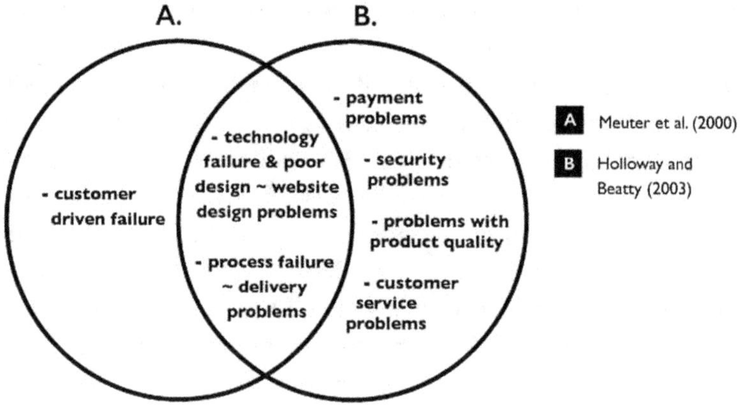

illustrates that of Holloway & Beatty (2003). The intersection of A and B represents the elements of two typologies that are similar to each other (Holloway & Beatty, 2003, p. 101). Given that the intersected section represents the most frequent failures identified by both studies, the intersection provides a good indicator of how online services might improve.

When the abovementioned typologies are reviewed on a macro level, the service failure typologies offered by scholars in blended traditional and online services are all to a large extent interrelated. Service failures can be visualised as a 'triangle' that encompasses the breakdown of the service itself, the breakdown of the service encounter, and the deviation from customer expectations. In contrast to research service recovery and research into service failure typologies, more academic focus has been given to the first two apexes of the triangle and less to the latter one. In support of this argument, it is easier to construct typologies subject to an analogy of service and service encounter breakdowns, rather than to focus purely on customer expectations. Conceptualising customer perceptions of expectation becomes even more complex when considering themes related to service failure recovery. To add clarity to discussions of customers' recovery expectations, a section in this chapter will provide explanations of service recovery as a process, together with discussions of customer responses to the recovery strategy.

SOCIAL MEDIA AND SERVICE RECOVERY

The multidimensional nature of social media provides great opportunities for service failure recovery (Barwise and Meehan, 2010; Azemi and Ozuem, 2015; Gregoire et al., 2015). However, a growing consensus across academics and practitioners is that if inappropriate service recovery is provided, social media can cause immense risks to the marketer (Pang et al., 2014; Gruber et al., 2015). The risk is associated with the speed that customers' complaint goes viral (Barwise and Meehan, 2010) and the lack of control businesses have over the flow of information (Kaplan and Haenlein, 2010). In this context, Barwise and Meehan (2010) suggest that social media has transferred the power from the marketer to the consumers (p. 80). This situation has been significantly explained through the 'United Breaks Guitars' story (Kietzmann et al., 2011). A customer whose guitar has been broken by United Airlines made the song 'United Breaks Guitars' as a revenge to the company, which has neglected the customer's recovery request, that is, to pay back for the broken guitar. This song has been uploaded on YouTube and has been viewed by almost 15 million people. This number means people worldwide are aware that United Airlines fails to recover and that its customers experience the double deviation effect. This is an example of how 'social media can turn a local event into a national or global story' (Gruber et al., 2015, p. 170).

The literature emphasises on a persistent online customer-provider relationship that starts well before the service failure happens, rather than one that emerges with the occurrence of the incident (Hanna et al., 2011). Hanna et al. (2011) suggest that if a company communicates online repetitively, 'social media enables both reach and engagement' stances (p. 268). Hanna et al.'s (2011) study does not explain the benefits of prior relationship in context with recovery strategy. However, if 'reach' and 'engagement' notions are explained from the failure recovery perspective, the former would have referred to the peak where the provider knows what the customer recovery requirements are and the latter to the customer's voluntary involvement into the recovery process. The literature on offline failure recovery has named customers' voluntary involvement the co-creation recovery strategy (Dong et al., 2008). The concept of co-creation strategy has yet to receive attention by online recovery strategy scholars. However, the omnidimensional nature of social media provides great opportunities for online co-creation.

The customer does not always convey a recovery recommendation through the online message, yet the message itself is an important source to understand the customer's recovery expectations. Today, many organisations have representatives that communicate with online customers in real time. Gu and Ye (2014) refer to this activity as online management response. Their study examines online management responses in hotel reviews. According to them, 'on average, 23% of customer reviews receive online management responses' (pp. 573–574), the majority of which go against the company (p. 574). This indicates that company representatives have a tendency to approach dissatisfied customers more than those with better evaluations. This isolation may generate frustration among the latter group. The aforementioned risk is highly possible considering Gu and Ye's (2014) proclamation that 40% of customers read other customers' online reviews prior to posting theirs (p. 574). It means social media is an open source to everyone, and the company is subject to monitoring. However, if the company manages the online communication well, the articulated information may be a well-embedded source to strategic decisions. Larivet and Brouard (2010) suggest that customer information is the core source of strategic intelligence. They define the strategic intelligence as the filter to articulate information external to organisation, which is essential in making strategic decisions (p.538), including recovery ones. Their explanations overcome the customer information perceived by means of online media. However, the abundance of information available through social media (Gu and Ye, 2014) seems to be the imperative foundation for strategic intelligence.

The literature on online service recovery has been specifically developed across nonfinancial recovery strategies, such as acknowledgement, apology, and explanation (Barwise and Meehan, 2010). Barwise and Meehan (2010) illustrate a successful application of the three aforementioned strategies through Procter & Gamble (P&G). A dissatisfied customer opened a Facebook account asking P&G to remove their diaper product from the market. This customer argued that the P&G diaper causes rushes to babies, and shortly after, she received significant online support from other customers. P&G publicly apologised for what has happened, acknowledged that 'a proportion of babies will always suffer from rushes' (p. 82), and explained that its product does not cause rushes. Such explanation was later reviled by the U.S. Consumer Product Safety Commission (see p. 82 for additional explanation on the case; Barwise and Meehan, 2010). Having been said that the explanation of P&G was in line with the Consumer Product

Safety Commission, it is revealed the importance of the 'company being sincere' through the recovery process. It can be argued that any contradiction between the Consumer Product Safety Commission and P&G explanations would have generated additional customer dissatisfaction.

The context of sincerity in the recovery response has also been considered by Xia (2013). This study examines the effectiveness of responses to customers' criticism in context with vulnerable and defensive responses. The former includes acknowledgement and apologising for the failure (p. 75), and the latter refers to disclaiming the failure to protect the company image (p. 75). This study suggests that the vulnerable response is associated with the sincere recovery; consequently, the recovery satisfies the customer. However, Xia's (2013) findings reveal that sincerity in recovery response is moderated by the brand personality, that is, perfect or sophisticated brands (p. 93). Customers of sophisticated brands consider that acknowledgement and apology reflect sincerity. This study fails to provide explanations on how 'sincerity' is transmitted across both vulnerable and defensive responses. The remaining unanswered question is this: what happens if a company correctly denies the online customer's criticisms, but it sounds insincere? This risk can be controlled through a social media strategy. In this context, Hobson (2012) recommends 'five tips' to use in social media: (1) recognize change, (2) make a deal with your employees to eliminate FUD, (3) be where your customers are, (4) listen, and (5) permit, not prohibit (pp. 4–12). These are greatly oriented towards empowering the employees to closely and repetitively monitor the online customers.

Additionally, research has considered the effectiveness of online recovery strategy in context with the recovery conveyer. Manika et al. (2013) have examined the effect of the CEO apologising publicly for a failure through a YouTube video. Their study is isolated to the case of BlackBerry. Their underlying suggestion is that CEO apologies are effective in keeping customers loyal. Manika et al.'s (2013) study seems to ignore the differences across online customers' evaluations. As explained by researchers on offline service failure (Ringberg et al., 2007; Schoefer and Diamantopoulos, 2009), customers are highly heterogeneous in recovery evaluations, and a structured approach of them leads to contradictory research findings and unsatisfactory recovery cases. Manika et al.'s (2013) study isolates customers' responses on a specific scale of variables, ignoring other explanations that customers may be associated with. Based on the comments posted by the video viewers, it seems that they highly question the CEO's message. These people (they may be BlackBerry's customers) seem to represent a contradictory sample of Manika et al.'s (2013) study. Consequently, their opinion doubts Manika et al.'s (2013) findings. A qualitative approach to customers may provide an enlarged explanation of customer perception to online service failure in general and to the CEO's apology in particular. Such an epistemological approach seems to have been highly excluded by scholars on online service recovery.

Kaplan and Hanlein (2010) suggest five criteria that companies must meet to benefit from social media: (1) be active, (2) be interesting, (3) be humble, (4) be unprofessional, and (5) be honest (pp. 66-67). These criteria underline an informal yet a sincere and repetitive online provider-customer relationship. The explanations on criteria are isolated to the measurements of avoiding online failures. If these criteria are followed, the provider easily understands customers' way of thinking and their perception on the online failure. This means they provide a great recovery guidance. The literature on *offline service failure and recovery strategy* associates the 'limited understanding of customers' to the main indicator of unsuccessful recoveries (Ringberg et al., 2007). Following this line of thought, if the company uses social media properly, it is a step closer to overcoming the key recovery challenge. This is supported by Gruber et al.'s (2015) study, which examines the case of the resignation of the president of the University of Virginia. Gruber et al. (2015) argue that social media meets two competences necessary during crises, namely, sensemaking and resilience (pp. 169–170). On general frames, the two terms refer to the understanding of crises through viral information (see pp. 169–170 for original roots/definitions of the concepts). This study perhaps regards the customer's debates on social media as the reasoning for optimum recovery decision choices.

Additionally, Gregoire et al. (2015) associate recovery-decision making to the customers' heterogeneity. They argue that customers differ across themselves and suggest that the timing of customers' engagement in online communication/complaint is associated with the individual service failure perception and recovery expectation and evaluation. This is in line with the ongoing debate of the literature on offline service failure and recovery strategy (Ringberg et al., 2007; Schoefer and Diamantapolous, 2011). The epistemological orientation, which undermines customers' individuality, overestimates the comfort of recovery-decision making that social media provides. Gregoire et al. (2015) recommend a typology with six types of customers complaining through social media: (1) directness, (2) boasting, (3) badmouthing, (4) tattling, (5) spite, and (6) feeding the vultures. The first two are attached to the customer's online word of mouth (WOM) after the service failure and the recovery paradox experience, respectively. The last four have grouped the customers' complaint after the double deviation encounter. These categories include anything between spreading negative WOM, complaining to a third party, and 'informally' assisting other companies to benefit from the failing company (see pp.175-178 for additional explanations).

The success of an online recovery strategy is greatly attributed to the provider's response speed (Pang et al., 2014). Essentially, engagement in conversation with the customer (Chaffey and Ellis-Chadwick, 2012) immediately after he/she uploads the complaint shortens the prerecovery phase. In terms of online recovery strategy, this perspective has yet to be empirically approached. However, practical examples of real-time conversation with customers have already proved satisfactory states (see Pang et al., 2014).

MANAGING SERVICE RECOVERY

Service recovery as a phenomenon has been prone to multiple realities for both academics and practitioners. One perspective in the extant literature articulates that if the provider chooses an adequate recovery strategy, the relationship with the customer will be strengthened. Conversely, minor failures can be altered into paramount issues for the company (Dong, Evans & Zou, 2008). The complexity in choosing an appropriate service recovery is concomitant to the myopic understanding of customer realities and the processes by which they assign meaning to the recovery encounter. Crucial in this study is understanding 'the moment of truth for the organization' (Smith & Bolton, 2002, p. 5). Customers want to 'receive' recovery attributes that 'match the type of failure they experience in amounts that are commensurate with the magnitude of the failure that occurs' (Smith, Bolton & Wagner, 1999, p. 356). However, the scope of conceptualising what customers see as a 'match state' is still anomalous, and the optimal 'moment of truth' experience achieved mutually by both the provider and the customer is still subject to enquiry.

In addition to the abovementioned argument, identifying the 'match state' is important. Consequently, the extant literature has considered service recovery discipline from polarised perspectives, including types of recovery strategies, typologies of customer response styles, antecedents that affect recovery evaluations, recovery postbehaviour, and others. Considering the complexity within the subject, service recovery is too convoluted to be approached semantically. The definitions below provide clarity to the phenomenon and assist a gradual conceptualisation of the following critical delineations. Recovery means 'to return to a normal state: to make whole again' (Bell & Zemke, 1987, p. 32). To gain a better insight into recovery phenomenon, Smith, Bolton & Wagner (1999, p. 357) imparted a conceptualisation on the service failure/recovery encounter:

We view a service failure/recovery encounter as a series of events in which a service failure triggers a procedure that generates economic and social interaction between the customer and the organization, through which an outcome is allocated to the customer. (p.357)

A set of recovery actions undertaken by the marketer after the occurrence of failure is known as 'the customer recovery process' (Chuang et al., 2012, p. 258). Miller, Craighead & Karwan (2000) were amongst the first to emphasise the importance of analysing recovery strategies from the perspective of operations management, and they called for further analysis of recovery strategies in operations research. They constructed a detailed framework (p. 388) on the domain of elements (i.e., the core elements: service recovery expectations, service recovery types, and follow-up service recovery outcome) compiled within the customer-provider encounter in the context of a failed service and endorsed the prior prototypes of findings as follows: if an appropriate recovery strategy is promptly provided, customers will return even when severe failures are experienced (p. 397). Additional findings show the influence of types of recovery strategies on customers. The recovery strategy typology suggested here is a twofold categorisation that encompasses both psychological and tangible recovery strategies. The former includes empathy and apology, whereas the latter includes compensation relative to the perceived failure and the value added (p. 390). The essence of the findings in the context of recovery types suggests that the provision of blended recovery strategies is useful, yet an apology alone will not be enough for the customer. Meanwhile, any extra compensation added enhances customer perceptions of justice (Miller et al., 2000, p. 397). In a macro analysis, the morphology of recovery strategies illustrates that this typology exemplifies *the main* and the most utilised recovery strategy type.

In analysing service recovery strategies, ample research has omitted the concept of co-creation as a component of recovery strategies (Dong, Evans & Zou, 2008). Exploiting a co-created service, that is, the self-service technology (SST), the conceptualisation of 'customer participation in service recovery' construct was explored by Dong et al. (2008, p. 123). Defined 'as the degree to which the customer is involved in taking actions to respond to a service failure' (p. 126), co-creation recovery strategies appear to be successful, particularly in co-created services. Such strategies have led to higher satisfaction, better recovery time management, and greater intention to co-create in the future. Dong et al.'s (2008) construct filled a lacuna in marketing research, yet it focused only on the customer's production of service (specifically, SST), and the findings probably cannot be generalised.

To comprehend the complexity of the abovementioned question, Roggeveen, Tsiros & Grewal (2012) undertook a 'reverse engineering' of Dong et al.'s (2008) construct by conducting a research into service in the airline industry. In the context of severe failures, the authors suggested that co-creation improves satisfaction, acquires the same or slightly better results as a compensation strategy, and enhances repurchase intention (p. 786). They also raised a very salient topic neglected by prior research: that of the customer's perception of co-creation. The authors suggested analysing the customer's perception of co-creation using a two-facet analogy. The first refers to the customer's positive stance, and the second indicates a negative conceptualisation that ties co-creation to the provider's gain from the customer's endeavour. Regardless of how the abovementioned analogy is comprehended, customer perceptions are viewed under a myopic stance primarily subject to the following uncertainty: when can a provider be cognizant of the customer's inclination to co-create, and of the effort level s/he is willing to provide for the recovery? This uncertainty has been probably illustrated by Roggeveen et al. (2012) with the 'negotiation process between the customer and the employee' (p. 787). Following this question, a 'black hole' derived from this study is contingent on understanding how customers generate meaning from service encounters and how they construct recovery expectations.

Further, Roggeveen et al. (2012) scrutinised the co-creation strategy in terms of breakdowns engendered from external factors. They suggest that to understand this strategy, it is critical to understand if customer behaviours and expectations of co-creation strategies are shaped by internal or external factors causing the breakdown. This means, it is important that providers understand the ontological stance of customers and how a customer's entity provides meaning to self and others. This is how providers will develop the 'co-created rule of thumb'. If appropriately constructed, the authors suggested that co-creation is a more 'cost-effective recovery strategy' to compensation (Roggeveen et al. 2012, p.787). Service recovery tends to be approached as a communication strategy often based on social comparison theory. This proposition was first scrutinised by Bonifield & Cole (2008), who examined the downward social comparison as a possible recovery strategy. They suggest that the downward social comparison happens when the provider compares a customer with other, less auspicious customers. 'Hirschman's 1970 typology of post-purchase' behavioural intentions, namely, exit and voice (i.e., complaining to management and complaining to a third party), is also relevant in this study (p. 566). Bonifield & Cole (2008) cautioned that 'it is true that a downward social comparison does not fix or compensate for a major failure' (pp. 573–574).

CUSTOMER SATISFACTION AND RECOVERY STRATEGY

In failure experiences prone to ambivalence in the context of 'situations where customers cannot be compensated for the loss arising from a service failure' (p. 574), to a large extent social comparison strategy appears to be a good replacement for compensation strategy (Bonifield & Cole, 2008). Following this argument, Bonifield & Cole (2008) discussed downward social comparison strategy from two points of view. First, if the provider appropriately uses the strategy, customers' anger will be reduced, thereby increasing their perception of a fair recovery distribution. Attenuating the effect of service failure on postpurchase behavioural intentions will also arise out of such strategies. The second viewpoint illustrates the risk of employing the strategy under dual dimensions, which are as follows: (a) If a provider exploits the downward social comparison strategy to a customer that has already been granted with a high level of compensation, a negative perception on downward social comparison strategy is emphasised. Being identified with the provider is manipulating me (p.573). (b) If a customer alludes to the company with the downward social comparison strategy, his/her fear of experiencing future comparisons will increase, reducing the overall evaluation of the recovery experience. To make use of the downward social comparison strategy, the employee must know when and how to utilise it. This is emphasised by the authors of this research, who recommended that service representatives undergo training programmes that prepare them to conceptualise the state of mind of their customers so they could better comprehend nonverbal signs of anger. Similar to the co-created strategy, downward social comparison, if employed successfully, can result in a cost-effective recovery strategy (Bonifield & Cole, 2008).

The perspective of service providers should be analysed in the context of employing adequate recovery strategy choice. When service failures occur, they all seek to achieve the service recovery paradox

(SRP). Matos, Henrique & Rossi (2007) proclaim that SRP 'refers to the effect that an outcome variable (e.g., satisfaction) is greater for a customer that has experienced a failure and a high recovery effort when compared to a customer that has experienced no failure' (p. 64). They have explored SRP in terms of numerous factors, including satisfaction, repurchase intent, WOM, image, trust, quality, intentions to complain, switching intentions, paying more intentions, and external responses (p. 65). They have analysed 319 articles published between 1987 and 2006 using a meta-analytical method. They identified four factors that can be considered by SRP scholars, and these factors are satisfaction, WOM, repurchase intent, and corporate image. The former factor is significantly encapsulated in SRP, whereas the latter showed no significant relationship with SRP. Following this study, the authors argued that the conflicting outcomes generated from SRP research are contingent on 'design (cross-sectional versus longitudinal), subject (student versus nonstudent), and service categories (hotel, restaurant, and others)' (Matos et al., 2007, pp. 70–71).

The core factor scrutinised by three elements that hinder the generation of a common outcome on SRP is 'the customer'. If this is valid, de facto, it is the customer that positions SRP under conflicted multifarious results, raising, first, the question: how can customers contrive meaning to a service recovery? Second is the emphasis on the necessity to understand the hermeneutic phenomenology of customers even by providers setting the self into Socratic dialogues, a delineation emphasised by Roulston (2010, pp. 16–19), who explained the original authors of these contexts.

Casado-Diaz & Nicolau-Gonzalbez (2009) suggest that when providing recovery strategies, the spectrum that providers attempt to always escape from is that of the double deviation scenario. Double deviation is the opposite of the recovery paradox context. These authors proclaim that if situated between the parameters of the double deviation, 'customers are doubly faced with a service failure, the initial service failure and the failed service recovery' (pp. 1659–1669). This situation directs the provider to decipher the mental encryption of the dissatisfied customers, and this is a very arduous activity. The authors have considered the literature on double deviation as it emerged from the mid-'90s, and have analysed 'the post-complaint customer behaviour in double deviation scenario' (p. 1666) using banking services as a research category. Validating their research approach based on previous research, they analysed four types of possible postfailure behaviours in the context of double deviation. These types of behaviours are no-action, complains, exits, and complains and exits simultaneously. Meanwhile, the variables they considered to examine the customer's postbehaviour in double deviation are the magnitude of service failure, recovery strategies, distributive and procedural justice, recovery-related emotions, and satisfaction with service recovery (p.1660-1662). All the abovementioned variables produce a significant effect on postbehaviour choices, and the satisfaction variable has the most significant effect. This variable emphasises 'the golden rule', that is, 'providers at once must provide the right recovery strategy'. The study results show that customers are prone to complain and exit instantly (Casado-Diaz & Nicolau-Gonzalbez, 2009), which again resonate with the golden rule.

One of the very first scholars who introduced the era of recovery strategies to justify strategy choices in the context of customer satisfaction were Bell & Zemke (1987). They suggested that the decision on what recovery strategy to utilise results from 'annoyance' and 'victimisation' (p.33). The former refers to the customer who feels inconvenience, irritation, and anger with the failure (p.33). The latter holds the customer dependent, and offering her/him some additional recovery effort is essential (p. 33). The 'recovery recipe' proposed by the authors encompasses five recovery ingredients. The first two, namely, *apology* and *urgent reinstatement*, are a requisite for annoyed customers (pp. 33-34). Three recovery strategies, namely, *empathy*, *symbolic atonement*, and *follow-up*, are added to the former list as vital for victimised customers (pp. 34-35). *Apology* refers to an immediate provider acknowledgement of service failure, and when it is 'delivered in the first person,' that is, 'I am sorry' rather than "We are sorry," it reflects a more sincere confession of the breakdown (p.33). The demonstration, which implies that the provider's main concern is the customer's interest, frames the *urgent reinstatement* recovery strategy (p. 34). Metaphorically, *empathy* alludes to 'a shoulder to cry on' and to 'a source of strength' (p. 34). The provider exploits empathy recovery strategies by conveying a common breakdown feeling to the customer through such responses as 'I know how you must feel', 'I care about you', 'I can relate to your misfortunate', and 'I can identify with what has happened' (p. 34). A further recovery approach from the latter strategy, *symbolic atonement* provides customers with a symbolic material reward for the failure, such as 'no charge', 'a coupon for next purchase', 'free drink', 'discounts', and others (p. 34). When the provider pursues the client, for example, through a phone call, to ask for her/his evaluation on the recovery granted, they use the *follow-up* recovery strategy (p. 35). Marketers exploit follow-up as a tool to promote themselves as providers who know how to make things right even when breakdowns occur (Bell & Zemke, 1987).

Shortly after Bell & Zemke's research, Singh (1990) heightened the vitality of comprehending customers' response styles to dissatisfaction. As a concept, 'response styles' refer to 'a unique set of responses that one or more consumers utilize to deal with a particular dissatisfying situation' (p. 58). However, as a phenomenon, response styles are prone to misconceptions, though essential to understand the consumer complaint behaviour (CCB) (p. 90), that is, to discern the service recovery expectations of customers and decide on what recovery strategy to exploit. Based on previous CCB studies, the first models on the typology of customer response styles, such as the 'activists' and 'passivists' model of Gronhaug and Zaltman (1981) and the 'complainers' and 'noncomplainers' model of Morganosky and Buckley (1986), were subject to a binary construct (p. 90). When dissatisfied with the provider, *activists* and *complainers* criticise the failure. By contrast, *passivists* and *noncomplainers* are part of a 'let the failure pass by' doctrine, which means that they ignore the failure. Arguing that 'consumers typically engage in multiple complaint responses, they in fact do not make a simple binary choice (e.g., to complain/not complain)' (p. 90). The author developed a typology of response styles with four labels, namely, 'passive', 'voicers', 'irates', and 'activists'. All of these labels resonate with previous research and are explained by the authors as follows: Voicers refer to customers who complain to the service provider but rarely switch the provider or spread negative WOM to private followers and third parties. Angry customers complain and tend to change the provider. The research under this model has been conducted with respect to 'demographic, personality/attitudinal, and episode-specific characteristics' (p.57). The latter variables (i.e., 'cost/benefit evaluations, attributions of blame, probability of successful redress, and the type of product or service involved in the dissatisfaction' [p. 83]) appeared to be the essential factors in consumer response styles. Drawing on this typology, the concept of 'segment-dissatisfied customers' (p. 92) provides a path to discern appropriate recovery strategies relevant to the failure. It is suggested that voicers are a 'perfect' source to detect fallacies in the provider's marketing plans, and rewards should be part of the recovery strategy when transacting with them (Singh, 1990, p. 92).

Another notion that provides meaning to how customers respond to recoveries in high-involvement encounters was framed by Ringberg et al. (2007). In their research recovery responses are expounded by customer expectations that are exemplified by the three cultural models: relational, oppositional, and utilitarian. This cultural approach is concerned with the 'heterogeneity' of customer preferences when facing service failure, that is, the three cultural models address the 'intrigue' of 'why one or more recovery initiatives (e.g., apology, empathy, compensation, replacement, explanation, timeliness, assurance of no recurrence) are indispensable in one situation but pointless in another' (p. 194). They summarised several presuppositions relating to the cultural model approach. They suggested that in the relational cultural model, people are identified with 'emotional ties' (p.197) to the provider, that is, regardless of the effect of failure, customers are concerned with maintaining a good interaction with the provider. Therefore, the recovery process is not subject to replacement or monetary compensation. Rather, customers seek to understand and to receive a sincere apology and recognition of the breakdown. When a satisfactory recovery is experienced, loyalty increases, directing the customer's state of mind to a 'recovery paradox' (p.202) status, that is, to a state whereby the satisfaction level after the recovery experience is higher than prior to the failure. It is natural for customers to blame themselves rather than the provider for the breakdown occurrence, yet in case of multiple failures, they are prone to switching providers. Oppositional customers settle under the 'caveat emptor' (p.204) principle, yet they play 'devil's advocate' to the provider through a consistent aggressive position, and they often believe that marketers are antagonists who seek to take advantage of and coerce the client. Oppositionists hold an ideological stance that is 'entirely skewed toward the negative vector of the consumer-provider interaction' (p. 204). When their personality is analysed, they are delightful to family and friends, yet they covet control and power over marketers. To encounter a successful recovery experience, the implicit indications reflect that marketers should provide control and power to oppositionists by providing them several recovery options, such as an apology, compensations, free service, and others. The utilitarian cultural model illustrates a more rational approach that suggests when a service failure occurs, the expectations of utilitarian customers stem from weighing the losses and gains. Thus, utilitarianism is a prototypical example of 'the ideal of rationality' and 'the subjective utility theory' (see p. 205 for original authors of the theories). A utilitarian customer calculates the service recovery output based on financial resources and time-related losses. These two variables, together with the cause of the failure (i.e., whether it is a provider's fault or not), shape the provider's recovery effort. When the provider causes the breakdown, a utilitarian expects a range of recovery strategies starting with an apology, and the provider acknowledges the problem by refunding or exchanging. If the failures occur out of external factors, rather than the company itself, utilitarians will literally ignore the failures but will never forget them, resulting in a decrease of expectations after each breakdown until they decide to move to another provider (Ringberg et al. 2007; Ozuem, Thomas and Lancaster, 2015).

The interest in this cultural approach has been enduring because, first, it is concerned with the development of a customer taxonomy based on expectations generated by the inner mechanism of the mind; thus, it is a cognitive tool that helps people to create a self of sense and provide meaning to failure and the self-provider encounter. Such an approach is a parallel conception to the perspective of the 'social constructivist'. Second, because cultural models barely change (p.195) (i.e., customers positioned in one of the three groups of the cultural model, regardless of the failure, have the tendency to remain there), they have provided some clarity to practitioners regarding the types of customer expectations and requirements that emerge when a service failure occurs (Ringberg et al., 2007).

SEGMENTING RECOVERY STRATEGIES

Schoefer & Diamantopoulos (2009) analysed the development of customer typologies relative to effective recovery programmes and argued that providers should be assiduous in contemplating emotional responses. They utilised Smith's (1998) relationship quality indicators, namely, 'satisfaction, trust, and commitment' (p. 294), and presented a typology of the emotional psychological state of customers, encompassing a four-clustered recovery formula. The first cluster, 'positivists prior to failure', possesses a high evaluation of quality indicators and exhibits positive emotions whilst encountering the recovery. Consistent with the rational group of Ringberg et al. (2007), if an effective recovery is provided to positivists, 'recovery paradox' (p.301) will be produced, thereby strengthening the quality relationship with the provider. Given that positivists prefer effective relationships instead of monetary compensation, the authors recommended a follow-up 'survey' (p.303) after the failure. 'Follow-up survey' will show the customer that the provider is willing to improve. Negativists, the second cluster, are pessimistic about service encounters. This attitude is manifested in limited or no satisfaction, trust, and commitment. If a poor recovery experience is manifested, negativists will undergo a 'double deviation effect' (p.302), that is, the relationship quality will be further destroyed after the recovery failure. To motivate repurchasing after the failure, the authors recommended that compensations such as a free offer or a voucher should be granted to negativists (pp. 302–303). With somewhat identical perceptions to the oppositional cluster of Ringberg et al. (2007), the third group, concerned customers, is subject to a weak provider-customer relationship, conveying ambiguity in making future purchases. The authors recommended offering guarantees as a recovery strategy to enhance relationship quality and encourage repurchasing. The final cluster, unemotionals, are customers for whom recovery has a 'negligible effect' (p. 302), manifesting in no emotions during and after recovery encounters. A discount on the next purchase is a suggested recovery tactic that can persuade unemotionals to strengthen the relationship quality (Schoefer & Diamantopoulos, 2009, p. 303).

According to Maxham & Netemeyer (2002), customers should be viewed as a single tablet and should not be examined as segmented into typologies. They argued that customer-provider relationships are ongoing activities and should be considered as such to conceptualise the true meaning of the recovery outcome. Underlining 'the role of failures severity, attributions of blame toward the firm, recovery expectations, failure similarity and type, and the time between failures' (p. 58), they provided some understanding of what recovery effects can be understood as across four variables. These effects are 'overall satisfaction with the firm, word-of-mouth, recommendations, and repurchase intent' (pp. 57–58). They noted that if no failures have been previously recorded and a satisfactory recovery was granted on the first breakdown, a paradox effect will reveal the former two and the latter variables. However, if two unsatisfactory recoveries are experienced, the double deviation effect is manifested. When customers are victimised by multiple failures, they explicitly attribute blame to the company, and their loathed ontological stance towards the provider is strongly indicated when similar failures within short periods occur (p. 67). With all concomitant dissatisfactions arising from failures, this study reveals that customers, and peculiarly those that previously received satisfactory recoveries, have high expectations after every failure (Maxham & Netemeyer, 2002).

Similar to Maxham & Netemeyer (2002), Wu & Lo (2012) illustrated that after consecutive service failures (i.e., two service failures), customers still have high expectations. However, this situation leads to the following question: what will be the risk outcome of reexperiencing a failure in the future? They suggested high involvement as a moderator of expectations. Other than high involvement, 'failure severity', rather than the customer's cognitive stance framed by societal factors, can be an important moderator of expectations in situations defined by multiple failures. Regardless of high expectations, they stated that customers post 'negative reviews' (p. 221) because of high negative emotions that resulted from the service failure. They emphasised the importance for providers to develop adequate strategies to recover breakdowns (Wu & Lo, 2012).

MANAGERIAL IMPLICATIONS AND CONCLUSION

Omitting employees from service encounter process 'ingredients' is a critical issue that can influence the treatments of service failure phenomenon (Bell & Zemke, 1987). Though research espouses the centrality of employee empowerment, it continues to be a salient theme in the literature but one that is perhaps overlooked by practitioners. Bitner et al. (1990) suggest that by its very nature, employee empowerment is identified as a form of 'knowledge' and 'control' (p.82). Knowledge refers to information imparted to employees (for example, on service standards, delivery process and service characteristics, amongst others), whereas the freedom of employees to make decisions is assigned to control. Further, they proclaim that knowledge will help the provider understand what is wrong with the service, whereas control will assign the right to recovery decisions to the employee. The endorsement that ''the customer is always right'' is not enough (p.82) - in fact, they can be wrong and can even be insulting, according to the authors (p. 82). Based on their arguments, customers can be very unpredictable. Therefore, employees should have adequate knowledge and the decision-making freedom to successfully handle the encounter (Bitner et al., 1990).

If a chronological examination of studies in this subject is undertaken, a key concern that may arise is how to situate, define and discuss failure and service recovery using a selective approach rather than considering the two comprehensively. Recently Sivakumar et al. (2014) questioned the researching of service failures alongside service recovery. They argued that most of the research approaching service failure focuses on types of recovery strategies, antecedents, mediators and recovery consequences (p.42). Prior to this work, to some extent, Choi & Mattila (2008) criticised conceptualisations of service failure in tandem with recovery outcomes. A comprehensive approach of service failure and recovery strategy helps scholars justify their studies. However, it leaves the literature prone to subjective interpretations of service failure and recovery strategy as separate topics. This does nothing to clarify discussions of what is ultimately a complex debate within the subject.

This paper suggests that service failure is highly significant to the provider. However, service failures can mitigate negative consequences through effective recovery strategies (Craighead et al., 2004). There are arguments that service recoveries can even enhance customer-provider relationships, yet extant 'research has shown that more than half of attempted recovery efforts only reinforce dissatisfaction' (Casado-Diaz & Nicolau-Gonzalbez, 2009, p. 1659). Today, social media seems to be an alternative channel to traditional recovery. If an adequate online recovery is provided, service recovery paradox is quite evident. On the contrary, social media adds greater risk to the provider, in case of ignored failures or unsuccessful recoveries. The latter is mitigated if the provider knows what the expectation and evaluation of customers are. Thus, service failure continues to be portrayed within unclear boundaries. Conceptualising service failure and identifying intrinsic recovery strategies to cope with it are useful to assess failure types alone so that a better understanding can be provided. Service failure typologies are essential for both the customer and the provider. The complexity within the service literature lies on the recovery strategies. At this point, there is no method within the existing literature that generates a definite reflection on what are the effective and efficient service recovery strategies for both the customer and the provider. Rather, different recovery expectations and satisfaction perceptions between the customer and the provider situate them into mutually exclusive fronts when recovery strategies are experienced. In the context of customer recovery perceptions, the research result differs across studies. The result suggests that customers are very heterogenic in their recovery expectations, and this condition makes the subject complex.

Considering this stance of the service failure and recovery strategy literature, future research should address the question: how do customers assign meaning to the service failure and the recovery strategy provided? As rhetorical as it may sound, it is complex at its core and divulges the necessity for further research under some new and previously ignored research paradigms.

REFERENCES

Argo, J. J., White, K., & Dahl, D. W. (2006). Social comparison theory and deception in the interpersonal exchange of consumption information. *The Journal of Consumer Research*, *33*(1), 99–108. doi:10.1086/504140

Azemi, Y., & Ozuem, W. (2015). Social media and SMEs in transition countries. In G. Bowen & W. Ozuem (Eds.), *Computer-mediated marketing strategies: social media and online brand communities* (pp. 114–133). Hershey, PA: IGI Global.

Barwise, P., & Meehan, S. (2010). The one thing you must get right when building a brand. *Harvard Business Review*, *88*(12), 80–84.

Bell, C. R., & Zemke, R. E. (1987). Service breakdown the road to recovery. *Management Review*, *76*(10), 32–35.

Bitner, M. J., Booms, B. H., & Tetreault, M. S. (1990). The service encounter: Diagnosing favorable and unfavorable incidents. *Journal of Marketing*, *54*(1), 71–84. doi:10.2307/1252174

Bonifield, C., & Cole, C. A. (2008). Better him than me: Social comparison theory and service recovery. *Journal of the Academy of Marketing Science*, *36*(4), 565–577. doi:10.1007/s11747-008-0109-x

Bougie, R., Pieters, R., & Zeelenberg, M. (2003). Angry customers don't come back, they get back: The experience and behavioral implications of anger and dissatisfaction in services. *Journal of the Academy of Marketing Science*, *31*(4), 377–393. doi:10.1177/0092070303254412

Bowen, G., & Ozuem, W. (Eds.). (2015). *Computer-mediated marketing strategies: Social media and online brand communities*. Hershey, PA: IGI Global. doi:10.4018/978-1-4666-6595-8

Casado-Diaz, A. B., & Nicolau-Gonzalbez, J. L. (2009). Explaining consumer complaining behaviour in double deviation scenarios: The banking services. *Service Industries Journal*, *29*(12), 1659–1668. doi:10.1080/02642060902793524

Chaffey, D., & Ellis-Chadwick, F. (2012). *Digital Marketing: Strategy, implementation and practice* (5th ed.). Harlow: Pearson Education Limited.

Choi, S., & Mattila, A. S. (2008). Perceived controllability and service expectations: Influences on customer reactions following service failure. *Journal of Business Research*, *61*(1), 24–30. doi:10.1016/j.jbusres.2006.05.006

Chuang, S. C., Cheng, Y. H., Chang, C. J., & Yang, S. W. (2012). The effect of service failure types and service recovery on customer satisfaction: A mental accounting perspective. *Service Industries Journal*, *32*(2), 257–271. doi:10.1080/02642069.2010.529435

Craighead, C. W., Karwan, K. R., & Miller, J. L. (2004). The effects of severity of failure and customer loyalty on service recovery strategies. *Production and Operations Management*, *13*(4), 307–321. doi:10.1111/j.1937-5956.2004.tb00220.x

Denzin, N. K., & Lincoln, Y. S. (2000). *Handbook of qualitative research* (2nd ed.). Thousand Oaks, CA: Sage Publications Inc.

Dong, B., Evans, K. R., & Zou, S. (2008). The effects of customer participation in co-created service recovery. *Journal of the Academy of Marketing Science*, *36*(1), 123–137. doi:10.1007/s11747-007-0059-8

Forbes, L. P., Kelley, S. W., & Hoffman, K. D. (2005). Typologies of e-commerce retail failures and recovery strategies. *Journal of Services Marketing*, *19*(5), 280–292. doi:10.1108/08876040510609907

Gregoire, Y., Salle, A., & Tripp, T. M. (2015). Managing social media crises with your customers: The good, the bad, and the ugly. *Business Horizons*, *58*(2), 173–182. doi:10.1016/j.bushor.2014.11.001

Gruber, D. A., Smerek, R. E., Thomas-Hunt, M. C., & James, E. H. (2015). The real-time power of twitter: Crises management and leadership in an age of social media. *Business Horizons*, *58*(2), 163–172. doi:10.1016/j.bushor.2014.10.006

Gu, B., & Ye, Q. (2014). First step in social media: Measuring the influence of online management responses on customer satisfaction. *Production and Operations Management*, *23*(4), 570–582. doi:10.1111/poms.12043

Hanna, R., Rohm, A., & Crittenden, V. L. (2011). We're all connected: The power of the social media ecosystem. *Business Horizons*, *54*(3), 265–273. doi:10.1016/j.bushor.2011.01.007

Hess, R. L. Jr, Ganesan, S., & Klein, N. M. (2003). Service failure and recovery: The impact of relationship factors on customer satisfaction. *Journal of the Academy of Marketing Science*, *31*(2), 127–145. doi:10.1177/0092070302250898

Hobson, N. (2012). Quick Recap. In C. Holloman (Ed.), *The social media MBA: Your competitive edge in social media strategy development & delivery* (pp. 3–13). Chichester, UK: John Wiley & Sons Ltd.

Hoffman, D. L., & Novak, T. P. (1996). Marketing in hypermedia computer-mediated environments: Conceptual foundations. *Journal of Marketing*, *60*(3), 50–68. doi:10.2307/1251841

Holloway, B. B., & Beatty, S. E. (2003). Service failure in online retailing: A recovery opportunity. *Journal of Service Research*, *6*(1), 92–105. doi:10.1177/1094670503254288

Hui, M. K., Ho, C. K. Y., & Wan, L. C. (2011). Prior relationships and consumer responses to service failures: A cross-cultural study. *Journal of International Marketing*, *19*(1), 59–81. doi:10.1509/jimk.19.1.59

Kaplan, A. M., & Haenlein, M. (2010). Users of the world, unite! The challenges and opportunities of social media. *Business Horizons*, *53*(1), 59–68. doi:10.1016/j.bushor.2009.09.003

Keaveney, S. M. (1995). Customer switching behavior in service industries: An exploratory study. *Journal of Marketing*, *59*(2), 71–82. doi:10.2307/1252074

Kietzmann, J. H., Hermkens, K., McCarthy, I. P., & Silvestre, B. S. (2011). Social media? Get serious! Understanding the functional building blocks of social media. *Business Horizons*, *54*(3), 241–251. doi:10.1016/j.bushor.2011.01.005

Kuo, Y., Yen, S., & Chen, L. (2011). Online auction service failures in Taiwan: Typologies and recovery strategies. *Electronic Commerce Research and Applications*, *10*(2), 183–193. doi:10.1016/j.elerap.2009.09.003

Larivet, S., & Brouard, F. (2010). Complaints are a firm's best friend. *Journal of Strategic Marketing*, *18*(7), 537–551. doi:10.1080/0965254X.2010.529155

Luo, J., Ba, S., & Zhang, H. (2012). The effectiveness of online shopping characteristics and well-designed websites on satisfaction. *Management Information Systems Quarterly*, *36*(4), 1131–1144.

Lusch, R. F., & Vargo, S. L. (2006). Service-dominant logic: Reactions, reflections and refinements. *Marketing Theory*, *6*(3), 281–288. doi:10.1177/1470593106066781

Mandle, J. (2009). *Rawls's a theory of justice: An introduction* (1st ed.). New York, NY: Cambridge University Press. doi:10.1017/CBO9780511814099

Manika, D., Papagiannidis, S., & Bourlakis, M. (2013, September 10-12). The effects of a CEO's YouTube apology for service failure on customers' behavioural intentions. *Proceedings of the British academy of management conference,* Liverpool. Retrieved from http://www.mbsportal.bl.uk/taster/subjareas/techinnov/bam2013/ebusinessandegovenment/full/156819contribution104.pdf

de Matos, C. A., Henrique, J. L., & Rossi, C. A. V. (2007). Service recovery paradox: A meta-analysis. *Journal of Service Research*, *10*(1), 60–77. doi:10.1177/1094670507303012

Maxham, J. G. III, & Netemeyer, R. G. (2002). A longitudinal study of complaining customers' evaluations of multiple service failures and recovery efforts. *Journal of Marketing*, *66*(4), 57–71. doi:10.1509/jmkg.66.4.57.18512

Meuter, M. L., Ostrom, A. L., Roundtree, R. I., & Bitner, M. J. (2000). Self-service technologies: Understanding customer satisfaction with technology-based service encounters. *Journal of Marketing*, *64*(3), 50–64. doi:10.1509/jmkg.64.3.50.18024

Miller, J. L., Craighead, C. W., & Karwan, K. R. (2000). Service recovery: A framework and empirical investigation. *Journal of Operations Management*, *18*(4), 387–400. doi:10.1016/S0272-6963(00)00032-2

Ozuem, W., Howell, K. E., & Lancaster, G. (2008). Communicating in the new interactive marketspace. *European Journal of Marketing*, *42*(9/10), 1059–1083. doi:10.1108/03090560810891145

Ozuem, W., & Lancaster, G. (2014). Recovery strategies in on-line service failure. In A. Ghorbani (Ed.), *Marketing in the cyber era: Strategies and emerging trends* (pp. 143–159). Hershey, PA: IGI Global. doi:10.4018/978-1-4666-4864-7.ch010

Ozuem, W., O'Keeffe, A., & Lancaster, G. (2015). Leadership Marketing: An exploratory study. *Journal of Strategic Marketing*. doi:10.1080/0965254X.2014.1001867

Ozuem, W., Thomas, T., & Lancaster, G. (2015). The influence of customer loyalty on small island economies: An empirical and exploratory study. *Journal of Strategic Marketing*. doi:10.1080/0965254X.2015.1011205

Ozuem, W., Thomas, T., & Lancaster, G. (2015). The influence of customer loyalty on small island economies: An empirical and exploratory study. *Journal of Strategic Marketing*. doi:10.1080/0965254X.2015.1011205

Pang, A., Hasan, N. B. B. A., & Chong, A. C. Y. (2014). Negotiating crises in the social media environment. *Corporate Communications: An International Journal*, *19*(1), 96–118. doi:10.1108/CCIJ-09-2012-0064

Ringberg, T., Odekerken-Schroder, G., & Christensen, G. L. (2007). A cultural models approach to service recovery. *Journal of Marketing*, *71*(3), 194–214. doi:10.1509/jmkg.71.3.194

Rio-Lanza, A. B. D., Vazquez-Casielles, R., & Diaz-Martin, A. M. (2009). Satisfaction with service recovery: Perceived justice and emotional responses. *Journal of Business Research*, *62*(8), 775–781. doi:10.1016/j.jbusres.2008.09.015

Roggeveen, A. L., Tsiros, M., & Grewal, D. (2012). Understanding the co-creation effect: When does collaborating with customers provide a lift to service recovery? *Journal of the Academy of Marketing Science*, *40*(6), 771–790. doi:10.1007/s11747-011-0274-1

Roulston, K. (2010). *Reflective interviewing: A guide to theory and practice*. London: Sage Publications Ltd.

Rust, R. T., & Oliver, R. L. (2000). Should we delight the customer? *Journal of the Academy of Marketing Science*, *28*(1), 86–94. doi:10.1177/0092070300281008

Schoefer, K., & Diamantopoulos, A. (2009). A typology of consumers' emotional response style during service recovery encounters. *British Journal of Management*, *20*(3), 292–308. doi:10.1111/j.1467-8551.2008.00589.x

Singh, J. (1990). A typology of consumer dissatisfaction response styles. *Journal of Retailing*, *66*(1), 57–99.

Sivakumar, K., Li, M., & Dong, B. (2014). Service quality: The impact of frequency, timing, proximity, and sequence of failure and delights. *Journal of Marketing*, *78*(1), 41–58. doi:10.1509/jm.12.0527

Smith, A. K., & Bolton, R. N. (2002). The effect of customers' emotional responses to service failures on their recovery effort evaluations and satisfaction judgments. *Journal of the Academy of Marketing Science*, *30*(1), 5–23. doi:10.1177/03079450094298

Smith, A. K., Bolton, R. N., & Wagner, J. (1999). A model of customer satisfaction with service encounters involving failure and recovery. *JMR, Journal of Marketing Research*, *36*(3), 356–372. doi:10.2307/3152082

Solomon, M. R., Surprenant, C., Czepiel, J. A., & Gutman, E. G. (1985). A role theory perspective on dyadic interactions: The service encounter. *Journal of Marketing*, *49*(1), 99–111. doi:10.2307/1251180

Tshin, E. Y. H., Tanakinjal, G. H., & Sondoh, S. L. Jr. (2014). The key dimensions of online service quality: A study of consumer perceptions. *IUP Journal of Marketing Management*, *13*(2), 7–18.

Wang, Y., Wu, Sh., Lin, H., & Wang, Y. (2011). The relationship of service failure severity, service recovery justice and perceived switching costs with customer loyalty in the context of e-tailing. *International Journal of Information Management*, *31*(4), 350–359. doi:10.1016/j.ijinfomgt.2010.09.001

Wu, C., & Lo, Y. H. (2012). Customer reactions to encountering consecutive service failures. *Journal of Consumer Behaviour*, *11*(3), 217–224. doi:10.1002/cb.1376

Xia, L. (2013). Effects of companies' responses to consumer criticism in social media. *International Journal of Electronic Commerce*, *17*(4), 73–99. doi:10.2753/JEC1086-4415170403

Zeelenberg, M., & Pieters, R. (2004). Beyond valence in customer dissatisfaction: A review and new findings on behavioral responses to regret and disappointment in failed services. *Journal of Business Research*, *57*(4), 445–455. doi:10.1016/S0148-2963(02)00278-3

Zeithaml, V. A., Bitner, M. J., & Gremler, D. D. (2013). *Services marketing: Integrating customer focus across the firm* (6th ed.). New York, NY: McGraw-Hill.

Zhu, Z., Nakata, C., Sivakumar, K., & Grewal, D. (2013). Fix it or leave it? Customer recovery from self-service technology failures. *Journal of Retailing*, *89*(1), 15–29. doi:10.1016/j.jretai.2012.10.004

KEY TERMS AND DEFINITIONS

Customer Postrecovery Behaviour: The actions, such as WOM and repurchase intent, undertaken by the customer after experiencing the service recovery. If the customer is satisfied with the recovery, his/her behaviour may be in favour of the provider.

Customer Recovery Evaluation: Customers evaluate *losses* from the failure against *gains* from the recovery experienced. The outcome from the 'losses versus gains' analysis directs the customer towards postrecovery behaviour.

Customer Recovery Expectation: Customers develop assumptions on the provider's recovery strategy choices to best overcome their losses from the failure.

Double Deviation Effect: The provider generates numerous unsuccessful recovery endeavours, resulting in highly dissatisfied customers.

Service Failure: The service provider performs below the customer's expectation, consequent to neglecting the promised service standard.

Service Recovery Paradox: The outcome of the service recovery, where the customer is more satisfied with the provider after experiencing the recovery than prior to the failure.

Service Recovery: Actions taken by the service provider to overcome the customer's dissatisfaction caused by the service failure, that is, to transform the dissatisfaction of the customer into satisfaction.

Chapter 7
State Fragility and Stakeholder Engagement:
New Media and Stakeholders' Voice Amplification in the Nigerian Petroleum Industry

Uzoechi Nwagbara
GSM, UK

Emeka Smart Oruh
Brunel University, UK

Carlton Brown
Rathbone Results Ltd, UK

ABSTRACT

In situations where government functions are in short supply as with most developing countries particularly Nigeria, issues concerning stakeholder engagement and stakeholder voice are usually on the back burner as a consequence. In this chapter, the authors argues that such landscape is midwifed and sustained by state fragility, which is a situation where government is incapacitated to provide basic social goods as well as infrastructures and enabling institutions that can facilitate corporate-stakeholder engagement and stakeholders' voice amplification. In the Nigerian petroleum industry, this contentious issue are redoubled, given the controversial dynamics of the sector. As this chapter contends, new media (as opposed to old media) has the potentials to facilitate better engagement in corporate-stakeholder dialectics, which can be a harbinger of amplification of stakeholders' voice for sustainable relations and engagement in the industry. In a fragile state, traditional media has a monopoly of information dissemination and sharing, which traditionally limits stakeholder engagement/voice thereby frustrating efforts towards ensuring corporate-stakeholder engagement, corporate responsibility and accountability. Thus, this dilemma can be surmounted with the aid of new media as it is a communication/engagement tool that democratises the discursive space for deliberative corporate-stakeholder relations. It is hoped that this contention will help to illuminate perspectives on how the lingering corporate-stakeholder Catch-22 in Nigeria's petroleum sector can be better managed. Methodologically, literature on main issues in this chapter will be explored and a conceptual framework – stakeholder voice amplification method (SVAM) – will be developed that has the potential to advance knowledge on better corporate-stakeholder engagement in a fragile state such as Nigeria.

DOI: 10.4018/978-1-4666-9776-8.ch007

INTRODUCTION: STATE FRAGILITY, NEW MEDIA, ENGAGEMENT PROCESSES, AND STAKEHOLDERS IN NIGERIA'S PETROLEUM INDUSTRY

Nigeria is a major crude oil exporter with equally huge prospect to be a key player in the global marketplace (Okonta & Douglas, 2003; Okoh, 2005). Nevertheless, this is sadly not the case, as the nation is enmeshed in stakeholder engagement discontents, corporate-stakeholder malaise and deepening conflict following oil exploration and modus operandi of corporate-stakeholder relations. Concomitantly, the Niger delta, which is the economic mainstay of Nigeria, where over 90% of the nation's revenue is generated through oil exploration as well as 90% of gross national product, is paradoxically embroiled in muffling of stakeholders' voice (Obi, 2010; Idemudia, 2010). Part of the reasons for this landscape is the scramble for ownership of oil, the black gold, which has precipitated a deliberate attempt to silence voice of key stakeholders for strategic gains by corporation operating in this region of the world. In a similar view, the world-renowned photojournalist, Ed Kashi, in his graphic distillation of oil and its associated consequences in the region, considers the contradictions that oil engenders in the Niger delta as the "curse of the black gold" (2008, p. 1), a remarkable manifestation of state fragility. Beyond the politics of oil extraction and distribution, there has arisen scholarly contemplation and elucidation on another key reason for Nigeria's postcolonial condition, which is verged on state fragility (Okome, 2013). This is the hub of this chapter. Before explaining state fragility, it is reasonable to touch upon stakeholder engagement process in the Niger delta region and thereafter impact of new media will be addressed.

Stakeholder engagement process in the Niger delta has been described as exclusive of external stakeholders and undemocratic rather than inclusive and empowering. As this chapter contends, this can be blamed on state fragility, which is a function of incapacity of the state to provide good governance in light of poor institutional and governance framework. More on this shall be dealt with presently. Given the negative impact of this state of affairs, stakeholder engagement mechanisms are rather primed to take cognisance of corporate interests rather than external stakeholders (Chester, 2007; Mangold & Faulds, 2009). This is the dilemma new media has come to confront as opposed to old media, which the state and the powers that be colonise to foreground discussions that will lead to their selfish interests as well as fulfilment of their strategic objectives particularly in the Nigerian petroleum industry with a history of narrowing of stakeholders' voice.

As a consequence, new media has come to the point of digital revolution which has essentially triggered freedom and easy flow of news and information dissemination from the technological constraints of old media (printing and broadcasting) (Aharony, 2009; Christensen, 2011). This revolution is reflected not only in the digitisation of networking, but also in the networking of data and information which are conveniently transformed into varieties of communication platforms between products and consumers (or communicator and the communicated) (Howard & Hussain, 2013). As a result, the shift in communication model of message execution has been drastically extended to recipient's amplified understanding and thereby impacting new media-customer relationship. This wave of innovation finds materiality in the dynamic and automated process of integrated communication, which essentially reinforces user's insight, cross-media amalgamation, multiple stakeholders' interactivity and overall efficiency in the management of global digital communication and relational engagement (Howard & Hussain, 2013; Mulheim, 2009). The urgency of this statement cannot be questioned, it does represent a bold call for new media to serve as platform within which future democracy and stakeholders' voice and engagement can be strengthened.

New media has been recognised as a valuable tool that can potentially foster accountability in governance in Nigeria, although there exists a long trajectory of the positive sides of this debate and its subsequent implementation, yet to be realised remains a critical factor in galvanising efforts towards corporate-stakeholder engagement, people's empowerment and confronting state fragility in Nigeria (Singh, Veron-Jackson & Cullinane, 2008). Whilst the global community is believed to be facing new media challenges given technological changes, the situation is critical for Africa – Nigeria – which has failed to tap into the energies and benefits of this emerging innovative reality. Such benefits include widening discursive space, distributed access to information/communication, expanded freedom of expression, and for the foremost part emancipation of the marginalised in Nigeria's Niger delta region (Christensen, 2011; Grayson, & Hodges, 2004).

Opinions however appear to be highly polarised with regards to how to use this platform – new media – to facilitate and sustain corporate-stakeholder dialogue and voice amplification. On one hand, it has been argued that access to new media as well as information and communication may only serve to trigger more conflict and tension in a fragile state. It is viewed that unfettered freedom of information and expression can potentially afford more strength to those voices that can exacerbate division, violence and overall state fragility. Conversely, it is also believed that this platform will rather accentuate a rethinking of democratised engagement, stakeholder empowerment and dialogic communication between corporate bodies and wider stakeholders in Nigeria's fragile state (Uzoechina, 2010; Nwagbara, 2010, 2013; Oruh, 2014). Thus, while new media technology remains a critical means of fostering accountability and people-oriented form of governance (Aharony, 2009), it is also creating both positive and negative tension in a fragile state such as Nigeria. Nevertheless, new media is a potent platform that can be utilised to tackle fragility of state as well as to foreground transparency and good governance (Ugwoji, 2014). Widening accessibility and utility of mobile technological devices including social media networks in fragile state has created a vista of openness within the public platform. Whilst information control remains more desirable than appears to be achievable in fragile state particularly, the heightening pressures associated with commercially driven operations often tend to stifle using new media to counter state fragility in developing countries such as Nigeria.

This syndrome is one of the features of Nigeria's Niger delta, the oil-producing region of Nigeria—and Nigeria by extension—where stakeholders' voice and mechanisms for engagement are in retreat consequent upon politics of oil extraction and distribution. This situation is rather not letting up in the petroleum industry, a sector habitually known for incessant conflict, controversy and corporate-stakeholder engagement dilemma (Nwagbara, 2010; 2013). In dealing with the poor engagement scenario as well as (possibly) rising above this intractable landscape, this chapter suggests that this can be realised via the instrumentality of new media – SVAM – which has the capacity to bring better engagement process (Ugwoji, 2014). This conception is premised on the contention that new media has been lauded as providing and sustaining virile and feasible platforms that can be used to widen the space of corporate-stakeholder debate as well as amplification of stakeholders' voice. It also has the tendency to democratise information dissemination, consumption and distribution that are vital for such engagement re-engineering. Such engagement reconfiguration if achieved, can help stakeholders (community people) to rise above the trammels of state fragility. To do this, we have conceptualised stakeholder voice amplification method (SVAM), a schema which we believe can facilitate a rethink of this process for better corporate-stakeholder engagement in Nigeria's petroleum industry. More elucidation of this conceptual framework is offered later in this chapter.

LITERATURE REVIEW: STATE FRAGILITY, THE NIGER DELTA, AND STAKEHOLDER VOICE/ENGAGEMENT IN THE NIGERIAN PETROLEUM INDUSTRY

In deepening the definitional contours of the concept state fragility as hinted earlier, it is a situation where government is weak in providing basic social commodities and infrastructural necessities that can facilitate democratic leadership/practice, human rights protection, social justice, rural capacity building and corporate-stakeholder engagement (Adeyeye, 2013). The term state fragility has been argued to be highly contentious. The nations that are classified as fragile states exhibit most of Paul Collier's theorisation in his now famous bottom billion dialectics as well as C. K. Prahalad's "bottom of the pyramid" thesis. These nations are stigmatised as weak to govern themselves including incapable of creating an enabling environment via leadership and governance that can facilitate corporate-stakeholder engagement and stakeholder empowerment (Nwagbara, 2013). In spite of diverse definitions that have been offered in explaining the nature and characteristics of this concept in management literature and extant literature on the phenomenon, there exist some basic features that underpin it. Some of these include loss of authority or legitimacy by the state, weak service provision and failure to make governance legitimate (Uzoechina, 2010). Fragile states can be further explained in informal and formal contexts in terms of their political architectonics, leadership structure and governance framework (Stewart & Brown. 2009). It is therefore necessary to note that state fragility can be defined based on the political and governance experimentation in a given society. From the perspective of Kaplan (2008), it describes borders that join identity grouping to operate together despite lack of common historic relationship. It also reflects a system of legal and political front with no values and belief in which the societal organisation systematically detaches itself from the public, and thus falls heavily short of satisfying or meeting the expectation of the population. In the words of Engberg-Pedersen, Andersen & Stepputat (2008) it entails, "institutional instability undermining the predictability, transparency and accountability of public decision processes and the provision of security and social services to the population" (p. 6). This is further characterised by poor stakeholder voice and engagement, constricted public sphere, increased authoritarian experimentation, heightened civil agitation and disobedience, weak civil society and control of information dissemination, and many more (Stewart & Brown, 2009).

In this direction, it is largely assumed that fragile states are susceptible to providing safe haven for bad governance, and this is based on the premise that the states are often not in adequate control of their terrains, given failure of leadership. Similarly, overall development and security at large are considered highly implicated in a state of fragility, which has culminated in the clarion call for a holistic approach (including military interventions) in addressing developmental challenges across these fragile states (Collier, 2009). It is against this backdrop that the OECD has strongly embarked on an agenda of Development Assistance Committee (DAC) which focus is directed mainly at institutional bases of fragile states. The underpinning of the DAC finds timbre in effective and long-term global engagement with fragile states – in which national reformers are stimulated with the view to effectively building and sustaining institutions of legitimacy and governance. These institutions in turn will help to engender high good governance, ethical leadership and inclusive engagement in the polity for sustainable development (OECD/DAC, 2007). The need to confront state fragility is becoming ever critical given the degree of effect it has on the global environment particularly in view of the highly envisaged realisation of the post 2015 Millennium Development Goal, eradication of global poverty, terrorist onslaughts, corporate-stakeholder engagement and good governance (OECD/DAC, 2007).

The characterisation of "fragile states" has been described as the necessity to understand the needs for better programming in states that have been directly or indirectly linked to international security issues as well as political and leadership problems (Uzoechina, 2010). However, debate continues to resound in relation to the definition of state fragility. The Organization for Economic Cooperation and Development contend that states are fragile "when governments and state structures lack capacity and/or political will to deliver safety and security, good governance, and poverty reduction to their citizens" (OECD/DAC, 2007). The OECD has been leading the debate in this area and has implemented policies which set out "Principles for Good International Engagement in Fragile States and Situations". Fragile states have also been characterised as a complex and dynamic ecosystems which are continually exposed to glacial change, and as such create a sense of fragility for both the citizens and the environment. They are both subject to and respond to gradual change in a seamless way. Whilst divergent events can activate shifts within states, recent studies show that a loss of resilience usually paves the way for a change to another adverse state.

Vallings & Torres (2005) posit that fragility is fundamentally a dynamic process. They contend that States do not always display signs of fragility and they are not always obvious indicators of fragility. There is no simple correlative process which determines a particular outcome or a set of interconnected variables of events and interactions. Whilst each determinant is dissimilar in nature and each have their own unique distinctive points, they are underpinned by common and interrelated factors that cause and sustain fragility as noted by Chester (2007).

- Weak political institutions that lack legitimacy, accountability and effectiveness.
- Economic decline or the inability or lack of will of the state to foster an environment conducive to equitable growth.
- Poverty or the lack of will or inability to meet basic human needs, and to secure citizens from violent conflict and control of their territories.
- Incapable institutions to provide social and political goods.

This would suggest that strategies for sustainable supervision of such state ecosystems should concentrate on sustainability. The stability and fragility of a state would characteristically depend on progressively changing variables. These variables may well be predicted, evaluated or adapted. Episodes that trigger state shifts are usually difficult to predict or control. The foregoing discussion has heightened stakeholders' perception of the activities of corporate organisations in Nigeria. An understanding of stakeholders will be appropriate in order to situate this chapter and to further educate clarity.

Extant literature educates that the concept of stakeholder (theory) emanated from Freeman's (1984) seminal treatise called *Strategic Management: A Stakeholder Approach* that popularised the theory as a useful heuristics that can be used to understand "contributors" to organisational wealth. Given the imperative of this line of argument, the discipline of management and social sciences are being inundated with growing reconceptualization and refuelling of this framework for better apprehension of societal concerns particularly in fragile states with limited legitimacy and more strategic operationalisation (Collier, 2009). Extant literature on stakeholder accountability and engagement (Morsing & Schultz, 2006; Nwagbara, 2010) suggests that each stakeholder group has a "stake" in the way organisations' wealth is shared (Freeman, 1984). Therefore, it is imperative that organisations look beyond their narrow confines of economic benefit and take into consideration other stakeholders' interests (Freeman, 1984). For this to happen communication is central as it is the medium via which conflicting interests can address their varying opinions for collegiality and participation (Nwagbara, 2013).

At the heart of stakeholders' agitation for widened discursive space are mode of relations between them and corporate bodies as well as social responsibility commitment of these corporations (Nwagbara, 2013). Thus, social responsibility and responsiveness of companies or corporate bodies to wider stakeholders are quite critical to managing relations and communication for collegial relations. Therefore, social responsibility and stakeholder engagement therefore dovetail with an organisation's commitment to engage in business but taking into consideration social and environmental impacts of their actions as a consequence for sustainability and accountability. To ensure plausibility of this process the modus operandi of stakeholder engagement is not only vital, it is critical in the wake of new media and its impacts on modern corporate-stakeholder relations.

Unambiguously, in the Niger delta region of Nigeria the oil and gas companies have reacted to these allegation and challenges by espousing their commitment to social responsible business venturing and policies and consequently doubling their community development spending (Idemudia, 2010; Obi, 2010). In instantiation this,

Shell Oil, for example, spent $100 million in 1995 alone on projects in Nigeria and more than $20 million on roads, health clinics, schools, scholarships, water projects, and agricultural support projects to help the people of the region, actions that did not seem to have been motivated by any legal duty to act. (Hartman & Desjardins, 2008, p. 153)

It is remarkable to note that notwithstanding such surge in community development spending, corporate-stakeholder relations in the Niger delta region has rather deteriorated in scale and intensity (Nwagbara, 2010). An essential facet of this situation finds ample expression in state fragility. A matter that this chapter is concerned with in relation to how new media can be used to transcend such malady in the Niger delta for better corporate-stakeholder engagement.

At this juncture, it is pertinent to look at how state fragility has facilitated the narrowing of stakeholders' voice and corporate-stakeholder engagement. But before going into that, the concept has to be defined within the purview of this chapter's logic. The word state fragility shall be used in this chapter as a generic term to underpin a continuum of multiplicities of state weakness and incapacity as well as state institutional collapse. By definition, state fragility is a state of affairs where the government cannot or will not deliver fundamental functions to the majority of its people, including the minorities (Adeyeye, 2013). In a similar mould Uzoechina (2008) considers state fragility as states that have fragile institutions of governance thereby making them precarious in their ability and preparedness to deliver public goods and services to their citizens. These states in this instance lack resilience in the face of conflict or political unpredictability. In this sense, there seems to be a strong, mutually reinforcing nexus between state fragility and stakeholder marginalisation and engagement with regard to argument bordering on corporate-stakeholder relations.

Deductively, state fragility resonates with incapacity of government to provide essential political and social good to its citizens as a result of weak institutional mechanism to make available these basic human needs as well as human rights. Thus, it is necessary to ask: what is the colour of leadership and engagement in a fragile sate? There are cardinal points or characteristics that underline state fragility. They include lack of stakeholder engagement, stifled stakeholder voice, contracted public sphere, poor democratic experimentation, weak civil society and monopoly of information dissemination (Stewart &

Brown, 2009). In his interesting book, *Beyond Corporate Social Responsibility*, George Frynas (2009) stated unequivocally that "oil companies have, until recently, rejected the notion that they should actively address macro-level governance issues. Governance in a society is ultimately related to the role of the government, and companies have been reluctant to become drawn into the sphere of politics … (p. 138-9). This position is in sharp contrast to the political role of corporations in today's changing world, where companies are urged to be part of governance as well as create enabling conditions that can advance engagement (Scherer & Palazzo, 2011). In a related ratiocination, both Idemudia (2010) and Obi (2010) have harped on how the mode operandi of petroleum industry's stakeholder engagement process has detoured developmental capacities and democratic sinews of Niger delta region as it constricts march towards corporate-stakeholder relations and stakeholder's voice amplification.

The Niger delta is located in the Southern part of Nigeria, West Africa. The Niger delta is one of the world's largest wetlands with total land area approximately 29, 100 km square; this excludes the continental shelf (Dhir, 2007). The region is made up of nine oil-producing states called the Niger delta states. These states include Abia, Imo, Akwa-Ibom, Bayelsa, Rivers, Cross River, Delta, Edo, and Ondo state. The map below shows the nine Niger delta states.

Although this is not a historical study, it is however pertinent to sketch some high points in the history of Niger delta as regards oil exploration and its attendant malaise in the region, as well as its environment and people. Since the discovery of oil in Nigeria's Nember Oloibiri (present Bayelsa State) in 1956, the Niger delta region has witnessed one of the worst forms of corporate-stakeholder malaise, environmental devastation, political conflict, minority marginalisation and other reverses (Agbiboa, 2012; Nwagbara, 2013; Watts, 2004).

The communities in this region that are haunted by "oil curse," paradox of plenty (Karl, 1997) have been vociferous in their condemnation of oil and gas companies actions. This is a situation that development economics consider to be negativities tied to oil blessings instead of positive outcomes of such

Figure 1. Map of Nigeria showing the Niger Delta State
Source: PIND (2012)

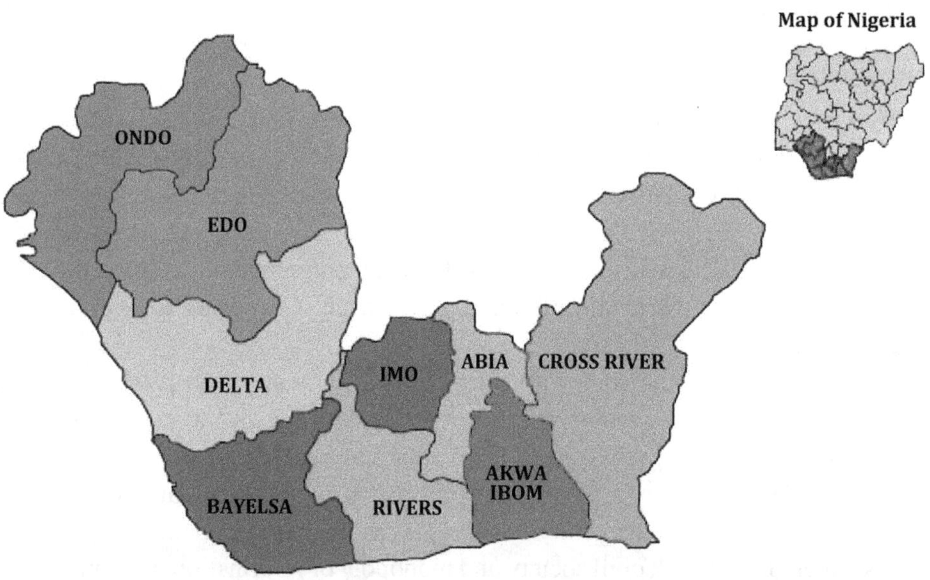

natural endowments. The communities in the Niger delta have blamed the companies operating in this region for not living up to their billings in corporate responsibility (CSR) (Frynas, 2009; Ite, 2004; Evuleocha, 2005; Eweje, 2007), provision of social amenities as government retreats (Idemudia, 2010), engaging stakeholders (Nwagbara, 2013) and taking issues of human rights seriously (Obi, 2010) for amplifies stakeholders' voice (Ugwoji, 2014). As this chapter opines, some of the strands of these lingering corporate-stakeholder impasse—particularly stakeholder engagement and voice amplifications—find resonance in the methods and processes in which corporate-stakeholder concept is conceived and practiced in this region. A look at how new media can help in recalibrating the architectonics of engagement in the region (given the limitations of old media) is addressed in the conceptual framework of this chapter.

CONCEPTUAL FRAMEWORK

The emergence of new technologies leading to reduced communication costs, amplified "richness" of communication and reduced travel cost, has propelled a reconsideration of stakeholder engagement that finds expression in new method of conceiving stakeholder voice and above all managing corporate-stakeholder conflict. In their book, *The Social Construction of Disability in New Media*, Goggin & Newell (2003) defined new media as

...new digital communications technologies that include the Internet and broadband networks (fast high-capacity data services), advanced telecommunications networks (offering services such as caller ID, digital mobile phones, third-generation mobile telecommunications, video telephones), and digital broadcasting (with digital television). (p. xiii)

Given its stretch, reach, speed and user-generated content application, new media technology has come to be seen as a kind of black swan theory – an unusual occurrence – which has reshaped communication history and engagement strategies. No other technological innovation has captured the interest and imagination of users with the speed, impact and effectiveness of the Internet (new media) (Peled, 2000). The Internet can be defined as the interconnection of a number of computer networks on a global magnitude through which information can be transmitted and retrieved. Through the connection of telephone and cable networks, which gives the Internet its unique feature, as a communication medium, it can be "owned" or "operated" by a particular body be it a single individual, corporation or government. This is what Cunningham (2010, p. 5) calls "personalisation of communication."

A recurring decimal in the discussion of virtual communities, which is a metonym for new media, is the extent to which they can mimic "real" communities (Komito & Bates, 2009, p. 233). Through this process of imitating the real, engagement can be launched. In exemplifying this, recent events in the world in which new media played pivotal roles in bringing social transformation as well as reconfiguring engagement are well documented. For example, the case in Arab Spring (Egypt), where by belonging to a Facebook group devoted to Khalid Said, the Egyptian programmer that was killed by the country's police forces, online protest was galvanised that transmuted into "real" protest. This singular incident was contributory to toppling the government of Egypt's erstwhile autocrat, Hosni Mubarak. This process is known as "slacktivism" (Livingston, 2010), which deals with doing something without having to do much at all – just by clicking the mouse. Another case is the Kryptonite Crisis, where poor and lack of immediate response to public relations issue by a company that sells bicycle locks, resulted to damaging PR outlook of the company. The birth of Facebook in 2004, YouTube in 2005 and Twitter in 2006, including other social networking sites have brought unparalleled wave of social activism and stakeholder engagement in human history. No matter the criticisms levelled against these mediums of engagement and interaction, they are powerful tools in advancing human rights issues, safeguarding rights of stakeholders, addressing corporate-stakeholder dilemma and specifically amplifying stakeholders' voice in times of conflicting interests (Eti, 2009). Given the innovative and flexible nature of new media, it has been observed that it is changing modes of information dissemination and sharing, as well as reshaping the whole gamut of stakeholder engagement in the Niger delta (Nwagbara, 2013; Kperogi, 2011).

In circumventing corporate-stakeholder dilemma in the Niger delta amongst stakeholders as well as foregrounding new media as an agent in facilitating greater engagement amongst stakeholders, this chapter unfolds a conceptual method called stakeholder voice amplification method (SVAM). It is a method of engagement with two basic parts: the traditional media and new media. The SVAM represents a journey from low engagement to high engagement via moving from the limiting tendencies of traditional media to new media to bring about high engagement and participatory relations. This method of high engagement is in congruence with what Xu & Thomas (2010) identified as "relationship-oriented behavior" (p. 404) in stakeholder relations. Consequently, in order to consolidate the amnesty deal in the post-conflict Niger delta, stakeholders can appropriate the energies of new media to deepen greater stakeholder engagement; this is also crucial for sustainability and social transformation. The ultimate goal here is to stimulate conversation and dialogue that allows stakeholders to change perception, as well as to bring collegiality, inclusiveness and objectivity to issues on corporate-stakeholder relations, stakeholder representation and CSR commitment. This is the hallmark of conceptualising a form of communication/engagement method that builds on authentic relationships amongst stakeholders by anticipating conflict including creating a framework for transcending it in order to consolidate peace and mutual sense-making and sense-giving (Morsing & Schultz, 2006; Aharony, 2009) in the region.

TRADITIONAL VS. NEW MEDIA: TOWARDS A NEW METHOD OF ENGAGEMENT

The new media (Internet) provides an alternative media that affords an opportunity for accessing more news items, as well as advancing alternative voices particularly that which might not be available through traditional media (Graham, 2002). It also provides a platform for wider access and dissemination of news and information against what the traditional media can offer (Youngs, 2010). To this end, many media outfits and individuals as well as television and radio stations such as CNN and BBC rely heavily on social platforms as significant sources of news items and information especially given its spontaneous information dissemination and diffusion. Arguably, the SVAM method apart from advancing alternative views can be instrumental in widening the discursive space for more democratised debate. To this end, the new form of engagement precipitated by SVAM "...could certainly be regarded as an indication of a modified public sphere approach, integrating new forms of horizontal (individualised) engagement with more traditional (collective) forms..." (Youngs, 2010, p. 133). This seemingly hybrid nature of SVAM that merges traditional media (vertical) with new media (horizontal) forms, has the capacity to transmute corporate-stakeholder engagement in the Niger delta.

The new media is characterised by the following: speedy information delivery and diffusion, unbounded retrieval system, user-generated application and "boundaryless" space. It is also underpinned by user interactivity, multimedia system, citizenship engagement, digital activism, reduced political editorialising and building of social momentum. In addition, new information and communications technologies are central to the processes of collective engagement. This is unlike the strategies that old media utilises, which are disempowering to external stakeholders. Thus in today's world, mediated communication is the leading instrument for constituting reality and managing corporate-stakeholder dilemma. This has precipitated a unique corporate exposure to the public regarding their CSR initiatives, weak stakeholder engagement and opaque communication process (Touri, 2009).

In addition to amplifying stakeholder voice and engagement, new media can fuel crisis and resistance amongst stakeholders (Mei, Bansal & Pang, 2010, p. 145). In consonance with this line of thinking, Hilse and Hoewner (1998) hypothesised the "internet crisis potential model", which identifies four broad Internet crisis classifications: 1. Competence crisis: Competence crisis can be seen where there is an appreciable level of disparity in competences between the aggressor (stakeholder) and the defender (corporations or companies) 2. Affecting crisis model: In this case, organisations are criticised by stakeholders to the point of public awareness with negative consequences. 3. Reinforcing crisis: In the case of affecting crisis, the Internet is essentially used in addition to the traditional media to catalogue stakeholders' views and opinions. 4. Absurd crisis: This typology is a function of uncontrollable and varied networks as well as contents that feed bizarre views circulated online. Based on the above four typologies (Hilse & Hoewner, 1998), we articulate a fifth approach to this schema, which is premised on using the new media to advance high stakeholder engagement. This resonates with transcending the dilemma of corporate-stakeholder engagement. In figure 2 – stakeholder voice amplification method (SVAM) – below, attempt is made to illustrate this process.

Figure 2. Stakeholder Voice Amplification Method (SVAM)

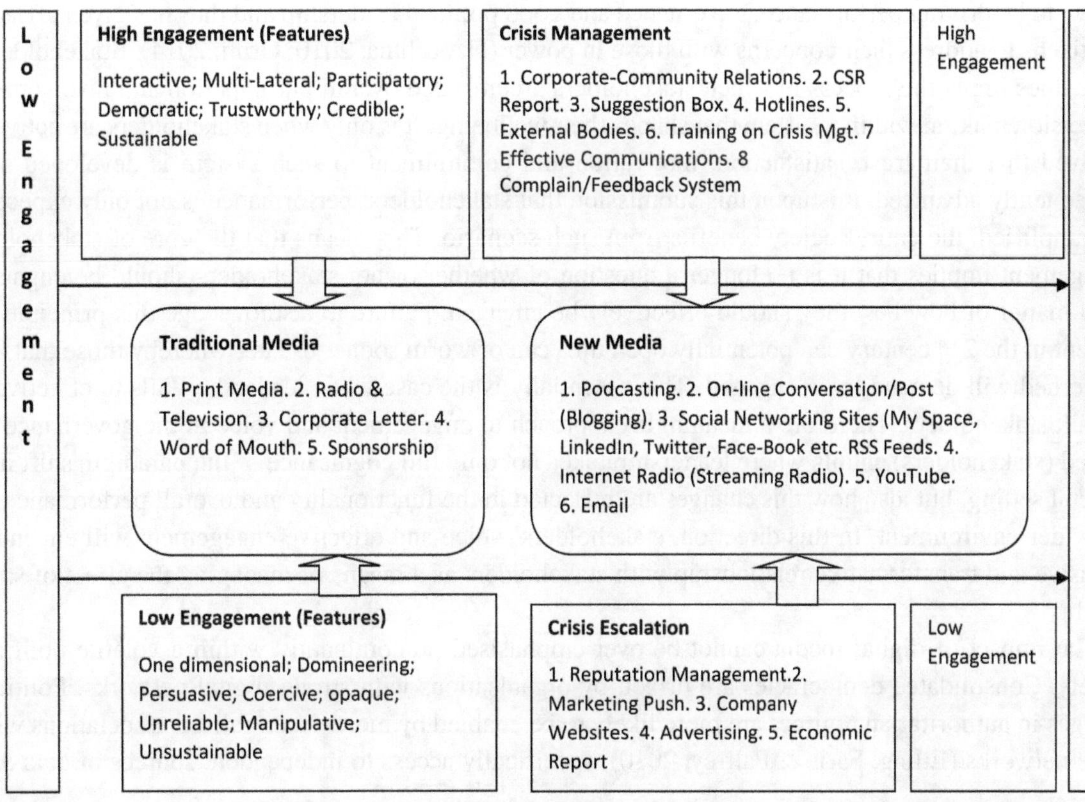

In the post-conflict era, when arms and ammunition are in retreat for dialogue to take place, SVAM is appropriate for sustainable and constructive engagement, rather than unilateral, self-serving and conflict-prone communication strategies. Figure 2 above gives a graphic picture of how stakeholders' voice can be amplified for better corporate-stakeholder engagement in the Niger delta and Nigeria in the final analysis. This is done via movement from old media to new media. The two facets of this engagement model have various features that help to designate the feasibility of the model. Thus, if new media has the capacity to escalate crisis, it could also be used to manage crisis. Thus, in the age of new media, immediate, emerging and sustained corporate-stakeholder engagement dilemma (Parson, 1996, p. 26) can be dealt with since it has the capacity to manage emotions via virtual community. The platform also has the tendency to negate content editorialising, which traditional media makes possible. Also, since new media is community-driven and interactive, it can facilitate lively conversations and citizen journalism, which is a platform for reinventing the social space and stakeholders' voice amplification. To this end, the new media is a "grassroots movement that may sow the seeds for new forms of journalism, public discourse, interactivity, and online communities ... more credible than traditional media" (Ko, Yin & Kuo, 2008, p. 542). The next section of this chapter looks at the challenges of state fragility as well as how it can be transcended for effective and empowering corporate-stakeholder engagement and amplified stakeholders' voice.

CHALLENGES OF STATE FRAGILITY AND THE IMPERATIVE OF NEW MEDIA: TOWARDS AMPLIFICATION OF STAKEHOLDERS' VOICE

Voice as an emerging concept has been defined as a key propeller of stakeholders' engagement commonly known to be driving performance, governance and good political leadership and thus has given afflatus to citizens to address their concerns with those in power (Uzoechina, 2010; Oruh, 2014). Stakeholders' voice does imply the process in which stakeholders are afforded overall participation and involvement in decision making within a system that shapes their wellbeing. It is only when stakeholders are actively involved that their trust, satisfaction, motivation and commitment to such system is developed and subsequently advanced. It is upon this submission that stakeholders' performance is not only expected and amplified, the entire society benefits from such scenario. This means that the core of stakeholder engagement implies that it is no longer a question of whether or not stakeholders should be engaged but a matter of how best they should effectively be engaged. Failure to acknowledge this principle as evident in the 21st century can potentially open up a can of worm sooner or later whereby those that are concerned will demand to be engaged. This essentially is the case when leadership fails to effectively consult stakeholders. Therefore a meaningful approach to engagement and voice in the governance of the led (stakeholders) entails where leadership takes not only full cognisance of the paradigm shift in a societal setting, but also how this changes are reflected in the functionality and overall performance of the wider environment. In this direction, stakeholders' voice and effective engagement will engender inclusive and transformative relationship with stakeholders as a means of managing the effect of state fragility.

The impact of digital media cannot be over-emphasised predominantly within a volatile political society. Consolidated democracies are driven by organisations with strong digital networks. Political changes in authoritarian regimes are more likely to be enabled by more decentralised associations with loose networks (Etling, Faris & Palfrey, 2010), specifically access to independent sources of data and unimpeded access to the Internet. The ability to access data through social media is acknowledged as a critical variable within a well-functioning democracy (Howard & Hussain, 2013). Unlimited access to information and an uninhibited press serve as a safety net against the state. It also facilitates transparency, diminishes corruptive behaviour and creates a platform for universal discussion, denigration and analysis of government decisions. This enables the citizens to contribute to the political process during the intervening period between elections and in building political leadership development.

The ability to have free unhindered access to social media has led to greater public engagement within the political arena, which has enabled all stakeholders in those debates to have a voice. Etling, Faris & Palfrey (2010) contend that the Internet has enabled new voices to enter the debate of the state by diminishing the control of gatekeepers and by facilitating the rise of citizen engagement. Howard & Hussain (2013) have postulated that the shift towards increased citizen participation within the political process has had a greater influence within state decision-making as a direct result of increased access to social media. Self-generated, socially constructed and shared data has been successful at unearthing corruption of government policies; it is often feared by autocratic leaders who have control of their social media, policies, and practices (Etling, et al, 2010). Additional voices, operating on alternative platforms, enable citizens to criticize the state, its leaders, policies and approach governance which affects the fragility of the state.

The fragility of the state is ever prevalent within the new digitised world in which they operate. The ability to spread information has thrived in a decentralised digital environment despite the efforts of many governments. Decentralised social organization has become a much more challenging proposition (Etling, Faris and Palfrey, 2010). This is evident within China and the Arab World, the Arab world has observed a dramatic increase in social media and its citizen engagement on the Internet and according to (Ghannam, 2011), it is expected to attract 100 million Arab users by 2015. The mobilisation of social media networks has seen an increase in transparency, which has ensured that states remain accountable and answerable. Ghannam (2011) goes on to suggest that social media is the most histrionic and unparalleled act of freedom of expression within modern Arab history. The fragility of the state has continued to be exacerbated as a result of the advent and adoption of social media.

Today there has been a dramatic shift in the way in which people communicate with each other and this is particularly relevant for consumers, as to how they collect and swap data about products or services they acquire, and how they consume them. The increase of new media has afforded consumers the opportunity to share information with virtual global spectators. It has been noted that "the digital innovations of the last decade made it effortless, indeed second nature, for audiences to talk back and talk to each other." New media has empowered society at large and given them the capacity and flexibility to promote themselves, products or services (Hilse & Hoewner, 1998). This has been achieved through various new media platforms such as Facebook, Twitter and YouTube. Individuals in essence have become their film/documentary makers via YouTube, photographs, Facebook and Instagram and blogging. According to Aharony (2009) user-generated content has become a global phenomenon, with Facebook, Myspace, YouTube, Wikipedia and Twitter all being listed among the Top 15 websites, accounting for more than 11 percent of global Internet traffic. This growth has pressurises, frightens and contributes to the fragility of established business models, and or States, particularly in comparison to traditional platforms such as newspapers and magazines, which are facing a major crisis. This is also noticed where regimes are fully in control of the media. This capability goes some way to threaten and undermine the regime as noted previously, within some Arab states. This can be replicated in Nigeria's

Niger delta, where incidence of undemocratic engagement has constituted a major roadblock to stifling the energies of state fragility, to say the least.

Barack Obama's Cairo speech in June 2009 and subsequent speech by Secretary of State – Hillary Clinton – on "Internet Freedom" in January 2010 pointed out that Arab activists confronted challenges with Internet freedom as they toil to confront Arab regimes. Many of these activists are allies with the United States, who have a long systematic track-record of adopting draconian measures to restrain online opposition. Social networking has transformed the society expectations of freedom of expression and the capacity for individuals and/or groups to communicate, mobilise and gain technical knowledge. This is expected to lead to even greater voice, political influence, and participation over the next few years for people globally, which will continue to lead to a greater level of dismantling the apparatuses of fragility within society (Ghannam, 2011).

Nearly six decades or so of decolonisation of most African country, there is no better time to assess the current position of media with respect to its impact on engagement and governance across the continent. This is particularly so in Nigeria, where incidence of corporate-stakeholder engagement is quite high. Based on the reports from those concerned with the effort of amplifying the development of the continent through stronger media development, the situation remains rather in retrogressive (Nwagbara, 2013). New media has been recognised as a valuable tool that can potentially foster accountability, populist-oriented governance and credible corporate-stakeholder engagement on the continent. Although there exists a long trajectory and positive debates of this initiative and its subsequent implementation, its materiality is yet to be seen. There remains lapses in concrete steps to ensure that this platform can be used to bring greater interests in providing social goods when the state retreats as seen in a fragile state such as Nigeria. Whilst the global community is believed to be facing new media challenges given technological changes in market environment, the situation is critical for Africa (Nigeria) which is failing to tap into the energies of this human and technological innovation. New media – social media – has the potentialities for distributed access to information and communication, expanded freedom of expression, economic growth and emancipation of the marginalised (Kperogi, 2011).

Operating in a fragile state can pose difficult and complex challenges to the new media actors both operationally and economically. Media operators in fragile states are faced with the challenges of being perceived as being politically motivated or biased (Nwagbara, 2013). Those supporting news media for instance are often accused of supporting one political group or the other. It is therefore important that media support should be directed towards public interest at large, which should be seen as promoting and supporting non-partisan approach to governance and corporate-stakeholder engagement. Given that media operators in fragile states face political challenges that are considerably different from those in the developed world for example imprisonment and violence, it is vital that they create enabling platforms upon which the development and growth of new media advancement are made possible. This can be done via social movements such as the Niger Delta Volunteer Force (NDVF) and the Movement for the Survival of the Ogoni People (MOSOP) among others (Oluwaniyi, 2011). This approach includes pressing for reformation of legal framework and processes that can support such engagement re-engineering. In this instance, the civil society and private people should galvanise support that will bring about concerted effort that can help in recalibrating corporate-stakeholder relations in Nigeria via new media and other forms of social activism precipitated by new media technology.

Business enterprise and organisation are constantly evolving and changing as a result of the dynamic technological environment in which they operate. As a consequence there has been a significant increase in the proliferation regarding use of new technologies within businesses, which is now universally referred to as new media (social media). This is also known as consumer generated media (Nwagbara, 2013), which is the integrated and interpersonal communication tool which utilises Internet-based platform. New media is content-based communication, based on a multitude of different web-based technologies. It is well known that most online adults/businesses are engaged with some form of social media, such as Facebook, LinkedIn and Twitter, each of which are used by hundreds of millions of people. McKinsey (2013) suggested that if Facebook were considered a country it would be the world's third largest population behind India and china, but they continue to argue that social media is still an enigma which continues to confound businesses.

Within the context of corporate-stakeholder engagement, social media is used as a constructive communication platform, which will often evoke positive messages amongst stakeholders (Morsing & Schultz, 2006). Engagement is consistently attributed to affirmative corporate virtues which has been argued benefits both internal and external stakeholders. This also finds expression in CSR, which is the propensity for an organisation to manage the economic, legal, ethical and social responsibilities towards a range of stakeholders each conveying diverse beliefs and expectations in regards to their relationship with the organisation (Frynas, 2009; Sen, 1981). However there appears to be an inherent dissonance between what managers or organisations particularly in the Niger delta region of Nigeria think about social media and the impact that it actually has on a businesses and other stakeholders for corporate-stakeholder engagement and sustainability. Nevertheless, most mangers contend that social media plays an important role within their business, which finds correspondence in McKinsey's (2013) forecast that the economic effect of social media could potentially exceed $1 trillion within the next few years, which would be derived from the efficiency gains delivered through better communication and collaboration within and outside the organisations. Interestingly one main reason for why new media's capacity to engender better corporate-stakeholder engagement is state fragility, which is a regular feature of most developing countries. This is essentially the case in Nigeria's petroleum sector, where oil and gas production has caused untold dissonance and social and political quandary. This landscape breeds muffling of stakeholders' voice in contributing to ways that can positively impact on the nation.

State fragility is increasingly becoming an issue of greater concern for the broader global community (Baliamoune-Lutz & McGillivray, 2008; Faria & Sherriff, 2009). This describes lack of will and ability by developing states to not only provide basic societal needs, but also to embark constructively on a healthy and dialogic engagement of mutuality with the stakeholders. In priming for new form of engagement in the petroleum industry new media is highly implicated in this process as it relates to two way communication stream, in which stakeholders are being communicated, listened to and collectively involved in decision making process in all form of governance or leadership (Morsing & Schultz, 2006). The underpinning of this process finds materiality in mutuality and genuine engagement, which includes not only the pursuit of greater functioning efficiency but also stakeholders' rights and views, which are not usually considered in a fragile state.

In this context, the need to confront state fragility cannot be overemphasised given the degree of effects it has on the community – particularly, in the context of the highly envisaged post 2015 millennium development framework attainment, domestic poverty eradication, sustainable development and democratic aspirations (Uzoechina, 2008). It is against this backdrop that the High Level Panel (HLP) advisers to the UN (which involves the UK, Indonesia and Liberian leaders, etc.) have embarked on a clarion call on the need for the global community to place at the centre of world development programme the fragile and conflict-ravaged states (Okome, 2013). For this effort to be achieved, effective stakeholder engagement and voice is highly crucial, and this is where a free and independent accessibility to media and information needs to be not only integrated into distributed and discursive engagement effort but also be committed to (Kahn & Kellner, 2004).). The logic of this line of thinking is underpinned by development of consensus that will help advance national identity upon which disjointed polity can co-exist as well as discordant voices in corporate-stakeholder engagement. This is essentially the view of Ugwoji (2014) in which an effectively functioning governance is described as that built on both shared interests and identity. To understand the imperatives of new media technology in addressing fragility particularly in the developing world, it is important that the principles of effective stakeholders' engagement needs to be critically understood. This is what our theoretical construct of engagement, SVAM, upholds.

CONCLUSION

Whilst diplomacy today is thought to be gaining amplified momentum towards addressing stakeholders' discontent and state fragility, there is still strident clamour for policy dialectics that addresses potential benefits accruable from new media communication technology in addressing state fragility in the 21st century. State fragility is increasingly becoming an issue of greater concern for the broader global community (Baliamoune-Lutz & McGillivray 2008; Faria and Sherriff, 2009). This describes apparent lack of will and ability by developing states such as Nigeria (Niger delta) to not only provide basic societal needs, but also to embark constructively on a healthy and dialogic engagement of mutuality with stakeholders (Caplan, 2009; Nwagbara, 2010). Similarly, stakeholders' voice is highly implicated in this construct as it relates to a two way communication stream, in which stakeholders are being communicated, listened to and collectively involved in decision-making process in corporate governance and stakeholder engagement that has the capacity to roll back the drawbacks of state fragility.

For this effort to be achieved, free, effective and independent accessibility to media and information needs to be not only integrated into distributed and discursive engagement effort but also resiliently committed to as this chapter proposes. The will help reinforce the development of a consensus that will advance corporate-stakeholder engagement and by extension national rebirth in the final analysis upon which Niger delta's disjointed polity can cohere. This is essentially the view of scholars and commentators on post-colonial Nigerian condition – this has been elucidated earlier in this chapter. Beyond this, new media can be used to effectively govern the functioning of government for shared interest and identity. To understand the imperatives of new media technology in addressing fragility particularly in the developing world, it is important that the principles of effective stakeholders' engagement and voice has to be critically understood. This is in the main a major argument that this chapter provokes.

Thus, it has been contended in this chapter that new media has great potential in redrawing the map of corporate-stakeholder engagement in a situation where government functions are in short supply, which is characteristic of fragile states such as Nigeria. In the Nigerian petroleum industry that is traditionally known for drawn-out corporate-stakeholder conundrum in the wake of state fragility that has muffled stakeholders' voice, new media has the capacity to engender democratised discourse, which as this chapter maintains can be midwifed via SVAM. SVAM is conceptual construct emanating from the interface of old media and new media premised on a movement from the former to the latter as demonstrated in figure 2. Thus, for better corporate-stakeholder engagement in the Niger delta region of Nigeria, this engagement method has the potential to recalibrate corporate-stakeholder relations. To this end, despite challenges facing appreciable realisation of using new media to facilitate engagement dialectics in developing nations such as Nigeria, it is a platform that has been lauded as having the energies to widen discursive space, which can be instrumental in amplifying stakeholders' voice in a fragile state, where old media has monopoly of information dissemination and sharing. Our hope in this chapter is that through an appreciation and consequent application of SVAM, the procedures and strategies of corporate-stakeholder relations in the Nigerian petroleum industry can be reworked for a more participatory corporate-stakeholder engagement in the Niger delta region.

REFERENCES

Adeyeye, A. I. (2013). Identity conflict, terror and the Nigerian state: Between fragility and failure. *Journal of Sustainable Development in Africa*, *15*(4), 116–129.

Agbiboa, D. E. (2012). Between corruption and development: The political economy of state robbery in Nigeria. *Journal of Business Ethics*, *108*(3), 325–345. doi:10.1007/s10551-011-1093-5

Aharony, N. (2009). An exploratory analysis of libraries' blogs: Their development, nature and changes. *Aslib Proceedings: New Information Perspectives*, *61*(6), 587–604. doi:10.1108/00012530911005535

Baliamoune-Lutz, M., & McGillivray, M. (2008). State Fragility Concept and Measurement. *UNU/WIDER Research Paper* No. 44.

Chester, J. (2007). *Digital destiny: New media and the future of democracy*. New York: New Press.

Christensen, C. (2011). Discourses of technology and liberation: State aid to net activists in an era of "Twitter Revolutions". *Communication Review*, *14*(3), 233–253. doi:10.1080/10714421.2011.597263

Collier, P. (2009). *Wars, Guns, and Votes: Democracy in Dangerous Places*. London: Bodley Head.

Cunningham, J. (2010). New workers, new workplaces? Getting the balance right. Viewpoint. *Strategic Direction*, *26*(1), 5–6. doi:10.1108/02580541011009725

Dhir, K. S. (2007). Stakeholder activism through non-violence. *Corporate Communication: An International Journal*, *12*(1), 75–93. doi:10.1108/13563280710723769

Engberg-Pedersen, L., Andersen, L., & Stepputat, F. (2008). *Fragile situations. DIIS Report 9*. Danish Institute for International Studies.

Eti, C. I. (2009). Objectivity and Balance in Conflict Reporting: Imperatives for the Niger Delta Press. *Journal of African Studies*, *3*, 391–104.

Etling, B., Faris, R., & Palfrey, J. (2010). Political change in the digital age: The fragility and promise of online organizing. *SAIS Review*, *30*(2), 37–49.

Evuleocha, S. U. (2005). Managing indigenous relations: Corporate social responsibility and corporate communication in a new age of activism. *Corporate Communications: an International Journal*, *10*(4), 328–340. doi:10.1108/13563280510630124

Eweje, G. (2007). Multinational oil companies' CSR initiatives in Nigeria. *Managerial Law*, *49*(5/6), 218–235. doi:10.1108/03090550710841340

Faria, F., & Sherriff, A. (2009). *EU Policies to Address Fragility in Sub-Saharan Africa. ECDPM* (pp. 1–19). Italy: European Report on Development.

Freeman, R. E. (1984). *Strategic management: a stakeholder approach.* Boston: Pitman.

Frynas, J. G. (2009). *Beyond Corporate Social Responsibility.* Oxford: Oxford University Press. doi:10.1017/CBO9780511581540

Ghannam, J. (2011). Social Media in the Arab World: Leading up to the Uprisings of 2011. *Centre for International Media Assistance, 3,* 1–44.

Goggin, G., & Newell, C. (2003). *The disability: The social construction of disability in new media.* New York: Rowman & Littlefield.

Graham, B. L. (2002). Why I weblog: A rumination on where the hell I'm going with this website. In J. Rodzvilla (Ed.), *We've got blog: How weblogs are changing our culture.* Retrieved from http://www.bradlands.com/words/maybe02.html

Grayson, D., & Hodges, A. (2004). *Corporate Social Opportunity, 7 Steps to make Corporate Social Responsibility work for your Business.* Sheffield: Greenleaf Publishing.

Hartman, L. P., & Desjardins, J. (2008). *Business ethics: Decision making for personal integrity and social responsibility.* New York: McGraw-Hill.

Hilse, M., & Hoewner, J. (1998). The communication crisis in the internet and what one can do against it. In M. Crimp (Ed.), *Interactive enterprise communication* (pp. 137–154). Frankfurt: IMK.

Howard, P. N., & Hussain, M. M. (2013). *Democracy's fourth wave? Digital media and the Arab spring.* Oxford: Oxford University Press. doi:10.1093/acprof:oso/9780199936953.001.0001

Idemudia, U. (2010). Corporate social responsibility and the rentier Nigerian state: Rethinking the role of government and the possibility of corporate social development in the Niger Delta. *Canadian Journal of Development Studies, 30*(1), 131–153.

Ite, U. (2004). Multinationals and corporate social responsibility in developing countries: A case study of Shell in Nigeria. *Corporate Social Responsibility and Environmental Management, 11*(1), 1–11. doi:10.1002/csr.49

Kahn, R., & Kellner, D. (2004). New media and internet activism: From the 'battle of Seattle' to blogging. *New Media & Society, 6*(1), 87–95. doi:10.1177/1461444804039908

Kaplan, S. (2008). *Fixing Fragile States – A New Paradigm for Development.* Westport, CT: Praeger Security International.

Karl, T. L. (1997). *The paradox of plenty: oil booms and petro-states.* California: University of California Press.

Kashi, E. (2008). *Curse of the black gold. 50 years of oil in the Niger delta.* New York: Powerhouse Publishers.

Ko, H.-C., Yin, C.-P., & Kuo, F.-Y. (2008). Exploring individual communication power in the bogosphere. *Internet Research*, *18*(5), 541–561. doi:10.1108/10662240810912774

Komito, L., & Bates, J. (2009). Virtual local: Social media and community among Polish nationals in Dublin. *Aslib Proceedings: New Information Perspectives*, *61*(3), 232–244. doi:10.1108/00012530910959790

Kperogi, F. A. (2011). Webs of resistance: The citizen online journalism of the Nigerian digital Diaspora [Doctoral Dissertation]. Georgia State University, Georgia, USA.

Livingston, G. (2010). *How to: Turn slackivists into activists with social media*. Mashable Social Media.

Mangold, W. G., & Faulds, D. J. (2009). Social media: The new hybrid element of the promotion mix. *Business Horizons*, *52*(4), 357–365. doi:10.1016/j.bushor.2009.03.002

McKinsey. (2013). Six social-media skills every leader needs. *The McKinsey Quarterly*, (February): 1–13.

Mei, J. S. A., Bansel, N., & Pang, A. (2010). New media: A new medium in escalating crisis. *Corporate Communication: An International Journal*, *15*(2), 143–155. doi:10.1108/13563281011037919

Morsing, M., & Schultz, M. (2006). Corporate social responsibility communication: Stakeholder information, response and involvement strategies. *Business Ethics (Oxford, England)*, *15*(4), 323–338. doi:10.1111/j.1467-8608.2006.00460.x

Mulhern, F. (2009). Integrated marketing communications: From media channels to digital connectivity. *Journal of Marketing Communications,* 15(2-3), 85-101.

Nwagbara, U. (2010). Towards a paradigm shift in the Niger Delta: Transformational leadership in the era of post amnesty deal. *Journal of Sustainable Development in Africa*, *12*(3), 387–400.

Nwagbara, U. (2013). *Leading sustainability in Nigeria: Problems, Processes and Prospects*. Saarbrucken: LAP.

Obi, C. (2010). Oil as the "curse" of conflict in Africa: Peering through the smoke and mirrors. *Review of African Political Economy*, *37*(126), 483–495. doi:10.1080/03056244.2010.530947

OECD/DAC (Organisation for Economic Co-operation and Development/Development Assistance Committee). (2007). *Principles for Good International Engagement in Fragile States and Situations*. Paris: OECD.

Okoh, R. N. (2005). Conflict management in the Niger delta region of Nigeria: A participatory approach. *African Journal of Conflict Resolution*, *5*, 24–37.

Okome, M. O. (2013). (Ed). State fragility, state formation, and human security in Nigeria. New Hampshire: Palgrave MacMillan.

Okonta, I., & Douglas, O. (2003). *Where vultures feast: Shell, human rights, and oil in the Niger delta*. London: Verso.

Oluwaniyi, O. O. (2011). Post-amnesty in the Niger delta: Challenges and prospects. *Conflict Trends*, *4*, 46–54.

Oruh, E. S. (2014). Giving voice to the people: Exploring the effect of new media on stakeholders' engagement in the Nigerian union movement. *Management Research and Practices*, *6*(3), 44–52.

Parson, W. (1996). Crisis communication. *Career Development International*, *1(5)*, 26–28.

Peled, A. (2000). Bringing the internet and multimedia revolution to the classroom. *Campus-Wide Information Systems*, *17*(1), 16–22. doi:10.1108/10650740010317023

Scherer, A., & Palazzo, G. (2011). The new political role of business in a globalized world: A review of a new perspective on CSR and its implications for the firm, governance, and democracy. *Journal of Management Studies*, *48*(4), 899–931. doi:10.1111/j.1467-6486.2010.00950.x

Sen, A. (1981). *Poverty and famine: An Essay on Entitlement and Deprivation*. Oxford: Clarendon Press.

Singh, T., Veron-Jackson, L., & Cullinane, J. (2008). Blogging: A new play in your marketing game plan. *Business Horizons*, *51*(4), 281–292. doi:10.1016/j.bushor.2008.02.002

Stewart, F., & Brown, G. (2009). Fragile States. *CRISE Working Paper No. 51*, University of Oxford, Oxford.

Touri, M. (2009). News blogs: Strengthening democracy through conflict prevention. *Aslib Proceedings: New Information Perspectives*, *61*(2), 170–184. doi:10.1108/00012530910946910

Ugwoji, A. C. (2014). Amplifying employees' voice in the Nigerian employment relations for better corporate governance: the imperative of new media. *Economic Insights – Trends & Challenges*, 3(3), 15-22.

Uzoechina, O. (2008). "State Fragility" and the Challenges of Development in West Africa: Moving from Reaction to Prevention. *ALC Research Report No. 3*. African Leadership Centre, King's College London.

Watts, M. (2004). Resource curse? Governmentality, oil and power in the Niger delta, Nigeria. *Geopolitics*, *9*(1), 50–80. doi:10.1080/14650040412331307832

Xu, J., & Cooper Thomas, H. (2011). How can leaders achieve high employee engagement? *Leadership and Organization Development Journal*, *32*(4), 399–416. doi:10.1108/01437731111134661

Youngs, G. (2007). Virtual democracy: An idea for our time. *Development*, 50, 23–27. doi:10.1057/palgrave.development.1100331 PMID:21115610

Chapter 8
Basics of Mobile Marketing Strategy

Wilson Ozuem
University of Gloucestershire, UK

Bibi Nafiisah Mulloo
London Metropolitan University, UK

ABSTRACT

Recent years have witnessed a rapid growth in internet-enabled devices, including smartphones which have facilitated the performance of many tasks online. One of the major activities taking place on such online platforms is shopping. Indeed, smartphones are redefining the landscape of consumption from visiting conventional physical shops to consuming products and services in a digital arena. Despite a proliferation of both theoretical and empirical studies on smartphones marketplace, there is still a paucity of studies on how mobile phone devices enhance and facilitate consumption from physical marketplace to online marketspace. This chapter aims to contribute to extant studies on how smartphones impact on the consumption process.

INTRODUCTION

The mobile revolution in the last decade has re-created a new era of an always-connected society which has reshaped the retail industry, including the clothing sector, in a major way (Euromonitor, 2013). Mobile devices becoming more powerful with their own operating systems, has given rise to a new marketing strategy enabling companies to connect to their consumers on the go and on a 24-hour basis (Emarketer, 2013). This new phenomenon has impacted on the purchasing behaviour of consumers in the clothing sector as well, who are increasingly adopting this new shopping medium. This emerging trend has resulted in all major clothing retailers working to gain online presence with a view to achieving a stronger customer relationship and sustaining a strong presence in the clothing industry which is becoming highly competitive (Keynote, 2009). With the rise of more sophisticated mobile devices, namely smartphones, this new convergence has resulted in powerful consumers who now have their stores in their hands (Abrams, 2013).

DOI: 10.4018/978-1-4666-9776-8.ch008

The purchasing habits of consumers have undergone a drastic shift from traditional physical high street shopping to home shopping (Keynote, 2013; Ozuem, Howell & Lancaster 2008). The role of salesmen and shopping displays has now been eclipsed with modern ways of shopping using technology. Research by Euromonitor (2013) identified consumers who increasingly favour seeking shopping information on their smartphones rather than consulting a salesperson or relying on adverts. The use of smartphones is thus not limited to buying online but rather it is that device which accompanies the consumers in their shopping experience such as browsing for product information, product reviews, price comparisons, consulting friends and families prior to shopping, or simply buying online. "This unique ability has transformed the social and spatial aspects of shopping for many consumers" (Brown *et al.*, 2003). In fact, the ongoing connectivity and exposure to shopping information are resulting in an 'always shopping' state of mind (Babbitts, 2013). If the art of mobile marketing is effectively and efficiently mastered by retailers, this can lead to strong positioning in their respective market. Although this new marketing trend has had a strong influence in different retail sectors, a survey carried out by Emarketer (2013) showed that consumers in the apparel sector still favour physical purchase or buying via the PC rather than smartphones when buying online. The main hindrance to buying via smartphones is usually a non-user friendly mobile site (Emarketer, 2013). The answer to successful retailing via smartphones relies on a strong technique and the application of mobile commerce (Branki *et al.*, 2008). Despite consumers showing a preference to shop or buy clothing in physical shops, being "creatures of convenience" there are billions reaching first for their phones when they think about shopping (Boyle, 2013). Much is assumed about the supposed effects of smartphones on the luxury fashion sector, but much research in the field suffers from epistemological and ontological incompatibility and can be interpreted in various conflicting ways. This chapter focuses on the impact of smartphones on consumer buying behaviour, particularly on the UK luxury fashion sector.

A rapid growth in internet-enabled devices including smartphones has taken place in recent years, allowing many tasks to be performed online (Euromonitor, 2013). One of the major activities taking place on these online platforms is shopping. Indeed, shopping has changed the landscape of consumption from visiting conventional physical shops to consuming products and services in a digital arena (San-Martin and Lopez-Catalan, 2013). Boyle (2013) posited that the number of consumers using smartphones to shop is expanding and consumers are now more willing to reach for their smartphones first when the idea of shopping strikes. This global phenomenon is affecting different parts of the world. A survey conducted in June 2013 by Emarketer (2013), shows that China is the leading country in terms of internet users purchasing via mobile devices followed by India and the United Kingdom. The UK was amongst the first nations to embrace digital shopping and buying and to date it continues to consume goods and services digitally at a pace greater than most other western European countries (Abrams, 2013). The UK's communications regulator Ofcom recently claimed that the UK leads among all other European countries with the highest number of smartphone users (Euromonitor, 2013). UK retail ecommerce sales are estimated to have risen from £38.48 billion in 2012 to £45.40 billion in 2013 with a further increase of 15% forecast for 2014 (Emarketer, 2013). This new trend in purchasing via mobile devices has initiated a new type of e-commerce commonly referred to as retail mobile commerce (m-commerce) which is defined by eMarketer (2013) as "products and services purchased using a browser or app via any mobile device, regardless of where fulfilment occurs." As the growth of m-commerce is overwhelming in the UK, shopping via mobile devices is becoming the norm for internet shoppers with smartphones: mobile commerce sales are forecast to more than double by 2017 (McCarthy, 2013). With such a proliferation of technologically advanced smartphones and the widespread availability of the internet in the UK, digital shoppers increasingly expect an enhanced mobile shopping experience (Boyle, 2013). This has highlighted the importance of mobile commerce for retailers as consumer buying behaviour has undergone a significant transformation (Persaud & Azhar, 2012). To survive in this new era, several retailers in the UK are at the forefront of m-commerce with major clothing retailers such as Net-a-Porter and Asos as two examples of fashion organisations with the most innovative websites and apps which help them to maintain customer relationships (Abrams, 2013). However, m-commerce is still considered to be in its infancy with most internet users favouring the PC to buy online (Emarketer, 2013). This new shopping trend with its ongoing challenge makes it interesting to investigate the effects of smartphone usage on users' purchase intentions.

THEORETICAL FRAMEWORK AND CONTEXT

Feature phones are now being gradually eclipsed by the proliferation of smartphones which are more sophisticated in terms of their functionality (Nokia, 2013; Li *et al.*, 2012; Kumar and Mukherjee, 2013, Holmes *et al.*, 2014). Technological advancement in mobile devices fuelled by the widespread availability of high-speed internet access has enhanced various features and the usage of mobile phones (Persaud & Azhar, 2012; Flint & Spaid, 2014; Schuster *et al.*, 2013). In fact, the rapid growth of internet-enabled mobile devices has redefined the primary purpose of phones, from devices primarily designed for call-making to a product capable of performing different functions such as web browsing, emailing, shopping and other tasks (Hu *et al.*, 2006; Ting *et al.*, 2011; Swilley *et al.*, 2012; Ozuem, O'Keeffe, & Lancaster 2015). A smartphone is a programmable phone which provides its user with advanced capabilities and features to enhance his/her daily work and personal life (Yang & Kim, 2012).

The rolling out of 3G and the EE 2012 launch of 4G in the UK has boosted mobile internet speed which enables users to have a more enriching browsing experience (BBC, 2012; Kumar & Zhan, 2003; Yang, 2012). Although UK mobile operators have restrained their generous unlimited mobile data offerings, mobile internet subscriptions and smartphone use are still witnessing constant growth (The Guardian, 2012). This can be attributed to the fact that consumers are now less reliant on mobile networks in the UK as the number of Wi-Fi spots available is increasing in cafes, transport hubs and other public places (Yang, 2012). The smartphone is now seen more and more as the must-have device that permits users to perform a multitude of tasks with no time or location constraints (Wong, 2012). The growing dependency on smartphones has revolutionised the lifestyle and behaviour of consumers in different sectors creating a digital landscape where consumers are engulfed in their own worlds anywhere and anytime (Elkin, 2012). For many individuals the smartphone is not only a personal device but it is "an extension of their personality and individuality" (Persaud & Azhar, p.418). A mobile device, for example in this study the smartphone, can be accessed anytime, anywhere, allowing access to the mobile web in more diverse contexts (Kim *et al.,* 2002). Thanks to its capacity of seamlessly integrating Bluetooth, GPS and other technologies, the smartphone is considered a useful tool that can provide a superior consumer experience (Swilley & Hofacker, 2006). Moreover, with smartphones at more affordable prices, the rate of adoption is ever-increasing with no signs of abating, thus emphasising the central importance smartphones are gradually and surely taking in consumers' decision making process (Pasqua & Elkin, 2013). The rapid development and deployment of internet-enabled mobile devices has led to the emergence of highly sophisticated applications commonly referred to as mobile commerce (m-commerce) (Wang *et al.*, 2007; Wheeler, 2013; San-Martin *et al.*, 2012; Wong, 2012).

Mobile commerce is commonly referred to as the ability to undertake commercial transactions through a wireless internet-enabled device (Swilley *et al.*, 2012). Most definitions of m-commerce focus on an extension of e-commerce (Frolick & Chen, 2004; Siau *et al.*, 2001; Dholakia & Dholakia, 2004). It is even considered an unprecedented business opportunity for e-commerce (Wang *et al.*, 2007; Yeh and Li, 2009; Wheeler, 2013). It is the medium through which retailers can develop their marketing strategies, as it is the channel that has the potential to initiate purchase intentions in consumers. However, m-commerce is not regarded as a replacement to e-commerce but rather as a supplement (Clarke, 2008). Mobile commerce in the UK has been effectively adopted due to the widespread availability of high-speed internet access via mobile devices which render mobile shopping readily accessible to consumers (Mintel, 2013). Research conducted by Ipsos and RetailMeNot.com in August 2013 suggest that UK remains the highest user of m-commerce among developed nations (eMarketer, 2013). In this respect, the importance of m-commerce cannot be ignored when conducting this research. Therefore, the ubiquity of smartphones and wireless technology are both important elements that indirectly affect consumers' purchase intentions.

Smartphones being the medium that has a growing influence on consumers purchase intention and buying habits, marketers have an increasing challenge to stay updated and on track about how to maximise consumer retention by adopting appropriate mobile marketing strategies (Elkin, 2013). Ranging from online advertisement, QR codes, Apps development and Geo-fencing, marketers have the enormous responsibility of deterring consumers from being influenced by showrooming (BBC, 2013). Showrooming is defined as the activity of going online while in-store to determine which competitors are offering a better deal for the product a consumer is currently looking to buy (Abrams, 2013). From search engines to deal sites, it has become crucial for companies to capitalise fully on the digital landscape to enhance their online presence (Ahrens *et al.*, 2013). This has become a necessity for the clothing sector as even though mobile shopping may not culminate in purchasing via mobiles, consumers in this sector still rely heavily on their smartphones to browse for product information, deals and purchase-related queries (Cho & Fiorito, 2009). This on-going thirst for information has emphasised to retailers the importance of enhancing their mobile commerce strategies to remain competitive in what is a highly digitalised shopping era (Skeldon, 2012).

The main activities undertaken by consumers on their smartphones include contacting friends about shopping matters, carrying out price checks, looking at product availability, finding out product information while in-store, accessing social media, acquiring / redeeming coupons, carrying out location-based search, consulting maps, using apps, buying products using devices and even buying products using devices while in-store. These suggest the powerful influence of effective mobile commerce on consumers' online shopping experience. For the purposes of this chapter, smartphones include all mobile phone devices which can access the internet via mobile networks or Wi-Fi spots. Mobile shopping and online consumer behaviour will be discussed further in this chapter in order to understand how smartphones can influence purchase intention.

Attitudes towards Technology

A number of studies have focused on research on key factors that influence the acceptance of new technologies (Ajzen, 1985; Davis *et al.*, 1989; Lu *et al.*, 2003). To understand how smartphones can affect consumers' purchase intentions and behaviour, it is indispensable to understand the user perception of the use of the technology (Kumar and Mukherjee, 2013). The Theory of Reasoned Action (TRA) suggests that the intention to undertake a behaviour is influenced by a person's attitudes towards that behaviour and a subjective norm (Fishbein & Ajzen, 1975). Attitude in this context is further defined by Spaid and Flint (2014) as an individual positive or negative feeling towards a specific behaviour. Fishbein and Ajzen (1975, p.302) refer to a subjective norm as "perception that most people who are important to him think that he should not perform the behaviour in question." The theory of reasoned action (TRA) implies that any factors that influence a person's behaviour do so through a change of attitudes, subjective norms or a combination of the two (Spaid & Flint, 2014). The theory of reasoned action (TRA) is considered fairly robust in predicting and explaining cognitively driven attitude (Spaid and Flint, 2014). To address some of the limitations of the TRA, Ajzen (1991) attributes the element of control as another determinant to behavioural intention and actual behaviour. The theory of planned behaviour (TPB) was thus created by Ajzen (1991) to study a perceived lack of control when it comes to certain behaviours. Both theories assist Spaid and Flint (2014) in understanding shoppers' attitudes towards mobile devices.

The TRA was further modified by Davis *et al.* (1989) where the element of subjective norm was dropped in the process. The Technology Acceptance Model (TAM) was thus devised where two main variables were added to the fundamental process of attitude, intention and behaviour. The TAM attempts to understand how users accept and use the technology (Lu *et al.*, 2003). The two main variables in the original TAM are "perceived usefulness" and "perceived ease of use" (Davis, 1989, cited in Kumar and Mukherjee, 2013, p. 25). These two determinants are considered useful indicators of the attitudes of users towards a new technologies and their eventual adoption or rejection (Lu et al, 2003). Perceived usefulness is described by Davis (1989, p.320) as "the degree to which a person believes that using a particular system would enhance his or her job performance." A system high in perceived usefulness is considered to positively influence adoption of the specific system (Davis, 1989). On the other hand, perceived ease of use is referred to as "the degree to which a person believes that using a particular system would be free of effort" (Davis, 1989, p.320). A system scoring high in ease of use will encourage users to use the system (Davis, 1989).

The TAM model has been used in various recent items of research into smartphones and mobile consumer behaviour (Holmes *et al.*, 2014). For instance, Lu and Su (2009) used the TAM model to explore factors affecting purchase intention in the context of mobile websites. Their research suggested that negative emotions such as anger have a negative impact on purchase intention whereas positive emotion such as enjoyment has a positive effect on purchase intention (Lamarre *et al.*, 2012; Ozuem, Thomas & Lancaster 2015). Although TAM is a model frequently cited by researchers, many have mixed opinions, regarding its applications as being limited (Lu *et al.*, 2003). Conversely to TRA, the TAM is criticised for lacking vigour and having limited variables (Davis *et al.*, 1992; Venkatesh *et al.*, 2013). Burton-Jones and Hubona (2006) stated that the original TAM can be modified to include external factors such as age, level of education and experience, which, according to their studies, can affect the use of technology. Mathieson (1991) on the other hand considers the TAM theoretical foundation to be poor and argues that there can be many uncertainties between the intention and adoption phase. However, the Technology Acceptance Model (TAM) remains a useful theoretical framework to assess users' acceptance or rejection of a particular technology (Davis, 1989 cited in Kumar and Mukherjee, 2013). Mobile shopping is an activity which involves interaction between the user and the technology, in this research, the smartphone hence the importance of the users' attitudes towards the said technology.

Researches in the past advocated that positive attitudes and purchase intentions are inter-related (Shim *et al.*, 2001; George, 2002; Goldsmiths & Bridges, 2005). Eagly and Chaiken (1993, p.1) define attitude as "a psychological tendency that is expressed by evaluating a particular entity with some degree of favour or disfavour." The many definitions of attitude emphasise the nature of the term and its connection with behaviour (Bohner & Bohner, 2001). For instance, Seock and Norton (2007) argue that consumers' attitudes towards a specific shopping channel will influence their likelihood to purchase through that channel. Therefore, consumers' perception of the mobile internet to search for information about products and services will eventually influence their intentions to undertake those searches via their smartphones and the likelihood to purchase online (Kim *et al.*, 2012). It has been argued further that attitude towards a technology (i.e. mobile internet) will determine the probability of a consumer using that technology (i.e. smartphones) as a medium to make a purchase. The consumers' intentions (Seock & Norton, 2007) and their objectives (Nysveen & Pedersen, 2005) will contribute towards a high-degree goal-oriented search mode which will influence the purchase intentions in an online mobile environment. As pointed out by both George (2002) and Seock and Norton (2007), a positive attitude towards online shopping will culminate in a positive purchase intention whereas a negative attitude towards online shopping will result in negative purchase intentions.

Smartphones and Mobile Shopping

Considerable evidence from industry sources reveals that mobile phones are playing a significant role in consumers' shopping processes (Skeldon, 2012; Seock & Norton, 2007). With the prediction of increased adoption of smartphones in future, there will inevitably be continuous growth in this new shopping trend. The use of smartphones for shopping is not restricted to purchasing but is more thoroughly used for activities such as searching for products, gathering production information, checking prices or reading reviews (Holmes *et al.*, 2014). The ability to conduct shopping activities on mobile devices has opened up opportunities for retailers to influence the purchase intentions of shoppers (Shankar *et al.*, 2011).

To understand the term mobile shopping, it is important to understand consumer buying behaviour. Consumer buying behaviour involves the process and activities entailed when consumers are searching, evaluating, analysing, buying, reviewing, rejecting, accepting products or services with a view to satisfying their personal needs. Solomon (2009, p.33) defines consumer behaviour as "the study of the processes involved when individuals or groups select, purchase, use, or dispose of products, services, ideas, or experiences to satisfy their needs and desires." According to Peter and Olson (1996), consumers' buying decisions are divided into interpretation, integration and behaviour. Interpretation deals with how consumers select information and derive meanings from particular information (Peter & Olson, 1996). Then, the integration happens when the consumer evaluates the product using various sources of information among other alternative behaviours towards the product (Peter & Olson, 1996). This is an important stage in the decision-making process that will eventually result in either the customer buying or rejecting the product (Peter & Olson, 1996). Nysveen and Pedersen (2005) identify the consumers' objectives as the ultimate factor that will influence the consumers search for a product and hereafter the buying behaviour. In their opinion, consumers with a high-degree goal-oriented search mode which is influenced by product knowledge, product risk and product involvement are more likely to complete a transaction than consumers with a low-degree search mode (Nysveen & Pedersen, 2005).

Mobile shopping is the process of consumers exhibiting particular buying behaviours in an online mobile environment (Skeldon, 2012). Easy access to internet on the go via smartphones has fuelled the ability of consumers to be more-goal oriented in their search for products (Nysveen & Pedersen, 2005). To assist them in their information search and in some cases buying process, smartphones are now the convenient medium. Increased adoption and functionality of smartphones means consumers are making ever greater use of their smartphones in the shopping process anywhere and anytime (Charlton, 2011). New technological developments in smartphones have indeed opened up opportunities for retailers to influence shopper attitudes and behaviours (Holmes *et al.*, 2014).

Online Shopping Motivations

Salomon and Rabolt (2006) describe motivation as the processes that drive people to behave in a particular manner. In the shopping context, motivations will be the behavioural factor that will ultimately drive shopping behaviour (Jim & Kim, 2003). Babin *et al.* (1994) identified two primary drivers of shopping motivations as being attributed to utilitarian and hedonic reasons. Adapting a traditional approach, shopping motivations were seen as highly task-related and rational from a utilitarian perspective (Kim, 2006). Babin *et al.* (1994), however, argued that shopping motivations are identified by the perception of shopping from the consumer point of view whether they see it as an activity of cognition or one of pleasure. Hence, the two perspectives of shopping motivations are identified as utilitarian and hedonic shopping motivations (Babin *et al.*, 1994). The utilitarian aspects of shopping considered shopping as a task to be performed in a timely and efficient manner (Childers *et al.*, 2001). These shoppers will use their mobiles to search for product information and offers online at their convenience to fulfill their motives, which plays an important role in shaping their shopping behaviour (Childers *et al.*, 2001).

Similarly, Babin *et al.* (1994) argue that shopping motivations need not be restricted to product or task-orientation but can also be hedonic. Consistent with these findings, Hoffman and Novak (1996) state that hedonic shopping motivation is associated with the entertainment and enjoyment derived from the shopping activity. Kim and Forsythe (2007) identify hedonic shoppers as those who seek pleasure and fun in the shopping process. Childers *et al.* (2001) state that the social activity for hedonic shoppers is not limited to product acquisitions but involves the activity of browsing or seeking excitement in surfing. Hedonic shoppers are considered as more apt to engage in online shopping, as their main motives are for non-economic reasons such as fun, social or emotional gratification (Park *et al.*, 2006). Arnold and Reynolds (2003) conducted research regarding the hedonic aspects of shopping which resulted in a range of motives from adventure, gratification, value, social, role and idea shopping motivations being identified. Although these two aspects are considered to offer contrasting conceptual approaches to shopping, they are both considered important in shaping consumer buying behaviour (Babin *et al.*, 1994). Scarpi (2006) suggests that consumers with a high level of hedonism tend to purchase on a frequent basis compared with consumers with a high level of utilitarianism. Childers *et al.* (2001) confirmed that both usefulness and enjoyment associated with purchasing a product have a positive effect on consumers' purchase intentions. Accordingly, these findings show that both hedonism and utilitarianism shape consumers' perceptions and adoption of online shopping (Babin *et al.*, 1994; Scarpi, 2006).

Establishing Trust in a Mobile Environment

Trust is an important element that can promote or deter consumers from using smartphones for shopping processes as emphasised by Yeh and Li (2008). Trust is an important element which can ensure consumers' satisfaction and which can thus lead to consumer retention for both online and offline retailers (Schiffman & Kanuk, 2010). Satisfaction and trust are closely related in the online shopping experience and to benefit from this consumers place high importance on website design, reliability, responsiveness, trust and personalisation when conducting online purchase (Yeh & Li, 2008). Satisfaction is a strong factor which will determine the level of trust established with consumers and this happens at the post-purchase stage (Yeh & Li, 2008). There should be a strong similarity in what consumers are expecting to be offered and what is being provided by the online service (Yeh & Li, 2008). Consequently, retailers need to focus on enhancing their mobile commerce with minimum hindrance in their mobile sites so as to encourage consumers to shop through their smartphones more frequently (Skeldon, 2011). Wang and Liao (2007) highlighted the fact that a successful online mobile experience will most likely encourage future online purchase. Other major concerns that influence consumers purchase intentions in a mobile environment are security and data protection (Yeh & Li, 2009). This is an on-going hindrance affecting purchase intentions on smartphones.

As mentioned earlier, consumers' attitudes towards their smartphones are an important consideration when studying the mobile shopping process. Consumers perceive their smartphones as personal and may consider it an intrusion if they are bombarded with commercials or advertising all the time (Holmes *et al.*, 2014). The element of trust is thus considered crucial as consumers are becoming more conscious about source credibility (Spaid & Flint, 2014). Consumers do intense research prior to purchase and thus online retailers need to provide genuine information to assist potential consumers (Solomon, 2009) The shopping experience via smartphones needs to be perceived as relevant, useful and timely and possibly funny, to establish a trust relationship (Hung *et al.*, 2012). Another factor that affects the trust element in consumers' willingness to adopt online shopping can be attributed to the quality of service they are being offered online (Chemingui & Lallouna, 2013). In the absence of a salesperson to guide them in their shopping process, it is crucial for the quality of service online to be perceived as exceptionally good (Chemingui & Lallouna, 2013). The first online shopping experience contributes towards building an initial trust relationship between the retailers and the shoppers which will lead to future online shopping (Zhou, 2011). In the apparel sector, although customisation of clothes is now possible with body-scanning technology, many consumers are reluctant to use this shopping format (Cho & Fiorito, 2009). Zhou (2011) further argues that it is even harder to establish a trust relationship in a virtual environment due to great uncertainty and trust. Therefore, it is important for retailers to concentrate on enhancing their mobile commerce strategies to maintain brand credibility and integrity (Chemingui & Lallouna, 2013). Considering that consumers still favour the PC and physical stores in the clothing sector, it is very interesting by conducting this research to see what affects their purchase intentions via smartphones and what changes they expect in the future. The element of trust is difficult to achieve in a mobile environment as the threats involved are considered very high and very difficult to eradicate.

Smartphones and Purchase Intentions

The rapid adoption and use of smartphones has driven many cultural changes including changes in consumers' shopping patterns and shopping behaviour (Spaid & Flint, 2014). Most existing studies have been focused on identifying the main variables responsible for consumers' purchasing behaviour in the mobile online environment (Kumar & Mukherjee, 2013; Spaid & Flint, 2014; Holmes *et al.*, 2014; Ting *et al.*, 2011). While some researchers attribute attitudes and consumers' perception as the main determinants that influence the use of smartphones as a shopping tool (Holmes *et al.*, 2014; Lu & Su, 2009; Lu *et al.*, 2003), others consider motivation as a major factor contributing towards the use of smartphones as a shopping channel (Childers *et al.*, 2001; Kim & Forsythe, 2007; Park *et al.*, 2006). Whichever the variables that determine the use of smartphones to conduct shopping activities may be, it is evident that smartphones and purchase intentions are inter-related (Seock & Norton, 2007; Skeldon, 2012; Elkin, 2013).

The technology acceptance model (TAM) is indeed a useful tool in assessing users' willingness to adopt smartphones as the new purchase channel (Kumar & Mukherjee, 2013; Spaid & Flint, 2014). This model had been used, and in certain research modified with a view to ascertaining a more defined understanding of how this new technology is continuously reshaping the shopping process. The common variables identified by a variety of research in this new field are attitudes, intention and behaviour (Spaid & Flint, 2014, Lu *et al.*, 2003; Seock & Norton, 2007; Holmes, 2014). Ting *et al.*.(2011) identified perception of and dependency on the smart device as major attributes that influence user's attitude towards using a smartphone. Due to a shortage of time, consumers find it convenient to use their smartphones anywhere and anytime to perform multiple tasks (Dibb & Carrigan, 2013). They perceive their smartphones as the ultimate device that performs the task of both a mobile phone and a laptop (Lu & Su, 2009). Consequently, consumers with a positive perception of the multi-usage capabilities of smartphones are identified as having a positive attitude towards the adoption of smartphones as a multitasking device (Kumar & Mukherjee, 2013; Ozuem & Lancaster 2014). Behavioural intention relates to the phase where an individual's attitude gradually controls or guides his or her behaviour (Ajzen, 1991). In the context of mobile shopping, attitude and motivation are considered the determinants of behavioural intention (Kim, 2006; Scarpi, 2006). Whether for utilitarian or hedonic reasons, positive motivation and initial attitude are believed to trigger the use of a smartphone as a shopping tool and henceforth purchase intention (Kim, 2006; Scarpi, 2006). The actual behaviour is the last phase of the technology acceptance model in which the users' decision to use the device culminates (Ajzen, 1991). In the context of this research, actual behaviour happens when consumers do in fact use the device for a shopping experience. Consumers' actual usage of this new shopping technology does not necessarily guarantee ultimate adoption of smartphones as a shopping channel (Yeh & Li, 2008). The first mobile shopping experience is considered as a crucial touchpoint that will initiate future purchase (Skeldon, 2012), hence, the growing importance of mobile commerce in this new digitalised marketplace (Zhou, 2011). The importance of a good mobile site, easy user interface, enhanced security and an overall sound mobile experience are the major contributors towards effective adoption of this new shopping tool (Yeh & Li, 2009). Considering the clothing sector, the challenge is even bigger as the sensory feelings of products constitute a major determinant of actual purchase (eMarketer, 2013). Moreover, as per research carried out by eMarketer (2013), although mobile commerce has shown considerable growth in the last few years, the personal desktop remains the most favoured device for online purchases.

The theory of reasoned action (TRA) and the theory of planned behaviour (TPB) are both attitudinal theories that will assist in gaining in-depth knowledge about shoppers' attitudes towards mobile technology (Ozuem, Borrelli, & Lancaster, 2015). The technology acceptance model remains the ultimate tool that will be used in this research to understand the different phase that constitutes the shopping process in a mobile environment. The main gap in the literature lies between the behavioural intention phase and actual behaviour. Though research has focused on different variables that might be integrated in the model to have a clearer picture on how shopping behaviour might be influenced in a mobile environment, little relates to how smartphones can influence purchase intention. Hence, the focus of the research will be to establish a link between smartphones and purchase intention with particular emphasis on those variables that affect the acceptance of this new shopping technology.

CONCLUSION AND MANAGERIAL IMPLICATIONS

Understanding the motivational factors and features that contribute to an effective and efficient mobile retail channel is of primary significance for retailers, including the clothing sector, with a view to selling their products successfully online and offline. For instance, consumers' pre-purchase activities using their smartphone are mainly directed towards deals and lower prices, both of which are driven by goal-oriented motivation. Therefore, marketers should revise their mobile commerce strategies to cater for and attract price-sensitive consumers. The challenge is to be the price leader with active promotional offers, deals and online discounts to attract consumers to their websites and to deter them from moving to competitors' websites.

Motivation is considered strategic to entertain consumers in a mobile retail setting. Whether the initial motive for shopping is task-related or for enjoyment, the objective of retailers is to ensure consumers' satisfaction at all stages of the shopping process. Therefore, marketers should develop marketing strategies aimed at encouraging consumers to conduct shopping activities online. Such strategies might include promotional offers, click-to-buy options, click-to-collect options, free delivery service, next day delivery service or online coupons which are commonly favoured by online shoppers.

Although many consumers conduct direct purchase on their smartphones, the majority use their devices for pre-purchase activities. These activities mostly include information enquiries regarding product specifications, product price, reviews and availability. In today's knowledge-based society, consumers are more willing to explore their personalised needs by using their smartphones prior to engaging in any form of transaction. Communications in the retail environment has evolved by involving consumers in the interactive platform of mobile commerce, targeted at providing information that meets consumers' expectation. Hence, marketers need to focus on the allocation of accurate and updated databases on their mobile sites to assist mobile shoppers with information queries at all times.

Trust is an important element that contributes to the establishment of a good rapport between consumers and retailers. This has emerged as a key variable within this study and constitutes a strategic element to encourage adoption of smartphones both for pre-purchase activities and for immediate purchase. Online retailers should thus ensure that consumers enjoy the mobile retail channel by implementing enhanced mobile commerce. This involves investment of resources towards a mobile site with user-friendly interface, easy access to commonly researched information and safe click-to-buy or click-to-collect in-store options. Furthermore, considering consumers' trustworthiness in social interaction for an authentic information, a mobile site needs to integrate features of social media to enhance consumers' experience and improve transparency in the mobile retail environment. Overall, consumers need to perceive mobile shopping as a convenient, safe shopping medium.

Intense innovation in features of smartphones and wireless technologies has freed users from the tethers that initially bounded them to their desks for online shopping. Convenience and flexibility are key features that initiate the use of smartphones for shopping irrespective of time and location. This is a golden opportunity for retailers to establish a mobile presence by making efficient use of mobile technology. Smartphones are now equipped with wide and high resolution screens which emphasise the need for marketers to implement a mobile site interface that closely matches the laptop or PC experience. Mobile sites need to improve navigation that will assist consumers whilst browsing for information they value at their convenience thus enriching their shopping experience. Marketers need to ensure that their mobile site is compatible and up-to-date with latest technologies such as fingerprint recognition, digital wallets, heartbeat rate, retinal recognition and other emerging technologies to attract and retain more consumers in the mobile environment. In successfully implementing such strategies, consumers will find it even more convenient to adopt mobile shopping and will also entertain a trusting relationship with the mobile retail channel.

By understanding the link between smartphone and purchase intention, marketers can adapt their marketing strategies to positively influence more users to conduct at least pre-purchase activities in a mobile environment. They need to acknowledge and analyse further variables valued by mobile consumers, and evaluate ways to improve these variables with a view of gaining and retaining mobile shoppers. Although the findings in this study are not exhaustive, they provide a snapshot into understanding the relationship between the smartphone and mobile shoppers' behavioural intention.

REFERENCES

Abrams, K. V. (2012). UK B2C Ecommerce: Mobile Takes Center Stage. *Emarketer.* Retrieved from http://www.emarketer.com/Article/Mobile-Gains-Speed-UK-Ecommerce-

Abrams, K. V. (2013). UK Digital Trends: Ecommerce, Video and Mobile Thrive, but Brands must work for loyalty and trust. *Emarketer.*

Abrams, K. V. (2013). Western Europe B2C Ecommerce: Solid Growth Continues as Mobile Gains Ground. *Emarketer.*

Ahrens, J., Coyle, J. R., & Strahilevitz, M. A. (2013). Electronic word of mouth: The effects of incentives on e-referrals by senders and receivers. *International Journal of Marketing*, *47*(7), 1034–1051.

Arnold, M. J., & Reynolds, K. E. (2003). Hedonic shopping motivations. *Journal of Retailing*, *79*(2), 77–95. doi:10.1016/S0022-4359(03)00007-1

Banerjee, S., & Dholakia, R. R. (2012). Location-based mobile advertisements and gender targeting. *Journal of Research in Interactive Marketing*, *6*(3), 198–214. doi:10.1108/17505931211274679

Barrutia, J. M., & Echebarria, C. (2013). Networks: A social marketing tool. *European Journal of Marketing*, *47*(1/2), 324–343. doi:10.1108/03090561311285574

BBC. (2012). *UK's first 4G mobile service launched in 11 cities by EE.* Retrieved from http://www.bbc.co.uk/news/technology-20121025

BBC. (2013). *The peril of "showrooming".* Retrieved from http://www.bbc.co.uk/news/magazine-22098575

Bohner, M., & Bohner, G. (2001). *Intrapersonal processes.* Oxford: Blackwell.

Boyatzis, R. E. (1998). *Transforming qualitative information: Thematic analysis and code development.* California: Sage Publications Inc.

Boyle, C. (2013). Retail Mobile Commerce Forecast: Shoppers Turn to Smartphones First. *Emarketer.* Retrieved from http://www.emarketer.com/Article/More-Shoppers-Reach-Mobile-Browse-Buy/1009615

Braun, V., & Clarke, V. (2006). Using thematic analysis in psychology. *Qualitative Research in Psychology*, *3*(2), 77–101. doi:10.1191/1478088706qp063oa

Brown, M., Pope, N., & Vogues, K. (2003). Buying or browsing?: An exploration of shopping orientations and online purchase intention. *European Journal of Marketing*, *37*(11/12), 1666–1684. doi:10.1108/03090560310495401

Bryman, A. (1988). *Contemporary Social Research Series*. London: Unwin Hyman Ltd.

Bryman, A. (1989). *Research Methods and Organization Studies*. London: Unwin Hyman Ltd. doi:10.4324/9780203359648

Burr, V. (2003). *Social Contructionism* (2nd ed.). London: Routledge.

Burton-Jones, A., & Hubona, G. S. (2006). The mediation of external variables in the technology acceptance model. *Information & Management*, *43*(6), 706–717. doi:10.1016/j.im.2006.03.007

Butler, P., & Peppard, J. (1998). Consumer Purchasing on the Internet: Processes and Prospects. *European Journal of Marketing*, *16*(5), 600–610.

Chan, F. T. S., & Yee-Loong Chong, A. (2013). Analysis of the determinants of consumers' m-commerce usage activities. *Online Information Review*, *37*(3), 443–461. doi:10.1108/OIR-01-2012-0012

Cheema, A., & Papatla, P. (2010). Relative importance of online versus offline information for Internet purchase: Product category and Internet experience effects. *Journal of Business Research*, *63*(9-10), 979–985. doi:10.1016/j.jbusres.2009.01.021

Chemingui, H., & Ben lallouna, H. B. (2013). Resistance, motivation, trust and intention to use mobile finance services. *International Journal of Bank Marketing*, *31*(7), 574–592. doi:10.1108/IJBM-12-2012-0124

Cheung, C. M. K., & Lee, M. K. O. (2012). What drives consumers to spread electronic word of mouth in online consumer-opinion platforms. *Decision Support Systems*, *53*(1), 218–225. doi:10.1016/j.dss.2012.01.015

Childers, T. L., Carr, C. L., Peck, J., & Carson, S. (2001). Hedonic and utilitarian motivations for online retail shopping behaviour. *Journal of Retailing*, *77*(4), 511–535. doi:10.1016/S0022-4359(01)00056-2

Cho, S., & Fiorito, S. S. (2009). Acceptance of online customization for apparel shopping. *International Journal of Retail & Distribution Management*, *37*(5), 389–407. doi:10.1108/09590550910954892

Clarke, I. (2008). Emerging Value Propositions for M-commerce. *The Journal of Business Strategy*, *25*(2), 41–57.

Clothing Retailing Market Report. (2013). Keynote. Retrieved from http://www.keynote.co.uk/market-intelligence/view/product/10792/clothing-retailing?highlight=clothing&utm_source=kn.reports.search

Collis, J., & Hussey, R. (2003). *Business Research: A practical guide for undergraduate and postgraduate students* (2nd ed.). New York: Palgrave Macmillan.

Collis, J., & Hussey, R. (2009). *Business Research: A Practical Guide for Undergraduate & Postgraduate Students* (3rd ed.). Hampshire: Palgrave Macmillan.

Constantinides, E., Lorenzo-Romero, G. M., & Gómez, M. A. (2010). Effects of web experience on consumer choice: A multicultural approach. *Internet Research*, *20*(2), 188–209. doi:10.1108/10662241011032245

Creswell, J. W. (1994). *Research design: Qualitative and Quantitative Approaches*. Thousand Oaks: Sage.

Davis, F. D., Bagozzi, R. P., & Warshaw, P. R. (1989). User acceptance of computer technology: A comparison of two theoretical models. *Management Science*, *35*(8), 982–1003. doi:10.1287/mnsc.35.8.982

Demangeot, C., & Broderick, A. J. (2007). Conceptualising consumer behaviour in online shopping environments. *International Journal of Retail & Distribution Management*, *35*(11), 878–894. doi:10.1108/09590550710828218

Denzin, N. K. (1970). *The Research Act: A theoretical Introduction to Sociological Methods*. New York: McGraw-Hill.

Denzin, N. K., & Lincoln, Y. S. (2000). *The Handbook of Qualitative Research* (2nd ed.). Thousand Oaks: Sage.

Dholakia, R. (1999). Going shopping: Key determinants of shopping behaviors and motivations. *International Journal of Retail & Distribution Management*, *27*(4), 140–165.

Dholakia, R. R., & Dholakia, N. (2004). Mobility and markets: Emerging outlines of m-commerce. *Journal of Business Research*, *57*(12), 1391–1396. doi:10.1016/S0148-2963(02)00427-7

Dibb, S., & Carrigan, M. (2013). Social marketing transformed. *European Journal of Marketing*, *47*(9), 1376–1398. doi:10.1108/EJM-05-2013-0248

Dittmar, H., & Drury, J. (2000). Self-image - is it in the bag? A qualitative comparison between 'ordinary' and 'excessive' consumers. *Journal of Economic Psychology*, *21*(2), 109–142. doi:10.1016/S0167-4870(99)00039-2

Eagly, A. H., & Chaiken, S. (1993). *The psychology of Attitudes*. Fort Worth, TX: HarcourtBrace Jovanovich.

Frolick, M. N., & Chen, L. (2004). Assessing M-Commerce Opportunities. *Information Systems Management*, *21*(2), 53–61. doi:10.1201/1078/44118.21.2.20040301/80422.8

Gamble, J., & Gilmore, A. (2013). A new era of consumer marketing? An application of co-creational marketing in the music industry. *European Journal of Marketing*, *47*(11/12), 1859–1888. doi:10.1108/EJM-10-2011-0584

George, J. F. (2002). Influence on the intent to make internet purchase. *Internet Research: Electronic networking Applications and Policy,* 12(2), 165-180.

Goldsmiths, R. E., & Bridges, E. (2000). E-tailing vs retailing: Using attitude to predict online buying behaviour. *Quarterly Journal of Electronic Commerce*, *1*(3), 245–253.

Gomm, R. (2004). *Social research methodology: a critical introduction.* Basingtoke: Palgrave Macmillan.

Guest, G., MacQueen, K. M., & Namey, E. E. (2012). *Applied Thematic Analysis*. Los Angeles: Sage publications Inc. doi:10.4135/9781483384436

Hartas, D. (2010). *Educational Research and Inquiry: Qualitative and Quantitative Approach*. London: Continuum International Publishing Group.

Hill, W. W., Beatty, S. E., & Walsh, G. (2013). A segmentation of adolescent users and shoppers. *Journal of Services Marketing*, *27*(5), 347–360. doi:10.1108/JSM-10-2011-0157

Hoffman, D. L., & Novak, T. P. (1996). Marketing in hype media computer-mediated environments: Conceptual foundations. *Journal of Marketing*, *60*(3), 50–68. doi:10.2307/1251841

Holmes, A., Byrne, A., & Rowley, J. (2014). Mobile shopping behaviour: Insights into attitudes, shopping process involvement and location. *International Journal of Retail & Distribution Management*, *42*(1), 25–39. doi:10.1108/IJRDM-10-2012-0096

Hsu, C. L., Lin, J. C. C., & Chiang, S. H. (2013). The effects of blogger recommendations on customers' online shopping intentions. *Internet Research*, *33*(1), 69–88. doi:10.1108/10662241311295782

Hu, W.-C., Yeh, J.-H., Fu, L., & Yang, H.-J. (2006). Handheld Computing and Programming for Mobile Commerce. *International Journal of Web Information Systems*, *2*(3/4), 164–175. doi:10.1108/17440080780000297

Hung, M. C., Yang, S. T., & Hsieh, T. C. (2012). An examination of the determinants of mobile shopping continuance. *International Journal of Electronic Business Management*, *10*(1), 29–37.

In-store Mobile Offers Still Finding Their Feet in the UK. (2013). *Emarketer.com*. Retrieved from http://www.emarketer.com/Article/Retail-Drives-UK-B2C-Ecommerce-Sales-Higher/1010106

Kelle, U. (2006). Combining qualitative and quantitative methods in research practice: Purpose and advantages. *Qualitative Research in Psychology*, *3*(4), 203–311.

Khalifa, M., & Shen, K. N. (2008). Explaining the adoption of transactional B2C mobile commerce. *Journal of Enterprise Information Management*, *21*(2), 110–124.

Kim, H., Kim, J. L. Y., Chae, M., & Choi, Y. (2002). *An empirical study of the use context and usability problems in mobile internet*. Hawaii: IEEE Computer Society.

Kim, H.-W., Xu, Y., & Gupta, S. (2012). Which is more important in Internet Shopping, perceived price or trust? *Electronic Commerce Research and Applications*, *11*(3), 241–252. doi:10.1016/j.elerap.2011.06.003

Kourouthanassis, P. E., & Giaglis, G. M. (2012). Introduction to the Special Issue Mobile Commerce: The Past, Present and Future of Mobile Commerce Research. *International Journal of Electronic Commerce*, *16*(4), 5–17. doi:10.2753/JEC1086-4415160401

Kumar, A., & Mukherjee, A. (2013). Shop while you talk: Determinants of purchase intentions through a mobile device. Mobile Marketing Association, 8(1), 23-37.

Kumar, S., & Zhan, C. (2003). Mobile communications: Evolution and the impact on business operations. *Technovation*, *23*(6), 515–520. doi:10.1016/S0166-4972(02)00120-7

Lamarre, A., Galarneau, S., & Boeck, H. (2012). Mobile Marketing and consumer Behaviour Current Research Trend. *International Journal of Latest Trends in Computing*, *3*(1), 1–9.

Li, M., Dong, Z. Y., & Chen, X. (2012). Factors influencing consumptions experience of mobile commerce. *Internet Research*, *22*(2), 120–141. doi:10.1108/10662241211214539

Lu, J., Yu, C.-S., Liu, C., & Yao, J. E. (2003). Technology acceptance model for wireless internet. *Internet Research: Electronic Networking Applications and Policy*, *13*(3), 206–222. doi:10.1108/10662240310478222

Markovic, M. (2006). Analysing Qualitative Data: Health care experiences of Women with Gynecological Cancer. *Field Methods*, *18*(4), 413–429. doi:10.1177/1525822X06293126

Marks, D., & Yardley, L. (2004). *Research methods for clinical and health psychology*. London: Sage.

Mathieson, K. (1991). Predicting user intentions: Comparing the technology acceptance model with the theory of planned behaviour. *Information Systems Research*, *2*(3), 173–191. doi:10.1287/isre.2.3.173

Miles, C. (2013). Persuasion, marketing, communication, and the metaphor of magic. *European Journal of Marketing*, *47*(11/12), 2002–2019. doi:10.1108/EJM-11-2011-0632

Mobile Cocooning: How Growing Reliance on Smart Devices is Influencing Consumer Behaviour. (2013). *Emarketer.com*. Retrieved from http://www.euromonitor.com/mobile-cocooning-how-growing-reliance-on-smart-devices-is-influencing-consumer-behaviour/report

Mobile's Share of UK Digital Retail Sales Doubles. (2013). *Emarketer.com*. Retrieved from http://www.emarketer.com/Article/Mobiles-Share-of-UK-Digital-Retail-Sales-Doubles/1010204

Moth, D. (2013). Mobile commerce now accounts for 23% of online sales: report. *Econsultancy.com*. Retrieved from https://econsultancy.com/blog/63338-mobile-commerce-now-accounts-for-23-of-online-sales-report

Nysveen, H., & Pedersen, P. E. (2005). Search mode and purchase intention in online shopping behaviour. *International Journal of Internet Marketing and Advertising*, *2*(4), 288–306. doi:10.1504/IJIMA.2005.008103

Online retail sales highest in two years as positive economic sign continues. (2013). Capgemini. Retrieved from http://www.uk.capgemini.com/online-retail-sales-highest-in-two-years-as-positive-economic-signs-continue

Ozuem, W., Borrelli, M., & Lancaster, G. (2015). Leveraging the co-evolution of offline and online video games: An empirical study. *Journal of Strategic Marketing*, 1–23. doi:10.1080/0965254X.2015.1076883

Ozuem, W., Howell, K. E., & Lancaster, G. (2008). Communicating in the new interactive marketspace. *European Journal of Marketing*, *42*(9/10), 1059–1083. doi:10.1108/03090560810891145

Ozuem, W., & Lancaster, G. (2014). Recovery strategies in on-line service failure. In A. Ghorbani (Ed.), *Marketing in the cyber era: strategies and emerging trends* (pp. 143–159). Hershey, PA: IGI Global.

Ozuem, W., O'Keeffe, A., & Lancaster, G. (2015). Leadership Marketing: An exploratory study. *Journal of Strategic Marketing*, 1–25. doi:10.1080/0965254X.2014.1001867

Ozuem, W., Thomas, T., & Lancaster, G. (2015). The Influence of customer loyalty on small island economies: An empirical and exploratory study. *Journal of Strategic Marketing*, 1–23. doi:10.1080/0965254X.2015.1011205

Parasuraman, A. (2000). Technology readiness index (TRI) a mutiple-item scale to measure readiness to embrace new technology. *Journal of Service Research, 2*(4), 307–320. doi:10.1177/109467050024001

Park, E. J., Kim, E. Y., & Forney, J. C. (2006). A structural model of fashion-oriented impulse buying behaviour. *Journal of Fashion Marketing and Management, 10*(4), 433–446. doi:10.1108/13612020610701965

Pasqua, R., & Elkin, N. (2013). *Mobile Marketing: An hour a day*. Indiana: John Wiley & Sons Inc.

Patton, M. Q. (2002). *Qualitative Research and Evaluation Methods* (3rd ed.). London: Sage Publications Ltd.

Persaud, A., & Azhar, I. (2012). Innovative mobile marketing via smartphones: Are consumers ready? *Marketing Intelligence & Planning, 30*(4), 418–443. doi:10.1108/02634501211231883

Peter, J. P., & Olson, J. (1996). *Consumer behaviour and marketing strategy*. Chicago: Irwin.

Qu, Z., Wang, Y., Wang, S., & Zhang, Y. (2013). Implications of online social activities for e-tailer's business performance. *European Journal of Marketing, 47*(8), 1190–1212. doi:10.1108/03090561311324282

Retail Drives UK B2C Ecommerce Sales Higher. (2013). *Emarketer.com.* Retrieved from http://www.emarketer.com/Article/Retail-Drives-UK-B2C-Ecommerce-Sales-Higher/1010106

Robson, C. (2011). *Real World Research: A Resource for Users of Social Research Methods in Applied settings* (3rd ed.). Cornwall: John Wiley & Sons Ltd.

Rogers, E. M. (1995). *Diffusion of Innovations*. New York: The Free Press.

San-Martin, S., & Lopez-Catalan, B. (2013). How can a mobile vendor get satisfied customers? *Industrial Management & Data Systems, 113*(2), 156–170. doi:10.1108/02635571311303514

San-Martin, S., Lopez-Catalan, B., & Ramon-Jeronimo, M. A. (2012). Factors determining firms' perceived performance of mobile commerce. *Industrial Management & Data Systems, 112*(6), 946–963. doi:10.1108/02635571211238536

Saunders, M., Lewis, P., & Thornhill, A. (2009). *Research methods for business students* (5th ed.). Harlow: Pearson Education Ltd.

Scarpi, D. (2006). Fashion stores between fun and usefulness. *Journal of Fashion Marketing and Management, 10*(1), 7–24. doi:10.1108/13612020610651097

Schiffman, L. G., & Kanuk, L. L. (2010). *Consumer Behaviour* (10th ed.). New Jersey: Pearson Education Inc.

Schuster, L., Drennan, J., & Lings, I. N. (2013). Consumer acceptance of m-wellbeing services: A social marketing perspective. *European Journal of Marketing, 47*(9), 1439–1457. doi:10.1108/EJM-10-2011-0556

Seock, Y. K., & Norton, M. (2007). Attitude towards internet websites, online information search and channel choices for purchasing. *Journal of Fashion Marketing and Management, 11*(4), 571–586. doi:10.1108/13612020710824616

Shim, S., Estlick, M. A., Lotz, S. L., & Warrington, P. (2001). An online prepurchase intentions model: The role of intention to search. *Journal of Retailing, 77*(2), 307–416.

Skeldon, P. (2011). *M-commerce: Boost your business with the power of mobile commerce*. Richmond: Crimson Publishing.

Solomon, M. R. (2009). *Consumer Behaviour: Buying, Having and Being* (8th ed.). New Jersey: Pearson Education Inc.

Spaid, B. I., & Flint, D. J. (2014). The meaning of shopping experiences augmented by mobile internet devices. *Journal of Marketing Theory and Practice*, *22*(1), 73–89.

Swilley, E., & Hofacker, C. F. (2006). Defining mobile commerce in a marketing context. *International Journal of Mobile Marketing*, *1*(2), 18–23.

Swilley, E., Hofacker, C. F., & Lamont, B. T. (2012). The Evolution of E-Commerce to M-Commerce: Pressures, Firm Capabilities and Competitive Advantage in Strategic Decision Making. *International journal of e-business research,* 8(1), 1-16.

Three of Four UK Mobile Users Own Smartphones by 2016. (2013). *Emarketer.com.* Retrieved from http://www.emarketer.com/Article/Three-of-Four-UK-Mobile-Users-Own-Smartphones-by-2016/1009614

Ting, D. H., Ling, S. F., Patanmacia, T. S., Low, C. G., & Ker, G. C. (2011). Dependency on smartphone and the impact on purchase behavior. *Young Consumers*, *12*(3), 193–203.

UK Online Clothing Shoppers Still Favor the PC. (2013). *Emarketer.com.* Retrieved from http://www.emarketer.com/Article/UK-Online-Clothing-Shoppers-Still-Favor-PC/1010274

Van Slyke, C., Belanger, F., & Comunale, C. L. (2004). Factors influencing the adoption of web-based shopping: The impact of trust. *ACM SIGMIS Database*, *35*(2), 32–49.

Venkatesh, V., Brown, S., & Bala, H. (2013). Bridging the Qualitative- Quantitative Divide: Guidelines for Conducting Mixed-Methodology Research in Information Systems. *Management Information Systems Quarterly*, *37*(1), 21–54.

Wang, M.-S., Chen, C. C., Chan, S.-C., & Yang, Y.-H. (2007). Effects of online shopping attitudes, subjective norms and control beliefs on online shopping intentions: A test of the theory of planned behaviour. *International Journal of Management*, *24*(2), 296–302.

Wang, Y., & Liao, Y. (2007). The conceptualization and measurement of m-commerce user satisfaction. *Computers in Human Behavior*, *23*(1), 381–398.

Wheeler, E. (2013). The emergence of M-Commerce and Geofencing. *Bloomberg.com.* Retrieved from http://www.bloomberg.com/video/from-e-commerce-to-m-commerce-bW0SIsCkRJaTiNTJ89zAnQ.html

Wong, S. H. R. (2012). Which platform do our users prefer: Website or mobile app? *RSR. Reference Services Review*, *40*(1), 113–115.

Yang, K., & Kim, H.-Y. (2012). Mobile shopping motivation: An application of multiple discriminant analysis. *International Journal of Retail & Distribution Management*, *40*(10), 778–789.

Yang, S. C. (2012). Mobile applications and 4G wireless networks: A framework for analysis. *Campus-Wide Information Systems*, *29*(5), 344–357.

Yeh, Y. S., & Li, Y.-M. (2009). Building trust in e-commerce: Contributions from quality and satisfaction. *Online Information Review*, *33*(6), 1066–1086.

Zhou, T. (2011). Examining the critical success factors of mobile site adoption. *Online Information Review*, *35*(4), 636–652.

Zhou, T. (2013). Understanding continuance usage of mobile site. *Industrial Management & Data Systems*, *113*(9), 1286–1299.

KEY TERMS AND DEFINITIONS

Mobile Commerce: Mobile commerce encompasses the buying and selling of goods and services online through wireless handheld devices usually smartphones or tablets.

Mobile Environment: The mobile environment is the move of the online environment towards the mobile platform to enable smartphones users to access and interact with online contents on the go.

Mobile Shopping: Mobile shopping refers to the action of using a smartphone to browse, compare or to shop for products and services online.

Mobile Storefront: Mobile storefront is when a business establishes an online presence by displaying their products and services on a mobile platform usually via a mobile website. It replaces the conventional storefront whereby consumers can browse for products' information and make purchases through their smartphones without having to physically go to a store.

Online Consumption: Online consumption refers to the action of using up resources, products and services in online environments or technology-enabled marketing platforms.

Showrooming: Showrooming is the action of using a smartphone to browse and compare goods and services online while being in a conventional store before considering a purchase.

Smartphones: A smartphone is an intelligent multi-functional handset capable of the traditional function of a mobile phone device (i.e making phone calls), along with highly advanced features such as internet access, high resolution cameras, GPS system and an operating system capable of running downloaded apps.

Chapter 9
The Roles of Social Media Marketing and Brand Management in Global Marketing

Kijpokin Kasemsap
Suan Sunandha Rajabhat University, Thailand

ABSTRACT

This chapter explains the roles of social media marketing and brand management in global marketing, thus describing the theoretical and practical concept of social media marketing, the overview of brand management, the significance of social media marketing, and the application of social media-related brand management in global marketing. The creation of social media marketing and brand management is necessary for modern organizations that seek to serve suppliers and customers, increase business performance, enhance competitiveness, and gain routine success in global business. Thus, it is vital for modern organizations to acknowledge their social media marketing and brand management utilization, establish a strategic plan to consistently evaluate their effective promotions, and immediately respond to social media marketing and brand management needs of customers. The chapter argues that applying social media marketing and brand management in global marketing has the potential to enhance organizational performance and achieve strategic goals in the digital age.

INTRODUCTION

The development of social media has facilitated communication of consumer to each other in global marketing (Abzari, Ghassemi, & Vosta, 2014). Due to the rising level of global competition as well as a fast-growing number of innovations organizations are forced to find new ways to attract, gain, and sustain loyal customers in order to stay competitive (Lorenzo-Romero, Constantinides, & Brünink, 2014). Social media has changed the power structures in the global marketplace (Constantinides, 2014). Social media is used as a platform to access potential customer and implement marketing campaign (Rawat

DOI: 10.4018/978-1-4666-9776-8.ch009

& Divekar, 2014). Social media offers opportunities to stimulate and to measure social interrelations among customers in global marketing (Chen, Chen, & Xiao, 2013).

The evolution of social media is challenging the ways that marketing academics and practitioners effectively conceptualize and manage the brands in modern organizations (Davis, Piven, & Breazeale, 2014). Brands have become instruments of status signaling, that satisfy consumer prevalence of a need for status (Han, Nunes, & Dreze, 2010). Understanding how brands should operate on social media is very important for contemporary marketing researchers and managers (Habibi, Laroche, & Richard, 2014). Brands have the power to communicate valuable information and can be used and perceived in many different ways by consumers (Catalin & Andreea, 2014). Concerning the advantages of social networks, brand management is practically able to implement brand communities with less time and financial effort (Zaglia, 2013).

The strength of this chapter is on the thorough literature consolidation of social media marketing and brand management. The extant literature of social media marketing and brand management provides a contribution to practitioners and researchers by describing a comprehensive view of the functional application of social media marketing and brand management to appeal to different segments of social media marketing and brand management in order to maximize the business impact of social media marketing and brand management in global marketing.

BACKGROUND

The use of social media has immensely grown over the past decade, with technological and Internet innovations like Facebook, Twitter, and YouTube achieving massive adoption in a few years. Social media is increasingly important in daily life and is an especially important social interaction mechanism for young people (Luchman, Bergstrom, & Krulikowski, 2014). Social media includes countless sites with very different functions or uses that fulfill different personal needs (Brandtzeg & Heim, 2009). Social media is defined as the perspective of technological innovations in terms of both hardware and software that facilitate inexpensive content creation, interaction, and interoperability by online users (Berthon, Pitt, Plangger, & Shapiro, 2012).

Labrecque et al. (2013) stated that the predictions of growing consumer power in the digital age are fueled by the rise of the Internet and reignited by social media With the proliferation in Web 2.0 technologies, many marketing educators are experimenting with new teaching and learning tools (i.e., Facebook, Twitter, YouTube, and Second Life) (Lowe, D'Alessandro, Winzar, Laffey, & Collier, 2013). A typical classification of social media includes collaborative projects (i.e. Wikipedia), blogs, user-generated content communities (i.e., Flickr, YouTube, and Youku/Toduo), virtual game worlds (i.e. EverQuest), and virtual social worlds (i.e. Second Life) (Kaplan & Haenlein, 2010).

SOCIAL MEDIA MARKETING AND BRAND MANAGEMENT IN GLOBAL MARKETING

This section describes the theoretical and practical concept of social media marketing, the overview of brand management, the significance of social media marketing, and the application of social media-related brand management in global marketing.

Concept of Social Media Marketing

The advent of the 21st century is marked by the introduction of a new generation of media in consumer's everyday life (Giannakis-Bompolis & Boutsouki, 2014). There is a growing use of the Internet for social interactions with a business purpose (Bauer, Grether, & Leach, 2002; Boyd & Spekman, 2004; Kandampully, 2003). Most popular social networks are Facebook, Youtube, and Twitter (Vásquez & Escamilla, 2014). Leeflang et al. (2014) stated that Internet usage continues to explode across the world with digital becoming an increasingly important source of competitive advantage. Kietzmann et al. (2011) indicated that Facebook is the most popular social media application, which offers many capabilities associated with social media toward sharing texts, pictures, videos, and blogging with other people.

Social media marketing is most prominent and plays a huge role in the fundamental level (Wen, 2013). Social media marketing establishes presence, increases brand exposure, and expands market size, thus opening up a room of opportunities for businesses to create and maintain their brand and consumer relationships (Wen, 2013). Social media facilitates marketing of products and services (Kaplan & Haenlein, 2010). Businesses utilize social influence marketing and advertisement programs to identify customers and communicate their philosophy (Jang, Sim, Lee, & Kwon, 2013). Businesses run social media pages to build familiarity and advertise their goods through steady communication with their customers (Mangold & Faulds, 2009). Consumers from diverse backgrounds are communicating more and exchanging abundant amount of information through social media (Piccoli, 2010).

Social media provides a forum for word-of-mouth (WOM) as an effective marketing strategy (Jang et al., 2013). WOM takes place within a variety of online environments, allowing information exchanges to be immediately available to a multitude of people and institutions (Hennig-Thurau, Gwinner, Walsh, & Gremler, 2004). Twitter has received increasing attention as a unique communication tool that facilitates electronic word-of-mouth (eWOM) (Kim, Sung, & Kang, 2014). The eWOM has materialized as a phenomenon of critical interest to global marketeers (Williams, Crittenden, Keo, & McCarty, 2012).

Social media provides a sharing platform with its tools, such as social networks, forums, e-mails, and blogosphere (Uzunoglu & Kip, 2014). The shared views, experiences and opinions of online users are eWOM (Cheung & Thadani, 2012; Filieri & McLeay, 2014) which are more trusted compared to other corporate messages, since these messages directly communicate what are perceived to be consumers' own experiences (Wu & Wang, 2011). Trusov et al. (2009) provided a precise perception of the relation between WOM and traditional media.

Social media is a suitable option to access and collect information from other consumers (Godes & Mayzlin, 2004). Bruyn and Lilien (2008) studied the effect of consumer communications to each other in the process of decision-making in the context of viral marketing. Social media provides an unparalleled platform for consumers to publicize their personal evaluations of purchased products and to facilitate WOM communication (Chen, Fay, & Wang, 2011). Computers are regarded as commonplace and the Internet serves as the main method for communication for the younger generations (Piccoli, 2010).

Social media represents a new trend, as it changes the rules of communication with customers by allowing firms to engage in timely and direct end-consumer contact at a relatively low cost and higher efficiency levels than with more traditional communication tools (Martini, Massa, & Testa, 2014). Social media shortens the distance between the company and users, thereby strengthening user involvement and engagement in the innovation process (Piller, Vossen, & Ihl, 2012).

Social media is a new way through which people are able to search and share information (Akar, 2011). Social media tools play an important role in transforming the characteristics of front-end innovation, changing its boundaries and knowledge distances, and making it more efficient and effective in certain circumstances (Afuah & Tucci, 2012; Bogers, Afuah, & Bastian, 2010; Jespersen, 2010). There is a distinction made between customer-initiated social media (i.e., reviews and blogs) and organization-initiated social media (i.e. brand communities) (de Vries, Gensler, & Leeflang, 2012).

The growing power of bloggers to influence their connected network has emerged as a new communication venue for brands (Uzunoglu & Kip, 2014). Marketing communications should be considered as an important determinant of brand equity (Simon & Sullivan, 1993). Marketing communications have a positive influence on brand equity, brand loyalty, brand awareness and brand value (Yoo, Donthu, & Lee, 2000). Positive and negative communications of user through social media as well as traditional advertising of the companies can influence consumers' attitudes toward a particular brand (Abzari et al., 2014).

Overview of Brand Management

Brands tend to influence more the high-involvement resolutions because they provide a valid method of identification (Catalin & Andreea, 2014). An economic perspective focuses on the brand's value (Motameni & Shahrokhi, 1998; Yoo et al., 2000), while a strategic perspective emphasizes understanding consumer-based market segments to improve overall marketing campaigns. The growing small and medium-sized enterprises (SMEs) have adopted market and brand orientations to a greater extent than have the stable or declining ones (Reijonen, Laukkanen, Komppula, & Tuominen, 2012).

Establishing a good brand relationship is necessary for brand management in emerging markets (Kasemsap, 2015a). Individuals who identify with a particular brand experience a positive psychological result in the form of improved self-esteem and are more likely to act favorably toward effective brand management (Donavan, Janda, & Suh, 2006). Brand primarily serves as the basis for the interactions and the benefits generated in high-quality customer-to-customer (C2C) interactions (Muniz & O'Guinn, 2001). Implementing the branding practices will increase the likelihood that consumers perceive the brand in question as fair, leading to an increase in brand loyalty and positive WOM (Chen, Nguyen, & Klaus, 2013).

As business-to-business (B2B) companies face large customer purchase volumes, it is essential for long-term B2B brand success to maintain and manage brand loyalty (Rauyruen, Miller, & Barrett, 2007). An increasing emphasis on branding activities is evident in B2B markets (Kalafatis, Riley, & Singh, 2014). B2B branding has received increasing attention from researchers in the last few years (Cassia & Magno, 2012). Continuous pioneering with a new brand leads to greater brand preferences when technological uncertainty is high (Chang & Park, 2013).

Theoretical and practical terms related to brand management in global marketing (i.e., brand equity, brand awareness, brand associations, perceived brand quality, brand loyalty, brand community, brand alliances, brand trust, and brand identification) are described.

Brand Equity

Most conceptualizations of brand equity come from a consumer's perspective considering consumers often drive a brand's success (Aitken & Campelo, 2011). Brand equity is a resource that influences the consumer's response to a branded organization's efforts to differentiate one brand from other (Lee & Griffith, 2012). Lieven et al. (2014) stated that brand personality has been suggested as an important source of consumer-based brand equity.

Consumer-based brand equity usually is evaluated for four dimensions: brand awareness, brand associations, perceived brand quality, and brand loyalty (Buil, Martinez, & de Chernatony, 2013). Brand managers utilize existing consumer-based brand equity scales (Yoo et al., 2000) in order to conduct holistic research into all of the brand equity elements via deployment to myriad stakeholder groups, thus transforming knowledge into marketing improvements.

Brand Awareness

Brand awareness indicates how well consumers recall the brand (Buil et al., 2013) and is a component of overall brand knowledge (Keller, 1993). Different studies stress the importance of advertising in brand awareness (Aaker, 1996; Buil et al., 2013; Kirmani & Wright, 1989), as well as the importance of brand awareness in the perception of brand quality (Aaker, 1996; Buil et al., 2013; Keller & Lehmann, 2003). Adolescents appear to have an awareness of the role of branding and advertising to form the brand consumption attitudes (Isaksen & Roper, 2012).

Brand Associations

Brand associations are the cognitive connections that a person has with the brand (Zavattaro, Daspit, & Adams, 2015). The most important step in creating and delivering a superior value to customers is by adding brand associations that create value beyond the intrinsic characteristics of a product. One of the most important characteristics of a brand is the self-expressive function (Keller, 2008).

Perceived Brand Quality

While consumers draw conclusions about the quality of a brand based on their evaluation of its intrinsic attributes (Shaharudin, Mansor, & Elias, 2011; Sule Alonso, Paquin, & Levy Mangin, 2002), its packaging (Lavenka, 1991) or its price (Cronley, Posavac, Meyer, Kardes, & Kellaris, 2005; Kardes, Cronley, Kellaris, & Posavac, 2004), one of the main elements concerning perception of a product's quality is brand name (Dawar & Parker, 1994). Perceived brand quality relates to a person's view of one brand or product versus another (Zavattaro et al., 2015).

Perceived value forms as a result of the consumer's experiences purchasing and consuming a brand (Cronin, Brady, & Hult, 2000). One of the key issues influencing the perceived quality of a brand is its brand awareness (Aaker, 1996; Buil et al., 2013; Keller & Lehman, 2003). Consumers assign high quality to prestigious brands (Rubio, Oubina, & Villasenor, 2014). Brands appreciate greater credibility and brand value for the consumer (Erdem & Swait, 1998; Erdem, Swait, & Louviere, 2002).

Brand Loyalty

Brand loyalty has developed into diverse areas from brand preference to brand community (Yoo & Bai, 2013). Brand loyalty is a long-term commitment to the brand, which is based on awareness, perceived brand quality, and brand associations (Zavattaro et al., 2015). Brand loyalty is a pre-economic target value and indicator of corporate as well as brand community success (Algesheimer, Dholakia, & Herrmann, 2005; Chaudhuri & Holbrook, 2001).

Customer value, customer satisfaction, and brand loyalty have the strengths to mediate positive effect on customer relationship management (CRM) performance (Kasemsap, 2015b). Attaching consumers to a brand is a cornerstone of relationship marketing as brand attachment effectively increases brand loyalty (Schmalz & Orth, 2012).

Brand Community

The concept of a brand community stems from the sociological notion of what constitutes an early community (Muniz & O'Guinn, 2001). Brand communities represent valuable marketing, innovation management, and CRM tools (Zaglia, 2013). Brand community consists of socially networked groups of individuals with mutual interests, who inhabit a common area in order to cope with routine tasks (Muniz & O'Guinn, 2001). Brand communities exist in the real world as well as in the virtual space of the Internet, utilizing chat, e-mail, and discussion forums as the virtual forms of communication and interaction media (Andersen, 2005; Muniz & O'Guinn, 2001; Schau, Muñiz, & Arnould, 2009).

Brand community can exist everywhere (Thompson & Sinha, 2008). Social interactions between brand community members effectively influence customers' relationship with brand (McAlexander, Schouten, & Koenig, 2002). The social formations offer many advantages (Brown, Kozinets, & Sherry, 2003), and serve as a tool to build strong relationships with customers (Algesheimer et al., 2005). The consumer engagement process comprises a range of sub-processes reflecting consumers' interactive experience within online brand communities among community participants (Brodie, Ilic, Juric, & Hollebeek, 2013). Businesses need to engage consumers in brand communications, which consumers perceive to be non-commercially driven within brand communities (Brodie et al., 2013).

The interactions between customers are characterized by mutual trust, which is of pivotal importance to B2B brand communities (Bruhn, Schnebelen, & Schäfer, 2014). Brand communities are characterized by the three constituent components: consciousness of kind; rituals and traditions; and a sense of moral responsibility (Muniz & O'Guinn, 2001). The opportunities that interactions in B2B brand communities offer companies as well as brand community members have been recognized by B2B firms, but are still an underexplored field of marketing research (Bruhn et al., 2014).

Brand Alliances

Brand alliances in the B2B domain are becoming popular (Kalafatis et al., 2014). Brand alliances benefit the business partners through reputation endorsement and access to resources and competencies, such as distribution and technology (Bengtsson & Servais, 2005; Cooke & Ryan, 2000; Erevelles, Horton, & Fukawa, 2008). Norris (1993) presented a case study of Intel, highlighting the benefits of its component branding strategy of Intel-inside. Bucklin and Sengupta (1993) indicated that successful brand alliances involve partners with equal power and managerial resources. Dahlstrom and Dato-on (2004) stated that both asymmetry and complementarity of company assets are the positive determinants of a firm's decision to co-brand.

Ghosh and John (2009) utilized the transaction cost economics to describe that original equipment manufacturers are more likely to use branded components when the brand name of components provides them with opportunities for important market differentiation. Gammoh and Voss (2013) explained that a company's propensity to engage in brand alliance activities is contingent on the extent and quality of related past experiences, managerial competence, and attitude toward brand alliance.

In the business-to-customer (B2C) brand alliance studies, context effects are recognized in the form of brand leveraging (Ghosh & John, 2009), resource allocation (Heide & John, 1990), feedback effect (Park, Jun, & Shocker, 1996), quality signals (Rao, Qu, & Ruekert, 1999), and are revealed to affect preference for familiar stimuli (Cooke & Mellers, 1998; Simonson & Tversky, 1992) and to help interpretation of unfamiliar stimuli (Sen, 1998; Wright & Rip, 1980).

Brand Trust

Brand trust is viewed as the essence of brand's value to consumers (Berry, 2000). Trust in the online environment is characterized by greater complexity (i.e., trust in the website versus trust in technology), need for structural assurances of security and privacy, and the lack of tangible brand cues (Pentina, Zhang, & Basmanova, 2013). Trust in the online community members should motivate the sharing of information (Ridings, Gefen, & Arinze, 2002). Previous studies on eWOM communication have indicated that people are more likely to pass along information when the source of it is perceived as trustworthy (Brown, Broderick, & Lee, 2007; Chiu, Hsieh, Kao, & Lee, 2007; Yeh & Choi, 2011).

An essential catalyst for establishing and maintaining long-term relationships is brand trust, defined as confidence in the brand's consistency, reliability, and honesty (Wang & Emurian, 2005). Trust facilitates customer satisfaction with a brand (Chaudhuri & Holbrook, 2001; Morgan & Hunt, 1994), thus determining customer intentions to maintain the relationship with other associated brands (Stewart, 2003). Morgan and Hunt (1994) identified trust and the resulting commitment as key mediators of successful buyer–seller relationships that lead to cooperation and reduce conflict and uncertainty in the B2B context. In the end-consumer domain, brand trust represents a manifestation of relationship quality (Crosby, Evans, & Cowles, 1990).

Previous studies found positive effects of trust on the likelihood of continuing the buyer–seller relationships (Crosby et al., 1990), long-term orientation of the trustor (Ganesan, 1994), and consumer intent to make a purchase (Doney & Cannon, 1997). Trust is critical for attracting traffic and completing successful online interactions, as well as maintaining online communities and virtual groups (Coppola, Hiltz, & Rotter, 2004).

Brand Identification

A brand's identity should be a clear and concise narrative that defines the brand's values and ideals (Reed & Botts, 2014). Brand relationships have traditionally been theorized as simulating interpersonal relationships, which are reflected in self-identity or self-expansion theory (Huang & Mitchell, 2014). The idea of brand identification suggests that community members identified with a brand tend to engage in pro-brand activities through their affiliation with the community and interactions with peer members (Algesheimer et al., 2005; Bagozzi & Dholakia, 2006; Carlson, Suter, & Brown, 2008).

Significance of Social Media Marketing in Global Marketing

The introduction of social media platforms has contributed to the development of a new era of customer empowerment enabling customers to interconnect worldwide and easily share and exchange personal, social, and scientific knowledge in the global marketplace (Lee, Olson, & Trimi, 2012). By having more information and alternatives where to buy a product or service, customers take a more influential role in the process of value creation forcing organizations to step away from their traditional organization-centric view to a more customer-centric view in order to be competitive (Prahalad & Ramaswamy, 2004; Sashi, 2012).

Social media tools that include social networking features are being utilized to allow users both inside and outside the organization to easily communicate and collaboratively design, manage, and launch new products and services (Marion, Barczak, & Hultink, 2014). The unique aspects of social media and its immense popularity have revolutionized marketing practices (Hanna, Rohm, & Crittenden, 2011) and consumer behavior from information acquisition to post purchase behavior (Mangold & Faulds, 2009; Powers, Advincula, Austin, & Graiko, 2012). The networked and social nature of social media allows like-minded people to gather in groups and subgroups with a specific common interest (Mangold & Faulds, 2009).

Social media makes customers more sophisticated and help them develop new marketing tactics in searching, evaluating, choosing and buying goods and services (Albors, Ramos, & Hervas, 2008). While social media and its marketing applications proliferate, developing distinctive strategies for effectively targeting and engaging users on each platform remains a work-in-progress (Pentina et al., 2013). Companies considering the Internet as a strategic communication tool have recognized the power of influential members of social media platform who frequently share their brand experiences on a regular basis (Uzunoglu & Kip, 2014).

Firms need to be connected to their technological business environment through social media because interacting with external sources of knowledge can improve their capabilities about industry benchmark and competitive advantage (Kasemsap, 2014a). The determinants of social media participation take a utility-based approach and investigate gratifications obtained (Park, Kee, & Valenzuela, 2009), perceived value, satisfaction, and habit (Barnes & Bohringer, 2011). Other studies utilize the technology acceptance model (TAM) (Pookulangara & Koesler, 2011) and the theory of planned behavior (Pelling & White, 2009) to explain participation and loyalty of social media users.

Social networking sites (SNSs) (i.e., Facebook, Twitter, Flickr, and MySpace) lead to increased brand reputation, a more open, transparent culture, and a more effective and efficient way of working (Kasemsap, 2014b). Among other online platforms, communities in SNSs have received much attention in recent years for their ability to accelerate eWOM for brands (Kim et al., 2014). SNSs serve as a powerful and ideal venue for eWOM, a marketing venue where consumers disseminate and seek out information from their established social networks through interpersonal interactions online (Boyd & Ellison, 2007; Vollmer & Precourt, 2008). Brand-related information and opinions that are shared among personal contacts in SNSs may be perceived as more credible and trustworthy than other forms of eWOM communication (Chu & Kim, 2011).

Social media has intensified instant personal interaction between the brand and its community (Nambisan & Watt, 2011). The ease of participating in online social communities removes both the physical and temporal barriers, increasing the likelihood of participation from consumers who may not have been able or inclined to do so previously (Davis et al., 2014). Social media access has moved beyond the fixed physical space of the computer screen to the ubiquitous mobile channel of the smartphone: instant consumption and interactivity is fueled by brand-related content from other connected channels of communication (i.e., radio and television) (Davis & Sajtos, 2008).

Companies utilize interpersonal messages in their Twitter posts to develop close relationships with their consumers (Kwon & Sung, 2011; Lin & Pena, 2011). Consumers generate brand-related tweets on Twitter to express their sentiments, complaints, and opinions concerning brands (Jansen, Zhang, Sobel, &

Chowdhury, 2009). Twitter is used as a social channel to promote communication and to help companies develop mutually beneficial relationships with consumers (Jansen et al., 2009). In SNS environments where consumers display themselves publicly to others, a consumer engaging in eWOM shapes and expresses brand identity (Taylor, Strutton, & Thompson, 2012).

Social media offers opportunities to create the brand trust and reach a large audience at a low cost (Leeflang et al., 2014). The effects of social networks on customer adoption have been recognized in multiple studies (Nitzan & Libai, 2011; Rahmandad & Sterman, 2008; Yoganarasimhan, 2012). Marketing users disseminate and share information via Twitter (Zhang, Jansen, & Chowdhury, 2011). Twitter has been found to offer relational benefits by allowing users to build perceptions of one another and establish common ground for future conversations, and by promoting a feeling of connectedness with one another (Zhao & Rosson, 2009), thus enhancing the power of eWOM. Marketing behaviors occurring on SNSs are considered customer investments in response to marketers' social media efforts (Hoffman & Fodor, 2010).

Application of Social Media-Related Brand Management in Global Marketing

Managing a brand in the 21st century is more complex than ever before due to the advancement in technology (Abratt & Kleyn, 2012; Balmer, 2012; Kaufmann, Vrontis, Czinkota, & Alvin Hadiono, 2012), faster innovation, growing competition, complexity and more demanding consumers (Kaufmann et al., 2012; Klaus, 2013; Maklan & Klaus, 2011). As a business moves toward globalization, shifting from marketing (product brand) to corporate branding becomes essential (Balmer, 2012; Hatch & Schultz, 2009; Kapferer, 2012).

Brands represent the instances of socially constructed identities, created by marketers and consumers (Muniz & O'Guinn, 2001), that reflect characteristics associated with the typical user, as well as with advertising images and associations (Poddar, Donthu, & Wei, 2009). Brands with high-intensity placements should encourage consumers to view with friends (Coker, Altobello, & Balasubramanian, 2013). The development of Internet technology enables service firms to obtain a high capability for brand information transmission as well as relative customer feedback data collection (Shirahada & Kosaka, 2012). Consumers possess almost unlimited opportunities to engage with brands (Christodoulides, Jevons, & Bonhomme, 2012; Helm & Jones, 2010). The results of the brand access practically mandate the changes in branding strategies toward engagement platforms (Naylor, Lamberton, & West, 2012; Verhoef, Reinartz, & Krafft, 2010).

A brand's Facebook page is a marketing communication tool (Brodmerkel & Carah, 2013). González-Benito et al. (2014) stated that retailers have worked to advance store-brand strategies, leading to greater success and higher congruence with the retailer's positioning. Consumers reflect their personalities by the brands they use, but the relationship between brand choice and symbolic dimensions (i.e., extraversion, agreeableness, neuroticism, and openness to experience) is much stronger than the relationship with functional dimensions (i.e. conscientiousness) (Huang, Mitchell, & Rosenaum-Elliott, 2012).

Corporate brand value is the brand promise of an organization which provides sameness and credibility about its organization to all its stakeholders (Balmer, 2012; Balmer & Gray, 2003; Knox, 2004). Consumers demand a great deal of information from a company before committing to a buying decision, thus leading a company to show greater transparency and integrity when delivering its services (Rowley, 2004). Brand consumption value is an uninterrupted social process of stakeholder interactions

(Merz, He, & Vargo, 2009). Brand consumption becomes the social co-production of shared meanings (de Chernatony & Segal-Horn, 2001; Tuominen, 2007).

Brands are perceived as social entities by consumers (Pentina et al., 2013). Consumers prefer brands with personality traits that are congruent with the social situations (Sung, Choi, & Lin, 2012). Consumers achieve the business meaning through their relationships with brands (Bagozzi, Bergami, Marzocchi, & Morandin, 2012; Brown et al., 2003; McAlexander et al., 2002). Aaker (1997) stated that consumers attribute human personality qualities to brands. Fournier (1998) identified the stages of interpersonal relationships toward developing brands.

The emergence of the Internet has a positive impact on building corporate brand (Kapferer, 2012; Shultz & de Chernatony, 2002; Stuart & Jones, 2004). Klaus et al. (2013) stated that the Internet is important as it influences the way businesses operate and people's lifestyles. Learning how to manage corporate brand through how consumers experience corporate websites will develop a long-term brand relationship (Klaus, 2013; Klaus & Maklan, 2013; Morgan-Thomas & Veloutsou, 2013).

The Internet is recognized as a useful way of delivering brand value to all stakeholders (Argyriou, Kitchen, & Melewar, 2006). The Internet responds to the dynamic environment, thus allowing greater involvement of brand experience and brand engagement in the brand communities through business interaction (de Chernatony & Christodoulides, 2004; Klaus et al., 2013; Stuart & Jones, 2004). By communicating corporate brand value on the Internet, the brand value is concise and defined (Balmer & Gray, 2003).

Marketing attempts have been made to describe online brand personalities (Okazaki, 2006), electronic brand personalities (Park, Choi, & Kim, 2005), and website personalities (Chen & Rodgers, 2006) using both pre-existing personality scales and lists of adjectives derived from qualitative research. The symbolic meaning of brands reflects attributes associated with groups using the brand and is used to enhance self-concept through brand adoption (McCracken, 1988). Brands recognize the power of bloggers, to directly influence their connected network by making suggestions, which result in the use of products (Flynn, Goldsmith, & Eastman, 1996).

Regarding social media marketing, online corporate brand is an important source of positioning and differentiation within the industry to effectively reach customers (de Chernatony, 2002; Melewar & Navalekar, 2002; Parasuraman, Zeithaml, & Malhotra, 2005). Corporate brand requires a dynamic interface between the actions of organization and the interpretation of customers (Balmer & Gray, 2003; de Chernatony, 2002).

Brand communities in social media have positive effects on the brand (Laroche, Habibi, Richard, & Sankaranarayanan, 2012). Choosing the appropriate brand community type, cultivating consumers' interaction, and staying tuned to social engagement are critical factors to gain brand outcomes (Zaglia, 2013). B2B brand communities offer great opportunities to promote profitability, brand loyalty, and economic success (Bruhn et al., 2014). B2B brand communities are able to meet the demands of customers in providing them with brand-related information through their interactions with other experienced customers (Andersen, 2005). Brand communities lead to improved value creation processes and service quality (Ellahi & Bokhari, 2013).

Marketers have been able to bring brands and their messages to the awareness of consumers, possessing full control over the message, but social media has changed this (Väisänen, 2015). Managers are creating their brands together with consumers by sharing experiences and opinions. Because this new type of branding process is dependent on consumers' opinions and perceptions of the brand image, managers need to listen what their customers are saying and engage consumers into the co-creation of their brands. This two-way communication has changed the ideology of branding online completely (Corstjens & Umblijs, 2012; Singh & Sonnenburg, 2012).

The biggest brands on Facebook within the area are media groups, closely followed by e-commerce and airlines (Prakash, 2012). Brand managers should begin thinking of social media as a massive data repository, a digitized focus group with millions of unpaid participants. This repository consists of huge amounts of unstructured data, which hold valuable insights about customer shopping habits, lifestyle interests, product use cases, even aspirations (Hamedi, 2014). Brand managers need to direct the channel toward achieving a specific marketing and brand goal, such as increasing brand awareness, brand loyalty and engagement, intelligence gathering, and new product development (Mount & Martinez, 2014).

Social media marketing can improve global business in terms of increased brand recognition, better brand loyalty, higher brand authority, more opportunities to convert, higher conversion rates, increased inbound traffic, decreased marketing costs, better search engine rankings, and improved customer insights (Forbes, 2014). Kraak and Story (2015) conducted a systematic review of five electronic databases (2000–2014) to identify experimental studies that measured how food companies' mascots and entertainment companies' media characters influence up to 12 diet-related cognitive, behavioral and health outcomes for children under 12 years. Eleven studies met the inclusion criteria. Studies used 21 media characters, but no brand mascots. Results suggest that cartoon media character branding can positively increase children's fruit intake compared with no character branding (Kraak & Story, 2015).

Ashley and Tuten (2015) studied the creative strategies in social media marketing are shared by a sample of top brands. The results reveal that social media channels and creative strategies in social media marketing are applied. Despite the value of creative approaches in social media marketing, most branded social content can be categorized as functional (Ashley & Tuten, 2015). Singh et al. (2012) documented global social media usage patterns based on a large-scale survey of 4,630 social media users around the world. Singh et al. (2012)'s empirical study provides the insights into how users in the European Union, United States, and BRIC (Brazil, Russia, India, and China) regions use social media for business and personal use. Social media is increasingly becoming the vehicle for the voice of people and consumers worldwide. From a business perspective, companies are actively leveraging social media to create brand communities, gain consumer insights, and enhance brand awareness in global marketing (Singh et al., 2012).

FUTURE RESEARCH DIRECTIONS

The strength of this chapter is on the thorough literature consolidation of social media marketing and brand management. The extant literature of social media marketing and brand management provides a contribution to practitioners and researchers by describing a comprehensive view of the functional application of social media marketing and brand management to appeal to different segments of social media marketing and brand management in order to maximize the business impact of social media marketing and brand management. The classification of the extant literature in the domains of social media marketing and brand management will provide the potential opportunities for future research. Future research direction should broaden the perspectives in the implementation of social media marketing and brand management to be utilized in the knowledge-based organizations.

Practitioners and researchers should recognize the applicability of a more multidisciplinary approach toward research activities in implementing social media marketing and brand management in terms of knowledge management-related variables (i.e., knowledge-sharing behavior, knowledge creation, organizational learning, learning orientation, and motivation to learn). It will be useful to bring additional disciplines together (i.e., strategic management, marketing, finance, and human resources) to support a more holistic examination of social media marketing and brand management in order to combine or transfer existing theories and approaches to inquiry in this area. The investigation of linkages among social media marketing, brand management, and business intelligence would seem to be workable for future research efforts.

CONCLUSION

This chapter explained the roles of social media marketing and brand management in global marketing, thus describing the theoretical and practical concept of social media marketing, the overview of brand management, the significance of social media marketing, and the application of social media-related brand management in global marketing. Social media marketing provides organizations with a way to connect with their customers. Social media marketing programs usually center on efforts to create content that attracts attention and encourages readers to share it across their social networks toward competition in the global marketplace. However, organizations must protect their business information as well as closely watch comments and concerns on the social media they use.

Companies on a global scale should recognize that one of the most promising paths to long-term longevity, a prosperous organization, and healthy profits is to create and manage strong brands for their products and services. Brand management is the analysis and planning on how that brand is perceived in the market. Knowing how consumers perceive a brand is essential to effective marketing. Executives and brand managers need to understand how customers perceive and select brands in specific product categories and market segments. Developing a good relationship with the target market is essential for brand management in global marketing.

The utilization of social media marketing effectively promotes and develops brand management in global marketing. The strategic uses of social media marketing and brand management can offer a greater competitive advantage in modern organizations. The creation of social media marketing and brand management is necessary for modern organizations that seek to serve suppliers and customers, increase business performance, enhance competitiveness, and gain routine success in global business. Thus, it is vital for modern organizations to acknowledge their social media marketing and brand management utilization, establish a strategic plan to consistently evaluate their effective promotions, and immediately respond to social media marketing and brand management needs of customers.

REFERENCES

Aaker, D. A. (1996). Measuring brand equity across products and markets. *California Management Review*, *38*(3), 102–120. doi:10.2307/41165845

Aaker, J. L. (1997). Dimensions of brand personality. *JMR, Journal of Marketing Research*, *34*(3), 347–356. doi:10.2307/3151897

Abratt, R., & Kleyn, N. (2012). Corporate identity, corporate branding and corporate reputations: Reconciliation and integration. *European Journal of Marketing*, *46*(7–8), 1048–1063.

Abzari, M., Ghassemi, R. A., & Vosta, L. N. (2014). Analysing the effect of social media on brand attitude and purchase intention: The case of Iran Khodro company. *Procedia: Social and Behavioral Sciences*, *143*, 822–826. doi:10.1016/j.sbspro.2014.07.483

Afuah, A., & Tucci, C. L. (2012). Crowdsourcing as a solution to distant search. *Academy of Management Review*, *37*(3), 355–375. doi:10.5465/amr.2010.0146

Aitken, R., & Campelo, A. (2011). The four Rs of place branding. *Journal of Marketing Management*, *27*(9–10), 913–933. doi:10.1080/0267257X.2011.560718

Akar, E., & Topçu, B. (2011). An examination of the factors influencing consumers' attitudes toward social media marketing. *Journal of Internet Commerce*, *10*(1), 35–67. doi:10.1080/15332861.2011.558456

Albors, J., Ramos, J. C., & Hervas, J. L. (2008). New learning network paradigm: Communities of objectives, crowdsourcing, wikis and open source. *International Journal of Information Management*, *28*(3), 194–202. doi:10.1016/j.ijinfomgt.2007.09.006

Algesheimer, R., Dholakia, U. M., & Herrmann, A. (2005). The social influence of brand community: Evidence from European car clubs. *Journal of Marketing*, *69*(3), 19–34. doi:10.1509/jmkg.69.3.19.66363

Andersen, P. H. (2005). Relationship marketing and brand involvement of professionals through web-enhanced brand communities: The case of Coloplast. *Industrial Marketing Management*, *34*(1), 39–51. doi:10.1016/j.indmarman.2004.07.002

Argyriou, E., Kitchen, P., & Melewar, T. C. (2006). The relationship between corporate websites and brand equity. *International Journal of Market Research*, *48*(5), 575–599.

Ashley, C., & Tuten, T. (2015). Creative strategies in social media marketing: An exploratory study of branded social content and consumer engagement. *Psychology and Marketing*, *32*(1), 15–27. doi:10.1002/mar.20761

Bagozzi, R. P., Bergami, M., Marzocchi, G. L., & Morandin, G. (2012). Customer-organization relationships: Development and test of a theory of extended identities. *Journal of Applied Psychology*, *97*(1), 63–76. doi:10.1037/a0024533 PMID:21766998

Balmer, J. M. T. (2012). Corporate brand management imperatives: Custodianship, credibility, and calibration. *California Management Review*, *54*(3), 6–33. doi:10.1525/cmr.2012.54.3.6

Balmer, J. M. T., & Gray, E. R. (2003). Corporate brands: What are they? What of them? *European Journal of Marketing*, *37*(7-8), 972–997. doi:10.1108/03090560310477627

Barnes, S. J., & Bohringer, M. (2011). Modeling use continuance behavior in microblogging services: The case of Twitter. *Journal of Computer Information Systems*, *51*(4), 1–10.

Bauer, H. H., Grether, M., & Leach, M. (2002). Building customer relations over the Internet. *Industrial Marketing Management*, *31*(2), 155–163. doi:10.1016/S0019-8501(01)00186-9

Bengtsson, A., & Servais, P. (2005). Co-branding on industrial markets. *Industrial Marketing Management, 34*(7), 706–713. doi:10.1016/j.indmarman.2005.06.004

Berry, L. L. (2000). Cultivating service brand equity. *Journal of the Academy of Marketing Science, 28*(1), 128–137. doi:10.1177/0092070300281012

Berthon, P. R., Pitt, L. F., Plangger, K., & Shapiro, D. (2012). Marketing meets Web 2.0, social media, and creative consumers: Implications for international marketing strategy. *Business Horizons, 55*(3), 261–271. doi:10.1016/j.bushor.2012.01.007

Bogers, M., Afuah, A., & Bastian, B. (2010). Users as innovators: A review, critique, and future research directions. *Journal of Management, 36*(4), 857–875. doi:10.1177/0149206309353944

Boyd, D. M., & Ellison, N. B. (2007). Social network sites: Definition, history, and scholarship. *Journal of Computer-Mediated Communication, 13*(1), 210–230. doi:10.1111/j.1083-6101.2007.00393.x

Boyd, D. E., & Spekman, R. E. (2004). Internet usage within B2B relationships and its impact on value creation: A conceptual model and research propositions. *Journal of Business-To-Business Marketing, 11*(1–2), 9–34. doi:10.1300/J033v11n01_03

Brandtzaeg, P. B., & Heim, J. (2011). A typology of social networking sites users. *International Journal of Web Based Communities, 7*(1), 28–51. doi:10.1504/IJWBC.2011.038124

Brodie, R. J., Ilic, A., Juric, B., & Hollebeek, L. (2013). Consumer engagement in a virtual brand community: An exploratory analysis. *Journal of Business Research, 66*(1), 105–114. doi:10.1016/j.jbusres.2011.07.029

Brodmerkel, S., & Carah, N. (2013). Alcohol brands on Facebook: The challenges of regulating brands on social media. *Journal of Public Affairs, 13*(3), 272–281. doi:10.1002/pa.1466

Brown, J., Broderick, A. J., & Lee, N. (2007). Word-of-mouth communication within online communities: Conceptualizing the online social network. *Journal of Interactive Marketing, 21*(3), 2–19. doi:10.1002/dir.20082

Brown, S., Kozinets, R. V., & Sherry, J. F. Jr. (2003). Teaching old brands new tricks: Retro branding and the revival of brand meaning. *Journal of Marketing, 67*(3), 19–33. doi:10.1509/jmkg.67.3.19.18657

Bruhn, M., Schnebelen, S., & Schäfer, D. (2014). Antecedents and consequences of the quality of e-customer-to-customer interactions in B2B brand communities. *Industrial Marketing Management, 43*(1), 164–176. doi:10.1016/j.indmarman.2013.08.008

Bruyn, A., & Lilien, G. L. (2008). A multi–stage model of word of mouth through viral marketing. *International Journal of Research in Marketing, 25*(3), 143–225. doi:10.1016/j.ijresmar.2008.03.004

Bucklin, L. P., & Sengupta, S. (1993). Organizing successful co-marketing alliances. *Journal of Marketing, 57*(2), 32–46. doi:10.2307/1252025

Buil, I., Martinez, E., & de Chernatony, L. (2013). The influence of brand equity on consumer responses. *Journal of Consumer Marketing, 30*(1), 62–74. doi:10.1108/07363761311290849

Carlson, B. D., Suter, T. A., & Brown, T. J. (2008). Social versus psychological brand community: The role of psychological sense of brand community. *Journal of Business Research*, *61*(4), 284–291. doi:10.1016/j.jbusres.2007.06.022

Cassia, F., & Magno, F. (2012). Business-to-business branding: A review and assessment of the impact of non-attribute-based brand beliefs on buyer's attitudinal loyalty. *Canadian Journal of Administrative Sciences*, *29*(3), 242–254. doi:10.1002/cjas.235

Catalin, M. C., & Andreea, P. (2014). Brands as a mean of consumer self-expression and desired personal lifestyle. *Procedia: Social and Behavioral Sciences*, *109*, 103–107. doi:10.1016/j.sbspro.2013.12.427

Chang, D. R., & Park, S. B. (2013). The effects of brand strategy and technological uncertainty on pioneering advantage in the multigenerational product market. *Journal of Product Innovation Management*, *30*(1), 82–95. doi:10.1111/j.1540-5885.2012.00988.x

Chaudhuri, A., & Holbrook, M. B. (2001). The chain of effects from brand trust and brand affect to brand performance: The role of brand loyalty. *Journal of Marketing*, *65*(2), 81–93. doi:10.1509/jmkg.65.2.81.18255

Chen, X., Chen, Y., & Xiao, P. (2013). The impact of sampling and network topology on the estimation of social intercorrelations. *JMR, Journal of Marketing Research*, *50*(1), 95–110. doi:10.1509/jmr.12.0026

Chen, Y., Fay, S., & Wang, Q. (2011). The role of marketing in social media: How online consumer reviews evolve. *Journal of Interactive Marketing*, *25*(2), 85–94. doi:10.1016/j.intmar.2011.01.003

Chen, J., Nguyen, B., & Klaus, P. (2013). Public affairs in China: Exploring the role of brand fairness perceptions in the case of Mercedes-Benz. *Journal of Public Affairs*, *13*(4), 403–414. doi:10.1002/pa.1493

Chen, Q., & Rodgers, S. (2006). Development of an instrument to measure web site personality. *Journal of Interactive Advertising*, *7*(1), 47–64. doi:10.1080/15252019.2006.10722124

Cheung, C. M. K., & Thadani, D. R. (2012). The impact of electronic word-of-mouth communication: A literature analysis and integrative model. *Decision Support Systems*, *54*(1), 461–470. doi:10.1016/j.dss.2012.06.008

Chiu, H. C., Hsieh, Y. C., Kao, Y. H., & Lee, M. (2007). The determinants of e-mail receivers' disseminating behaviors on the Internet. *Journal of Advertising Research*, *47*(4), 524–534. doi:10.2501/S0021849907070547

Christodoulides, G., Jevons, C., & Bonhomme, J. (2012). Memo to marketers: Quantitative evidence for change. How user-generated content really affects brands. *Journal of Advertising Research*, *52*(1), 53–64. doi:10.2501/JAR-52-1-053-064

Chu, S. C., & Kim, Y. (2011). Determinants of consumer engagement in electronic word-of-mouth (eWOM) in social networking sites. *International Journal of Advertising*, *30*(1), 47–75. doi:10.2501/IJA-30-1-047-075

Coker, K. K., Altobello, S. A., & Balasubramanian, S. K. (2013). Message exposure with friends: The role of social context on attitudes toward prominently placed brands. *Journal of Consumer Behaviour*, *12*(2), 102–111. doi:10.1002/cb.1423

Constantinides, E. (2014). Foundations of social media marketing. *Procedia: Social and Behavioral Sciences*, *148*, 40–57. doi:10.1016/j.sbspro.2014.07.016

Cooke, A. D., & Mellers, B. A. (1998). Multiattribute judgment: Attribute spacing influences single attributes. *Journal of Experimental Psychology. Human Perception and Performance*, *24*(2), 496–504. doi:10.1037/0096-1523.24.2.496

Cooke, S., & Ryan, P. (2000). Brand alliances: From reputation endorsement to collaboration on core competencies. *Irish Marketing Review*, *13*(2), 36–41.

Coppola, N. W., Hiltz, S. R., & Rotter, N. G. (2004). Building trust in virtual teams. *IEEE Transactions on Professional Communication*, *47*(2), 95–104. doi:10.1109/TPC.2004.828203

Corstjens, M., & Umblijs, A. (2013). The power of evil: The damage of negative social media strongly outweigh positive contributions. *Journal of Advertising Research*, *52*(4), 433–449. doi:10.2501/JAR-52-4-433-449

Cronin, J. J. Jr, Brady, M. K., & Hult, G. T. M. (2000). Assessing the effects of quality, value, and customer satisfaction on customer behavioral intentions in service environments. *Journal of Retailing*, *76*(2), 193–218. doi:10.1016/S0022-4359(00)00028-2

Cronley, M. L., Posavac, S. S., Meyer, T., Kardes, F. R., & Kellaris, J. J. (2005). A selective hypothesis testing perspective on price-quality inference and inference-based choice. *Journal of Consumer Psychology*, *15*(2), 159–169. doi:10.1207/s15327663jcp1502_8

Crosby, L. A., Evans, K. R., & Cowles, D. (1990). Relationship quality in services selling: An interpersonal influence perspective. *Journal of Marketing*, *54*(3), 68–81. doi:10.2307/1251817

Dahlstrom, R., & Dato-on, M. (2004). Business-to-business antecedents to retail co-branding. *Journal of Business-To-Business Marketing*, *11*(3), 1–22. doi:10.1300/J033v11n03_01

Davis, R., Piven, I., & Breazeale, M. (2014). Conceptualizing the brand in social media community: The five sources model. *Journal of Retailing and Consumer Services*, *21*(4), 468–481. doi:10.1016/j.jretconser.2014.03.006

Davis, R., & Sajtos, L. (2008). Measuring consumer interactivity in response to campaigns coupling mobile and television media. *Journal of Advertising Research*, *48*(3), 375–391. doi:10.2501/S0021849908080409

Dawar, N. J., & Parker, P. (1994). Marketing universals: Consumers' use of brand name, price, physical appearance and retailer reputation as signals of product quality. *Journal of Marketing*, *58*(2), 81–95. doi:10.2307/1252271

de Chernatony, L. (2002). Would a brand smell any sweeter by a corporate name? *Corporate Reputation Review*, *5*(2-3), 114–132. doi:10.1057/palgrave.crr.1540169

de Chernatony, L., & Christodoulides, G. (2004). Taking the brand promise online: Challenges and opportunities. *Interactive Marketing*, *5*(3), 238–251. doi:10.1057/palgrave.im.4340241

de Chernatony, L., & Segal-Horn, S. (2001). Building on services' characteristics to develop successful service brand. *Journal of Marketing Management*, *17*(7–8), 645–669. doi:10.1362/026725701323366773 de Vries, L., Gensler, S., & Leeflang, P. S. H. (2012). Popularity of brand posts on brand fan pages: An investigation of the effects of social media marketing. *Journal of Interactive Marketing*, *26*(2), 83–91. doi:10.1016/j.intmar.2012.01.003

Donavan, T. D., Janda, S., & Suh, J. (2006). Environmental influences in corporate brand identification and outcomes. *Journal of Brand Management*, *14*(1–2), 125–136. doi:10.1057/palgrave.bm.2550057

Doney, P. M., & Cannon, J. P. (1997). An examination of the nature of trust in buyer–seller relationships. *Journal of Marketing*, *61*(2), 35–51. doi:10.2307/1251829

Ellahi, A., & Bokhari, R. H. (2013). Key quality factors affecting users' perception of social networking websites. *Journal of Retailing and Consumer Services*, *20*(1), 120–129. doi:10.1016/j.jretconser.2012.10.013

Erdem, T., & Swait, J. (1998). Brand equity as a signaling phenomenon. *Journal of Consumer Psychology*, *7*(2), 131–157. doi:10.1207/s15327663jcp0702_02

Erdem, T., Swait, J., & Louviere, J. (2002). The impact of brand credibility on consumer price sensitivity. *International Journal of Research in Marketing*, *19*(1), 1–19. doi:10.1016/S0167-8116(01)00048-9

Erevelles, S., Horton, V., & Fukawa, N. (2008). Understanding B2C brand alliances between manufacturers and suppliers. *Marketing Management Journal*, *18*(2), 32–46.

Filieri, R., & McLeay, F. (2014). E-WOM and accommodation: An analysis of the factors that influence travelers' adoption of information from online reviews. *Journal of Travel Research*, *53*(1), 44–57. doi:10.1177/0047287513481274

Flynn, L. R., Goldsmith, R. E., & Eastman, J. K. (1996). Opinion leaders and opinion seekers: Two new measurement scales. *Journal of the Academy of Marketing Science*, *24*(2), 137–147. doi:10.1177/0092070396242004

Forbes. (2014). *The top 10 benefits of social media marketing*. Retrieved from http://www.forbes.com/sites/jaysondemers/2014/08/11/the-top-10-benefits-of-social-media-marketing/

Fournier, S. (1998). Consumer and their brands: Developing relationship theory in consumer research. *Journal of Consumer Research*, *24*(4), 343–353. doi:10.1086/209515

Gammoh, B. S., & Voss, K. E. (2013). Alliance competence: The moderating role of valence of alliance experience. *European Journal of Marketing*, *47*(5/6), 964–986. doi:10.1108/03090561311307029

Ganesan, S. (1994). Determinants of long–term orientation in buyer–seller relationships. *Journal of Marketing*, *58*(2), 1–19. doi:10.2307/1252265

Ghosh, M., & John, G. (2009). When should original equipment manufacturers use branded component contracts with suppliers? *JMR, Journal of Marketing Research*, *46*(5), 597–611. doi:10.1509/jmkr.46.5.597

Giannakis-Bompolis, C., & Boutsouki, C. (2014). Customer relationship management in the era of social web and social customer: An investigation of customer engagement in the Greek retail banking sector. *Procedia: Social and Behavioral Sciences*, *148*, 67–78. doi:10.1016/j.sbspro.2014.07.018

Godes, D., & Mayzlin, D. (2004). Using online conversations to study word-of-mouth communication. *Marketing Science*, *23*(4), 545–560. doi:10.1287/mksc.1040.0071

González-Benito, Ó., Martos-Partal, M., & Fustinoni-Venturini, M. (2014). Retailers' price positioning and the motivational profiling of store-brand shoppers: The case of Spain. *Psychology and Marketing*, *31*(2), 115–125. doi:10.1002/mar.20680

Habibi, M. R., Laroche, M., & Richard, M. (2014). Brand communities based in social media: How unique are they? Evidence from two exemplary brand communities. *International Journal of Information Management*, *34*(2), 123–132. doi:10.1016/j.ijinfomgt.2013.11.010

Hamedi, J. (2014, April 25). How social media will transform brand management. *Direct Marketing News*. Retrieved from http://www.dmnews.com/how-social-media-will-transform-brand-management/article/343917/

Hamzah, Z. L., Syed Alwi, S. F., & Othman, M. N. (2014). Designing corporate brand experience in an online context: A qualitative insight. *Journal of Business Research*, *67*(11), 2299–2310. doi:10.1016/j.jbusres.2014.06.018

Han, Y. J., Nunes, J. C., & Dreze, X. (2010). Signaling status with luxury goods: The role of brand prominence. *Journal of Marketing*, *74*(4), 15–30. doi:10.1509/jmkg.74.4.15

Hanna, R., Rohm, A., & Crittenden, V. L. (2011). We're all connected: The power of the social media ecosystem. *Business Horizons*, *54*(3), 265–273. doi:10.1016/j.bushor.2011.01.007

Hatch, M. J., & Schultz, M. (2009). Of bricks and brands: From corporate to enterprise branding. *Organizational Dynamics*, *38*(2), 117–130. doi:10.1016/j.orgdyn.2009.02.008

Heide, J. B., & John, G. (1990). Alliances in industrial purchasing: The determinants of joint action in buyer–supplier relationships. *JMR, Journal of Marketing Research*, *27*(1), 24–36. doi:10.2307/3172548

Helm, C., & Jones, R. (2010). Brand governance: The new agenda in brand management. *Journal of Brand Management*, *17*(8), 545–547. doi:10.1057/bm.2010.20

Hennig-Thurau, T., Gwinner, K. P., Walsh, G., & Gremler, D. D. (2004). Electronic word-of-mouth via consumer-opinion platforms: What motivates consumers to articulate themselves on the Internet? *Journal of Interactive Marketing*, *18*(1), 38–52. doi:10.1002/dir.10073

Hoffman, D. L., & Fodor, M. (2010). Can you measure the ROI of your social media marketing? *MIT Sloan Management Review*, *52*(1), 41–50.

Huang, H. H., & Mitchell, V. W. (2014). The role of imagination and brand personification in brand relationships. *Psychology and Marketing*, *31*(1), 38–47. doi:10.1002/mar.20673

Huang, H. H., Mitchell, V. W., & Rosenaum-Elliott, R. (2012). Are consumer and brand personalities the same? *Psychology and Marketing*, *29*(5), 334–349. doi:10.1002/mar.20525

Isaksen, K. J., & Roper, S. (2012). The commodification of self-esteem: Branding and British teenagers. *Psychology and Marketing*, *29*(3), 117–135. doi:10.1002/mar.20509

Jang, H. J., Sim, J., Lee, Y., & Kwon, O. (2013). Deep sentiment analysis: Mining the causality between personality-value-attitude for analyzing business ads in social media. *Expert Systems with Applications*, *40*(18), 7492–7503. doi:10.1016/j.eswa.2013.06.069

Jansen, B. J., Zhang, M., Sobel, K., & Chowdury, A. (2009). Twitter power: Tweets as electronic word of mouth. *Journal of the American Society for Information Science and Technology*, *60*(11), 2169–2188. doi:10.1002/asi.21149

Jespersen, K. R. (2010). User-involvement and open innovation: The case of decision-maker openness. *International Journal of Innovation Management*, *14*(3), 471–489. doi:10.1142/S136391961000274X

Kalafatis, S. P., Riley, D., & Singh, J. (2014). Context effects in the evaluation of business-to-business brand alliances. *Industrial Marketing Management*, *43*(2), 322–334. doi:10.1016/j.indmarman.2013.09.002

Kandampully, J. (2003). B2B relationships and networks in the Internet age. *Management Decision*, *41*(5), 443–451. doi:10.1108/00251740310479296

Kapferer, J. N. (2012). *The new strategic brand management: Advanced insights and strategic thinking*. London, UK: Kogan Page.

Kaplan, A. M., & Haenlein, M. (2010). Users of the world, unite! The challenges and opportunities of social media. *Business Horizons*, *53*(1), 59–68. doi:10.1016/j.bushor.2009.09.003

Kardes, F. R., Cronley, M. L., Kellaris, J. J., & Posavac, S. S. (2004). The role of selective information processing in price-quality inference. *The Journal of Consumer Research*, *31*(2), 368–374. doi:10.1086/422115

Kasemsap, K. (2014a). The role of social media in the knowledge-based organizations. In I. Lee (Ed.), *Integrating social media into business practice, applications, management, and models* (pp. 254–275). Hershey, PA: IGI Global. doi:10.4018/978-1-4666-6182-0.ch013

Kasemsap, K. (2014b). The role of social networking in global business environments. In P. Smith & T. Cockburn (Eds.), *Impact of emerging digital technologies on leadership in global business* (pp. 183–201). Hershey, PA: IGI Global. doi:10.4018/978-1-4666-6134-9.ch010

Kasemsap, K. (2015a). The role of brand management in emerging markets. In *Marketing and consumer behavior: Concepts, methodologies, tools, and applications* (pp. 2006–2023). Hershey, PA: IGI Global. doi:10.4018/978-1-4666-7357-1.ch099

Kasemsap, K. (2015b). The role of brand loyalty on CRM performance: An innovative framework for smart manufacturing. In *Marketing and consumer behavior: Concepts, methodologies, tools, and applications* (pp. 413–446). Hershey, PA: IGI Global. doi:10.4018/978-1-4666-7357-1.ch019

Kaufmann, H. R., Vrontis, D., Czinkota, M., & Alvin Hadiono, A. (2012). Corporate branding and transformational leadership in turbulent times. *Journal of Product and Brand Management*, *21*(3), 192–204. doi:10.1108/10610421211228810

Keller, K. L. (1993). Conceptualizing, evaluating, and managing customer–based brand equity. *Journal of Marketing*, *57*(1), 1–22. doi:10.2307/1252054

Keller, K. L. (2008). *Strategic brand management: Building, measuring and managing brand equity*. Upper Saddle River, NJ: Prentice Hall.

Keller, K. L., & Lehmann, D. R. (2003). How do brands create value? *Marketing Management, 12*(3), 27–31.

Kietzmann, J. H., Hermkens, K., McCarthy, I. P., & Silvestre, B. S. (2011). Social media? Get serious! Understanding the functional building blocks of social media. *Business Horizons, 54*(3), 241–251. doi:10.1016/j.bushor.2011.01.005

Kim, E., Sung, Y., & Kang, H. (2014). Brand followers' retweeting behavior on Twitter: How brand relationships influence brand electronic word-of-mouth. *Computers in Human Behavior, 37*, 18–25. doi:10.1016/j.chb.2014.04.020

Kirmani, A., & Wright, P. (1989). Money talks: Perceived advertising expense and expected product quality. *Journal of Consumer Research, 16*(3), 344–353. doi:10.1086/209220

Klaus, Ph. (2013). The Case of Amazon.com: Towards a conceptual framework of online customer service experience (OCSE) using emerging consensus technique (ECT). *Journal of Services Marketing, 27*(6), 443–457. doi:10.1108/JSM-02-2012-0030

Klaus, P., Gorgoglione, M., Buonamassa, D., Panniello, U., & Nguyen, B. (2013). Are you providing the "right" experiences? The case of Banca Popolare di Bari. *International Journal of Bank Marketing, 31*(7), 506–528. doi:10.1108/IJBM-02-2013-0019

Klaus, Ph., & Maklan, S. (2013). Towards a better measure of customer experience. *International Journal of Market Research, 55*(2), 227–246. doi:10.2501/IJMR-2013-021

Knox, S. (2004). Positioning and branding your organization. *Journal of Product and Brand Management, 13*(2), 105–115. doi:10.1108/10610420410529735

Kraak, V. I., & Story, M. (2015). Influence of food companies' brand mascots and entertainment companies' cartoon media characters on children's diet and health: A systematic review and research needs. *Obesity Reviews, 16*(2), 107–126. doi:10.1111/obr.12237 PMID:25516352

Kwon, E. S., & Sung, Y. (2011). Follow me! Global marketers' Twitter use. *Journal of Interactive Advertising, 12*(1), 4–16. doi:10.1080/15252019.2011.10722187

Labrecque, L. I., vor dem Esche, J., Mathwick, C., Novak, T. P., & Hofacker, C. F. (2013). Consumer power: Evolution in the digital age. *Journal of Interactive Marketing, 27*(4), 257–269. doi:10.1016/j.intmar.2013.09.002

Laroche, M., Habibi, M. R., Richard, M. O., & Sankaranarayanan, R. (2012). The effects of social media based brand communities on brand community markers, value creation practices, brand trust and brand loyalty. *Computers in Human Behavior, 28*(5), 1755–1767. doi:10.1016/j.chb.2012.04.016

Lavenka, N. M. (1991). Measurement of consumers' perceptions of product quality, brand name, and packaging: Candy bar comparisons by magnitude estimation. *Marketing Research, 3*(2), 38–46.

Lee, H., & Griffith, D. (2012). Transferring corporate brand image to local markets: Governance decisions for market entry and global branding. *Advances in International Marketing*, *23*(1), 39–65. doi:10.1108/S1474-7979(2012)0000023006

Lee, S. M., Olson, D. L., & Trimi, S. (2012). Co-innovation: Convergenomics, collaboration, and co-creation for organizational values. *Management Decision*, *50*(5), 817–831. doi:10.1108/00251741211227528

Leeflang, P. S. H., Verhoef, P. C., Dahlstrom, P., & Freundt, T. (2014). Challenges and solutions for marketing in a digital era. *European Management Journal*, *32*(1), 1–12. doi:10.1016/j.emj.2013.12.001

Lieven, T., Grohmann, B., Herrmann, A., Landwehr, J. R., & van Tilburg, M. (2014). The effect of brand gender on brand equity. *Psychology and Marketing*, *31*(5), 371–385. doi:10.1002/mar.20701

Lin, J. S., & Pena, J. (2011). Are you following me? A content analysis of TV networks' brand communication on Twitter. *Journal of Interactive Advertising*, *12*(1), 17–29. doi:10.1080/15252019.2011.10722188

Lorenzo-Romero, C., Constantinides, E., & Brünink, L. A. (2014). Co-creation: Customer integration in social media based product and service development. *Procedia: Social and Behavioral Sciences*, *148*, 383–396. doi:10.1016/j.sbspro.2014.07.057

Lowe, B., D'Alessandro, S., Winzar, H., Laffey, D., & Collier, W. (2013). The use of Web 2.0 technologies in marketing classes: Key drivers of student acceptance. *Journal of Consumer Behaviour*, *12*(5), 412–422. doi:10.1002/cb.1444

Luchman, J. N., Bergstrom, J., & Krulikowski, C. (2014). A motives framework of social media website use: A survey of young Americans. *Computers in Human Behavior*, *38*, 136–141. doi:10.1016/j.chb.2014.05.016

Maklan, S., & Klaus, Ph. (2011). Customer experience: Are we measuring the right things? *International Journal of Market Research*, *53*(6), 771–792. doi:10.2501/IJMR-53-6-771-792

Mangold, W. G., & Faulds, D. J. (2009). Social media: The new hybrid element of the promotion mix. *Business Horizons*, *52*(4), 357–365. doi:10.1016/j.bushor.2009.03.002

Marion, T. J., Barczak, G., & Hultink, E. J. (2014). Do social media tools impact the development phase? An exploratory study. *Journal of Product Innovation Management*, *31*(S1), 18–29. doi:10.1111/jpim.12189

Martini, A., Massa, S., & Testa, S. (2014). Customer co-creation projects and social media: The case of Barilla of Italy. *Business Horizons*, *57*(3), 425–434. doi:10.1016/j.bushor.2014.02.003

McAlexander, J. H., Schouten, J. W., & Koenig, H. F. (2002). Building brand community. *Journal of Marketing*, *66*(1), 38–54. doi:10.1509/jmkg.66.1.38.18451

McCracken, G. (1988). *Culture and consumption*. Bloomington, IN: Indiana University Press.

Melewar, T. C., & Navalekar, A. (2002). Leveraging corporate identity in the digital age. *Marketing Intelligence & Planning*, *20*(2), 96–103. doi:10.1108/02634500210418518

Merz, M. A., He, Y., & Vargo, S. L. (2009). The evolving brand logic: A service-dominant logic perspective. *Journal of the Academy of Marketing Science*, *37*(3), 328–344. doi:10.1007/s11747-009-0143-3

Morgan, R. M., & Hunt, S. D. (1994). The commitment-trust theory of relationship marketing. *Journal of Marketing*, *58*(3), 20–38. doi:10.2307/1252308

Morgan-Thomas, A., & Veloutsou, C. (2013). Beyond technology acceptance: Brand relationships and online brand experience. *Journal of Business Research*, *66*(1), 21–27. doi:10.1016/j.jbusres.2011.07.019

Motameni, R., & Shahrokhi, M. (1998). Brand equity valuation: A global perspective. *Journal of Product and Brand Management*, *7*(4), 275–290. doi:10.1108/10610429810229799

Mount, M., & Martinez, M. G. (2014, June 17). Rejuvenating a brand through social media. *MIT Sloan Management Review*. Retrieved from http://sloanreview.mit.edu/article/rejuvenating-a-brand-through-social-media/

Muniz, A. M. Jr, & O'Guinn, T. C. (2001). Brand community. *The Journal of Consumer Research*, *27*(4), 412–432. doi:10.1086/319618

Nambisan, P., & Watt, J. H. (2011). Managing customer experiences in online product communities. *Journal of Business Research*, *64*(8), 889–895. doi:10.1016/j.jbusres.2010.09.006

Naylor, R. W., Lamberton, C. P., & West, P. M. (2012). Beyond the like button: The impact of mere virtual presence on brand evaluations and purchase intentions in social media settings. *Journal of Marketing*, *76*(6), 105–120. doi:10.1509/jm.11.0105

Nitzan, I., & Libai, B. (2011). Social effects on customer retention. *Journal of Marketing*, *75*(6), 24–38. doi:10.1509/jm.10.0209

Norris, D. G. (1993). Intel inside: Branding a component in a business market. *Journal of Business and Industrial Marketing*, *8*(1), 14–24. doi:10.1108/08858629310027560

Okazaki, S. (2006). Excitement or sophistication? A preliminary exploration of online brand personality. *International Marketing Review*, *23*(3), 279–303. doi:10.1108/02651330610670451

Parasuraman, A., Zeithaml, V. A., & Malhotra, A. (2005). e-SERVQUAL: A multiple-item scale for assessing electronic service quality. *Journal of Service Research*, *7*(3), 213–233. doi:10.1177/1094670504271156

Park, S. E., Choi, D., & Kim, J. (2005). Visualizing e-brand personality: Exploratory studies on visual attributes and e-brand personalities in Korea. *International Journal of Human-Computer Interaction*, *19*(1), 7–34. doi:10.1207/s15327590ijhc1901_3

Park, C. W., Jun, S. Y., & Shocker, A. D. (1996). Composite branding alliances: An investigation of extension and feedback effects. *JMR, Journal of Marketing Research*, *33*(4), 453–466. doi:10.2307/3152216

Park, N., Kee, K., & Valenzuela, S. (2009). Being immersed in social networking environment: Facebook groups, uses and gratifications, and social outcomes. *CyberPsychology & Behavior*, *12*(6), 729–733. doi:10.1089/cpb.2009.0003 PMID:19619037

Pelling, E. L., & White, K. M. (2009). The theory of planned behavior applied to young people's use of social networking web sites. *CyberPsychology & Behavior*, *12*(6), 755–759. doi:10.1089/cpb.2009.0109 PMID:19788377

Pentina, I., Zhang, L., & Basmanova, O. (2013). Antecedents and consequences of trust in a social media brand: A cross-cultural study of Twitter. *Computers in Human Behavior*, *29*(4), 1546–1555. doi:10.1016/j.chb.2013.01.045

Piccoli, G. (2010). Information technology and the future of hospitality brand management. Retrieved from http://content.ebscohost.com.ezproxy.library.unlv.edu/pdf25 26/pdf/2010/

Piller, F. T., Vossen, A., & Ihl, C. (2012). From social media to social product development: The impact of social media on co-creation of innovation. *Die Unternehmung*, *66*(1), 7–27. doi:10.5771/0042-059X-2012-1-7

Poddar, A., Donthu, N., & Wei, Y. (2009). Web site customer orientations, web site quality, and purchase intentions: The role of web site personality. *Journal of Business Research*, *6*(4), 441–450. doi:10.1016/j.jbusres.2008.01.036

Pookulangara, S., & Koesler, K. (2011). Cultural influence on consumers' usage of social networks and its impact on online purchase intentions. *Journal of Retailing and Consumer Services*, *18*(4), 348–354. doi:10.1016/j.jretconser.2011.03.003

Powers, T., Advincula, D., Austin, M. S., & Graiko, S. (2012). Digital and social media in the purchase-decision process: A special report from the advertising research foundation. *Journal of Advertising Research*, *52*(4), 479–489. doi:10.2501/JAR-52-4-479-489

Prahalad, C. K., & Ramaswamy, V. (2004). Co-creation experiences: The next practice in value creation. *Journal of Interactive Marketing*, *18*(3), 5–14. doi:10.1002/dir.20015

Prakash, N. (2012, December 8). How the Middle East, North Africa are using Facebook for marketing. *Mashable*. Retrieved from http://mashable.com/2012/12/07/facebook-middle-east-africa/

Rahmandad, H., & Sterman, J. D. (2008). Heterogeneity and network structure in the dynamics of diffusion: Comparing agent-based and differential equation models. *Management Science*, *54*(5), 998–1014. doi:10.1287/mnsc.1070.0787

Rao, A. R., Qu, L., & Ruekert, R. W. (1999). Signaling unobservable product quality through a brand ally. *JMR, Journal of Marketing Research*, *36*(2), 258–268. doi:10.2307/3152097

Rauyruen, P., Miller, K. E., & Barret, N. J. (2007). Relationship quality as a predictor of B2B customer loyalty. *Journal of Business Research*, *60*(1), 21–31. doi:10.1016/j.jbusres.2005.11.006

Rawat, S., & Divekar, R. (2014). Developing a social media presence strategy for an e-commerce business. *Procedia Economics and Finance*, *11*, 626–634. doi:10.1016/S2212-5671(14)00228-7

Reed, A., & Botts, S. (2014). Building identity loyalty through social media. *Think with Google*. Retrieved from https://www.thinkwithgoogle.com/columns/building-identity-through-social-media.html

Reijonen, H., Laukkanen, T., Komppula, R., & Tuominen, S. (2012). Are growing SMEs more market-oriented and brand-oriented? *Journal of Small Business Management*, *50*(4), 699–716. doi:10.1111/j.1540-627X.2012.00372.x

Ridings, C. M., Gefen, D., & Arinze, B. (2002). Some antecedents and effects of trust in virtual communities. *The Journal of Strategic Information Systems*, *11*(3–4), 271–295. doi:10.1016/S0963-8687(02)00021-5

Rowley, J. (2004). Online branding. *Online Information Review*, *28*(2), 131–138. doi:10.1108/14684520410531637

Rubio, N., Oubina, J., & Villasenor, N. (2014). Brand awareness–Brand quality inference and consumer's risk perception in store brands of food products. *Food Quality and Preference*, *32*, 289–298. doi:10.1016/j.foodqual.2013.09.006

Sashi, C. M. (2012). Customer engagement, buyer-seller relationships, and social media. *Management Decision*, *50*(2), 253–272. doi:10.1108/00251741211203551

Schau, H. J., Muñiz, A. M. Jr, & Arnould, E. J. (2009). How brand community practices create value. *Journal of Marketing*, *73*(5), 30–51. doi:10.1509/jmkg.73.5.30

Schmalz, S., & Orth, U. R. (2012). Brand attachment and consumer emotional response to unethical firm behavior. *Psychology and Marketing*, *29*(11), 869–884. doi:10.1002/mar.20570

Sen, S. (1998). Knowledge, information mode and the attraction effect. *Journal of Consumer Research*, *25*(1), 64–77. doi:10.1086/209527

Shaharudin, M. R., Mansor, S. W., & Elias, S. J. (2011). Food quality attributes among Malaysia's fast food customer. *International Business and Management*, *2*(1), 198–208.

Shirahada, K., & Kosaka, M. (2012). Evaluation method for service branding using word-of-mouth data. *Electronics and Communications in Japan*, *95*(12), 21–28. doi:10.1002/ecj.11442

Shultz, M., & de Chernatony, L. (2002). Introduction the challenges of corporate branding. *Corporate Reputation Review*, *5*(2/3), 105–112. doi:10.1057/palgrave.crr.1540168

Simon, C. J., & Sullivan, M. W. (1993). The measurement and determinants of brand equity: A financial approach. *Marketing Science*, *12*(1), 28–52. doi:10.1287/mksc.12.1.28

Simonson, I., & Tversky, A. (1992). Choice in context: Trade-off contrast and extremeness aversion. *JMR, Journal of Marketing Research*, *29*(3), 281–295. doi:10.2307/3172740

Singh, N., Lehnert, K., & Bostick, K. (2012). Global social media Usage: Insights into reaching consumers worldwide. *Thunderbird International Business Review*, *54*(5), 683–700. doi:10.1002/tie.21493

Singh, S., & Sonnenburg, S. (2012). Brand performances in social media. *Journal of Interactive Marketing*, *26*(4), 189–197. doi:10.1016/j.intmar.2012.04.001

Stewart, K. J. (2003). Trust transfer on the World Wide Web. *Organization Science*, *14*(1), 5–17. doi:10.1287/orsc.14.1.5.12810

Stuart, H., & Jones, C. (2004). Corporate branding in market space. *Corporate Reputation Review*, *7*(1), 84–93. doi:10.1057/palgrave.crr.1540213

Sule Alonso, M. A., Paquin, J. P., & Levy Mangin, J. P. (2002). Modelling perceived quality in fruit products: Their extrinsic and intrinsic attributes. *Journal of Food Products Marketing*, *8*(1), 29–49. doi:10.1300/J038v08n01_03

Sung, Y., Choi, S. M., & Lin, J. S. (2012). The interplay of culture and situational cues in consumers' brand evaluation. *International Journal of Consumer Studies*, *36*(6), 696–701. doi:10.1111/j.1470-6431.2011.01047.x

Taylor, D. G., Strutton, D., & Thompson, K. (2012). Self-enhancement as a motivation for sharing online advertising. *Journal of Interactive Advertising*, *12*(2), 13–28. doi:10.1080/15252019.2012.10722193

Thompson, S. A., & Sinha, R. K. (2008). Brand communities and new product adoption: The influence and limits of oppositional loyalty. *Journal of Marketing*, *72*(6), 65–80. doi:10.1509/jmkg.72.6.65

Trusov, M., Bucklin, R. E., & Pauwels, K. (2009). Effects of word-of-mouth versus traditional marketing, findings from an internet social networking site. *Journal of Marketing*, *73*(9), 90–102. doi:10.1509/jmkg.73.5.90

Tuominen, P. (2007). Emerging metaphors in brand management: Towards a relational approach. *Journal of Communication Management*, *11*(2), 182–191. doi:10.1108/13632540710747398

Uzunoglu, E., & Kip, S. M. (2014). Brand communication through digital influencers: Leveraging blogger engagement. *International Journal of Information Management*, *34*(5), 592–602. doi:10.1016/j.ijinfomgt.2014.04.007

Väisänen, J. (2015, January 15). Threats of brand management in social media why strong social media presence magnifies brand weaknesses and how international brand managers can address this: Part 1. *Brand Management for a Wired World*. Retrieved from http://www.brandba.se/blog/2014/8/14/threats-of-brand-management-in-social-media-why-strong-social-media-presence-magnifies-brand-weaknesses-and-how-international-brand-managers-can-address-this-part-1

Vásquez, G. A. N., & Escamilla, E. M. (2014). Best practice in the use of social networks marketing strategy as in SMEs. *Procedia: Social and Behavioral Sciences*, *148*, 533–542. doi:10.1016/j.sbspro.2014.07.076

Verhoef, P. C., Reinartz, W. J., & Krafft, M. (2010). Customer engagement as a new perspective in customer management. *Journal of Service Research*, *13*(3), 247–252. doi:10.1177/1094670510375461

Vollmer, C., & Precourt, G. (2008). *Always on: Advertising, marketing, and media in an era of consumer control*. New York, NY: McGraw–Hill.

Wen, Q. (2013, July 2). Using social media for brand management. *Megaphone Marketing*. Retrieved from http://megaphonemarketing.com.au/using-social-media-for-brand-management/

Williams, D. L., Crittenden, V. L., Keo, T., & McCarty, P. (2012). The use of social media: An exploratory study of usage among digital natives. *Journal of Public Affairs*, *12*(2), 127–136. doi:10.1002/pa.1414

Wright, P., & Rip, P. (1980). Product class advertising effects on first-time buyers' decision strategies. *Journal of Consumer Research*, *7*(2), 776–788. doi:10.1086/208805

Wu, P. C. S., & Wang, Y. (2011). The influences of electronic word-of-mouth message appeal and message source credibility on brand attitude. *Asia Pacific Journal of Marketing and Logistics*, *23*(4), 448–472. doi:10.1108/13555851111165020

Yeh, Y. H., & Choi, S. M. (2011). Mini-lovers, maxi-mouths: An investigation of antecedents to eWOM intention among brand community members. *Journal of Marketing Communications*, *17*(3), 145–162. doi:10.1080/13527260903351119

Yoganarasimhan, H. (2012). Impact of social network structure on content propagation: A study using YouTube data. *Quantitative Marketing and Economics*, *10*(1), 111–150. doi:10.1007/s11129-011-9105-4

Yoo, M., & Bai, B. (2013). Customer loyalty marketing research: A comparative approach between hospitality and business journals. *International Journal of Hospitality Management*, *33*, 166–177. doi:10.1016/j.ijhm.2012.07.009

Yoo, B., Donthu, N., & Lee, S. (2000). An examination of selected marketing mix elements and brand equity. *Journal of the Academy of Marketing Science*, *28*(2), 195–211. doi:10.1177/0092070300282002

Zaglia, M. E. (2013). Brand communities embedded in social networks. *Journal of Business Research*, *66*(2-2), 216–223. doi:10.1016/j.jbusres.2012.07.015 PMID:23564989

Zavattaro, S. M., Daspit, J. J., & Adams, F. G. (2015). Assessing managerial methods for evaluating place brand equity: A qualitative investigation. *Tourism Management*, *47*, 11–21. doi:10.1016/j.tourman.2014.08.018

Zhang, M., Jansen, B. J., & Chowdhury, A. (2011). Business engagement on Twitter: A path analysis. *Electronic Markets*, *21*(3), 161–175. doi:10.1007/s12525-011-0065-z

Zhao, D., & Rosson, M. B. (2009). How and why people Twitter: The role that microblogging plays in informal communication at work. Paper presented at the ACM 2009 International Conference on Supporting Group Work, New York, NY. doi:10.1145/1531674.1531710 doi:10.1145/1531674.1531710

ADDITIONAL READING

Antorini, Y. M., Muniz, A. M., & Askildsen, T. (2012). Collaborating with customer communities: Lessons from the Lego group. *MIT Sloan Management Review*, *53*(3), 73–79.

Bao, Y., Bao, Y., & Sheng, S. (2011). Motivating purchase of private brands: Effects of store image, product signatureness, and quality variation. *Journal of Business Research*, *64*(2), 220–226. doi:10.1016/j.jbusres.2010.02.007

Gensler, S., Völckner, F., Liu-Thompkins, Y., & Wiertz, C. (2013). Managing brands in the social media environment. *Journal of Interactive Marketing*, *27*(4), 242–256. doi:10.1016/j.intmar.2013.09.004

Hansen, D. L., Shneiderman, B., & Smith, M. A. (2011). *Analyzing social media networks with Nodexl.* Burlington, MA: Elsevier.

Healy, J. C., & McDonagh, P. (2013). Consumer roles in brand culture and value co-creation in virtual communities. *Journal of Business Research*, *66*(9), 1528–1540. doi:10.1016/j.jbusres.2012.09.014

Hollebeek, L. D., Glynn, M. S., & Brodie, R. J. (2014). Consumer brand engagement in social media: Conceptualization, scale development and validation. *Journal of Interactive Marketing*, *28*(2), 149–165. doi:10.1016/j.intmar.2013.12.002

Hsu, Y. H., & Tsou, H. T. (2011). Understanding customer experiences in online blog environments. *International Journal of Information Management*, *31*(6), 510–523. doi:10.1016/j.ijinfomgt.2011.05.003

Kalafatis, S. P., Remizova, N., Riley, D., & Singh, J. (2012). The differential impact of brand equity on B2B co-branding. *Journal of Business and Industrial Marketing*, *27*(8), 623–634. doi:10.1108/08858621211273574

Kuksov, D., Shachar, R., & Wang, K. (2013). Advertising and consumers' communications. *Marketing Science*, *32*(2), 294–309. doi:10.1287/mksc.1120.0753

Lee, T. Y., & BradLow, E. T. (2011). Automated marketing research using online customer reviews. *JMR, Journal of Marketing Research*, *48*(5), 881–894. doi:10.1509/jmkr.48.5.881

Lipsman, A., Mudd, G., Rich, M., & Bruich, S. (2012). The power of "like": How brands reach (and influence) fans through social-media marketing. *Journal of Advertising Research*, *52*(1), 40–52. doi:10.2501/JAR-52-1-040-052

Liu, F., Li, J., Mizerski, D., & Soh, H. (2012). Self–congruity, brand attitude, and brand loyalty: A study on luxury brands. *European Journal of Marketing*, *46*(7–8), 922–937.

Mann, B. J. S., & Kaur, M. (2013). Exploring branding strategies of FMCG, services and durables brands: Evidence from India. *Journal of Product and Brand Management*, *22*(1), 6–17. doi:10.1108/10610421311298650

Marzocchi, M., Morandin, G., & Bergami, M. (2013). Brand communities: Loyal to the community or the brand? *European Journal of Marketing*, *47*(1-2), 93–114. doi:10.1108/03090561311285475

Mayzlin, D., & Yoganarasimhan, H. (2012). Link to success: How blogs build an audience by promoting rivals. *Management Science*, *58*(9), 1651–1668. doi:10.1287/mnsc.1110.1510

Moe, W. M., & Schweidel, D. A. (2012). Online product opinions: Incidence, evaluation, and evolution. *Marketing Science*, *31*(3), 372–386. doi:10.1287/mksc.1110.0662

Noble, C. H., Bing, M. N., & Bogoviyeva, E. (2013). The effects of brand metaphors as design innovation: A test of congruency hypotheses. *Journal of Product Innovation Management*, *30*, 126–141. doi:10.1111/jpim.12067

Olsen, L. E., & Lanseng, E. J. (2012). Brand alliances: The role of brand concept consistency. *European Journal of Marketing*, *46*(9), 1108–1126. doi:10.1108/03090561211247874

Onishi, H., & Manchanda, P. (2012). Marketing activity, blogging and sales. *International Journal of Research in Marketing*, *29*(3), 221–234. doi:10.1016/j.ijresmar.2011.11.003

Pongsakornrungsilp, S., & Schroeder, J. (2011). Understanding value co-creation in a co-consuming brand community. *Marketing Theory*, *11*(3), 303–324. doi:10.1177/1470593111408178

Quintal, V., & Phau, I. (2013). Brand leaders and me-too alternatives: How do consumers choose? *Marketing Intelligence & Planning*, *31*(4), 367–387. doi:10.1108/02634501311324852

Romaniuk, J., & Nenycz-Thiel, M. (2013). Behavioral brand loyalty and consumer brand associations. *Journal of Business Research*, *66*(1), 67–72. doi:10.1016/j.jbusres.2011.07.024

Schnittka, O., Sattler, H., & Zenker, S. (2012). Advanced brand concept maps: A new approach for evaluating the favorability of brand association networks. *International Journal of Research in Marketing*, *29*(3), 265–274. doi:10.1016/j.ijresmar.2012.04.002

Sharifi, S. S. (2014). Impacts of the trilogy of emotion on future purchase intentions in products of high involvement under the mediating role of brand awareness. *European Business Review*, *26*(1), 43–63. doi:10.1108/EBR-12-2012-0072

Smock, A. D., Ellison, N. B., Lampe, C., & Wohn, D. Y. (2011). Facebook as a toolkit: A uses and gratification approach to unbundling feature use. *Computers in Human Behavior*, *27*(6), 2322–2329. doi:10.1016/j.chb.2011.07.011

Stahl, F., Heitmann, M., Lehmann, D. R., & Neslin, S. A. (2012). The impact of brand equity on customer acquisition, retention, and profit margin. *Journal of Marketing*, *76*(4), 44–63. doi:10.1509/jm.10.0522

Wang, X., Yu, C., & Wei, Y. (2012). Social media peer communication and impacts on purchase intentions: A consumer socialization framework. *Journal of Interactive Marketing*, *26*(4), 198–208. doi:10.1016/j.intmar.2011.11.004

KEY TERMS AND DEFINITIONS

Brand: An identifying symbol, words, or mark that distinguishes a product or company from its competitors.

Brand Loyalty: The extent of the faithfulness of consumers to a particular brand, expressed through their repeat purchases.

Brand Management: The process of maintaining, improving, and upholding a brand so that the name is associated with positive results.

Brand Strategy: The long-term marketing support for a brand, based on the definition of the characteristics of the target consumers.

Facebook: The name of a social networking service and website, launched in 2004.

Marketing: The management process through which goods and services move from concept to the customer.

Marketing Strategy: An organization's strategy that combines all of its marketing goals into one comprehensive plan.

Social Media: The Internet or cellular phone based applications and tools to share information among people.

Twitter: A social networking website, which allows users to publish short messages that are visible to other social media users.

Chapter 10
Using Social Media Marketing for Competitive Advantage

Amir Manzoor
Bahria University, Pakistan

ABSTRACT

Social media provides companies innovative ways to market their products and services to their customers. The social media tools, such as Facebook, provides new ways to reach customers. With increasing number of people being connected to social media, businesses of all types are targeting social media as a new platform to reach their customers and strengthen customer relationships. Still, many companies are unsure as to how they can use social media for their advantage. There is lack of resources and fear of failure that hold many companies back from using social media in their marketing campaigns. Companies need a set of guidelines to understand how they can develop long-term, successful marketing strategies that involve social media as a significant component. This chapter analyzes use of social media marketing to suggest some ways companies can use social media to generate value both for them and their customers. This chapter also discusses how companies can develop a social media marketing strategy.

INTRODUCTION

Social Media

Social networking is a generally new idea. As such, social media experts keep on debating a legitimate meaning of the term, and choosing a universally accepted definition may be unimaginable (Solis, 2009). However, definitions from a few social media experts may help provide a reasonable definition—one that precisely portrays the core motivation behind social media.

According to Safko and Brake (2009), social media "refers to activities, practices, and behaviors among communities of people who gather online to share information, knowledge, and opinions using conversational media" (p. 6). According to Weinberg (2009), social media "relates to the sharing of information, experiences, and perspectives throughout community-oriented websites" (p. 1). Comm (2009) suggests that social media is "content that has been created by its audience" (p. 3). The Universal

DOI: 10.4018/978-1-4666-9776-8.ch010

McCann report (2008) suggests social media as "online applications, platforms and media which aim to facilitate interaction, collaboration, and the sharing of content" (p. 10).

The previous definitions, though depict different aspects of social media, fails to identify the essence of social media. Zarrella (2010) provides a basic definition of social media by suggesting that social media consists of online technologies that facilitate the creation and distribution of content. This compact and straightforward definition establishes the framework to properly understand additional aspects of social media.

Categories of Social Media

Social media includes a vast array of online resources each having unique features that appeal different people. In this chapter, we shall discuss some of the most important categories of social media such as social networking, blogging, microblogging, social news, social bookmarking, and media sharing.

Social Networking Site

According to Weinberg (2009), social networking sites and social networks "are generic terms for sites that are used to connect users with similar backgrounds and interests" (p. 149). Most social networks provide the same essential features such as an individual profile, the ability to include friends, photographs, and various ways to collaborate with friends. In general, there exist two categories of social networking sites: popular sites or niche sites. Popular sites, such as Facebook, attract a broader set of audience and have millions of active users. LinkedIn is another example of a general purpose popular site that attracts all types of professionals. In contrast, niche social networking sites, such as Sharecipe, attracts people interested in cooking. The site provides its users with many recipes and cooking tips. For the Love of Film (fan.tcm.com) is another niche site that is a place for movie lovers to gather. ActiveRain is another niche site that brings together land experts.

Blog

According to (Zarrella 2010), a blog is "a kind of substance administration framework that makes it simple for anybody to distribute short articles called posts" (p. 9). Blogs have become very popular recently due to the fat that virtually anyone with Internet access can start a blog using a variety of freely available tools (Safko & Brake, 2009). Mainstream blogging platforms include WordPress (http://wordpress.org), Movable Type (http://www.movabletype.com), and Google's Blogger (http://www.blogger.com). Some regular features of blogs include comments, which permits readers to leave remarks on various blog posts; the blogroll, a list of other suggested blogs; and Really Simple Syndication (RSS), an innovative technology that empowers users to effortlessly see summary of blog posts.

Microblog

A microblog is a kind of site in which posts have a restricted length. The essential example of a microblogging platform is Twitter, which restricts the length of every post to 140 characters. Numerous individuals mistakenly mention Twitter as a social networking site due to its similarities to prevalent social networking sites. Microblogging encourages concise discussions. Individuals consider microblogging valuable to share interesting web site links, make statements, and provide status updates (O'Reilly

& Milstein, 2009). Different examples of microblogging sites include Jaiku (http://www.jaiku.com), which is comparable to Twitter; and Yammer (http://www.yammer.com), an internal communication platform for enterprises.

Social News Site

On a social news site, users can submit and vote on content. It might be said, a social news website serves as a channel that filters compelling content from everyday content on the Web. When users discover content that interests them (for example, an article, feature, picture, and so forth.), they can submit the content to a social news site. In the event that the online community finds the content intriguing they will vote likewise and drive the content to a more visible place on the new website. At present, the most well known social news site is Digg (digg.com). Other famous social news sites are Reddit (reddit.com) and Mixx (mixx.com). These sites serve broad audience and cover extensive variety of subjects. There are numerous specialty social news sites, for example, Tip'd (tipd.com), which focuses on investment/finance and business, and Slashdot (slashdot.org), which focuses on science and innovation.

Social Bookmarking Site

A social bookmarking site is like a social news site. According to Zarrella (2010), for a social bookmarking site, "the value presented to users is focused on allowing them to collect and store interesting links they've found and may wish to revisit"(p. 103). Basically, users use web links or bookmarks to share organized content from the web. Voting on submitted bookmarks is used to determine the bookmarks which will be shown prominently on the bookmarking site. Social news sites and social bookmarking sites both focus on helping users find desired information. As such, individuals frequently confuse these two different types of sites. The most prevalent social bookmarking sites are Delicious (delicious.com) and StumbleUpon (stumbleupon.com). Diigo (diigo.com) is an specialty social bookmarking site which concentrates on collaboration and research.

Media-Sharing Site

A media-sharing site enables clients to upload video, images, podcasts and other forms of multimedia (Zarrella, 2010). This part of social media has is especially powerful through video-sharing sites, for example, YouTube (youtube.com). Photograph sharing sites, for example, Flickr (flickr.com), let users upload their own pictures and scan a large number of pictures that others have uploaded. Presentation-sharing sites, for example, SlideShare (slideshare.net), let users upload and share presentations. A typical feature of media-sharing sites is that a tag can be associated with a user's content. A tag is essentially a descriptive word that helps individuals find the content (Zarrella, 2010).

Significance of Social Media

To establish the impact and potential of social media, we can take example of the case of Iranian presidential elections of 2009. In June 2009, Iran was reeling from the political turmoil of a disputed presidential elections. Protestors had been pouring into the streets for a long time when a 26-year-old Iranian lady, Neda, chose to go to the anti-government rally in Tehran, the capital of Iran. Soon after touching base close to the scene of the rally, a shooter fired a shot that that struck in her heart. Neda died on the spot (Fathi, 2009).

The terrible story of Neda's sudden demise shortly went worldwide. More shockingly, the phenomenal coverage of her demise came not from professional journalists but individuals using social media. The publicity of this incident on social media was so extensive that traditional mainstream media eventually covered the story (Cashmore, 2009). The timeline of the events on social media made it possible to compile and report the events as they occurred (Parr, 2009).

The disruptive consequence of the Iranian election exhibited the extensive potential and impact of social media. In another case, the Australian Network Ten newsreader Natarsha Belling took to the airwaves to present the channel's current affair show Eyewitness News over the weekend, wearing a fetching 'phallic-shaped neckline' green jacket over her black top. Her act caused social media meltdown. It all started with Facebook user Ruben Haywood, and from there the comments just kept on coming. Social media was quick to respond after Facebook user Ruben Haywood posted a snap of the newsreader online – with some pointing out it was hard to 'unsee' Natarsha's top once you'd had a look. Within few days the show went on air, Natarsha Belling became the No. 1 trending Facebook topic and the post garnered more than 113,000 likes (Blidner, 2015).

By 2008, a very large number of Internet users were reading blogs, viewing multimedia content, and taking part in different types of social media (Universal McCann., 2008). In 2007, one in four online American adults visited social networking sites at least a month (Li & Bernoff, 2008). Facebook doubled its active users base to 400 million users by 2010 (Zuckerberg, 2010).

Social Media Marketing

Barefoot and Szabo (2010) offers a basic definition of social media marketing by saying that social media marketing is "using social media channels to promote your company and its products" (p. 13). An expanded definition provided by Weinberg (2009) describes social media marketing as "a process that empowers individuals to promote their websites, products, or services through online social channels and to communicate with and tap into a much larger community that may not have been available via traditional advertising channels" (p. 3). The focus of this definition on communication with the community is in line with Hunt (2009) who maintains that community marketing is synonymous with social media marketing.

The tremendous development of social media has numerous implications. One of these implications is the way social media transform business. Social media represents some genuine difficulties to organizations as clients and workers progressively rush to social media sites (Ross, 2009). Exceptionally compelling is the impact of social media on marketing. By 2014, social media marketing was expected to grow annually at a rate of 34%, outpacing all other forms of online marketing (VanBoskirk, 2009). The huge number of individuals utilizing social media sites provides one explanation behind this trend. Marketers now have a very large customer base. An alternate explanation is the users ability to engage in instant communication with other users. Unfortunately, for numerous organizations social media is still a mystery as they remain uncertain of how to integrate social media in their marketing efforts (Li & Bernoff, 2008).

Social media technologies continually change. However, the desire of companies to use social media for engaging in meaningful interactions with customers is yet a dream to come true for many companies. As such, the social media tools themselves could change but social media marketing principles would remain relevant for the time to come. One reason why many companies are reluctant to integrate social media in their marketing efforts is the examples of many failed social media marketing campaigns. These campaigns failed despite the availability of magnitude of resources and brought serious consequences for the companies. It is therefore crucial for companies to understand how they can develop a social media marketing campaign that will be successful in the long run and help companies create and capture value. The objective of this chapter is explore the social media marketing phenomenon and social media marketing principles. The chapter further explores ways companies can use to create and capture value using social media marketing and discuss how companies should formulate a social media marketing strategy.

CONSUMER AND BUSINESS ADOPTION OF SOCIAL MEDIA

There is a need to understand why consumers and businesses have enthusiastically adopted social media. Such an understanding would not only help to explain the social media phenomenon but also demonstrate the permanency of social media.

Reasons behind Consumers Use of Social Media

The individual's desire to connect with other people and belong to a community is the most fundamental reason why people adopt social media. As Barefoot and Szabo (2010) notes "From [bulletin board systems] to chat rooms, forums, and blogs, human nature is at the heart of creating and building online communities" (p. 3). This reason applies to all forms of online communities. This trend is clearly demonstrated by the explosion of online communities. Barefoot and Szabo (2010) further notes that consumers now know the power social media has provided them to communicate, share, and collaborate with greater efficiency. The projects of open source web browser, such as Firefox, and open source operating systems, such as Ubuntu Linux, are developed and managed by online communities.

By relying on social networking to connect with loved ones, individuals build up an emotional and personal affection to social media. Chase (2009) notes that "If your experience with a social catalyst, be it either a brand or a website, is something that enhances your life or deepens your bonds with friends and associates, you will also become bonded with that social catalyst" (p. 285). Many a times, users don't understand their reliance on social media service until a blackout abruptly happens. As an interesting illustration, the US State Department asked Twitter and other online networking sites to put on hold their schedule maintenance in order avoid any downtime of these services during the crisis of Iranian presidential elections of 2009.

In this situation, getting information through the social media sites was the primary reason that forced US authorities to contact the social networking sites (Labott, 2009). Businesses must comprehend the idea that individuals appreciate utilizing social media fundamentally because its use satisfy their intrinsic desire to connect with other individuals. According to Powell (2009), the businesses bears the obligation of "comprehension that need, arranging it, and utilizing that code to better succeed in business" (p. 6).

An alternate explanation for the user acceptance of social media is the radical shift of power from the business to the customer. An indication of this critical shift was the dotcom bubble burst in late 2001. This dotcom bubble burst resulted in the emergence of Web 2.0. Basically, Web 2.0 technologies present interactive, dynamic, content as opposed to static content (Google, 2008). Earlier, users passively observed the Web; now they can actively contribute content to the Web through social media. Threadless (threadless.com), an online apparel store, figured out how to use the capability of online users to contribute content. The organization keeps up a flourishing online community of T-shirts designers. The members submit designs to Threadless, and other members vote in favor of their most favorite design. Threadless then takes the designs getting most votes and produces a limited quantity of these designs, offering T-shirts to the community that designed them. Members get involved by submitting shirt designs as well as by posting pictures, taking part in community, and writing slogans. Voting play a vital role in the community and members are encouraged to distinguish quality content from mundane content. The Threadless site serves as the nucleus for all these activities. The Threadless's methodology appears to have met expectations, particularly since it almost doubled its revenue and registered around half a minion users by 2009. (Hunt, 2009).

Media, used to be top-down, is another aspect of this power shift from business to consumer (Comm, 2009; Powell, 2009). Social media is making the media bottom-up and empowering media consumers to both create media and communicate with media creators (Szabo & Barefoot, 2010). Companies have historically relied on traditional media channels for their marketing efforts. According to Hunt (2009), these media channels present few potential problems such as too much advertising, lack of trust, and too many choices. The story of Thomas Hawke a blogger, is an illustration of this power shift into the hands of consumer. Thomas Hawk wrote a blog post about PriceRitePhoto when the company denied to ship him the camera he purchase if he didn't buy the accessories. His post sparked a firestorm of online criticism on PriceRitePhoto. The scale of criticism was so massive that traditional media giants, such as New York Times and Forbes, eventually covered this story. PriceRitePhoto went out of business shortly and all this happened because of the influence of just one blogger (Powell, 2009).

Organizations must comprehend that consumers are utilizing one another to discover what they need, when they need it, and how they need it. Li and Bernoff (2008) portray this phenomenon as the groundswell. A groundswell, according to Li and Bernoff (2008), is a "social trend in which people use technologies to get the things they need from each other, rather than from traditional institutions like corporations" (p. 9). Chase (2009) says, "the majority of our buying decisions have always been through word of mouth. However…thanks to the proliferation of online communities, our personal networks have gotten *bigger*, much bigger" (p. 36). The basic premise is that buyers are making purchase decisions in which friends recommendations have lot more weight than the product recommendations provided by the businesses.

Reasons behind Businesses Use of Social Media

Business world now understand the intensity of social media use by the consumers. As a result, marketers have come up with a variety of reasons for engaging in social media marketing. Two reasons mentioned earlier are the large number of social media users and instant communication with the consumers. However, these two reasons need to be looked at great depth in order provide a more helpful explanation of social media phenomenon.

To start, more individuals are utilizing the Internet than ever before. BY 2009, there were more than 1.7 billion Internet users and this user base grew at a rate of 380% from year 2000 to 2009. People were spending more time than ever using Internet. According to Bloomberg (2009b), adult users were "spending an average of thirteen hours a week online" (p. 1). This was more than double the amount of time adult users spent in 2002. The influx of Internet users has sparked an exponential growth in social media users. As of 2009, there were about 625 million active users of social media. Out of these 625 millions users, 83% watched online videos, 71% visited a friend's page on a social networking site, and 63% crated a profile on social networking sites (Universal McCann., 2009). Forrester (2009) reported that "marketing budgets are following the innovation trail—social media spending in the US will grow from $716 million this year to more than $3.1 billion in 2014" (p. 1).

Marketing is about fulfilling people's needs. According to Weinberg (2009), 58% of individuals use Internet to address their problem and issues. Wikis and online repositories receive millions of visitors searching for answers. There exist an enormous opportunity to influence consumer purchase decisions. Take example of Home Depot, a US retailer of home improvement and construction products and services. Home Depot uses YouTube to share demonstrations of do-it-yourself home projects. The topics may include home improvement and energy efficiency. The Home Depot also make use of Twitter to deliver announcements and resolve customer queries. During the 2008 hurricane Gustav in USA, the Home Depot used Twitter to provide helpful safety information to the users (Weinberg, 2009).

Customers are already using Internet to engage in conversations about products, services, and brands. Participation in these conversations can be beneficial for companies (Zarrella, 2010). Active participation in these conversations can help companies attract customers and provide useful information to the customers (Hunt, 2009). Scott (2009) notes that "where organizations get into trouble is in failing to participate at all" (p. 121). Hewlett Packard (HP) made an intensive effort by hosting many executive blogs on industry-related topics. The objective of this effort was to stay in touch with its target customers. Using these blogs, HP was able to respond to customers through comments customers posted on these blogs. With these blogs, HP was able to build trust and encourage conversations with the customers by showing them that HP was willing to have conversation with them and listen to their concerns.

The financial barriers to social media marketing are not high and many social media tools are free even for businesses to use. Companies with limited budgets can run successful social media marketing campaigns. Blendtec, a manufacturer of blenders, used a $50 initial marketing budget to create a video series called 'Will it Blend?' The video series received millions of viewers in a short period of time (Weinberg, 2009).

CREATING AND CAPTURING VALUE WITH SOCIAL MEDIA

Companies use a variety of methods/techniques of creating and capturing value with social media. A wide variety of social media tools are available and companies can use them to reach their customers in many ways. Social media is like a large toolbox in which blogs, social networks, and social news sites are unique tools. These tools are most effective in different situations. It is important for marketers to learn the capabilities of each tool and when to use each tool. The practical experience of marketers is, therefore, very important for formulating a successful social media marketing campaign.

Principles of Social Media Marketing

Each social media marketing campaign is governed by certain principle. These principles relate to community, content, conversation, and transparency. Each principle is crucial in supporting the effectiveness of social media marketing. Social media cannot be truly social without conversations and without transparency these conversations cannot be constructive. Social media would not be a media if content is missing and this content cannot be relevant without a community (Perdue, 2010).

Community

A community should be the hub of company's social media marketing campaigns. This is important because social media marketing is about meaningful connections with groups of people and connecting with people having similar interests is important tool. According to Barefoot and Szabo (2010), "social media tools enable like- minded people—be they bird watchers, Québécois undertakers, or Vietnam veterans—to find each other. This is a key benefit of social media marketing" (p.7). Companies generally are more successful when they target specific online communities. Companies can either target existing communities or build a new online community around its products and services. To build a community, however, a core customer is important (Hunt, 2009). With increasing number of people publishing their preferences on social network sites, the markets served by the companies can become narrower. We can see the emergence of 'socialgraphics' i.e. the segmenting of people based on their memberships of groups, their preferences, their public wish lists, and the topics of their discussions with their friends and family.

Content

Social media are tools that facilitate the creation and distribution of content. When companies publish content using social media, they need to decide both the type and purpose of the content to be created. According to Safko and Brake (2009), there are four pillars of social media marketing strategies to engage in online communities. These four pillars are communication, collaboration, education, and entertainment (Perdue, 2010). Put it simply, content is the main element companies use to communicate with its customers, facilitate collaboration with customers, and educate/entertain the customers. A company also need to make significant efforts to develop creative content i.e. the type of content that attracts people and encourage them to share it with others (Scott, 2009). The 'Will it Blend' video series attracted a large number of people because it was based on providing people with information they needed in their daily lives. As Weinberg (2009) notes, "instead of making ads, think of making content" (p. 30).

Conversations

By nature, social media is interactive. A company can participate in online conversations and engage with online communities related to its products and services. This conversation and engagement is not meant to provide advertising and promotion but to provide information to the customers by answering questions, posting tips, or just make comments.

Transparency

According to principle of transparency, a company's participation in social media must be authentic. Weinberg (2009) notes that "when it comes to social media marketing, the rules of engagement are different. Altruism rules above all. Authentic online relationships can further your cause and help foster real relationships that can flourish offline" (p. 323). In its social media marketing, a company attempts for the ultimate transparency in all of its online interactions. Those companies who do not do so can end up distancing themselves from customer communities and lose their trust. In its every type or level of social media interaction, a company needs to keep focus on reaching out online communities, creating attractive content for the communities, participating in online conversations, and be transparent in all of its online interactions.

Techniques of Creating and Capturing Value through Social Media

There are many techniques/methods marketers can use to develop profitable social media marketing campaigns. Not all methods result in direct sales but certainly do add value by providing indirect sales. All of these techniques/methods possess huge potential to have meaningful engagements with the customers.

Online Reputation Management

Online reputation management involves building a positive perception of a company's brands. It is achieved by interacting with customers and responding to negative perceptions about the company and its brands. Weinberg (2009) notes, "you can manage relationships, but you can't manage reputation" (p. 30). The online reputation management is important because the Internet has significantly enhanced people's ability to affect company's reputation. Scott (2009) notes that "the power of the Internet makes it easier for people to fall in love with you faster. But beware—it also makes it easier for them to fall out of love with you faster. It's a double-edged sword" (p. 11). Companies may adopt a passive approach to online reputation management. In passive approach, company simply ignores what people say about it online. However, this approach is not recommended. Companies can use social media to actively participate in online conversations related to company or its brands. Beal (2008) suggests that to monitor their reputation, companies should monitor their name, brands, company's executives, slogans, competitions, intellectual property etc. Monitoring so many things can be tricky. According to Brogan and Smith (2009), reputation management is "is a burgeoning field right now because the process of checking everything is so daunting that large companies often need entire smaller companies to deal with it" (p. 172). Many online tracking tools are available. Some are free while other are fee-based. Companies need to select those tools that best meet their needs. Some examples of free tools include Google Alerts and Technorati (a blog search engine). Some examples of commercial fe-based tools include Radian6, Trackur, and Buzzlogic. All these tools provide detailed dashboards that can aggregate real-time information and help in quick understanding of people perception of the company (Schawbel, 2009).

A good example of the power of effective online reputation management is a serious ethical failure at Network Solutions. Network Solutions is an Internet domain registrar company. In this case, Network Solutions bought those domain names that users searched on its website. Network Solutions did so with a hope that users would be forced to use its services to acquire those domain names. Such unethical behavior resulted in a very negative reputation and Network Solutions, in an attempt to regain customer trust, started to listen to, participate in, and add value to online communities of its customers. These efforts proved successful and during next six months company witnessed a significant decrease in negative comments and increase in positive comments about the company (Weinberg, 2009).

Brand Awareness

Social media marketing can also be used to increase brand awareness. Brand awareness may not necessarily result in immediate sales but can help increase future customer recall of company's products and services to make a purchase (Weinberg, 2009). According to Immediate Future (2008), active participation across social media sites positively impacts a company's brand awareness. Today, customers are expecting an established social media presence of their favorite companies. At the same times, customers are also continually coming across many companies on social media sites. According to Weinberg (2009), one of the major focuses of brand awareness is to simultaneously target multiple audience across various social media sites on which users spend time. However, social media presence of a company should be relevant to each online community they participate in. Companies should also increase their social media presence beyond popular social media sites to cover relevant niche social media sites (Weinberg, 2009). In social media, identity theft is now common place where someone claims a user name that should belong to someone else such as a company. KnowEm (knowem.com) is a service companies can use to prevent social media identity theft. Companies can also target influencers in online communities they participate in to increase brand awareness. Companies should be careful while deliberately transforming these influencers into their brand ambassadors. These brand ambassadors would be individuals passionate about the products and services of the company. The company can use these brand ambassadors to indirectly access potential customers in online communities they enter (Safko & Brake, 2009). Burger King, a famous fast food chain in USA, released a Facebook App called 'Whopper Sacrifice' in 2009. Users of the app were promised a free whopper if they remove ten of their Facebook friends from their account. As a result, users removed about 234,000 of their friends. Eventually, Facebook removed this app but by that time the app was already mentioned by more than 13,000 blogs around the globe. This example illustrates an unusual attempt by a company to increase its brand awareness using social media (Weinberg, 2009).

Social Capital Management

Social media marketing can increase a company's social capital. According to Powell (2009), social capital is "both the network of relationships you have and the access to resources provided therein" (p. 77). In other words, a company builds social capital by developing and maintaining relationships with its customers. One strong reason why companies should focus on increasing social capital and not the financial capital is that social capital can provide indirect and vital increase in financial capital (Powell, 2009). According to Hunt (2009), there are four important reasons for companies to focus on increasing social capital. First, meaningful customer relationships can develop into long-term customer loyalty. Second, the companies can spread word of mouth by having customers talk favorably about their products and services and company itself. Third, building relationships with customers online is relatively inexpensive. Fourth, the companies cannot afford to lag behind in increasing social capital while all their competitors are in the race to increase social capital. If a company lags behind in increasing social capital it can be difficult for the company to build customer loyalty because customers may already have established their loyalties. According to Hunt (2009), one way to raise social capital in an increasingly uncertain online world is "about recognizing how to find your community and potential community and interact on a level that will benefit everyone" (p. 282). Companies need to look genuine in their interaction with the online communities and provide compelling content. A US-based wine store 'Shopper's discount liquors' started a Wine Library TV video podcast. In less than three years since its start, the TV series became so successful that the wine store developed into a multi-million dollar global business and increased its employee base from ten to one hundred employees. This excellent example of raising social capital was made possible by listening to store customers and having conversations with them using social media (i.e. video podcasts). Viewers found the podcast series very interesting and within one year of its launch 15,000 downloads were made and each podcast received around hundred comments (Hunt, 2009).

Viral Marketing

Companies can also take advantage of viral marketing power of the social media. Viral marketing on social media sites revolves around the content created by companies. According to Powell (2009), whether or not that content will go viral depends on if "the content resonate with people enough that they want to share it with their friends?" (p. 93). To start a viral marketing campaign, a company first needs to identify those aspects of a product or service that resonate with people. According to Scott (2009), "If you can boil your message down to just its syrupy goodness, you can achieve lift—the irresistible force of millions of customers selling your product for you" (p. 43). The concept behind marketing is that companies use its own customers to promote its products and services. As Scott (2009) notes "potential customers are eager to hear from people like them, and they pay close attention to how others have been helped by a product or service" (p. 149). After determining a core concept of a product or service, a company must use some creative content to demonstrate that concept in an appealing way. Use of videos is very common for delivering content (Scott, 2009).

Approva is an enterprise software solution provider that deals in solutions to identify and prevent fraud. Approva started a company blog named 'Audit Trail' and posted a video celebrating fifth birthday of the Sarbanes-Oxley Act. The humorous video was enjoyed by many who understood the complexities of the act and were able to relate to the humor presented in the video. This video soon went viral and spread by many bloggers. During the first six months of the posting of video, Approva blog received many more visitors than the visitors to the Approva's official website (Scott, 2009).

Customer and Media Communication

Social media can be used by businesses to communicate with their customers as well as media. Use of social media for communication provides companies opportunities of personal communication with customers. Twitter is a popular microblogging tool to reach out customers in a personal way. According to O'Reilly and Milstein (2009), "the biggest opportunity Twitter gives you is the chance to show the personality and humanness behind your organization" (p. 197). Tools like Twitter can be used by companies to communicate with customers they previously communicated using traditional media. Companies can also open communication with bloggers because of their influence in the online world. Scott (2009) also recognizes importance of bloggers by noting that "bloggers are likely already talking about *your* organization, too. Why not cultivate a relationship with them?" (p. 98). Companies should remember that social media is not simply a platform to make product announcements but can also be used to participate in online conversations with the customers. Companies can also use social media to report problems or inform customers of resolution of issues (O'Reilly & Milstein, 2009). Companies can maintain close and direct communication with their loyal customers who can help promote the company and get the attention of mainstream media (Scott, 2009; Perdue, 2010). In 2007, Dell (dell.com) implemented IdeaStorm (ideastorm.com) as a platform to gather ideas from users. The IdeaStorm was implemented after a disaster that involved poor product performance. Dell used IdeaStorm to communicate with users and get their support. By 2008, IdeaStorm received over 7,000 ideas from users (Li & Bernoff, 2008).

Other Techniques/Methods

There are other techniques/methods available to create and capture value using social media. According to Hunt (2009), social media can be a good platform to market research because social media encourages a "continuous flow of information to and from your customers" (p.1). With increasing number of businesses establish social media presence, companies can use social media to monitor their competitors and review their social media tactics. Companies can also use social media to drive traffic to their websites and improve search engine visibility (Weinberg, 2009). Companies can use social media to get deeper insight of their target markets, discover new distribution channels, generate leads, find joint venture opportunities, and improve their customer service (Carleton, 2009; Perdue, 2010). Since social media is still at its nascent stages, companies should continue to look for innovative ways to use social media in their marketing efforts.

PRACTICAL/MANAGERIAL IMPLICATIONS AND RECOMMENDATIONS

Without a strategy to use social media marketing, an understanding of the social media phenomenon and ways of creating and capturing value with social media marketing would be of little value for companies. This strategy is needed in order provide coherence among different methods of creating and capturing value using social media marketing. Some preliminary considerations are also important before a company develop and use a social media marketing strategy.

First, companies should understand that social media marketing requires a significant investment of time. It would be unwise for a company to start with handful social media resources and hope to realize enormous returns. Second, social media marketing is complementary to traditional marketing. Social media marketing doesn't require companies to stop using traditional marketing methods (Barefoot & Szabo, 2010). There may be few exceptions where companies may be able to successfully rely on social media marketing alone. The marketer's goal should be to discover the best marketing mix-one that involves both traditional and social media marketing. Third, use of social media marketing may not get approval from all stakeholders of the company. This is because it empowers consumers. Therefore, a company must address any internal concerns about the use of social media first. In addition, many managers may see potential problems with employees using social media because they feel that employee could leak secret information through social media (Scott, 2009). Companies may opt to develop social computing guidelines for employees similar to the ones developed by IBM (IBM, 2011).

Developing the Strategy

Keeping these preliminary consideration in mind, companies should proceed to develop their social media marketing strategy. According to Li and Bernoff (2008), "technology is shifting so quickly—chasing it is like trying to jump on a speeding merry-go-round" (p. 67). Li and Burnoff (2008), further suggests that companies should focus their social media marketing strategy around four aspects: people, objectives, strategy, and technology.

People

It is important for companies to know who their customers are, what kinds of social media they are already using, and what they are most willing to do online using social media. Companies may still succeed without this knowledge but as Li and Burnoff (2008) points out that "you might also build a whole social networking strategy only to find that your customers are more likely to write reviews than join social networks" (p. 67) this customer knowledge would be necessary to build a strong foundation of social media marketing and gain competitive advantage.

Objectives

A company should have clearly defined objectives for its social media marketing campaign. These objectives could relate to the social media marketing methods used to create and capture value. However, one general objective of company's social media marketing campaign should be expanding the company's web presence (Barefoot & Szabo, 2010). In addition, companies may have specific short-term and long-term objectives (Zarrella, 2010).

Strategy

According to Li and Bernoff (2008), the strategy aspect of social media marketing answers the question "How do you want relationships with your customers to change?" (p. 68). The ultimate objective of company's social media marketing is to develop and sustain customer relationships. Li and Bernoff (2008) identified five basic strategies companies could use in their social media marketing campaigns. These include *listening* (i.e. knowing what the customers saying about your products and services), *talking* (i.e. using social media to communicate with customers), *energizing* (i.e. encouraging customers to become your), *supporting* (i.e. helping customers), and *embracing* (i.e. gain customer support to achieve company's goals).

Technology

This aspect refers to company's selection and use of technology to achieve its goals and reach customers. Companies should consider current and popular technologies. Companies must not forget that selection of technology or tool (such as Facebook) should not be solely based on familiarity with the technology or tool. According to Weinberg (2009), use of a single technology or tool in a social media marketing campaign with not produce optimal results. Companies should analyze a variety of available social media tools and choose the ones that will optimize company's performance in social media marketing campaign. According to Weinberg (2009), regardless of the type of tools used, a company should clearly identify itself on all social media sites that it participates in. Doing so, companies can promote their transparency in the online community and establish their identity and aims.

Integration of Tools

Since companies can have different combinations of customer, objectives, strategies, and technologies, their individual approaches to social media marketing can be different as well. However, a focus of social media marketing campaign of a company should be to integrate company's message across all social media platforms in order achieve coherence and success in their strategy. According to Zarrella (2010), "users of one kind of social media are likely to be users of other types; it makes sense to invite those who interact with you on Twitter to join your page on Facebook" (p. 199). Similarly, companies should operate a company blog that would become the central platform for their social media marketing campaign. This is because blogs can integrate with many types of social media platforms.

Social Media Marketing Metrics

To measure the success of the social media marketing campaigns, companies generally are eager to measure the ROI (Return on Investment) of the campaign. Companies should also consider using metrics in their social media marketing campaigns. A metric is a unit of measurement. Metrics can be classified into two broad categories: on-site metrics and off-site metrics. According to Zarrella (2010), "on- site metrics measure activity that takes place directly on your site, whereas off-site metrics measure activity that happens on other sites where you and your customers interact" (p. 207). Within these two categories, there can be many other metrics that can be used to measure the ROI of social media marketing campaign. According to Barefoot and Szabo (2010), companies should measure eight metrics namely visitors, incoming links, social network activity, conversations and contributions, references in the blogosphere, views on social media sites, RSS subscribers, and social bookmarking. For visitors, companies should know both number and types of visitors in order identify visitors that engage with company and its products. Analytic software, such as Google Analytics, can be used in this regard. More incoming links help establish a company's authority and expertise and stir up talks about up company. Social network activity can be measured by counting Friends on social media (such as Facebook friends or Twitter followers). Conversations and contributions can be measured by tracking the frequency and quality of customer interaction with the company. This interaction can occur through comments the customer post on company's blog, Facebook pages, Twitter followings etc. The purpose of this measurement is to ensure company's meaningful conversations with the target customer population. To keep track of references in the blogosphere, companies can measure the frequency with which other blogs provide reference to company's blog. It also involves analyzing whether these references actually result in customers conversations about company. Knowing both the number of conversations as well as the quality of conversations can be very helpful. To keep track of customer views on social media sites, companies can measure number of hits on the content posted to social media sites. For example, a company could measure how many times a video posted by the company on YouTube was watched by users or measure the number of Facebook likes on a post made by the company. To keep track of RSS subscribers, companies can use tools (such as FeedBurner) to count subscribers, track subscribers origin, and learn their preferences. With this information, a company can be in a better position to understand what people are looking for and deliver the appropriate content. Using social book marking sites, companies can measure the number of links about the company that users post to various social media sites. A low number may indicate a lack of customer interest in content posted by company.

FUTURE RESEARCH AREAS

There exist some additional social media categories that worth mentioning. These sites include rating and review sites, forums, and virtual worlds. Further research in these areas may yield helpful thoughts for social media marketing. However, organizations may get good advantage from concentrating on these forms of social media due to their tremendous prominence.

CONCLUSION

The phenomenon of social media is rapidly affecting all aspects of business and marketing is no exception. It is clear that a good grasp on meaning and capabilities of social media provide companies a decisive advantage in their marketing capabilities. Individuals are spending more time on the Internet and progressively spending their online time utilizing social networking. As communities of people establish and the force of social networking builds relentlessly, organizations must consider their active involvement. The companies who avoid doing as such or just defer progressing onto the social networking scene—are prone to pay a high cost. While a huge number of Internet users are rushing to social networking sites, organizations all over still struggle to discover methods for contacting them so as to grow their customer base. There exist variety of techniques to create and capture value using social media in marketing. However, building an effective social media marketing strategy based on four aspects i.e. people, objectives, strategy, and technology, is essential to gain the competitive advantage through social media marketing. Individuals change and technology changes but standards don't. Organizations who base their social media marketing campaigns on these four aspects can gain stability and progress in a business environment that is increasingly complex and challenging. This chapter contributes to the existing knowledge base of social media marketing and provide a practical approach to using social media marketing to better serve customers and gain competitive advantage.

REFERENCES

Barney, J. B. (1999). How a firm's capabilities affect boundary decisions. *Sloan Management Review*, *40*(3), 137–145.

Beal, A. (2008, April 10). 12 Reputations Every Company Should Monitor Online | Marketing Pilgrim. Retrieved from http://www.marketingpilgrim.com/2008/04/online-reputation-monitoring-campaign.html

Bharadwaj, A., El Sawy, O. A., Pavlou, P. A., & Venkatraman, N. (2013). Digital business strategy: Toward a next generation of insights. *Management Information Systems Quarterly*, *37*(2), 471–482.

Blidner, R. (2015, March 17). Australian news anchor goes viral with penis-shaped neckline. Retrieved from http://www.nydailynews.com/entertainment/tv/australian-news-anchor-viral-penis-shaped-neckline-article-1.2151861

Brogan, C., & Smith, J. (2010). *Trust Agents: Using the Web to Build Influence, Improve Reputation, and Earn Trust* (2nd ed.). Hoboken, N.J: Wiley.

Carleton, D. (2009, June 25). The Top 20 Business Reasons To Use Social Media Marketing. Retrieved from http://www.examiner.com/article/the-top-20-business-reasons-to-use-social-media-marketing

Cashmore, P. (2009, June 21). Neda: YouTube Video Too Distressing to Ignore. *Mashable.com*. Retrieved from http://mashable.com/2009/06/21/neda/

Cashmore, P. (n.d.). Neda: YouTube Video Too Distressing to Ignore. Retrieved July 29, 2014, from http://mashable.com/2009/06/21/neda/

The World Factbook. (2014). Central Intelligence Agency (CIA). Retrieved from https://www.cia.gov/library/publications/the-world-factbook/rankorder/2119rank.html

Chan, J. M., & Yazdanifard, R. (2014). How social media marketing can influence the profitability of an online company from a consumer point of view. *Journal of Research in Marketing*, *2*(2), 157–160. doi:10.17722/jorm.v2i2.55

Comm, J. (2010). *Twitter Power 2.0: How to Dominate Your Market One Tweet at a Time* (2nd ed.). Hoboken, NJ: Wiley.

Correia, A. (2013). Social Information: Gaining Competitive and Business Advantage Using Social Media Tools. *Online Information Review*, *37*(1), 151–152. doi:10.1108/14684521311311720

Fathi, N. (2009, June 23). In a Death Seen Around the World, a Symbol of Iranian Protests. *The New York Times*. Retrieved from http://www.nytimes.com/2009/06/23/world/middleeast/23neda.html

Fathi, N. (2009, June 23). In a Death Seen Around the World, a Symbol of Iranian Protests. *The New York Times*. Retrieved from http://www.nytimes.com/2009/06/23/world/middleeast/23neda.html

Forrester Marketing Forum: Social Technologies Allow For More. (2009a, April 24). *Bloomberg*. Retrieved from http://www.bloomberg.com/apps/news?pid=newsarchive&sid=ax9.YmVPxwMg

Forrester Research. (2009). Forrester marketing forum: Social technologies allow for more accessible innovation in down economy. Retrieved from http://www.forrester.com/ER/Press/Release/0,1769,1274,00.html

The top brands in social media report 2008. (2008). *Immediate Future*. Retrieved from http://www.immediatefuture.co.uk/the-top-brands-in-social-media-report-2008

Web 2.0: The new face of the Web. (2008). Google. Retrieved from www.google.com/a/help/intl/en/security/pdf/web_2_new_face.pdf

He, W., Zha, S., & Li, L. (2013). Social media competitive analysis and text mining: A case study in the pizza industry. *International Journal of Information Management*, *33*(3), 464–472. doi:10.1016/j.ijinfomgt.2013.01.001

Hunt, T. (2009). *The whuffie factor: Using the power of social networks to build your business*. Crown Pub.

Hunt, T. (2010a). *The power of social networking: Using the whuffie factor to build your business*. Crown Business.

Hunt, T. (2010b). *The Power of Social Networking: Using the Whuffie Factor to Build Your Business* (1st ed.). New York: Crown Business.

IBM Social Computing Guidelines [CT402]. (2011, August 3). *IBM*. Retrieved from http://www.ibm.com/blogs/zz/en/guidelines.html

IBM Social Computing Guidelines [CT402]. (2011, August 3). IBM. Retrieved from http://www.ibm.com/blogs/zz/en/guidelines.html

Internet Users Now Spending an Average of 13 Hours a Week Online. (2009b, December 23). *Bloomberg*. Retrieved from http://www.bloomberg.com/apps/news?pid=newsarchive&sid=aQrAoB85tDvs

Internet Users Spend an Average of 13 Hours a Week Online, Survey Finds. (2009). eWeek. Retrieved from http://www.eweek.com/c/a/Midmarket/Internet-Users-Spend-an-Average-of-13-Hours-a-Week-Online-Survey-Finds-485147

Internet Users Spend an Average of 13 Hours a Week Online, Survey Finds. (2009). eWeek. Retrieved from http://www.eweek.com/c/a/Midmarket/Internet-Users-Spend-an-Average-of-13-Hours-a-Week-Online-Survey-Finds-485147

Internet usage statistics: The Internet big picture. (2009). *Internet World Stats*. Retrieved from http://www.internetworldstats.com/stats.htm

Kogut, B. (1985). Designing global strategies: Comparative and competitive value added chains. *Sloan Management Review*, *26*(4).

Labott, E. (2009, June 16). State Department to Twitter: Keep Iranian tweets coming. Retrieved from http://ac360.blogs.cnn.com/2009/06/16/state-department-to-twitter-keep-iranian-tweets-coming/

Li, C. (2010). Groundswell. Winning in a world transformed by social technologies. *Strategic Direction*, *26*(8).

Mangold, W. G., & Faulds, D. J. (2009). Social media: The new hybrid element of the promotion mix. *Business Horizons*, *52*(4), 357–365. doi:10.1016/j.bushor.2009.03.002

Michaelidou, N., Siamagka, N. T., & Christodoulides, G. (2011). Usage, barriers and measurement of social media marketing: An exploratory investigation of small and medium B2B brands. *Industrial Marketing Management*, *40*(7), 1153–1159. doi:10.1016/j.indmarman.2011.09.009

O'Reilly, T., & Milstein, S. (2009). *The twitter book*. O'Reilly Media, Inc.

Parr, B. (2009, June 21). #IranElection Crisis: A Social Media Timeline. *Mashable.com*. Retrieved from http://mashable.com/2009/06/21/iran-election-timeline/

Perdue, D. J. (2010). Social media marketing: Gaining a competitive advantage by reaching the masses (Paper 127). *Senior Honors Papers*.

Piskorski, M. J., Casciaro, T., & Kivel, M. (2013). Social Strategy: Why Social Media Platforms Work and How to Leverage them for Competitive Advantage. Princeton, NJ: Princeton University Press.

Powell, J. (2009). *33 Million people in the room: How to create, influence, and run a successful business with social networking*. Que Publishing.

Ross, J. (2009). A corporate guide for social media. Retrieved from http://www.forbes.com/2009/06/30/social-media-guidelines-intelligenttechnology-oreilly.html

Safko, L., & Brake, D. K. (2009). *The social media bible: Tactics, tools & strategies for business success*. Hoboken, NJ: John Wiley & Sons.

Schaupp, L. C., & Bélanger, F. (2014). The Value of Social Media for Small Businesses. *Journal of Information Systems*, *28*(1), 187–207. doi:10.2308/isys-50674

Schawbel, D. (2008, December 29). Top 10 Reputation Tracking Tools Worth Paying For. *Mashable.com*. Retrieved from http://mashable.com/2008/12/29/brand-reputation-monitoring-tools/

Scott, D. M. (2009). *World wide rave: Creating triggers that get millions of people to spread your ideas and share your stories*. Hoboken, NJ: John Wiley & Sons. doi:10.1002/9781118258286

Power to the people: Social media tracker wave 3. (2008). *Universal McCann*. Retrieved from http://www.universalmccann.com/Assets/UM%20Wave%203%20Final_20080505110444.pdf

Power to the people: Social media tracker wave 4. (2009). *Universal McCann*. Retrieved from http://universalmccann.bitecp.com/wave4/Wave4.pdf

VanBoskirk, S. (2009, July 7). Interactive marketing nears $55 billion; advertising overall delines. Retrieved from http://blogs.forrester.com/

Weinberg, T. (2009). The new community rules: Marketing on the social web. O'Reilly Sebastopol, CA.

Zarrella, D. (2010). *The social media marketing book*. O'Reilly Media, Inc.

Zuckerberg, M. (2009, April 8). 200 million strong. Retrieved from http://blog.facebook.com/blog.php?post=72353897130

Zuckerberg, M. (2010, February 4). Six years of making connections. Retrieved from http://blog.facebook.com/blog.php?post=287542162130

Chapter 11
Search Engine Marketing:
An Outlining of Conceptualization and Strategic Application

Azizul Hassan
Cardiff Metropolitan University, UK

Sumesh S. Dadwal
Glyndwr University London Campus, UK

ABSTRACT

The most common feature of Search Engine Marketing (SEM) is the pay-per-click concept that outlines the conceptual understanding of the human-computer interaction (HCI) in marketing. In this type of marketing, the three active actors act simultaneously: the service provider, the search engine as the platform and the individual user base. On the assumption that technology will dominate future marketing channels, this study will explore the conceptualisations of SEM, in relation to HCI in tourism marketing. This paper asserts that strategically, a congenial and accepted level of interaction is much required between the service provider and consumers. Also, this is outlined that the customization of a tourism industry led application and adoption of SEM is possible on ground of the Unified theory of Acceptance and Use of Technology (UTAUT) where, factors like age, gender, experience and voluntariness of use are attached with performance expectancy (Venkatesh et al., 2003).

INTRODUCTION

In tourism marketing, technology as deemed to become more in practice and in effect as opposite to conventional marketing strategies. The reliability and usability of such tools are in fact focused to fill the demands of consumers those remain as inconsistent due to the availability of offers and the individual mind-set. On the other side, technology enabled marketing strategies can hardly be confined within geographical boundaries and inaccessible for global consumer bases. There is also general understanding that, technology supported marketing tools are required in such a situation where, almost every aspects of human life is intertwined with technology and technology backed innovations. The application of

DOI: 10.4018/978-1-4666-9776-8.ch011

technology in tourism or related areas of business can become diverse and may not follow the similar pace of advancements as they require. This is mainly an interaction between consumers and services or product providers. Thus, if marketing strategies remain as more rigid, inaccessible and incompatible to absorb, the level of acceptance will also remain as lower than the expectation. The common understanding that, technology should remain as more rewarding and accessible for consumers becomes more convincing. SEM is gradually becoming a major concept in the present world. There are very few or almost none example that can reveal the significance or bottlenecks of SEM. Also, the relevancies to reveal applications and uses of technologies become crucial to some extent. SEM is an unavoidable element of online marketing that is mostly attached with technological advancements. The necessities to applause technological applications in wider forms of the societal structure render importance. This type of marketing is getting popular in numerous societies covering both relatively developed and less developed market settings and structures. Search engine is an element of a system as part of the technological intervention within the humans. This has been getting modified over years through the involvement of organisations and institutions of diverse types. Online platforms as part of technological advancements are essential components of technological applications. Marketing methods on the internet concentrates on ads purchase that appears on search engine result pages like Google. The number of search engines is not huge but characteristically, the rate of payment as offered by an advertiser settles the frequency of appearance on the page. Simply, advertisement of that particular company or service provider will appear more that pays more. However, due to limited display capacities a sort of competition always remains between advertisers or service providers.

SEM is relatively new in research areas in tourism research as in past the research was focused on technical aspects of Search Engine Optimisation (SEO) and confined to computer and information science (Pan et al., 2011). The internet has affected five competitive forces in the tourisms, on supply side tourism business has adopted this, on demand sides now most of customers rely on internet, the entry barriers are decreasing, threats of new substitutes offering is increasing and industry rivalry is become very fierce and just a click away (Pan et al., 2011). As a result, there is a constant struggle among tourism sector players to engage with potential tourist as well be on the top of organic searches as Search Engine Result Pages (SERPs). So, this research attempts to answer the questions related to how tourism and destination marketing organisations should use SEO as a CRM tool and create competitive advantages.

Search engine marketing (SEM) is a tool of customer relationship management (CRM) strategy that predominantly aims at acquiring new customers. Due to competitive dynamics of the tourism industry and customers' movement to online platforms for decision making, SEM has a great role as a tool of CRM strategy. This research article aims at critically analysing and synthesising researches and practices in search engine marketing (SEM). The implications of research findings for tourism marketers are discussed. SEM has potentials as a multi-billion dollar industry. As per research by Piper Jaffray, search is second most used application on the web and the industry amounts about $44.5 billion worldwide (Jarboe, 2007). Its' actual emergence dates back for decades as related to the availability and access of internet. This is a form of marketing that initiates with the consumer's search for a specific product or service that is termed as the 'hunt mode'. The consumer then indulges in research as passing through the 'buying cycle'. Marketers target the traffic through paid advertising post and normal search engine result page listings. Both segments of SEM as organic (free) and inorganic (paid) are dominated by giant market players as Google, Bing, Yahoo and few others and are used by millions of companies or business firms worldwide. **:** Technically, SEM is a type of wider internet marketing platform that attaches the use of advertising and optimization. This form of marketing is concerned with promoting websites through increasing appearances on the search engine results page or SERPs. Currently, SEM includes paid listings, SEO, relevant search engine services or activities as supportive to increase the traffic or exposure to the advertised website. This paper aims to outline the strategic relationship between consumers and service providers through conceptualizing the human –computer interaction (HCI). On ground of the Unified Theory of Acceptance and Use of Technology (UTAUT) (Venkatesh et al., 2003), the paper also concentrates on SEM in particular areas of tourism industry.

LITERATURE AND BACKGROUND

Search Engine Marketing: The Concept

The concept of SEM is relatively new and has been evolving over the years due to the introduction of more sophisticated technologies. In tourism sector, SEM is using technology as tool of marketing by enhancing visibility and search-ability of tourism products and services in paid or non-paid form (Moran & Hunt, 2005). Google, Bing, Nexis/Lexis, travel reservation systems, private search databases or even electronic card catalogue are all some sort of search engines at present. Technological experts had a strong sense of wit as most of such programmes were named after a book character 'Archie' that followed Veronica, Jughead and Gopher (this was a non-comic character). As soon as browser was invented to display information graphically, this became a major search interface.

There are differences between Search Engine Marketing (SEM) and Search Engine. *Search Engine Marketing, or SEM, is a form of Internet Marketing that seeks to promote brands and websites by increasing their visibility in the Search Engine results pages (SERPs) and has a proven positive ROI (Return on Investment).*

Theoretically three main SEM types are:

1. **Organic Search Tools or Search Engine Optimization (SEO):** 'Search Engine Optimization (SEO) is the process of improving the ranking, volume and quality of traffic to a web site from search engines via "natural" ("organic" or "algorithmic") search results, when a consumers inputs some key search words. Usually, the earlier a site is presented in the search results, or the higher it "ranks", the more searchers will visit that site. SEO can also target different kinds of search, including image search, local search, and industry-specific vertical search engines' (Dealerspan, 2014).
2. **Paid Placement or Search Engine Advertising:** Buying a paid position on web space page from companies like Google AdWords, Yahoo! Precision (e.g.: Google displays paid advertisements on the top and right side); and
3. **Paid Inclusion:** Paying search engine companies to appear on the top.

Other sources, including the New York Times define SEM as the practice of buying paid search listings, different from SEO which seeks to obtain better free search listings. (Dealerspan, 2014)

Travel information searchers are the potential tourists searching or hunting online for travel related information. Online tourism domains are the combinations of links, domain names, and web pages that contain texts, images, and audio/video files related to travel and tourism (Xiang et al., 2007). Thus, when search engines receive a tourist's queries, they retrieve related documents found in the searchable indexes created by indexer. Search engines then produce snippets with web address, a short description, similar pages, and cache, and display them in an Organic Listing (ranked order) on the SERPs. Conceptually, SEM is relatively simple and functions as 'hunt mode' that is, a business person or consumer searches for particular information by either clicking a directory hierarchy or the text box. This mode is important as it is concerned with indication that a person is searching for information that can be both indirect commercial or direct commercial type. 'Hunt mode' is the representation that a consumer is on any step of a buying cycle to research product or service to satisfy or try an urgent or potential demand. This shows the importance of SEM realize that a search engine normally generates the best sources of target traffic. This can be generated from either paid advertising listings or 'organic' unpaid search listings.

The webpage ranking depends on used URL keywords, keywords frequency and font size, presences of keywords in link anchor texts, substituting texts fir imagers, meta-tags as keywords in titles and descriptions, frequency of inbound link structures, age of the site, site updating frequency, page loading time, and the numbers of clicks on a result on

SERPs (Pan et al., 2011). In order to control the power that is attached with sources of target traffic, marketers have to realize effective uses of both organic and paid SEM and to achieve their expectations. Search engine traffic is exceptional as this is a non-invasive method of internet marketing because most of both offline and online advertisers invade the audiences and interrupt their functions. The traffic on search engines originates from audience focused and voluntary activities that are visitors on a search engine are influenced by results of the listings as shown. The exact moment for helping visitors to select a particular product or service is commonly known as 'Just-in-time Marketing'. A fixed inventory generates search engine traffic and to qualify as search engine traffic, a particular website has to be displayed before the consumers that they can access either by search query box filling or by clicking a search link in a directory style portal. However, contextual link inventory remains as an exception.

'Organic Search Listings' or 'Organic Search Engine Marketing' accumulates the best examples of usability, technology, online PR and linguistics or copy. Basic reason for this is that, numerous search engines ground their relevancy algorithms as combined with what are appeared on a page or site with external components as user preferences or behaviours and links. Net Ratings and Media Metrix have ranked 15 search engines and in SEM, marketers can purchase text-link search results. This is a major shift as before 1998, no search engines were able to include paid listings within search results. Paid search results very soon attained huge popularity within marketers as well as an attribution to search engine's revenue sources that persuaded marketers to make more requests for search results traffic with the high value of traffic as generated through search results. Organic or algorithmic or unpaid search engine traffic was easier to get but, the situation changed dramatically when more 3 billion documents engaged in competition to get attention in the search engine databases. A number of marketers believe in existence of some 'tricks' to support improving sites' relevancy within search engines in shapes of crawler or spider based. However, out of all of these tricks, not necessarily that these entire tricks act as expected. A number of these can also generate negative consequences that result in punishing marketers those tend to manipulate relevance and rankings.

From a more technical angle, some reasons persist for placing justifiable efforts to back organic SEO and mainly in site design, copy optimization, HTML formatting or even severe platform amendments. Paid listings have created a long lasting impact on most of the marketers' mindset in last the decade mainly for enlarging screen real estate. XML (Per-URL) Paid Inclusion, Paid Placement, Directory Paid

Inclusion, Shopping Search and Graphical (Rich Media) Search Inventory are some of the most popular paid listings. Organic Search Engine Optimization or SEO is very often compared to public relation due to its significant importance for a business organisation. In both PR and SEO, marketers enjoy freedom to hire internal staff, employ consultants or even to use outside agencies to serve purposes. Similar activities can take place for paid SEM, as well. In many cases, large paid search engine campaigns demand the engagement of bid management technology or campaign optimization for combining with both external and internal expertises. SEM has arguably established itself as an essential component of a complete or integrated campaign as participated by both direct marketers and branders. A kind of dialogue can benefit marketers and searchers in case of emergency purchase or information. A brief history of search engines is available on the iProspect website (iProspect, 2009). The costs of SEM is around one sixth of online add displays and one eighth of email marketing. Sonenclar (2005) found that most of the organisational outsource SEM companies require to concentrate on to work more efficiently, lack of updated knowledge of technologies, time pressures, not having in-house tools, issues with SEM provider contacts, complications and complexities of managing in-house SEM.

Tourists search for travel related information from search engines at different stages of their pre, during and post trip and tourism product consumption. Also, tourists search for all relevant information that fall in domains of tourism industry/sector/network (i.e.: suppliers, tour operators, governments, destination marketing organizations, substitutes, players, destinations, tourism products, hotels, cities, tourist reviews, social media sites, activities and supports needed during all phases of buying and consumption of tourism products, related links, domain names, web pages containing texts, images, and audio/video information (Pan et al., 2011). Several studies have explored the dynamic triad- relationship among three parties namely: customers of information as tourists, search engines and tourism sector domain. These studies have argued that relationships between these parties are not linear but, complex. Dynamics with each component has effect on other two and vice versa. Hence, one sole management says that search engine will not only provide an effective SEM strategy. The needs and goals of each of three parties of the triad and their relationship impacts should be understood and addressed by appropriate SEM strategies to co-evolve relationships. It is important to understand tourists' behaviour while, using search engine through stages like; formulating search queries in form of key words, thinking about goals of information and transactions, making decisions out of alternatives and taking actions. Researchers have also argued that user-search engine interactions influence their clicking behaviour. Studies have found that tourists usually use 3-4 key words to search for information and mostly do not go beyond second page of search results. In one study related to 'eye movements' on pages, it was found that users prefer to look into only upper left triangular area of page with boundaries at top-left side up to half of the page (up to top 7-10 listings) and only 1-2 top lines of right side of the page (Sonenclar, 2005). While searching, users 'switch' between broader search (e.g.: city) and narrow focused (e.g.: hotel or destination brand) using few distinct vocabularies like London hotels, London attractions, Hotels near London eye' etc. The organic listing is more trusted. Users click 1-2 top, then 8th-10th listings. Ranking 6th-7th is the least preferred clicking place (Pan et al., 2011). Even in order to maintain credibility, search engines continually change their algorithms and Universal Search (e.g.: images blending, blogs, videos and other formats) to avoid biases, misuses, cheating of systems by the destination marketing domains or tourists.

SEARCH ENGINE MARKETING AND ADSENSE: WHAT ARE THESE ALL ABOUT?

Information system research demands non-conventional methods as hermeneutic method (Butler, 1998). This is one of the most under researched area and can possibly be a better match for the eMediaries. According to Google (2014), the concept of free and flexible AdSense advertisement deviates from the Google Adwords advertisers and these advertisers provide AdSense to Google to show on appropriate sites. AdSense typically cover tests, videos, graphic advertisements or even advertisements for feeds and can be available both mobiles, domains and others. Marketers should be offered to explore opportunities (Miller, 2010). AdSense, typically reveal more solutions for earning. However, it's potential to become a valid marketing instrument is questionable. Still, as argued by Buhalis and Wagner (2013), the less researched areas should be offered priorities in the academic domain to explore the potentials.

AdSense is a concept that can be relatively unfamiliar to most of the general users of internet. However, this is undoubtedly common among those who frequently use the internet as reliable platform to generate income and earnings. AdSense is a useful means of internet based marketing and is capable to reach a wider segment of potential customers across the world. This is Google's online platform of advertisement. This is useful to identify the target group of customers using their geographical locality, feature and content of the website that they use. Through this process, Google can manage to understand the taste, choice or preferences of identified group of potential customers and thus to offer them the most suitable product of service options. Through AdSense, Google becomes able to spot and thus to deliver advertisement to them. For the online marketers, this is a solid and useful platform to fulfil their desire to reach the potential customers with the product or service offers through the use of advertisement. AdSense has enabled the online marketers to answer the queries with information of their services or products with details of information. AdSense is turning as a reliable platform to reach the target customer base and thus to allow them to get sufficient information of their desired products or services and then finally, maximizing the future use of this advertisements based marketing.

This is very often unclear the ways through which AdSense is able to reach the wider segments of customers across the world, regardless of geographical boundaries. The engagement with customer base is not an easy job to perform and rather a difficult or complex type of responsibility. Online marketers are mostly lacking the availability of a ground or platform that can be relied or used as efficient and AdSense has managed to fill this gap with their strong presence. Google is attached with the availability of information sharing for the relevant customers. For example, if the selected business is linked with garments accessories and when any customer will search on the website about garments, the advertisement of that specific business organisation will appear. This thus will offer them to select and get response from them with details of the services or products they offer through their website. This also works with locality that is Google helps to find out local customers to get access to this specific business organisation. This is the general pattern within which AdSense normally works. There are also other types applicability of this platform those are more complex and expertise tailored. Google through AdSense thus makes and turns a selected business enterprise to become available to certain groups of customers and allow them to avail the offered products or services. This certainly helps in expanding the scopes of business with a possible ground of generating future potentials. The introduction of AdSense by Google thus can be identified as an efficient platform to understand the capacity, necessity and application of such platform for generating business prospects. Thus the use of AdSense cannot be ignored in the current and future marketing world.

AdSense is attached with customer responses and this is important that marketers are required to follow and adopt. However, the patterns of understanding generated responses are required to be monitored and followed carefully. Where, marketers need to adopt and embrace diversities in offering objectives of AdSense marketing. There is a requirement that AdSense marketers have to rely on sustainable forms of responses. In AdSense marketing, the selection of keywords on the advertisements those should direct the customers to a certain goal of purchasing the advertised products or services. AdSense is a click and pay and thus is based on customer responses. AdSense is thus required to be attached with keyword searches to allow customers to get clear ideas about the demands and offerings of that business organisation. The advertisements as are mostly well informative offer better and information on key areas that are not general and widely descriptive. Marketers are required to generate valid and reasonable reasons or motivations for customers those should attract customers to view their advertisements, motivated and thus become well persuaded to avail the services or products those are made available for them. The blogs those advertisers create for customers should be concise, short and clear to attract the potential customers. There should be a combination of information those are mostly attractive and from diverse sources are normally placed on the blog prepared by the marketer. This is very natural and common that in many times customers does not even see the best advertisement and this is thus natural that attractive and graphically enriched advertisements cannot always attract potential customers in the same pattern and in similar features. There should be well-balanced blends of information; design and attractiveness are required for an effective type of AdSense marketing. The frequency and amount of revenue generation also mainly depends on this with the basic conceptual acceptability of AdSense. AdSense is responsible for generating interests of potential customers, persuade them about the offered products or services and then based on the blogs created by the marketers take decisions on purchasing those advertised products or services. AdSense normally creates opportunities by direct purchases and in addition, creates more chances for future businesses in other related ways those are mostly concerned with the similar business enterprise. The types of diversity and opportunities those AdSense can produce and generate can be immense and can also lead that business to become more able to make profitability.

Google AdSense is a programme that is concerned with advertisement on the internet and allows the marketers to ensure financial gain through click and pay concept. AdSense is linked with a certain website of an identified marketer that is linked with blog to offer the customers on details of their products or services. This is simple in one sense that is the click and pay system. On the other side, there are complexities in terms of technology adoption and selecting the most suitable for using in a volatile market structure or situation. The success of AdSense relies on numerous factors and is related with diverse factors or issues. This is very often believed that Google AdSense allows users to earn money in a relatively easier way. However, a proper understanding of pros and cons of such online platform is essential for the purpose and without this; this cannot always generate money for users. This happens mainly due to closer involvement of numerous customer bases with diverse characteristics or typologies. The management of Google AdSense programmes are also bit difficult for the clients. Google AdSense cannot generate income for users in many cases where they believe that this would be supportive for their earning through easier ways of money earning but, in many cases, the result appear as reverse and do not necessarily match with their expectations. A considerable number of users cannot reap the maximum outcome from this Google AdSense and find it difficult in the practical ground of turning it as a reliable source of earning. This is important that Google has its own set of policies and procedures in some cases; these can be restricted to others and mainly to users. This is similarly true for AdSense as well where; user can violate the set terms and conditions of use. This in turn can create complexities and potentially lead to defamation and legal penalties. Computer webmasters with vast expertise in relevant areas should attempt to make the rules and regulations to potential users for getting benefit from Google AdSense. Still, many webmasters violate these mainly due to their negligence and carelessness. However, this brings reverse result that is if Google's policies are not respected, Google also cannot respect those websites aimed to generate money through using AdSense. The basic criterion of making benefit from Google AdSense is to attract diverse sets interest groups. This is purely related to traffic. This is particularly important because, the success of making money from Google AdSense largely relies on loads of oncoming traffic to the user's website that is there have to be some users for clicking on the website. Without these clicks, there cannot be effective results. Pay per click that is commonly known as PPC is also the outcome of the website's attractiveness with the contents and outlooks. These contents need to attract the advertisements and the interested and potential users, as well. At this stage, the web pages need to be blended in with website of the users. Colour matching, resolutions, contrasts are all important for an effective website that can create appeal to users as well as capable of attracting advertisements from diverse groups of clients. The attraction has to be meaningful that is attracting the potential traffic and thus to persuade them to click simultaneously. This sequence is essential because, without a clear intention, no user would like to click on the website that does not completely persuade them to click rather than having a glimpse of viewing only. The demand of potential users or traffic needs to be carefully outlined that is Google AdSense is simply linked with clicking and this needs to be ensured in practice.

THE DIFFUSION OF ADSENSE IN TOURISM MARKETING BY eMEDIARIES

AdSense is turning as a useful and more acceptable platform for online marketing. This is very common and anticipated that this will enhance the areas of online marketing. Following the origin and characteristics of AdSense, this is produced from Google Adwords advertisers and Google is the main organization responsible for type of technology marketing. Adwords deliver AdSense to Google for showing on sites those it find as relevant for the purpose. AdSense has typical features in variety and incredible in terms of providing advertisement to targeted customers or marketers. Thus this is relevant that customers will look for selected advertisements and the revealed advertisements. AdSense very often appears in diverse forms with the use of text, graphics or even audio-visuals. The typology of AdSense included graphics, videos or audio advertisements. Also, AdSense advertisements for domains, mobile phones or feeds are also beneficial for both of the marketers or customers. This thus becomes apparent that there are various ways to reach messages to audiences or customers and to help to bring out the maximum from them. This is thus very well established that AdSense is capable to offer the maximum benefits from using online platforms and to produce some sort of general benefits or freedom for them. AdSense is customer and user friendly that is, after signing up as a user of AdSense, users are allowed to design, prepare and to view the appearance of their proposed advertisement. There is a close relationship between website, advertisement and micro or blogging, to be used for practices. AdSense has capacities to appear and to be used as a reliable platform of online marketing. As blogs are relevant with AdSense, these should appear in form to offer the customers to offer the maximum possible information and to persuade them to get the offered products or services. Blogs are required to appear with information and non-detailed contents with representing the sources those can be numerous and diverse. AdSense is attached with payments that is, this pays for per click and this is the reason for which AdSense marketers required to create a serial of blogs concerned with such marketing with updated forms of information. This thus turns AdSense as difficult for marketers where, Google has placed more restrictions. This is in fact obvious that Google is cracking down AdSense constantly in relation to the mini blog phenomenon that Google considers as spams. The marketing process with AdSense is rewarding and has to follow a systematic way of procedures. Marketers are required to become aware that AdSense can become beneficial for the entire business through exploring and utilizing the relatively wide ground of online marketing sources. In order to become more aware with AdSense to ensure financial gains, marketers are required to follow some specific types of actions and these should be more realistic and should meet the demands of existing demands. The use and application of AdSense for promotion and marketing activities, there is a requirement of following an effective set of procedures for getting the most possible outcome of AdSense marketing.

SEARCH ENGINE MARKETING: IS IT A SYNCHRONIZATION OF DIGITAL MARKETING?

The meaning of digital marketing in tourism is still to get an appropriate academic shape. There are scopes to introduce, develop and to circulate a workable definition of this for helping to understand the central theme. A more industry tailored and relevant outlining with the existing tourism market structures is also much desired. In a very general understanding, digital marketing refers to a pattern of marketing that uses technology as the main platform to reach the target consumers bases. There are numerous professional and practical techniques to apply technologies in tourism markets where, digital marketing is entirely technology based. A wider selection of tourism products or services coupled with marketing tactics like branding or promotions are presented before consumers to allow them to reach a positive purchase decision.

Digital marketing has unparalleled dependency on internet and thus very often is termed as internet marketing. Internet is the central base of digital tourism while, television-radio or even the mobile telephone devices are used to serve purposes. The use of internet is relatively far more effective to reach wider consumer segments and thus to persuade them to purchase a selected or available offers, services or products. Unlike conventional patterns of marketing, this internet based marketing is more focused, targeted and comprehensive. This type of marketing moves in aligned with dynamic technological innovations, changes and thus to enhance the capacities of consumers. This also supports consumers to get expanded knowledge on form of products or services selection (Ardichvili, 2008).

Digital marketing is getting related to tourism marketing in recent times where, tourism business enterprises use digital marketing campaigns or tools for marketing. Certain number of advanced options becomes available for digital marketing, other than, email, sms, mms or social networking. Display supported digital marketing can offer realistic experiences to consumers and thus to help them select products or services in a more convenient way. The introduction of Smartphones has enabled digital tourism marketers and consumers to reach a mutual standpoint of both offerings and acceptances. Digital marketing is faster than conventional marketing, that is the message can pass over within a very short time to numerous consumer bases across the world. However, evidently, digital tourism marketing requires expert knowledge on certain areas and on technical issues. Digital marketing is also advancing and this pace of advancement is overwhelming. Basic advantages of digital marketing are phenomenal and thus almost all over the world this type of marketing are managing to get sufficient responses. These are mostly positive. In comparison with direct marketing, digital marketing has specific advantages that mostly come in numerous forms. The main factor of personal attention of consumers is crucial and is related to the interaction with customers. Also, digital marketing tends to focus individually on each of the customers and thus creates more possibility to generate direct responses.

In digital marketing, this is very often manageable and possible to create personalised message to individual customer. Each customer can be addressed and greeted separately and uniformly. This thus promotes personalised service or product marketing that is more effective than other conventional forms. Also, digital marketing supports the response measurements from customers in forms like replies or reactions. Responses are quicker from messages sent to each customer. This is important to understand the customer bases and their responses or mindsets. Digital marketing necessarily require specialized forms of knowledge on marketing and technology. This is more customer-tailored and relevant to meet their demands more satisfactorily. Digital marketing can become an important addition to any existing or potential business enterprise in tourism industry. This helps both the marketers and customers to achieve a target that is more focused and realistic. There is a gap between traditional and digital forms of marketing and this gap is gradually increasing over the years due to the availability of more advanced types of technologies. These advancements are continuously beating the older forms. Digital marketing is the productive outcome of internet and online progresses. This is much supported by diverse forms of technological innovations. Also, this is convincing that digital marketing keeps on evolving over the coming years through the adoption of more advanced technological modernizations. This is a way to support, promote and expand an existing business enterprise and to reach the target customer bases. In addition, this is important to ensure that the business enterprise is getting the maximum from digital forms of marketing even within a complex market setting. Digital marketing is believed to have very good possibility to become popular in tourism industry.

Digital marketing has simply turned as a necessity of today's business world that is supported by technologies than ever before. The demand of technology adoption is enormous in tourism industry where, this is required to have practical knowledge in marketing and technology. This form of tourism deals with both of the supply and demand sides and thus the interests of both parties are also involved. Digital marketing is beneficial and rewarding for marketing and technology applications.

Customers are stayed connected and thus the response generation becomes more obvious than conventional marketing. The activity operations and successes of a tourism business enterprise depend on specific marketing factors. These also are related to many types of business functionalities including understanding the targeted customer bases and becoming able to realize their responses in a purposeful manner. The success of digital marketing relies on specific strategies or factors. Unlike, conventional marketing approach, in digital marketing, there has to be specific business targets. The basic intention should entail to ensure accomplishments in a selected business enterprise. The more number of customers is involved with a business enterprise, the more attentions on each of these customers are required. This is also essential to have a gross business aim and to ensure that the business is directed towards the desired goal. Digital marketing is particularly imperative for any business to have achievements within the shortest possible timeframe. Understanding the market situations and the business policies are very essential for effective marketing. Again, the creation and use of marketing tools is important. These help to bring products or services closer to customers to purchase. Tools in marketing are very essential as without their presence there are very little or even no scopes to let customers purchase the services or products. Marketing tools help to convert undecided person into customers. Certain business strategies are required to ensure that the marketing tools are in operation and effective.

SEARCH ENGINE MARKETING IN TOURISM BUSINESS MANAGEMENT STRATEGIES

The practices and management of strategies those are aligned with non-conventional marketing strategies can be outlined as to develop a conceptual sketch aimed to capitalize strategic advantages. Futures marketing areas can be overwhelming where; the interaction and introduction of technology supported marketing tools can appear as basic concerns. This is natural that newer forms of marketing strategies will replace the existing ones and with their effective interaction that particular marketplace will gradually develop to attain a certain position. The shaping and formation of technology based market place is a part of global marketing strategies. This can become truly effective where, the emergence of relatively innovative forms of strategies are adopted and placed in practice. Evidently, development of marketing channels or tools in tourism is becoming more appealing to those who rely on technology transfer. As the process of development and growth of market place moves in a faster pace than predicted even few decades ago, this is also natural that consumers will adopt and capitalize the outcomes of technological innovations. The patterns of technology supported marketing tools and their diffusion relies on some specific criteria as part of the strategic policy formulation and their implementation process. Resources and capacities those are considered as static need to be more available and flexible to access and to enhance the level of acceptance. The excellence in operation, designing process, development of services or products, portfolio analysis, effective management of supply chains are more focused on rationalization of strategy formulation and implementation. This supports to bring effectiveness to certain types of marketing strategies or policies. Conventional models, channels or tools of marketing can very often appear as risky in market places those are relatively new, unknown and technology demanding. This is where; technology supported marketing tools can have affectivity, in relation to outline the marketing channels, enterprise development, both online and offline marketing communication generation. Such type marketing tools, channels or platforms can initiate more opportunities and capacities to bring efficiency and effectiveness. This can also reduce the level of dependency on a single specific marketing channel or tool.

THE HUMAN – COMPUTER INTERACTION: AN ANALOGY

The human-computer interaction is concerned with studies, design, planning and uses of interaction that take place between computers as machine with humans as users. This notion as developed by Card, Moran and Newell (1983), in their book *The Psychology of Human-Computer Interaction* found its way in behavioural sciences, designing, media studies, computer sciences and many more. This concept outlines that a computer can have many uses and engages in open ended conversation between the computer and users as different from general tools as useful driving nails, hammers or similar). In tourism, consumers' nature and intention to look for information of diverse types are innate. This has found ways in many times and in many parameters or angles. Thus Search Engine turns as an unavoidable part of human societal system. These are interfaces through which consumers tend to search for desired information or data of products or services as per their demands. The types and mindsets of consumers are different by character or feature analysis. Thus the importance of adopting and applying technological developments are mostly common as related to their attachments or applications. The attitudes or motives of consumers' can appear as simple to complex depending on their types, natures and sector based applications. This is also the part of a wider system or framework that necessitates the use of advanced technologies. The uses of Search Engine are phenomenal with the introduction of more advanced features. Over the years, the features and types of search engines have modified and have taken more advanced shapes. These have helped to create more opportunities in relation to application of technologies. There are also ways that effect the interaction between technologies and human usage. Consumers can search for data and information from diverse perspectives and backgrounds that have made search engines as more accessible to almost all types of consumers. Search engines are not huge in numbers and capacities rather they are very few and mostly the outcomes of technologically strong nations in the world. The global marketplace is constantly changing with more interaction of technology and actors as active in the entire process. Conventional means of communication between businesses and the beneficiaries are dramatically getting changed over the years with introduction of more devices and gadgets. The platforms on which business activities normally take place are getting more updated with advanced forms and diversities of applications including internet based outcomes. Thus this is very true that conventional platforms are constantly getting changed and is getting replaced by non-conventional and more technology centric gadgets or applications. Before, consumers tend to search for information on non-technological interfaces. However, these have changed as long as technologies have intervened that also sharpened the entire process and modes of searching platforms. Thus this is strongly suggested that internet based search engines are playing crucial role in taking places within the consumers' mind-set that in turn helps in getting access and control over the pursuit of their knowledge and information.

THE UNIFIED THEORY OF ACCEPTANCE AND USE OF TECHNOLOGY (UTAUT)

The Unified theory of acceptance and use of technology (UTAUT) is a model of technology acceptance as proposed by Venkatesh, Morris, Davis and Davis (2003) in *User acceptance of information technology: Toward a unified view*. According to the UTAUT, a user intends to use a system of information with subsequent usage behaviour. The UTAUT is constructed with four key constructs as: performance expectancy, effort expectancy, social influence and facilitating conditions. The first three constructs act as direct determinants of use intention and behaviour while, the fourth acts as the direct determinant of use behaviour. Age, gender, experience and voluntariness of use are hypothesised to advance effects of the four key constructs on usage intention and behaviour. The UTAUT as a theory was introduced on the basis of consolidations and reviews of the constructs of eight models. These constructs were used is previous researches to outline information system usage behaviour. The eight models were: technology acceptance model, theory of reasoned action, theory of planned behaviour, diffusion of innovations theory, social cognitive theory, motivational model, a combined theory of planned behaviour/technology acceptance model and model of personal computer use. Consequent validation by Venkatesh et al. (2003) of UTAUT in a longitudinal study explored it to account for 70% of the variance in behavioural intention and about 50% in actual use.

Figure 1.

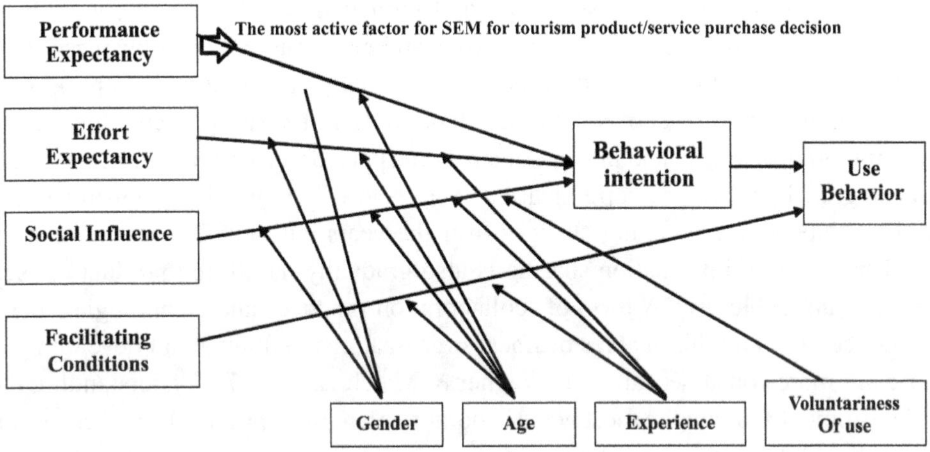

SEARCH ENGINE MARKETING, THE UNIFIED THEORY OF ACCEPTANCE AND USE OF TECHNOLOGY (UTAUT) IN TOURISM

Any marketing tool or channel needs to be effective, reliable and dynamic. The global marketplace is competitive and hence, this is more expected that potential marketing tools have more capacities to generate results those are innovative, more user friendly and supportive for the growth and development of a specific business enterprise as well as the entire market structure. The gradual move from conventional to more advanced marketing strategies is viewed as demand realization backed by necessity information. The progression of technologies can be extraordinary in terms of their conceptualizations and applications. Technologies in many cases can even reshape the organizational structure of a business enterprise. This is expected that traditional marketing tools or channels are also shifted to more acceptable and reliable forms those are supported by technologies with an example of the Word of Mouth (WOM) to Electronic Word of Mouth (eWOM) (Wasko & Faraj, 2000). The interrelationship between service or product providers with consumers needs to be congenial that in return can become more effective with effective applications.

Information and communication technologies in the last few decades have witnessed dramatic improvements and have transformed into diverse consumer segments. The trend has updated choices of conventional users to get access and utilize the features regardless of any geographical area. Impacts of such advancements allow a wider spectrum of interconnections between consumers and service or product providers. The introduction of technological gadgets like the tourism related applications have in fact revolutionised the entire industry. These otherwise could remain static and without any digitalized format for coming several hundreds of years. Information and communication technologies have created a ground that has turned as the hub for those who are involved with the process of technology transfer. This has appeared in shapes of creating a link between different types of service or product providers in these identified areas with general consumers. Information and communication technology type data coupled with video and voice sources are getting enormously popular and essential to generate new models or themes for accelerating the process of forming social or business enterprises (Salesforce, 2014). The interrelationship between stakeholders and recipients are also benefitted through communication, supply chains, management and exchange opportunities. Creation of new forms media and enterprises offers opportunities for furthering both subjective and applied knowledge. These should be in line with solving disputes with existing theoretical frameworks and corporate or social business strategies. The strategic aspects of relationships with consumers are gradually changing and adopting newer dimensions those are relatively newer set of policies and tend to back the base of technology diffusions. The relevancy and importance of data and information become part for the growth of infrastructures in cyber domains for integrated performance optimization. The patterns within which consumers and business service providers interact are attaining changes over the years with involvement of technologies and information. The nature of information sharing is also gradually modifying products or services data offer in a more manageable way. A form of 'collaboration practices and technologies' is replacing of being 'customer centric' and this enables business organizations to think about developing products or services those are more consumer tailored (Wagner & Majchrzak, 2007). Understanding the demands and needs of customer bases are the most generic point to plan for improvised products or services than the existing ones. Newer forms of marketing innovations are appearing in business and most of these can be beneficial and effective to generate positive outcomes (Abernathy & Clark, 1985).

MANAGEMENT IMPLICATIONS FOR TOURISM

Technology is affecting management practices in tourism. Proper applications of technologies are getting in use and their influences are also becoming useful mainly in areas of promoting the channels and strategies as used in management and marketing activities in tourism. The level of acceptance and their applications of technologies in management and marketing typically follow different typologies and strategic grounds. However, on the points of their affectivity, this needs to be generalized.

The application of technologies in management and marketing should be accelerated by supportive innovations. These should help in outlining basic features of tourism management structure to become more effective and thus to appear as more reliable, in terms of their validity and effectiveness. Different parts of the world are advancing differently, in terms of their capacities and benefit generations. There are also factors as related to management outline that technology supported management communications can create more opportunities to be termed as beneficial for effective strategies formulations. The demand for advanced technology supported management and marketing channels or tools can be universal in almost every sector of business where, tourism cannot be viewed as different.

Technology adoption and its use need to be highly emphasized. The acceptance is also related with the perception and decision making process of consumers and these normally influence the aspects of digitalised form of technology transfer in tourism. The development of technology supported gadgets need to be considered as another driving factor for this sector and part of the entire conceptualisation of development. Tourism industry is booming rapidly with huge amount of investment both from private and public sector and importance needs to be placed on technology application. Technological infrastructures should also be given scopes to rise to numerous industries as related to tourism those have turned as part of this industry at present and their possible contributions will grow in coming years. Tourism as a ground should be managed to attract attention of certain number of tourists and industry experts those have played crucial roles in the process of advancing this sector.

CONCLUSION

As outlined from discussions, the relevancy of Human-Computer Interaction and Search Engine Marketing are important in tourism business where, technology will dominate almost all of the future marketing channels. The Unified theory of Acceptance and Use of Technology (UTAUT) also beholds importance in tourism marketing where, factors like age, gender, experience and voluntariness of use are attached with performance expectancy and level of use of tourism products or services (Venkatesh et al., 2003). The background and history of technology transfer in marketing is not that old as they assume to be. However, the process managed to get acceleration on the basis of their outcomes and capacities. The transfer of technologies in tourism marketing is pivotal to accelerate the shift of an identified business sector to turn it as more benefitting. The transfer of technologies and their relevancies are essential to create more business opportunities, to smooth marketing operations and thus to view them as valid in changing market situations. There are potentials that technology supported marketing channels, tools and related means can ensure to bring dynamism. On the other side, there are also ways on which marketing policy planning process can rely and become capable to offer more positive outcomes, in terms of their capacities and application. The use of data, information with factors as voice and video recording capacities are incorporating to become able to be considered as effective platforms of marketing. A harmonized form of interrelationship between these facts is helping to flourish the global market place of technology supported marketing innovations. On the other side, the potentials are also enhanced and scopes are created to capitalize newer forms of marketing channels those tend to be more effective, in relation to their abilities and possibilities. There is no single consideration that can be identified as responsible for technology supported innovations but, the reality is that potentials are created and these need to be utilized in almost all areas of business and thus to turn marketing as beneficial and rewarding. Marketing channels and tools those are based on technologies are more reliable, faster and effective as believed and these can generate better opportunities in a changing marketplace. The transfer of technology supports is narrowing the world to a certain extent and has been turning as essential components for the operational and managerial aspects of marketing. There are also relevant benefits of technology transfer as they can offer spaces to communicate from any part of the world and at any time regardless of worrying geographical distances. The wider engagements of technology transfers are playing crucial roles in building technology enabled infrastructures and thus to allow the creation of platforms those can benefit the entire marketing place. Consumers are also more inclined to get the services of product offers through technology supported platforms those can be viewed as more dynamic and rewarding. On the other side, workplaces in the present world are getting more dependent on technologies and the generated impacts can also become beneficial in many ways. The use of gadgets like mobile phones and other devices are frequently used by marketers while, opportunities are created to grasp the outcome of these advancements more closely. Still, the claim is more agreeable that business managers and strategists in technology enabled office spaces will prefer to communicate through mediums those are technology based, more convenient and accessible that validates the existence of technology transfer. Search engine marketing and application of the Unified theory of Acceptance and Use of Technology (UTAUT) in tourism still remains under researched where, the lack of relevant literature is acute. Basic limitation of this study is its type as a conceptual paper. An empirical type research could have present more arguments. This paper suggests conducting more researches in future in areas of technology penetration in tourism business to outline the future trends of technology adoption in marketing.

REFERENCES

Albernathy, W. J., & Clark, K. B. (1985). *Innovation: mapping the winds of creative destruction. North Holland*. Elsevier Science Publishers B.V.

Ardichvili, A. (2008). Learning and knowledge sharing in virtual communities of practice: Motivators, barriers, and enablers. *Advances in Developing Human Resources*, *10*(4), 541–554. doi:10.1177/1523422308319536

Butler, T. (1998). Towards a hermeneutic method for interpretive research in information systems. *Journal of Information Technology*, *13*(4), 285–300. doi:10.1057/jit.1998.7

Card, S. K., Moran, T. PNewell, A. (1980). The keystroke-level model for user performance time with interactive systems. *Communications of the ACM*, *23*(7), 396–410. doi:10.1145/358886.358895

Dealerspan (2014). *Home*. Retrieved from http://bit.ly/1wEqnOO

Google. (2014). *Google AdSense*. Retrieved from http://bit.ly/n3XpnY

iProspect (2009). *Search Engine marketing and online display advertising integration study*. Retrieved from http://bit.ly/1qhYjee

Jarboe, G. (2007). *SE watch*. Retrieved from http://bit.ly/1HNQ6Hx

McLure Wasko, M., & Faraj, S. (2000). "It is what one does": Why people participate and help others in electronic communities of practice. *The Journal of Strategic Information Systems*, *9*(2-3), 155–173. doi:10.1016/S0963-8687(00)00045-7

Moran, M., & Hunt, B. (2005). *Search Engine Marketing, Inc.: Driving search traffic to your company's web site*. Upper Saddle River, NJ: IBM Press.

Pan, B., Xiang, Z., Law, R., & Fesenmaier, D. R. (2011). *The dynamics of search engine marketing for tourist destinations*. Retrieved from http://bit.ly/1FGKL2Y

Sonenclar, K. (2005). *Search-engine marketing: Growth companies in play*. Retrieved from http://bit.ly/1rI5J9q

Venkatesh, V., Morris, M. G., Davis, G. B., & Davis, F. D. (2003). User acceptance of information technology: Toward a unified view. *Management Information Systems Quarterly*, *27*(3), 425–478.

Wagner, C., & Majchrzak, A. (2007). Enabling customer-centricity using wikis and the wiki way. *Journal of Management Information Systems*, *23*(3), 17–43. doi:10.2753/MIS0742-1222230302

Xiang, Z., Hyun, K., Wöber, K., & Fesenmaier, D. R. (2007, June 17-20). Online representation of tourism: An analysis of search engine results from a major search engines. *Proceedings of the Travel and Tourism Research Association (TTRA) Annual Conference*. Las Vegas, NV.

Chapter 12
The Intersection of Social Media and Customer Retention in the Luxury Beauty Industry

Ellen Stokinger
London Metropolitan University, UK

Wilson Ozuem
Regents University, London UK

ABSTRACT

Debates regarding the ontological relationship between Social Media and customer retention have attracted considerable attention, particularly in the luxury beauty industry. The use of Social Media in the luxury beauty industry has caused many heated debates as it is seen as a form of interference in the exclusivity of luxury brands by limiting the physical and sensual contact between brand and customer. The purpose of this chapter is to provide some insights into how social media impacts on the cosmetics industry. Further, we provide evidence that the effective application of social media in the luxury beauty industry could lead to wider market share, and customer retention. The chapter concludes with some strategies that practitioners and researchers can adopt to develop effective marketing communication strategies, using social media platforms.

INTRODUCTION

The concept of social media and its relevance to effective marketing communications has gained much attention (Bolton et al., 2013; Brennan & Croft, 2012; Hamid, Akhir & Cheng, 2013; Hanna, Rohm & Crittenden, 2011; Hoffman & Fodor, 2010; Mangold & Faulds, 2009; Ozuem & Tan, 2014). The evolution of Social Media has led to the democratisation of corporate communications, with power shifting from advertising departments towards the opinions of individuals and communities, who like or dislike, comment upon and share content (Kietzmann, Hermkens, McCarthy & Silvestre, 2011; Dann & Dann, 2011). The online social landscape has converted the standard one-to-many media monologue into many-to-many dialogue. Social Media has increasingly become a product of consumers (Berthon, Pitt,

DOI: 10.4018/978-1-4666-9776-8.ch012

Plangger & Shapiro, 2012). Online conversations have become the new fuel and forefront of customer-firm relationships. Practitioners of the Cluetrain Manifesto (Levine, Locke, Searle &Weinberger, 2011) even describe conversations as "new products" that are part of a marketplace of organisations that permanently pitch to each other. As the rise of Social Media offers great opportunities to connect with consumers, Mangold and Faulds (2009) have made a case for the long-term incorporation of Social Media in a company's integral Marketing Communications strategy.

Bain and Company (2013), the leading strategy consultancy in the global luxury goods industry, expects the worldwide market of luxury goods to continue its double-digit growth, accounting for a total of £208 billion sales by 2015. In the UK specifically, the Walpole (2013), a non-profit association representing more than 180 British luxury brands such as Harrods, the Royal Opera House and Selfridges, reports an estimated growth of 12 per cent in the UK luxury industry, reaching an estimated record of £11.5 billion in the year 2017. With regard to beauty in particular, the global luxury beauty market outpaced mass-market beauty growth by 1.6 per cent in 2012 (BW Confidential). The luxury beauty industry in the UK is especially unique, as the nation's beauty market grew by 5 per cent to £2.2bn in 2012, propelling the UK to the third biggest luxury beauty market in Europe after France and Italy (Euromonitor International, 2013). The luxury beauty market in the UK is forecasted to be the fastest growing developed market in Western Europe with a growth rate of 6 per cent over the next five years, compared with an average growth of 2 per cent in the region (Euromonitor International, 2013).

The rise in the standard of living and consumer education about products has led to a democratisation of what were originally considered the most exclusive products (Garland, 2008). Globalisation has furthermore contributed to an increased level of competition, leading companies to create more exclusive products in order to differentiate from each other (Vickers & Renand, 2003). Many companies seek to add value to their brand by simply adding the term "luxury" or by extending their product portfolio with a luxury range, whilst others have created a truly luxury-oriented brand as their core business proposition. This study focuses on the last group, luxury brands that authentically carry the original meaning of luxury. We differentiate our approach by highlighting the principal theoretical starting points of this rapidly burgeoning literature related to social media and customer retention in the luxury beauty industry.

THEORETICAL CONTEXT AND FOUNDATIONS

The growing desire of consumers for exclusivity and personalisation motivates luxury retailers to strongly invest in beauty. Evidence for this can be seen in for example the new "Beauty Workshop" area in Selfridges, the recently opened "Beauty Mart" section in Harvey Nichols in London or the new Luxury Beauty store on Amazon. Nowadays luxury beauty brands increasingly use Social Media to give consumers a more actively engaging brand experience. Despite the growing popularity of online shopping, so far only one in five women purchases beauty products via the Internet and many consumers are still uncomfortable about buying beauty products online, as the preference to explore, assess and test the products prior to purchase still holds true (YouGov, 2012). Some scholars, for example, Kane, Alavi, Labianca & Borgatti (2014) suggested that social media provide users and companies with capabilities that they do not possess in traditional offline social networks, such as visualising network structure and searching for content in a network without using relational ties. Others have cautioned that social media's impressive rise comes with meaningful challenges in the social media world. One of the challenges is that whereas good information travels quickly, bad information can even more quickly (Goldenberg, 2015; Holloman, 2013)

Social Media has become an integrated part of everyday life, but its entry into the luxury goods industry has been far from easy. The use of Social Media in the luxury beauty industry has caused many heated debates as it is seen as interference to the exclusivity of a luxury brand by limiting the physical and sensual contact between the customer and the luxury brand (Choo,Moon, Kim & Yoon,2012; Dall'Olmo Riley & Lacroix, 2003; Dubois & Paternault, 1995; Khang, Ki & Ye, 2012;Okonkwo, 2010; Seung-A, 2013; Smith, 2009). However, as the number of affluent customers purchasing online increases, luxury brands face the challenge of retaining their customer base in order to create more sustainable revenue streams (Bolton, 1998; Buttle, 2009). Companies have reacted to this recent evolution in the marketing landscape and almost every luxury brand has adopted Social Media to connect with customers (Kim & Ko, 2010). A survey by the Luxury Interactive Conference's research team reported that 78 per cent of digital marketing executives for luxury brands increased their spend on Social Media in 2012, with 73 per cent of those surveyed planning to further increase their Social Media spend in 2013 (Alston, 2012).

The last decade has seen the production of a vast range of literature about Social Media. Topics of preference have so far included communication (Ozuem, Howell & Lancaster, 2008; Quinton & Harridge-March, 2010; Powers, Advincula, Austin, Graiko & Snyder,2012), the impact of word of mouth (Kozinets, Valck, Wojnicki & Wilner, 2010; Hennig-Thurau, Gwinner, Walsk & Gremler, 2004, Prendergast & Yuen, 2010), purchase intentions (Naylor, Walker, Cait & West, 2012) and service creation (Jarvenpaa & Tuunainen, 2013; Onook, Manish & Raghave, 2013; Trainor, 2012). Some of the literature focuses on how Social Media influences customer relations (Katsioloudes, Grant & McKechnie, 2007; Kim & Ko, 2010; Clark & Melancon, 2013; Laroche, Habibi, & Richard, 2013; Hennig-Thurau et al., 2010).

Most of these studies have focused on customer loyalty (Clark & Melancon, 2013; Gummerus, Liljander, Weman & Pihlström, 2012; Hawkins & Vel, 2013; Laroche et al., 2013; Ozuem & Lancaster 2014) yet Hennig-Thurau et al. (2010) considered customer retention as the outcome of engagement with new media. Their observations, however, were out-with the context of the UK luxury beauty industry. Blattberg, Getz and Thomas (2001) emphasised the need to clearly distinguish between customer loyalty and customer retention. Just because a customer is retained does not automatically imply that the individual is also loyal to a brand. Whereas customer loyalty is a customer reward that occurs once customers have changed their hearts and minds in favour of a particular product or service, customer retention is an organisational reward and focuses on how to keep customers without first having to change their hearts or minds (The Customer Institute, 2010).

Furthermore, Kim and Ko (2010) identified the impact of Social Media on customer equity, thereby emphasising the correlation between purchase intention and customer equity. Referring to the financially driven customer equity model as described by Blattberg et al. (2001), customer equity consists of three steps – customer acquisition, customer retention and add-on selling. It can thus be argued that evaluating the impact of Social Media marketing on customer equity jumps to the end without considering important hurdles in between such as customer retention. Therefore, instead of directly measuring customer equity or focusing on customer loyalty, this study recommends first analysing the extent to which Social Media impacts on customer retention. Whilst Social Media is often viewed as a positive lever in the customer-firm relationship, few studies refer to the luxury industry and fewer yet speak to the context of the UK luxury beauty industry.

Kim and Ko (2010; 2012) have made a substantial contribution to the literature on Social Media in the luxury market. However, as with many other studies, the researchers primarily focus on the luxury fashion industry (Choo et al., 2012; Kim & Ko, 2010; Kim & Ko, 2012; Jin, 2012; Moore & Doyle, 2010; Phan, Thomas & Heine, 2011). In contrast to the consumption of luxury fashion, buying luxury beauty products involves a high level of pre-purchase testing, which raises the question of whether or not Social Media provides an adequate tool to retain customers, as product testing is difficult and complex to implement online. This study therefore aims to identify the extent to which Social Media is a convenient tool to support the retention of luxury beauty customers and in which ways a brand's communication via Social Media can impact on customer retention.

The proliferation of Social Media is closely related to and facilitated by the development of Web 2.0 technologies (Berthon et al., 2012; Brennan & Croft, 2012; Fieseler & Fleck, 2013; Kaplan & Haenlein, 2010; Laroche et al., 2013; Tuten, 2008; Ozuem, Borrelli & Lancaster, 2015). The term "Web 2.0" was first introduced by the American media company O'Reilly and can be thought of as a set of technological innovations including hardware and software, which have the aim of empowering the user instead of the firm by allowing for content creation and increased interaction (Berthon et al., 2012; O'Reilly, 2005). While its predecessor, Web 1.0, had already laid the foundation for connecting people online via email and chat, Web 2.0 takes connectivity to another level by providing a variety of tools which enable the user to create, publish and share content and give recommendations to online friends and followers (Atta & Mahmoud, 2012; Evans & McKee, 2010).

This development has allowed for a new and disruptive marketing platform: Social Media and this was quickly identified as a revolution of the online generation and it has thus attracted the interest of researchers whose definitions bring Social Media into contact with different aspects such as the power of "social sharing" behaviour (Kaplan & Haenlein, 2010, Jevons & Gabbott, 2000; Nair, 2011; Safko & Brake, 2009; Stokes, 2008), interconnectivity (Dann & Dann, 2011; Hoffman & Novak, 2012; Laroche et al., 2013), influence (Brown & Fiorella, 2013), education (Blackshaw & Nazzarro 2004, Mangold & Faulds, 2009) and comparisons with traditional marketing (Mangold & Faulds, 2009; Zarella, 2010; Ozuem, O'Keeffe & Lancaster, 2015).

The most widespread definition of Social Media was originated by Kaplan and Haenlein (2010), who suggested that Social Media refers to a range of internet-based applications that build on the foundation of Web 2.0 and enable users to create and exchange User Generated Content (UGC). UGC is the engine of today's participative web and to "count" as UGC it must be published, creative and produced outside the professional context (Daugherty, Eastin &Bright, 2008; OECD, 2007). Many researchers emphasise the importance of exchanging and sharing UGC (Jevons & Gabbott, 2000; Nair, 2011; Safko & Brake, 2009; Stokes, 2008), after all the "social" in Social Media already promises a high degree of contact and exchange with other people.

Stokes (2008) sees the sense of Social Media in its ability to make users share content. Safko and Brake (2009) develop this further and define Social Media as a tool that allows users to share information, knowledge and opinions by engaging in online dialogues. On Social Media platforms, users have the opportunity to create a specific image of themselves, which is maintained through the sharing of posts, pictures, videos, liking certain posts and groups and extending the network of online friends. However, one might have the impression that some users pursue purely narcissistic interests (Nair, 2011), which can then quickly evoke negative attitudes towards users, brands or companies. In addition, the opportunity for self-expression might not be available to such an extent offline (Hoffman & Novak, 2012) and can thus result in some exaggeration of the personal self.

It is undisputed that Social Media can bring together like-minded people and businesses (Hagel & Armstrong, 1997; Wellman & Gulia, 1999) and hence it satisfies a need rooted deeply in human nature for a sense of belonging, (Maslow, 1943; Gangadharbhatla, 2008). Hoffman and Novak (2012) describe this as another revolutionising aspect of Social Media, as it is a tool that enables users to connect and re-connect even over long distances. Social Media allows for interconnectivity between users and between content and communication technologies (Dann & Dann, 2011). In the context of interconnectivity Tuten (2008) describes Social Media as an online community categorised as either social networks or virtual worlds that are participatory, conversational and fluid. Significantly, an online community "promotes the individual while also emphasizing an individual's relationship to the community" (Tuten, 2008, p.20). The motivation to engage in an online community derives from the need for contact comfort, also referred to as a need for affiliation, and a need for entertainment (Tuten, 2008). A brand community in particular is defined as a "specialised, non-geographically bound community, based on a structured set of relations among admirers of a brand" (Muniz & O'Guinn, 2001, p.412). Brands are referred to fundamentally as social entities (Muniz & O'Guinn, 2001) created through the inter-play of consumers and marketers (Firat & Venkatesh, 1995), which can thus be leveraged through the utilisation of Social Media.

Enabling users to talk to each other can be considered as an extension to traditional word-of-mouth communication (Divol, Edelman & Sarrazin, 2012; Mangold & Faulds, 2009). Amongst online users, some establish a more dominant position than others by sharing more information and opinions and thus procuring more buzz around them. Marketers have quickly discovered the power of targeting Social Media communities and they recognise that such groups gave rise to a new form of "influence marketing" (Williams & Cothrell, 2000; Brown & Fiorella, 2013). As well as exerting influence, Social Media also impacts upon persuasive acts, as persuasion is based on social connections and cultural assumptions (Noor Al-Deen & Hendricks, 2012).

Furthermore, the emergence of Social Media has led to a shift in power asymmetry from the marketer to the consumer, who now has a greater mandate over media consumption than ever before (Vollmer & Precourt, 2008). Social Media can spur consumer education about brands, products and services (Blackshaw & Nazzaro, 2004; Mangold & Faulds, 2009, Hoffman & Novak, 2012). Since Social Media is about sharing, consumers can use the web as a way to educate themselves and to contribute to the education of others within their network. In addition to collecting information from Social Media sources, users also see Social Media as a service channel that enables them to remain in easy touch with organisations (Leggat, 2010).

Whereas Social Media has all the hallmarks of the traditional paths of communication between company and consumer, it has also evolved as a new communication channel between consumer and consumer and it can thus be considered as a hybrid addition to the promotional mix (Mangold & Faulds, 2009). Mangold and Faulds (2009) therefore stress the permanent incorporation of Social Media in every company's Integral Marketing Communication's strategy. However, only implementing Social Media in the promotional mix does not guarantee success, as it is also crucial that public relations practitioners adapt their strategies to newly evolving media (Pavlik, 2007). Kietzmann et al. (2011) furthermore suggest that a firm's performance on Social Media (if done passionately and appropriately) can significantly impact upon reputations, turnover and even survival but it can cause damage if done half-heartedly (Kietzmann et al., 2011).

Dimensions of Social Media

The variety of Social Media allows for many different kinds of users and marketers have to distinguish between these different Social Media users if they want to target them effectively (Hanna et al., 2011).

Sukoco and Wu (2010) have identified two kinds of interests groups in Social Media communities. One group seeks to fulfil a self-related interest including knowledge and enjoyment and another follows socially-related interests which refer to their search for affiliation and social status. Humans generally want to create a specific image of themselves and want to control how other people perceive this image (Goffmann, 1959) by disclosing selected pieces of their daily lives to the public.

Cavazza (2013) suggests another model to categorise the motivations of online consumers according to four categories (sharing, discussing, networking and publishing). Whereas these categories adequately describe the most common online behaviour of today's user, it is doubtful if users already know the exact action they undertake during a browsing session. This study argues that users are more likely to know only the general purpose of what they want from their Social Media visit instead of planning the exact action beforehand. Rather than already knowing what exactly to discuss with other users prior to browsing, customers are more likely to first seek to satisfy general needs such as entertainment once only and find an inspiring article which they spontaneously decide to share. In examining Social Media platforms, the current paper identifies four different kinds of Social Media users and allocates the most appropriate Social Media tools aligned to each of these users.

The trefoil model (figure 1) distinguishes between four purposes of the users' online activity, their desire for status, entertainment, knowledge or business. In most cases the users' online activity has at

Figure 1. The trefoil model of Social Media users and tools
Source: Researcher

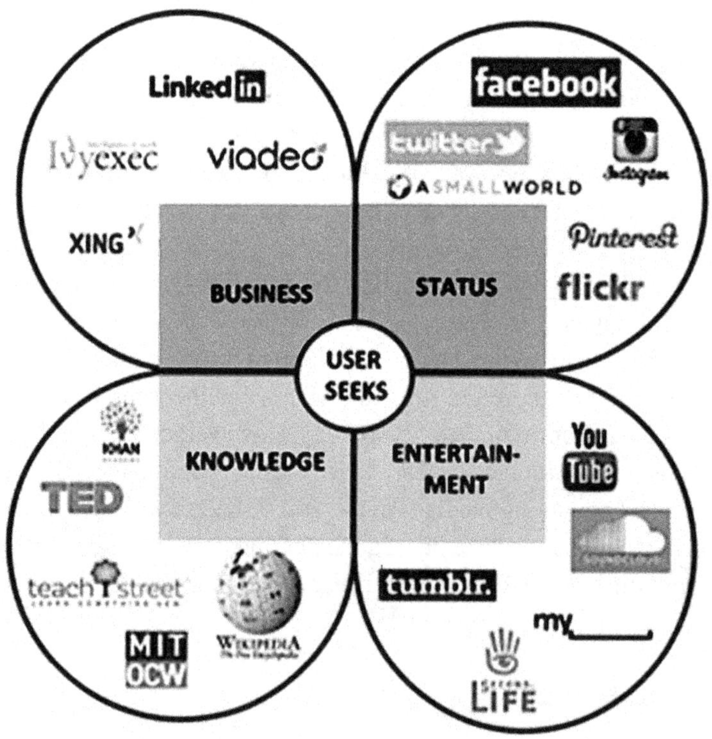

***All logos are trademarked.**

least one and at maximum all four identified purposes. During browsing on Social Media the user might spontaneously switch between the purposes.

- *Status-seekers* generally use social networking sites and visual Social Media, which allows them to construct a certain image through tweeting, sharing pictures with sophisticated filters and following particular brands. Examples include Facebook, twitter, Instagram, Pinterest and Flickr.
- *Entertainment-seekers* visit Social Media in order to have a good experience, to feel better through browsing. They seek platforms, which cover a certain topic of interest, such as music-focused Social Media platforms including YouTube, my space and Soundcloud, or, according to hobby and interest through organised blogs like Tumblr.
- *Knowledge-seekers* have the goal of extending their knowledge whilst using Social Media and so they target science-based learning platforms such as Wikipedia, TED or the Khan Academy.
- *Business-seekers* generally use Social Media because they want to leverage their career perspectives, either indirectly, through extending their professional network and updating their online CV, or even directly by applying for positions using, for example, their LinkedIn profiles.

Social Media is growing at a phenomenal speed and the increasing number of platforms provides challenges for companies to decide which newly developed media are sustainable and which are not (Kaplan & Haenlein, 2010). Possibly the most successful example of a sustainable medium is Facebook. Founded in 2004 by Harvard student Mark Zuckerberg Facebook has become the world's number one social medium in just under 10 years with 1 billion active users (Kirckpatrick, 2010; Socialmediatoday, 2013). Another example of a Social Medium that successfully re-shaped the communication landscape of today is Twitter. This micro-blog was launched as a secondary project in 2006 by a San-Francisco-based podcasting company but it quickly turned into a major project when it reached 215 million monthly active users and 500 million tweets a day in 2013 (Geron, 2013; O'Reilly & Milstein, 2012). However, not every Social Medium is qualified to survive in the long-term and even Apple's music sharing platform Ping has not managed to find success (Hof, 2012).

With such a rich amount of Social Media types it is useful to categorise these in order to afford an overview. Kaplan and Haenlein (2010) divide Social Media into six types comprising of collaborative projects, blogs, content communities, social networking sites, virtual game worlds, and virtual social worlds. However, new Social Media tools frequently emerge and in this context Kaplan and Haenlein's (2010) categorisation seems to offer only a limited perspective of the vast array of Social Media types. Mangold and Faulds (2009) provide a more detailed understanding of different Social Media types and tools, and their list is broken down and allocated to the appropriate user in the previously identified trefoil model of Social Media users and tools (Table 1).

For now the trefoil model of Social Media users and tools in combination with Mangold and Faulds' (2009) adjusted categorisation of Social Media tools and types provides a comprehensive overview about today's Social Media landscape. However, Social Media tools evolve quickly and the model therefore requires regular updates.

Critics have already raised the argument that text-based Social Media such as posts on Facebook and Twitter are outdated and are being replaced by visual-based Social Media (Walpole, 2013; Moritz, 2012). The latest development in Social Media supports this critique. Instagram, the photo-sharing networking service, has garnered 7,302,000 users and overtook Twitter with 6,868,000 users in August 2012. Pinterest, another content sharing service, has emerged as the 4th largest driver of traffic worldwide (Moritz, 2012).

Table 1. Examples of Social Media types and tools

Status-seekers • Social networking sites (Myspace, Facebook) • Invitation only social networks (ASmallWorld.net) • Photo sharing sites (Flickr)
Entertainment-seekers • Creative work sharing sites: - Video sharing sites (YouTube) - Music sharing sites (Soundcloud) - Content sharing combined with assistance (Piczo) - General intellectual property sharing sites (Creative Commons) • Virtual worlds (Second Life) • Commerce communities (EBay, Amazon) • Social bookmarking sites allowing users to recommend music, videos (Digg) • Open Source Software communities (Linux)
Knowledge-seekers • User-sponsored blogs (The Unofficial Apple Weblog, Cnet.com) • Company-sponsored websites/blogs (Apple) • Company-sponsored cause/help sites (click2quit) • Collaborative websites (Wikipedia) • Podcasts • News delivers sites • Educational materials sharing (MIT OpenCourseWare)
Business-seekers • Business networking sites (LinkedIn)

Source: Mangold and Faulds, 2009, p.358.

Mapping of Social Media for Marketing

The first predecessor of today's Social Media was introduced in 1979, when Tom Truscott and Jim Ellis from Duke University created "Usenet" (Kaplan & Haenlein, 2010). By allowing its users to post public messages this platform served as a Bulletin Board System (BBS) similar to today's forums (Kaplan & Haenlein, 2010). In addition to Usenet, the Internet ran a variety of protocols such as email, the chat system IRC and Gopher, a system to browse files (Rettberg, 2008). Towards the end of 1990 Tim Berners-Lee, a CERN scientist, implemented the first graphical web browser, which allowed for text with embedded images at the same time (Rettberg, 2008). This gave rise to the construction of the first webpages, both private and corporate, which (retrospectively considered) were the precursors of today's blogs (Rettberg, 2008). In 1998 Bruce and Susan Abelson launched the first social networking site "Open Diary", which connected online diary writers together in one community and gave them the opportunity to comment on other bloggers' opinions (Kaplan & Haenlein, 2010; Safko, 2012).

The development of high-speed Internet was the break-through of the constantly changing and evolving Social Media environment. Critics formulated doubts as to whether Social Media could survive in today's fast-paced media environment and labelled it as short-term trend. However, in 2012 there were 1.43 billion social network users worldwide (Arno, 2012) and many additional email and search engine users deliver sufficient proof that Social Media is a permanent, integrated part of life for young and old users. The serious advancement of Social Media leads to a shift in marketing thinking. Transactional marketing, which was identified by McCarthy's (1960) 4P model of Product, Price, Promotion and Place is now being replaced by the more relevant notion of relational marketing, which aims to satisfy the unique needs of each individual customer (Bhatnagar, 2012). To understand the different desires of every consumer, marketers need to involve them from early on in product development (Hoffman, Kopalle & Novak, 2010). Taking this into consideration, Lauterborn (1990) complements the concept of the 4Ps with the 4Cs including Consumer wants and needs, Cost to satisfy, Convenience to buy and Communication (Lauterborn, 1990). While the 4C concept provides a better fit with today's marketing environment, both the concepts were introduced before the take-off of Social Media.

In the meantime, the development of new technologies has challenged traditional ways of communication between companies and consumers (Ozuem et al., 2008). Instead of one-way communication directed by the company and with a passively receptive customer, consumers are now actively involved in a dialogue with companies. Brown and Fiorella (2013) acknowledge that the Internet and Social Media have disrupted direct communication between brands, its influencers and their followers. Nowadays, companies can no longer rely on the bandwagon effect of appealing directly to the influencers of a marketplace to win more consumers. The researchers conclude that the facilitation of word-of-mouth and the enormous amount of noise have proven to be critical to consumer trust in brands, which is the basis for a successful online marketing campaign. Brown and Fiorella (2013) thus suggest the 4As model, a concept specifically suitable for an increasingly word-of-mouth-based marketing environment (figure 2).

Regardless of which kind of Social Media a company chooses it must ensure that the audience receives the message. Google's Pay Per Click and Facebook's Insight algorithm help to ensure that the right audience is targeted. In order to accept the message, the user must trust the chosen medium. This can be achieved by social influencer endorsements and a seamless application of the brand's message by planning every step. Amplification is a further success factor for Social Media marketing, as people thrive on the sharing and multiplication of messages. Brown and Fiorella (2013, p.43) furthermore state that Social Media have completely changed the "ballgame" of marketing to consumers. An important aspect thereof is the impact of Social Media on customer service. Companies can no longer afford to ignore criticism and customer apathy. The conversation-enabling nature of Social Media spreads negative word-of-mouth very rapidly, which, in the worst case, can lead to complete consumer detachment from a company with accompanying loss of revenue (Khammash & Griffiths, 2010; Sandes & Urdan, 2013).

For marketers the emergence of Social Media implies one dominant benefit: the forming of close relationships with the consumer. Information exchange with a brand's followers and amongst followers

Figure 2. Paradigm shifts in technologically-induced environments
Source: McCarthy, 1960; Lauterborn, 1990; Brown and Fiorella, 2013.

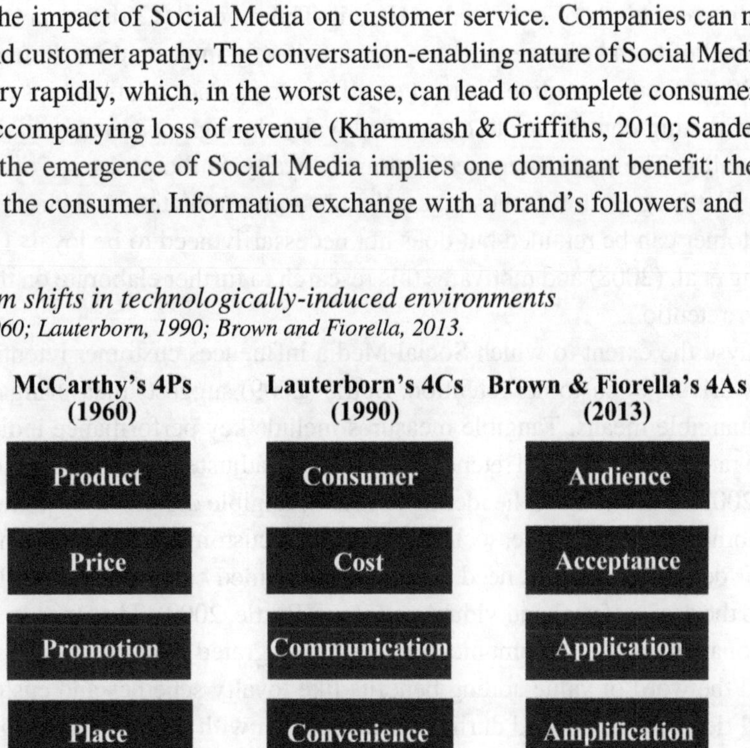

themselves on Social Media uncovers the way consumers think and feel about a product. Gunelius (2011) remarks that online conversations between users are beneficial for companies in the sense that they build brand awareness, brand recognition and brand loyalty. Literature increasingly recognises the importance of co-creation and collaboration with customers online (Vargo & Lusch, 2004). Sharing details about the brand's history, lifestyle, product range and events keeps the consumer close and allows for the creation of emotional bonds (Quinton & Harridge-March, 2010). The researchers suggest that social bonding with the customer results in a sense of loyalty and the more participative the nature of these social bonds, the less the consumer is stimulated to look elsewhere. Trainor (2012) thus remarks that the utilisation of Social Media represents a competitive advantage for companies as it helps to generate superior customer value and increased profitability for the firm. Tuten (2008) identifies further advantages of a brand's presence on Social Media, including strengthening its personality and extending its ethos as well as providing a positive contribution to brand equity through internationalisation.

Many advocates of Social Media are convinced that the recent development has completely replaced traditional media. Whereas this can be confirmed to some extent, the 2012 CMO survey provides evidence of some contradiction (The CMO survey, 2013). Even though marketers can increase their Social Media spend in the next five years to around three times the current level, Social Media spend will only account for 20% of the Marketing budget with the remaining 80% still being spent on traditional media advertising (The CMO survey, 2013).

SOCIAL MEDIA AND CUSTOMER RETENTION INTERPLAY

Studies on the emergence of Social Media and its impact on customer retention are scarce. In analysing the effects of ten different kinds of new media, Hennig-Thurau et al. (2010) conclude that new media releases a higher level of brand engagement and thus positively impacts on customer retention. Liang, Chen and Wang (2008) focus on online, instead of offline, customer relationships and predict that online relationship marketing contributes to customer loyalty through perceived relationship investment and relationship quality. The researchers see customer loyalty as the precursor of customer retention and cross-buying. Blattberg et al. (2001) suggest that customer retention and customer loyalty are not the same, as a customer can be retained but does not necessarily need to be loyal. This contradicts the conception of Liang et al. (2008) and motivates this research to further elaborate on the impact of Social Media on customer retention.

In order to analyse the extent to which Social Media influences customer retention, it is crucial to understand the key drivers of customer retention. Buttle (2009) suggests measuring customer retention by tangible and intangible means. Tangible measures include key performance indicators such as raw customer retention rates, sales-adjusted retention rates, profit-adjusted retention rates or cost of customer retention (Buttle, 2009). Furthermore, he identifies four intangible drivers of customer retention as customer delight, customer perceived value, social and structural customer bonds and customer engagement. To create customer delight companies need to introduce detailed customer knowledge systems, which address and exceed the desire of each individual customer (Buttle, 2009). The emergence of Social Media provides an additional channel of communication and if integrated with other channels, marketers can more easily spread the word of value adding benefits like loyalty schemes and customer clubs. Social bonds are personal ties that are created during the interaction with others and the virtual world can be considered as distant at first, so companies need to consider their online interfaces with customers in order to transmit vividly what the brand stands for (Srinivasan, Anderson&Ponnavolu.2002; Wilson, 1995). Structural bonds exist when the company and the customer dedicate resources to the relationship (Buttle, 2009). Moreover, customer engagement involves commitment and experience and significantly contributes towards the formation of competitive advantage (Buttle, 2009).

Referring to the tangible and intangible measures of customer retention, Hoffman and Fodor (2010) remark that many marketers still focus solely on return numbers, such as Buttle's (2009) tangible customer retention KPIs, which the researchers consider to be short-term oriented and only suitable for traditional media. The emergence of Social Media comes with a set of unconventional and more intangible characteristics and marketers need to adjust their measurement schemes to this. Hoffman and Fodor (2010) provide four strategic options to measure Social Media effectiveness and these are presented below (figure 3).

The aim for every company should be to move away from fuzzy measurement attempts to more quantifiable metrics in the direction of the upper right quadrant. At first sight, many intangible factors might seem immeasurable, but Hoffmann and Fodor (2010) stress that marketers need to implement metrics for intangible factors as well, such as brand awareness, brand engagement and word-of-mouth in order to create successful campaigns.

Literature on customer retention cannot be considered complete without citing further intangible drivers such as customer satisfaction and customer loyalty (Crosby, 1990; Ozuem, Thomas & Lancaster, 2015). Satisfaction has been identified as one of the key influencing factors of customer retention (Gustafsson, Johnson& Roos2005; Liang et al., 2008; Sashi, 2012; Buttle, 2009) due to the long-term impact on customer behaviour (Oliver, 1980; Yi, 1990). Customer satisfaction generally refers to a customer's impression of product quality, service quality and price equity (Bolton & Lemon, 1999; Fornell, 1992).

Figure 3. Strategic options for Social Media measurement
Source: Hofmann and Fodor, 2010, p.47.

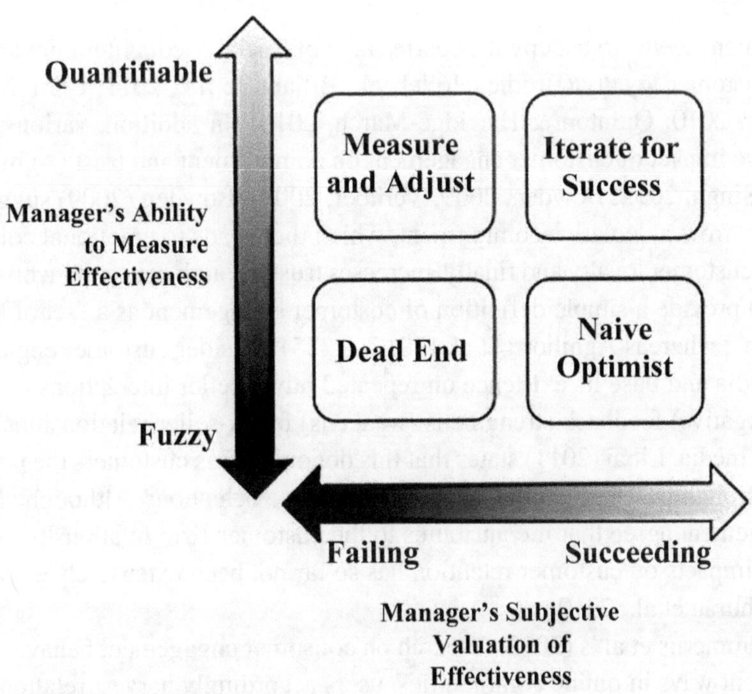

The more satisfied a customer is with a brand experience, the greater the retention rate (Anderson & Sullivan, 1993; Ranaweera & Prabhu, 2003).

The quality of a product can be divided into three levels; basic quality, which the customer routinely expects, linear quality, which the customer more or less wants and attractive quality, which surprises, delights and excites the customer (Kano, 1995). Delight, which can be traced back to satisfaction, therefore is another key driver of customer retention (Buttle, 2009). The advance of Social Media has found appeal in the literature of satisfaction as it gives customers the opportunity to communicate faster with a company, and likewise it allows companies to respond faster to customer complaints and thus enhances the level of customer service (Krishna, Dangayach & Jain, 2011; Clark & Melancon, 2013).

Morgan and Hunt (1994) define trust as one party's confidence in another party's reliability and integrity. Chaudhuri and Holbrook (2001) refer to trust as the willingness of consumers to rely on the brand to perform its intended function. Satisfaction alone is not enough to retain customers (Danesh, Nasab & Kwek, 2012), and it has been widely discussed in literature that satisfaction goes hand in hand with customer trust in a company (Crosby, Ewans & Cowles, 1990; Dwyer, Schurr & Oh, 1987; Hart & Johnson, 1999; Liang et al., 2008). According to Betrand (2013), the emergence of Social Media has had a strong impact on customer trust.

The level of online word-of-mouth is multiplied and as consumers generally trust personal sources to a higher extent than they trust non-personal sources (Weber, 2007), companies have an additional opportunity to influence their customers (Brown & Fiorella, 2013). Trust in online environments was found to reduce the cognitive uncertainty related to online purchasing (Dash & Saji, 2007) and instead increased customer retention (Abhamid, Akhir& Cheng, 2013). However, the uncertainty of the Internet in terms of e-commerce (Pavlou, 2003) and personal information (Flavian & Guinaliu, 2006; Kelly & Erickson, 2004) provides challenges to the long-term preservation of customer trust.

Social Media and Customer Engagement

Customer engagement seems to occupy the centre stage of Social Media literature and is often referred to as impacting customer loyalty (Brodie, Hollebeek, Biljana & Ilic, 2011; Clark & Melancon, 2013; Hoffman & Fodor, 2010; Quinton & Harridge-March, 2010). In addition, various studies have shed light on the positive impact of customer engagement on commitment and trust (Agnihotri, Kothandaraman, Kashyap & Singh, 2012; Bowden, 2009; Verhoef, 2003). Bowden (2009) suggests that customer engagement results from calculative commitment, which then leads to emotional commitment forming the foundation for customer loyalty and finally, increases trust through constant involvement. Gummerus et al.(2012, p.857) provide a simple definition of customer engagement as a "set of behavioural activities towards a firm", whereas Agnihotri et al. (2012, p.335) consider customer engagement in the new light of Social Media and base its existence on repeated buyer-seller interactions on Social Media, "in which positive (negative) feedback strengthens (weakens) buyer-seller relationships". Referring to the emergence of new media, Libai (2011) states that this not only gives customers the possibility to engage with a company through purchase, but also via non-purchase behaviour. Although all these definitions of customer engagement agree that it contributes to the customer-firm relationship to some extent, the extent to which it impacts on customer retention has so far not been extensively elaborated upon in literature (Hennig-Thurau et al., 2010).

In addition, Gummerus et al.'s (2012) research on consumer engagement behaviour suggests that by engaging in different ways in online communities, users accordingly harvest relationship benefits such as entertainment. Dholakia, Bagozzi, & Pearo (2004) and Nonnecke, Andrews & Preece (2006) credit the entertainment of customers to relaxation, fun, community participation and online services. Adding to customer engagement impact on entertainment, Prahalad and Ramaswamy (2004) and Brodie et al. (2011) consider customer engagement as something formed by interactive customer experiences and as an important step in the co-creation of value, which is especially promoted through the participative nature of Social Media (Atwal & Williams, 2009; Kumar et al., 2010).

MANAGERIAL IMPLICATIONS AND RECOMMENDATIONS

The current paper proposes a number of managerial implications. Before beginning with a Social Media presence, luxury beauty brands need to first reflect upon their core values and their vision and mission. They must develop a clear and succinct Social Media strategy based on these factors. This strategy needs to include not only obvious objectives such as sales, cost efficiencies and product development, but also needs to consider objectives such as brand awareness, customer engagement and word-of-mouth. It is important that all the objectives are assessable. In the future, retailing will increasingly follow an Omni-channel approach, focusing on a seamless provision of experiences through whichever channel, digital or offline, the brand participates in. In order to make this work, the Social Media strategy needs to be integrated within the corporate strategy. Every department and every employee has to be aligned with it in order to convey authentic experiences through every single touch point.

For a Social Media strategy to be successful, a continuous budget needs to be ensured. It is therefore crucial to equip every objective of the Social Media strategy with measurable key performance indicators. Every campaign on Social Media is different and in order to continuously improve their activities, luxury beauty brands need to measure the effect of each campaign on customer retention by looking at conversion rates, positive sentiment analysis and successful customer complaints rates amongst others. Picking up the Omni-channel trend cited above, luxury beauty brands would greatly benefit from integrating online and offline data about customers. Customers nowadays expect companies to know when they have previously purchased from them and combining these two databases does not only open up an entirely new dimension to customer experiences but also enables a more complete measurement of customer retention, which ultimately allows for a more personalised communication with customers.

Without investing in traditional media a luxury beauty brand cannot expect any form of engagement from its customers. Prior to a participating in Social Media, customers have to be made aware of the brand's existence. Therefore luxury beauty brands need to continue investing in advertising, whilst at the same time balancing this with content creation. Whereas under-investment in advertising and over-creation of content lead to a brand's unknown exposure in the market place, vice versa, over-investment in advertising and under-creation of content can provoke a customer expectation gap, ultimately leading to customer disappointment and rejection of the brand. Luxury beauty brands have to find the right balance between advertising and content creation to achieve maximum brand exposure.

Customers aspire to luxury beauty brands. The products are highly coveted for their exclusivity and this is influenced by the brand's story and price point. Therefore, luxury beauty brands should not engage their customers via promotions, as this removes part of the exclusivity from the brand and can even lead to customer disappointment, realising that the brand is not as luxurious as expected when the same promotion tools as in the mass market are applied. The luxury beauty customer is not a value-for-money customer and their involvement starts with the brand's roots, the story. Therefore, luxury beauty brands should engage customers via value-adding content, such as previews, 'How to'- videos, beauty expert interviews - giving customers exclusive content they cannot get anywhere else, delighting them by going the unexpected extra mile. Beauty is fun and so is Social Media, now the brands need to leverage this by being innovative and having the courage to try things out. Luxury beauty brands should not be afraid to fail; mistakes contribute to the learning curve and prevent becoming rooted in a comfort zone.

Luxury beauty brands participating on Social Media should be aware that growth is incredibly fast-paced. Some already consider the Facebook social network, founded in 2004, as out-dated. An array of new, visual-based Social Media tools is on the rise. Whereas text-based Social Media are convenient for customer service purposes, and therefore have to remain a part of the strategy, visual Social Media allow for a more vivid and luxurious presentation of the brand. A healthy mix of text and visual-based Social Media is necessary. Text-based Social Media communications should have the aim of leveraging customer dialogue via reviews and posts, whereas communication through visual Social Media should increase emotional engagement by encouraging customers to share photos of important and meaningful moments. To further humanise the image of luxury beauty brands it is important to relax the communication and to not always share perfectly retouched pictures but to allow for natural and more imperfect looks. The aim of every luxury beauty company should be to become truly customer-centred. The participative nature of Social Media implies that word-of-mouth, and especially negative word-of-mouth, can spread very fast. Therefore luxury beauty companies need to have sufficient resources at hand to follow what their customers say about the brand in each channel and to immediately react to issues in an authentic and transparent manner. Only when the company proves to be reactive and honest will customers feel valued and able to establish a feeling of trust towards the brand. A customer that trusts a brand will ultimately come back.

REFERENCES

5 Surprising Social Media Statistics for 2013. (2013, October 12). *Social Media Today*. Retrieved from http://socialmediatoday.com/docmarkting/1818611/five-surprising-social-media-statistics-2013

Abhamid, N. R., Akhir, R. M., & Cheng, A. Y. (2013). Social media: An emerging dimension of marketing communication. *Journal of Management and Marketing Research*, *12*, 4–11.

Agnihotri, R., Kothandaraman, P., Kashyap, R., & Singh, R. (2012). Bringing 'Social' into Sales: The Impact of Salespeople's Social Media Use on Service Behaviours and Value Co-creation. *Journal of Personal Selling & Sales Management*, *XXXII*(3), 333–348. doi:10.2753/PSS0885-3134320304

Alston, M. (2012, October 5). 78% of Luxury Marketers Spent More on Social Media in 2012 Than 2011, Luxury Interactive. Retrieved from http://finance.yahoo.com/news/78-luxury-marketers-spent-more-141500809.html

Anderson, E. W., & Sullivan, M. W. (1993). The antecedents and consequences of customer satisfaction for firms. *Marketing Science*, *12*(2), 125–143. doi:10.1287/mksc.12.2.125

Annie Jin, S.-A. (2012). The potential of social media for luxury brand management. *Marketing Intelligence & Planning*, *30*(7), 687–699. doi:10.1108/02634501211273805

Arno, C. (2012, December 26).Worldwide Social Media Usage Trends in 2012, Search Engine Watch. Retrieved from http://searchenginewatch.com/article/2167518/Worldwide-Social-Media-Usage-Trends-in-2012

Atta, A., & Mahmoud, A. (2012). Web 2.0: A Movement within the Learning Community. *Information Management and Business Review*, *4*(12), 625–631.

Atwal, G., & Williams, A. (2009). Luxury brand marketing – The experience is everything! *Brand Management*, *16*(5-6), 338–346. doi:10.1057/bm.2008.48

Worldwide luxury goods continues double-digit annual growth; global market now tops €200 billion, finds Bain & Company. (2013, March 16). *Bain & Company*. Retrieved from http://www.bain.com/about/press/press-releases/worldwide-luxury-goods-continues-double-digit-annual-growth.aspx

Beauty Customer Journey. (2012). *YouGov*. Retrieved from http://d25d2506sfb94s.cloudfront.net/cumulus_uploads/document/wa32oxme7c/Beauty%20Customer%20Journey.pdf

Berthon, P. R., Pitt, L. F., Plangger, K., & Shapiro, D. (2012). Marketing meets Web 2.0, social media, and creative consumers: Implications for international marketing strategy. *Business Horizons*, *55*(3), 261–271. doi:10.1016/j.bushor.2012.01.007

Bertrand, G. (2013). Socialmedia research: Developing a trust metric in the social age. *International Journal of Market Research*, *55*(3), 333–335. doi:10.2501/IJMR-2013-032

Bhatnagar, N. (2012). Customer Relationship Marketing: Customer-Centric Processes for Engendering Customer- Firm Bonds and Optimizing Long-Term Customer Value. *Intechopen*. Retrieved from http://cdn.intechopen.com/pdfs/35309/InTech-Customer_relationship_marketing_customer_centric_processes_for_engendering_customer_firm_bonds_and_optimizing_long_term_customer_value.pdf

Blackshaw, P., & Nazzaro, M. (2004). Consumer-Generated Media (CGM) 101: Word-of-mouth in the age of the Webfortified consumer. *Intelliseek*. Retrieved from http://www.brandchannel.com/images/papers/222_cgm.pdf

Blattberg, R., Getz, G., & Thomas, J. S. (2001). *Customer Equity: Building and Managing Relationships as Valuable Assets*. Boston: Harvard Business School Press.

Bolton, R. N. (1998). A Dynamic Model of the Duration of the Customer's Relationship with a Continuous Service Provider: The Role of Satisfaction. *Marketing Science*, *17*(1), 45–65. doi:10.1287/mksc.17.1.45

Bolton, R. N., & Lemon, K. N. (1999). Dynamic Model of Customers' Usage of Services: Usage as an Antecedent and Consequence of Satisfaction. *The Journal of Consumer Research*, *36*(2), 171–186.

Bolton, R. N., Parasuraman, A., Hoefnagels, A., Migchels, N., Kabadayi, S., Gruber, T., & Solnet, D. et al. (2013). Understanding Generation Y and their use of social media: A review and research agenda. *Journal of Service Management*, *24*(3), 245–267. doi:10.1108/09564231311326987

Bowden, J. L. H. (2009). The process of customer engagement: A conceptual framework. *Journal of Marketing Theory and Practice*, *17*(1), 63–74. doi:10.2753/MTP1069-6679170105

Brennan, R., & Croft, R. (2012). The use of social media in B2B marketing and branding: An exploratory study. *Journal of Consumer Behaviour, 11*(2), 101–115. doi:10.1362/147539212X13420906144552

Brodie, R. J., Hollebeek, L. D., Juric, B., & Ilic, A. (2011). Customer engagement: Conceptual domain, fundamental propositions, and implications for research. *Journal of Service Research, 14*(3), 252–271. doi:10.1177/1094670511411703

Brown, D., & Fiorella, S. (2013). Influence Marketing, US: Que Publishing.

Buttle, F. (2009). *Customer relationship management – concepts and technologies* (2nd ed.). Oxford: Elsevier.

Chaudhuri, A., & Holbrook, M. B. (2001). The chain of effects from brand trust and brand affect to brand performance: The role of brand loyalty. *Journal of Marketing, 65*(2), 81–93. doi:10.1509/jmkg.65.2.81.18255

Choo, H., Moon, H., Kim, H., & Yoon, N. (2012). Luxury customer value. *Journal of Fashion Marketing and Management, 16*(1), 81–101. doi:10.1108/13612021211203041

Clark, M., & Melancon, J. (2013). The Influence of Social Media Investment on Relational Outcomes: A Relationship Marketing Perspective. *International Journal of Marketing Studies, 5*(4), 132–142. doi:10.5539/ijms.v5n4p132

Crosby, L. A., Evans, K. R., & Cowles, D. (1990). Relationship quality in services selling: An interpersonal influence perspective. *Journal of Marketing, 54*(3), 68–81. doi:10.2307/1251817

Dall'Olmo Riley, F., & Lacroix, C. (2003). Luxury branding on the internet: Lost opportunity or impossibility? *Marketing Intelligence & Planning, 21*(2), 96–104. doi:10.1108/02634500310465407

Danesh, S. N., Nasab, S. A., & Kwek, C. L. (2012). The Study of Customer Satisfaction, Customer Trust and Switching Barriers on Customer Retention in Malaysia Hypermarkets. *International Journal of Business and Management, 7*(7), 141–150.

Dann, S., & Dann, S. (2011). *E-marketing: theory and application.* Basingstoke, England: Palgrave Macmillan.

Dash, S., & Saji, K. B. (2008). The role of consumer self-efficacy and website social presence in customers' adoption of B2C online shopping: An empirical study in the Indian context. *Journal of International Consumer Marketing, 20*(2), 33–48. doi:10.1300/J046v20n02_04

Daugherty, T., Eastin, M., & Bright, L. (2008). Exploring Consumer Motivations for creating User-Generated Content. *Journal of Interactive Advertising, 8*(2), 16–25. doi:10.1080/15252019.2008.10722139

Dholakia, U. M., Bagozzi, R. P., & Pearo, L. K. (2004). A social influence model of consumer participation in network- and small-group-based virtual communities. *International Journal of Research in Marketing, 21*(3), 241–263. doi:10.1016/j.ijresmar.2003.12.004

Divol, R., Edelman, D., & Sarrazin, H. (2012). Demystifying social media. *The McKinsey Quarterly, 2*, 66–77.

Dubois, B., & Paternault, C. (1995). Observations: Understanding the world of international luxury brands. *Journal of Advertising Research*, *35*(4), 69–76.

Dwyer, F. R., Schurr, P. H., & Oh, S. (1987). Developing buyer–seller relationships. *Journal of Marketing*, *51*(2), 11–27. doi:10.2307/1251126

Europe's Prestige Beauty Market 2012. *BW Confidential*. (2013). Retrieved from http://www.bwconfidential.com/en/europe-s-prestige-beauty-market-2012,article-1875.html

Evans, D., & McKee, J. (2010). *Social Media Marketing – The Next Generation of Business Engagement*. Indianapolis: Wiley Publishing Inc.

Fieseler, C., & Fleck, M. (2013). The Pursuit of Empowerment through Social Media: Structural Social Capital Dynamics in CSR-Blogging. *Journal of Business Ethics*, *118*(4), 759–775. doi:10.1007/s10551-013-1959-9

Firat, A. F., & Venkatesh, A. (1995). Liberatory Postmodernism and the Reenchantment of Consumption. *The Journal of Consumer Research*, *22*(3), 239–267. doi:10.1086/209448

Flavian, C. & Guinaliu, M. (2006). Consumer trust, perceived security and privacy policy: Three basic elements of loyalty to a web site. *Industrial Management + Data Systems, 106(5)*, 601-620.

Fornell, C. (1992). A National Customer Satisfaction Barometer: The Swedish Experience. *Journal of Marketing*, *56*(1), 6–21. doi:10.2307/1252129

Gangadharbhatla, H. (2008). Facebook me: Collective self esteem, need to belong and Internet self efficacy as predictors of the I-generations attitudes toward social networking sites. *Journal of Interactive Advertising*, *8*(2), 5–15. doi:10.1080/15252019.2008.10722138

Garland, E. (2008). The experience economy: The high life of tomorrow. *The Futurist*. Retrieved from http://mestovetra.files.wordpress.com/2008/06/experience-economy.pdf

Geron, T. (2013, March 10). Twitter Reveals Long-Awaited IPO Plans With 215 Million Users. *Forbes*. Retrieved from http://www.forbes.com/sites/tomiogeron/2013/10/03/twitter-reveals-long-awaited-ipo-plans-253m-revenue-in-first-half-of-2013/

Goffman, E. (1959). *The presentation of self in everyday life*. New York: Doubleday Anchor Books.

Goldenberg, B. (2015). *The Definitive Guide to Social CRM: maximizing customer relationships with Social Media to gain market insights, customers, and profits*. Harlow: Pearson.

Gummerus, J., Liljander, V., Weman, E., & Pihlström, M. (2012). Customer engagement in a Facebook brand community. *Management Research Review*, *35*(9), 857–877. doi:10.1108/01409171211256578

Gunelius, S. (2011). *30 minute Social Media Marketing: Step by Step Techniques to Spread the Words about your Business*. USA: McGraw-Hill.

Gustafsson, A., Johnson, M. D., & Roos, I. (2005). The Effects of Customer Satisfaction, Relationship Commitment Dimensions, and Triggers on Customer Retention. *Journal of Marketing*, *69*(10), 210–218. doi:10.1509/jmkg.2005.69.4.210

Hagel, J., & Armstrong, A. G. (1997). *Net gain: Expanding markets through virtual Communities*. Boston: Harvard Business School Press.

Hanna, R., Rohm, A., & Crittenden, V. L. (2011). We're all connected: The power of the social media ecosystem. *Business Horizons*, *54*(3), 265–273. doi:10.1016/j.bushor.2011.01.007

Hart, C. W., & Johnson, M. D. (1999). Growing the trust relationship. *Marketing Management*, *8*(1), 8–19.

Hawkins, K., & Vel, P. (2013). Attitudinal loyalty, behavioural loyalty and social media: An Introspection. *Marketing Review*, *13*(2), 125–141. doi:10.1362/146934713X13699019904605

Hennig-Thurau, T., Gwinner, K., Walsh, G., & Gremler, D. (2004). Electronic word of-mouth via consumer-opinion platforms: What motivates consumers to articulate themselves on the Internet? *Journal of Interactive Marketing*, *18*(1), 38–52. doi:10.1002/dir.10073

Hennig-Thurau, T., Malthouse, E., Friege, C., Gensler, S., Lobschat, L., Rangaswamy, A., & Skiera, B. (2010). The Impact of New Media on Customer Relationships. *Journal of Service Research*, *13*(3), 311–330. doi:10.1177/1094670510375460

Hof, R. (2012, September 2). Google+'s Success and Failure, in Two Images. *Forbes*. http://www.forbes.com/sites/roberthof/2012/02/09/googles-success-and-failure-in-two-images/

Hoffman, D. L., & Fodor, M. (2010). Can you measure the ROI of your social media marketing? *MIT Sloan Management Review*, *52*(1), 41–49.

Hoffman, D. L., Kopalle, P. K., & Novak, T. P. (2010). A New Marketing Paradigm for Electronic Commerce. *JMR, Journal of Marketing Research*, *XLVII*, 854–865. doi:10.1509/jmkr.47.5.854

Hoffman, D. L., & Novak, T. P. (2012, January 17). Why Do People Use Social Media? Empirical Findings and a New Theoretical Framework for Social Media Goal Pursuit. *Social Science Research Network*. Retrieved from http://ssrn.com/abstract=1989586

Holloman, C. (2013). *The Social Media MBA in practice*. Chichester: Wiley.

Jarvenpaa, S., & Tuunainen, V. K. (2013). How Finnair Socialized Customers for Service Co-Creation with SocialMedia. *MIS Quarterley Executive*, *12*(3), 125–136.

Jevons, C., & Gabbott, M. (2000). Trust, Brand Equity and Brand Reality in Internet Business Relationships: An Interdisciplinary Approach. *Journal of Marketing Management*, *16*(6), 619–634. doi:10.1362/026725700785045967

Kane, G, & Alavi, M, Labianca &Borgatti. (2014). What's different about Social Media Networks? A Framework and Research Agenda. *Management Information Systems Quarterly*, *38*(1), 275–304.

Kano, N. (1995). Upsizing the organization by attractive quality creation. In G.K. Kanji (Ed.), Total Quality Management: Proceedings of the First World Congress. London: Chapman & Hall. doi:10.1007/978-94-011-0539-2_6

Kaplan, A., & Haenlein, M. (2010). Users of the world, unite! The challenges and opportunities of Social Media. *Business Horizons*, *53*(1), 59–68. doi:10.1016/j.bushor.2009.09.003

Katsioloudes, M., Grant, J., & McKechnie, D. S. (2007). Social marketing: Strengthening company-customer bonds. *The Journal of Business Strategy*, *28*(3), 56–64. doi:10.1108/02756660710746283

Kelly, E. P., & Erickson, G. S. (2004). Legal and privacy issues surrounding customer databases and e-merchant bankruptcies: Reflections on Toysmart.com. *Industrial Management & Data Systems*, *104*(3), 209–217. doi:10.1108/02635570410525762

Khammash, M., & Griffiths, G. H. (2011). Arrivederci CIAO.com, Buongiorno Bing. Com - electronic word-of-mouth (eWOM), antecedences and consequences. *International Journal of Information Management*, *31*(1), 82–87. doi:10.1016/j.ijinfomgt.2010.10.005

Khang, H., Ki, E., & Ye, L. (2012). Social Media Research in Advertising, Communication, Marketing, and Public Relations. *Journalism & Mass Communication Quarterly*, *89*(2), 279–298. doi:10.1177/1077699012439853

Kietzmann, J. H., Hermkens, K., McCarthy, I. P., & Silvestre, B. S. (2011). Social media? Get serious! Understanding the functional building blocks of social media. *Business Horizons*, *54*(3), 241–251. doi:10.1016/j.bushor.2011.01.005

Kim, A. J., & Ko, E. (2010). Impacts of Luxury Fashion Brand's Social Media Marketing on Customer Relationship and Purchase Intention. *Journal of Global Fashion Marketing*, *1*(3), 164–171. doi:10.1080/20932685.2010.10593068

Kim, A. J., & Ko, E. (2012). Do Social Media marketing activities enhance customer equity? An empirical study of luxury fashion brand. *Journal of Business Research*, *65*(10), 1480–1486. doi:10.1016/j.jbusres.2011.10.014

Kirkpatrick, D. (2010). *The Facebook effect: The inside story of the company that is connecting the world*. New York: Simon & Schuster.

Kozinets, R., deValck, K., Wojnicki, A., & Wilner, S. (2010). Networked Narratives: Understanding Word-of-Mouth Marketing in Online Communities. *Journal of Marketing*, *74*(2), 71–89. doi:10.1509/jmkg.74.2.71

Krishna, A., Dangayach, G., & Jain, R. (2011). A Conceptual Framework for the Service Recovery Paradox. *The Marketing Review*, *11*(1), 41–56. doi:10.1362/146934711X565288

Kumar, V., Aksoy, L., Donkers, B., Venkatesan, R., Wiesel, T., & Tillmanns, S. (2010). Undervalued or Overvalued Customers: Capturing Total Customer Engagement Value. *Journal of Service Research*, *13*(3), 297–310. doi:10.1177/1094670510375602

Laroche, M., Habibi, M. R., & Richard, M. O. (2013). To be or not to be in social media: How brand loyalty is affected by social media? *International Journal of Information Management*, *33*(1), 76–82. doi:10.1016/j.ijinfomgt.2012.07.003

Lauterborn, B. (1990). New Marketing Litany: Four P's Passe: C-Words Take Over. *Advertising Age*, *61*(41), 26.

Leggatt, H. (2010, October 19). Rebuild Brand Loyalty with Social Media. Bizreport. Retrieved from http://www.bizreport.com/2010/08/price-sensitiveshoppers-still-seeking-out-deals.html

Levine, R., Locke, C., Searle, D., & Weinberger, D. (2001). *The Cluetrain Manifesto: The end of business as usual*. New York: Basic Books.

Liang, C. L., Chen, H. J., & Wang, W. H. (2008). Does online relationship marketing enhance customer retention and cross-buying? *Service Industries Journal*, *28*(6), 769–787. doi:10.1080/02642060801988910

Libai, B. (2011). Comment: The perils of focusing on highly engaged customers. *Journal of Service Research*, *14*(3), 275–276. doi:10.1177/1094670511414583

Loyalty Versus Retention - Is There a Difference? (2010, April 9). The Customer Institute. Retrieved from http://thecustomerinstitute.blogspot.co.uk/2010/04/loyalty-versus-retention-is-there.html

Luxury Beauty Having a Love Affair with the UK. (2013). *Euromonitor International*. Retrieved from http://www.euromonitor.com/

Mangold, W. G., & Faulds, D. J. (2009). Social media: The new hybrid element of the promotion mix. *Business Horizons*, *52*(4), 357–365. doi:10.1016/j.bushor.2009.03.002

Maslow, A. H. (1943). A theory of human motivation. *Psychological Review*, *50*(4), 370–396. doi:10.1037/h0054346

McCarthy, E. J. (1960). *Basic Marketing - A Managerial Approach*. Homewood: Richard D. Irwin.

Moore, C. M., & Doyle, S. A. (2010). The evolution of a luxury brand: The case of Prada. *International Journal of Retail & Distribution Management*, *38*(11), 915–927.

Morgan, R. M., & Hunt, S. (1994). The commitment-trust theory of relationship marketing. *Journal of Marketing*, *58*(3), 20–38. doi:10.2307/1252308

Moritz, D. (2012, December 15).The Shift to Visual Social Media – 6 Tips for Business, Socially Sorted. Retrieved from http://sociallysorted.com.au/shift-to-visual-social-media-6-tips-for-business-infographic/

Muniz, M. A. Jr, & O'Guinn, C. T. (2001). Brand community. *The Journal of Consumer Research*, *27*(4), 412–432. doi:10.1086/319618

Nair, M. (2011). Understanding and Measuring the Value of Social Media. *Journal of Corporate Accounting & Finance*, *22*(3), 45–51. doi:10.1002/jcaf.20674

Naylor, R., Walker, L., Cait, P., & West, P. M. (2012). Beyond the 'Like' Button: The impact of Mere Virtual Presence on Brand Evaluations and Purchase Intentions in Social Media Settings. *Journal of Marketing*, *76*(6), 105–120. doi:10.1509/jm.11.0105

Nonnecke, B., Andrews, D., & Preece, J. (2006). Non-public and public online community participation: Needs, attitudes and behaviour. *Electronic Commerce Research*, *6*(1), 7–20. doi:10.1007/s10660-006-5985-x

Noor Al-Deen, H. S., & Hendricks, J. A. (2012). *Social Media – usage and impact*. Plymouth: Lexington Books.

O'Reilly, T. (2005, September 30). What is Web 2.0? Design Patterns and Business Models for the Next generation of Software. *O'Reilly*. Retrieved from http://www.im.ethz.ch/education/HS08/OReilly_What_is_Web2_0.pdf

O'Reilly, T., & Milstein, S. (2012). *The Twitter Book*. Sebastopol: O'Reilly Media Inc.

Working Party on the Information Economy – Participative Web: User-created content. (2007, April 12). OECD, Organisation for Economic Co-operation and Development. Retrieved from http://www.oecd.org/sti/38393115.pdf

Okonkwo, U. (2010). Luxury Online. New York: Palgrave Macmillan.

Oliver, R. L. (1980). A Cognitive Model of the Antecedents and Consequences of Satisfaction Decisions. *JMR, Journal of Marketing Research, 17*(4), 460–469. doi:10.2307/3150499

Onook, O., Manish, A., & Raghave, R. H. (2013). Community intelligence and social media services: A rumor theoretic analysis of tweets during social crisis. *Management Information Systems Quarterly, 37*(2), 407–A7.

Ozuem, W., Borrelli, M., & Lancaster, G. (2015). Leveraging the co-evolution of offline and online video games: An empirical study. *Journal of Strategic Marketing*, 1–23. doi:10.1080/0965254X.2015.1076883

Ozuem, W., Howell, K. E., & Lancaster, G. (2008). Communicating in the new interactive marketspace. *European Journal of Marketing, 42*(9/10), 1059–1083. doi:10.1108/03090560810891145

Ozuem, W., & Lancaster, G. (2014). Recovery strategies in on-line service failure. In A. Ghorbani (Ed.), *Marketing in the cyber era: strategies and emerging trends* (pp. 143–159). Hershey, PA, USA: IGI Global. doi:10.4018/978-1-4666-4864-7.ch010

Ozuem, W., O'Keeffe, A., & Lancaster, G. (2015). Leadership Marketing: An exploratory study. *Journal of Strategic Marketing*, 1–25. doi:10.1080/0965254X.2014.1001867

Ozuem, W., Thomas, T., & Lancaster, G. (2015). The Influence of customer loyalty on small island economies: An empirical and exploratory study. *Journal of Strategic Marketing*, 1–23. doi:10.1080/0965254X.2015.1011205

Pavlik, J. V. (2007, June 4). Mapping the consequences of technology of public relations, Institute for public relations. Institute for Public Relations. Retrieved from http://www.instituteforpr.org/topics/mapping-technology-consequences/

Pavlou, P. A. (2003). Consumer acceptance of electronic commerce: Integrating trust and risk with the technology acceptance model. *International Journal of Electronic Commerce, 7*(3), 101–134.

Phan, M., Thomas, R., & Heine, K. (2011). Social Media and Luxury Brand Management: The Case of Burberry. *Journal of Global Fashion Marketing, 2*(4), 213–222. doi:10.1080/20932685.2011.10593099

Powers, T., Advincula, D., Austin, M., Graiko, S., & Snyder, J. (2013). Digital and Social Media in the Purchase Decision Process. *Journal of Advertising Research, 52*(4), 479–489. doi:10.2501/JAR-52-4-479-489

Prahalad, C. K., & Ramaswamy, V. (2004). Co-creation experiences: The next practice in value creation. *Journal of Interactive Marketing*, *18*(3), 5–14. doi:10.1002/dir.20015

Prendergast, G., Ko, D., & Yuen, S. Y. V. (2010). Online word of mouth and consumer purchase intentions. *International Journal of Advertising*, *29*(5), 687–708. doi:10.2501/S0265048710201427

Quinton, S., & Harridge-March, S. (2010). Relationships in online communities: The potential for marketers. *Journal of Research in Interactive Marketing*, *4*(1), 59–73. doi:10.1108/17505931011033560

Ranaweera, C., & Prabhu, J. (2003). The influence of satisfaction, trust and switching barriers on customer retention in a continuous purchasing setting. *International Journal of Service Industry Management*, *14*(4), 374–395. doi:10.1108/09564230310489231

Rettberg, J. W. (2008). *Blogging – Digital Media and Society Series*. Malden: Polity.

Safko, L. (2012). *The Social Media Bible– Tools, Tactics and Strategies for Business Success* (3rd ed.). New Jersey: John Wiley & Sons Inc.

Safko, L., & Brake, D. K. (2009). *The Social Media Bible*. New Jersey: John Wiley & Sons, Inc.

Sandes, F. S., & Urdan, A. T. (2013). Electronic Word-of-Mouth Impacts on Consumer Behaviour: Exploratory and Experimental Studies. *Journal of International Consumer Marketing*, *25*(3), 181–197. doi:10.1080/08961530.2013.780850

Sashi, C. M. (2012). Customer engagement, buyer-seller relationships and Social Media. *Management Decision*, *50*(2), 253–272. doi:10.1108/00251741211203551

Smith, T. (2009). The Social Media Revolution. *International Journal of Market Research*, *51*(4), 559–561. doi:10.2501/S1470785309200773

Social Media Landscape 2013. (2013, April 17). *Fred Cavazza*. Retrieved from http://www.fredcavazza.net/2013/04/17/social-media-landscape-2013/

Srinivasan, S. S., Anderson, R., & Ponnavolu, K. (2002). Customer loyalty in e-commerce: An exploration of its antecedents and consequences. *Journal of Retailing*, *78*(1), 41–50. doi:10.1016/S0022-4359(01)00065-3

Stokes, R. (2008).E-marketing: The essential guide to online marketing, South Africa: Quirk eMarketing (Pty) Ltd.

Sukoco, B. & Wu, W. (2010). The personal and social motivation of customers' participation in brand community. *African journal of business management, 4(5)*, 614-622.

Highlights and Insights February 2013. (2013, February). The CMO Survey. Retrieved from http://cmosurvey.org/files/2013/02/The_CMO_Survey_Highlights_and_Insights_Feb-2013-Final2.pdf

Annie Jin, S.-A. (2012). The potential of Social Media for luxury brand management. *Marketing Intelligence & Planning*, *30*(7), 687–699. doi:10.1108/02634501211273805

Trainor, K. (2012). Relating SocialMedia Technologies to Performance: A Capabilities-Based Perspective. *Journal of Personal Selling & Sales Management*, *32*(3), 317–331. doi:10.2753/PSS0885-3134320303

Tuten, T. L. (2008). *Advertising 2.0 – Social Media Marketing in a Web 2.0 World.* Westport: Praeger Publishers.

Vargo, S. L., & Lusch, R. F. (2004). Evolving to a new Dominant Logic for Marketing. *Journal of Marketing*, *68*(1), 1–17. doi:10.1509/jmkg.68.1.1.24036

Verhoef, P. C. (2003). Understanding the Effect of Customer Relationship Management Efforts on Customer Retention and Customer Share Development. *Journal of Marketing*, *67*(4), 30–45. doi:10.1509/jmkg.67.4.30.18685

Vickers, J. S., & Renand, F. (2003). The Marketing of Luxury Goods: An exploratory study – three conceptual dimensions. *The Marketing Review*, *3*(4), 459–478. doi:10.1362/146934703771910071

Vollmer, C., & Precourt, G. (2008). *Always on: Advertising, marketing, and media in an era of consumer control.* New York: McGraw-Hill.

Walpole (2013). British Luxury Showcase.

Weber, L. (2007). *Marketing to the Social Web: How Digital Customer Communities Build Your Business.* New Jersey: John Wiley & Sons Inc.

Wellman, B., & Gulia, M. (1999). Net-surfers don't ride alone: Virtual communities as communities. In B. Wellman (Ed.), Networks in the global village (pp. 331-366). Boulder: Westview.

Williams, L., & Cothrell, J. (2000). Four smart ways to run online communities. *Sloan Management Review*, *41*(4), 81–91.

Wilson, D. T. (1995). An integrated model of buyer–seller relationships. *Journal of the Academy of Marketing Science*, *23*(4), 335–345. doi:10.1177/009207039502300414

Yi, Y. (1990). A critical review of consumer satisfaction, In V.A. Zeithaml (Ed.), Review of Marketing (pp. 68-123). Chicago: American Marketing Association.

Zarella, D. (2010). *The social media marketing book.* California: O'Reilly Media Inc.

ADDITIONAL READING

Baer, J. (2013). *Youtility*. New York: Penguin Group.

Brown, D., & Fiorella, S. (2013). Influence Marketing. US: Que Publishing.

Clark, M., & Melancon, J. (2013). The Influence of Social Media Investment on Relational Outcomes: A Relationship Marketing Perspective. *International Journal of Marketing Studies*, *5*(4), 132–142. doi:10.5539/ijms.v5n4p132

Hoffman, D. L., & Fodor, M. (2010). Can you measure the ROI of your social media marketing? *MIT Sloan Management Review*, *52*(1), 41–49.

Sandes, F. S., & Urdan, A. T. (2013). Electronic Word-of-Mouth Impacts on Consumer Behaviour: Exploratory and Experimental Studies. *Journal of International Consumer Marketing*, *25*(3), 181–197. doi:10.1080/08961530.2013.780850

KEY TERMS AND DEFINITIONS

Cosmetics: A cosmetic product is applied on the human body with the purpose of cleaning, protecting, maintaining or perfuming it.

Customer Retention: Customer retention describes a company's activities in order to ensure that the customer repeatedly comes back to repurchase from the company and does not move on to the competition.

Loyalty: Customer loyalty is expressed through an attitudinal and behavioural preference for one brand.

Luxury Beauty Industry: The luxury beauty industry belongs to the consumer products industry. It provides premium products in a set of different subcategories such as colour cosmetics, skin care, fragrances, sun care, hair care and men's grooming.

Marketing Communications: Marketing communications are coordinated messages through which a company reaches out to its target audience.

Social Media: Social media is the totality of different online channels and platforms, which enable online users not only to receive but also to create and share content.

Word of Mouth: Word-of-mouth is a powerful form of advertising based on peer-to-peer recommendations.

Compilation of References

(n. d.). Retrieved from http://www.acxiom.fr/ideas-and-innovation/glossary/fid%C3%A9lisation-client

(n.d.). Retrieved from http://www.escpap.net/conferences/marketing/2008_cp/Materiali/Paper/Fr/Janouri_Gharbi.pdf

5 Surprising Social Media Statistics for 2013. (2013, October 12). *Social Media Today*. Retrieved from http://socialmediatoday.com/docmarkting/1818611/five-surprising-social-media-statistics-2013

Aaker, D. A. (1996). Measuring brand equity across products and markets. *California Management Review*, *38*(3), 102–120. doi:10.2307/41165845

Aaker, J. L. (1997). Dimensions of brand personality. *JMR, Journal of Marketing Research*, *34*(3), 347–356. doi:10.2307/3151897

Abdelmoula, S. N., Ben Lallouna, H. H., Skandrani, H., & Zghal, M. (2007). Transactionnel, relationnel ou hybride pour l'acquisition d'un avantage concurrentiel? Cas des entreprises tunisiennes. 75éme congrès de l'ACFAS, Québec.

Abhamid, N. R., Akhir, R. M., & Cheng, A. Y. (2013). Social media: An emerging dimension of marketing communication. *Journal of Management and Marketing Research*, *12*, 4–11.

Abrams, K. V. (2012). UK B2C Ecommerce: Mobile Takes Center Stage. *Emarketer*. Retrieved from http://www.emarketer.com/Article/Mobile-Gains-Speed-UK-Ecommerce-

Abrams, K. V. (2013). UK Digital Trends: Ecommerce, Video and Mobile Thrive, but Brands must work for loyalty and trust. *Emarketer*.

Abrams, K. V. (2013). Western Europe B2C Ecommerce: Solid Growth Continues as Mobile Gains Ground. *Emarketer*.

Abratt, R., & Kleyn, N. (2012). Corporate identity, corporate branding and corporate reputations: Reconciliation and integration. *European Journal of Marketing*, *46*(7–8), 1048–1063.

Abzari, M., Ghassemi, R. A., & Vosta, L. N. (2014). Analysing the effect of social media on brand attitude and purchase intention: The case of Iran Khodro company. *Procedia: Social and Behavioral Sciences*, *143*, 822–826. doi:10.1016/j.sbspro.2014.07.483

Adams, D. A., Nelson, R. R., & Todd, P. A. (1992). Perceived usefulness, ease of use, and usage of information technology: A replication. *Management Information Systems Quarterly*, *16*(2), 227–247. doi:10.2307/249577

Adeyeye, A. I. (2013). Identity conflict, terror and the Nigerian state: Between fragility and failure. *Journal of Sustainable Development in Africa*, *15*(4), 116–129.

Adjei, M., Noble, S., & Noble, C. (2010). The influence of C2C communications in online brand communities on customer purchase behavior. *Journal of the Academy of Marketing Science*, *38*(5), 634–653. doi:10.1007/s11747-009-0178-5

Afuah, A., & Tucci, C. L. (2012). Crowdsourcing as a solution to distant search. *Academy of Management Review*, *37*(3), 355–375. doi:10.5465/amr.2010.0146

Agarwal, R., & Prasad, J. (1997). The role of innovation characteristics and perceived voluntariness in acceptance of information technologies. *Decision Sciences*, *28*(3), 557–582. doi:10.1111/j.1540-5915.1997.tb01322.x

Agarwal, R., & Prasad, J. (1999). Are individual differences germane to the acceptance of new information technologies? *Decision Sciences*, *30*(2), 361–391. doi:10.1111/j.1540-5915.1999.tb01614.x

Agbiboa, D. E. (2012). Between corruption and development: The political economy of state robbery in Nigeria. *Journal of Business Ethics*, *108*(3), 325–345. doi:10.1007/s10551-011-1093-5

Aggarwal, R., Gopal, R., Gupta, A., & Singh, H. (2012). Putting Money Where the Mouths Are: The Relation between Venture Financing and Electronic Word-of-Mouth. *Information Systems Research*, *23*(3), 976–992. doi:10.1287/isre.1110.0402

Aggarwal, R., Gopal, R., Sankaranarayanan, R., & Singh, P. V. (2012). Blog, Blogger, and the Firm: Can Negative Employee Posts Lead to Positive Outcomes? *Information Systems Research*, *23*(2), 306–322. doi:10.1287/isre.1110.0360

Aggarwal, R., & Singh, H. (2013). Differential Influence of Blogs across Different Stages OF Decision Making: The Case of Venture Capitalists. *Management Information Systems Quarterly*, *37*(4), 1093–1112.

Aghaei, S., Nematbakhsh, A. N., & Farsani, H. K. (2012). Evolution of the World Wide Web: From Web 1.0 to Web 4.0. *International Journal of Web & Semantic Technology*, *3*(1), 1–10. doi:10.5121/ijwest.2012.3101

Agnihotri, R., Kothandaraman, P., Kashyap, R., & Singh, R. (2012). Bringing 'Social' into Sales: The Impact of Salespeople's Social Media Use on Service Behaviours and Value Co-creation. *Journal of Personal Selling & Sales Management*, *XXXII*(3), 333–348. doi:10.2753/PSS0885-3134320304

Aharony, N. (2009). An exploratory analysis of libraries' blogs: Their development, nature and changes. *Aslib Proceedings: New Information Perspectives*, *61*(6), 587–604. doi:10.1108/00012530911005535

Ahrens, J., Coyle, J. R., & Strahilevitz, M. A. (2013). Electronic word of mouth: The effects of incentives on e-referrals by senders and receivers. *International Journal of Marketing*, *47*(7), 1034–1051.

Aitken, R., & Campelo, A. (2011). The four Rs of place branding. *Journal of Marketing Management*, *27*(9–10), 913–933. doi:10.1080/0267257X.2011.560718

Ajzen, I., & Fishbein, M. (1980). Understanding Attitudes and Predicting Social Behavior, Prentice-Hall Inc, NJ. Englewood Cliffs.

Akar, E., & Topçu, B. (2011). An examination of the factors influencing consumers' attitudes toward social media marketing. *Journal of Internet Commerce*, *10*(1), 35–67. doi:10.1080/15332861.2011.558456

Albernathy, W. J., & Clark, K. B. (1985). *Innovation: mapping the winds of creative destruction. North Holland.* Elsevier Science Publishers B.V.

Albors, J., Ramos, J. C., & Hervas, J. L. (2008). New learning network paradigm: Communities of objectives, crowdsourcing, wikis and open source. *International Journal of Information Management*, *28*(3), 194–202. doi:10.1016/j.ijinfomgt.2007.09.006

Algesheimer, R., Dholakia, U. M., & Herrmann, A. (2005). The social influence of brand community: Evidence from European car clubs. *Journal of Marketing*, *69*(3), 19–34. doi:10.1509/jmkg.69.3.19.66363

Alhaiou, T., Irani, Z., & Ali, M. (2009, July 13-14). The relationship between e-CRM implementation and e-loyalty at different adoption stages of transaction cycle: a conceptual framework and hypothesis. *Proceedings of theEuropean and Mediterranean Conference on Information Systems EMCIS '09*, Izmir.

Allen, N. J., & Meyer, J. P. (1990). The measurement and antecedents of affective, continuance and normative commitment to the organization. *Journal of Occupational Psychology*, 63(1).

Alston, M. (2012, October 5). 78% of Luxury Marketers Spent More on Social Media in 2012 Than 2011, Luxury Interactive. Retrieved from http://finance.yahoo.com/news/78-luxury-marketers-spent-more-141500809.html

Andersen, P. H. (2005). Relationship marketing and brand involvement of professionals through web-enhanced brand communities: The case of Coloplast. *Industrial Marketing Management*, *34*(1), 39–51. doi:10.1016/j.indmarman.2004.07.002

Anderson, E. W., & Sullivan, M. W. (1993). The antecedents and consequences of customer satisfaction for firms. *Marketing Science*, *12*(2), 125–143. doi:10.1287/mksc.12.2.125

Andrews, R. L., & Manrai, A. K. (1998). Simulation Experiments in Choice Simplification: The Effects of Task and Context on Forecasting. *JMR, Journal of Marketing Research*, *35*(2), 198–209. doi:10.2307/3151848

Andrews, R. L., & Srinivasan, T. C. (1995). Studying Consideration Effects in Empirical Choice Models Using Scanner Panel Data. *JMR, Journal of Marketing Research*, *32*(1), 30–41. doi:10.2307/3152108

Angel, R., & Sexsmith, J. (2009), Social networking: The view from the c-suite. *Ivey Business Journal Online*. Retrieved from http://www.iveybusinessjournal.com/topics/strategy/social-networking-theview-from-the-c-suite

Annie Jin, S.-A. (2012). The potential of social media for luxury brand management. *Marketing Intelligence & Planning*, *30*(7), 687–699. doi:10.1108/02634501211273805

Ardichvili, A. (2008). Learning and knowledge sharing in virtual communities of practice: Motivators, barriers, and enablers. *Advances in Developing Human Resources*, *10*(4), 541–554. doi:10.1177/1523422308319536

Argo, J. J., White, K., & Dahl, D. W. (2006). Social comparison theory and deception in the interpersonal exchange of consumption information. *The Journal of Consumer Research*, *33*(1), 99–108. doi:10.1086/504140

Argyriou, E., Kitchen, P., & Melewar, T. C. (2006). The relationship between corporate websites and brand equity. *International Journal of Market Research*, *48*(5), 575–599.

Arno, C. (2012, December 26).Worldwide Social Media Usage Trends in 2012, Search Engine Watch. Retrieved from http://searchenginewatch.com/article/2167518/Worldwide-Social-Media-Usage-Trends-in-2012

Arnold, M. J., & Reynolds, K. E. (2003). Hedonic shopping motivations. *Journal of Retailing*, *79*(2), 77–95. doi:10.1016/S0022-4359(03)00007-1

Artegic.com. (2014). *What Social Media Can Do for Your Dialogue Marketing*. Retrieved from https://www.artegic.com/eCRM/0,215645635f6964092d0933333734/EN/news/d0.html

Ashley, C., & Tuten, T. (2015). Creative strategies in social media marketing: An exploratory study of branded social content and consumer engagement. *Psychology and Marketing*, *32*(1), 15–27. doi:10.1002/mar.20761

Atta, A., & Mahmoud, A. (2012). Web 2.0: A Movement within the Learning Community. *Information Management and Business Review*, *4*(12), 625–631.

Atwal, G., & Williams, A. (2009). Luxury brand marketing – The experience is everything! *Brand Management*, *16*(5-6), 338–346. doi:10.1057/bm.2008.48

Au, K. M., & Enderwick, P. (2000). A cognitive model on attitude toward technology adoption. *Journal of Managerial Psychology*, *15*(4), 266–282. doi:10.1108/02683940010330957

Azemi, Y., & Ozuem, W. (2015). Social media and SMEs in transition countries. In G. Bowen & W. Ozuem (Eds.), *Computer-mediated marketing strategies: social media and online brand communities* (pp. 114–133). Hershey, PA: IGI Global. doi:10.4018/978-1-4666-6595-8.ch005

Bagozzi, R. P., Bergami, M., Marzocchi, G. L., & Morandin, G. (2012). Customer-organization relationships: Development and test of a theory of extended identities. *Journal of Applied Psychology*, *97*(1), 63–76. doi:10.1037/a0024533 PMID:21766998

Bahri, N., & Mzoughi, N. (2007). Impact of the Intranet on the Performance of Marketing Information System: Empirical Investigation in the Pharmaceutical Industry. *Online Journal of Management research, OJMR, e-Journal of PCTE.*

Bahri-Ammari, N. (2014). The Role of Loyalty Program (LP) in Establishing Brand Attachment and Word-of-Mouth Intentions: An Empirical Investigation in the Mobile Sector. *International Journal of Customer Relationship Marketing and Management*, *5*(3), 49–68. doi:10.4018/ijcrmm.2014070104

Baird, C. H., & Parasnis, G. (2011). From social media to Social CRM: Reinventing the customer relationship. *Strategy and Leadership*, *39*(6), 27–34. doi:10.1108/10878571111176600

Baker, B. (2009). Your customer is talking—to everyone: Social media is the new channel for customer connection. *Information Management Journal*, *19*(4), 20.

Balasubramanian, S., & Mahajan, V. (2001). The economic leverage of the virtual community. *International Journal of Electronic Commerce*, *5*(3), 103–138.

Baliamoune-Lutz, M., & McGillivray, M. (2008). State Fragility Concept and Measurement. *UNU/WIDER Research Paper* No. 44.

Balkundi, P., & Harrison, D. A. (2006). Ties, leaders, and time in teams: Strong inference about network structure's effects on team viability and performance. *Academy of Management Journal*, *49*(1), 49–68. doi:10.5465/AMJ.2006.20785500

Balmer, J. M. T. (2012). Corporate brand management imperatives: Custodianship, credibility, and calibration. *California Management Review*, *54*(3), 6–33. doi:10.1525/cmr.2012.54.3.6

Balmer, J. M. T., & Gray, E. R. (2003). Corporate brands: What are they? What of them? *European Journal of Marketing*, *37*(7-8), 972–997. doi:10.1108/03090560310477627

Banerjee, S., & Dholakia, R. R. (2012). Location-based mobile advertisements and gender targeting. *Journal of Research in Interactive Marketing*, *6*(3), 198–214. doi:10.1108/17505931211274679

Barki, H., & Hartwick, J. (1994). Measuring user participation, user involvement, and user attitude. *Management Information Systems Quarterly*, *18*(1), 59–82. doi:10.2307/249610

Barnes, S. J., & Bohringer, M. (2011). Modeling use continuance behavior in microblogging services: The case of Twitter. *Journal of Computer Information Systems*, *51*(4), 1–10.

Barney, J. B. (1999). How a firm's capabilities affect boundary decisions. *Sloan Management Review*, *40*(3), 137–145.

Barrutia, J. M., & Echebarria, C. (2013). Networks: A social marketing tool. *European Journal of Marketing*, *47*(1/2), 324–343. doi:10.1108/03090561311285574

Barry, C., Markey, R., Almquist, E., & Brahm, C. (2011). Putting Social Media to work. Retrieved from http://www.bain.com/publications/articles/putting-social-media-to-work.aspx

Barwise, P., & Meehan, S. (2010). The one thing you must get right when building a brand. *Harvard Business Review*, *88*(12), 80–84.

Bauer, H. H., Grether, M., & Leach, M. (2002). Building customer relations over the Internet. *Industrial Marketing Management*, *31*(2), 155–163. doi:10.1016/S0019-8501(01)00186-9

BBC. (2012). *UK's first 4G mobile service launched in 11 cities by EE*. Retrieved from http://www.bbc.co.uk/news/technology-20121025

BBC. (2013). *The peril of "showrooming"*. Retrieved from http://www.bbc.co.uk/news/magazine-22098575

BBC. (2014a). Obesity crisis: Future projections 'underestimated'. Retrieved from http://www.bbc.co.uk/news/health-25708278

BBC. (2014b). What are the health risks of obesity? Retrieved from http://www.bbc.co.uk/science/0/21702372

Beal, A. (2008, April 10). 12 Reputations Every Company Should Monitor Online | Marketing Pilgrim. Retrieved from http://www.marketingpilgrim.com/2008/04/online-reputation-monitoring-campaign.html

Beal, V. (2014). *Electronic Commerce (ecommerce)*. Retrieved from http://www.webopedia.com/TERM/E/electronic_commerce.html

Beauty Customer Journey. (2012). *YouGov*. Retrieved from http://d25d2506sfb94s.cloudfront.net/cumulus_uploads/document/wa32oxme7c/Beauty%20Customer%20Journey.pdf

Beech, L. (1990). *Image theory: Decision making in Personal and Organizational Contexts*. New York, NY: John Wiley and Sons.

Belch, G. E., Belch, M. A., Kerr, G., & Powell, I. (2009). *Advertising and Promotion: An Integrated Marketing Communication Perspective*. Sydney, Australia: McGraw Hill.

Bell, C. R., & Zemke, R. E. (1987). Service breakdown the road to recovery. *Management Review*, *76*(10), 32–35.

Ben Issa, H. (2011). « Une approche socio-économique du maintien de la relation: Prestataire de service-Consommateur », Acte du 27éme Congrès de l'AFM, Bruxelles.

Bengtsson, A., & Servais, P. (2005). Co-branding on industrial markets. *Industrial Marketing Management*, *34*(7), 706–713. doi:10.1016/j.indmarman.2005.06.004

Bernoff, J., & Li, C. (2008). Harnessing the power of the oh-so-social web. *Sloan Management Review*, *49*(3), 36–42.

Berry, A. J. (2000). Leadership in a new millennium: The challenge of the 'risk society'. *Leadership and Organization Development Journal*, *21*(1), 5–12. doi:10.1108/01437730010310686

Berry, L. L. (2000). Cultivating service brand equity. *Journal of the Academy of Marketing Science*, *28*(1), 128–137. doi:10.1177/0092070300281012

Berthon, P. R., Pitt, L. F., Plangger, K., & Shapiro, D. (2012). Marketing meets Web 2.0, social media, and creative consumers: Implications for international marketing strategy. *Business Horizons*, *55*(3), 261–271. doi:10.1016/j.bushor.2012.01.007

Bertrand, G. (2013). Socialmedia research: Developing a trust metric in the social age. *International Journal of Market Research*, *55*(3), 333–335. doi:10.2501/IJMR-2013-032

Bettman, J. R., Luce, M. F., & Payne, J. W. (1998). Constructive Consumer Choice Processes. *The Journal of Consumer Research*, *25*(12), 187–217. doi:10.1086/209535

Bettman, J. R., & Park, C. W. (1980). Effects of Prior Knowledge and Experience and Phase of the Choice Process on Consumer Decision Processes: A Protocol Analysis. *The Journal of Consumer Research*, *7*(3), 234–248. doi:10.1086/208812

Bharadwaj, A., El Sawy, O. A., Pavlou, P. A., & Venkatraman, N. (2013). Digital business strategy: Toward a next generation of insights. *Management Information Systems Quarterly*, *37*(2), 471–482.

Bhatnagar, N. (2012). Customer Relationship Marketing: Customer-Centric Processes for Engendering Customer- Firm Bonds and Optimizing Long-Term Customer Value. *Intechopen*. Retrieved from http://cdn.intechopen.com/pdfs/35309/InTech-Customer_relationship_marketing_customer_centric_processes_for_engendering_customer_firm_bonds_and_optimizing_long_term_customer_value.pdf

Bhattacherjee, A., & Sanford, C. (2006). Influence processes for information technology acceptance: An elaboration likelihood model. *Management Information Systems Quarterly*, *30*(4), 805–825.

Bickart, B., & Schindler, R. (2001). Internet forums as influential sources of consumer information. *Advances in Consumer Research. Association for Consumer Research (U. S.)*, *28*(1), 134.

Bigdoor.com. (2014). *A Marketers Guide to Customer Loyalty*. Retrieved from http://bigdoor.com/resources/marketers-guide-to-customer-loyalty/

Bigné-Alcañiz, E., Currás-Pérez, R., Ruiz-Mafé, C., & Sanz-Blas, S. (2012). Cause-related marketing influence on consumer responses: The Moderating effect of Cause-brand fit. *Journal of Marketing Communications*, *18*(4), 265–283. doi:10.1080/13527266.2010.521358

Bitner, M. J., Booms, B. H., & Tetreault, M. S. (1990). The service encounter: Diagnosing favorable and unfavorable incidents. *Journal of Marketing*, *54*(1), 71–84. doi:10.2307/1252174

Blackshaw, P., & Nazzaro, M. (2004). *Consumer-generated media (CGM) 101: Word-of-mouth in the age of the Web fortified consumer*. Retrieved from http://www.nielsen-online.com/downloads/us/buzz/nbzm_wp_CGM101.pdf

Blackshaw, P., & Nazzaro, M. (2004). Consumer-Generated Media (CGM) 101: Word-of-mouth in the age of the Web-fortified consumer. *Intelliseek*. Retrieved from http://www.brandchannel.com/images/papers/222_cgm.pdf

Blattberg, R., Getz, G., & Thomas, J. S. (2001). *Customer Equity: Building and Managing Relationships as Valuable Assets*. Boston: Harvard Business School Press.

Blidner, R. (2015, March 17). Australian news anchor goes viral with penis-shaped neckline. Retrieved from http://www.nydailynews.com/entertainment/tv/australian-news-anchor-viral-penis-shaped-neckline-article-1.2151861

Bogers, M., Afuah, A., & Bastian, B. (2010). Users as innovators: A review, critique, and future research directions. *Journal of Management*, *36*(4), 857–875. doi:10.1177/0149206309353944

Bohner, M., & Bohner, G. (2001). *Intrapersonal processes*. Oxford: Blackwell.

Bolton, R. N. (1998). A Dynamic Model of the Duration of the Customer's Relationship with a Continuous Service Provider: The Role of Satisfaction. *Marketing Science*, *17*(1), 45–65. doi:10.1287/mksc.17.1.45

Bolton, R. N., & Lemon, K. N. (1999). Dynamic Model of Customers' Usage of Services: Usage as an Antecedent and Consequence of Satisfaction. *The Journal of Consumer Research*, *36*(2), 171–186.

Bolton, R. N., Parasuraman, A., Hoefnagels, A., Migchels, N., Kabadayi, S., Gruber, T., & Solnet, D. et al. (2013). Understanding Generation Y and their use of social media: A review and research agenda. *Journal of Service Management*, *24*(3), 245–267. doi:10.1108/09564231311326987

Bolton, R., Kannan, P. K., & Bramlett, M. (2000). Implications of loyalty program membership and service experiences for customer retention and value. *Journal of the Academy of Marketing Science*, *28*(1), 95–108. doi:10.1177/0092070300281009

Bone, P. F. (1992). Determinants of Word-of-Mouth communication during product consumption. *Advances in Consumer Research. Association for Consumer Research (U. S.)*, *19*, 579–583.

Bone, P. F. (1995). Word of Mouth effects on short-term and long-term product judgments. *Journal of Business Research*, *32*(3), 213–223. doi:10.1016/0148-2963(94)00047-I

Bonifield, C., & Cole, C. A. (2008). Better him than me: Social comparison theory and service recovery. *Journal of the Academy of Marketing Science*, *36*(4), 565–577. doi:10.1007/s11747-008-0109-x

Booth, N., & Matic, J. A. (2011). Mapping and leveraging influencers in social media to shape corporate brand perceptions. *Corporate Communications: An International Journal*, *16*(3), 184–191. doi:10.1108/13563281111156853

Borden, N. H. (1964). The Concept of the Marketing Mix. In G. Schwartz (Ed.), Science in Marketing. New York, NJ: John Wiley.

Borison, A., & Hamm, G. (2010). Prediction Markets: A New Tool for Strategic Decision Making. *California Management Review*, *52*(4), 125–141. doi:10.1525/cmr.2010.52.4.125

Bougie, R., Pieters, R., & Zeelenberg, M. (2003). Angry customers don't come back, they get back: The experience and behavioral implications of anger and dissatisfaction in services. *Journal of the Academy of Marketing Science*, *31*(4), 377–393. doi:10.1177/0092070303254412

Bowden, J. L. H. (2009). The process of customer engagement: A conceptual framework. *Journal of Marketing Theory and Practice*, *17*(1), 63–74. doi:10.2753/MTP1069-6679170105

Bowen, G., & Ozuem, W. (Eds.). (2015). *Computer-mediated marketing strategies: Social media and online brand communities*. Hershey, PA: IGI Global. doi:10.4018/978-1-4666-6595-8

Boyatzis, R. E. (1998). *Transforming qualitative information: Thematic analysis and code development*. California: Sage Publications Inc.

Boyce, J. (2002). *Market Research in Practice*. Sydney, Australia: McGraw Hill.

Boyd, D. E., & Spekman, R. E. (2004). Internet usage within B2B relationships and its impact on value creation: A conceptual model and research propositions. *Journal of Business-To-Business Marketing*, *11*(1–2), 9–34. doi:10.1300/J033v11n01_03

Boyd, D. M., & Ellison, N. B. (2007). Social network sites: Definition, history, and scholarship. *Journal of Computer-Mediated Communication*, *13*(1), 210–230. doi:10.1111/j.1083-6101.2007.00393.x

Boyle, C. (2013). Retail Mobile Commerce Forecast: Shoppers Turn to Smartphones First. *Emarketer.* Retrieved from http://www.emarketer.com/Article/More-Shoppers-Reach-Mobile-Browse-Buy/1009615

Bradbury, T., & Coons, D. (2007). *Customer Touchpoints – Your Brand in Action.* Retrieved from http://www.thesmartbuilder.com/whitepapers/SMART_Whitepaper_-_Touchpoints.pdf

Brandtzaeg, P. B., & Heim, J. (2011). A typology of social networking sites users. *International Journal of Web Based Communities*, *7*(1), 28–51. doi:10.1504/IJWBC.2011.038124

Brass, D. J., Galaskiewicz, J., Greve, H. R., & Tsai, W. P. (2004). Taking stock of networks and organizations: A multilevel perspective. *Academy of Management Journal*, *47*(6), 795–817. doi:10.2307/20159624

Bratucu, R., Gheorghe, I. R., Radu, A., & Purcarea, V. L. (2014). The relevance of netnography to the harness of Romanian health care electronic word-of-mouth. *Journal of Medicine and Life*, *7*(3), 363–367. PMID:25408755

Braun, V., & Clarke, V. (2006). Using thematic analysis in psychology. *Qualitative Research in Psychology*, *3*(2), 77–101. doi:10.1191/1478088706qp063oa

Brennan, R., & Croft, R. (2012). The use of social media in B2B marketing and branding: An exploratory study. *Journal of Consumer Behaviour*, *11*(2), 101–115. doi:10.1362/147539212X13420906144552

Brodie, R. J., Hollebeek, L. D., Juric, B., & Ilic, A. (2011). Customer engagement: Conceptual domain, fundamental propositions, and implications for research. *Journal of Service Research*, *14*(3), 252–271. doi:10.1177/1094670511411703

Brodie, R. J., Ilic, A., Juric, B., & Hollebeek, L. (2013). Consumer engagement in a virtual brand community: An exploratory analysis. *Journal of Business Research*, *66*(1), 105–114. doi:10.1016/j.jbusres.2011.07.029

Brodie, R., Coviello, R., Brookes, R., & Little, V. (1997). Towards a Paradigm Shift in Marketing? An Examination of Current Marketing Practices. *Journal of Marketing Management*, *13*(5), 383–406. doi:10.1080/0267257X.1997.9964481

Brodmerkel, S., & Carah, N. (2013). Alcohol brands on Facebook: The challenges of regulating brands on social media. *Journal of Public Affairs*, *13*(3), 272–281. doi:10.1002/pa.1466

Brogan, C., & Smith, J. (2010). *Trust Agents: Using the Web to Build Influence, Improve Reputation, and Earn Trust* (2nd ed.). Hoboken, N.J: Wiley.

Brown, D., & Fiorella, S. (2013). Influence Marketing, US: Que Publishing.

Brown, J. J., & Reingen, P. H. (1987). Social ties and Word-of- Mouth referral behavior. *The Journal of Consumer Research*, *14*(3), 350–362. doi:10.1086/209118

Brown, J., Broderick, A., & Lee, N. (2007). Word of mouth communication within online communities: Conceptualizing the online social network. *Journal of Interactive Marketing*, *21*(3), 2–20. doi:10.1002/dir.20082

Brown, M., Pope, N., & Vogues, K. (2003). Buying or browsing?: An exploration of shopping orientations and online purchase intention. *European Journal of Marketing*, *37*(11/12), 1666–1684. doi:10.1108/03090560310495401

Brown, S., Kozinets, R. V., & Sherry, J. F. Jr. (2003). Teaching old brands new tricks: Retro branding and the revival of brand meaning. *Journal of Marketing*, *67*(3), 19–33. doi:10.1509/jmkg.67.3.19.18657

Bruhn, M., Schnebelen, S., & Schäfer, D. (2014). Antecedents and consequences of the quality of e-customer-to-customer interactions in B2B brand communities. *Industrial Marketing Management*, *43*(1), 164–176. doi:10.1016/j.indmarman.2013.08.008

Bruner, G. C. II, & Kumar, A. (2005). Explaining consumer acceptance of handheld internet devices. *Journal of Business Research*, *58*(5), 553–558. doi:10.1016/j.jbusres.2003.08.002

Bruyn, A., & Lilien, G. L. (2008). A multi–stage model of word of mouth through viral marketing. *International Journal of Research in Marketing*, *25*(3), 143–225. doi:10.1016/j.ijresmar.2008.03.004

Bryman, A. (1988). *Contemporary Social Research Series*. London: Unwin Hyman Ltd.

Bryman, A. (1989). *Research Methods and Organization Studies*. London: Unwin Hyman Ltd. doi:10.4324/9780203359648

Buckinx, W., & Van-den Poel, D. (2005). Customer base analysis: Partial defection of behaviourally loyal clients in a non-contractual FMCG retail setting. *European Journal of Operational Research*, *164*(1), 252–268. doi:10.1016/j.ejor.2003.12.010

Bucklin, L. P., & Sengupta, S. (1993). Organizing successful co-marketing alliances. *Journal of Marketing*, *57*(2), 32–46. doi:10.2307/1252025

Buda, R., & Zhang, Y. (2000). Consumer product evaluation: The interactive effect of message framing, presentation order, and source credibility. *Journal of Product and Brand Management*, *9*(4), 229–242. doi:10.1108/10610420010344022

Buderi, R., & Huang, G. T. (2006). Guanxi, New York: Simon & Schuster.

Bughin, J. (2013). Brand success in the era of digital Darwinism. *Journal of Brand Strategy*, 2(4), 355–365.

Buil, I., Martinez, E., & de Chernatony, L. (2013). The influence of brand equity on consumer responses. *Journal of Consumer Marketing*, *30*(1), 62–74. doi:10.1108/07363761311290849

Bukszar, E. (2003). Does overconfidence lead to poor decisions? A comparison of decision making and judgment under uncertainty. *Journal of Business Management*, *9*, 33–43.

Bumell, P. (2013). What happened to charity credit cards? *News archive*. Retrieved from http://www.affinitymarketing.co.uk

Burez, J., & Van-den, Poel, D. (2007). CRM at a pay-TV company: Using analytical models to reduce customer attrition by targeted marketing for subscription services. *Expert Systems with Applications*, *32*(2), 277–288. doi:10.1016/j.eswa.2005.11.037

Burg, N. (2013). *How to Measure Your Social Media Return on Investment*. Retrieved from http://www.forbes.com/sites/capitalonespark/2013/04/25/how-to-measure-your-social-media-return-on-investment/

Burr, V. (2003). *Social Contructionism* (2nd ed.). London: Routledge.

Burton-Jones, A., & Hubona, G. S. (2006). The mediation of external variables in the technology acceptance model. *Information & Management*, *43*(6), 706–717. doi:10.1016/j.im.2006.03.007

Butler, P., & Peppard, J. (1998). Consumer Purchasing on the Internet: Processes and Prospects. *European Journal of Marketing*, *16*(5), 600–610.

Butler, T. (1998). Towards a hermeneutic method for interpretive research in information systems. *Journal of Information Technology*, *13*(4), 285–300. doi:10.1057/jit.1998.7

Buttle, A. F. (1998). Word-of-mouth: Understanding and managing referral marketing. *Journal of Strategic Marketing*, *6*(3), 241–254. doi:10.1080/096525498346658

Buttle, F. (2009). *Customer relationship management – concepts and technologies* (2nd ed.). Oxford: Elsevier.

Calabrese, R. L., Sally, J., & Zepeda, S. J. (1999). Decision-making assessment: Improving principal performance. *International Journal of Educational Management*, *13*(1), 6–13. doi:10.1108/09513549910253428

Campbell, D. T. (1963). C.W. Harris (Ed.), From descriptions to experimentation: interpreting trends as quasi experiments in Problems in measuring change. Madison university of Wisconsin.

Card, S. K., Moran, T. PNewell, A. (1980). The keystroke-level model for user performance time with interactive systems. *Communications of the ACM*, *23*(7), 396–410. doi:10.1145/358886.358895

Carleton, D. (2009, June 25). The Top 20 Business Reasons To Use Social Media Marketing. Retrieved from http://www.examiner.com/article/the-top-20-business-reasons-to-use-social-media-marketing

Carlson, B. D., Suter, T. A., & Brown, T. J. (2008). Social versus psychological brand community: The role of psychological sense of brand community. *Journal of Business Research*, *61*(4), 284–291. doi:10.1016/j.jbusres.2007.06.022

Carroll, J., & Johnson, S. (1990). *Decision Research: A Field Guide*. Newbury Park, CA: Sage Press.

Caru, A., & Cova, B. (2008). Small versus big stories in framing consumption experiences. *Qualitative Market Research: An International Journal*, *11*(2), 166–176. doi:10.1108/13522750810864422

Casado-Diaz, A. B., & Nicolau-Gonzalbez, J. L. (2009). Explaining consumer complaining behaviour in double deviation scenarios: The banking services. *Service Industries Journal*, *29*(12), 1659–1668. doi:10.1080/02642060902793524

Cashmore, P. (2009, June 21). Neda: YouTube Video Too Distressing to Ignore. *Mashable.com*. Retrieved from http://mashable.com/2009/06/21/neda/

Cashmore, P. (n.d.). Neda: YouTube Video Too Distressing to Ignore. Retrieved July 29, 2014, from http://mashable.com/2009/06/21/neda/

Cassia, F., & Magno, F. (2012). Business-to-business branding: A review and assessment of the impact of non-attribute-based brand beliefs on buyer's attitudinal loyalty. *Canadian Journal of Administrative Sciences*, *29*(3), 242–254. doi:10.1002/cjas.235

Catalin, M. C., & Andreea, P. (2014). Brands as a mean of consumer self-expression and desired personal lifestyle. *Procedia: Social and Behavioral Sciences*, *109*, 103–107. doi:10.1016/j.sbspro.2013.12.427

Catillo, M. (2014). Sensa, L'Occitane, LeanSpa, HGG Diet Direct fined by FTC for false advertising. Retrieved from http://www.cbsnews.com/news/sensa-loccitane-leanspa-hcg-diet-direct-fined-by-ftc-for-false-advertising/

Cciq.com.au. (2012). *2012 Digital Readiness Study*. Retrieved from http://www.cciq.com.au/assets/Documents/Digital/DigitalReadiness-Report-final-web.pdf

Cciq.com.au. (2013). *2013 Digital Readiness Survey*. Retrieved from http://www.cciq.com.au/industries/technology/digital-readiness-study/

Chaffey, D., & Ellis-Chadwick, F. (2012). *Digital Marketing: Strategy, implementation and practice* (5th ed.). Harlow: Pearson Education Limited.

Chaffey, D., Ellis-Chadwick, F., Johnson, K., & Mayer, R. (2006). *Internet Marketing Strategy, Implementation and Practice* (3rd ed.). Harlow, UK: Prentice Hall FT.

Chaffey, D., & Smith, P. R. (2008). *EMarketing Excellence Planning and optimizing your digital marketing* (3rd ed.). London, UK: Elsevier.

Chan, F. T. S., & Yee-Loong Chong, A. (2013). Analysis of the determinants of consumers' m-commerce usage activities. *Online Information Review*, *37*(3), 443–461. doi:10.1108/OIR-01-2012-0012

Chang, D. R., & Park, S. B. (2013). The effects of brand strategy and technological uncertainty on pioneering advantage in the multigenerational product market. *Journal of Product Innovation Management*, *30*(1), 82–95. doi:10.1111/j.1540-5885.2012.00988.x

Chan, J. M., & Yazdanifard, R. (2014). How social media marketing can influence the profitability of an online company from a consumer point of view. *Journal of Research in Marketing*, *2*(2), 157–160. doi:10.17722/jorm.v2i2.55

Chaudhuri, A., & Holbrook, M. B. (2001). The chain of effects from brand trust and brand affect to brand performance: The role of brand loyalty. *Journal of Marketing*, *65*(2), 81–93. doi:10.1509/jmkg.65.2.81.18255

Chau, P. Y. K., & Hu, P. (2004). Investigating health care professionals decisions to accept telemedicine technology: An empirical test of competing theories. *Information & Management*, *39*(4), 705–719.

Cheema, A., & Papatla, P. (2010). Relative importance of online versus offline information for Internet purchase: Product category and Internet experience effects. *Journal of Business Research, 63*(9-10), 979–985. doi:10.1016/j.jbusres.2009.01.021

Chemingui, H., & Ben lallouna, H. B. (2013). Resistance, motivation, trust and intention to use mobile finance services. *International Journal of Bank Marketing, 31*(7), 574–592. doi:10.1108/IJBM-12-2012-0124

Chen, J., Nguyen, B., & Klaus, P. (2013). Public affairs in China: Exploring the role of brand fairness perceptions in the case of Mercedes-Benz. *Journal of Public Affairs, 13*(4), 403–414. doi:10.1002/pa.1493

Chen, J., Xu, H., & Whinston, A. (2011). Moderated online communities and quality of user-generated content. *Journal of Management Information Systems, 28*(2), 237–268. doi:10.2753/MIS0742-1222280209

Chen, Q., & Rodgers, S. (2006). Development of an instrument to measure web site personality. *Journal of Interactive Advertising, 7*(1), 47–64. doi:10.1080/15252019.2006.10722124

Chen, Q., & Wells, W. D. (2002). Attitude toward the site II: New information. *Journal of Advertising Research, 42*(2), 33–46.

Chen, X., Chen, Y., & Xiao, P. (2013). The impact of sampling and network topology on the estimation of social intercorrelations. *JMR, Journal of Marketing Research, 50*(1), 95–110. doi:10.1509/jmr.12.0026

Chen, Y., Fay, S., & Wang, Q. (2011). The role of marketing in social media: How online consumer reviews evolve. *Journal of Interactive Marketing, 25*(2), 85–94. doi:10.1016/j.intmar.2011.01.003

Chester, J. (2007). *Digital destiny: New media and the future of democracy*. New York: New Press.

Cheung, C. M. K., & Lee, M. K. O. (2012). What drives consumers to spread electronic word of mouth in online consumer-opinion platforms. *Decision Support Systems, 53*(1), 218–225. doi:10.1016/j.dss.2012.01.015

Cheung, C. M. K., & Thadani, D. R. (2012). The impact of electronic word-of-mouth communication: A literature analysis and integrative model. *Decision Support Systems, 54*(1), 461–470. doi:10.1016/j.dss.2012.06.008

Cheung, C., Lee, M., & Rabjohn, N. (2008). The impact of electronic word-of-mouth: The adoption of online opinions in online customer communities. *Internet Research, 18*(3), 229–247. doi:10.1108/10662240810883290

Cheung, M. Y., Luo, C., Sia, C. L., & Chen, H. (2009). Credibility of electronic word-of-mouth: Informational and normative determinants of on-line consumer recommendations. *International Journal of Electronic Commerce, 13*(4), 9–38. doi:10.2753/JEC1086-4415130402

Chevalier, J. A., & Mayzlin, D. (2006). The Effect of Word of Mouth on Sales: Online Book Reviews. *JMR, Journal of Marketing Research, 43*(3), 345–354. doi:10.1509/jmkr.43.3.345

Childers, T. L., Carr, C. L., Peck, J., & Carson, S. (2001). Hedonic and utilitarian motivations for online retail shopping behavior. *Journal of Retailing, 77*(4), 511–536. doi:10.1016/S0022-4359(01)00056-2

Chintagunta, P. K., Gopinath, S., & Venkataraman, S. (2010). The effects of online user reviews on movie box office performance: Accounting for sequential rollout and aggregation across local markets. *Marketing Science, 29*(5), 944–957. doi:10.1287/mksc.1100.0572

Chiu, H. C., Hsieh, Y. C., Kao, Y. H., & Lee, M. (2007). The determinants of e-mail receivers' disseminating behaviors on the Internet. *Journal of Advertising Research, 47*(4), 524–534. doi:10.2501/S0021849907070547

Choi, S., & Mattila, A. S. (2008). Perceived controllability and service expectations: Influences on customer reactions following service failure. *Journal of Business Research, 61*(1), 24–30. doi:10.1016/j.jbusres.2006.05.006

Choo, H., Moon, H., Kim, H., & Yoon, N. (2012). Luxury customer value. *Journal of Fashion Marketing and Management, 16*(1), 81–101. doi:10.1108/13612021211203041

Cho, S., & Fiorito, S. S. (2009). Acceptance of online customization for apparel shopping. *International Journal of Retail & Distribution Management, 37*(5), 389–407. doi:10.1108/09590550910954892

Choudhury, M. M., & Harrigan, P. (2012, July 2-4). Technology Acceptance Model and the Social CRM: A Model for Customer Engagement. Proceedings of the Academy of Marketing Conference, Southampton, UK.

Christensen, C. (2011). Discourses of technology and liberation: State aid to net activists in an era of "Twitter Revolutions". *Communication Review, 14*(3), 233–253. doi:10.1080/10714421.2011.597263

Christodoulides, G., Jevons, C., & Bonhomme, J. (2012). Memo to marketers: Quantitative evidence for change. How user-generated content really affects brands. *Journal of Advertising Research, 52*(1), 53–64. doi:10.2501/JAR-52-1-053-064

Chuang, S. C., Cheng, Y. H., Chang, C. J., & Yang, S. W. (2012). The effect of service failure types and service recovery on customer satisfaction: A mental accounting perspective. *Service Industries Journal, 32*(2), 257–271. doi:10.1080/02642069.2010.529435

Chu, S. C., & Kim, Y. (2011). Determinants of consumer engagement in electronic word-of-mouth (eWOM) in social networking sites. *International Journal of Advertising, 30*(1), 47–75. doi:10.2501/IJA-30-1-047-075

Clarke, I. (2008). Emerging Value Propositions for M-commerce. *The Journal of Business Strategy, 25*(2), 41–57.

Clark, M., & Melancon, J. (2013). The Influence of Social Media Investment on Relational Outcomes: A Relationship Marketing Perspective. *International Journal of Marketing Studies, 5*(4), 132–142. doi:10.5539/ijms.v5n4p132

Clickzintel.com. 2014a. *The Value of Social Data.* Retrieved from http://www.clickzintel.com/download/getting-true-value-social-20281

Clickzintel.com. 2014b. *Conversion: Along the Suspect to Advocate Journey.* Retrieved from http://www.clickzintel.com/abstract/conversion-suspect-advocate-journey-22997

Clothing Retailing Market Report. (2013). Keynote. Retrieved from http://www.keynote.co.uk/market-intelligence/view/product/10792/clothing-retailing?highlight=clothing&utm_source=kn.reports.search

CMOSurvey.org. (2014). *CMO Survey Report: Highlights and Insights, August 2014.* Retrieved from http://cmosurvey.org/files/2014/09/The_CMO_Survey-Highlights_and_Insights-Aug-2014.pdf

Coker, K. K., Altobello, S. A., & Balasubramanian, S. K. (2013). Message exposure with friends: The role of social context on attitudes toward prominently placed brands. *Journal of Consumer Behaviour, 12*(2), 102–111. doi:10.1002/cb.1423

Collier, P. (2009). *Wars, Guns, and Votes: Democracy in Dangerous Places.* London: Bodley Head.

Collis, J., & Hussey, R. (2003). *Business Research: A practical guide for undergraduate and postgraduate students* (2nd ed.). New York: Palgrave Macmillan.

Collis, J., & Hussey, R. (2009). *Business Research: A Practical Guide for Undergraduate & Postgraduate Students* (3rd ed.). Hampshire: Palgrave Macmillan.

Comm, J. (2010). *Twitter Power 2.0: How to Dominate Your Market One Tweet at a Time* (2nd ed.). Hoboken, NJ: Wiley.

Connolly, M., & James, C. (2006). Collaboration for school improvement: A resource dependency and institutional framework of analysis. *Educational Management Administration & Leadership, 34*(1), 69–87. doi:10.1177/1741143206059540

Constantinides, E. (2014). Foundations of social media marketing. *Procedia: Social and Behavioral Sciences*, *148*, 40–57. doi:10.1016/j.sbspro.2014.07.016

Constantinides, E., Lorenzo-Romero, G. M., & Gómez, M. A. (2010). Effects of web experience on consumer choice: A multicultural approach. *Internet Research*, *20*(2), 188–209. doi:10.1108/10662241011032245

Convinceandconvert.com. (2014). *Social Circles Use Social Media to Build a Touchpoint Corral*. Retrieved from http://www.convinceandconvert.com/social-media-strategy/social-circles-use-social-media-to-build-a-touchpoint-corral/

Cooke, A. D., & Mellers, B. A. (1998). Multiattribute judgment: Attribute spacing influences single attributes. *Journal of Experimental Psychology. Human Perception and Performance*, *24*(2), 496–504. doi:10.1037/0096-1523.24.2.496

Cooke, S., & Ryan, P. (2000). Brand alliances: From reputation endorsement to collaboration on core competencies. *Irish Marketing Review*, *13*(2), 36–41.

Cook, N. (2008). *Enterprise 2.0*. Burlington, VT: Gower Publishing Limited.

Coppola, N. W., Hiltz, S. R., & Rotter, N. G. (2004). Building trust in virtual teams. *IEEE Transactions on Professional Communication*, *47*(2), 95–104. doi:10.1109/TPC.2004.828203

Correia, A. (2013). Social Information: Gaining Competitive and Business Advantage Using Social Media Tools. *Online Information Review*, *37*(1), 151–152. doi:10.1108/14684521311311720

Corstjens, M. & Umblijs, A. (2012). The Power of Evil – The Damage of Negative Social Media Strongly Outweigh Positive Contributions. *Journal of Advertising Research*, December, 52(4), 433-449.

Corstjens, M., & Umblijs, A. (2013). The power of evil: The damage of negative social media strongly outweigh positive contributions. *Journal of Advertising Research*, *52*(4), 433–449. doi:10.2501/JAR-52-4-433-449

Craighead, C. W., Karwan, K. R., & Miller, J. L. (2004). The effects of severity of failure and customer loyalty on service recovery strategies. *Production and Operations Management*, *13*(4), 307–321. doi:10.1111/j.1937-5956.2004.tb00220.x

Creswell, J. W. (1994). *Research design: Qualitative and Quantitative Approaches*. Thousand Oaks: Sage.

Cronin, J. J. Jr, Brady, M. K., & Hult, G. T. M. (2000). Assessing the effects of quality, value, and customer satisfaction on customer behavioral intentions in service environments. *Journal of Retailing*, *76*(2), 193–218. doi:10.1016/S0022-4359(00)00028-2

Cronley, M. L., Posavac, S. S., Meyer, T., Kardes, F. R., & Kellaris, J. J. (2005). A selective hypothesis testing perspective on price-quality inference and inference-based choice. *Journal of Consumer Psychology*, *15*(2), 159–169. doi:10.1207/s15327663jcp1502_8

Crosby, L. A., Evans, K. R., & Cowles, D. (1990). Relationship Quality in Services Selling: An Interpersonal Influence Perspective. *Journal of Marketing*, *54*(3), 68–81. doi:10.2307/1251817

Crowdtap (2014). Millennials heart UGC. Retrieved from http://blog.crowdtap.it/2014/04/millennials-heart-ugc-infographic/

Culnan, M. J., McHugh, P. J., & Zubillaga, J. I. (2010). How Large U.S. Companies Can Use Twitter and Other Social Media to Gain Business Value. *MIS Quarterly Executive*, *9*(4), 243–259.

Cunningham, J. (2010). New workers, new workplaces? Getting the balance right. Viewpoint. *Strategic Direction*, *26*(1), 5–6. doi:10.1108/02580541011009725

Curran, J. M., & Meuter, M. L. (2005). Self-service technology adoption: Comparing three technologies. *Journal of Services Marketing*, *19*(2), 103–113. doi:10.1108/08876040510591411

Dabholkar, P. A., & Bagozzi, R. P. (2002). An attitudinal model of technology based self-service: Moderating effects of consumer traits and situational factors. *Journal of the Academy of Marketing Science*, *30*(3), 184–201. doi:10.1177/0092070302303001

Dahlstrom, R., & Dato-on, M. (2004). Business-to-business antecedents to retail co-branding. *Journal of Business-To-Business Marketing*, *11*(3), 1–22. doi:10.1300/J033v11n03_01

Dall'Olmo Riley, F., & Lacroix, C. (2003). Luxury branding on the internet: Lost opportunity or impossibility? *Marketing Intelligence & Planning*, *21*(2), 96–104. doi:10.1108/02634500310465407

Danesh, S. N., Nasab, S. A., & Kwek, C. L. (2012). The Study of Customer Satisfaction, Customer Trust and Switching Barriers on Customer Retention in Malaysia Hypermarkets. *International Journal of Business and Management*, *7*(7), 141–150.

Dann, S. (2010). Redefining social marketing with contemporary commercial marketing definitions. *Journal of Business Research*, *63*(2), 147–153. doi:10.1016/j.jbusres.2009.02.013

Dann, S., & Dann, S. (2011). *E-marketing: theory and application*. Basingstoke, England: Palgrave Macmillan.

Dash, S., & Saji, K. B. (2008). The role of consumer self-efficacy and website social presence in customers' adoption of B2C online shopping: An empirical study in the Indian context. *Journal of International Consumer Marketing*, *20*(2), 33–48. doi:10.1300/J046v20n02_04

Daugherty, T., Eastin, M., & Bright, L. (2008). Exploring Consumer Motivations for creating User-Generated Content. *Journal of Interactive Advertising*, *8*(2), 16–25. doi:10.1080/15252019.2008.10722139

Davis, S., & Longoria, T. (2003). *Harmonizing your Touchpoints*. Retrieved October 16, 2014, from https://www.prophet.com/downloads/articles/Harmonizing%20Your%20Touchpoints%20(SD%20TL).pdf

Davis, F. D. (1989). Perceived usefulness, perceived ease of use, and user acceptance of information technology. *Management Information Systems Quarterly*, *13*(3), 319–340. doi:10.2307/249008

Davis, F. D., Bagozzi, R. P., & Warshaw, P. R. (1989). User acceptance of computer technology: A comparison of two theoretical models. *Management Science*, *35*(8), 982–1003. doi:10.1287/mnsc.35.8.982

Davis, R., Piven, I., & Breazeale, M. (2014). Conceptualizing the brand in social media community: The five sources model. *Journal of Retailing and Consumer Services*, *21*(4), 468–481. doi:10.1016/j.jretconser.2014.03.006

Davis, R., & Sajtos, L. (2008). Measuring consumer interactivity in response to campaigns coupling mobile and television media. *Journal of Advertising Research*, *48*(3), 375–391. doi:10.2501/S0021849908080409

Dawar, N. J., & Parker, P. (1994). Marketing universals: Consumers' use of brand name, price, physical appearance and retailer reputation as signals of product quality. *Journal of Marketing*, *58*(2), 81–95. doi:10.2307/1252271

de Chernatony, L. (2002). Would a brand smell any sweeter by a corporate name? *Corporate Reputation Review*, *5*(2-3), 114–132. doi:10.1057/palgrave.crr.1540169

de Chernatony, L., & Christodoulides, G. (2004). Taking the brand promise online: Challenges and opportunities. *Interactive Marketing*, *5*(3), 238–251. doi:10.1057/palgrave.im.4340241

de Chernatony, L., & Segal-Horn, S. (2001). Building on services' characteristics to develop successful service brand. *Journal of Marketing Management*, *17*(7–8), 645–669. doi:10.1362/026725701323366773

De Clerck, J.-P. (2014). *Is Touchpoint Marketing the Only Marketing Left?* Retrieved from http://www.i-scoop.eu/touchpoint-marketing-marketing-left/

de Matos, C. A., Henrique, J. L., & Rossi, C. A. V. (2007). Service recovery paradox: A meta-analysis. *Journal of Service Research*, *10*(1), 60–77. doi:10.1177/1094670507303012

De Valck, K., Van Bruggen, G., & Wierenga, B. (2009). Virtual communities: A marketing perspective. *Decision Support Systems*, *47*(3), 185–203. doi:10.1016/j.dss.2009.02.008

de Vries, L., Gensler, S., & Leeflang, P. S. H. (2012). Popularity of brand posts on brand fan pages: An investigation of the effects of social media marketing. *Journal of Interactive Marketing*, *26*(2), 83–91. doi:10.1016/j.intmar.2012.01.003

Dealerspan (2014). *Home*. Retrieved from http://bit.ly/1wEqnOO

Deans, P. C., & Miles, J. B. (2011), "A framework for understanding social media trends in China", Proceedings of the 11th International DSI and APDSI Joint Meeting, Taipei, Taiwan, July pp. 12–16.

Deans, P. C. (2012). Integration of Study Abroad with Social Media Technologies and Decision-making Applications. *Decision Sciences Journal of Innovative Education*, *10*(3), 299–336. doi:10.1111/j.1540-4609.2012.00344.x

Deetz, S., & Brown, D. (2004). Conceptualising involvement, participation and workplace decision processes – a communication theory perspective. In D. Tourish & O. Hargie (Eds.), *Key Issues in Organisational Communication* (pp. 172–187). London: Routledge.

Dellarocas, C. (2003). The digitization of word of mouth: Promise and challenges of online feedback mechanisms. *Management Science*, *49*(10), 1407–1424. doi:10.1287/mnsc.49.10.1407.17308

Dellarocas, C., Zhang, X., & Awad, N. F. (2008). Exploring the Value of Online Product Reviews in Forecasting Sales: The Case of Motion Pictures. *Journal of Interactive Marketing*, *21*(4), 23–45. doi:10.1002/dir.20087

Demangeot, C., & Broderick, A. J. (2007). Conceptualising consumer behaviour in online shopping environments. *International Journal of Retail & Distribution Management*, *35*(11), 878–894. doi:10.1108/09590550710828218

Denzin, N. K. (1970). *The Research Act: A theoretical Introduction to Sociological Methods*. New York: McGraw-Hill.

Denzin, N. K., & Lincoln, Y. S. (2000). *Handbook of qualitative research* (2nd ed.). Thousand Oaks, CA: Sage Publications Inc.

Denzin, N. K., & Lincoln, Y. S. (2000). *The Handbook of Qualitative Research* (2nd ed.). Thousand Oaks: Sage.

Derbaix, C., & Brée, J. (2000). *Comportement du consommateur, présentation de textes choisis*. Paris: Editions Economica.

Dhar, V., & Chang, E. (2009). Does chatter matter? The impact of user-generated content on music sales. *Journal of Interactive Marketing*, *23*(4), 300–307. doi:10.1016/j.intmar.2009.07.004

Dhir, K. S. (2007). Stakeholder activism through non-violence. *Corporate Communication: An International Journal*, *12*(1), 75–93. doi:10.1108/13563280710723769

Dholakia, R. (1999). Going shopping: Key determinants of shopping behaviors and motivations. *International Journal of Retail & Distribution Management*, *27*(4), 140–165.

Dholakia, R. R., & Dholakia, N. (2004). Mobility and markets: Emerging outlines of m-commerce. *Journal of Business Research*, *57*(12), 1391–1396. doi:10.1016/S0148-2963(02)00427-7

Dholakia, U. M., Bagozzi, R. P., & Pearo, L. K. (2004). A social influence model of consumer participation in network- and small-group-based virtual communities. *International Journal of Research in Marketing*, *21*(3), 241–263. doi:10.1016/j.ijresmar.2003.12.004

Dibb, S., & Carrigan, M. (2013). Social marketing transformed. *European Journal of Marketing*, *47*(9), 1376–1398. doi:10.1108/EJM-05-2013-0248

Dichter, E. (1966). How Word-of-Mouth Advertising Works. *Harvard Business Review*, *44*, 147–157.

Dimarca.com.au. (2012). *Build the Brand Experience Through Touch Points*. Retrieved from http://www.dimarca.com.au/brand-touch-points.aspx

Dittmar, H., & Drury, J. (2000). Self-image - is it in the bag? A qualitative comparison between 'ordinary' and 'excessive' consumers. *Journal of Economic Psychology*, *21*(2), 109–142. doi:10.1016/S0167-4870(99)00039-2

Divol, R., Edelman, D., & Sarrazin, H. (2012). Demystifying social media. *The McKinsey Quarterly*, *2*, 66–77.

Donavan, T. D., Janda, S., & Suh, J. (2006). Environmental influences in corporate brand identification and outcomes. *Journal of Brand Management*, *14*(1–2), 125–136. doi:10.1057/palgrave.bm.2550057

Doney, P. M., & Cannon, J. P. (1997). An examination of the nature of trust in buyer–seller relationships. *Journal of Marketing*, *61*(2), 35–51. doi:10.2307/1251829

Dong, B., Evans, K. R., & Zou, S. (2008). The effects of customer participation in co-created service recovery. *Journal of the Academy of Marketing Science*, *36*(1), 123–137. doi:10.1007/s11747-007-0059-8

Doob, L. W. (1947). The behavior of attitudes. *Psychological Review*, *54*(3), 135–156. doi:10.1037/h0058371 PMID:20240010

Dorie, C. (2012). The End of the Expert: Why no one in marketing knows what they are doing. *Forbes News archive*. Retrieved from http://www.forbes.com

Drucker, P. F. (1993). *Post-capitalist Society*. New York, NY: Harper Collins.

Duan, W., Gu, B., & Whinston, A. B. (2008). The dynamics of online word-of-mouth and product sales: An empirical investigation of the movie industry. *Journal of Retailing*, *84*(2), 233–242. doi:10.1016/j.jretai.2008.04.005

Dubois, B., & Paternault, C. (1995). Observations: Understanding the world of international luxury brands. *Journal of Advertising Research*, *35*(4), 69–76.

Duhan, D. F., Johnson, S. D., Wilcox, J. B., & Harrell, G. D. (1997). Influences on consumer use of Word-of-Mouth recommendation sources. *Journal of the Academy of Marketing Science*, *25*(4), 283–295. doi:10.1177/0092070397254001

Dulyalak, P., & Settapong, M. (2005, August 4-7). A study of behavioral intention for 3G mobile Internet technology: Preliminary research on mobile learning. *Proceedings* of *the second international conference on e-learning for knowledge based society*, Bangkok, Thailand.

Dwyer, F. R., Schurr, P. H., & Oh, S. (1987). Developing buyer–seller relationships. *Journal of Marketing*, *51*(2), 11–27. doi:10.2307/1251126

Eagly, A. H., & Chaiken, S. (1993). *The psychology of attitudes*. Fort Worth, TX: Harcourt Bracce Jovanovich College Publishers.

Eagly, A. H., & Chaiken, S. (1993). *The psychology of Attitudes*. Fort Worth, TX: HarcourtBrace Jovanovich.

Economist Intelligence Unit. (2014). *EIU Survey Report: Customer Service, Marketing and Technology: Mastering the Customer Journey*. Retrieved from http://www.cio.co.uk/cmsdata/whitepapers/3508924/Customer_service_marketing_and_technology_Mastering_the_customer_journey.pdf

Eisend, M. (2006). Source credibility dimensions in marketing communication – A generalized solution. *Journal of Empirical Generalisations in Marketing*. Retrieved from http://www.empgens.com/resources/SourceCredibility.pdf

Ellahi, A., & Bokhari, R. H. (2013). Key quality factors affecting users' perception of social networking websites. *Journal of Retailing and Consumer Services*, *20*(1), 120–129. doi:10.1016/j.jretconser.2012.10.013

Ellison, N., Steinfeld, C., & Lampe, C. (2007). The benefits of Facebook "friends": Social capital and college students' use of online social network sites. *Journal of Computer-Mediated Communication*, *12*(4), 1143–1168. doi:10.1111/j.1083-6101.2007.00367.x

eMarketer.com. (2014). *In Australia, Mobile Propels More Time Spent on Social*. Retrieved from http://www.emarketer.com/Articles/Print.aspx?R=1009951

Engberg-Pedersen, L., Andersen, L., & Stepputat, F. (2008). *Fragile situations. DIIS Report 9*. Danish Institute for International Studies.

Erdem, T., & Swait, J. (1998). Brand equity as a signaling phenomenon. *Journal of Consumer Psychology*, *7*(2), 131–157. doi:10.1207/s15327663jcp0702_02

Erdem, T., Swait, J., & Louviere, J. (2002). The impact of brand credibility on consumer price sensitivity. *International Journal of Research in Marketing*, *19*(1), 1–19. doi:10.1016/S0167-8116(01)00048-9

Erevelles, S., Horton, V., & Fukawa, N. (2008). Understanding B2C brand alliances between manufacturers and suppliers. *Marketing Management Journal*, *18*(2), 32–46.

Eti, C. I. (2009). Objectivity and Balance in Conflict Reporting: Imperatives for the Niger Delta Press. *Journal of African Studies*, *3*, 391–104.

Etling, B., Faris, R., & Palfrey, J. (2010). Political change in the digital age: The fragility and promise of online organizing. *SAIS Review*, *30*(2), 37–49.

Ettenson, R. Eduardo, C. & Knowles, J. (2013). Rethinking the 4Ps. *Harvard Business Review*, 91(1), 26.

Euromonitor International. (2011, March). Global Market Information Database GMID - Country Sector Briefing – credit cards London, UK.

Euromonitor International. (2014). Consumer health trends, developments and prospects. Retrieved from http://www.euromonitor.com/consumer-health-trends-developments-and-prospects/report

Europe's Prestige Beauty Market 2012. *BW Confidential*. (2013). Retrieved from http://www.bwconfidential.com/en/europe-s-prestige-beauty-market-2012,article-1875.html

Evans, D., & McKee, J. (2010). *Social Media Marketing – The Next Generation of Business Engagement*. Indianapolis: Wiley Publishing Inc.

Evuleocha, S. U. (2005). Managing indigenous relations: Corporate social responsibility and corporate communication in a new age of activism. *Corporate Communications: an International Journal*, *10*(4), 328–340. doi:10.1108/13563280510630124

Eweje, G. (2007). Multinational oil companies' CSR initiatives in Nigeria. *Managerial Law*, *49*(5/6), 218–235. doi:10.1108/03090550710841340

Fan, Y., Miao, Y., Fang, Y., & Lin, R. (2013). Establishing the adoption of electronic word-of-mouth through consumers' perceived credibility. *International Business Research, 6*(3). Retrieved from http://ccsenet.org/journal/index.php/ibr/article/view/24217/15334

Faria, F., & Sherriff, A. (2009). *EU Policies to Address Fragility in Sub-Saharan Africa. ECDPM* (pp. 1–19). Italy: European Report on Development.

Fathi, N. (2009, June 23). In a Death Seen Around the World, a Symbol of Iranian Protests. *The New York Times*. Retrieved from http://www.nytimes.com/2009/06/23/world/middleeast/23neda.html

Fetherstonhaugh, B. (2009). *The 4Ps are out, the 4Es are in.* OgilvyOne worldwide- New York, Retrieved from http// www.ogilvyone.com.ph/downloads/The4PsAreOutthe4EsAreIn.pdf

Fieseler, C., & Fleck, M. (2013). The Pursuit of Empowerment through Social Media: Structural Social Capital Dynamics in CSR-Blogging. *Journal of Business Ethics, 118*(4), 759–775. doi:10.1007/s10551-013-1959-9

Filieri, R., & McLeay, F. (2014). E-WOM and accommodation: An analysis of the factors that influence travelers' adoption of information from online reviews. *Journal of Travel Research, 53*(1), 44–57. doi:10.1177/0047287513481274

Finaccord. (2010). *Affinity and Partnership Marketing in UK Payment Cards and Consumer Finance*. London: UK. April 2010

Financial-dictionary.thefreedictionary.com. (2014). *Dialogue Marketing*. Retrieved from http://financial-dictionary.thefreedictionary.com/Dialogue+Marketing

Firat, A. F., & Venkatesh, A. (1995). Liberatory Postmodernism and the Reenchantment of Consumption. *The Journal of Consumer Research, 22*(3), 239–267. doi:10.1086/209448

Fishbein, M. A., & Ajzen, I. (1975). *Belief, attitude, intention and behavior: an introduction to theory and research, Reading*. MA: Addison Wesley.

Flavian, C. & Guinaliu, M. (2006). Consumer trust, perceived security and privacy policy: Three basic elements of loyalty to a web site. *Industrial Management + Data Systems, 106(5)*, 601-620.

Fletcher, K., & Wright, G. (1995). Organisational, Strategic and Technical Barriers to Successful Implementation of Database Marketing. *International Journal of Information Management, 15*(2), 115–126. doi:10.1016/0268-4012(95)00005-R

Flynn, L. R., Goldsmith, R. E., & Eastman, J. K. (1996). Opinion leaders and opinion seekers: Two new measurement scales. *Journal of the Academy of Marketing Science, 24*(2), 137–147. doi:10.1177/0092070396242004

Forbes. (2014). *The top 10 benefits of social media marketing.* Retrieved from http://www.forbes.com/sites/jaysondemers/2014/08/11/the-top-10-benefits-of-social-media-marketing/

Forbes, L. P., Kelley, S. W., & Hoffman, K. D. (2005). Typologies of e-commerce retail failures and recovery strategies. *Journal of Services Marketing, 19*(5), 280–292. doi:10.1108/08876040510609907

Forman, C., Ghose, A., & Wiesenfeld, B. (2008). Examining the Relationship Between Reviews and Sales: The Role of Reviewer Identity Disclosure in Electronic Markets. *Information Systems Research, 19*(3), 291–313. doi:10.1287/isre.1080.0193

Fornell, C. (1992). A National Customer Satisfaction Barometer: The Swedish Experience. *Journal of Marketing, 56*(1), 6–21. doi:10.2307/1252129

Forrester Marketing Forum: Social Technologies Allow For More. (2009a, April 24). *Bloomberg*. Retrieved from http://www.bloomberg.com/apps/news?pid=newsarchive&sid=ax9.YmVPxwMg

Forrester Research. (2009). Forrester marketing forum: Social technologies allow for more accessible innovation in down economy. Retrieved fromhttp://www.forrester.com/ER/Press/Release/0,1769,1274,00.html

Fournier, S. (1998). Consumer and their brands: Developing relationship theory in consumer research. *Journal of Consumer Research, 24*(4), 343–353. doi:10.1086/209515

Franchise.edu.au. (2014). *2014 Franchising Australia Report.* Retrieved from https://www.franchise.edu.au/__data/assets/pdf_file/0009/657063/FranchisingAustralia2014_webversion.pdf?bustCache=93366477&webSyncID=ab0cfc4d-39e7-41ad-b380-0eda5d1b3503&sessionGUID=08846ed5-e354-4c7e-aa14-4a24feb9b611

Franchisemarketingsystems.com. (2014). *Franchise Marketing Systems will sell your franchise for you.* Retrieved from http://www.franchisemarketingsystems.com/services/franchise-sales/

Frazer, L., Weaven, S., & Bodey, K. (2012). *Franchising Australia 2012 Report.* Retrieved from http://www.franchise.org.au/images/FranchisingAustralia2012fullreport.pdf

Freeman, R. E. (1984). *Strategic management: a stakeholder approach.* Boston: Pitman.

Frolick, M. N., & Chen, L. (2004). Assessing M-Commerce Opportunities. *Information Systems Management, 21*(2), 53–61. doi:10.1201/1078/44118.21.2.20040301/80422.8

Frynas, J. G. (2009). *Beyond Corporate Social Responsibility.* Oxford: Oxford University Press. doi:10.1017/CBO9780511581540

Gambetti, R. C., & Graffigna, G. (2010). The concept of Engagement: A Systematic Analysis of the Ongoing Marketing Debate. *International Journal of Market Research, 52*(6), 801–826. doi:10.2501/S147078531020166

Gamble, J., & Gilmore, A. (2013). A new era of consumer marketing? An application of co-creational marketing in the music industry. *European Journal of Marketing, 47*(11/12), 1859–1888. doi:10.1108/EJM-10-2011-0584

Gammoh, B. S., & Voss, K. E. (2013). Alliance competence: The moderating role of valence of alliance experience. *European Journal of Marketing, 47*(5/6), 964–986. doi:10.1108/03090561311307029

Ganesan, S. (1994). Determinants of long–term orientation in buyer–seller relationships. *Journal of Marketing, 58*(2), 1–19. doi:10.2307/1252265

Gangadharbhatla, H. (2008). Facebook me: Collective self esteem, need to belong and Internet self efficacy as predictors of the I-generations attitudes toward social networking sites. *Journal of Interactive Advertising, 8*(2), 5–15. doi:10.1080/15252019.2008.10722138

Garland, E. (2008). The experience economy: The high life of tomorrow. *The Futurist.* Retrieved from http://mestovetra.files.wordpress.com/2008/06/experience-economy.pdf

Gartner. (2013). *Gartner Survey Shows U.S. Digital Marketing Budgets Average 2.5 Percent of Company Revenue,* Stamford, CT, USA. Retrieved from http://www.gartner.com/newsroom/archive/

Gefen, D., & Straub, D. W. (1997). Gender differences in perception and adoption of e-mail: An extension to the Technology Acceptance Model. *Management Information Systems Quarterly, 21*(4), 389–400. doi:10.2307/249720

Gensch, D. H. (1987). A Two-Stage Disaggregate Attribute Choice Model. *Marketing Science, 6*(3), 223–239. doi:10.1287/mksc.6.3.223

George, J. F. (2002). Influence on the intent to make internet purchase. *Internet Research: Electronic networking Applications and Policy,* 12(2), 165-180.

Geron, T. (2013, March 10). Twitter Reveals Long-Awaited IPO Plans With 215 Million Users. *Forbes*. Retrieved from http://www.forbes.com/sites/tomiogeron/2013/10/03/twitter-reveals-long-awaited-ipo-plans-253m-revenue-in-first-half-of-2013/

Ghannam, J. (2011). Social Media in the Arab World: Leading up to the Uprisings of 2011. *Centre for International Media Assistance*, *3*, 1–44.

Ghoshal, S., & Bartlett, C. A. (1995). Changing the role of the top management: Beyond structure to process. *Harvard Business Review*, (January-February): 86–96.

Ghosh, M., & John, G. (2009). When should original equipment manufacturers use branded component contracts with suppliers? *JMR, Journal of Marketing Research*, *46*(5), 597–611. doi:10.1509/jmkr.46.5.597

Giannakis-Bompolis, C., & Boutsouki, C. (2014). Customer relationship management in the era of social web and social customer: An investigation of customer engagement in the Greek retail banking sector. *Procedia: Social and Behavioral Sciences*, *148*, 67–78. doi:10.1016/j.sbspro.2014.07.018

Gigerenzer, G. (2000). *Adaptive Thinking: Rationality in the Real World*. New York, NY: Oxford University Press.

Gigerenzer, G., & Todd, P. M.ABC Research Group. (1999). *Simple Heuristics that Make Us Smart*. New York, NY: Oxford University Press.

Glasman, N. S., & Biniaminov, I. (1981). Input-output Analyses of Schools. *Review of Educational Research*, *51*(4), 509–539. doi:10.3102/00346543051004509

Glasman, N. S., & Fuller, J. (1992). Assessing the Decisionmaking Patterns of School Principals. *International Journal of Educational Management*, *6*(3), 22–30. doi:10.1108/09513549210014178

Godes, D., & Mayzlin, D. (2004). Using online conversations to study word-of-mouth communication. *Marketing Science*, *23*(4), 545–560. doi:10.1287/mksc.1040.0071

Goffman, E. (1959). *The presentation of self in everyday life*. New York: Doubleday Anchor Books.

Goggin, G., & Newell, C. (2003). *The disability: The social construction of disability in new media*. New York: Rowman & Littlefield.

Goldenberg, B. (2015). *The Definitive Guide to Social CRM: maximizing customer relationships with Social Media to gain market insights, customers, and profits*. Harlow: Pearson.

Goldsmiths, R. E., & Bridges, E. (2000). E-tailing vs retailing: Using attitude to predict online buying behaviour. *Quarterly Journal of Electronic Commerce*, *1*(3), 245–253.

Gomm, R. (2004). *Social research methodology: a critical introduction*. Basingtoke: Palgrave Macmillan.

Gong, M. Y., & Yu, Y. (2004). An enhanced technology acceptance model for web-based learning. *Journal of Information Systems Education*, *15*(4), 365–374.

Gonzales, A. (2014). *The Eight Touchpoints of a Customers Consideration Phase*. Retrieved from http://www.marketingprofs.com/opinions/2014/24455/the-eight-touchpoints-of-a-customers-consideration-phase

González-Benito, Ó., Martos-Partal, M., & Fustinoni-Venturini, M. (2014). Retailers' price positioning and the motivational profiling of store-brand shoppers: The case of Spain. *Psychology and Marketing*, *31*(2), 115–125. doi:10.1002/mar.20680

Goodwin, P. (2014). Getting Real about Uncertainty. *Foresight*, *33*(Spring Iss.), 4–7.

Google. (2014). *Google AdSense*. Retrieved from http://bit.ly/n3XpnY

Gorton, R. A. (1987). School Leadership and Administration. Brown, Wm C, Dubugne.

Goyette, I., L.Ricard, J. Bergeron et F. Marticotte (2010), « e-WOM scale: Une échelle de mesure du bouche-à-oreille dans un contexte de services électroniques », *Revue canadienne des sciences de l'administration,* 27: 5–23 (2010).

Grabner-Kraeuter, S., & Moedritscher, G. (2002). Alternative Approaches Toward Measuring CRM Performance. 6 th Research Conference on Relationship Marketing and Customer relationship Management, *Atlanta,* 9-12 Juin, 1-16.

Grabner-Kraeuter, S., & Moedritscher, G. (2002, June 9-12). Alternative Approaches Toward Measuring CRM Performance. *Proceedings of the 6thResearch Conference on Relationship Marketing and Customer relationship Management*, Atlanta.

Graham, B. L. (2002). Why I weblog: A rumination on where the hell I'm going with this website. In J. Rodzvilla (Ed.), *We've got blog: How weblogs are changing our culture*. Retrieved from http://www.bradlands.com/words/maybe02.html

Grayson, D., & Hodges, A. (2004). *Corporate Social Opportunity, 7 Steps to make Corporate Social Responsibility work for your Business*. Sheffield: Greenleaf Publishing.

Gregoire, Y., Salle, A., & Tripp, T. M. (2015). Managing social media crises with your customers: The good, the bad, and the ugly. *Business Horizons*, *58*(2), 173–182. doi:10.1016/j.bushor.2014.11.001

Griffith.edu.au. (2012). *2012 Franchising Australia Report*. Retrieved from https://www.griffith.edu.au/__data/assets/pdf_file/0005/571793/Franchising-Australia-2012-full-report-compressed.pdf

Grônroos, C. (1996). Relationship Marketing: Strategic and Tactical Implications. *Management*, 34/3, 5-14.

Grônroos, C. (1994). From marketing mix to relationship marketing: Towards a paradigm shift in marketing. *Australasian Marketing Journal*, *2*(August), 9–29. doi:10.1016/S1320-1646(94)70275-6

Gross, T. S. (2012). *Social Relationship Management ...Is In Your Future*. Retrieved from http://www.forbes.com/sites/prospernow/2012/02/20/social-relationship-management-is-in-your-future/

Gruber, D. A., Smerek, R. E., Thomas-Hunt, M. C., & James, E. H. (2015). The real-time power of twitter: Crises management and leadership in an age of social media. *Business Horizons*, *58*(2), 163–172. doi:10.1016/j.bushor.2014.10.006

Gruen, T., Osmonbekov, T., & Czaplewski, A. (2007). Customer-to-customer exchange: Its MOA antecedents and its impact on value creation and loyalty. *Journal of the Academy of Marketing Science*, *35*(4), 537–549. doi:10.1007/s11747-006-0012-2

Gu, B., & Ye, Q. (2014). First step in social media: Measuring the influence of online management responses on customer satisfaction. *Production and Operations Management*, *23*(4), 570–582. doi:10.1111/poms.12043

Guest, G., MacQueen, K. M., & Namey, E. E. (2012). *Applied Thematic Analysis*. Los Angeles: Sage publications Inc. doi:10.4135/9781483384436

Gummerus, J., Liljander, V., Weman, E., & Pihlström, M. (2012). Customer engagement in a Facebook brand community. *Management Research Review*, *35*(9), 857–877. doi:10.1108/01409171211256578

Gummesson, E. (1999). *Total Relationship Marketing*. Oxford: Butterworth Heinemann.

Gunelius, S. (2011). *30 minute Social Media Marketing: Step by Step Techniques to Spread the Words about your Business*. USA: McGraw-Hill.

Gustafsson, A., Johnson, M. D., & Roos, I. (2005). The Effects of Customer Satisfaction, Relationship Commitment Dimensions, and Triggers on Customer Retention. *Journal of Marketing*, *69*(10), 210–218. doi:10.1509/jmkg.2005.69.4.210

Habibi, M. R., Laroche, M., & Richard, M. (2014). Brand communities based in social media: How unique are they? Evidence from two exemplary brand communities. *International Journal of Information Management*, *34*(2), 123–132. doi:10.1016/j.ijinfomgt.2013.11.010

Hagel, J., & Armstrong, A. G. (1997). *Net gain: Expanding markets through virtual communities*. Boston, MA: Harvard Business School.

Hagel, J., & Armstrong, A. G. (1997). *Net gain: Expanding markets through virtual Communities*. Boston: Harvard Business School Press.

Hamedi, J. (2014, April 25). How social media will transform brand management. *Direct Marketing News*. Retrieved from http://www.dmnews.com/how-social-media-will-transform-brand-management/article/343917/

Hamon, C., Lézin, P., & Toullec, A. (2004). *Gestion des Clientèles*. Edition DUNOD.

Hamzah, Z. L., Syed Alwi, S. F., & Othman, M. N. (2014). Designing corporate brand experience in an online context: A qualitative insight. *Journal of Business Research*, *67*(11), 2299–2310. doi:10.1016/j.jbusres.2014.06.018

Hanna, R., Rohm, A., & Crittenden, V. L. (2011). We're all connected: The power of the social media ecosystem. *Business Horizons*, *54*(3), 265–273. doi:10.1016/j.bushor.2011.01.007

Han, Y. J., Nunes, J. C., & Dreze, X. (2010). Signaling status with luxury goods: The role of brand prominence. *Journal of Marketing*, *74*(4), 15–30. doi:10.1509/jmkg.74.4.15

Harrigan & Choudhury. M. M. (2012). *Social Media Technologies for CRM* (Working Paper). University of Southampton.

Hartas, D. (2010). *Educational Research and Inquiry: Qualitative and Quantitative Approach*. London: Continuum International Publishing Group.

Hart, C. W., & Johnson, M. D. (1999). Growing the trust relationship. *Marketing Management*, *8*(1), 8–19.

Hartman, L. P., & Desjardins, J. (2008). *Business ethics: Decision making for personal integrity and social responsibility*. New York: McGraw-Hill.

Hatch, M. J., & Schultz, M. (2009). Of bricks and brands: From corporate to enterprise branding. *Organizational Dynamics*, *38*(2), 117–130. doi:10.1016/j.orgdyn.2009.02.008

Hautz, J., Füller, J., Hutter, K., & Thürridl, C. (2013). Let users generate your video ads? The impact of video source and quality on consumers' perceptions and intended behaviors. *Journal of Interactive Marketing*, *28*(1), 1–15. doi:10.1016/j.intmar.2013.06.003

Hawkins, K., & Vel, P. (2013). Attitudinal loyalty, behavioural loyalty and social media: An Introspection. *Marketing Review*, *13*(2), 125–141. doi:10.1362/146934713X13699019904605

Heck, M. (2009). Telepresence shatters communication barriers. *Infoworld*. Retrieved from http://www.infoworld.com/d/hardware/telepresence-shatters-communication-barriers-657

Heck, R. S., & Marcoulides, G. A. (1991). The Effects of Organisational Size on Principal Decision Making. *International Journal of Educational Management*, *5*(1), 4–12. doi:10.1108/EUM0000000001966

Heck, R., Larsen, T., & Marcoulides, G. (1990). Instructional Leadership and School Achievement: Validation of a Causal Model. *Educational Administration Quarterly*, *26*(2), 94–125. doi:10.1177/0013161X90026002002

Heck, R., Marcoulides, G., & Glasman, N. (1989). The Application of Causal Modeling Techniques to Administrative Decision-making: The Case of Teacher Allocation. *Educational Administration Quarterly*, *25*(3), 253–267. doi:10.1177/0013161X89025003003

Heide, J. B., & John, G. (1990). Alliances in industrial purchasing: The determinants of joint action in buyer–supplier relationships. *JMR, Journal of Marketing Research*, *27*(1), 24–36. doi:10.2307/3172548

Helm, C., & Jones, R. (2010). Brand governance: The new agenda in brand management. *Journal of Brand Management*, *17*(8), 545–547. doi:10.1057/bm.2010.20

Hennig-Thurau, T., Gwinner, K., Walsh, G., & Gremler, D. (2004). Electronic word-of-mouth via consumer-opinion platforms: What motivates consumers to articulate themselves on the Internet? *Journal of Interactive Marketing*, *18*(1), 38–52. doi:10.1002/dir.10073

Hennig-Thurau, T., Malthouse, E. C., Friege, C., Gensler, S., Lobschat, L., Rangaswamy, A., & Skiera, B. (2010). The Impact of New Media on Customer Relationships. *Journal of Service Research*, *13*(3), 311–330. doi:10.1177/1094670510375460

Hess, R. L. Jr, Ganesan, S., & Klein, N. M. (2003). Service failure and recovery: The impact of relationship factors on customer satisfaction. *Journal of the Academy of Marketing Science*, *31*(2), 127–145. doi:10.1177/0092070302250898

He, W., Zha, S., & Li, L. (2013). Social media competitive analysis and text mining: A case study in the pizza industry. *International Journal of Information Management*, *33*(3), 464–472. doi:10.1016/j.ijinfomgt.2013.01.001

Highlights and Insights February 2013. (2013, February). The CMO Survey. Retrieved from http://cmosurvey.org/files/2013/02/The_CMO_Survey_Highlights_and_Insights_Feb-2013-Final2.pdf

Hill, W. W., Beatty, S. E., & Walsh, G. (2013). A segmentation of adolescent users and shoppers. *Journal of Services Marketing*, *27*(5), 347–360. doi:10.1108/JSM-10-2011-0157

Hilse, M., & Hoewner, J. (1998). The communication crisis in the internet and what one can do against it. In M. Crimp (Ed.), *Interactive enterprise communication* (pp. 137–154). Frankfurt: IMK.

Hobson, N. (2012). Quick Recap. In C. Holloman (Ed.), *The social media MBA: Your competitive edge in social media strategy development & delivery* (pp. 3–13). Chichester, UK: John Wiley & Sons Ltd.

Hoffman, D. L., & Novak, T. P. (2012, January 17). Why Do People Use Social Media? Empirical Findings and a New Theoretical Framework for Social Media Goal Pursuit. *Social Science Research Network*. Retrieved from http://ssrn.com/abstract=1989586

Hoffman, D. L., & Fodor, M. (2010). Can you measure the ROI of your social media marketing? *MIT Sloan Management Review*, *52*(1), 41–50.

Hoffman, D. L., Kopalle, P. K., & Novak, T. P. (2010). A New Marketing Paradigm for Electronic Commerce. *JMR, Journal of Marketing Research*, *XLVII*, 854–865. doi:10.1509/jmkr.47.5.854

Hoffman, D. L., & Novak, T. P. (1996). Marketing in hypermedia computer-mediated environments: Conceptual foundations. *Journal of Marketing*, *60*(3), 50–68. doi:10.2307/1251841

Hof, R. (2012, September 2). Google+'s Success and Failure, in Two Images. *Forbes*. http://www.forbes.com/sites/roberthof/2012/02/09/googles-success-and-failure-in-two-images/

Hogan, R., Curphy, G. J., & Hogan, J. (1994). What we know about leadership. *The American Journal of Psychology*, *49*(6), 493–504. doi:10.1037/0003-066X.49.6.493 PMID:8042818

Holloman, C. (2013). *The Social Media MBA in practice*. Chichester: Wiley.

Holloway, B. B., & Beatty, S. E. (2003). Service failure in online retailing: A recovery opportunity. *Journal of Service Research*, *6*(1), 92–105. doi:10.1177/1094670503254288

Holmes, A., Byrne, A., & Rowley, J. (2014). Mobile shopping behaviour: Insights into attitudes, shopping process involvement and location. *International Journal of Retail & Distribution Management*, *42*(1), 25–39. doi:10.1108/IJRDM-10-2012-0096

Honoré E. (2011). *The role of Information Communication Technology in Philanthropy*, Centre of charitable giving and philanthropy NCVO/CAF.

Horne, S., Naudé, P., & Worthington, S. (2000). Knowledge Gaps between Participants in a Triadic Relationship. *International Journal of Bank Marketing*, *18*(6), 287–293. doi:10.1108/02652320010358706

Howard, B. (2012, January 28). Cancer charity loses out as bank ends credit card deal. BBC News – Business. London, UK.

Howard, P. N., & Hussain, M. M. (2013). *Democracy's fourth wave? Digital media and the Arab spring*. Oxford: Oxford University Press. doi:10.1093/acprof:oso/9780199936953.001.0001

Hoy, W. K., & Tarter, C. J. (2010). Swift and smart decision making: Heuristics that work. *International Journal of Educational Management*, *24*(4), 351–358. doi:10.1108/09513541011045272

Hsu, C. L., Lin, J. C. C., & Chiang, S. H. (2013). The effects of blogger recommendations on customers' online shopping intentions. *Internet Research*, *33*(1), 69–88. doi:10.1108/10662241311295782

Huang, E. (2005). The acceptance of women-centric web sites. *Journal of Computer Information Systems*, *45*(4), 75–83.

Huang, H. H., & Mitchell, V. W. (2014). The role of imagination and brand personification in brand relationships. *Psychology and Marketing*, *31*(1), 38–47. doi:10.1002/mar.20673

Huang, H. H., Mitchell, V. W., & Rosenaum-Elliott, R. (2012). Are consumer and brand personalities the same? *Psychology and Marketing*, *29*(5), 334–349. doi:10.1002/mar.20525

Huang, L. (2010). Cross-cultural communication in business negotiations. *International Journal of Economics and Finance*, *2*(2), 196–199. doi:10.5539/ijef.v2n2p196

Huang, Y., Singh, P. V., & Ghose, A. (2010, December 12-15). Show Me the Incentives: A Dynamic Structural Model of Employee Blogging Behavior.*Proceedings of the 31st International Conference of Information Systems*, Saint Louis, MO, USA.

Hui, M. K., Ho, C. K. Y., & Wan, L. C. (2011). Prior relationships and consumer responses to service failures: A cross-cultural study. *Journal of International Marketing*, *19*(1), 59–81. doi:10.1509/jimk.19.1.59

Hung, M. C., Yang, S. T., & Hsieh, T. C. (2012). An examination of the determinants of mobile shopping continuance. *International Journal of Electronic Business Management*, *10*(1), 29–37.

Hunt, T. (2009). *The whuffie factor: Using the power of social networks to build your business*. Crown Pub.

Hunt, T. (2010a). *The power of social networking: Using the whuffie factor to build your business*. Crown Business.

Hunt, T. (2010b). *The Power of Social Networking: Using the Whuffie Factor to Build Your Business* (1st ed.). New York: Crown Business.

Husted, S. W., & Whitehouse, F. R. Jr. (2002). Cause-Related Marketing via the World Wide Web: A Relationship Marketing Strategy. *Journal of Nonprofit & Public Sector Marketing*, *10*(1), 3–22. doi:10.1300/J054v10n01_02

Hu, W.-C., Yeh, J.-H., Fu, L., & Yang, H.-J. (2006). Handheld Computing and Programming for Mobile Commerce. *International Journal of Web Information Systems*, *2*(3/4), 164–175. doi:10.1108/17440080780000297

Iab.net. (2014). *Digital Content Newfronts: Video Ads Spend Study April 2014*. Retrieved from http://www.iab.net/media/file/2014_IAB_Digital_NewFronts.pdf

IBM Social Computing Guidelines [CT402]. (2011, August 3). *IBM*. Retrieved from http://www.ibm.com/blogs/zz/en/guidelines.html

Idemudia, U. (2010). Corporate social responsibility and the rentier Nigerian state: Rethinking the role of government and the possibility of corporate social development in the Niger Delta. *Canadian Journal of Development Studies*, *30*(1), 131–153.

Igbaria, M., Parasuraman, S., & Baroudi, J. J. (1996). A motivational model of microcomputer usage. *Journal of Management Information Systems*, *13*(Summer), 127–143. doi:10.1080/07421222.1996.11518115

Iglesias, O., Singh, J., & Batista-Foguet, J. (2011). The role of brand experience and affective commitment in determining brand loyalty. *Journal of Brand Management*, *18*(8), 570–582. doi:10.1057/bm.2010.58

In-store Mobile Offers Still Finding Their Feet in the UK. (2013). *Emarketer.com*. Retrieved from http://www.emarketer.com/Article/Retail-Drives-UK-B2C-Ecommerce-Sales-Higher/1010106

International Advertising Bureau IBA. (2014). Advertising Revenue Report HY 2014 DOC.

Internet Society. (2015). Global Internet user survey 2012. Retrieved from https://www.internetsociety.org/internet/global-internet-user-survey-2012

Internet usage statistics: The Internet big picture. (2009). *Internet World Stats*. Retrieved from http://www.internetworldstats.com/stats.htm

Internet Users Now Spending an Average of 13 Hours a Week Online. (2009b, December 23). *Bloomberg*. Retrieved from http://www.bloomberg.com/apps/news?pid=newsarchive&sid=aQrAoB85tDvs

Internet Users Spend an Average of 13 Hours a Week Online, Survey Finds. (2009). eWeek. Retrieved from http://www.eweek.com/c/a/Midmarket/Internet-Users-Spend-an-Average-of-13-Hours-a-Week-Online-Survey-Finds-485147

Inwise.com. (2011). *What is Digital Marketing?* Retrieved from http://www.inwise.com/about/what's-digital-marketing.aspx

iProspect (2009). *Search Engine marketing and online display advertising integration study*. Retrieved from http://bit.ly/1qhYjee

Isaksen, K. J., & Roper, S. (2012). The commodification of self-esteem: Branding and British teenagers. *Psychology and Marketing*, *29*(3), 117–135. doi:10.1002/mar.20509

Ite, U. (2004). Multinationals and corporate social responsibility in developing countries: A case study of Shell in Nigeria. *Corporate Social Responsibility and Environmental Management*, *11*(1), 1–11. doi:10.1002/csr.49

Jackson, C. M., Chow, S., & Leitch, R. A. (1997). Toward an understanding of the behavioral intention to use an information System. *Decision Sciences*, *28*(2), 357–389. doi:10.1111/j.1540-5915.1997.tb01315.x

Jang, H. J., Sim, J., Lee, Y., & Kwon, O. (2013). Deep sentiment analysis: Mining the causality between personality-value-attitude for analyzing business ads in social media. *Expert Systems with Applications*, *40*(18), 7492–7503. doi:10.1016/j.eswa.2013.06.069

Janouri, F., & Gharbi, J.E. (2008). Affrontement entre le risque perçu et le capital marque dans la formation de la confiance dans un site marchand.

Jansen, B. J., Zhang, M., Sobel, K., & Chowdury, A. (2009). Twitter power: Tweets as electronic word of mouth. *Journal of the American Society for Information Science and Technology*, *60*(11), 2169–2188. doi:10.1002/asi.21149

Jarboe, G. (2007). *SE watch*. Retrieved from http://bit.ly/1HNQ6Hx

Jarvenpaa, S., & Tuunainen, V. K. (2013). How Finnair Socialized Customers for Service Co-Creation with SocialMedia. *MIS Quarterley Executive*, *12*(3), 125–136.

Jespersen, K. R. (2010). User-involvement and open innovation: The case of decision-maker openness. *International Journal of Innovation Management*, *14*(3), 471–489. doi:10.1142/S136391961000274X

Jevons, C., & Gabbott, M. (2000). Trust, Brand Equity and Brand Reality in Internet Business Relationships: An Interdisciplinary Approach. *Journal of Marketing Management*, *16*(6), 619–634. doi:10.1362/026725700785045967

Johnson, B. (2014). *Revenue, Staffing, Stocks and Digital Show Growth for Agencies in 2014 Report*. Retrieved from http://adage.com/article/agency-news/2014-agency-report-revenue-staffing-stocks-digital/292849/

Jolley, B., Mizerski, R., & Doina, O. (2006). How Habit and Satisfaction Affects Player Retention for Online Gambling. *Journal of Business Research*, *59*(12), 770–777. doi:10.1016/j.jbusres.2006.01.017

Jones, R. (2009). *Social Media Marketing 101, Part 1*. Retrieved from http://sbinfocanada.about.com/gi/o.htm?zi=1/XJ&zTi=1&sdn=sbinfocanada&cdn=money&tm=1059&gps=451_10_1887_1024&f=00&tt=8&bt=6&bts=6&zu=http%3A//searchenginewatch.com/3632809

Jordan, W.G., & Krumwiede, K.R. (1999). ERP? Implementation, Beware. *Cost Management Update, (March),* 1-4.

Jöreskog, K. G., Sörbom, D., Du-Toit, S., & Du-Toit, M. (1999). *LISREL 8: NEW Statistical Feature*. Chicago, IL: Scientific Software International Inc.

Kahneman, D. K., Solvic, P., & Tversky, A. (1982). *Judgment under Uncertainty, Heuristics and Biases*. Cambridge: Cambridge University Press. doi:10.1017/CBO9780511809477

Kahneman, D. K., & Tversky, A. (1973). On the psychology of prediction. *Psychological Review*, *80*(4), 251–273. doi:10.1037/h0034747

Kahneman, D., & Klein, G. (2010). Conditions for intuitive expertise: A failure to disagree. *The American Journal of Psychology*, *64*(6), 515–526. doi:10.1037/a0016755 PMID:19739881

Kahn, R., & Kellner, D. (2004). New media and internet activism: From the 'battle of Seattle' to blogging. *New Media & Society*, *6*(1), 87–95. doi:10.1177/1461444804039908

Kalafatis, S. P., Riley, D., & Singh, J. (2014). Context effects in the evaluation of business-to-business brand alliances. *Industrial Marketing Management*, *43*(2), 322–334. doi:10.1016/j.indmarman.2013.09.002

Kandampully, J. (2003). B2B relationships and networks in the Internet age. *Management Decision*, *41*(5), 443–451. doi:10.1108/00251740310479296

Kane, G, & Alavi, M, Labianca &Borgatti. (2014). What's different about Social Media Networks? A Framework and Research Agenda. *Management Information Systems Quarterly*, *38*(1), 275–304.

Kano, N. (1995). Upsizing the organization by attractive quality creation. In G.K. Kanji (Ed.), Total Quality Management: Proceedings of the First World Congress. London: Chapman & Hall. doi:10.1007/978-94-011-0539-2_6

Kapferer, J. N. (2012). *The new strategic brand management: Advanced insights and strategic thinking*. London, UK: Kogan Page.

Kaplan, A. M., & Haenlein, M. (2010). Users of the world, unite! The challenges and opportunities of Social Media. *Business Horizons*, *53*(1), 59–68. doi:10.1016/j.bushor.2009.09.003

Kaplan, S. (2008). *Fixing Fragile States – A New Paradigm for Development*. Westport, CT: Praeger Security International.

Kardes, F. R., Cronley, M. L., Kellaris, J. J., & Posavac, S. S. (2004). The role of selective information processing in price-quality inference. *The Journal of Consumer Research*, *31*(2), 368–374. doi:10.1086/422115

Karl, T. L. (1997). *The paradox of plenty: oil booms and petro-states*. California: University of California Press.

Kasemsap, K. (2014a). The role of social media in the knowledge-based organizations. In I. Lee (Ed.), *Integrating social media into business practice, applications, management, and models* (pp. 254–275). Hershey, PA: IGI Global. doi:10.4018/978-1-4666-6182-0.ch013

Kasemsap, K. (2014b). The role of social networking in global business environments. In P. Smith & T. Cockburn (Eds.), *Impact of emerging digital technologies on leadership in global business* (pp. 183–201). Hershey, PA: IGI Global. doi:10.4018/978-1-4666-6134-9.ch010

Kasemsap, K. (2015a). The role of brand management in emerging markets. In *Marketing and consumer behavior: Concepts, methodologies, tools, and applications* (pp. 2006–2023). Hershey, PA: IGI Global. doi:10.4018/978-1-4666-7357-1.ch099

Kasemsap, K. (2015b). The role of brand loyalty on CRM performance: An innovative framework for smart manufacturing. In *Marketing and consumer behavior: Concepts, methodologies, tools, and applications* (pp. 413–446). Hershey, PA: IGI Global. doi:10.4018/978-1-4666-7357-1.ch019

Kashi, E. (2008). *Curse of the black gold. 50 years of oil in the Niger delta*. New York: Powerhouse Publishers.

Katsioloudes, M., Grant, J., & McKechnie, D. S. (2007). Social marketing: Strengthening company-customer bonds. *The Journal of Business Strategy*, *28*(3), 56–64. doi:10.1108/02756660710746283

Katz, E., & Lazarsfeld, P. F. (1955). *Personal Influence, 2*. New York: The Free Press.

Kaufmann, H. R., Vrontis, D., Czinkota, M., & Alvin Hadiono, A. (2012). Corporate branding and transformational leadership in turbulent times. *Journal of Product and Brand Management*, *21*(3), 192–204. doi:10.1108/10610421211228810

Keaveney, S. M. (1995). Customer switching behavior in service industries: An exploratory study. *Journal of Marketing*, *59*(2), 71–82. doi:10.2307/1252074

Keller, E. (2007). Unleashing the power of word of mouth: Creating brand advocacy to drive growth. *Journal of Advertising Research*, *47*(4), 448–452. doi:10.2501/S0021849907070468

Keller, K. L. (1993). Conceptualizing, evaluating, and managing customer–based brand equity. *Journal of Marketing*, *57*(1), 1–22. doi:10.2307/1252054

Keller, K. L. (2008). *Strategic brand management: Building, measuring and managing brand equity*. Upper Saddle River, NJ: Prentice Hall.

Keller, K. L., & Lehmann, D. R. (2003). How do brands create value? *Marketing Management*, *12*(3), 27–31.

Kelle, U. (2006). Combining qualitative and quantitative methods in research practice: Purpose and advantages. *Qualitative Research in Psychology*, *3*(4), 203–311.

Kelly, E. P., & Erickson, G. S. (2004). Legal and privacy issues surrounding customer databases and e-merchant bankruptcies: Reflections on Toysmart.com. *Industrial Management & Data Systems*, *104*(3), 209–217. doi:10.1108/02635570410525762

Khalifa, M., & Shen, K. N. (2008). Explaining the adoption of transactional B2C mobile commerce. *Journal of Enterprise Information Management*, *21*(2), 110–124.

Khalil, M.N., & Pearson, J.M. (2007). The Influence of Trust on Internet Banking Acceptance. *Journal of internet banking and commerce*,12(2).

Khammash, M., & Griffiths, G. H. (2011). Arrivederci CIAO.com, Buongiorno Bing. Com - electronic word-of-mouth (eWOM), antecedences and consequences. *International Journal of Information Management*, *31*(1), 82–87. doi:10.1016/j.ijinfomgt.2010.10.005

Khang, H., Ki, E., & Ye, L. (2012). Social Media Research in Advertising, Communication, Marketing, and Public Relations. *Journalism & Mass Communication Quarterly*, *89*(2), 279–298. doi:10.1177/1077699012439853

Kietzmann, J. H., Hermkens, K., McCarthy, I. P., & Silvestre, B. S. (2011). Social Media? Get serious! Understanding the functional building blocks of social media. *Business Horizons*, *54*(3), 241–251. doi:10.1016/j.bushor.2011.01.005

Kim, A. J., & Ko, E. (2010). Impacts of Luxury Fashion Brand's Social Media Marketing on Customer Relationship and Purchase Intention. *Journal of Global Fashion Marketing*, *1*(3), 164–171. doi:10.1080/20932685.2010.10593068

Kim, A. J., & Ko, E. (2012). Do Social Media marketing activities enhance customer equity? An empirical study of luxury fashion brand. *Journal of Business Research*, *65*(10), 1480–1486. doi:10.1016/j.jbusres.2011.10.014

Kim, B. Y. (2008). Mediated Effects of Customer Orientation on Customer Relationship Management Performance. *International Journal of Hospitality & Tourism Administration*, *9*(2), 192–218. doi:10.1080/15256480801909089

Kim, E., Sung, Y., & Kang, H. (2014). Brand followers' retweeting behavior on Twitter: How brand relationships influence brand electronic word-of-mouth. *Computers in Human Behavior*, *37*, 18–25. doi:10.1016/j.chb.2014.04.020

Kim, H., Kim, J. L. Y., Chae, M., & Choi, Y. (2002). *An empirical study of the use context and usability problems in mobile internet*. Hawaii: IEEE Computer Society.

Kim, H.-W., Xu, Y., & Gupta, S. (2012). Which is more important in Internet Shopping, perceived price or trust? *Electronic Commerce Research and Applications*, *11*(3), 241–252. doi:10.1016/j.elerap.2011.06.003

Kinard, B. R., & Capella, M. L. (2006). Relationship marketing: The influence of consumer involvement on perceived benefits. *Journal of Services Marketing*, *20*(6), 359–368. doi:10.1108/08876040610691257

King, R., Racherla, P., & Bush, V. (2014). What we know and don't know about online word-of-mouth: A review and synthesis of the literature. *Journal of Interactive Marketing*, *28*(3), 167–183. doi:10.1016/j.intmar.2014.02.001

King, S. F., & Burgess, T. F. (2008). Understanding success and failure in customer relationship management. *Industrial Marketing Management*, *37*(4), 421–431. doi:10.1016/j.indmarman.2007.02.005

Kinnear, T. C., & Taylor, J. R. (1988). *Marketing Research: An Applied Approach* (3rd ed.). Singapore: McGraw Hill.

Kirkpatrick, D. (2010). *The Facebook effect: The inside story of the company that is connecting the world.* New York: Simon & Schuster.

Kirmani, A., & Wright, P. (1989). Money talks: Perceived advertising expense and expected product quality. *Journal of Consumer Research*, *16*(3), 344–353. doi:10.1086/209220

Klaus, P., Gorgoglione, M., Buonamassa, D., Panniello, U., & Nguyen, B. (2013). Are you providing the "right" experiences? The case of Banca Popolare di Bari. *International Journal of Bank Marketing*, *31*(7), 506–528. doi:10.1108/IJBM-02-2013-0019

Klaus, Ph. (2013). The Case of Amazon.com: Towards a conceptual framework of online customer service experience (OCSE) using emerging consensus technique (ECT). *Journal of Services Marketing*, *27*(6), 443–457. doi:10.1108/JSM-02-2012-0030

Klaus, Ph., & Maklan, S. (2013). Towards a better measure of customer experience. *International Journal of Market Research*, *55*(2), 227–246. doi:10.2501/IJMR-2013-021

Knox, S. (2004). Positioning and branding your organization. *Journal of Product and Brand Management*, *13*(2), 105–115. doi:10.1108/10610420410529735

Kogut, B. (1985). Designing global strategies: Comparative and competitive value added chains. *Sloan Management Review*, *26*(4).

Ko, H.-C., Yin, C.-P., & Kuo, F.-Y. (2008). Exploring individual communication power in the bogosphere. *Internet Research*, *18*(5), 541–561. doi:10.1108/10662240810912774

Komito, L., & Bates, J. (2009). Virtual local: Social media and community among Polish nationals in Dublin. *Aslib Proceedings: New Information Perspectives*, *61*(3), 232–244. doi:10.1108/00012530910959790

Koreatimes.co.kr. (2013). *Dialogue Marketing: Having a Two-way Conversation*. Retrieved from http://www.koreatimes.co.kr/www/news/biz/2014/03/331_131812.html

Kotler, P., Brown, L., Adam, S., Burton, S., & Armstrong, G. (2007). *Marketing* (7th ed.). Sydney, Australia: Pearson Education.

Kourouthanassis, P. E., & Giaglis, G. M. (2012). Introduction to the Special Issue Mobile Commerce: The Past, Present and Future of Mobile Commerce Research. *International Journal of Electronic Commerce*, *16*(4), 5–17. doi:10.2753/JEC1086-4415160401

Kozinets, R. V. (1999). E-tribalized marketing?: The strategic implications of virtual communities of consumption. *European Management Journal*, *17*(3), 252–264. doi:10.1016/S0263-2373(99)00004-3

Kozinets, R. V. (2002). The field behind the screen: Using netnography for marketing research in online communities. *JMR, Journal of Marketing Research*, *39*(1), 61–72. doi:10.1509/jmkr.39.1.61.18935

Kozinets, R. V., de Valck, K., Wojnicki, A. C., & Wilner, S. J. S. (2010). Networked narratives: Understanding word-of-mouth marketing in online communities. *Journal of Marketing*, *74*(2), 71–89. doi:10.1509/jmkg.74.2.71

Kperogi, F. A. (2011). Webs of resistance: The citizen online journalism of the Nigerian digital Diaspora [Doctoral Dissertation]. Georgia State University, Georgia, USA.

Kraak, V. I., & Story, M. (2015). Influence of food companies' brand mascots and entertainment companies' cartoon media characters on children's diet and health: A systematic review and research needs. *Obesity Reviews*, *16*(2), 107–126. doi:10.1111/obr.12237 PMID:25516352

Krishna, A., Dangayach, G., & Jain, R. (2011). A Conceptual Framework for the Service Recovery Paradox. *The Marketing Review*, *11*(1), 41–56. doi:10.1362/146934711X565288

Kumar, A., & Mukherjee, A. (2013). Shop while you talk: Determinants of purchase intentions through a mobile device. Mobile Marketing Association, 8(1), 23-37.

Kumar, R. (1996). *Research Methodology: A Step-by-Step Guide for Beginners*. Melbourne, Australia: Addison Wesley Longman.

Kumar, S., & Zhan, C. (2003). Mobile communications: Evolution and the impact on business operations. *Technovation*, *23*(6), 515–520. doi:10.1016/S0166-4972(02)00120-7

Kumar, V., Aksoy, L., Donkers, B., Venkatesan, R., Wiesel, T., & Tillmanns, S. (2010). Undervalued or Overvalued Customers: Capturing Total Customer Engagement Value. *Journal of Service Research*, *13*(3), 297–310. doi:10.1177/1094670510375602

Kuo, Y., Yen, S., & Chen, L. (2011). Online auction service failures in Taiwan: Typologies and recovery strategies. *Electronic Commerce Research and Applications*, *10*(2), 183–193. doi:10.1016/j.elerap.2009.09.003

Kwon, E. S., & Sung, Y. (2011). Follow me! Global marketers' Twitter use. *Journal of Interactive Advertising*, *12*(1), 4–16. doi:10.1080/15252019.2011.10722187

Labott, E. (2009, June 16). State Department to Twitter: Keep Iranian tweets coming. Retrieved from http://ac360.blogs.cnn.com/2009/06/16/state-department-to-twitter-keep-iranian-tweets-coming/

Labrecque, L. I., vor dem Esche, J., Mathwick, C., Novak, T. P., & Hofacker, C. F. (2013). Consumer power: Evolution in the digital age. *Journal of Interactive Marketing*, *27*(4), 257–269. doi:10.1016/j.intmar.2013.09.002

Lagrosen, S. O., & Grunden, K. (2014). Social media marketing in the wellness industry. *The TQM Journal*, *26*(3), 253–260. doi:10.1108/TQM-12-2013-0129

Laing, A., Harris, F., & Mekonnen, A. (2004). Deconstructing affinity relationships: Consumers and affinity marketing. *Journal of Customer Behaviour*, *3*(2), 215–228. doi:10.1362/1475392041829500

Lamarre, A., Galarneau, S., & Boeck, H. (2012). Mobile Marketing and consumer Behaviour Current Research Trend. *International Journal of Latest Trends in Computing*, *3*(1), 1–9.

Lam, D., & Mizerski, D. (2005). The effects of locus of control on word-of-mouth communication. *Journal of Marketing Communications*, *11*(3), 215–228. doi:10.1080/1352726042000333180

LaPointe, P. (2012). Mind Over Metrics Measuring Facebook's Impact on Marketing The proverbial Hits the Fan. *Journal of Advertising Research*, *52*(3), 286–287. doi:10.2501/JAR-52-3-286-287

Laran, J., & Tsiros, M. (2013). An Investigation of the Effectiveness of Uncertainty in Marketing Promotions Involving Free Gifts. *Journal of Marketing*, *77*(2), 112–123. doi:10.1509/jm.11.0255

Larivet, S., & Brouard, F. (2010). Complaints are a firm's best friend. *Journal of Strategic Marketing*, *18*(7), 537–551. doi:10.1080/0965254X.2010.529155

Larivière, B., & Van-den Poel, D. (2005). Predicting Customer Retention and Profitability by Using Random Forests and Regression Forests Techniques. *Expert Systems with Applications*, *29*(2), 472–484. doi:10.1016/j.eswa.2005.04.043

Laroche, M., Habibi, M. R., & Richard, M. O. (2013). To be or not to be in social media: How brand loyalty is affected by social media? *International Journal of Information Management*, *33*(1), 76–82. doi:10.1016/j.ijinfomgt.2012.07.003

Laroche, M., Habibi, M. R., Richard, M. O., & Sankaranarayanan, R. (2012). The effects of social media based brand communities on brand community markers, value creation practices, brand trust and brand loyalty. *Computers in Human Behavior*, *28*(5), 1755–1767. doi:10.1016/j.chb.2012.04.016

Lars, M. W. (2007). The Effects of Loyalty Programs on Customer Lifetime Duration and Share of Wallet. *Journal of Retailing*, *83*(2), 223–236. doi:10.1016/j.jretai.2007.01.002

Laudon, K., & Travis, C. (2013). *E-Commerce 2013: Global Edition* (9th ed.). Harlow, UK: Pearson Education.

Lauterborn, B. (1990). New Marketing Litany: Four P's Passe: C-Words Take Over. *Advertising Age*, *61*(41), 26.

Lauterborn, R. (1990). New Marketing Litany: 4Ps Passé; C-Words Take Over. *Advertising Age*, *61*(41), 26–28.

Lavenka, N. M. (1991). Measurement of consumers' perceptions of product quality, brand name, and packaging: Candy bar comparisons by magnitude estimation. *Marketing Research*, *3*(2), 38–46.

Lavidge, R. J., & Steiner, G. A. (1961). A Model for Predictive Measurements of Advertising Effectiveness. *Journal of Marketing*, *25*(6), 59–62. doi:10.2307/1248516

Lawer, E. (1999). Employee involvement makes a difference. *Journal for Quality and Participation*, *22*(5), 18–20.

Le Roux, J.-B. (2013). Le nombre de smartphones dans le monde pourrait atteindre 3,3 milliards d'ici 2018. *Economiematin.fr*. Retrieved from http://www.economiematin.fr/ecoquick/item/3977-smartphones-utilisation-monde-reseau-operateurs-mobiles

Lee Yahn, D. (2013). *Brand Touchpoint Wheel – Worksheet*. Retrieved from http://deniseleeyohn.com/wp-content/uploads/2013/12/WGBD-Download-Brand-Touchpoint-Wheel-Worksheet.pdf

Lee, D. (2010). *Korean Consumer Society Growing Popularity of Social Media and Business Strategy Samsung Economic Research Institute (SERI)* (pp. 112–117).

Leeflang, P. S. H., Verhoef, P. C., Dahlstrom, P., & Freundt, T. (2014). Challenges and solutions for marketing in a digital era. *European Management Journal*, *32*(1), 1–12. doi:10.1016/j.emj.2013.12.001

Lee, H., & Griffith, D. (2012). Transferring corporate brand image to local markets: Governance decisions for market entry and global branding. *Advances in International Marketing*, *23*(1), 39–65. doi:10.1108/S1474-7979(2012)0000023006

Lee, S. M., Olson, D. L., & Trimi, S. (2012). Co-innovation: Convergenomics, collaboration, and co-creation for organizational values. *Management Decision*, *50*(5), 817–831. doi:10.1108/00251741211227528

Leggatt, H. (2010, October 19). Rebuild Brand Loyalty with Social Media. Bizreport. Retrieved from http://www.bizreport.com/2010/08/price-sensitiveshoppers-still-seeking-out-deals.html

Legris, P., Ingham, J., & Collerette, P. (2003). Why do people use information technology? A critical review of the technology acceptance mode. *Information & Management*, *40*(3), 191–204. doi:10.1016/S0378-7206(01)00143-4

Leroy, R. J. R., Marshall, G. W., & Stamps, M. B. (2005). Sales force use of technology: Antecedents to technology acceptance. *Journal of Business Research*, *58*(5), 553–280.

Levine, R., Locke, C., Searle, D., & Weinberger, D. (2001). *The Cluetrain Manifesto: The end of business as usual*. New York: Basic Books.

Li, C. (2010). Groundswell. Winning in a world transformed by social technologies. *Strategic Direction, 26*(8).

Liang, T., Ho, Y., Li, Y. & Turton E. (2011). What Drives Social Commerce: The Role of Social Support and Relationship Quality. *International Journal of Electronic Commerce,* 16(2), 69–90.

Liang, C. L., Chen, H. J., & Wang, W. H. (2008). Does online relationship marketing enhance customer retention and cross-buying? *Service Industries Journal*, *28*(6), 769–787. doi:10.1080/02642060801988910

Libai, B. (2011). Comment: The perils of focusing on highly engaged customers. *Journal of Service Research*, *14*(3), 275–276. doi:10.1177/1094670511414583

Li, C., & Bernoff, J. (2008). *Groundswell: Winning in a world transformed by social technologies.* Boston, MA: Forrester Research, Inc.

Lieven, T., Grohmann, B., Herrmann, A., Landwehr, J. R., & van Tilburg, M. (2014). The effect of brand gender on brand equity. *Psychology and Marketing, 31*(5), 371–385. doi:10.1002/mar.20701

Li, H., & Kannan, P. K. (2014). Attributing Conversions in a Multichannel Online Marketing Environment: An Empirical Model and a Field Experiment. *JMR, Journal of Marketing Research, 51*(1), 40–56. doi:10.1509/jmr.13.0050

Li, J., & Zhan, L. (2011). Online persuasion: How the written word drives WOM—Evidence from consumer-generated product reviews. *Journal of Advertising Research, 51*(1), 239–257. doi:10.2501/JAR-51-1-239-257

Li, M., Dong, Z. Y., & Chen, X. (2012). Factors influencing consumptions experience of mobile commerce. *Internet Research, 22*(2), 120–141. doi:10.1108/10662241211214539

Limayem, M., & Rowe, F. (2006). Comparaison des facteurs influençant les intentions d'achat à partir du web à Hong Kong et en France: Influence sociale, risque et aversion pour la perte de contact. *Revue Française du Marketing, 209*, 4–5.

Lindon, D., & Jallat, F. (2002). *Le Marketing*. Paris: Édition DUNOD.

Lin, J. S., & Pena, J. (2011). Are you following me? A content analysis of TV networks' brand communication on Twitter. *Journal of Interactive Advertising, 12*(1), 17–29. doi:10.1080/15252019.2011.10722188

Litchfield, E. (1956). Notes on a general theory of administration. *Administrative Science Quarterly, 1*(1), 3–29. doi:10.2307/2390838

Liu, Y., Chen, Y., Lusch, R. F., Chen, H., Zimbra, D., & Zeng, S. (2010). User-Generated Content on Social Media: Predicting New Product Market Success from Online Word-of-Mouth. *IEEE Intelligent Systems, 25*(1), 75–78.

Livingston, G. (2010). *How to: Turn slackivists into activists with social media.* Mashable Social Media.

Lorenzo-Romero, C., Constantinides, E., & Brünink, L. A. (2014). Co-creation: Customer integration in social media based product and service development. *Procedia: Social and Behavioral Sciences, 148*, 383–396. doi:10.1016/j.sbspro.2014.07.057

Lowe, B., D'Alessandro, S., Winzar, H., Laffey, D., & Collier, W. (2013). The use of Web 2.0 technologies in marketing classes: Key drivers of student acceptance. *Journal of Consumer Behaviour, 12*(5), 412–422. doi:10.1002/cb.1444

Loyalty Versus Retention - Is There a Difference? (2010, April 9). The Customer Institute. Retrieved from http://thecustomerinstitute.blogspot.co.uk/2010/04/loyalty-versus-retention-is-there.html

Luchman, J. N., Bergstrom, J., & Krulikowski, C. (2014). A motives framework of social media website use: A survey of young Americans. *Computers in Human Behavior, 38*, 136–141. doi:10.1016/j.chb.2014.05.016

Lu, J., Yu, C.-S., Liu, C., & Yao, J. E. (2003). Technology acceptance model for wireless internet. *Internet Research: Electronic Networking Applications and Policy, 13*(3), 206–222. doi:10.1108/10662240310478222

Luo, J., Ba, S., & Zhang, H. (2012). The effectiveness of online shopping characteristics and well-designed websites on satisfaction. *Management Information Systems Quarterly, 36*(4), 1131–1144.

Lusch, R. F., & Vargo, S. L. (2006). Service-dominant logic: Reactions, reflections and refinements. *Marketing Theory, 6*(3), 281–288. doi:10.1177/1470593106066781

Luxury Beauty Having a Love Affair with the UK. (2013). *Euromonitor International.* Retrieved from http://www.euromonitor.com/

Macchiette, B., & Roy, A. (1992). Affinity Marketing: What is it and How does it Work? *Journal of Services Marketing*, *6*(3), 47–67. doi:10.1108/08876049210035935

Mackie, D. M., & Worth, L. T. (1989). Processing deficits and the mediation of positive affect in persuasion. *Journal of Personality and Social Psychology*, *57*(1), 27–40. doi:10.1037/0022-3514.57.1.27 PMID:2754602

Maklan, S., & Klaus, Ph. (2011). Customer experience: Are we measuring the right things? *International Journal of Market Research*, *53*(6), 771–792. doi:10.2501/IJMR-53-6-771-792

Malhotra, N., & Mac, C. D. (2001). A cross-cultural comparison of behavioral intention models: Theoretical consideration and en empirical investigation. *International Marketing Review*, *18*(3), 235–269. doi:10.1108/02651330110396505

Mandle, J. (2009). *Rawls's a theory of justice: An introduction* (1st ed.). New York, NY: Cambridge University Press. doi:10.1017/CBO9780511814099

Mangold, W. G., & Faulds, D. J. (2009). Social media: The new hybrid element of the promotion mix. *Business Horizons*, *52*(4), 357–365. doi:10.1016/j.bushor.2009.03.002

Manika, D., Papagiannidis, S., & Bourlakis, M. (2013, September 10-12). The effects of a CEO's YouTube apology for service failure on customers' behavioural intentions. *Proceedings of the British academy of management conference*, Liverpool. Retrieved from http://www.mbsportal.bl.uk/taster/subjareas/techinnov/bam2013/ebusinessandegovenment/full/156819contribution104.pdf

Manrai, A. K. (1995). Mathematical Models of Brand Choice Behavior. *European Journal of Operational Research*, *82*(1), 1–17. doi:10.1016/0377-2217(94)00236-6

Mansfield, E. (1968). *Industrial Research and Technological innovation. New-York.* Norton.

Marion, T. J., Barczak, G., & Hultink, E. J. (2014). Do social media tools impact the development phase? An exploratory study. *Journal of Product Innovation Management*, *31*(S1), 18–29. doi:10.1111/jpim.12189

Marketingcharts.com. (2014a). *Marketing Budget Shifts from Traditional to Digital Media Might be Slowing*. Retrieved from http://www.marketingcharts.com/online/marketing-budget-shifts-from-traditional-to-digital-media-may-be-slowing-42159/

Marketingcharts.com. (2014b). *Are Young People Watching less TV?* Retrieved from http://www.marketingcharts.com/television/are-young-people-watching-less-tv-24817/

Markovic, M. (2006). Analysing Qualitative Data: Health care experiences of Women with Gynecological Cancer. *Field Methods*, *18*(4), 413–429. doi:10.1177/1525822X06293126

Marks, D., & Yardley, L. (2004). *Research methods for clinical and health psychology*. London: Sage.

Martini, A., Massa, S., & Testa, S. (2014). Customer co-creation projects and social media: The case of Barilla of Italy. *Business Horizons*, *57*(3), 425–434. doi:10.1016/j.bushor.2014.02.003

Maslow, A. H. (1943). A theory of human motivation. *Psychological Review*, *50*(4), 370–396. doi:10.1037/h0054346

Mathieson, K. (1991). Predicting user intentions: Comparing the technology acceptance model with the theory of planned behaviour. *Information Systems Research*, *2*(3), 173–191. doi:10.1287/isre.2.3.173

Maxham, J. G. III, & Netemeyer, R. G. (2002). A longitudinal study of complaining customers' evaluations of multiple service failures and recovery efforts. *Journal of Marketing*, *66*(4), 57–71. doi:10.1509/jmkg.66.4.57.18512

McAfee, A. (2006). Enterprise 2.0: The dawn of emergent collaboration. *Sloan Management Review*, *47*(3), 21–28.

McAfee, A. (2009). Shattering the myths about Enterprise 2.0. *Harvard Business Review*, *87*(11), 120–124.

McAlexander, J. H., Schouten, J. W., & Koenig, H. F. (2002). Building brand community. *Journal of Marketing*, *66*(1), 38–54. doi:10.1509/jmkg.66.1.38.18451

McCarthy, E. J. (1960). *Basic Marketing - A Managerial Approach*. Homewood: Richard D. Irwin.

McColl-Kennedy, J. R., & Kiel, G. C. (2000). *Marketing – A Strategic Approach*. Melbourne, Australia: Nelson Thompson Learning.

McCracken, G. (1988). *Culture and consumption*. Bloomington, IN: Indiana University Press.

McKinsey. (2013). Six social-media skills every leader needs. *The McKinsey Quarterly*, (February): 1–13.

McLure Wasko, M., & Faraj, S. (2000). "It is what one does": Why people participate and help others in electronic communities of practice. *The Journal of Strategic Information Systems*, *9*(2-3), 155–173. doi:10.1016/S0963-8687(00)00045-7

Mehra, A., Dixon, A. L., Brass, D. J., & Robertson, B. (2006). The social network ties of group leaders: Implications for group performance and leader reputation. *Organization Science*, *17*(1), 64–79. doi:10.1287/orsc.1050.0158

Mei, J. S. A., Bansel, N., & Pang, A. (2010). New media: A new medium in escalating crisis. *Corporate Communication: An International Journal*, *15*(2), 143–155. doi:10.1108/13563281011037919

Mekonnen, A. (2012). *Customer-service provider relationship dissolution: the case of affinity marketing*. Thesis ((Doctoral dissertation). Open University, UK. Available from ProQuest Dissertations and Theses database. (U581639)

Mekonnen, A., Harris, F., & Laing, A. (2008). Linking products to a cause or affinity group: Does this really make them more attractive to consumers? *European Journal of Marketing*, *42*(1/2), 135–153. doi:10.1108/03090560810840943

Melewar, T. C., & Navalekar, A. (2002). Leveraging corporate identity in the digital age. *Marketing Intelligence & Planning*, *20*(2), 96–103. doi:10.1108/02634500210418518

Merz, M. A., He, Y., & Vargo, S. L. (2009). The evolving brand logic: A service-dominant logic perspective. *Journal of the Academy of Marketing Science*, *37*(3), 328–344. doi:10.1007/s11747-009-0143-3

Meuter, M. L., Ostrom, A. L., Roundtree, R. I., & Bitner, M. J. (2000). Self-service technologies: Understanding customer satisfaction with technology-based service encounters. *Journal of Marketing*, *64*(3), 50–64. doi:10.1509/jmkg.64.3.50.18024

Michaelidou, N., Siamagka, N. T., & Christodoulides, G. (2011). Usage, barriers and measurement of social media marketing: An exploratory investigation of small and medium B2B brands. *Industrial Marketing Management*, *40*(7), 1153–1159. doi:10.1016/j.indmarman.2011.09.009

Miles, C. (2013). Persuasion, marketing, communication, and the metaphor of magic. *European Journal of Marketing*, *47*(11/12), 2002–2019. doi:10.1108/EJM-11-2011-0632

Miller, D., & Lee, J. (2001). The people make the process: Commitment to employees, decision making and performance. *Journal of Management*, *2*(2), 163–189. doi:10.1177/014920630102700203

Miller, J. L., Craighead, C. W., & Karwan, K. R. (2000). Service recovery: A framework and empirical investigation. *Journal of Operations Management*, *18*(4), 387–400. doi:10.1016/S0272-6963(00)00032-2

Mintel. (2000). *Affinity and Store Cards October 2000*. London, UK Mintel.

Mintel. (2004). *Affinity Marketing UK 2004*. London, UK: Mintel.

Mobile Cocooning: How Growing Reliance on Smart Devices is Influencing Consumer Behaviour. (2013). *Emarketer.com.* Retrieved from http://www.euromonitor.com/mobile-cocooning-how-growing-reliance-on-smart-devices-is-influencing-consumer-behaviour/report

Mobile's Share of UK Digital Retail Sales Doubles. (2013). *Emarketer.com.* Retrieved from http://www.emarketer.com/Article/Mobiles-Share-of-UK-Digital-Retail-Sales-Doubles/1010204

Mohanty, S. N., & Suar, D. (2014). Decision Making Under Uncertainty and Information Processing In Positive and Negative Mood States. *Psychological Reports: Employment Psychology & Marketing*, *115*(1), 91–105. doi:10.2466/20.04.PR0.115c16z2 PMID:25153952

Monk, D. (1987). Assigning Elementary Pupils to their Teachers. *The Elementary School Journal*, *88*(2), 167–187. doi:10.1086/461531

Moore, C. M., & Doyle, S. A. (2010). The evolution of a luxury brand: The case of Prada. *International Journal of Retail & Distribution Management*, *38*(11), 915–927.

Moore, G. C., & Benbasat, I. (1991). Development of an instrument to measure the perceptions of adopting an information technology innovation. *Information Systems Research*, *2*(3), 192–222. doi:10.1287/isre.2.3.192

Moran, M., & Hunt, B. (2005). *Search Engine Marketing, Inc.: Driving search traffic to your company's web site*. Upper Saddle River, NJ: IBM Press.

Morgan, R. M., & Hunt, S. D. (1994). The commitment-trust theory of relationship marketing. *Journal of Marketing*, *58*(3), 20–38. doi:10.2307/1252308

Morgan-Thomas, A., & Veloutsou, C. (2013). Beyond technology acceptance: Brand relationships and online brand experience. *Journal of Business Research*, *66*(1), 21–27. doi:10.1016/j.jbusres.2011.07.019

Morin, S. P. (1983, February 28). Influentials advising their friends to sell lots of high-tech gadgetry. *Wall Street Journal*, 30(8), 982-1003.

Moritz, D. (2012, December 15).The Shift to Visual Social Media – 6 Tips for Business, Socially Sorted. Retrieved from http://sociallysorted.com.au/shift-to-visual-social-media-6-tips-for-business-infographic/

Morsing, M., & Schultz, M. (2006). Corporate social responsibility communication: Stakeholder information, response and involvement strategies. *Business Ethics (Oxford, England)*, *15*(4), 323–338. doi:10.1111/j.1467-8608.2006.00460.x

Motameni, R., & Shahrokhi, M. (1998). Brand equity valuation: A global perspective. *Journal of Product and Brand Management*, *7*(4), 275–290. doi:10.1108/10610429810229799

Moth, D. (2013). Mobile commerce now accounts for 23% of online sales: report. *Econsultancy.com.* Retrieved from https://econsultancy.com/blog/63338-mobile-commerce-now-accounts-for-23-of-online-sales-report

Mount, M., & Martinez, M. G. (2014, June 17). Rejuvenating a brand through social media. *MIT Sloan Management Review*. Retrieved from http://sloanreview.mit.edu/article/rejuvenating-a-brand-through-social-media/

Mudambi, S., & Schuff, D. (2010). What makes a helpful online review? A study of customer reviews on amazon.com. *Management Information Systems Quarterly*, *34*(1), 185–200.

Mulhern, F. (2009). Integrated marketing communications: From media channels to digital connectivity. *Journal of Marketing Communications,* 15(2-3), 85-101.

Muniz, A. M. Jr, & O'Guinn, T. C. (2001). Brand Community. *The Journal of Consumer Research*, *27*(4), 412–432. Retrieved from http://search.ebscohost.com/login.aspx?direct=true&AuthType=ip,shib&db=buh&AN=5244454&site=ehost-live doi:10.1086/319618

Nahapiet, J., & Ghoshal, S. (1998). Social capital, intellectual capital, and the organizational advantage. *Academy of Management Review*, *23*(2), 242–266.

Nair, M. (2011). Understanding and Measuring the Value of Social Media. *Journal of Corporate Accounting & Finance*, *22*(3), 45–51. doi:10.1002/jcaf.20674

Nambisan, P., & Watt, J. H. (2011). Managing customer experiences in online product communities. *Journal of Business Research*, *64*(8), 889–895. doi:10.1016/j.jbusres.2010.09.006

Nasco, S., Kulviwat, S., Kumar, A.G., & Bruner, C. (2008). The CAT model: extensions and moderators of dominance in technology acceptance. *Psychology & marketing*, 25(10), 987-1005.

Nations, D. (2014). *What is Social Media?* Retrieved from http://webtrends.about.com/od/web20/a/social-media.htm

Naylor, R. W., Lamberton, C. P., & West, P. M. (2012). Beyond the like button: The impact of mere virtual presence on brand evaluations and purchase intentions in social media settings. *Journal of Marketing*, *76*(6), 105–120. doi:10.1509/jm.11.0105

Neal, C., Quester, P. G., & Hawkins, D. (2002). *Consumer Behaviour – Implications for Marketing Strategy* (3rd ed.). Sydney, Australia: McGraw-Hill Irwin.

Nielsen. (2007). Trust in advertising, a global Nielsen consumer report. Retrieved from www.nielsen.com/solutions/TrustinAdvertisingOct07.pdf

Nitzan, I., & Libai, B. (2011). Social effects on customer retention. *Journal of Marketing*, *75*(6), 24–38. doi:10.1509/jm.10.0209

Nonnecke, B., Andrews, D., & Preece, J. (2006). Non-public and public online community participation: Needs, attitudes and behaviour. *Electronic Commerce Research*, *6*(1), 7–20. doi:10.1007/s10660-006-5985-x

Noor Al-Deen, H. S., & Hendricks, J. A. (2012). *Social Media – usage and impact*. Plymouth: Lexington Books.

Norris, D. G. (1993). Intel inside: Branding a component in a business market. *Journal of Business and Industrial Marketing*, *8*(1), 14–24. doi:10.1108/08858629310027560

Nuccio, L. (2013). *Social Dialogue Marketing Metrics Drives Word-of-Mouth*. Retrieved from http://www.meltwater.com/social-media-blog/social-dialogue-marketing/

Nummela, N., Saarenketo, S., Jokela, P., & Loane, S. (2014). Strategic Decision-Making of a Born Global: A Comparative Study from Three Small Open Economies. *Management International Review*, *54*(4), 527–550. doi:10.1007/s11575-014-0211-x

Nwagbara, U. (2010). Towards a paradigm shift in the Niger Delta: Transformational leadership in the era of post amnesty deal. *Journal of Sustainable Development in Africa*, *12*(3), 387–400.

Nwagbara, U. (2013). *Leading sustainability in Nigeria: Problems, Processes and Prospects*. Saarbrucken: LAP.

Nysveen, H., & Pedersen, P. E. (2005). Search mode and purchase intention in online shopping behaviour. *International Journal of Internet Marketing and Advertising*, *2*(4), 288–306. doi:10.1504/IJIMA.2005.008103

Nysveen, H., Perdersen, P. E., & Thorbjornsen, H. (2005). Explaining intention to use mobile services: Antecedents and cross-service comparisons. *Journal of the Academy of Marketing Science, 33*(3), 330–346. doi:10.1177/0092070305276149

O'Reilly, T. (2005, September 30). What is Web 2.0? Design Patterns and Business Models for the Next generation of Software. *O'Reilly*. Retrieved from http://www.im.ethz.ch/education/HS08/OReilly_What_is_Web2_0.pdf

O'Reilly, T., & Milstein, S. (2009). *The twitter book*. O'Reilly Media, Inc.

O'Reilly, T., & Milstein, S. (2012). *The Twitter Book*. Sebastopol: O'Reilly Media Inc.

Obi, C. (2010). Oil as the "curse" of conflict in Africa: Peering through the smoke and mirrors. *Review of African Political Economy, 37*(126), 483–495. doi:10.1080/03056244.2010.530947

O'Cass, A., & French, T. (2003). Web Retailing Adoption: Exploring the nature of Internet Users Web Retailing Behaviour. *Journal of Retailing and Consumer Services, 10*(2), 81–94. doi:10.1016/S0969-6989(02)00004-8

OECD/DAC (Organisation for Economic Co-operation and Development/Development Assistance Committee). (2007). *Principles for Good International Engagement in Fragile States and Situations*. Paris: OECD.

Ohanian, R. (1990). Construction and validation of a scale to measure celebrity endorsers' perceived expertise, trustworthiness, and attractiveness. *Journal of Advertising, 19*(3), 39–52. doi:10.1080/00913367.1990.10673191

Okazaki, S. (2006). Excitement or sophistication? A preliminary exploration of online brand personality. *International Marketing Review, 23*(3), 279–303. doi:10.1108/02651330610670451

Okoh, R. N. (2005). Conflict management in the Niger delta region of Nigeria: A participatory approach. *African Journal of Conflict Resolution, 5*, 24–37.

Okome, M. O. (2013). (Ed). State fragility, state formation, and human security in Nigeria. New Hampshire: Palgrave MacMillan.

Okonkwo, U. (2010). Luxury Online. New York: Palgrave Macmillan.

Okonta, I., & Douglas, O. (2003). *Where vultures feast: Shell, human rights, and oil in the Niger delta*. London: Verso.

Oliver, R. L. (1980). A Cognitive Model of the Antecedents and Consequences of Satisfaction Decisions. *JMR, Journal of Marketing Research, 17*(4), 460–469. doi:10.2307/3150499

Oluwaniyi, O. O. (2011). Post-amnesty in the Niger delta: Challenges and prospects. *Conflict Trends, 4*, 46–54.

Online retail sales highest in two years as positive economic sign continues. (2013). Capgemini. Retrieved from http://www.uk.capgemini.com/online-retail-sales-highest-in-two-years-as-positive-economic-signs-continue

Onook, O., Manish, A., & Raghave, R. H. (2013). Community intelligence and social media services: A rumor theoretic analysis of tweets during social crisis. *Management Information Systems Quarterly, 37*(2), 407–A7.

Oruh, E. S. (2014). Giving voice to the people: Exploring the effect of new media on stakeholders' engagement in the Nigerian union movement. *Management Research and Practices, 6*(3), 44–52.

Ostrow, A. (2011). *Kindle Books Now Outselling Paperbacks at Amazon*. Retrieved from http://mashable.com/2011/01/27/kindle-books-outselling-paperbacks/

Ozuem, W., Borrelli, M., & Lancaster, G. (2015). Leveraging the co-evolution of offline and online video games: An empirical study. *Journal of Strategic Marketing*. doi:10.1080/0965254X.2015.1076883

Ozuem, W., Howell, K. E., & Lancaster, G. (2008). Communicating in the new interactive marketspace. *European Journal of Marketing*, *42*(9/10), 1059–1083. doi:10.1108/03090560810891145

Ozuem, W., & Lancaster, G. (2014). Recovery strategies in on-line service failure. In A. Ghorbani (Ed.), *Marketing in the cyber era: strategies and emerging trends* (pp. 143–159). Hershey, PA: IGI Global. doi:10.4018/978-1-4666-4864-7.ch010

Ozuem, W., O'Keeffe, A., & Lancaster, G. (2015). Leadership Marketing: An exploratory study. *Journal of Strategic Marketing*. doi:10.1080/0965254X.2014.1001867

Ozuem, W., Thomas, T., & Lancaster, G. (2015). The influence of customer loyalty on small island economies: An empirical and exploratory study. *Journal of Strategic Marketing*. doi:10.1080/0965254X.2015.1011205

Paffenback, M. (2011). *How To Identify Your Brand Touchpoints*. Retrieved from http://www.touchpointers.com/2011/10/11/how-to-identify-your-brand-touchpoints/

Pan, B., Xiang, Z., Law, R., & Fesenmaier, D. R. (2011). *The dynamics of search engine marketing for tourist destinations*. Retrieved from http://bit.ly/1FGKL2Y

Pang, B., & Lee, L. (2005). Seeing stars: Exploiting class relationships for sentiment categorization with respect to rating scales. Proceedings of the Association for Computational linguistics (pp. 115–124). Retrieved from http://www.cs.cornell.edu/home/llee/papers/pang-lee-stars.home.html doi:10.3115/1219840.1219855

Pang, A., Hasan, N. B. B. A., & Chong, A. C. Y. (2014). Negotiating crises in the social media environment. *Corporate Communications: An International Journal*, *19*(1), 96–118. doi:10.1108/CCIJ-09-2012-0064

Parasuraman, A. (2000). Technology readiness index (TRI) a mutiple-item scale to measure readiness to embrace new technology. *Journal of Service Research*, *2*(4), 307–320. doi:10.1177/109467050024001

Parasuraman, A., Zeithaml, V. A., & Malhotra, A. (2005). e-SERVQUAL: A multiple-item scale for assessing electronic service quality. *Journal of Service Research*, *7*(3), 213–233. doi:10.1177/1094670504271156

Park, C. W., Jun, S. Y., & Shocker, A. D. (1996). Composite branding alliances: An investigation of extension and feedback effects. *JMR, Journal of Marketing Research*, *33*(4), 453–466. doi:10.2307/3152216

Park, E. J., Kim, E. Y., & Forney, J. C. (2006). A structural model of fashion-oriented impulse buying behaviour. *Journal of Fashion Marketing and Management*, *10*(4), 433–446. doi:10.1108/13612020610701965

Park, N., Kee, K., & Valenzuela, S. (2009). Being immersed in social networking environment: Facebook groups, uses and gratifications, and social outcomes. *CyberPsychology & Behavior*, *12*(6), 729–733. doi:10.1089/cpb.2009.0003 PMID:19619037

Park, S. E., Choi, D., & Kim, J. (2005). Visualizing e-brand personality: Exploratory studies on visual attributes and e-brand personalities in Korea. *International Journal of Human-Computer Interaction*, *19*(1), 7–34. doi:10.1207/s15327590ijhc1901_3

Parr, B. (2009, June 21). #IranElection Crisis: A Social Media Timeline. *Mashable.com*. Retrieved from http://mashable.com/2009/06/21/iran-election-timeline/

Parson, W. (1996). Crisis communication. *Career Development International*, *1(5)*, 26–28.

Pasqua, R., & Elkin, N. (2013). *Mobile Marketing: An hour a day*. Indiana: John Wiley & Sons Inc.

Patterson, B. (1984). Perceptions of Efficacy in Effective and Ineffective Principals [Unpublished PhD dissertation]. University of California, Santa Barbara, CA, USA.

Patton, M. Q. (2002). *Qualitative Research and Evaluation Methods* (3rd ed.). London: Sage Publications Ltd.

Pavlik, J. V. (2007, June 4). Mapping the consequences of technology of public relations, Institute for public relations. Institute for Public Relations. Retrieved from http://www.instituteforpr.org/topics/mapping-technology-consequences/

Pavlou, P. A. (2003). Consumer acceptance of electronic commerce: Integrating trust and risk with the technology acceptance model. *International Journal of Electronic Commerce*, *7*(3), 101–134.

Pawar, B., & Sharda, R. (1997). Obtaining Business Intelligence on the Internet. *Long Range Planning*, *30*(1), 110–121. doi:10.1016/S0024-6301(96)00100-8

Pearson, N., Larson, E. W., & Gray, C. F. (2013). *Project Management in Practice* (1st ed.). Sydney, Australia: McGraw-Hill Education.

Peled, A. (2000). Bringing the internet and multimedia revolution to the classroom. *Campus-Wide Information Systems*, *17*(1), 16–22. doi:10.1108/10650740010317023

Pelling, E. L., & White, K. M. (2009). The theory of planned behavior applied to young people's use of social networking web sites. *CyberPsychology & Behavior*, *12*(6), 755–759. doi:10.1089/cpb.2009.0109 PMID:19788377

Pentina, I., Zhang, L., & Basmanova, O. (2013). Antecedents and consequences of trust in a social media brand: A cross-cultural study of Twitter. *Computers in Human Behavior*, *29*(4), 1546–1555. doi:10.1016/j.chb.2013.01.045

Perdue, D. J. (2010). Social media marketing: Gaining a competitive advantage by reaching the masses (Paper 127). *Senior Honors Papers*.

Perrigot, R., & Penard, T. (2013, Spring). Determinants of Economic Strategy in Franchising: A Resources –Based View in Franchising. *International Journal of Electronic Commerce*, *17*(3), 109–130. doi:10.2753/JEC1086-4415170305

Persaud, A., & Azhar, I. (2012). Innovative mobile marketing via smartphones: Are consumers ready? *Marketing Intelligence & Planning*, *30*(4), 418–443. doi:10.1108/02634501211231883

Persson, J. (2012). *Brand Touchpoint Matrix*. Retrieved from http://brandtouchpointmatrix.com/

Peter, J. P., & Olson, J. (1996). *Consumer behaviour and marketing strategy*. Chicago: Irwin.

Petersen, M., Grone, F., Kammer, K., & Kirscheneder, J. (2010). *Multi-Channel Customer Management: Delighting Consumers, Driving Efficiency*. Retrieved from http://www.strategyand.pwc.com/media/uploads/Multi-Channel_Customer_Management.pdf

Petty, R. E., & Cacioppo, J. T. (1986). *Communication and persuasion: Central and peripheral routes to attitude change*. New York, NY: Springer-Verlag. doi:10.1007/978-1-4612-4964-1

Phan, M., Thomas, R., & Heine, K. (2011). Social Media and Luxury Brand Management: The Case of Burberry. *Journal of Global Fashion Marketing*, *2*(4), 213–222. doi:10.1080/20932685.2011.10593099

Piccoli, G. (2010). Information technology and the future of hospitality brand management. Retrieved from http://content.ebscohost.com.ezproxy.library.unlv.edu/pdf25 26/pdf/2010/

Piller, F. T., Vossen, A., & Ihl, C. (2012). From social media to social product development: The impact of social media on co-creation of innovation. *Die Unternehmung*, *66*(1), 7–27. doi:10.5771/0042-059X-2012-1-7

Piskorski, M. J., Casciaro, T., & Kivel, M. (2013). Social Strategy: Why Social Media Platforms Work and How to Leverage them for Competitive Advantage. Princeton, NJ: Princeton University Press.

Poddar, A., Donthu, N., & Wei, Y. (2009). Web site customer orientations, web site quality, and purchase intentions: The role of web site personality. *Journal of Business Research*, *6*(4), 441–450. doi:10.1016/j.jbusres.2008.01.036

Pookulangara, S., & Koesler, K. (2011). Cultural influence on consumers' usage of social networks and its impact on online purchase intentions. *Journal of Retailing and Consumer Services*, *18*(4), 348–354. doi:10.1016/j.jretconser.2011.03.003

Porter, M. E. (2001). Strategy and the Internet. *Harvard Business Review*, *79*(3), 62–78. PMID:11246925

Powell, J. (2009). *33 Million people in the room: How to create, influence, and run a successful business with social networking*. Que Publishing.

Power to the people: Social media tracker wave 3 . (2008). *Universal McCann*. Retrieved from http://www.universalmccann.com/Assets/UM%20Wave%203%20Final_20080505110444.pdf

Power to the people: Social media tracker wave 4. (2009). *Universal McCann*. Retrieved from http://universalmccann.bitecp.com/wave4/Wave4.pdf

Powers, T., Advincula, D., Austin, M. S., & Graiko, S. (2012). Digital and social media in the purchase-decision process: A special report from the advertising research foundation. *Journal of Advertising Research*, *52*(4), 479–489. doi:10.2501/JAR-52-4-479-489

Prahalad, C. K., & Ramaswamy, V. (2004). Co-creation experiences: The next practice in value creation. *Journal of Interactive Marketing*, *18*(3), 5–14. doi:10.1002/dir.20015

Prahalad, C. K., & Ramaswamy, V. (2004). *The future of competition: Co-creating unique value with customers*. Boston, MA: Harvard Business School Press.

Prakash, N. (2012, December 8). How the Middle East, North Africa are using Facebook for marketing. *Mashable*. Retrieved from http://mashable.com/2012/12/07/facebook-middle-east-africa/

Prendergast, G., Ko, D., & Yuen, S. Y. V. (2010). Online word of mouth and consumer purchase intentions. *International Journal of Advertising*, *29*(5), 687–708. doi:10.2501/S0265048710201427

Quinton, S., & Harridge-March, S. (2010). Relationships in online communities: The potential for marketers. *Journal of Research in Interactive Marketing*, *4*(1), 59–73. doi:10.1108/17505931011033560

Qu, Z., Wang, Y., Wang, S., & Zhang, Y. (2013). Implications of online social activities for e-tailer's business performance. *European Journal of Marketing*, *47*(8), 1190–1212. doi:10.1108/03090561311324282

Qu, Z., Wang, Y., Wang, S., & Zhang, Y. (2013). Implications of online social activities for e-tailers' business performance. *European Journal of Management*, *47*(8), 1190–1212.

Rahmandad, H., & Sterman, J. D. (2008). Heterogeneity and network structure in the dynamics of diffusion: Comparing agent-based and differential equation models. *Management Science*, *54*(5), 998–1014. doi:10.1287/mnsc.1070.0787

Ranaweera, C., & Prabhu, J. (2003). On the relative importance of customer satisfaction and trust as determinants of customer retention and positive word of mouth. *Journal of Targeting Measurement and Analysis of Marketing*, *12*(1), 82–90. doi:10.1057/palgrave.jt.5740100

Ranaweera, C., & Prabhu, J. (2003). The influence of satisfaction, trust and switching barriers on customer retention in a continuous purchasing setting. *International Journal of Service Industry Management*, *14*(4), 374–395. doi:10.1108/09564230310489231

Rao, A. R., Qu, L., & Ruekert, R. W. (1999). Signaling unobservable product quality through a brand ally. *JMR, Journal of Marketing Research*, *36*(2), 258–268. doi:10.2307/3152097

Rauyruen, P., Miller, K. E., & Barret, N. J. (2007). Relationship quality as a predictor of B2B customer loyalty. *Journal of Business Research*, *60*(1), 21–31. doi:10.1016/j.jbusres.2005.11.006

Rawat, S., & Divekar, R. (2014). Developing a social media presence strategy for an e-commerce business. *Procedia Economics and Finance*, *11*, 626–634. doi:10.1016/S2212-5671(14)00228-7

Reed, A., & Botts, S. (2014). Building identity loyalty through social media. *Think with Google.* Retrieved from https://www.thinkwithgoogle.com/columns/building-identity-through-social-media.html

Reijonen, H., Laukkanen, T., Komppula, R., & Tuominen, S. (2012). Are growing SMEs more market-oriented and brand-oriented? *Journal of Small Business Management*, *50*(4), 699–716. doi:10.1111/j.1540-627X.2012.00372.x

Retail Drives UK B2C Ecommerce Sales Higher. (2013). *Emarketer.com.* Retrieved from http://www.emarketer.com/Article/Retail-Drives-UK-B2C-Ecommerce-Sales-Higher/1010106

Rettberg, J. W. (2008). *Blogging – Digital Media and Society Series*. Malden: Polity.

Reynolds, L. A., & Hrudey, S. E. (2006). Managing uncertainty in environmental decision-making: The risky business of establishing a relationship between science and law. *International Journal of Risk Assessment and Management*, *6*(1-3), 1–249. doi:10.1504/IJRAM.2006.007889

Ricard, L., & Perrien, J. (1999). Explaining and evaluating the implementation of organizational relationship marketing in the banking industry: Clients' perception. *Journal of Business Research*, *45*(2), 199–209. doi:10.1016/S0148-2963(97)00226-9

Richardson, M., & Lane, K. (1994). Reforming principal preparation from training to learning.Catalyst, Winter, 14-18.

Ricks, D. A. (2006). *Blunders in international business*. Malden, MA: Blackwell Publishing.

Ridings, C. M., Gefen, D., & Arinze, B. (2002). Some antecedents and effects of trust in virtual communities. *The Journal of Strategic Information Systems*, *11*(3–4), 271–295. doi:10.1016/S0963-8687(02)00021-5

Rifkin, G. (2006). Building better global managers. Harvard Management Update, March, pp. 3–6.

Ringberg, T., Odekerken-Schroder, G., & Christensen, G. L. (2007). A cultural models approach to service recovery. *Journal of Marketing*, *71*(3), 194–214. doi:10.1509/jmkg.71.3.194

Rio-Lanza, A. B. D., Vazquez-Casielles, R., & Diaz-Martin, A. M. (2009). Satisfaction with service recovery: Perceived justice and emotional responses. *Journal of Business Research*, *62*(8), 775–781. doi:10.1016/j.jbusres.2008.09.015

Roberts, J. H., & Lattin, J. M. (1991). Development and Testing of a Model of Consideration Set Composition. *JMR, Journal of Marketing Research*, *28*(4), 429–440. doi:10.2307/3172783

Roberts, J. H., & Lattin, J. M. (1997). Consideration: Review of Research and Prospects for Future Insights. *JMR, Journal of Marketing Research*, *34*(3), 406–410. doi:10.2307/3151902

Robson, C. (2011). *Real World Research: A Resource for Users of Social Research Methods in Applied settings* (3rd ed.). Cornwall: John Wiley & Sons Ltd.

Rogers, E. M. (1983). *Diffusion of Innovations* (3rd ed.). London: The Free Press.

Rogers, E. M. (1995). *Diffusion of innovations* (4th ed.). New York: Free Press.

Roggeveen, A. L., Tsiros, M., & Grewal, D. (2012). Understanding the co-creation effect: When does collaborating with customers provide a lift to service recovery? *Journal of the Academy of Marketing Science*, *40*(6), 771–790. doi:10.1007/s11747-011-0274-1

Ross, J. (2009). A corporate guide for social media. Retrieved from http://www.forbes.com/2009/06/30/social-media-guidelines-intelligenttechnology-oreilly.html

Ross, J. K., Patterson, L., & Stutts, M. A. (1992). Consumer Perceptions of Organisations that Use Cause-Related Marketing. *Journal of the Academy of Marketing Science*, *20*(1), 93–97. doi:10.1007/BF02723480

Roulston, K. (2010). *Reflective interviewing: A guide to theory and practice*. London: Sage Publications Ltd.

Rouse, M. (2014). *Big Data*. Retrieved from http://searchcloudcomputing.techtarget.com/definition/big-data-Big-Data

Rowley, J. (2004). Online branding. *Online Information Review*, *28*(2), 131–138. doi:10.1108/14684520410531637

Ruane, L., & Wallace, E. (2013). Generation Y females online: Insights from brand narratives. *Qualitative Market Research: An International Journal*, *16*(3), 315–335. doi:10.1108/13522751311326125

Rubin, G. (2014). *Effective National Marketing Policies for Your Local Franchisees*. Retrieved from http://www.franchising.com/articles/effective_national_marketing_policies_for_your_local_franchisees.html

Rubio, N., Oubina, J., & Villasenor, N. (2014). Brand awareness–Brand quality inference and consumer's risk perception in store brands of food products. *Food Quality and Preference*, *32*, 289–298. doi:10.1016/j.foodqual.2013.09.006

Rust, R. T., & Oliver, R. L. (2000). Should we delight the customer? *Journal of the Academy of Marketing Science*, *28*(1), 86–94. doi:10.1177/0092070300281008

Ryan, D., & Jones, C. (2012). *Understanding Digital Marketing* (2nd ed.). London, UK: Kogan Page.

Safko, L. (2012). *The Social Media Bible– Tools, Tactics and Strategies for Business Success* (3rd ed.). New Jersey: John Wiley & Sons Inc.

Safko, L., & Brake, D. K. (2009). *The Social Media Bible*. New Jersey: John Wiley & Sons, Inc.

Safko, L., & Brake, D. K. (2009). *The social media bible: Tactics, tools & strategies for business success*. Hoboken, NJ: John Wiley & Sons.

Saiti, A., & Eliophotou-Menon, M. (2009). Educational decision making in a centralised system: The case of Greece. *International Journal of Educational Management*, *23*(6), 446–455. doi:10.1108/09513540910980998

Salley, C., McPherson, B., & Baehr, M. (1979). *National Occupational Analysis of the School Principalship*. Chicago: Industrial Relations Center, University of Chicago Press.

Sandes, F. S., & Urdan, A. T. (2013). Electronic Word-of-Mouth Impacts on Consumer Behaviour: Exploratory and Experimental Studies. *Journal of International Consumer Marketing*, *25*(3), 181–197. doi:10.1080/08961530.2013.780850

San-Martin, S., & Lopez-Catalan, B. (2013). How can a mobile vendor get satisfied customers? *Industrial Management & Data Systems*, *113*(2), 156–170. doi:10.1108/02635571311303514

San-Martin, S., Lopez-Catalan, B., & Ramon-Jeronimo, M. A. (2012). Factors determining firms' perceived performance of mobile commerce. *Industrial Management & Data Systems*, *112*(6), 946–963. doi:10.1108/02635571211238536

Sanou, B. (2014). *ICT Facts and Figures, International Telecommunication Union (ICT)*. Publication.

Sashi, C. M. (2012). Customer engagement, buyer-seller relationships, and social media. *Management Decision*, *50*(2), 253–272. doi:10.1108/00251741211203551

Saunders, M., Lewis, P., & Thornhill, A. (2009). *Research methods for business students* (5th ed.). Harlow: Pearson Education Ltd.

Scarpi, D. (2006). Fashion stores between fun and usefulness. *Journal of Fashion Marketing and Management*, *10*(1), 7–24. doi:10.1108/13612020610651097

Schau, H. J., Muñiz, A. M. Jr, & Arnould, E. J. (2009). How brand community practices create value. *Journal of Marketing*, *73*(5), 30–51. doi:10.1509/jmkg.73.5.30

Schaupp, L. C., & Bélanger, F. (2014). The Value of Social Media for Small Businesses. *Journal of Information Systems*, *28*(1), 187–207. doi:10.2308/isys-50674

Schawbel, D. (2008, December 29). Top 10 Reputation Tracking Tools Worth Paying For. *Mashable.com.* Retrieved from http://mashable.com/2008/12/29/brand-reputation-monitoring-tools/

Scherer, A., & Palazzo, G. (2011). The new political role of business in a globalized world: A review of a new perspective on CSR and its implications for the firm, governance, and democracy. *Journal of Management Studies*, *48*(4), 899–931. doi:10.1111/j.1467-6486.2010.00950.x

Schiffman, L. G., & Kanuk, L. L. (2010). *Consumer Behaviour* (10th ed.). New Jersey: Pearson Education Inc.

Schlegelmilch, B. B., & Woodruffe, H. (1995). A comparative analysis of the affinity card market in the USA and the UK. *International Journal of Bank Marketing*, *13*(5), 12–23. doi:10.1108/02652329510092176

Schmalz, S., & Orth, U. R. (2012). Brand attachment and consumer emotional response to unethical firm behavior. *Psychology and Marketing*, *29*(11), 869–884. doi:10.1002/mar.20570

Schoefer, K., & Diamantopoulos, A. (2009). A typology of consumers' emotional response style during service recovery encounters. *British Journal of Management*, *20*(3), 292–308. doi:10.1111/j.1467-8551.2008.00589.x

Schultz, D.E., (1996, December 18). Integration and the Internet. *Marketing News*, No. 12.

Schuster, L., Drennan, J., & Lings, I. N. (2013). Consumer acceptance of m-wellbeing services: A social marketing perspective. *European Journal of Marketing*, *47*(9), 1439–1457. doi:10.1108/EJM-10-2011-0556

Scott, D. M. (2007). *The New Rules of Marketing and PR*. Hoboken, New Jersey: John Wiley & Sons, Inc.

Scott, D. M. (2009). *World wide rave: Creating triggers that get millions of people to spread your ideas and share your stories*. Hoboken, NJ: John Wiley & Sons. doi:10.1002/9781118258286

Scott, D. M. (2011). *The New Rules of Marketing & PR*. Hoboken, NJ: Wiley.

Selby, E. (2014). *The Big Misunderstanding About Social Media Marketing*. Retrieved from http://www.maxxdesignblog.co.uk/integrated-marketing/social-media-marketing/social-media-berkshire/

Sen, A. (1981). *Poverty and famine: An Essay on Entitlement and Deprivation*. Oxford: Clarendon Press.

Senach, B. (1990). Evaluation ergonomique des IHM. *Revue de la littérature*, rapport Inria N° 1180.

Sen, S. (1998). Knowledge, information mode and the attraction effect. *Journal of Consumer Research*, *25*(1), 64–77. doi:10.1086/209527

Sensis.com.au. (2014). *Yellow Social Media Report*. Retrieved from https://www.sensis.com.au/content/dam/sas/PDF-directory/Yellow-Social-Media-Report-2014.pdf

Seock, Y. K., & Norton, M. (2007). Attitude towards internet websites, online information search and channel choices for purchasing. *Journal of Fashion Marketing and Management*, *11*(4), 571–586. doi:10.1108/13612020710824616

Shaharudin, M. R., Mansor, S. W., & Elias, S. J. (2011). Food quality attributes among Malaysia's fast food customer. *International Business and Management*, *2*(1), 198–208.

Shim, S., Estlick, M. A., Lotz, S. L., & Warrrington, P. (2001). An online prepurchase intentions model: The role of intention to search. *Journal of Retailing*, *77*(2), 307–416.

Shirahada, K., & Kosaka, M. (2012). Evaluation method for service branding using word-of-mouth data. *Electronics and Communications in Japan*, *95*(12), 21–28. doi:10.1002/ecj.11442

Shultz, M., & de Chernatony, L. (2002). Introduction the challenges of corporate branding. *Corporate Reputation Review*, *5*(2/3), 105–112. doi:10.1057/palgrave.crr.1540168

Siddiqi, A. (2014). *From Monologue to Dialogue With the Right Technology and the 4 C's of Social Media Marketing*. Retrieved from http://www.mediabuzz.com.sg/asian-emarketing/Social-Media/1855-from-monologue-to-dialogue-with-the-right-technology-and-the-four-cs-of-social-media-marketing

Simon, C. J., & Sullivan, M. W. (1993). The measurement and determinants of brand equity: A financial approach. *Marketing Science*, *12*(1), 28–52. doi:10.1287/mksc.12.1.28

Simon, H. A. (1960). *New Science of Management Decisions*. New York, NY: Harper and Row. doi:10.1037/13978-000

Simonson, I., & Tversky, A. (1992). Choice in context: Trade-off contrast and extremeness aversion. *JMR, Journal of Marketing Research*, *29*(3), 281–295. doi:10.2307/3172740

Singh, J. (1990). A typology of consumer dissatisfaction response styles. *Journal of Retailing*, *66*(1), 57–99.

Singh, N., Lehnert, K., & Bostick, K. (2012). Global social media Usage: Insights into reaching consumers worldwide. *Thunderbird International Business Review*, *54*(5), 683–700. doi:10.1002/tie.21493

Singh, P. V., Sahoo, N., & Mukhopadhyay, T. (2010). Seeking Variety: A Dynamic Model of Employee Blog Reading Behavior.*Proceedings of the Workshop on Information Systems Economics*, Saint Louis, MO. doi:10.2139/ssrn.1617405

Singh, S., & Sonnenburg, S. (2012). Brand performances in social media. *Journal of Interactive Marketing*, *26*(4), 189–197. doi:10.1016/j.intmar.2012.04.001

Singh, T., Veron-Jackson, L., & Cullinane, J. (2008). Blogging: A new play in your marketing game plan. *Business Horizons*, *51*(4), 281–292. doi:10.1016/j.bushor.2008.02.002

Sivakumar, K., Li, M., & Dong, B. (2014). Service quality: The impact of frequency, timing, proximity, and sequence of failure and delights. *Journal of Marketing*, *78*(1), 41–58. doi:10.1509/jm.12.0527

Skeldon, P. (2011). *M-commerce: Boost your business with the power of mobile commerce*. Richmond: Crimson Publishing.

Smedescu, D. A. (2013). Social Media Marketing Tools. *Romanian Journal of Marketing*.

Smith, C. (2014). *One-Third of Marketers Generate a Return on Their Social Media Efforts*. Retrieved from http://www.businessinsider.com.au/one-third-of-marketers-generate-a-return-on-their-social-media-efforts-2014-1

Smith, A. K., & Bolton, R. N. (2002). The effect of customers' emotional responses to service failures on their recovery effort evaluations and satisfaction judgments. *Journal of the Academy of Marketing Science*, *30*(1), 5–23. doi:10.1177/03079450094298

Smith, A. K., Bolton, R. N., & Wagner, J. (1999). A model of customer satisfaction with service encounters involving failure and recovery. *JMR, Journal of Marketing Research*, *36*(3), 356–372. doi:10.2307/3152082

Smith, J. B., & Colgate, M. (2007). Customer value creation: A practical framework. *Journal of Marketing Theory and Practice*, *15*(1), 7–23. doi:10.2753/MTP1069-6679150101

Smith, T. (2009). The Social Media Revolution. *International Journal of Market Research*, *51*(4), 559–561. doi:10.2501/S1470785309200773

Snyder, B., & Barzilay, R. (2007). Multiple Aspect Ranking using the Cood Crief Algorithm. *Proceedings of the Joint Human Language Technology/North American Chapter of the ACL Conference* (HLT-NAACL) (pp. 300-307).

Social Media Landscape 2013. (2013, April 17). *Fred Cavazza*. Retrieved from http://www.fredcavazza.net/2013/04/17/social-media-landscape-2013/

Solomon, M. R. (2009). *Consumer Behaviour: Buying, Having and Being* (8th ed.). New Jersey: Pearson Education Inc.

Solomon, M. R., Surprenant, C., Czepiel, J. A., & Gutman, E. G. (1985). A role theory perspective on dyadic interactions: The service encounter. *Journal of Marketing*, *49*(1), 99–111. doi:10.2307/1251180

Sonenclar, K. (2005). *Search-engine marketing: Growth companies in play*. Retrieved from http://bit.ly/1rI5J9q

Spaid, B. I., & Flint, D. J. (2014). The meaning of shopping experiences augmented by mobile internet devices. *Journal of Marketing Theory and Practice*, *22*(1), 73–89.

Srinivasan, S. S., Anderson, R., & Ponnavolu, K. (2002). Customer loyalty in e-commerce: An exploration of its antecedents and consequences. *Journal of Retailing*, *78*(1), 41–50. doi:10.1016/S0022-4359(01)00065-3

Stalker, R. (2010). *The Rise and Rise of Social Media*. Retrieved from http://www.franchise.net.au/issues/the-rise-and-rise-of-social-media

Stambouli, K., & Briones, E. (2002). *Buzz marketing: les stratégies de bouche à oreille*. Paris: Éditions d'Organisation.

Steinmetz, A. (1997). *The Art of Conversation: Dialogue Marketing and the Business-to-Business Relationship*. Retrieved from http://www.adlittle.com/downloads/tx_adlprism/1997_q4_27-32.pdf

Stelzner, M. (2013). Social media marketing industry report: How Marketers Are Using Social Media to Grow Their Business. *Social Media Examiner*. Retrieved from http://www.socialmediaexaminer.com/socialmedia-marketing-report-2013

Stephen, A. T., & Toubia, O. (2010). Deriving value from social commerce networks. *JMR, Journal of Marketing Research*, *47*(2), 215–228. doi:10.1509/jmkr.47.2.215

Stewart, F., & Brown, G. (2009). Fragile States. *CRISE Working Paper No. 51*, University of Oxford, Oxford.

Stewart, K. J. (2003). Trust transfer on the World Wide Web. *Organization Science*, *14*(1), 5–17. doi:10.1287/orsc.14.1.5.12810

Stokes, R. (2008).E-marketing: The essential guide to online marketing, South Africa: Quirk eMarketing (Pty) Ltd.

Stone, R., & Jacobs, R. (2001). *Successful Direct Marketing Methods* (7th ed.). New York, NJ: McGraw Hill.

Storbacka, K., Strandvik, T., & Grönroos, C. (1994). Managing Customer Relationships for Profit: The Dynamics of Relationship Quality. *International Journal of Service Industry Management*, *5*(5), 21–38. doi:10.1108/09564239410074358

Strauss, J., & Frost, R. (2014). *E-marketing* (6th ed.). New Jersey: Pearson Education Limited.

Stuart, H., & Jones, C. (2004). Corporate branding in market space. *Corporate Reputation Review*, *7*(1), 84–93. doi:10.1057/palgrave.crr.1540213

Sukoco, B. & Wu, W. (2010). The personal and social motivation of customers' participation in brand community. *African journal of business management, 4(5)*, 614-622.

Sule Alonso, M. A., Paquin, J. P., & Levy Mangin, J. P. (2002). Modelling perceived quality in fruit products: Their extrinsic and intrinsic attributes. *Journal of Food Products Marketing*, *8*(1), 29–49. doi:10.1300/J038v08n01_03

Sung, Y., Choi, S. M., & Lin, J. S. (2012). The interplay of culture and situational cues in consumers' brand evaluation. *International Journal of Consumer Studies*, *36*(6), 696–701. doi:10.1111/j.1470-6431.2011.01047.x

SurveyMonkey.com. (2014). *How To Identify Your Customer Touchpoints*. Retrieved October 17, 2014, from https://www.surveymonkey.com/blog/en/identify-customer-touchpoints/

Sussman, S., & Siegal, W. (2003). Informational influence in organizations: An integrated approach to knowledge adoption. *Information Systems Research*, *14*(1), 47–65. doi:10.1287/isre.14.1.47.14767

Swilley, E., Hofacker, C. F., & Lamont, B. T. (2012). The Evolution of E-Commerce to M-Commerce: Pressures, Firm Capabilities and Competitive Advantage in Strategic Decision Making. *International journal of e-business research,* 8(1), 1-16.

Swilley, E., & Hofacker, C. F. (2006). Defining mobile commerce in a marketing context. *International Journal of Mobile Marketing*, *1*(2), 18–23.

Szajna, B. (1996). Empirical Evaluation of the Revised Technology Acceptance Model. *Management Science*, *42*(1), 85–92. doi:10.1287/mnsc.42.1.85

Taylor, D. G., Strutton, D., & Thompson, K. (2012). Self-enhancement as a motivation for sharing online advertising. *Journal of Interactive Advertising*, *12*(2), 13–28. doi:10.1080/15252019.2012.10722193

Taylor, S., & Todd, P. A. (1995). Understanding information technology usage: A test of competing models. *Information Systems Research*, *6*(2), 144–176. doi:10.1287/isre.6.2.144

The top brands in social media report 2008. (2008). *ImmediateFuture*. Retrieved fromhttp://www.immediatefuture.co.uk/the-top-brands-in-social-media-report-2008

The World Factbook. (2014). Central Intelligence Agency (CIA). Retrieved from https://www.cia.gov/library/publications/the-world-factbook/rankorder/2119rank.html

Thompson, S. A., & Sinha, R. K. (2008). Brand communities and new product adoption: The influence and limits of oppositional loyalty. *Journal of Marketing*, *72*(6), 65–80. doi:10.1509/jmkg.72.6.65

Three of Four UK Mobile Users Own Smartphones by 2016. (2013). *Emarketer.com*. Retrieved from http://www.emarketer.com/Article/Three-of-Four-UK-Mobile-Users-Own-Smartphones-by-2016/1009614

Tian, K., Sautter, P., Fisher, D., Fischbach, S., Luna-Nevarez, C., Boberg, K., & Vann, R. et al. (2014). Transforming health care: Empowering therapeutic communities through technology-enhanced narratives. *The Journal of Consumer Research*, *41*(2), 237–260. doi:10.1086/676311

Ting, D. H., Ling, S. F., Patanmacia, T. S., Low, C. G., & Ker, G. C. (2011). Dependency on smartphone and the impact on purchase behavior. *Young Consumers*, *12*(3), 193–203.

Tjosvold, D., Peng, A. C., Chen, N. Y., & Fang, S. S. (2012). Individual Decision-Making in Organizations: Contribution of Uncertainty and Controversy in China.

Torsten, G. J., Rams, W., & Schindler, A. (2001). Customer Retention, Loyalty, and Satisfaction in the German Mobile Cellular Telecommunication Market. *Telecommunications Policy*, *25*(4), 249–269. doi:10.1016/S0308-5961(00)00097-5

Touri, M. (2009). News blogs: Strengthening democracy through conflict prevention. *Aslib Proceedings: New Information Perspectives*, *61*(2), 170–184. doi:10.1108/00012530910946910

Trainor, K. (2012). Relating SocialMedia Technologies to Performance: A Capabilities-Based Perspective. *Journal of Personal Selling & Sales Management*, *32*(3), 317–331. doi:10.2753/PSS0885-3134320303

Trusov, M., Bucklin, R. E., & Pauwels, K. (2009). Effects of word-of-mouth versus traditional marketing, findings from an internet social networking site. *Journal of Marketing*, *73*(9), 90–102. doi:10.1509/jmkg.73.5.90

Tshin, E. Y. H., Tanakinjal, G. H., & Sondoh, S. L. Jr. (2014). The key dimensions of online service quality: A study of consumer perceptions. *IUP Journal of Marketing Management*, *13*(2), 7–18.

Tuominen, P. (2007). Emerging metaphors in brand management: Towards a relational approach. *Journal of Communication Management*, *11*(2), 182–191. doi:10.1108/13632540710747398

Tuten, T. L. (2008). *Advertising 2.0 – Social Media Marketing in a Web 2.0 World.* Westport: Praeger Publishers.

Tyebjee, T. T., & Bruno, A. V. (1984). A Model of Venture Capitalist Investment Activity. *Management Science*, *30*(9), 1051–1066. doi:10.1287/mnsc.30.9.1051

Ugwoji, A. C. (2014). Amplifying employees' voice in the Nigerian employment relations for better corporate governance: the imperative of new media. *Economic Insights – Trends & Challenges*, 3(3), 15-22.

UK Online Clothing Shoppers Still Favor the PC. (2013). *Emarketer.com.* Retrieved from http://www.emarketer.com/Article/UK-Online-Clothing-Shoppers-Still-Favor-PC/1010274

United States Government Accountability Office. (2014). CREDIT CARDS: Marketing to College Students Appears to Have Declined (GAO-14-225).

Uzoechina, O. (2008). "State Fragility" and the Challenges of Development in West Africa: Moving from Reaction to Prevention. *ALC Research Report No. 3*. African Leadership Centre, King's College London.

Uzunoglu, E., & Kip, S. M. (2014). Brand communication through digital influencers: Leveraging blogger engagement. *International Journal of Information Management*, *34*(5), 592–602. doi:10.1016/j.ijinfomgt.2014.04.007

Väisänen, J. (2015, January 15). Threats of brand management in social media why strong social media presence magnifies brand weaknesses and how international brand managers can address this: Part 1. *Brand Management for a Wired World.* Retrieved from http://www.brandba.se/blog/2014/8/14/threats-of-brand-management-in-social-media-why-strong-social-media-presence-magnifies-brand-weaknesses-and-how-international-brand-managers-can-address-this-part-1

Valsecchi, M., Renga, F. M., & Rangone, A. (2007). Mobile customer relationship management: An exploratory analysis of Italian applications. *Business Process Management Journal*, *13*(6), 755–770. doi:10.1108/14637150710834532

Van Doorn, J., Lemon, K. N., Mittal, V., Nass, S., Pick, D., Pirner, P., & Verhoef, P. C. (2010). Customer Engagement Behavior: Theoretical Foundations and Research Directions. *Journal of Service Research*, *13*(3), 253–266. doi:10.1177/1094670510375599

Van Slyke, C., Belanger, F., & Comunale, C. L. (2004). Factors influencing the adoption of web-based shopping: The impact of trust. *ACM SIGMIS Database*, *35*(2), 32–49.

VanBoskirk, S. (2009, July 7). Interactive marketing nears $55 billion; advertising overall delines. Retrieved from http://blogs.forrester.com/

Varadarajan, P., & Menon, A. (1988). Cause-Related Marketing: A Coalignment of Marketing Strategy and Corporate Philanthropy. *Journal of Marketing*, *52*(3), 58–74. doi:10.2307/1251450

Vargo, S. L., & Lusch, R. F. (2004). Evolving to a new Dominant Logic for Marketing. *Journal of Marketing*, *68*(1), 1–17. doi:10.1509/jmkg.68.1.1.24036

Vásquez, G. A. N., & Escamilla, E. M. (2014). Best practice in the use of social networks marketing strategy as in SMEs. *Procedia: Social and Behavioral Sciences*, *148*, 533–542. doi:10.1016/j.sbspro.2014.07.076

Vela-McConnell, J. A. (1999). *Who is my neighbour?: Social affinity in a modern world.* Albany, NY: New York Press.

Venkatesh, V., Brown, S., & Bala, H. (2013). Bridging the Qualitative- Quantitative Divide: Guidelines for Conducting Mixed-Methodology Research in Information Systems. *Management Information Systems Quarterly*, *37*(1), 21–54.

Venkatesh, V., & Davis, F. D. (2000). A theoretical extension of the technology acceptance model: Four longitudinal field studies. *Management Science*, *46*(2), 186–204. doi:10.1287/mnsc.46.2.186.11926

Venkatesh, V., & Davis, F. D.VenKkatesh. (1996). A Model of the perceived ease of use: Development and test. *Decision Sciences*, *27*(3), 451–481. doi:10.1111/j.1540-5915.1996.tb01822.x

Venkatesh, V., Morris, M. G., Davis, G. B., & Davis, F. D. (2003). User acceptance of information technology: Toward a unified view. *Management Information Systems Quarterly*, *27*(3), 25–47.

Verhoef, P. C. (2003). Understanding the Effect of Customer Relationship Management Efforts on Customer Retention and Customer Share Development. *Journal of Marketing*, *67*(4), 30–45. doi:10.1509/jmkg.67.4.30.18685

Verhoef, P. C., Reinartz, W. J., & Krafft, M. (2010). Customer engagement as a new perspective in customer management. *Journal of Service Research*, *13*(3), 247–252. doi:10.1177/1094670510375461

Vesel, P., & Zabkar, V. (2009). Managing customer loyalty through the mediating role of satisfaction in the DIY retail loyalty program. *Journal of Retailing and Consumer Services*, *16*(5), 396–406. doi:10.1016/j.jretconser.2009.05.002

Vickers, J. S., & Renand, F. (2003). The Marketing of Luxury Goods: An exploratory study – three conceptual dimensions. *The Marketing Review*, *3*(4), 459–478. doi:10.1362/146934703771910071

Vollmer, C., & Precourt, G. (2008). *Always on: Advertising, marketing, and media in an era of consumer control.* New York, NY: McGraw–Hill.

Wafi, T. (2014). *From 4Ps to SAVE – A Theoretical Analysis of Various Marketing Mix Models.* Retrieved from http://www.academia.edu/3834304/FROM_4PS_TO_SAVE_A_THEORITICAL_ANALYSIS_OF_VARIOUS_MARKETING_MIX_MODELS

Wagner, C., & Majchrzak, A. (2007). Enabling customer-centricity using wikis and the wiki way. *Journal of Management Information Systems*, *23*(3), 17–43. doi:10.2753/MIS0742-1222230302

Walpole (2013). British Luxury Showcase.

Walters, J. (2013). *What is a Customer Touchpoint?* Retrieved from http://360connext.com/customer-touchpoint/

Wang, H.-F., & Hong, W. (2006). Managing Customer Profitability in a Competitive Market by Continuous Data Mining. *Industrial Marketing Management*, *35*(6), 715–723. doi:10.1016/j.indmarman.2005.06.005

Wang, M.-S., Chen, C. C., Chan, S.-C., & Yang, Y.-H. (2007). Effects of online shopping attitudes, subjective norms and control beliefs on online shopping intentions: A test of the theory of planned behaviour. *International Journal of Management*, *24*(2), 296–302.

Wang, Y., & Liao, Y. (2007). The conceptualization and measurement of m-commerce user satisfaction. *Computers in Human Behavior*, *23*(1), 381–398.

Wang, Y., Wu, Sh., Lin, H., & Wang, Y. (2011). The relationship of service failure severity, service recovery justice and perceived switching costs with customer loyalty in the context of e-tailing. *International Journal of Information Management*, *31*(4), 350–359. doi:10.1016/j.ijinfomgt.2010.09.001

Wathen, C. N., & Burkell, J. (2002). Believe it or not: Factors influencing credibility on the Web. *Journal of the American Society for Information Science and Technology*, *53*(2), 134–144. doi:10.1002/asi.10016

Wattal, S., Schuff, D., Mandviwalla, M., & Williams, C. B. (2010). Web 2.0 and Politics: The 2008 U.S. Presidential Election and an E-Politics Research Agenda. *Management Information Systems Quarterly*, *34*(4), 669–688.

Watts, M. (2004). Resource curse? Governmentality, oil and power in the Niger delta, Nigeria. *Geopolitics*, *9*(1), 50–80. doi:10.1080/14650040412331307832

Web 2.0: The new face of the Web. (2008). Google. Retrieved from www.google.com/a/help/intl/en/security/pdf/web_2_new_face.pdf

Web Analytics Association (2008), *Web Analytics Definitions*. Draft for Public Comment, September 22nd 2008.

Weber, L. (2007). *Marketing to the Social Web: How Digital Customer Communities Build Your Business*. New Jersey: John Wiley & Sons Inc.

Weber, L. (2009). *Marketing To The Social Web: How Digital Customer Communities Build Your Business* (2nd ed.). Hoboken, New Jersey: John Wiley & Sons. doi:10.1002/9781118258125

Webster, G. B., & Hume, M. (2015). Defining the Role of Social Media as a Contemporary LAM Technique in Franchising. In G. Bowen & W. Ozuem (Eds.), *Computer-mediated strategies: social media and online brand communities* (pp. 223–251). Hershey, PA: IGI Global.

Weinberg, T. (2009). The new community rules: Marketing on the social web. O'Reilly Sebastopol, CA.

Weinberg, T. (2009). *The new community rules: Marketing on the social web*. Sebastopol, CA: O'Reilly Media, Inc.

Wellman, B., & Gulia, M. (1999). Net-surfers don't ride alone: Virtual communities as communities. In B. Wellman (Ed.), Networks in the global village (pp. 331-366). Boulder: Westview.

Wen, Q. (2013, July 2). Using social media for brand management. *Megaphone Marketing*. Retrieved from http://megaphonemarketing.com.au/using-social-media-for-brand-management/

Westbrook, R. A. (1987). Product/consumption-based affective responses and post-purchase processes. *JMR, Journal of Marketing Research*, *24*(3), 258–270. doi:10.2307/3151636

Wheeler, E. (2013). The emergence of M-Commerce and Geofencing. *Bloomberg.com*. Retrieved from http://www.bloomberg.com/video/from-e-commerce-to-m-commerce-bW0SIsCkRJaTiNTJ89zAnQ.html

Wicker, A. W. (1969). Attitudes versus actions: The relationship of verbal overt behavioral responses to attitude objects. *The Journal of Social Issues*, *25*(4), 41–78. doi:10.1111/j.1540-4560.1969.tb00619.x

Wiedmann, K. P., Langner, S., & Hennings, N. (2007). Collaborated Marketing. In H. Bauer, D. Grosse-Leege, & J. Rösger (Eds.), Interactive Marketing in Web 2.0 – Konzepte und Anwendungen für ein erfolgreiches Marketing management in Internet. Munich: Vahlen.

Williams, D., Crittenden, V., Keo, T., & McCarty, P. (2012). The use of social media: An exploratory study of usage among digital natives. *Journal of Public Affairs*, *12*(2), 127–136. doi:10.1002/pa.1414

Williams, L., & Cothrell, J. (2000). Four smart ways to run online communities. *Sloan Management Review*, *41*(4), 81–91.

Willis, J. (2011). *8 Characteristics of Effective Social Media Campaigns*. Retrieved from http://www.searchenginepeople.com/blog/effective-social-media-campaigns.html

Wilson, D. T. (1995). An integrated model of buyer–seller relationships. *Journal of the Academy of Marketing Science, 23*(4), 335–345. doi:10.1177/009207039502300414

Wilson, J. J., & Morgan, J. E. (2011). Friends or Freeloaders? Encouraging brand conscience and introducing the concept of emotion-based consumer loss mitigation. *Journal of Brand Management, 18*(9), 659–676. doi:10.1057/bm.2011.4

Wong, S. H. R. (2012). Which platform do our users prefer: Website or mobile app? *RSR. Reference Services Review, 40*(1), 113–115.

Working Party on the Information Economy – Participative Web: User-created content. (2007, April 12). OECD, Organisation for Economic Co-operation and Development. Retrieved from http://www.oecd.org/sti/38393115.pdf

Worldwide luxury goods continues double-digit annual growth; global market now tops €200 billion, finds Bain & Company. (2013, March 16). *Bain & Company*. Retrieved from http://www.bain.com/about/press/press-releases/worldwide-luxury-goods-continues-double-digit-annual-growth.aspx

Worthington, S. (1997). Affinity Credit Card Issuers and their Relationship with their Alumni Affinity Group Partners. *International Journal of Bank Marketing, 15*(2), 39–47. doi:10.1108/02652329710160448

Worthington, S. (2001). Affinity credit cards: A critical review. *International Journal of Retail & Distribution Management, 29*(11), 485–512. doi:10.1108/EUM0000000006174

Worthington, S., & Horne, S. (1992). Affinity Credit Cards in the United Kingdom – Card Issuer Strategies and Affinity Group Aspirations. *International Journal of Bank Marketing, 10*(7), 3–10. doi:10.1108/02652329210021113

Wright, P., & Rip, P. (1980). Product class advertising effects on first-time buyers' decision strategies. *Journal of Consumer Research, 7*(2), 776–788. doi:10.1086/208805

Wu, C., & Lo, Y. H. (2012). Customer reactions to encountering consecutive service failures. *Journal of Consumer Behaviour, 11*(3), 217–224. doi:10.1002/cb.1376

Wu, P. C. S., & Wang, Y. (2011). The influences of electronic word-of-mouth message appeal and message source credibility on brand attitude. *Asia Pacific Journal of Marketing and Logistics, 23*(4), 448–472. doi:10.1108/13555851111165020

Xia, L. (2013). Effects of companies' responses to consumer criticism in social media. *International Journal of Electronic Commerce, 17*(4), 73–99. doi:10.2753/JEC1086-4415170403

Xiang, Z., Hyun, K., Wöber, K., & Fesenmaier, D. R. (2007, June 17-20). Online representation of tourism: An analysis of search engine results from a major search engines. *Proceedings of theTravel and Tourism Research Association (TTRA) Annual Conference*. Las Vegas, NV.

Xue, F., & Phelps, J. (2004). Internet-facilitated consumer-to-consumer communication: The moderating role of receiver characteristics. *International Journal of Internet Marketing and Advertising, 1*(2), 121–136. doi:10.1504/IJIMA.2004.004016

Xu, J., & Cooper Thomas, H. (2011). How can leaders achieve high employee engagement? *Leadership and Organization Development Journal, 32*(4), 399–416. doi:10.1108/01437731111134661

Xun, J., & Reynolds, J. (2010). Applying netnography to market research: The case of the online forum. *Journal of Targeting. Measurement and Analysis for Marketing, 18*(1), 17–31. doi:10.1057/jt.2009.29

Yadav, M. S., & Pavlou, P. A. (2014). Marketing in Computer-Mediated Environments: Research Synthesis and New Directions. *Journal of Marketing*, *78*(1), 20–40. doi:10.1509/jm.12.0020

Yang, K., & Kim, H.-Y. (2012). Mobile shopping motivation: An application of multiple discriminant analysis. *International Journal of Retail & Distribution Management*, *40*(10), 778–789.

Yang, S. C. (2012). Mobile applications and 4G wireless networks: A framework for analysis. *Campus-Wide Information Systems*, *29*(5), 344–357.

Yastrow, S. (n. d.). *Touchpoint Mapping Exercise*. Retrieved from http://www.yastrow.com/downloads/touchpoint-map.pdf

Yeh, Y. H., & Choi, S. M. (2011). Mini-lovers, maxi-mouths: An investigation of antecedents to eWOM intention among brand community members. *Journal of Marketing Communications*, *17*(3), 145–162. doi:10.1080/13527260903351119

Yeh, Y. S., & Li, Y.-M. (2009). Building trust in e-commerce: Contributions from quality and satisfaction. *Online Information Review*, *33*(6), 1066–1086.

Yen, T. F., Hung, C. J., & Liu, H. H. J. (2014). The Effects of Perceived Uncertainty on Tourists' Decision-Making to Agritourism in Taiwan. *The International Journal of Organizational Innovation*, *6*(4), 236–247.

Yi, Y. (1990). A critical review of consumer satisfaction, In V.A. Zeithaml (Ed.), Review of Marketing (pp. 68-123). Chicago: American Marketing Association.

Yoganarasimhan, H. (2012). Impact of social network structure on content propagation: A study using YouTube data. *Quantitative Marketing and Economics*, *10*(1), 111–150. doi:10.1007/s11129-011-9105-4

Yoo, B., Donthu, N., & Lee, S. (2000). An examination of selected marketing mix elements and brand equity. *Journal of the Academy of Marketing Science*, *28*(2), 195–211. doi:10.1177/0092070300282002

Yoo, M., & Bai, B. (2013). Customer loyalty marketing research: A comparative approach between hospitality and business journals. *International Journal of Hospitality Management*, *33*, 166–177. doi:10.1016/j.ijhm.2012.07.009

Youngs, G. (2007). Virtual democracy: An idea for our time. *Development*, 50, 23–27. doi:10.1057/palgrave.development.1100331 PMID:21115610

Zagenczyk, T. J., Gibney, R., Murrell, A. J., & Boss, S. R. (2008). Friends don't make friends good citizens, but advisors do. *Group & Organization Management*, *33*(6), 760–780. doi:10.1177/1059601108326806

Zaglia, M. E. (2013). Brand communities embedded in social networks. *Journal of Business Research*, *66*(2-2), 216–223. doi:10.1016/j.jbusres.2012.07.015 PMID:23564989

Zaoui, I., & Akremi, A. E. (2003, May 21-23). l'intention d'achat du consommateur sur Internet: Déterminants et rôle modérateur de la confiance. Cas du site marchand du magasin général. Proceedings of the*8th AIM conference*, Grenoble, France.

Zarrella, D. (2010). *The social media marketing book*. Sebastopol, CA: O'Reilly Media, Inc.

Zavattaro, S. M., Daspit, J. J., & Adams, F. G. (2015). Assessing managerial methods for evaluating place brand equity: A qualitative investigation. *Tourism Management*, *47*, 11–21. doi:10.1016/j.tourman.2014.08.018

Zeelenberg, M., & Pieters, R. (2004). Beyond valence in customer dissatisfaction: A review and new findings on behavioral responses to regret and disappointment in failed services. *Journal of Business Research*, *57*(4), 445–455. doi:10.1016/S0148-2963(02)00278-3

Zeithaml, V. A., Bitner, M. J., & Gremler, D. D. (2013). *Services marketing: Integrating customer focus across the firm* (6th ed.). New York, NY: McGraw-Hill.

Zhang, M., Jansen, B. J., & Chowdhury, A. (2011). Business engagement on Twitter: A path analysis. *Electronic Markets*, *21*(3), 161–175. doi:10.1007/s12525-011-0065-z

Zhao, D., & Rosson, M. B. (2009). How and why people Twitter: The role that microblogging plays in informal communication at work. Paper presented at the ACM 2009 International Conference on Supporting Group Work, New York, NY. doi:10.1145/1531674.1531710 doi:10.1145/1531674.1531710

Zhou, T. (2011). Examining the critical success factors of mobile site adoption. *Online Information Review*, *35*(4), 636–652.

Zhou, T. (2013). Understanding continuance usage of mobile site. *Industrial Management & Data Systems*, *113*(9), 1286–1299.

Zhu, Z., Nakata, C., Sivakumar, K., & Grewal, D. (2013). Fix it or leave it? Customer recovery from self-service technology failures. *Journal of Retailing*, *89*(1), 15–29. doi:10.1016/j.jretai.2012.10.004

Zikmund, W. G., Ward, S., Lowe, B., & Winzar, H. (2007). *Marketing Research* (A. Pacific, Ed.). Melbourne, Australia: Thomson Learning.

Zineldin, M. (2000). Beyond relationship marketing: Technologicalship marketing. *Management Intelligence & planning*, 18(1), 9-23.

Zuckerberg, M. (2009, April 8). 200 million strong. Retrieved fromhttp://blog.facebook.com/blog.php?post=72353897130

Zuckerberg, M. (2010, February 4). Six years of making connections. Retrieved from http://blog.facebook.com/blog.php?post=287542162130

Zulkifli, Z., & Tahir, I. M. (2012). Developing and validating Customer Relationship Management (CRM) practices construct. *International Journal of Business and Behavioral Sciences*, *2*(1), 35–48.

About the Contributors

Wilson Ozuem is Associate Professor of Digital Marketing at Regent's University London (UK). His research interests include the implications of information technology for decision making by marketers and consumers. The results of his research have been published in scholarly journals and international conference papers, including *European Journal of Marketing, Journal of Strategic Marketing, Journal of Information Technology and Management, Education + Training*. Dr. Ozuem teaches in a number of UK universities, including University of Gloucestershire, University of Hertfordshire, University of West London, University of East London, Lincoln University, CAPA: The Global Education Network (London). Dr. Wilson holds a visiting professorial fellowship at the University of Tirana (Albania). Currently, he teaches MSc and MBA courses in marketing communications, Internet marketing, research methodology, and marketing management. He is a Fellow of the Chartered Institute of Marketing (FCIM) and has worked as a marketing consultant for several companies and organisations. He received his BA in Business from the University of Portsmouth, MA Marketing from University of West London, MBA from London Metropolitan University, MEd (Educational leadership and Management) from Open University (UK), Doctorate from Anglia Ruskin University, and Postgraduate Degree in Educational Research from University of Cambridge.

Gordon Bowen has a Doctorate in Business (University of Hull) and is a Chartered Marketer from the Chartered Institute of Marketing (UK). He is an Associate Lecturer at various universities and higher education institutions, including University of Gloucestershire, Regent's University London, Ulster University, University of Hertfordshire and Grenoble Graduate Business School. His research interests are strategy, marketing, digital marketing, and SMEs, and he supervises PhD and DBA students in these areas. Gordon has held senior positions in the telecommunications industry, including strategy development, business development and training. He has also advised SMEs on business matters.

* * *

Yllka Azemi is a PhD candidate at Cardiff Metropolitan University, Wales (UK). Her research interests include online service failure and recovery strategies, social media marketing, and brand relationships. She received her bachelor degree from Rochester Institute of Technology, USA and Master's degree from University of Wales. She is an Assistant Professor in the College of International Management Globus, Kosovo, where she teaches a wide range of management courses, including strategic management and human resource management.

Nedra Bahri-Ammari is a permanent assistant professor (*equivalent to associate professor in Europe*) of marketing at IHEC of Carthage, Tunisia and a member of the LARIME research center. She holds a Doctorate in marketing and a master degree in Marketing from ISG of Tunisia, University of Tunis. She is a graduate of marketing from ISG of Tunis, University of Tunis. Dr. Bahri's researches include: business-to-customer and business-to-business marketing, customer relationships management (CRM), social-CRM, customer satisfaction, loyalty, retention, technology's implementation, firm profitability, enterprise Resource Planning (ERP) and Supply Chain Management. She has published in International peer-reviewed academic journals such as: *International Journal of Contemporary Hospitality Management; Journal of Hospitality and Tourism Technology*; *Journal of Research in Marketing and Entrepreneurship; International Journal of Customer Relationship Marketing and Management;* An *International Journal of Science, Engineering and Technology.* She has published a book on CRM and loyalty strategy also participated in the writing of books on tourism and social CRM. She has also been published in international and national academic conference proceedings (EUROMED, World Research Summit for Hospitality and Tourism, Marketing Trends, WASET, IBIMA, Academy of Marketing Science).

Deidre Bowen holds a Masters in Applied Management (Henley Business School) with distinction, is a qualified solicitor and completed her degree at Oxford University. She is currently a Regional Manager for a charity, specializing in safeguarding and business development. Her research interests are strategy, social media, SMEs sustainability and leadership. More recently, Deidre has explored how business effectiveness is impacted in recessionary conditions, with particular focus on the role of employee engagement.

Carlton Brown, PHD, MBA, PGDip, FISMM & MCMi, is an accomplished consultant, marketer and entrepreneur. Dr Brown is ''scratch to £1 million turnover'' start-up entrepreneur. His experiences over the last 25 years, 15 at director level, have led to Dr Brown becoming a sought-after lecturer, trainer, speaker and coach. He is frequently described as creative, diligent, innovative, energetic and motivational. He is a Member of the British Management Association (BAM), a Fellow of the Institute of Sales and Marketing Management (FLISMM) and Member of the Chartered Management Institute (CMI). He is also an author with articles on *Leadership and Emotional Intelligence* and *Communication and Conflict* which have been published in peer-reviewed international academic journals. Besides teaching, Dr Brown is a partner with Rathbone Results Limited, a blue-chip UK consultancy firm.

Sumesh Dadwal has 15 years of experience in business & academic research, teaching, eLearning, educational quality management in wide range of business subjects. As Senior Lecturer, assessor/examiner, quality auditor and Programme Leader of Business PGs, Dr. Sumesh has lead a team of experts in teaching & research, academics, research design, and actively participates at university assessment boards. He has also been associated with QAA for Reviewer for Educational Oversight. Dr. Sumesh also possess years of hands on industrial experience in constructions and agricultural supply chain. He is also PhD research Leader, supervisor as well as external examiner for PhD thesis. Dr. Sumesh has supervised graduate and postgraduate students, and also involved in PhD supervision. His core research areas include International Strategic Marketing & Globalisation, Strategic Management, consumer behaviour & misbehaviour, product launches, prosumers & experience economy, service encounters & sensational experiences, Research methods & Quantitative techniques.

Azizul Hassan is a member of the Tourism Consultants Network of the Tourism Society, UK, and is currently working towards a PhD at Cardiff Metropolitan University. Hassan attended more than thirty four training workshops covering diverse aspects of research including the 'International Workshop – Fielding challenges, challenging the field: The methodologies of mobility' organized at the University of Oxford, UK. With his participation as the 'Engaged Participant', this workshop uniquely explored how ethnographers are responding methodologically to new questions being raised in the study of mobility and migration. His main areas of research are: technology-supported marketing in tourism; innovative marketing dynamics; destination branding in tourism; cultural heritage tourism; heritage interpretation; and sustainable management/marketing alternatives for cultural heritage industries. He is a regular reviewer of Tourism Analysis, the International Journal of Human Resource Management, the International Journal of Ecotourism, the eReview of Tourism Research (eRTR) and The International Interdisciplinary Business-Economics Advancement Journal.

Margee Hume is a Professor in the School of Business and Law at the University of Central Queensland. She researches in innovation in health, professional services, process mapping and service innovation. She has extensive skills in business operations/marketing strategy, interactive technology and strategic marketing. She has an impressive and extensive list of publications in prestigious journals and outlets. Her teaching interest includes service strategy, innovation and digital technology in particular health-care interactive/digital technology. She specialises in novel methods including application of operations management techniques in a services paradigm. Margee is the leader of the Service Industry Innovation and work stream of the Centre for Tourism and Regional Opportunities and leads the funded research group service innovation and work supporting a collaborative group of national researchers.

Kijpokin Kasemsap received his BEng degree in Mechanical Engineering from King Mongkut's University of Technology Thonburi, his MBA degree from Ramkhamhaeng University, and his DBA degree in Human Resource Management from Suan Sunandha Rajabhat University. He is a Special Lecturer at Faculty of Management Sciences, Suan Sunandha Rajabhat University based in Bangkok, Thailand. He is a Member of International Association of Engineers (IAENG), International Association of Engineers and Scientists (IAEST), International Economics Development and Research Center (IEDRC), International Association of Computer Science and Information Technology (IACSIT), International Foundation for Research and Development (IFRD), and International Innovative Scientific and Research Organization (IISRO). He also serves on the International Advisory Committee (IAC) for International Association of Academicians and Researchers (INAAR). He has numerous original research articles in top international journals, conference proceedings, and book chapters on business management, human resource management, and knowledge management published internationally.

Amir Manzoor holds a bachelor's degree in engineering from NED University, Karachi, an MBA from Lahore University of Management Sciences (LUMS), and an MBA from Bangor University, United Kingdom. He has many years of diverse professional and teaching experience working at many renowned national and internal organizations and higher education institutions. His research interests include electronic commerce and technology applications in business.

Aster Mekonnen is a Lecturer in Marketing at GSM London (Partner of Plymouth University). Her research interests include Digital Marketing, Consumer Behaviour & Insight, Services Marketing, and Affinity Marketing. Aster is also a member of a number of professional associations (Fellow of the Academy of Marketing Science, Member of Chartered Institute of Marketing and Member of the Academy of Marketing). Aster is a former researcher at the Open University Business School (OUBS) Marketing and Strategy Unit, and holds a master degree in Marketing from the University of Leicester. Prior to her research she has acquired extensive experience in the service industry.

Bibi Nafiisah Mulloo is an ACCA affiliate and was awarded her MBA in Financial Management from London Metropolitan University, United Kingdom. Her research interest lies primarily in finance and marketing, with particular interest in the influence of technology on consumer's behaviour. After her MBA studies, she progressed in her career as an accounts executive and is now the finance manager in a London law firm.

Uzoechi Nwagbara earned both BA and MA in English (Nigeria), MSc in Human Resource Management and PhD in Management (Corporate Social Responsibility & Sustainability Accounting) from University of Wales. He is author of four books as well as over one hundred publications in peer-reviewed international journals such as *Thunderbird International Business Review*, *East-West Journal of Economics & Business*, *International Journal of Technology & Sustainable Development*, *Polish Journal of Management Studies*, *Nordic Journal of African Studies*, *African Identities*, *Leadership*, *Leadership Review*, and *Journal of International Women's Studies*, among others. Dr Nwagbara is on the editorial boards of six international journals and acts as member advisory board to *Journal of Sustainable Development in Africa* (Clarion University, Pennsylvania, USA). Dr Nwagbara is management lecturer, consultant and writer. He teaches at Greenwich School of Management London as well as Visiting Professor at London School of Commerce (LSC). Dr Nwagbara has professional affiliations including British Academy of Management (BAM), European Association for the Study of Literature, Culture and the Environment (EASLCE), Postcolonial Studies Association (PSA) & Royal African Society (RAS), among others.

Emeka Smart Oruh obtained BSc in Management and Information Technology and MBA in Human Resource Management both from Plymouth University, UK. He is currently undertaking doctoral studies in Management at Brunel University. Mr Oruh has authored a number of academic articles including "*Towards Sustainable Human Resource Information Systems (HRIS) in the Nigerian Banking Sector: The Role of New Media*" and "*Giving Voice to the People: Exploring the Effects of New Media on Stakeholder Engagement in the Nigerian Trade Union*". His book reviews have appeared in *Journal of Pan African Studies* and *African Studies Quarterly*. He has attended and presented at (academic) conferences including the 2015 British Academy of Management (BAM) conference at Portsmouth University.

Celia Almeida Pinho completed her Master of Business Administration (MBA) at the University of West London. Her dissertation primarily focused on informational and normative influences of consumer generated content and its perceived customer value within online environments. Her general research interests include the field of digital marketing, in particular, consumer behaviour and branding strategies in online marketing environments. She is currently working for Guardian News and Media.

Ellen Stokinger holds a Master of Science in Strategic Marketing and Sales Management (with distinction) from London Metropolitan University, a Bachelor of Arts in Business Administration from Lancaster University (UK), and a Bachelor of Science Degree in International Management from European School of Business in Germany. Her research interests lie primarily in social media and online brand communities, particularly the influence of social media on the luxury beauty brands. Ellen has worked for a number of cosmetics companies, including L'Oréal and Estée Lauder. Ellen is now working in the digital customer experience team at Burberry.

Geoffrey Webster is a Doctoral student at the Central Queensland University (Australia). His research pursuits include the comparative study of social media as well as other community and local area marketing techniques, contemporary versus traditional as used by small to medium enterprises, particularly amongst franchise businesses. Geoffrey holds an Education Master's degree in Training and Development from Griffith University, a bachelor of Applied Science, Built Environment, from Queensland University of Technology. Prior to his PhD programme, Geoff was the marketing director of a plastics manufacturing and fabrication company.

Index